Cryptography and Secure Communications

Man Young Rhee

Hanyang University
Seoul, Korea

McGRAW-HILL BOOK CO.

Singapore Auckland Bogotá Caracas
Lisbon London Madrid Mexico
Milan Montreal New Delhi New York
Paris San Juan San Fransisco St Louis
Sydney Tokyo Toronto

Library of Congress Cataloging-in-Publication Data

Rhee, Man Young.
Cryptography and secure communications / Man Young Rhee.
p. cm. -- (McGraw-Hill series on computer communications)
Includes bibliographical references and index.
ISBN 0-07-112502-7 (hardcover)
1. Computer security. 2. Telecommunication systems--Security measures. 3. Cryptography. I. Title. II. Series.
QA76.9.A25R44 1994
005.8--dc20 94-10752
CIP

2 3 4 5 6 7 8 9 JBW FC 9 8 7 6 5 4

When ordering this title, use ISBN 0-07-112502-7

Printed in Singapore

ABOUT THE AUTHOR

Man Young Rhee is professor emeritus of electrical engineering at Hanyang University, Seoul, Korea. At present he is president of Korea Institute of Information Security and Cryptology. He received his B.S.E.E. degree from Seoul National University and his M.S.E.E. and Ph.D. degrees from the University of Colorado, Boulder, Colorado.

In the United States, Dr. Rhee taught at Virginia Polytechnic Institute and State University as a professor and was employed at the Jet Propulsion Laboratory, California Institute of Technology as a member of research staff. In Korea he was vice president of the Agency for Defence Development, Ministry of National Defence, Republic of Korea; president of the Korea Telecommunications Company (a government cooperation where the ESS telephone exchange system was first developed under contract with ITT/BTM); and president of Samsung Semiconductor and Telecommunications Company.

Dr. Rhee is the author of *Error Correcting Coding Theory* published by McGraw-Hill in the United States and is a recipient of the academic achievement prize from the National Academy of Sciences, Republic of Korea. His current interest is in the research area of error control coding, cryptography and its relevant applications.

Contents

Preface

Secure communications for preventing the unauthorized interception of sensitive information data is a legitimate need of not only institutions in the military and government, but also the business sector and private individuals. Data privacy, authentication, digital signature, and file security are the various elements that need to be examined for protecting data in computer and communication systems from unauthorized disclosure and modification. If a noninterceptable means for data storage and transmission were available, then all messages and data in the communications as well as in the data storage unit could obviously be secured. One such possible system is a cryptographic cipher system which can conceal the contents of every message by transforming (enciphering) it before transmission or storage.

There are several situations where the information should be kept confidential, and where an opponent (eavesdropper) can intercept vital information by monitoring the communications network. In such situations, necessary steps should be taken to conceal and protect the information contents. The role of the cryptographer will be recognized and appreciated if adequate measures are taken: (i) to protect valuable data in computer systems for processing and storing of data; (ii) to prevent the unauthorized extraction or deletion of information from messages transmitted over the open channel; and (iii) to prevent the unauthorized injection or addition of false data into the open channel. From the standpoint of data security, data processing systems should not be vulnerable to any attack. In addition, one must be aware that transmitted data could be intercepted and data could be modified, deleted, or added to a system. Therefore, data system designers are increasingly becoming aware of these threats, and most of them now recognize that cryptography is an important factor in the design of secure systems.

Data security has evolved rapidly after the National Bureau of Standards (NBS) adopted the Data Encryption Standard (DES) as a Federal standard in 1977. Since experts the world over recognize that encrypted messages (ciphertext) can be intercepted by wiretapping during transmission and that encrypted data files can be copied or stolen from their storage medium, there is little doubt that the problem of protecting data and securing communications will receive growing attention in the years to come. With the advent of modern computer and communication technologies, the need for cryptographic protection has become widely recognized and the direction of research has changed drastically. In the early seventies, only symmetrical (single-key) cryptography was known, and classified researches in cryptography discouraged cryptologists who sought to discover new cryptosystems. However, there has been an explosive growth in unclassified research in all aspects of cryptology since 1976. Since 1980, cryptanalysis has become one of the most active areas of research and a large set of mathematical tools useful for cryptanalysis has been developed with the progress in computational complexity.

The book is designed for students and professional engineers as an introduction to cryptography and information security. The main aim is to introduce cryptographic operation principles and algorithms for communication security and data privacy, and to relate the relevant protocols to practical security systems. This book is suitable for first-year graduate students or those attending an advanced senior course, and can also be used as a reference for electronics and communication engineers and computer scientists. The following is a summary of the contents of each chapter.

Chapter 1 presents a short survey of cryptologic evolution along with an overview of cryptographic cipher systems. We abstractly introduce classical ciphers that were formerly in use as well as modern cryptosystems being used presently with historical and bibliographical remarks.

Chapter 2 introduces the algebraic framework of number theory, which is particularly useful for public-key algorithms as well as zero-knowledge interactive proofs.

Chapter 3 covers in detail the Data Encryption Standard as a block cipher algorithm. The scope of analysis includes (i) distribution, transposition, and substitution of plaintext and key bits, (ii) analysis and design of substitutions (S-boxes), (iii) intersymbol dependence of ciphertext bits on data and key bits, (iv) encipherment at each round of DES, and (v) deciphering process for recovering the plaintext.

Chapter 4 presents a stream cipher by which the ciphertext can be obtained by Exclusive-ORing of the plaintext and the key-bit stream generated from a keystream generator called a linear feedback shift register (LFSR). There are two types of stream ciphers—synchronous and self-synchronizing. A key-autokey cipher is a typical synchronous cipher. The key-bit stream in this ciphersystem is generated independently of the plaintext bits. Therefore, synchronous stream ciphers do not propagate errors because each ciphertext block is independently enciphered under the key-bit block of the same length. Thus, each ciphertext block corrupted in transmission noise will precisely result in one erroneously deciphered plaintext block. The self-synchronizing stream ciphers usually employ ciphertext feedback or plaintext feedback. On the other hand, self-synchronizing stream ciphers propagate errors and exhibit an error-containing cryptogram because each key character is functionally dependent on the entire preceding ciphertext or plaintext block. In a ciphertext autokey system, an erroneous or lost ciphertext character causes only a fixed number of errors in the deciphered plaintext, after which the correct plaintext is again produced. However, in a plaintext autokey system, an erroneous ciphertext block causes indefinite error propagation in the deciphered plaintext blocks.

In this chapter, key-autokey synchronous ciphers, autokey ciphers with ciphertext feedback, autokey ciphers with plaintext feedback, and error propagation due to the errors caused in ciphertext during transmission are discussed and anlayzed in detail. Keystream generators employ nonlinear filtering in order to achieve high unpredictability of the generated bitstream. Therefore, this chapter also includes an analysis of nonlinear combinations of linear feedback shift register.

Chapter 5 deals with public-key cryptosystems, often called asymmetric two-key cryptosystems. The invention of public-key cryptosystems appeared to satisfy the commercial need for provable security that overcame some of the disadvantages of conventional multiple-key management problems. All works relating to public-key cryptosystems begin with the classic paper by Diffie and Hellman (1976). Subsequently, Rivest, Shamir, and Adleman (1978) discovered the RSA scheme which depends on the difficulty of factoring large integers, and Merkle and Hellman (1978) produced another two-key cryptosystem which is based on the trapdoor knapsack problem. The eighties were the first full decade of public-key cryptography and zero-knowledge interactive proofs. Many systems were proposed and many were broken. This chapter includes realistic examples, based on several schemes, such as the public-key distribution system, Merkle-Hellman knapsack cryptosystems, the RSA two-key cryptosystem, McEliece's algebraic codes cryptosystem, and others.

Chapter 6 presents the arithmetic operating circuits over the finite field GF (2^m) that perform addition, multiplication, multiplicative inverse, squaring and computation of square roots according to standard basis, normal basis, and dual basis. Gate-array fabrications, such as cellular or systolic arrays, exhibit a high degree of regularity and ease of generalization, and are able to perform effective logical operations. Therefore, VLSI fabrication makes possible some arrays of logic devices to perform such functions.

Chapters 7 and 8 present the important classes of BCH and Reed-Solomon codes for multiple-error correction. Since detailed discussions on these error-correcting codes were fully covered in my earlier book *Error Correcting Coding Theory* published by McGraw-Hill in 1989, only the new decoding algorithms and implementation methods that have appeared in the literature in the eighties are discussed here.

Chapter 9 mainly describes error correction for various stream cipher systems by providing a detailed coverage on ciphertext protection against illegal deletion of information or injection of false data by an opponent during data transmission or storage.

Chapter 10 deals with various problems relating to authentication, signature, and cryptologic applications. Authentication and signature problems relate to preventing an opponent from injecting false data into the channel or altering messages so that their meanings would change. In computerized communication networks, it is important to provide an adequate method by which communicators can identify themselves to each other in an unforgeable manner. The validity of business contracts and agreements, or military command and control orders should be required and guaranteed by signatures. In this chapter, our attention will be focussed on examining several authentication schemes built using public-key cryptosystems as well as conventional symmetric cryptosystems; and discussing several signature schemes which are applied to conformation of the alleged messages. The ID-based cryptosystems and zero-knowledge interactive proofs, being recent applications, are also included in this chapter.

Chapter 11 presents key management schemes for communication or file security. Key management is one of the important factors for designing secure cryptosystems. For data encryption and authentication it is necessary to manage a large set of cryptographic keys. Such keys are enciphered and sent to suitable users in the form of cryptograms. The function of key management is to securely distribute and update keys wherever required for cryptographic protection of data transmission or file security. This chapter mainly deals with key management for such a conventional symmetric cryptosystem as DES in order to provide secure communications. In addition, the key distribution protocol for implementing public-key algorithms and secret key sharing methods are also described here.

The theory and techniques of cryptography have been developed in a clear and understandable manner. Numerous examples included in each chapter are designed to enhance and augment the materials presented in this book.

The book can be used as a text for an introductory course on cryptography and secure communications for graduate students who have an adequate background on computer, communication, and coding. It is recommended that the instructor covers Chapters 2, 3, 4, 5, 10, and 11 for such a course. The book can serve for a one-semester course in cryptography for senior students with Chapters 2, 3, 4, and 5. It could also serve as a reference book or for a short course for practising engineers and computer scientists. This book contains both cryptology and error-control coding. Since Chapters 6 through 9 mainly cover error-control coding, the instructor can well choose to teach error-correction coding in one semester and cover cryptology using the rest of the chapters.

I am thankful to my former students Dr. Heung Y. Youm and Dr. Jae M. Kim who read the manuscript and provided numerous comments and suggestions.

I am deeply grateful to the Ministry of Communications and the Ministry of Science and Technology, Republic of Korea, Korea Telecom, and Electronics and Telecommunications Research Institute for their continuing support of my interest and research in the area of cryptography and information security.

Man Young Rhee

List of Symbols

A, B, C	Arbitrary elements of GF (2^m) in vector form
$A(\alpha), B(\alpha), Z(\alpha)$	Arbitrary elements of GF (2^m) in polynomial form
$\mathbf{B}_1$	32–bit output of S-boxes after round one
B^{-1}	Multiplicative inverse of element B
$\mathbf{c} = (c_0, c_1, \ldots, c_{n-1})$	An n-bit code word
$c(x)$	Code polynomial
$\mathbf{C}_X$	Encoded plaintext
$\mathbf{C}_Y$	Encoded ciphertext
$\mathbf{d}$	Information vector
d_0	Designed distance of the code
$d(x)$	Information polynomial
$d_{\min}$	Minimum distance of a algebraic code
d_n	nth discrepancy
D	Delay operator
$e(x)$	Error polynomial or error pattern
$E(\mathbf{R}_0)$	The 32-bit $\mathbf{R}_0$ is spread out and scrambled into 48 bits with E-table
E_k (IA)	Encryption function to identifier IA

$f(x)$	Arbitrary nonlinear function
$g(x)$	Generator polynomial
$\mathbf{G}$	A $(k \times n)$ generator matrix
$\mathbf{G}' = \mathbf{SGP}$	$(k \times n)$ public generator matrix
$\mathbf{H}$	Parity-check matrix
H_i	Host i
ID_A	User A's identity
j_λ	Error location
$\mathbf{k}$	External key vector
$\mathbf{K}$	Key-bit stream
k	Number of information bits in a block code
K_{AB}	Common key between users A and B
K_F	File key
K_{ij}	Common key between users i and j
$k(\mathrm{D})$	Key input in polynomial form
K_M	Master key
K_{MH}	Host master key
K_{MHi}	Variant of host master key
K^*_{MH}	Old host master key
K^*_{MHi}	Variant of old host master key
K_{Mi}	Variant of master key
K_{MT}	Terminal master key
K_{MTi}	i's terminal master key
K_N	Secondary key
K_{NFij}	Secondary file key from node i to node j
$\mathbf{K}_p$	Trapdoor knapsack vector
K'_{PA}	A's public key
K'_p	Superincreasing integer knapsack vector
K_S	Secret key
$K_s^k,\ 0 \le k \le j$	Iterative secret key generation

K_{SC}	Secondary communication key
K_{SCij}	Secondary communication key from domain i to domain j
K_{SF}	Secondary file key
$\mathbf{L}_1$	Left-half output after round one, $\mathbf{L}_1 = \mathbf{R}_0$
$\mathbf{M}_i^j$	A 64 × 64 matrix for investigation of data intersymbol dependence $\mathbf{M}_i^j = \begin{bmatrix} \mathbf{M}_{L_i}^{L_j} & \mathbf{M}_{R_i}^{L_j} \\ \mathbf{M}_{L_i}^{R_j} & \mathbf{M}_{R_i}^{R_j} \end{bmatrix}$ for $1 \le i \le 15, \quad 1 \le j \le 16$
m,w	Two large secret integers with gcd $(w,m) = 1$
$\mathbf{m} = (m_0, m_1, \ldots, m_{k-1})$	A k-bit message
$\mathbf{M}_v$	Symmetrical matrix
$\mathbf{M}$	Syndrome component matrix
$m(x)$	Minimal polynomial
n	Code length of a block code
$\mathbf{N}_i$	A 64 × 56 matrix for investigation of key intersymbol dependence $\mathbf{N}_i = \begin{bmatrix} \mathbf{N}_i^L \\ \mathbf{N}_i^R \end{bmatrix}$ for $1 \le i \le 16$
$\mathbf{N}_v$	A matrix composed by deleting the first row and first column of $\mathbf{M}_v$
$\mathbf{P}$	A random $(n \times n)$ permutation matrix
P	Prover
p,q	Two large primes
$P(B_1)$	Permutation function of B_1
$p(x)$	Irreducible primitive polynomial
$q(x)$	Quotient polynomial
$\mathbf{Q}_v$	Matrix of syndrome

r	Composite integer, $r = pq$
r	Remainder or residue
$\mathbf{r}$	Received word
$r(x)$	Received polynomial
$\mathbf{R}_1$	Right-half output after round one, $\mathbf{R}_1 = P(\mathbf{B}_1) + \mathbf{L}_0$
RN_i	Pseudorandom number
RQ_i	i's request
$\mathbf{s}$	Syndrome of the code
S_i	S-boxes
S_i^j	Symbol for substitution operations on S-boxes
$S(x)$	Register contents of LFSR or seed polynomial
$s(x)$	Syndrome polynomial
$\mathbf{s}$	Initial state vector
$\mathbf{S}$	A random $(k \times k)$ non-singular matrix in McEliece scheme
s_k	Syndrome component
t	Error correcting capability
$\mathbf{T}$	Tap generating matrix or characteristic matrix
T(D)	Transfer function of encoding circuit
$\mathbf{U}$	Final key-bit stream of DES
$\mathbf{u}$	Matrix composed of vector u_i corresponding to state bit $s_i = 1$
$u(t)$	Deciphered output as a function of t
v	Multiplicative inverse of w modulo m, i.e. $v = w^{-1}$
V	Verifier

X	Plaintext or message; Subliminal message
$x(t)$	Plaintext as a function of t
Y	Ciphertext or cryptogram
Y'	Transformed ciphertext, $Y' \equiv w^{-1} Y \pmod{m}$
$y(t)$	Ciphertext as a function of t
Y_k, e_{j_k}	Error value
Z	Encoded keystream, the f-output vector
$Z(D)$	Output keystream in polynomial form
Z_k, x^{j_k}	Error-location number
Z^*_n	Reduced residue system $\{1, 2, \ldots, n-1\}$ (mod n)
α	Root of primitive polynomial
α	Primitive element of GF (2^m)
$\alpha^{j_\lambda}, \beta_\lambda$	Error-location numbers
β	Primitive element of GF (q)
$\gamma(x)$	Remainder polynomial
$\mathbf{\Gamma}_i$	Key-dependent function $\mathbf{\Gamma}_i = E(\mathbf{R}_0) + \mathbf{K}_j$ which are arguments to S-boxes S_1 through S_8
$\{\mu_j\}$	Dual basis
$\lvert\rho_v\rvert$	Vandermonde determinant
$\sigma(x)$	Error-locator polynomial
σ_k	Coefficients of error-locator polynomial
$\sigma^{(n)}(x)$	Minimal solution polynomial at the nth step of iteration
$\phi(n)$	Euler's totient function
$\Phi(x)$	Error-locator polynomial in the frequency domain

$\Omega(x)$	Error-evaluator polynomial
BFM	Blum, Feldman, and Micali
CF	Cryptographic facility
CKDF	Centrailized key distribution facility
DC	Data compression
DCPH	Decipher data
DFT	Discrete Fourier transform
DMP	De Sautis, Micali, and Persiano
DSEC	Double-symbol error correction
ECPH	Encipher data
EFT	Electronic funds transfer
EID	Extended identity
EM	Electronic mail
EMK	Encipher under master key
FEAL	Fast Data Encipherment Algorithm
FS	Fiat-Shamir
GMR	Goldwasser, Micali, and Rackoff
GMW	Goldwasser, Micali, and Wigderson
IP	Interactive proof
IP	Initial permutation
KD	Key directory
KDC	Key distribution center
KPS	Key predistribution system
LCM	Least common multiple
NIZK	Noninteractive zero knowledge
OSS	Ong, Schnorr, and Shamir
PIN	Personal Identification Number
RFMK	Reencipher from master key
RSA	Rivest, Shamir and Adleman
RTMK	Reencipher to master key
SMK	Set master key

TCF	Terminal's cryptographic facility
ZKIP	Zero-knowledge interactive proofs
$a \mid b$	a divides b
$a \nmid b$	a cannot divide b
(a/p)	Legendre symbol
$(b/p) = \prod_{i=1}^{s} (b/p_i)$	Jacobi symbol
$(\mathbf{C}_0, \mathbf{D}_0)$	Two 28-bit initial key contents
$(\mathbf{C}_i, \mathbf{D}_i)$	Concatenated key blocks $(\mathbf{C}_1, \mathbf{D}_1)$, $(\mathbf{C}_2, \mathbf{D}_2)$, . . ., $(\mathbf{C}_{16}, \mathbf{D}_{16})$
DC(X)	Data digest of the message X
gcd(a,p)	Greatest common divisor of a and p
$\gcd(n_i, n_j) = 1$ for $i \neq j$	The moduli are pairwise coprime
GCD[$a(x)$, $b(x)$]	Great common divisor of two polynomials $a(x)$ and $b(x)$
GF(2^m)	Galois field of 2^m binary symbols
$(\mathbf{L}_0, \mathbf{R}_0)$	Two 32-bit initial blocks of plaintext after the initial permutation
SG(**X**)	Signature of the message plaintext **X**
Tr(β)	Trace for an element β in GF(p^m)
$\equiv$	Symbol for congruence
$\not\equiv$	Not congruence to

Chapter

1

Introduction

There have been widespread applications of data storage and transmission in recent times. Such data teleprocessing runs the risk of making sensitive or valuable information vulnerable to unauthorized access while in storage and transmission. Until the late 1970s, cryptographic technology was exclusively used for military and diplomatic purposes. But of late business sectors and private individuals have recognized the need to protect valuable information in computer communication networks against unauthorized interception, and the use of some types of cryptosystems. Cryptography is the study of cryptosystems by which privacy and authentication of data can be ensured.

In this chapter, we shall discuss cryptographic cipher systems, operation techniques, symmetric and asymmetric algorithms, and applications of cryptography together with communication security and file security problems.

1.1 FUNDAMENTAL CONCEPT OF CRYPTOSYSTEMS

Cryptosystems are used to ensure privacy and authentication of data in computer-communication systems. An unprotected message is called a plaintext. The process by which message plaintext is transformed into ciphertext (or cryptogram) of an unintelligible form is called encryption or encipherment. A deciphering algorithm is used for decryption or decipherment in order to restore the original plaintext. The ciphering facilities for conversion of plaintext into ciphertext and vice versa comprise what is known as a cryptographic system or simply cryptosystem. In a cryptosystem, a set of parameters that selects a specific ciphering transformation is called a key set. Both encryption and decryption are controlled by a cryptographic key or keys. In general, the enciphering and deciphering keys need not be identical, depending on what kinds of cryptographic systems are used. In symmetric cryptosystems (or one-key ciphers), the enciphering and deciphering keys are in principle identical, but one also can be derived from the other. These keys must be kept secret. This is the reason why a symmetric cryptosystem is often called a secret-key ciphersystem. The number of keys generally required are $\binom{n}{2} = n\,(n-1)/2$ keys for n users. For example, the Data Encryption Standard (DES) and rotor ciphers belong to symmetric ciphersystems. In asymmetric ciphersystems (two-key or public-key cryptosystems), two different keys are used. One key used for enciphering can be made public, while the other used for deciphering is kept secret. All kinds of public-key cryptosystems (for example, the Merkle-Hellman scheme, RSA scheme, ElGamal scheme, etc) are classified as asymmetric ciphers.

Eavesdropping (or wiretapping) means the interception of information data by an unauthorized individual or a third party monitoring a communication channel. If the opponent listens to or records information being transmitted, it is called a passive attack; whereas if the opponent modifies transmitted information or injects false data into the communication channel it is called an active attack. Any attempt by an eavesdropper to decrypt a ciphertext (i.e. to break a cipher) without knowledge of the key is called cryptanalysis. A breakable cipher is one for which it is possible to determine the plaintext or key or both from the ciphertext using finite computational resources. Cryptanalysis is the science of breaking ciphers, and cryptology is the science of cryptography and cryptanalysis.

Figure 1.1 illustrates the flow of information plaintext in a general cryptosystem. The enciphering and deciphering operations are generally described by

$$Y = E_{K_E}(X) \qquad \text{(Encryption)}$$

$$X = D_{K_D}(Y) \qquad \text{(Decryption)}$$

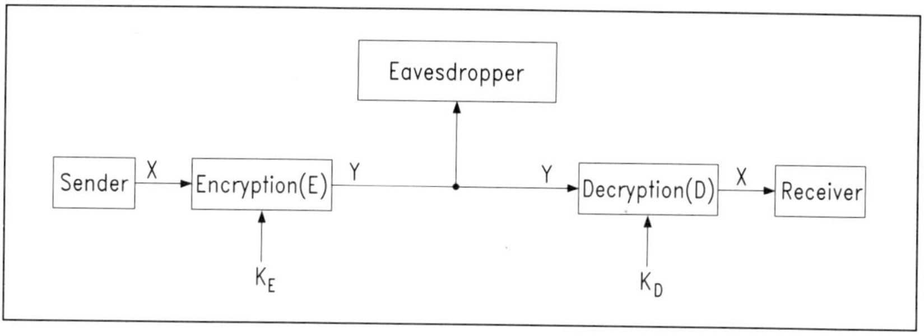

Fig. 1.1 General cryptosystems

where X denotes message plaintext, Y represents ciphertext (cryptogram), and K_E and K_D stand for enciphering and deciphering keys.

1.2 HISTORICAL REVIEW OF CLASSICAL CIPHERS

There are three important types of ciphers, namely, transposition, substitution, and product ciphers. Since transposition or substitution ciphers need the simplest encryption technique, they are of little use nowadays, but are important components of more complex product ciphers. First, we will introduce various classical ciphers which were formerly used, and then discuss modern cryptosystems currently in use.

1.2.1 Transposition Ciphers

Transposition ciphers are block ciphers that change the positions of characters or bits of message plaintext. The oldest known transposition cipher is the Scytale cipher used by the ancient Greeks as early as 400 B.C. One typical transposition cipher belonging to this category is the depth-k cipher whose plaintext pattern is rearranged in k-row decomposition to conceal the message. Consider the encryption process of this particular cipher. If the message plaintext "CRYPTOGRAPHY AND DATA SECURITY" is enciphered into the cryptogram by using depth-3 row decomposition, it may be shown as follows:

C				T				A				A				A				E				I		
	R		P		O		R		P		Y		N		D		T		S		C		R		T	
		Y				G				H				D				A				U				Y

Since depth-3 for $k = 3$ becomes a cryptographic key, the following ciphertext results from row-by-row arrangement.

C T A A A E I R P O R P Y N D T S C R T Y G H D A U Y

Thus, transposition ciphers consist of rearrangements of the positions of plaintext letters rather than those of the alphabet. The key used in transforming the plaintext can be recovered from the cryptogram alone.

1.2.2 Substitution Ciphers

There are four types of substitution ciphers, namely, monoalphabetic, homophonic, polyalphabetic, and polygram.

A simple substitution cipher is called monoalphabetic because there is a one-to-one correspondence between a character and its substitute. In other words, a monoalphabetic cipher is one which replaces a character in the plaintext by another character. Thus, a simple one-to-one mapping from plaintext to ciphertext character is used to encipher an entire message. There are $26! = 4 \times 10^{26}$ different monoalphabetic ciphers corresponding to the permutations of the English alphabet. The key is a permuted alphabet. As is well known, simple substitution ciphers involving small letters of the English alphabet, or the ASCII code offer little protection to the given plaintext.

Substitution ciphertext may be deciphered by making use of frequency tables of characters, which help identification of plaintext characters corresponding to the ones in the cryptogram. Thus, simple substitution ciphers define that each letter in the English alphabet shifts forward by k positions, where k is the key to the cipher. As an example, the so-called Caesar cipher is a fixed-key monoalphabetic substitution cipher with the ith letter replaced by the $(i + k)$th letter modulo 26. Julius Caesar used it with $k = 3$.

The following example illustrates Caesar's encryption:

Plaintext : CRYPTOGRAPHY AND DATA SECURITY

Key : Use $k = 3$ with 26 letters of the English alphabet

Ciphertext : FUBSWRJUDSKB DQG GDWD VHFXULWB

Besides the Caesar cipher, there are more complex transformations of the plaintext alphabet.

Ciphers based on multiplication involve the multiplication of each character by a key k such that

$$f(x) \equiv kx \pmod{n}, \quad \gcd(k, n) = 1 \qquad \text{(relatively prime)}$$

Ciphers based on shifting and multiplication are given an affine transformation such that

$$f(x) \equiv k_1 x + k_0 \pmod{n}$$

where k_0 is a constant and gcd $(k_1, n) = 1$ [3].

Ciphers obtained with polynomial transformations of degree t, such as shown in the following, are called higher-order transformations.

$$f(x) \equiv k_0 + k_1x + k_2x^2 + \cdots + k_{t-1}x^{t-1} + k_tx^t \pmod n$$

Caesar ciphers are polynomial transformations of degree 0; while affine transformations are of degree 1.

A homophonic substitution cipher maps each character x of the plaintext alphabet into a set of ciphertext elements $f(x)$ called homophones. Thus, the mapping f from plaintext to ciphertext is one-to-many. The Beale cipher (1880s) is an example of a homophonic cipher. Such ciphers are far more difficult to solve than simple substitution ciphers. However, a homophonic cipher may be broken if the statistical properties of the plaintext are apparent in the ciphertext.

Polyalphabetic substitution ciphers are multiple-substitution ciphers involving the use of different keys. The development of polyalphabetic ciphers began with Leon Alberti in 1568 who invented a cipher disk that defined multiple substitutions. Most polyalphabetic ciphers are periodic substitution ciphers based on a period p. For instance, if a message plaintext is

$$X = x_1 x_2 \cdots x_p x_{p+1} \cdots x_{2p} \cdots$$

then the ciphertext by encryption becomes

$$E_k(X) = f_1(x_1) f_2(x_2) \cdots f_p(x_p) f_{p+1}(x_{p+1}) \cdots f_{2p}(x_{2p}) \cdots$$

where x_i denotes plaintext letters. For $p = 1$, the cipher is monoalphabetic and equivalent to simple substitution.

A popular form of a periodic substitution cipher based on shifted alphabets is the Vigenère cipher invented by French cryptologist Blaise de Vigenère in the 16th Century.

Let the key K be specified by a sequence as

$$K = k_1k_2 \cdots k_p$$

where k_i for $1 \le i \le p$ represents the amount of shift in the ith alphabet. Then the ciphertext character $y_i(x)$ becomes

$$y_i(x) \equiv x + k_i \pmod n$$

The Beaufort cipher, named after the English admiral Sir Francis Beaufort, is similar to the Vigenère cipher and is based on the formula

$$y_i(x) \equiv k_i - x \pmod n$$

The variant Beaufort cipher uses the substitution

$$y_i(x) \equiv x - k_i \pmod{n}$$

which shows really the inverse of the Vigenère cipher. Since $(x - k_i) \bmod n \equiv (x + (n - k_i)) \bmod n$, the variant Beaufort cipher is equivalent to a Vigenère cipher with the key character $(n - k_i)$.

Letter-frequency analysis alone is not sufficient to meet the minimum requirement for breaking polyalphabetic ciphers. The Kasiski method, introduced in 1863 by a Prussian officer, Friedrich W. Kasiski, analyzes repetitions in the ciphertext to determine the exact period. Hence, using this method, the period can be found first and then a set of monoalphabetic ciphers may be solved.

In an effort to remove the weaknesses of periodic polyalphabetic ciphers, cryptologists turned to running key ciphers which are aperiodic polyalphabetics. It is generally accepted that the security of a substitution cipher increases with key length. A running-key cipher, designed for complete concealment of information, has a key sequence as long as the message plaintext, with a view to foiling a Kasiski attack. Using running key ciphers, the message and key letters are added modulo 26 and a key as long as the message is used. Therefore, one may expect a running key cipher to be unbreakable. However this is not always true. A Kasiski solution is no longer possible due to the aperiodic selection of the 26 letters of the alphabet used. But Bazeries solved this problem in the late 1890s. If the key has a redundancy, the cipher may be broken using Friedman's method (1918). This method searches for an accidental match between the plaintext and key and breaks the running-key cipher by exploiting the redundancy and other statistical properties of the English language.

The Hagelin machine (M–209) and all rotor ciphers are polyalphabetic substitution ciphers generating a stream with a long period. The Hagelin C–48 machine was widely used as an American field cipher during World War II, under its military designation M–209. Kahn gives a complete mechanical description of this machine in his highly readable book [6]. The M–209 combines the plaintext, character by character, with the pseudorandom keystream to produce the ciphertext in much the same manner as Vigenère or running key ciphers. The plaintext, the keystream, and the ciphertext are all written in a 26-character alphabet. In fact, the plaintext X is subtracted from the keystream K modulo 26, to make the following encryption.

$$Y \equiv K - X \pmod{26}$$

The rotor ciphers were the most important cryptographic devices used in World War II, and remained dominant at least until the late 1950s. The American Sigaba (M–134), the British Typex, the German Enigma, and the Japanese Purple, were all rotor ciphers, and undoubtedly many are still in use today. The Hagelin and all rotor machines are polyalphabetic ciphers generating a stream with a large period. Since the sequences generated by the above machines are not random, cryptanalysis is possible, and some were successfully broken during World War II.

Another important substitution cipher is the one-time pad in which the key is a random sequence of characters and is not repeated. One-time pads are unbreakable because there is not enough information in the ciphertext to determine the message or the key uniquely. For a one-time pad the key required grows linearly with message length, which limits their use for practical purposes. The one-time pad was first used in the Vernam cipher, designed by Gilbert Vernam in 1917, in which the key bits were added modulo 2 to plaintext bits on a bit-by-bit basis. If $X = x_1 x_2 x_3 \cdots$ denotes a plaintext-bit stream and $K = k_1 k_2 k_3 \cdots$ a key-bit stream, then the Vernam cipher produces a ciphertext-bit stream $Y = E_k(X) = y_1 y_2 y_3 \cdots$ where $y_i \equiv (x_i + k_i) \bmod 2$ for $i = 1, 2, 3, \cdots$. The Vernam cipher can be efficiently implemented by introducing the Exclusive-OR of each pair of plaintext-key bits such that $y_i = x_i \oplus k_i$. One application of such mechanisms is a stream cipher which uses a linear feedback shift register (LFSR) as a key-bit generator.

Up to this point, all substitution ciphers encipher a single character of plaintext at a time. But in polygram ciphers, several characters are enciphered at the same time using one key. The Playfair cipher is a 2–gram substitution cipher, whereas the Hill cipher is a more general N–gram substitution cipher employing linear transformations. The Playfair cipher named after the English scientist Lyon Playfair, but actually invented by Charles Wheatstone in 1854, was used by the British during World War I [6]. The Hill cipher (1929) performs a linear transformation on ν plaintext characters to obtain ν ciphertext characters.

1.2.3 Classical Product Ciphers

A product cipher is a composition of two or more ciphers such that the ciphertext space of one cipher becomes the message plaintext space of the next. The combination of ciphers, called cascaded superencipherment, is done in such a manner that the final product is superior to either of its components. In fact, the principle of product ciphers is evident in all rotor ciphers which use several steps of encryption. A product cipher involves the steps of both substitution and transposition. An early product cipher is the German ADFGVS cipher used in World War I. It used a table having six rows and six columns labelled with letters A, D, F, G, V, X as illustrated in Table 1.1. The ADFGVX table contained 26 letters (A, B, C, ···, Z) and 10 digits (0, 1, 2, ···, 9) inserted in a random order.

Consider an example of the ADFGVX product cipher. Let the plaintext be CRYPTOGRAPHY and the key be SECURITY. Encryption is accomplished by replacing each plaintext letter by a pair of letters from the top row and the leftmost column of ADFGVX in Table 1.1. The intermediate text is then obtained as DG AG GF FG XV VD FV AG GV FG VG GF. The intermediate text is arranged in transposition rectangle as shown below.

Table 1.1 The ADFGVX Table

Row / Column	A	D	F	G	V	X
A	K	Z	W	R	1	F
D	9	B	6	C	L	5
F	Q	7	J	P	G	X
G	E	V	Y	3	A	N
V	8	O	D	H	0	2
X	U	4	1	S	T	M

D	G	A	G	G	F	F	G
X	V	V	D	F	V	A	G
G	V	F	G	V	G	G	F

Key :	S	E	C	U	R	I	T	Y
Sorted numerical key :	5	2	1	7	4	3	6	8

The sorted alphabetical order for the key SECURITY becomes CEIRSTUY which is equivalent to the numerical order 1, 2, 3, 4, 5, 6, 7, 8. Writing column-by-column according to the numerical key order, we obtain the ciphertext as AVF GVV FVG GFV DXG FAG GDG GGF.

Although the ADFGVX product cipher was designed for increasing cryptographic strength, this cipher is actually a weak algorithm, because substitution and transposition are used only once and the substitution is not under control of a key. Repetition of the substitution and permutation process several times increases cryptographic strength. The Data Encryption Standard (DES) is a strong modern product cipher. Its algorithm consists of 16 alternate rounds of key-controlled substitution and fixed permutation. Modern product ciphers will be discussed in detail in Section 1.4.

1.3 CRYPTANALYTIC ATTACKS AND CRYPTOSYSTEMS SECURITY

A cipher may be broken if it is possible to determine the plaintext or key from the intercepted ciphertext, or to determine the key from plaintext-ciphertext pairs. Therefore, the design of a cryptosystem is determined by its security against the types of threat to which it may be subjected. Of course, it is impossible to state absolutely that a cryptographic algorithm is free from all possible attacks. There are three types of attack for breaking a cipher. These basic methods of attack are a ciphertext-only attack, a known plaintext attack, and chosen text attack.

A ciphertext-only attack is a cryptanalytic attack in which the cryptanalyst possesses only ciphertext. The cryptanalyst has nothing available to him but the intercepted information, knowledge of the general encryption system, certain probable words and statistical properties of the language in use. The decryption has to be done based on probabilities, characteristics of the available ciphertext, plus publicly available knowledge. Such an attack is the weakest threat to which a system can be subjected.

A known plaintext attack is a cryptanalytic attack in which the cryptanalyst possesses a substantial amount of plaintext and corresponding ciphertext. The cryptanalyst can either approximate or guess the plaintext because of the redundancy and statistics of the plaintext language or the highly structured formats of the plaintext in other applications. All ciphers should be designed to resist this type of attack because it is thought to occur often in practice.

In the chosen text attack, it is assumed that the cryptanalyst can obtain either the plaintext or the ciphertext of his choice. Therefore, this type of attack is difficult to achieve in practice, but can be approximated. A chosen plaintext attack is a cryptanalytic attack in which the cryptanalyst can submit an unlimited number of plaintext messages of his own choosing and examine the resulting cryptograms. The chosen plaintext attack is powerful and is considered the most favorable to the cryptanalyst. In a chosen ciphertext attack, the encryption algorithm and ciphertext may be available to the cryptanalyst. The cryptanalyst can run the encryption algorithm on massive amounts of plaintext to determine one plaintext message. The purpose of a chosen ciphertext attack is to deduce the encryption key in order to decipher future messages by applying the decryption key to intercepted ciphertext.

If the cipher resists all attacks, it can be considered secure in practice. In most cases, it is not possible to prove that a cipher is secure. Ciphers are either unconditionally or computationally secure. A cryptosystem is called unconditionally secure if the ciphertext does not contain sufficient information for the cryptanalyst to solve it, no matter how much computing power is available. The one-time pad is the only known unconditionally secure cipher which requires keys as long as the messages. This key is never reused. Since an extremely large keyspace is required for perfect secrecy, practical cipher design is concerned with techniques to expand smaller keys into seemingly large keys to approximate the one-time pad.

A cryptosystem is said to be computationally secure when the cryptanalyst's task is made computationally infeasible. In other words, a computationally secure cipher is one which requires an infeasible amount of computing resources to break. Even if a successful cryptanalysis is achieved with a finite amount of computation, the computing resources required for this task may yet be beyond cryptanalytic control. The theory of computational complexity is still inadequate to demonstrate the computational infeasibility of any cipher system. As an alternative, cipher security is established on the basis of certification methods which involve subjecting the cipher to various cryptanalytic attacks under circumstances considered most favourable to the cryptanalyst. The cryptosystem is then certified to be secure from the specific type of attack. In fact, the cryptanalyst's attempts to break ciphers and computational resources available are crucial factors in the determination of cipher security.

1.4 MODERN CRYPTOSYSTEMS

We shall now introduce the various modern cryptosystems in use. The central issue of cryptanalysis is to determine to what extent a secure cipher system is immune against all kinds of attack. Classical ciphers are of little use today owing to the simplest encryption technique, but are important components in more complex product ciphers. Since the 1970s, research in cryptology has shifted dramatically from the study of classical ciphers to the development of modern cryptosystems.

1.4.1 Data Encryption Standard (DES)

By the late 1960s, threats to communication and computer data had caused much anxiety in the private sector. With the advent of VLSI technology, any complex crypto-algorithm could be implemented on a single chip. Therefore, strong product ciphers were developed and used between 1968 and 1976. The DES algorithm based on the Lucifer block cipher designed by Horst Feistel was developed at IBM under the leadership of W.H. Tuchman in 1972. This algorithm, approved by the National Bureau of Standard (NBS) after assessment by the National Security Agency (NSA), was adopted as a Federal Standard in 1977.

The DES, which is a block cipher, is the most widely known encryption algorithm. In block encryption, the plaintext is divided into blocks of fixed length which are then enciphered using the same key. The DES is the algorithm with which a 64-bit block of plaintext is enciphered into a 64-bit ciphertext under the control of a 56-bit internal key. The iterated process consists of 16 rounds of encipherment, while the deciphering process is exactly the same as the process of encryption except that the keys are used in reverse order. The central technique governing DES implementation involves the design of DES permutation (P-box), substitutions (S-boxes), and key schedules.

The plaintext block X is first transposed under an initial permutation (IP), giving $X_0 = \mathrm{IP}(X) = (L_0, R_0)$. After passing through 16 rounds of substitution and transposition, it is transposed under the inverse permutation (IP^{-1}) to yield the ciphertext Y. If $X_i = (L_i, R_i)$, where L_i and R_i are 32-bit sub-blocks, denotes the result of the ith round iteration, then it gives $L_i = R_{i-1}$ and $R_i = L_{i-1} + f(R_{i-1}, K_i)$. But care should be taken at the last 16th round to ensure that the left and right halves are not exchanged, i.e., the concatenated block (R_{16}, L_{16}) becomes the preoutput to the final permutation IP^{-1}. In practice, many more than five rounds are used to provide an adequate level of security.

The key schedule begins with an initial permutation which selects 56 bits out of the 64-bit external key, by stripping off the 8-parity bits. These 56 key bits are loaded into two 28-bit shift registers and are subsequently shifted one or two positions to the left according to the shift schedule for encipherment. Since a 56-bit key selects one of the 2^{56} possible transformations, the key space contains 2^{56} different keys.

S-box functions must be designed for enhancement of cryptographic strength and for easy incorporation onto a single chip. With such S-boxes, a total of $(2^{64})!$ different transformations from plaintext to ciphertext are possible. In fact, the design of S-box structure becomes an important subject of study for establishing a strong DES. Since a single huge S-box is impossible to construct, S-box substitutions in DES are divided into several small S-boxes. Each S-box has 6-bit input and 4-bit output. Implementing S-box design using the minimum number of logic circuits has to be the subject of research for increasing cryptographic strength and reducing complexity.

Each bit of the ciphertext produced by DES is a complex function for all plaintext bits and all key bits. The dependence of each ciphertext-bit on all bits of the plaintext as well as key is called intersymbol dependence. In a well-designed cipher system, an output bit depends on more and more input bits as the number of rounds increases so that rapid intersymbol dependence can be achieved. This measure of dependency plays an important role in the enhancement of cryptographic strength [7].

The Data Encryption Standard, which is classified as a block cipher algorithm, is currently the only certified encryption standard. It has been widely used in the area of banking and electronic funds transfer (EFT).

1.4.2 Stream Cipher Systems

There are two types of stream ciphers—one for which the key-bit stream is independent of the plaintext and the other for which the key-bit stream is a function of either the plaintext or ciphertext. The former is called a synchronous cipher and the latter is often known as a self-synchronizing cipher. The key-bit stream, which is a coded sequence generated from an m-stage shift register with linear feedback, is modulo-2 added to the plaintext to produce the ciphertext. Therefore, stream ciphers operate on a bit-by-bit basis, combining the plaintext with a key stream.

A cryptosystem which can resist any cryptanalytic attack, no matter how much computation is allowed, is said to be unconditionally secure. The one-time pad is the only unconditionally secure cipher in use. One of the most remarkable ciphers is the one-time pad in which the ciphertext is the bit-by-bit modulo-2 sum of the plaintext and a nonrepeating keystream of the same length. However, the one-time pad is impractical for most applications because of the large size of the nonrepeating key.

The key-bit stream in a synchronous stream cipher is generated independently of the plaintext. The loss of a bit in ciphertext causes loss of synchronization and all ciphertext following the loss is decrypted incorrectly. We also know that synchronous stream ciphers can be broken when the key-bit stream is repeated periodically. For this reason, synchronous stream ciphers have limited applicability to file and database encryption. However, synchronous stream ciphers protect the ciphertext to some extent against search by opponents, because identical blocks in the plaintext are enciphered in different parts of the keystream. They also protect the system against injection of false ciphertext, replay, and ciphertext deletion, because insertion or deletion in ciphertext causes loss of synchronization. Synchronous stream ciphers have an advantage in that there is no error propagation. In fact, a transmission error affecting one bit will not affect subsequent bits. But this fact may be a disadvantage because it is easier for an opponent to modify a single bit of ciphertext rather than a block of bits. The key-autokey cipher is a typical synchronous stream cipher.

Self-synchronizing stream cipher systems are another class of stream ciphers and are categorized as ciphertext autokey ciphers and plaintext autokey ciphers. A ciphertext autokey cipher is one in which the key is derived from the ciphertext and is called a self-synchronizing stream cipher with ciphertext feedback. Since each key bit is computed from the preceding ciphertext bit, it is functionally dependent on all preceding bits in the plaintext plus the priming key. This makes cryptanalysis more difficult because the statistical properties of the plaintext are diffused across the ciphertext. A plaintext autokey cipher is one in which the key is derived from the plaintext to be enciphered. However, in plaintext autokey cipher system, an erroneous ciphertext block causes indefinite error propagation in the deciphered plaintext blocks.

As running-key generators in stream ciphers, PN-sequences generated by LFSRs with a nonlinear combining function have been studied by several cryptologists for cryptographic applications. PN-sequences are well known in respect of their statistical properties and linear complexity. These properties are largely governed by the number of memory cells and the feedback connections in the shift register. However, a simple LFSR device has low linear complexity because it can be easily analyzed. Therefore, many cryptologists have attempted to find nonlinear combination techniques of LFSR sequences capable of producing an output sequence with good pseudorandom properties as well as high linear complexity. The purpose of nonlinear combination is to produce an equivalent system that withstands any cryptanalytic attack.

1.4.3 Public-key Cryptosystems

The invention of public-key cryptosystems in the late 1970s considerably altered the course of cryptologic research. A solution to the key-distribution problem was suggested by Diffie and Hellman in 1976. Since then, asymmetric cryptosystems using two different keys have been proposed. One key used for enciphering can be made public, while the other meant for deciphering is kept secret. The two keys are generated in such a manner that it is computationally infeasible to deduce the secret key from the public key. The RSA public-key cryptosystem was invented by Rivest, Shamir, and Adleman in 1978, and McEliece proposed the algebraic codes cryptosystem in 1978.

Public-key cryptosystems generally use a public key for encryption and a secret key for decryption. If user A wants to communicate with user B, A can use B's public key from a public directory to encipher the plaintext. Only B can decipher the ciphertext because he alone possesses the secret deciphering key.

A cryptographic system is said to be secure if and only if computing logarithms over GF (p) is infeasible. The public key distribution algorithm proposed by Diffie and Hellman appears to be difficult for computing discrete logarithms over GF (p) with p elements [4].

Consider a pair of inverse functions over a finite field GF (p) such that

$$Y \equiv \alpha^{X} \pmod{p}$$

$$X \equiv \log_{\alpha} Y \pmod{p}$$

where $1 \leq X, Y \leq p-1, p$ is a prime, and α is a primitive element of GF (p). The calculation of Y from X is easy and requires O (log p) operations, whereas the computation of X from Y is more difficult and requires approximately $O(\exp\sqrt{\ln p \ln(\ln p)})$ operations. Hence, in the Diffie-Hellman key exchange protocol, security is based on the difficulty of taking discrete logarithms which reverse the process of exponentiations in the finite field GF (p).

To derive a common key between two users i and j, user i selects a secret key X_i from the set of integers $\{1, 2, \cdots, p-1\}$ and places a public key $Y_i \equiv \alpha^{X_i} \pmod{p}$ in a public directory. Then, two users can communicate with each other by computing their common key K_{ij}. User i computes K_{ij} as follows:

$$\begin{aligned} K_{ij} &\equiv Y_j^{X_i} && \pmod{p} \\ &\equiv \left(\alpha^{X_j}\right)^{X_i} && \pmod{p} \\ &\equiv \alpha^{X_j X_i} && \pmod{p} \end{aligned}$$

Similarly, user j computes

$$\begin{aligned} K_{ji} &\equiv Y_i^{X_j} && \pmod{p} \\ &\equiv \alpha^{X_i X_j} && \pmod{p} \end{aligned}$$

To find the common key K_{ij}, a cryptanalyst must compute

$$K_{ij} \equiv (Y_i)^{\log_{\alpha} Y_j} \pmod{p}$$

which can be made to be computationally infeasible if p contains 10^3 bits.

Shortly after Diffie and Hellman introduced the idea of a public-key distribution system, Rivest, Shamir and Adleman (RSA) proposed the most promising public-key cryptosystem. The RSA algorithm employs the discrete logarithm and factorization of the product of two large primes. In this scheme, either the public key e or secret key d is an integer selected at random. Two large primes p and q are generated and the sender calculates their product $n = pq$. Then the sender finds integers e and d such that

$$e \cdot d \equiv 1 \mod \phi(n)$$

where $\phi(n) = (p - 1)(q - 1)$ is called Euler's totient function, and $\gcd(\phi(n), e) = 1$. Thus, the public key (n, e) can be placed in a public directory, whereas the secret key d must be kept privately. A message plaintext is encrypted as

$$Y \equiv X^e \pmod{n}$$

where $e = K_p$ is the public key and is relatively prime to $\phi(n)$. If a cryptanalyst can factor a composite n, then the cryptogram can be deciphered. For decryption, the secret key d is used to restore the message plaintext X such that

$$X \equiv Y^d \pmod{n}$$

Integer factorization has advanced considerably in the last decade and the largest hard integer up to almost 90 decimal integers in length has been factored. Only a machine capable of factoring 150-digit integers, can break the RSA cryptosystem. Several integer-factoring algorithms have been proposed by Lenstra and Lenstra (1989), Pomerance (1987), and Gordon (1985). Even though the original RSA cryptosystem is virtually immune to all attacks, that is not true for all variants of it. Kravity and Reed (1982) have proposed using an irreducible polynomial over GF(2) in place of the primes p and q. That is, the public modulus is the polynomial $r(z) = p(z)q(z)$ which indicates the product of polynomials of degree t and s, and the key exponent $e = K_p$ is chosen to be relatively prime to $(2^t - 1)(2^s - 1)$. This system can be broken by factoring $r(z)$. The weaknesses of this system have been extensively studied by Delsart and Piret (1982) and by Gait (1982). The RSA scheme is only a system used for secrecy and authentication.

In 1978, Merkle and Hellman proposed an M-H public key cryptosystem based on the trapdoor knapsack problem. A simple knapsack vector $K_p' = (k_1', k_2', \cdots k_n')$ where k_i' for $1 \le i \le n$ are integers, is a superincreasing vector. The designer chooses two large secret integers m and w such that $m > w$ and $\gcd(m, w) = 1$. Moreover, m must be an integer larger than $\sum k_i'$, i.e. $m > \sum k_i'$ for $1 \le i \le n$. Now, the trapdoor knapsack vector K_p is calculated from the simple knapsack vector k_p' via v which is the multiplicative inverse of w modulo m such that $vw \equiv 1 \pmod{m}$, where $v = w^{-1}$. Thus, a trapdoor knapsack K_p is generated by multiplying each component of a simple knapsack vector K_p' by w such that

$$k_i \equiv wk_i' \pmod{m}, \qquad 1 \le i \le m$$

or

$$K_p \equiv wK_p' \pmod{m}$$

Thus, a trapdoor knapsack vector K_p is published by the user as his public key, whereas the parameters $v \equiv w^{-1}$ and m, and a knapsack vector K_p' are kept as his secret keys.

It was supposed until 1982 that the public-key algorithms for solving the knapsack problem are of exponential computational complexity because the knapsack problem is NP-complete. Particularly the iterated Merkle-Hellman scheme was claimed to be secure. However, the basic Merkle-Hellman additive knapsack system was shown by Shamir (1982) to be easy to crack. Subsequently, Adleman (1983) proposed attacks on the iterated Merkle-Hellman cryptosystem by cracking the enciphering key obtained using the Graham-Shamir knapsack, but Adleman's attack on the multiple iterated knapsack did not really succeed. Brickell, Lagarias, and Odlyzko (1984) have evaluated the Adleman attacks on the multiple iterated knapsack system. In addition, Desmedt, Vandewalle, and Govaerts (1982, 1984) claimed that the iterated Merkle-Hellman systems are insecure, since an enciphering key can be cracked. A multiple-iterated knapsack scheme is the cryptosystem relying on modular multiplications which are used for disguising an easy knapsack. Lagarias (1984) and Brickell (1985) have performed an intensive study of these systems by using simultaneous diophantine approximation. Goodman-McAuley (1985) proposed another knapsack cryptosystem using modular multiplication to disguise an easy knapsack, but this system is substantially different from those mentioned above. However, this cryptosystem can still be broken using lattice basis reduction. Pieprzyk (1985) designed a knapsack system which is similar to the Goodman-McAuley knapsack except that integers are replaced by polynomials over GF(2).

Brickell (1984) and Lagarias and Odlyzko (1985) proposed the algorithms for solving knapsacks of low density. Schnorr (1988) developed the more efficient lattice basis reduction algorithm capable of succeeding on knapsacks of much higher density.

In 1978 McEliece proposed a public-key cryptosystem based on error correcting codes. His cryptosystem is based on the Goppa code with the generator matrix **G** and then transform this matrix into $\mathbf{G}' = \mathbf{SGP}$ which is the public key of this system. McEliece scrambles **G** by selecting a random $(k \times k)$ non-singular matrix **S** and a random $(n \times n)$ permutation matrix $\mathbf{P}.\mathbf{G}'$ is published as the encryption key, but its component matrices $\mathbf{G}, \mathbf{S}$, and **P** are all secret. Now, the sender encrypts a k-bit plaintext **m** into an n-bit ciphertext **c** according to the formula

$$\mathbf{c} = \mathbf{mSGP} + \mathbf{e}$$

where **e** is the error pattern due to the additive noise. On receipt of **c**, the received ciphertext $\mathbf{c}'$ becomes

$$\mathbf{c}' = \mathbf{c}P^{-1} = (\mathbf{mS})\,\mathbf{G} + \mathbf{e}'$$

where $\mathbf{e}' = \mathbf{e}P^{-1}$. A decoding algorithm for the original code should remove the error vector $\mathbf{e}'$ and recover the vector **mS**. Thus, the message plaintext **m** is then easily determined using the formula

$$\mathbf{m} = (\mathbf{mS})\,\mathbf{S}^{-1}$$

The McEliece scheme has two drawbacks: the key is quite large and increases the bandwidth, and a ciphertext would be twice as long as a plaintext. Adams and Meijer (1987) showed that for $n = 1024$ (code length), $t = 37$ (error correcting capability) is the optimum value and the expected number of operations is about $2^{84.1}$.

1.5 AUTHENTICATION, DIGITAL SIGNATURE, AND ID-BASED CRYPTOSYSTEMS

Data security embraces problems pertaining to both privacy and authentication. The privacy problem is concerned with preventing an opponent from extracting the message information from the channel; whereas the authentication problem is related to preventing an opponent from injecting false data into the channel or altering messages to change their meaning.

In computer communication networks, it is important to provide an adequate method by which communicators can identify themselves to each other in a manner that cannot be forged. Authentications can be classified as user authentication and message authentication. The validity of business contracts and agreements is guaranteed by signature. Business applications, such as bank transactions, military command and control orders, and contract negotiations using computer communication networks, will require digital signatures. The digital signature scheme can be classified into one of two categories, namely arbitrated signatures and true signatures.

We outline a general authentication protocol between users A and B using a conventional secret-key cryptosystem, where A and B use a common secret key K to encipher the message plaintext and decipher the cryptogram.

1. B picks a random identifier IB and sends its encryption function E_k (IB) to A.
2. A deciphers E_k (IB) first and picks a random identifier IA. After these steps, A sends its encryption function E_k (IB, IA) to B.
3. B deciphers E_k (IB, IA) to obtain IB′ and IA′ and compare IB with IB′. If they match, i.e. IB = IB′, then B determines the identity of A as the legitimate user. B subsequently sends E_k (IA′) to A.
4. A deciphers E_k (IA′) to get IA′. If IA = IA′, then A confirms receipt to B.

Thus, users A and B have identified themselves to each other.

Public-key cryptosystems make authentication easy owing to the simplification of key distribution. An authentication protocol using a public-key cryptosystem is described in the following.

1. A sends to B the cryptogram E_{K_pB} (IA, A) encrypted with public key K_pB of B.
2. B deciphers $E_{K_p\mathrm{B}}$ (IA, A) using its secret key K_sB and obtains IA and A. B then sends $E_{K_p\mathrm{A}}$ (IA, IB) to A.
3. A deciphers $E_{K_p\mathrm{A}}$ (IA, IB) using its secret key K_sA to get IA′ and IB′. If IA = IA′, then A confirms the identity of B. A next sends $E_{K_p\mathrm{B}}$ (IB) to B.
4. B deciphers $E_{K_p\mathrm{B}}$ (IB) using its secret key K_sB and compares IB with IB′. If IB = IB′, then B confirms the identity of A.

Thus, users A and B have identified themselves to each other, because IAs and IBs are matched.

In an arbitrated signature scheme, signed messages produced by the sender S are sent to the receiver R via an arbitrator A, who serves as a witness. In a true signature scheme, S sends signed messages directly to R, who checks their validity and authenticity. Both conventional secret-key and public-key cryptosystems can be applied to produce true signatures.

Let us review some authentication schemes built using public-key cryptosystems as well as conventional symmetric cryptosystems. ElGamal's algorithm (1985) for authentication relies on the difficulty of computing discrete logarithms over a finite field GF (p), where p is a prime. Ong, Schnorr, and Shamir (1984) proposed a signature scheme based on a polynomial equation modulo 2. However Pollard (1987) broke the quadratic and cubic OSS schemes. The Okamoto-Shiraishi signature scheme (1985) relies on the difficulty of determining approximate kth roots modulo n. Their original scheme was for $k = 2$. Not only the $k = 2$ case, but the $k = 3$ case also was quickly broken by Brickell and DeLawrentis in 1986. The cryptanalysis of Shamir's fast signature scheme (1978) is somewhat similar to the attacks on the multiplicative knapsack system. In 1984, Odlyzko showed a method of attack to break Shamir's scheme which was designed for authentication. The Rabin signature scheme (1978) is based on symmetric crypto-operations. Cryptographic operations used in the Diffie-Lamport scheme (1979) are based on symmetric encryption and decryption. The drawback of the Diffie-Lamport scheme is the excessive length of signatures. To overcome this weakness, the compression method can be used for reduction of signature length. The signature scheme invented by Matyas and Meyer in 1981 is based on the DES algorithm.

The 1980s were the first full decade of public key cryptography. Many systems were proposed and many were broken. But no one can deny the success of asymmetric two-key cryptosystems over this period.

In 1984, Shamir proposed a novel cryptographic scheme—the ID-based cryptosystem and signature scheme. This system enables two communicators to exchange their messages securely and to verify each other's signatures without exchanging secret or public keys. Consequently this scheme does not require the user to keep a key directory, nor does it involve service from a third party. But it requires an individual smart card to be provided to each user, enabling him to sign and encrypt messages to be transmitted and decrypt and verify messages received. Even though the scheme is based on a public-key cryptosystem, the user can use any combination of his name, social security number, telephone number, or network address as his public key without the generation of a random pair of public and secret keys. The secret key is computed by a key generation center and issued to the user in the form of a smart card when he first joins the network.

Since Shamir introduced ID-based cryptosystems in 1984, several cryptologists have investigated this area. In 1986, Desmedt and Quisquater proposed a public-key cryptosystem based on the difficulty of tampering. Tsujii and Itoh (1989) presented a paper on an ID-based cryptosystem based on the discrete logarithm problem. Okamoto and

Tanaka (1989) introduced an ID-based information security management system for personal computer networks. Matsumoto and Imai (1990) discussed the security of some key sharing schemes. Akiyama, Torii, and Hasabe (1990) presented a paper on an ID-based key management system using discrete exponentiation calculation. Recently, Youm and Rhee published a paper on an ID-based cryptosystem and digital signature scheme using the discrete logarithm problem in 1991. Most of the research papers based upon published algorithms in this area are due to Japanese authors.

Nowadays, the banking community is attempting to improve its services by applying the Electronic Funds Transfer (EFT) technology in order to attract new customers. Theoretically, every customer can have access to his funds at terminals via the EFT system by utilizing the bank's own computer network. Terminals must, of course, provide several services such as withdrawal of cash, encashing traveller's checks, paying bills, booking flights, and so on. However, there are many security measures which have to be solved before the EFT network is installed. In fact, customers face problems of identification before transaction and those of ensuring authenticity and integrity of transaction.

The Personal Identification Number (PIN) is a secret number assigned to, or selected by, the cardholder used in an Electronic Funds Transfer (EFT) network. The PIN also helps the cardholder establish his identity within the EFT system. The PIN is basically the cardholder's electronic signature, and serves the same role in an EFT transaction as a written signature serves in a conventional financial transaction. PIN secrecy is of the utmost importance. Therefore, the protection of both the PIN and the bank card is crucial to EFT security. Bank cards may be lost, stolen or forged. In such cases, the only existing countermeasure against an unauthorized access is the secret PIN. This is why only the legitimate cardholder should know his clear form of the PIN. The PIN should never be stored or transmitted within the EFT system. PINs and relevant bank cards are treated as signatures of cardholders. Usually, to initiate a transaction, cardholders who use the EFT terminal insert their cards in a special slot and enter their PINs using the keyboard of the terminal. If the PIN matches the account number imprinted on the magnetic strip of the card, the transaction is initiated and the cardholder can proceed further.

We have merely introduced the general outlook on the security problem with regard to an EFT system. But there are several different applications to ensure cryptographic protection. There is a variety of articles on cryptographic application in computer networks. Among others are the following services meant to enhance cryptographic protection. They are database protection, unforgeable ID card using smart cards, one-way ciphers and passwords, an automatic teller machine, notary services, and so on.

1.6 ZERO-KNOWLEDGE INTERACTIVE PROOFS (ZKIP)

Since 1985, considerable interest has been shown in the establishment of zero-knowledge proofs. This new area provides cryptologists with fascinating protocols for obtaining provably secure communications. A basic question in complexity theory is how much knowledge should be yielded to convince a polynomial-time verifier about the validity of a theorem. In 1985, issues in complexity theory and cryptography motivated Goldwasser, Micali, and Rackoff to introduce the concept of an interactive proof system. Since then, zero-knowledge interactive proofs (ZKIP) have been the focus of much attention.

Goldrich, Micali, and Wigderson (1986) showed that any language in NP has a computational zero-knowledge proof, and presented a methodology of cryptographic protocol design. In 1988, Ben-Or, Goldreich, Goldwasser, Håstad, Kilian, Micali and Rogaway extended the result of Goldreich, Micali and Wigderson that, under the same assumption, all of NP admits zero-knowledge interactive proofs. They also showed that every language that admits an interactive proof admits a perfect zero-knowledge interactive proof. A multi-prover interactive proof is an extension of an interactive proof. Ben-Or, Goldwasser, Kilian, and Wigderson (1988) introduced the idea of multi-prover interactive proofs, in order to show how to achieve perfect zero-knowledge interactive proofs without resorting to any interactability assumptions.

Crepeau (1987) described a zero-knowledge poker protocol that achieves confidentiality of the player's strategy. In other words, it makes for an electronic poker face. Chaum, Evertse, Van der Graaf, and Peralta (1987) showed how to demonstrate possession of a discrete logarithm without revealing it. Several practical protocols have been proposed for this type of knowledge proof without revealing any actual information related to the secret. Some numerical problems belonging to this category are related to demonstrating knowledge of square roots modulo n (a composite) and discrete logarithm modulo p (a prime). Tompa and Woll (1987) showed that any random self-reducible problem has a zero-knowledge interactive proof. They proved that the computation of both square roots modulo n (a composite) and discrete logarithms modulo p (a prime) are in the random self-reducible class. Shizuya, Koyama, and Itoh (1990) presented an interactive protocol demonstrating that (1) the prover actually knows two factors a and b (not necessarily primes) of a composite n, and showing that (2) it is really a ZKIP. The security of this protocol is based on the difficulty of computing a discrete logarithm modulo a large prime. As an extension of this protocol, they have also shown that two or more factors are known by the prover and illustrated that the extended protocol is applicable to a weighted membership protocol with hierarchical classes within a group.

1.7 KEY MANAGEMENT FOR CRYPTOSYSTEMS

Key management is an important aspect of the design of secure cryptosystems. For data encryption and authentication, a large set of cryptographic keys is required. Key management provides communication and file security for such a conventional symmetric cipher as DES. The key distribution protocol for implementing public-key algorithms is also important. Cryptographic keys are enciphered and sent to suitable users (or nodes) in the form of cryptograms. The function of key management is to securely distribute and update keys whenever required for cryptographic protection of data transmission or file security.

The key hierarchy is composed of key layers at each host node, i.e. one master key and two of its variants at the highest level, key encryption keys at the second level, and data encryption keys at the third level. Each host includes the highest level of key organization which creates one master key and two of its variants. The second level comprises the secondary keys which are stored in the form of cryptograms encrypted by variants of the master key. The third level is created by the data encryption keys which are protected by applying the key encryption keys or the host master key. The data encryption keys, sometimes called primary keys or session keys, are used to protect large amounts of data or messages in symmetric cryptosystems such as DES. The key encryption keys are, in turn, protected under the variants of the host master key. The master key is used to encrypt the key encryption keys when information has to be stored outside a secure cryptographic facility, such as disk. Since the master key protects all other keys at the host processor, special care should be taken to ensure that it is generated and installed in the cryptographic facility in a secure manner.

Let us consider a communication network in which cryptographic protection is based on either a symmetric or an asymmetric algorithm. Either of these two algorithms requires a key control center that verifies the authenticity of keys and initiates communication between users. However, the key distribution problems for symmetric cryptographic algorithms are more sensitive to illegal activity because a key distribution center stores all cryptographic keys. All keys are stored in the form of cryptograms which have been generated under the master key and its variants. Whereas, with an asymmetric algorithm, a key directory distributes public keys whose protection is not needed.

Key distribution based on conventional symmetric cryptosystems may be either centralized or decentralized. The former is controlled by a single host computer, and the latter by a group of host computers. However, in a network with symmetric algorithm protection, all keys are stored in the form of cryptograms obtained using the host master key. When cryptographic protection is based on asymmetric algorithms, we employ the key distribution protocol for public-key cryptosystems. The problem of key transmission via an insecure channel has been solved after the invention of cryptography with public keys.

Undoubtedly, common key distribution is extremely important for providing privacy and authenticity. Therefore, the secret key sharing method has been studied by several researchers in an effort to provide a unique common key for each user pair in open communication networks.

REFERENCES

1. Ayoub, F. and K. Singh: "Cryptographic Techniques and Network Security," *IEE Proc.*, vol. 131, no. 7, Dec. 1984.
2. *The Beale Ciphers*, The Beale Cipher Association, Nedfield, MA, 1978.
3. Denning, D.E.: *Cryptography and Data Security*, Addison Wesley, Reading, Mass., 1982.
4. Diffie, W. and M.E. Hellman: "Privacy and Authentication: An Introduction to Cryptography," *Proc. IEEE*, vol. 67, no. 3, pp 397-427, Mar. 1979.
5. Friedman, W.: "Methods for the Solution of Running-Key Ciphers," *Riverbank Publ.* 16, Riverbank Labs, Geneva, 1918.
6. Kahn, D.: *The Codebreakers*, Macmillan, New York, 1967.
7. Meyer, C.H. and S.M. Matyas: *Cryptography: A New Dimension in Computer Data Security*, John Wiley, New York, 1982.
8. Seberry, J. and J. Pieprzyk: *Cryptography: An Introduction to Computer Security*, Prentice-Hall of Australia, Sydney, 1989.
9. Vernam, G.: "Cipher Printing Telegraphy Systems for Secret Wire and Radio Telegraphic Communications," *J. AIEE*, vol. 45, pp 109-115, 1926.

Chapter

2

Number Theory

This chapter discusses the theory of numbers. A basic understanding of this theory is essential for the comprehension of cryptographic algorithms. It will be particularly helpful to those involved with secure communications, data privacy, and file security. Basic theorems of number theory with proofs in terms of modular arithmetic will benefit readers unfamiliar with them. Ore [6], Dudley [2] and Burton [1] are probably the most easily understandable texts on number theory.

2.1 CONGRUENCES

Carl F. Gauss (1801) introduced the concept of congruence and notation using the symbol ≡.

Two integers a and b are said to be congruent modulo n, expressed as

$$a \equiv b \pmod{n}$$

if and only if n divides $a - b$ (symbolically $n \mid (a - b)$), that is, provided $a - b = k\,n$ for some integer k. Hence, the congruence $a \equiv b \pmod{n}$ signifies that the numbers a and b differ by a multiple of n. In general, "a is congruent to b modulo n" denotes $a \equiv b \pmod{n}$ in symbols if and only if $n \mid (a - b)$ for some integer $n > 0$. Customarily, $a \mid b$ denotes that a divides b if and only if there is an integer d such that $ad = b$. For example, $2 \mid 6$, $17 \mid 34$, and $4 \mid (-32)$. But $a \nmid b$ indicates that a cannot divide b. For example, $3 \nmid 4$ and $4 \nmid 5$. Also the symbol $\not\equiv$ means "not congruent to". For example, $4 \not\equiv 8 \pmod{12}$.

■ **Example 2.1** Consider $n = 9$.

$5 \equiv 32 \pmod 9$, because $5 - 32 = -27 = (-3)(9)$.
$48 \equiv 3 \pmod 9$, because $48 - 3 = 45 = (5)(9)$.
$42 \not\equiv 7 \pmod 9$, since 9 fails to divide $42 - 7 = 35$.

If $a \equiv r \pmod n$, then $n \mid (a - r)$. Hence, there is $a - r = qn$ or $a = qn + r$, $0 < r < n$. The remainder r is called a residue of $a \pmod n$. A set of n integers $\{a_i\} = \{a_1, a_2, \ldots a_n\}$ is said to form a complete set of residues $\{r_i\} = \{0, 1, 2, \ldots, n - 1\}$ modulo n if every a_i in the set of n integers is congruent modulo n to any r_i in the residue system $\{0, 1, 2, \ldots, n - 1\}$ in some order. Thus, for any integer a, there exists a congruence

$$a \equiv r \pmod n$$

where r is a unique one among the numbers in a complete set of residues. There are many residue systems such that every integer is congruent $(\text{mod } n)$ to a unique number in the residue system to which it belongs.

■ **Example 2.2** Since $-14 \equiv 1 \pmod 5$, $12 \equiv 2 \pmod 5$, $19 \equiv 4 \pmod 5$, $48 \equiv 3 \pmod 5$, and $65 \equiv 0 \pmod 5$, the integer set $\{-14, 12, 19, 48, 65\}$ constitutes a complete residue system $\{1, 2, 4, 3, 0\}$ modulo 5.

Thus we see that every integer is congruent $(\text{mod } n)$ to exactly one of $0, 1, 2, \ldots, n - 1$.

Theorem 2.1 For any integers a and b, $a \equiv b \pmod n$ if and only if a and b leave the same remainder when divided by n.

Proof If a and b leave the same remainder r on division by n, then

$$a = q_1 n + r \quad \text{and} \quad b = q_2 n + r$$

for some integers q_1 and q_2. Thus it follows that

$$a - b = (q_1 n + r) - (q_2 n + r) = (q_1 - q_2)\, n$$

which implies that $n \mid (a - b)$. From the definition of congruence, we conclude that $a \equiv b \pmod n$. To prove the converse, take $a \equiv b \pmod n$, so that $a = b + kn$ for some integer k. Since b leaves a certain remainder r upon division by n, $b = qn + r$ for $0 \le r < n$. Therefore,

$$a = b + kn = (qn + r) + kn = (q + k)\, n + r$$

which implies that a has the same remainder r as b. This proves the theorem.

■ **Example 2.3** $-32 \equiv 17 \pmod 7$ implies that -32 and 17 have the same remainder 3 when divided by 7 such that

$$-32 = (-5)(7) + 3, \; 17 = (2)(7) + 3$$

Since there exist numbers that correspond to the same remainder r when divided by n, they form a residue class (mod n). For a given remainder r, the residue class to which it belongs consists of the numbers r, $r \pm n$, $r \pm 2n$, ... Consider next the set of all numbers a for which the congruence $a \equiv 0 \pmod n$ is fulfilled. In this case, we have the zero residue class (mod n) 0, $\pm n$, $\pm 2n$, ... In addition, for a given modulo n, the reduced set of residues is the set of $n - 1$ elements 1, 2, . . . , $(n - 1)$ except for 0.

Theorem 2.2 If gcd $(a, n) = 1$, then the least residues of the integer sequence $a, 2a, 3a, \ldots, (n-1)a \pmod n$ are $1, 2, 3, \ldots, (n-1)$ in some order.

Proof Since there is no congruence to 0 (mod n), the number of integers in the sequence is $n - 1$. But each integer is congruent (mod n) to one of its residues. If no two integers in the sequence are congruent (mod n), then their least residues (mod n) will be all different, that is, a permutation of $1, 2, 3, \ldots, (n-1)$, taken in some order. Suppose two of the integers are congruent (mod n). We then have

$$ra \equiv sa \pmod n, \; 1 \le r < s \le n - 1$$

Since gcd $(a, n) = 1$

$$r \equiv s \pmod n$$

But because r and s are least residues, it follows that $r = s$, which is impossible. This proves the theorem.

Theorem 2.3 Let $n > 0$ be fixed, and let a and b be any integers. Prove that $a^k \equiv b^k \pmod n$ for any positive integer k if $a \equiv b \pmod n$.

Proof For $k = 1$, the theorem certainly holds because $a \equiv b \pmod n$. For $k = 2$, it can be proved as shown below.

$$a = b + k_1 n$$

$$c = d + k_2 n$$

from which
$$\begin{aligned} ac &= (b + k_1 n)(d + k_2 n) \\ &= bd + (bk_2 + dk_1 + k_1 k_2 n) n \end{aligned}$$

If $a = c$ and $b = d$,

$$a^2 = b^2 + [(k_1 + k_2) b + k_1 k_2 n] n$$

Since $(k_1 + k_2) b + k_1 k_2 n$ is an integer, $a^2 - b^2$ is divisible by n. Consequently $a^2 \equiv b^2 \pmod{n}$. For $k > 2$, $a^k \equiv b^k \pmod{n}$ can also be proved by taking the induction steps. Finally, since $a \equiv b \pmod{n}$ and $a^k \equiv b^k$ (mod n), it follows that $aa^k \equiv bb^k \pmod{n}$, or $a^{k+1} \equiv b^{k+1} \pmod{n}$.

This is the form of congruence modulo n for $k + 1$. Thus the induction argument is completed.

■ **Example 2.4** Show that 41 divides $2^{20} - 1$.

Since $2^5 \equiv -9 \pmod{41}$, $(2^5)^4 \equiv (-9)^4 \pmod{41}$ by Theorem 2.3.
Hence it follows that $2^{20} \equiv (81)(81) \pmod{41}$. Knowing that $81 \equiv -1$ (mod 41), we have $(81)(81) \equiv (-1)(-1) \equiv 1$ mod (41). Thus we arrive at $2^{20} - 1 \equiv 1 - 1 \equiv 0 \pmod{41}$. Thus $41 \mid (2^{20} - 1)$, as expected.

Theorem 2.4 If $ac \equiv bc \pmod{n}$ and $\gcd(c, n) = 1$, then $a \equiv b \pmod{n}$.

Proof If $ac \equiv bc \pmod{n}$, then $n \mid c(a-b)$. Since $\gcd(n, c) = 1$, $(a - b)$ must be a multiple of n, i.e. $n \mid (a - b)$. This implies that $a \equiv b \pmod{n}$. Thus, we see that a factor c on both sides of a congruence can be cancelled if c is relatively prime to mod n.

■ **Example 2.5** Consider the congruence $39 \equiv 15 \pmod{8}$. It can be expressed $(3)(13) \equiv (3)(5) \pmod{8}$. But since $\gcd(3, 8) = 1$, Theorem 2.4 leads to the conclusion that $13 \equiv 5 \pmod{8}$.

Theorem 2.5 If $ac \equiv bc \pmod{n}$ and $\gcd(c, n) = d$, then $a \equiv b$ (mod n/d).

Proof If $ac \equiv bc \pmod{n}$, then $n \mid c(a - b)$, or $c(a - b) = kn$ for some integer k. Since $\gcd(c, n) = d$, there exist relatively prime integers r and s such that $c = dr$ and $n = ds$. Thus, from $c(a - b) = kn$, $dr(a - b) = k(ds)$, or $r(a - b) = ks$. Hence $s \mid r(a - b)$ and $\gcd(r, s) = 1$. From Theorem 2.4, this gives $s \mid (a - b)$ which implies $a \equiv b \pmod{s}$. Because $n = ds$ or $s = n/d$, we have $a \equiv b \pmod{n/d}$, which completes the proof of the theorem.

■ **Example 2.6** Consider the congruence $39 \equiv 21 \pmod{9}$. Since $(3)(13) \equiv (3)(7) \pmod{9}$ and $\gcd(3, 9) = 3$, Theorem 2.5 leads to the conclusion that $13 \equiv 7 \pmod{3}$. Similarly, the congruence $220 \equiv 1180 \pmod{96}$ gives the common factor $c = 20$, and $\gcd(20, 96) = 4$. Therefore, after cancellation with $c = 20$, there remains $11 \equiv 59 \pmod{24}$.

2.2 LINEAR CONGRUENCES

Consider the simplest linear congruence $ax \equiv b \pmod{n}$ involving an unknown x. The congruence $ax \equiv b \pmod{n}$ has a solution if and only if there are integers x and k such that $ax = b + kn$. However, the linear congruence $ax \equiv b \pmod{n}$ may have no solution, exactly one solution, or many solutions. In fact, the linear congruence $ax \equiv b \pmod{n}$ has d solutions, where $d = \gcd(a, n)$, if and only if $d \mid b$. For example, $2x \equiv 1 \pmod{4}$ has no solution, because $4 \nmid (2x - 1)$ owing to the fact that $(2x - 1)$ is odd. The congruence $2x \equiv 1 \pmod{3}$ has just one solution $x = 2$, because $d = \gcd(2, 3) = 1$ which surely divides 1. The congruence $6x \equiv 9 \pmod{15}$ has three solutions $x = 4, 9$, and 14, because $d = \gcd(6, 15) = 3$ which shows the existence of exactly three solutions.

Theorem 2.6 If $\gcd(a, n) \nmid b$, then $ax \equiv b \pmod{n}$ has no solutions.

Proof Suppose $ax \equiv b \pmod{n}$ has a solution. Hence it must be $\gcd(a, n) \mid b$. If it is assumed that σ is a solution, then $a\sigma \equiv b \pmod{n}$, that is, $n \mid (a\sigma - b)$ or $a\sigma - b = kn$ for some k. Since $\gcd(a, n) \mid a$ and $\gcd(a, n) \mid kn$, it follows that $\gcd(a, n) \mid b$ which contradicts our assumption.

For example, $4x \equiv 1 \pmod{10}$ has no solution, because $\gcd(4, 10) = 2$ cannot divide 1, i.e. $2 \nmid 1$.

Theorem 2.7 If $\gcd(a, n) = 1$, then $ax \equiv b \pmod{n}$ has exactly one solution.

Proof Since $\gcd(a, n) = 1$, it can be expressed as $a\lambda + n\gamma = 1$ (Euclidean algorithm) for some integers λ and γ. Multiplying by b gives

$$a\lambda b + n\gamma b = b$$

from which $a(\lambda b) \equiv b \pmod{n}$, because $a\lambda b - b$ is a multiple of n. Thus the least residue of λb modulo n is a solution of the linear congruence. Let us now show that there does not exist more than one solution. Assume that both λ and γ are solutions. Then we have

$$a\lambda \equiv b \pmod{n} \quad \text{and} \quad a\gamma \equiv b \pmod{n}$$

from which it follows that $a\lambda \equiv a\gamma \pmod{n}$. Since $\gcd(a, n) = 1$, the last congruence gives, using Theorem 2.5, we get $\lambda \equiv \gamma \pmod{n}$ by cancelling the common factor a. Hence we know that $n \mid (\lambda - \gamma)$. Since λ and γ are least residues (mod n), it follows that $0 \le \lambda < n$ and $0 \le \gamma < n$. Thus $-n < \lambda - \gamma < n$. Since $n \mid (\lambda - \gamma)$, $-1 < (\lambda - \gamma)/n < 1$, the solution must be $\lambda - \gamma = 0$, or $\lambda = \gamma$. Thus if two least residues (mod n) are congruent (mod n), then they are equal, and the solution is unique.

■ **Example 2.7** Consider the linear congruence $ax \equiv b \pmod{n}$. Continue to add n to b until cancellation is possible. Let us solve $14x \equiv 27 \pmod{31}$. Add 31 to 27 for obtaining the first cancellation such that $14x \equiv 58 \pmod{31}$, or $7x \equiv 29 \pmod{31}$. The second cancellation is found by adding 31 to 29 repeatedly until we can cancel 7 as follows:

$$7x \equiv 60 \equiv 91 \pmod{31}$$

from which we get $x \equiv 13 \pmod{31}$, and 13 is surely the solution.

Theorem 2.8 If $\gcd(a, n) \mid b$, then $ax \equiv b \pmod{n}$ has exactly $d = \gcd(a, n)$ solutions.

Proof If we substitute a by $d\alpha$, b by $d\beta$, and n by dm, then we have $\alpha x \equiv \beta \pmod{m}$ and $\gcd(\alpha, m) = 1$, which implies the condition for just one solution (see Theorem 2.7). If r is the solution, then the reduced residue class to which it belongs consists of the d numbers $r, r + m, r + 2m, \ldots, r + (d - 1)m$. These d numbers will be all the solutions of $ax \equiv b \pmod{n}$. Since each of these numbers satisfies the congruence (mod m), we have $a(r + km) = d\alpha(r + km) = \alpha\, dr + \alpha k(dm)$. Because $\alpha r \equiv \beta \pmod{m}$ and $dm = n$, it follows that

$$\alpha\, dr + \alpha k(dm) \equiv \beta d + \alpha kn \equiv \beta d \equiv b \pmod{n}$$

Hence we have

$$a(r + km) \equiv b \pmod{n}.$$

Each member of the above residue class for $k = 0, 1, \ldots, d - 1$ is a least residue (mod n). Therefore $0 \le r + km \le r + (d - 1)m = dm = n$. Since the numbers in the residue class are distinct least residues, no two of the numbers in the system are congruent (mod n). Thus, the linear congruence $ax \equiv b \pmod{n}$ has $d = \gcd(a, n)$ solutions, and the theorem is proved.

■ **Example 2.8** Consider the linear congruence $5x \equiv 10 \pmod{15}$. Determine the number of solutions of this congruence. According to Theorem 2.8, this congruence has exactly $d = \gcd(5, 15) = 5$ solutions. Cancelling 5 yields $x \equiv 2 \pmod{3}$.
Thus, the integers included in $x \equiv 2 \pmod{3}$ are least residues (mod 15), that is, 2, 5, 8, 11, and 14. Hence they are the five solutions.

2.3 FERMAT'S THEOREM

Fermat's theorem (1640) was fundamental to the development of the theory of numbers and is extremely helpful in the study of quadratic congruences. Almost 100 years were to elapse before Euler published the first proof of Fermat's theorem in 1736.

Theorem 2.9 (Fermat's Theorem) If p is a prime and gcd $(a, p) = 1$, then $a^{p-1} \equiv 1 \pmod{p}$.

Proof Given any prime p and gcd $(a, p) = 1$, consider the integers of the first $p - 1$ positive multiples of a, viz. $a, 2a, 3a, \ldots, (p-1)\,a$. None of these integers is congruent modulo p to any order, nor is any congruent to zero. Hence, the least residues of the $p - 1$ multiples of a, i.e. ka $(1 \le k \le p - 1)$ are a permutation of $1, 2, 3, \ldots, p - 1$, taken in some order. Multiplying all these congruences together gives $a \cdot 2a \cdot 3a \ldots (p-1)a \equiv 1 \cdot 2 \cdot 3 \ldots (p-1) \pmod{p}$, or $a^{p-1}(p-1)! \equiv (p-1)! \pmod{p}$. Since p and $(p - 1)!$ are relatively prime, the last congruence gives

$$a^{p-1} \equiv 1 \pmod{p}$$

which is Fermat's theorem.

Fermat's theorem has many applications in certain calculations as demonstrated in the following.

■ **Example 2.9** Verify that $3^{16} \equiv 1 \pmod{17}$.
Knowing the congruence $3^3 \equiv 10 \pmod{17}$, we proceed in steps by reducing modulo 17 as follows:
Squaring the congruence above yields

$$3^6 \equiv 100 \equiv -2 \pmod{17}$$

Squaring again gives

$$3^{12} \equiv 4 \pmod{17}$$

Thus, we have $3^{16} \equiv 3^{12} \cdot 3^3 \cdot 3 \equiv (4)\,(10)\,(3) \equiv 120 \equiv 1 \pmod{17}$.

■ **Example 2.10** Verify that $18^6 \equiv 1 \pmod{49}$.

$$18^2 \equiv 324 \equiv 30 \pmod{49}$$

$$18^4 \equiv 900 \equiv 18 \pmod{49}$$

$$18^6 \equiv 18^4 \cdot 18^2 \equiv 18 \cdot 30 \equiv 540 \equiv 1 \pmod{49}$$

2.4 WILSON'S THEOREM

Waring (1770) published Wilson's idea without proof. But Lagrange (1771) had given the first proof of Wilson's theorem and observed that the converse also holds. Wilson's theorem is also helpful in the study of quadratic congruences and is particularly remarkable because it establishes a condition for a number to be prime.

Theorem 2.10 (Wilson's Theorem) p is a prime if and only if $(p-1)! \equiv -1 \pmod{p}$.

Proof This theorem obviously holds good for the cases $p = 2$ and $p = 3$, because $1 \equiv -1 \pmod{2}$ and $2 \equiv -1 \pmod{3}$, respectively. Consider the case when $p > 3$.

Let α denote the solution of $ax \equiv 1 \pmod{p}$, $1 \le a \le p-1$. Since gcd $(a, p) = 1$, this linear congruence admits a unique solution α $(1 \le \alpha \le p-1)$ modulo p, satisfying $a\alpha \equiv 1 \pmod{p}$. Since p is prime, $a = \alpha$ if and only if $a = 1$ or $a = p-1$.

Let r be any solution of $x^2 \equiv 1 \pmod{p}$. Since p is prime, the congruence $r^2 - 1 \equiv (r-1)(r+1) \equiv 0 \pmod{p}$ gives $p \mid (r-1)(r+1)$, which implies $p \mid (r-1)$ or $p \mid (r+1)$. Hence $r - 1 \equiv 0 \pmod{p}$ or $r + 1 \equiv 0 \pmod{p}$. Since r is a least residue modulo p, it follows that either $r - 1 \equiv 0 \pmod{p}$, in which case $r = 1$, or $r + 1 \equiv 0 \pmod{p}$, in which case $r = p - 1$.

Deleting the numbers 1 and $p-1$, we could group the remaining integers $2, 3, \ldots, p-2$ into $(p-3)/2$ pairs (a, α), where $a \ne \alpha$, such that $a\alpha \equiv 1 \pmod{p}$. In fact, the product of the two integers in each pairs (a, α) is a congruence to $1 \pmod{p}$. When these $(p-3)/2$ pairs are multiplied together and the factors rearranged, we get

$$2 \cdot 3 \ldots (p-2) \equiv 1 \pmod{p}$$

or

$$(p-2)! \equiv 1 \pmod{p}$$

Multiplying by $p-1$ gives the congruence $(p-1)! \equiv p - 1 \equiv -1 \pmod{p}$ Thus, Wilson's theorem is proved.

■ **Example 2.11** Consider $(p-1)! \equiv -1 \pmod{p}$, with $p = 13$. Verify $12! \equiv -1 \pmod{13}$ in order to clarify the proof of Wilson's theorem.

Let us divide the integers $2, 3, \ldots, 11$ into $(p-3)/2 = 5$ pairs (a, α) each of whose products is congruent to 1 modulo 13, as shown below.

a	2	3	4	5	6
α	7	9	10	8	11
$a\alpha$	14	27	40	40	66

It is easily seen that $a\alpha \equiv 1 \pmod{13}$ in each case.

$$2 \cdot 7 \equiv 14 \equiv 1 \pmod{13}$$

$$3 \cdot 9 \equiv 27 \equiv 1 \pmod{13}$$

$$4 \cdot 10 \equiv 40 \equiv 1 \pmod{13}$$

$$5 \cdot 8 \equiv 40 \equiv 1 \pmod{13}$$

$$6 \cdot 11 \equiv 66 \equiv 1 \pmod{13}$$

Multiplying together the above set of congruences, we have

$$11! \equiv (2 \cdot 7)(3 \cdot 9)(4 \cdot 10)(5 \cdot 8)(6 \cdot 11) \equiv 1 \pmod{13}$$

Now multiply by 12 to obtain the congruence

$$12! \equiv 12 \equiv -1 \pmod{13}$$

Taking all the values of a in the range $1 \le a \le 12$, it will be found that the set of numbers in the second row is a permutation of the set of numbers in the first. But it may be seen that $a \equiv \alpha \pmod{13}$ only when $a = 1$ or 12.

2.5 EULER'S THEOREM AND ϕ–FUNCTION

Euler (1707-1783) was the key figure in the 18th century mathematics. Recall that the basic role to prove Fermat's theorem is that "If gcd $(a, p) = 1$, then the least residues (mod p) of $a, 2a, \ldots, (p-1)\,a$ are a permutation of $1, 2, \ldots\ p-1$. This fact is also the key to Euler's generalization of Fermat's theorem. Euler in 1760 proved his landmark result "If gcd $(a, n) = 1$, then $a^{\phi(n)} \equiv 1 \pmod{n}$." This is Euler's theorem and ϕ function is called Euler's totient function.

2.5.1 Euler's ϕ-function

Euler's ϕ-function is defined such that $\phi(n)$ for $n \ge 1$ denotes the number of positive integers not exceeding n that are relatively prime to n. Considering $\phi(n)$ for $n = 1, 2, 3, \ldots, 10$, Euler's ϕ-function may be expressed as follows:

$$\phi(1) = 0 \qquad \phi(6) = 2$$
$$\phi(2) = 1 \qquad \phi(7) = 6$$
$$\phi(3) = 2 \qquad \phi(8) = 4$$
$$\phi(4) = 2 \qquad \phi(9) = 6$$
$$\phi(5) = 4 \qquad \phi(10) = 4$$

■ **Example 2.12** Determine $\phi(20)$. The positive integers that do not exceed 20 are the numbers from 1 to 19. Among these positive integers, there are $\phi(20) = 8$ which are relatively prime to 20.

If n is a prime number, then every integer less than n is relatively prime to n. Thus, it follows that $\phi(n) = n - 1$ if and only if n is prime.

■ **Example 2.13** $\phi(3) = 2$, $\phi(5) = 4$, $\phi(7) = 6$, $\phi(11) = 10$, $\phi(13) = 12$, $\phi(17) = 16$, $\phi(19) = 18$, $\phi(23) = 22$, $\phi(29) = 28, \ldots$

Theorem 2.11 If $n = pq$ is composite and p and q are prime, then $\phi(n) = \phi(p)\,\phi(q) = (p-1)(q-1)$.

Proof Consider the complete set of residues $\{0, 1, \ldots, pq-1\}$ modulo n. All of these residues are relatively prime to n except for the $p-1$ elements $\{q, 2q, \ldots, (p-1)q\}$, the $q-1$ elements $\{p, 2p, \ldots, (q-1)p\}$, and 0. Therefore we have $\phi(n) = pq - \{(p-1) + (q-1) + 1\} = pq - p - q + 1 = (p-1)(q-1)$.

■ **Example 2.14** Find $\phi(35)$.

Since $35 = 5 \cdot 7$, $\phi(35) = \phi(5)\,\phi(7) = 4 \cdot 6 = 24$. Thus, there are 24 positive integers which are relatively prime to 35.

Theorem 2.12 If p is a prime and $k > 0$, then $\phi(p^k) = p^k - p^{k-1} = p^{k-1}(p-1)$.

Proof The positive integers less than or equal to p^k which are not relatively prime to p^k are the integral multiples of p, namely, p, $2p$, $3p, \ldots, (p^{k-1})\,p$. There are p^{k-1} positive integers between 1 and p^k which are divisible by p. Thus, the residue set $\{1, 2, 3, \ldots, p^k\}$ contains exactly $p^k - p^{k-1}$ integers which are relatively prime to p^k. Thus, it follows that $\phi(p^k) = p^k - p^{k-1} = p^{k-1}(p-1)$.

■ **Example 2.15** Since $\phi(16) = \phi(2^4) = 2^4 - 2^3 = 16 - 8 = 8$, the eight integers less than and relatively prime to 16 are 1, 3, 5, 7, 9, 11, 13, and 15. Similarly, we have that, since $\phi(9) = \phi(3^2) = 3^2 - 3 = 6$, the six prime integers less than 9 are 1, 2, 4, 5, 7 and 8. $\phi(25) = \phi(5^2) = 5^2 - 5 = 20$ and the 20 integers less than and relatively prime to 25 are 1, 2, 3, 4, 6, 7, 8, 9, 11, 12, 13, 14, 16, 17, 18, 19, 21, 22, 23 and 24.

Theorem 2.13 The function $\phi(mn)$ is multiplicative, that is, $\phi(mn) = \phi(m)\,\phi(n)$ whenever $\gcd(m, n) = 1$.

Proof It is required to show that $\phi(mn) = \phi(m)\,\phi(n)$ whenever $\gcd(m,n) = 1$. Write the number in the following array from 1 to mn in

m columns of n entries each, as follows:

1	2	...	m
$m+1$	$m+2$	...	$2m$
$2m+1$	$2m+2$	...	$3m$
.	.		.
.	.		.
.	.		.
$(n-1)m+1$	$(n-1)m+2$	...	nm

Let $\phi(n)$ denote numbers relatively prime to mn in each of the columns that have first elements relatively prime to m. Since there exist $\phi(m)$ such columns, the number of integers in the above array that are relatively prime to mn is $\phi(m)\,\phi(n)$. Thus, $\phi(mn) = \phi(m)\,\phi(n)$, whenever $\gcd(n,m) = 1$. But consider the entries in the rth column, namely, r, $m+r$, $2m+r, \ldots, (n-1)\,m + r$. It is required to verify that their least residues (mod n) are a permutation of $0, 1, 2, \ldots, (n-1)$. Since $\gcd(qm + r, m) = \gcd(r,m)$, the numbers in the rth column are relatively prime to m if and only if r itself is relatively prime to m. Suppose $km + r \equiv jm + r \pmod{n}$, with $0 \le k < j < n$. Then $km \equiv jm \pmod{n}$, and since $\gcd(m,n) = 1$, we arrive at $k \equiv j \pmod{n}$, which is a contradiction. Hence the numbers in the rth column are congruent modulo n to $0, 1, 2, \ldots, n-1$ in some order. Thus, the total number of entries in the array that are relatively prime to both m and n is $\phi(m)\,\phi(n)$. This is enough to complete the proof of the theorem.

■ **Example 2.16** Consider the following array for $n = 5$ and $m = 6$.

1	2	3	4	5	6
7	8	9	10	11	12
13	14	15	16	17	18
19	20	21	22	23	24
25	26	27	28	29	30

Notice that the first element in each of the 2nd, 3rd, 4th, and 6th columns is not relatively prime to $m = 6$. Also, observe that no element in these columns in the array is relatively prime to $mn = 30$. However, all numbers (except 25 and 5) relatively prime to $mn = 30$ are found only in the first and fifth columns as below.

1	5	1	0
7	11	2	1
13	17	3	2
19	23	4	3
25	29	0	4

The least residues (mod 5) of the numbers in these two columns that include all elements relatively prime to mn = 30 are shown in the right group. Each column contains ϕ (5) = 4 numbers relatively prime to 30, there being ϕ (6) = 2 such columns. Thus $\phi(30) = \phi(5)\,\phi(6) = 4 \cdot 2 = 8$.

Theorem 2.14 If $\phi(n)$ is a multiplicative function and the prime factorization of n is $p_1^{k_1} p_2^{k_2} \ldots p_r^{k_r}$, then $\phi(n) = \phi(p_1^{k_1})\,\phi(p_2^{k_2}) \ldots \phi(p_r^{k_r})$.

Proof The theorem can be proved by induction on r. Suppose it is true for $r = \lambda$. Since gcd $(p_1^{k_1} p_2^{k_2} \ldots p_\lambda^{k_\lambda} p_{\lambda+1}^{k_{\lambda+1}}) = 1$, it follows, from the definition of a multiplicative function, that

$$\phi((p_1^{k_1} p_2^{k_2} \ldots p_\lambda^{k_\lambda})\, p_{\lambda+1}^{k_{\lambda+1}}) = \phi\left(p_1^{k_1} p_2^{k_2} \ldots p_\lambda^{k_\lambda}\right) \phi\left(p_{\lambda+1}^{k_{\lambda+1}}\right)$$

From the induction principle, the first factor on the right gives

$$\phi\left(p_1^{k_1} p_2^{k_2} \ldots p_\lambda^{k_\lambda}\right) = \phi\left(p_1^{k_1}\right) \phi\left(p_2^{k_2}\right) \ldots \phi\left(p_\lambda^{k_\lambda}\right)$$

Thus, $\phi(n)$ can be determined by substitution of this result into the preceding equation, such that

$$\phi(n) = \phi\left(p_1^{k_1}\right) \phi\left(p_2^{k_2}\right) \ldots \phi\left(p_\lambda^{k_\lambda}\right) \phi\left(p_{\lambda+1}^{k_{\lambda+1}}\right)$$

and this completes the proof.

Theorem 2.15 If $n > 1$ has a prime-power decomposition given by $n = p_1^{k_1} p_2^{k_2} \ldots p_r^{k_r}$, then

$$\begin{aligned}\phi(n) &= \left(p_1^{k_1} - p_1^{k_1-1}\right)\left(p_2^{k_2} - p_2^{k_2-1}\right) \ldots \left(p_r^{k_r} - p_r^{k_r-1}\right) \\ &= n\left(1 - \frac{1}{p_1}\right)\left(1 - \frac{1}{p_2}\right) \ldots \left(1 - \frac{1}{p_r}\right)\end{aligned}$$

Proof Since r is the number of distinct prime factors of n, $\phi(n)$ is multiplicative due to Theorem 2.14 such that $\phi(n) = \phi(p_1^{k_1})\,\phi(p_2^{k_2}) \ldots \phi\left(p_r^{k_r}\right)$. Using Theorem 2.12, namely, $\phi(p^k) = p^k(1 - (1/p))$, it gives

$$\begin{aligned}\phi(n) &= p_1^{k_1}\left(1 - \frac{1}{p_1}\right) p_2^{k_2}\left(1 - \frac{1}{p_2}\right) \cdots p_r^{k_r}\left(1 - \frac{1}{p_r}\right) \\ &= n\left(1 - \frac{1}{p_1}\right)\left(1 - \frac{1}{p_2}\right) \cdots \left(1 - \frac{1}{p_r}\right)\end{aligned}$$

This completes the proof.

■ **Example 2.17** Calculate the value of $\phi(2700)$. The prime-power factorization of 2700 is $2^2 \cdot 3^2 \cdot 5^2$. From Theorem 2.15, it follows that

$$\begin{aligned}\phi(2700) &= \phi(2^2)\,\phi(3^3)\,\phi(5^2)\\ &= 2700\left(1-\frac{1}{2}\right)\left(1-\frac{1}{3}\right)\left(1-\frac{1}{5}\right)\\ &= (2700)(1/2)(2/3)(4/5) = 720\end{aligned}$$

2.5.2 Euler's Theorem

Euler was the first to publish a proof of Fermat's theorem in 1736. Considerably later in 1760, Euler gave a more generalized version of Fermat's theorem from the case of prime p to an arbitrary integer n. Euler's theorem is helpful in reducing large powers modulo n.

Theorem 2.16 (Euler's theorem) If $n \geq 2$ is a positive integer and $\gcd(a,n) \equiv 1$, then $a^{\phi(n)} = 1 \pmod{n}$, where $\phi(n)$ denotes the number of positive integers less than and relatively prime to n.

Proof Let $r_1, r_2, \ldots, r_{\phi(n)}$ be the $\phi(n)$ positive integers less than n which are relatively prime to n. Consider the least residues (mod n) of the $\phi(n)$ numbers $ar_1, ar_2, \ldots, ar_{\phi(n)}$. For the least residues of these $\phi(n)$ numbers to be a permutation of $r_1, r_2, \ldots, r_{\phi(n)}$ in a certain order, these $\phi(n)$ numbers should all be distinct and relatively prime to n. To show that no two of the integers of the $\phi(n)$ numbers are congruent modulo n, we set

$$ar_i \equiv ar_j \pmod{n}, \quad 1 \leq i < j \leq \phi(n)$$

Since $\gcd(a,n) = 1$, it follows that $r_i \equiv r_j \pmod{n}$ by the cancellation law. Since r_i and r_j are least residues (mod n), it implies that $r_i = r_j$, which is a contradiction. Furthermore, if $r_i \neq r_j$, then $ar_i \not\equiv ar_j \pmod{n}$, and so the $\phi(n)$ numbers are all distinct. To prove that all $\phi(n)$ numbers ar_i, $i = 1, 2, \ldots, \phi(n)$, are relatively prime to n, suppose p is a prime common divisor of ar_i and n for some $i, 1 \leq i \leq \phi(n)$. Since p is a prime, either $p \mid a$ or $p \mid r_i$. Thus either p is a common divisor of a and n or of r_i and n. But these two cases will never happen, because $\gcd(a,n) = \gcd(r_i, n) = 1$. Therefore, $\gcd(ar_i, \text{n})$ must be 1 for each i, $1 \leq i \leq \phi(n)$. Thus we see that

$$(ar_1)(ar_2)\ldots(ar_{\phi(n)}) \equiv r_1 r_2 \ldots r_{\phi(n)} \pmod{n}$$

or

$$a^{\phi(n)}(r_1 r_2 \ldots r_{\phi(n)}) \equiv r_1 r_2 \ldots r_{\phi(n)} \pmod{n}$$

Since gcd $(r_i, n) = 1$, with $i = 1, 2, \ldots, \phi(n)$, it follows that their product is also relatively prime to n, i.e. gcd $(r_1 r_2 \ldots r_{\phi(n)}, n)$, = 1.

Thus, the product factor can be cancelled out in the last congruence, which leaves us with $a^{\phi(n)} \equiv 1 \pmod{n}$.

■ **Example 2.18** Let $n = 7$. The positive integers less than and relatively prime to 7 are 1, 2, 3, 4, 5, 6 which correspond to $r_1, r_2, r_3, r_4, r_5, r_6$. If $a = -3$, then the ϕ (7) numbers ar_i, $1 \le i \le \phi(7)$ are −3, −6, −9, −12, −15, −18, and when with modulo 7, $-3 \equiv 4$, $-6 \equiv 1$, $-9 \equiv 5$, $-12 \equiv 2$, $-15 \equiv 6$, and $-18 \equiv 3$. When the above congruences (mod 7) are all multiplied together.

$$(-3)(-6)(-9)(-12)(-15)(-18) \equiv 4 \cdot 1 \cdot 5 \cdot 2 \cdot 6 \cdot 3 \pmod{7}$$

which becomes

$$(1)(-3) \cdot (2)(-3) \cdot (3)(-3) \cdot (4)(-3) \cdot (5)(-3) \cdot (6)(-3) \equiv 1 \cdot 2 \cdot 3 \cdot 4 \cdot 5 \cdot 6 \pmod{7}$$

$$(1 \cdot 2 \cdot 3 \cdot 4 \cdot 5 \cdot 6)(-3)^6 \equiv (1 \cdot 2 \cdot 3 \cdot 4 \cdot 5 \cdot 6) \pmod{7}$$

Knowing that 720 is relatively prime to 7, the product of six integers $(1 \cdot 2 \cdot 3 \cdot 4 \cdot 5 \cdot 6)$ can be cancelled to give

$$(-3)^6 \equiv 1 \pmod{7}$$

2.6 CHINESE REMAINDER THEOREM AND SIMULTANEOUS CONGRUENCES

Having considered a single linear congruence, it is appropriate to turn to the problem of solving a system of simultaneous linear congruences.

$$a_r x \equiv b_r \pmod{n_r}, 1 \le r \le k$$

where the moduli n_r are relatively prime in pairs. The Chinese Remainder Theorem is the rule for obtaining a solution for simultaneous congruences.

Theorem 2.17 (Chinese Remainder Theorem) Let $n_1, n_2, \ldots, n_k$ be positive integers such that gcd $(n_i, n_j) = 1$ for $i \ne j$. Then the system of linear congruences

$$x \equiv a_r \pmod{n_r}, \qquad r = 1, 2, \ldots, k$$

has a unique solution modulo $n_1 n_2 \ldots n_k$.

Proof Let us show by induction that the simultaneous congruence system has a solution. When $k = 1$, it results in $x \equiv a_1 \pmod{n_1}$. Therefore, $x = a_1 + k_1 n_1$ for some k_1. If $x \equiv a_2 \pmod{n_2}$ for $k = 2$, then

$$a_1 + k_1 n_1 \equiv a_2 \pmod{n_2}$$

or

$$k_1 n_1 \equiv a_2 - a_1 \pmod{n_2}$$

Since gcd $(n_2, n_1) = 1$ due to pairwise coprime we see that this congruence has a unique solution modulo n_2 with the unknown k_1 such that $k_1 = \lambda + k_2 n_2$ for some k_2. Thus, we have

$$x = a_1 + (\lambda + k_2 n_2) n_1 \equiv a_1 + \lambda n_1 \pmod{n_1 n_2}$$

which satisfies both congruences.

Suppose the given system has a solution (mod $n_1 n_2 \ldots n_k$) for $k = \mu - 1$. Then there is a solution σ to the system

$$x \equiv a_r \pmod{n_r}, r = 1, 2, \ldots, \mu - 1$$

But the system

$$x \equiv \sigma \pmod{n_1 n_2 \ldots n_{\mu-1}}$$

$$x \equiv a_\mu \pmod{n_\mu}$$

has a solution modulo $n_1 n_2 \ldots n_{\mu-1}$, because gcd $(n_1 n_2 \ldots n_k) = 1$.

Next, let us show the solution is unique. If μ and σ are both solutions of the given simultaneous congruences, then

$$\mu \equiv \sigma \equiv a_r \pmod{n_r}, r = 1, 2, \ldots, k$$

whence $n_r \mid (\mu - \sigma)$, $1 \le r \le k$. Thus, we see that $\mu - \sigma$ is a common multiple of $n_1, n_2, \ldots, n_k$. Since the moduli are pairwise coprime, that is, gcd $(n_i, n_j) = 1$ for $i \ne j$, we have $n_1 n_2 \ldots n_k \mid (\mu - \sigma)$. But since μ and σ are least residues modulo $n_1 n_2 \ldots n_k$, $-n_1 n_2 \ldots n_k < (\mu - \sigma) < n_1 n_2 \ldots n_k$, where $\mu - \sigma = 0$.

■ **Example 2.19** Find the unique solution of x satisfying the system of simultaneous congruences $x \equiv 3 \pmod 5$, $x \equiv 5 \pmod 7$, and $x \equiv 7 \pmod{11}$.

The first congruence gives $x = 3 + 5k_1$ for some k_1. Substituting this in the second congruence, it follows that $3 + 5k_1 \equiv 5 \pmod 7$, from which we obtain $k_1 \equiv 6 \pmod 7$, or $k_1 = 6 + 7k_2$ for some k_2. Thus we have $x = 3 + 5k_1 = 3 + 5(6 + 7k_2) = 33 + 35k_2$ which must satisfy the first two congruences. If x satisfies the third congruence, we must have $33 + 35k_2 \equiv 7 \pmod{11}$, which implies $k_2 \equiv 9 \pmod{11}$ or $k_2 \equiv 9 + 11k_3$. Substituting this k_2 into the above third congruence results in $x = 33 + 35(9 + 11k_3) \equiv 348 + 385k_3 \pmod{11}$. Thus, $x \equiv 348 \pmod{385}$ must satisfy the three congruences. Hence, 348 is the unique solution modulo 385.

This unique solution can be proved as follows. The solution modulo is $n = (5)(7)(11) = (5)(77) = (7)(55) = (11)(35)$. Since $(77)(3) \equiv 1 \pmod 5$, $(55)(6) \equiv 1 \pmod 7$, and $(35)(6) \equiv 1 \pmod{11}$, the unique solution of this simultaneous congruences is

$$x \equiv (3)(77)(3) + (5)(55)(6) + (7)(35)(6) \pmod{385}$$

$$\equiv 3813 \pmod{385} \equiv 348 \pmod{385}, \text{ as expected}$$

2.7 QUADRATIC CONGRUENCES

We considered linear congruences in Sec. 2.2. Let us now learn how to solve quadratic congruences

$$Az^2 + Bz + C \equiv 0 \pmod m$$

where m is an odd prime or composite, i.e. $m = p_1^{e_1} p_2^{e_2} \ldots p_k^{e_k}$ and $A \not\equiv 0 \pmod p$. For m an odd prime p, there is an inverse A' of A, that is, $AA' \equiv 1 \pmod p$. Consequently, the quadratic congruence in the preceding becomes

$$z^2 + A'Bz + A'C \equiv 0 \pmod p$$

for modulo an odd prime p. If $A'B$ is even, the above congruence becomes

$$\left(z + \frac{A'B}{2}\right)^2 \equiv \left(\frac{A'B}{2}\right)^2 - A'C \pmod p$$

whereas if $A'B$ is odd, $p + A'B$ becomes even and consequently the quadratic congruence can be expressed as

$$z^2 + (p + A'B)z + A'C \equiv 0 \pmod p$$

or

$$\left(z + \frac{p + A'B}{2}\right)^2 \equiv \left(\frac{p + A'B}{2}\right)^2 - A'C \pmod p$$

In either case, we can express an equivalent form as

$$x^2 \equiv a \pmod p, \gcd(a, p) = 1$$

■ **Example 2.20** Find the solution for the quadratic congruence $x^2 \equiv 1 \pmod 3$. Since $1^2 \equiv 1 \pmod 3$ and $2^2 \equiv 1 \pmod 3$, two solutions of this quadratic congruence are

$$x \equiv 1 \pmod 3 \qquad \text{and} \qquad x \equiv 2 \pmod 3$$

■ **Example 2.21** Convert $2x^2 + 3x + 1 \equiv 0 \pmod{5}$ into quadratic congruence. Since $2A' \equiv 1 \pmod{5}$, $A' = 3$. Therefore, we have $x^2 + 4x + 3 \equiv 0 \pmod{5}$. Since $A'B = 4$ is even, this quadratic congruence becomes $(x + 2)^2 \equiv 1 \pmod{5}$.

Next, consider the case of composite moduli. Let $p_1^{e_1} p_2^{e_2} \ldots p_k^{e_k}$ be the prime-power decomposition of m. As is well known, the quadratic congruence $x^2 \equiv a \pmod{p}$ can also hold for composite m. Thus, quadratic congruences modulo $m = p_1^{e_1} p_2^{e_2} \ldots p_k^{e_k}$ are solved by evaluating k simultaneous congruences modulo the coprime factors of m as follows:

$$
\begin{aligned}
x^2 &\equiv a \pmod{p_1^{e_1}} \\
x^2 &\equiv a \pmod{p_2^{e_2}} \\
&\cdot \\
&\cdot \\
&\cdot \\
x^2 &\equiv a \pmod{p_k^{e_k}}
\end{aligned}
$$

Therefore, these k simultaneous congruences may be compactly expressed in the following form.

$$x^2 \equiv a \pmod{p_r^{e_r}}, r = 1, 2, \ldots, k$$

Now we shall see how to solve these simultaneous congruences for all primes p_r and positive integers e_r.

■ **Example 2.22** Solve $x^2 \equiv 9 \pmod{28}$. The prime-power decomposition of 28 turns out to be 2^2 and 7. Therefore, the simultaneous congruences are

$$x^2 \equiv 9 \pmod{4}$$

$$x^2 \equiv 9 \pmod{7}$$

The first congruence has solutions 1 and 3, and the second 3 and 4. Thus, there are four sets of solutions as follows:

$$x \equiv 1 \pmod{4} \quad \text{and} \quad x \equiv 3 \pmod{7}$$

$$x \equiv 1 \pmod{4} \quad \text{and} \quad x \equiv 4 \pmod{7}$$

$$x \equiv 3 \pmod{4} \quad \text{and} \quad x \equiv 3 \pmod{7}$$

From these four sets of congruence, the solutions to $x^2 \equiv 9 \pmod{28}$ are 17, 25, 3, and 11.

2.8 QUADRATIC RESIDUES, LEGENDRE SYMBOL, AND JACOBI SYMBOL

Consider a simple quadratic congruence

$$x^2 \equiv a \pmod{p}, \qquad \gcd(a, p) = 1$$

For a solution to $x^2 \equiv a \pmod{p}$ to exist, a has to be a quadratic residue (mod p). In other words, if $x^2 \equiv a \pmod{p}$ has a solution, then a is called a quadratic residue (mod p). If $x^2 \equiv a \pmod{p}$ has no solution, then a is called a quadratic nonresidue (mod p). In other words, if a is a quadratic nonresidue, then there is no solution.

■ **Example 2.23** Consider the case of $p = 13$ which is an odd prime. Pick the quadratic residues a of p from the reduced residue system $Z_{13}^* = \{1, 2, \ldots, 12\}$. Substituting the squares of integers $x = 1, 2, 3, \ldots,$ 12 in $x^2 \equiv a \pmod{13}$, it is possible to find the quadratic residues of p even though this procedure is long and rather tedious. The squares of the integers 1, 2, 3, . . ., 12 for modulo 13 may be computed as follows:

$$\begin{aligned}
1^2 &\equiv 1 \pmod{13} \\
2^2 &\equiv 4 \pmod{13} \\
3^2 &\equiv 9 \pmod{13} \\
4^2 &= 16 = (13)(1) + 3 \equiv 3 \pmod{13} \\
5^2 &= 25 = (13)(1) + 12 \equiv 12 \pmod{13} \\
6^2 &= 36 = (13)(2) + 10 \equiv 10 \pmod{13} \\
7^2 &= 49 = (13)(3) + 10 \equiv 10 \pmod{13} \\
8^2 &= 64 = (13)(4) + 12 \equiv 12 \pmod{13} \\
9^2 &= 81 = (13)(6) + 3 \equiv 3 \pmod{13} \\
10^2 &= 100 = (13)(7) + 9 \equiv 9 \pmod{13} \\
11^2 &= 121 = (13)(9) + 4 \equiv 4 \pmod{13} \\
12^2 &= 144 = (13)(11) + 1 \equiv 1 \pmod{13}
\end{aligned}$$

As a result, the quadratic residues of 13 are 1, 3, 4, 9, 10, and 12; while the quadratic nonresidues are 2, 5, 6, 7, 8, and 11. Thus, you can see that the set $Z_{13}^* = \{1, 2, \ldots, 12\}$ is equally divided into quadratic residues and nonresidues.

In general, if modulo p is an odd prime, there are precisely $(p-1)/2$ quadratic residues and $(p-1)/2$ quadratic nonresidues of p.

Let p be an odd prime and gcd $(a, p) = 1$. The Legendre symbol (a/p) is defined as

$$(a/p) = \begin{cases} 1 & \text{if } a \text{ is quadratic residue of } p \\ -1 & \text{if } a \text{ is a quadratic nonresidue of } p \end{cases}$$

Thus, (a/p), a symbol introduced by Legendre in his Essai sur la Théore des Nombres (1798), is called the Legendre symbol for expressing whether or not a is quadratic residue modulo p.

Euler devised a simple criterion (Theorem 2.19) for deciding whether an integer a is a quadratic residue of an odd prime p. Before discussing this criterion, we would prefer to introduce the conceptual relation between the order of an integer and a primitive root modulo p. Let as show how this works in a specific example.

■ **Example 2.24** The following table exhibits the order of 3 modulo 7.

n	1	2	3	4	5	6	7	8	9	10	...
3^n	3	9	27	81	243	729	2187	6561	19683	59049	...
3^n (mod 7)	3	2	6	4	5	1	3	2	6	4	...
	←			a period		→					

Here the period after which the sequence is repeated for the first time is obviously 6. Therefore, we say that the integer 3 has order 6 modulo 7, or that the order 3 modulo-7 is 6. Thus, we call 3 a primitive root modulo 7, because the primitive root generates the reduced residue system Z_7^* over a period in some permutation.

Theorem 2.18 If p is an odd prime, then there exists a primitive root g of p such that

$$g^{(p-1)/2} \equiv -1 \pmod{p}$$

Proof Since $g^{p-1} \equiv 1 \pmod{p}$ from Fermat's theorem, we have

$$(g^{(p-1)/2} - 1)(g^{(p-1)/2} + 1) \equiv g^{p-1} - 1 \equiv 0 \pmod{p}$$

Hence we have either $g^{(p-1)/2} \equiv 1 \pmod{p}$ or $g^{(p-1)/2} \equiv -1 \pmod{p}$. But, since the order of g is $p-1$, $g^{(p-1)/2} \not\equiv 1 \pmod{p}$. It must therefore satisfy $g^{(p-1)/2} \equiv -1 \pmod{p}$, because a quadratic nonresidue of p does not satisfy $g^{(p-1)/2} \equiv 1 \pmod{p}$.

Theorem 2.19 (Euler's Criterion)
Let p be an odd prime and gcd $(a, p) = 1$. Then a is a quadratic residue of p if and only if $a^{(p-1)/2} \equiv 1 \pmod{p}$: it is a quadratic nonresidue if and only if $a^{(p-1)/2} \equiv -1 \pmod{p}$.

Proof According to Fermat's theorem $a^{p-1} \equiv 1 \pmod{p}$ for $\gcd(a, p) = 1$. Let g be a primitive root of the odd prime p and $a \equiv g^n \pmod{p}$ for some n. If $n = 2k$ (even), then $x^2 \equiv a \pmod{p}$ becomes

$$a \equiv g^{2k} \pmod{p} \equiv (g^k)^2 \pmod{p}$$

Hence we have

$$a^{(p-1)/2} \equiv (g^{p-1})^k \equiv 1^k \equiv 1 \pmod{p}$$

Thus, the solution of $x^2 \equiv a \pmod{p}$ is $x \equiv g^k \pmod{p}$. Consequently, a is a quadratic residue.

If $n = 2k + 1$ (odd), i.e. for a equal to an odd power of a primitive root, then $a^{(p-1)/2} \equiv (g^{2k+1})^{(p-1)/2} \equiv (g^{p-1})^k \cdot g^{(p-1)/2} \equiv 1^k \cdot g^{(p-1)/2} \equiv -1 \pmod{p}$. Thus, using Theorem 2.18, a is a quadratic nonresidue.

■ **Example 2.25** Choose $p = 11$. Using the reduced residue system $Z_{11}^* = \{1, 2, \ldots, 10\}$, the quadratic residues are computed as follows:

$$\begin{aligned} 1^2 &\equiv 10^2 \equiv 1 \pmod{11} \\ 2^2 &\equiv 9^2 \equiv 4 \pmod{11} \\ 3^2 &\equiv 8^2 \equiv 9 \pmod{11} \\ 4^2 &\equiv 7^2 \equiv 5 \pmod{11} \\ 5^2 &\equiv 6^2 \equiv 3 \pmod{11} \end{aligned}$$

Thus, the quadratic residues of 11 are 1, 3, 4, 5, 9: whereas the quadratic nonresidues of 11 are 2, 6, 7, 8, 10. Hence, using the Legendre symbol, the results of quadratic residues and nonresidues can be expressed as

$$(1/11) = (3/11) = (4/11) = (5/11) = (9/11) = 1$$

and

$$(2/11) = (6/11) = (7/11) = (8/11) = (10/11) = -1$$

The next theorem concerning the Legendre symbol exhibits simple but important properties.

Theorem 2.20 Let p be an odd prime and a and b be integers which are relatively prime to p. Then the Legendre symbol has the following properties.

(A) If $a \equiv b \pmod{p}$, then $(a/p) = (b/p)$

(B) If $\gcd(a, p) = 1$, then $(a/p) \equiv a^{(p-1)/2} \pmod{p}$

(C) If $\gcd(a, p) = 1$, then $(a^2/p) = 1$

(D) If both $\gcd(a, p) = 1$ and $\gcd(b, p) = 1$, then $(ab/p) = (a/p)(b/p)$

(E) When p is an odd prime, $(-1/p) = (-1)^{(p-1)/2}$ and $(1/p) = 1$

Proof (A) Suppose $x^2 \equiv a \pmod p$ has a solution. If $a \equiv b \pmod p$, then $x^2 \equiv b \pmod p$ also has a solution. If $(a/p) = 1$ and $a \equiv b \pmod p$, then $(b/p) = 1$. Similarly, if $(a/p) = -1$ and $a \equiv b \pmod p$, then $(b/p) = -1$. Thus $(a/p) = (b/p)$ is proved.

(B) Using Euler's criterion in terms of the Legendre symbol, we have $(a/p) = 1$ if $a^{(p-1)/2} \equiv 1 \pmod p$ and $(a/p) = -1$ if $a^{(p-1)/2} \equiv -1 \pmod p$. Combining these two relations into a single expression, we have

$$(a/p) \equiv a^{(p-1)/2} \pmod p$$

This is simply Euler's criterion rephrased in terms of the Legendre symbol.

(C) $x^2 \equiv a^2 \pmod p$ clearly has a solution. Hence $(a^2/p) = 1$. But, using $(a/p) \equiv a^{(p-1)/2} \pmod p$ in (B), it can be shown that

$$(a^2/p) \equiv (a^2)^{(p-1)/2} \equiv a^{p-1} \equiv 1 \pmod p$$

by Fermat's theorem.

(D) Using the property (B), we have

$$(ab/p) \equiv (ab)^{(p-1)/2} \equiv a^{(p-1)/2} \cdot b^{(p-1)/2} \equiv (a/p)(b/p) \pmod p$$

However, if $(ab/p) \neq (a/p)\,(b/p)$, we could have $1 \equiv -1 \pmod p$ or $2 \equiv 0 \pmod p$ due to the fact that the Legendre symbol takes only the values 1 or -1. But, since $p > 2$, $2 \equiv 0 \pmod p$ does not hold. Since both sides of the congruence are either 1 or -1, the only way the two members can be congruent modulo p is their being equal. Therefore, $(ab/p) \equiv (a/p)(b/p) \pmod p$ is proved.

(E) Using the property (B), we obtain $(-1/p) \equiv (-1)^{(p-1)/2} \pmod p$ by setting $a = -1$. Since $(-1/p)$ and $(-1)^{(p-1)/2}$ are either 1 or -1, the resulting congruence $(-1/p) \equiv (-1)^{(p-1)/2} \pmod p$ implies that $(-1/p) = (-1)^{(p-1)/2}$. And the second equality in (E), namely $(1/p) = 1$, is a special case of (C) for $a = 1$.

The definition of the Jacobi symbol will be introduced in the following. Let b and p be relatively prime integers with an odd prime $p > 1$. If $p = p_1 p_2 \ldots p_s$ is the decomposition of p into odd primes, but p_i and p_j are not necessarily distinct, then the Jacobi symbol is defined as

$$(b/p) = (b/p_1)(b/p_2)\ldots(b/p_s) = \prod_{i=1}^{s} (b/p_i)$$

where the symbols (b/p_i) for $i = 1, 2, \ldots, s$ are Legendre symbols.

■ **Example 2.26** Let us consider whether the quadratic congruence $x^2 \equiv 2 \pmod 9$ is solvable. The coprime factors of 9 are 3 and 3. From the Jacobi symbol, $(2/9) = (2/3)\,(2/3)$, where the Legendre symbol is $(2/3) \equiv 2^{(3-1)/2} \pmod 3 \equiv 2 \pmod 3 \equiv -1$. This gives $(2/9) = (-1)\,(-1) = 1$. Therefore, $x^2 \equiv 2 \pmod 9$ seems to be solvable. However, we have

$$\begin{aligned} 1^2 \equiv 8^2 &\equiv 1 \pmod 9 \\ 2^2 \equiv 7^2 &\equiv 4 \pmod 9 \\ 3^2 \equiv 6^2 &\equiv 0 \pmod 9 \\ 4^2 \equiv 5^2 &\equiv 7 \pmod 9 \end{aligned}$$

which indicates no solution for $x^2 \equiv 2 \pmod 9$.

Therefore, for $x^2 \equiv b \pmod p$ to be solvable, where $p = p_1\,p_2 \ldots p_s$, the following conditions have to be satisfied.

$$\begin{aligned} (b/p_1) &= 1 \\ (b/p_2) &= 1 \\ &\vdots \\ (b/p_s) &= 1 \end{aligned}$$

REFERENCES

1. Burton, D.M. : *Elementary Number Theory*, Allyn and Bacon, Boston, Mass., 1976.
2. Dudley, U. : *Elementary Number Theory*, W.H. Freeman and Company, San Francisco, Cal., 1969.
3. Ireland, K. and M. Rosen : *Elements of Number Theory : Including an Introduction to Equations over Finite Fields*, Bogden and Quigley, Tarrytown-on-Hudson, New York, 1972.
4. Niven, I. and H. Zuckerman, *An Introduction to the Theory of Numbers*, Wiley, New York, 1972.
5. Ore, O. : *Number Theory and Its History*, McGraw-Hill, New York, 1948.
6. Ore, O. : *Introduction to Number Theory*, Random House, New York, 1967.
7. Starke, H. : *An Introduction to Number Theory*, Markham Publishing Company, Chicago, Ill., 1970.

Chapter

3

Data Encryption Standard as Block Cipher Algorithm

Private key cryptosystems are commonly classified as block and stream ciphers. Block ciphers divide the plaintext into blocks of fixed size, and operate on each block independently. A block cipher provides secrecy by use of encryption—plaintext is transformed into ciphertext with the aid of the enciphering key. The ciphertext should be unintelligible without the secret deciphering key. Using the deciphering key, the ciphertext is transformed back into the original plaintext.

The Data Encryption Standard (DES), which is classified as a block cipher system, is currently the only certified encryption standard. It has been widely used in the area of banking and electronic funds transfer (EFT). In this chapter, DES is the main subject to be analysed in detail.

3.1 DATA ENCRYPTION STANDARD (DES)

The DES algorithm based on LUCIFER designed by Horst Feistel was developed at IBM under the leadership of W.L. Tuchman in 1972. This algorithm approved by the National Bureau of Standards (NBS) after assessment of DES strength by the National Security Agency

(NSA), became effective as a Federal Standard in 1977. The DES, which belongs to a secret key cryptosystem, is the most widely known encryption algorithm. Figure 3.1 shows the sketch of the DES algorithm. The plaintext block $\mathbf{X}$ is first transposed under an initial permutation IP, giving $\mathbf{X}_0 = \text{IP}(\mathbf{X}) = (\mathbf{L}_0, \mathbf{R}_0)$. After passing through 16 rounds of substitution and transposition, it is transposed under the inverse permutation IP^{-1} to give the ciphertext $\mathbf{Y}$. If $\mathbf{X}_i = (\mathbf{L}_i, \mathbf{R}_i)$ denotes the result of the ith round (iteration), then $\mathbf{L}_i = \mathbf{R}_{i-1}$ and $\mathbf{R}_i = \mathbf{L}_{i-1} \oplus f(\mathbf{R}_{i-1}, \mathbf{K}_i)$. But care should be taken at the last round (i.e. the 16th iteration) such that the left and right halves are not exchanged, that is, the concatenated block $(\mathbf{R}_{16}, \mathbf{L}_{16})$ becomes the preoutput to the final permutation IP^{-1}.

DES is the algorithm with which a 64-bit block of plaintext is enciphered into a 64-bit ciphertext by means of a 56-bit of cryptographic key. The encryption process consists of 16 rounds of encipherment, while the deciphering process is identical to that of encryption except that the keys are used in reverse order. The central techniques governing DES implementation involve the design of DES's permutation (P-box), substitutions (S-boxes), and key schedules.

Each bit of the ciphertext produced by DES is a complex function for all plaintext bits and all key bits. The permutation schedule must ensure that each bit of ciphertext be a function of all plaintext and key bits after a minimum number of rounds.

S-box functions must be designed in such a way that cryptographic strength is enhanced and easy implementation onto a single chip can be achieved. With such S-boxes, a total of $(2^{64})!$ different transformations from plaintext to ciphertext are possible. Therefore, the design of S-box structure becomes an important issue that will be raised as part of an independent study for DES. However, at the present time, there is no better S-box design than the one currently used by DES. The achievement of minimum number of logic circuits needed to implement S-box design will be the subject of study for increasing cryptographic strength and reducing complexity.

The key schedule begins with an initial permutation (PC–1) which selects 56-bits out of the 64-bit external key, by stripping off the 8 parity bits. These 56 key bits are loaded into two 28-bit shift registers and are shifted one or two positions to the left according to the shift schedule for encipherment. The key space contains 2^{56} keys.

The dependence of each ciphertext bit on all bits of plaintext and key is called intersymbol dependence. In a well designed cipher system, an output bit depends on more and more input bits as the number of

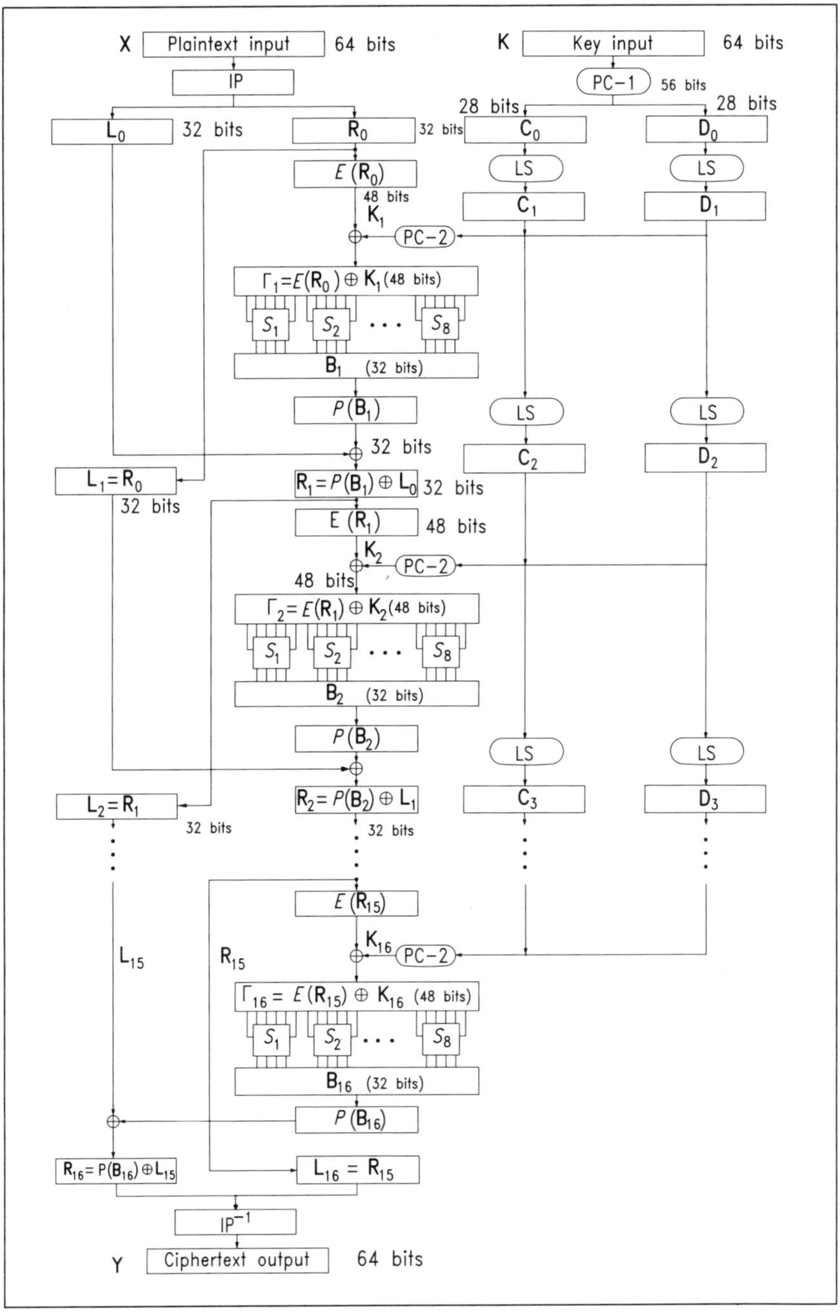

Fig. 3.1 Block cipher design used by DES

rounds increases. Many applications can take advantage of this property which should be analyzed by evaluating how fast intersymbol dependence can be achieved as a function of the number of rounds. This dependency measure plays an important role in the enhancement of cryptographic strength.

Although DES has been discussed for over 15 years, the theoretical background required for understanding it will make it difficult for the beginner to follow. A more detailed analysis of the DES algorithm is given in this chapter to facilitate easy understanding DES's operation. The scope of analysis will be (i) the permutation, distribution and substitution of plaintext data and key bits, (ii) analysis and implementation of substitutions (*S*-boxes), (iii) intersymbol dependencies of data and key bits, (iv) enciphering process at each round of DES, and (v) deciphering process for recovering the plaintext.

A detailed analysis of enciphering and deciphering processes will be presented with a numerical example of a two-round DES system, as shown in Fig. 3.1. The analysis will be done under the assumption that the 64-bit plaintext $\mathbf{X} = (x_1, x_2, \ldots, x_{64}) = (3\ 5\ 7\ 0\ E\ 2\ F\ 1\ B\ A\ 4\ 6\ 8\ 2\ C\ 7)$, in hexadecimal notation, enciphers into the 64-bit ciphertext $\mathbf{Y} = (y_1, y_2, \ldots, y_{64})$ under the control of a 64-bit externally entered key $\mathbf{K} = (k_1, k_2, \ldots, k_{64}) = (5\ 8\ 1\ F\ B\ C\ 9\ 4\ D\ 3\ A\ 4\ 5\ 2\ E\ A)$ including 8 parity bits.

3.2 KEY SCHEDULE

The key schedule starts with an initial permuted choice 1 (PC−1). The 8-bit parity vector $(k_8, k_{16}, k_{24}, k_{32}, k_{40}, k_{48}\ k_{56}, k_{64})$ must be removed prior to PC−1. 1 bit in each 8-bit byte of the key may be utilized for error detection in key generation, distribution, and storage. The parity bits $k_8, k_{16}, \ldots, k_{64}$ help ensure that each byte is of odd parity. Thus, 56 of the 64 external key bits are loaded into two 28-bit shift registers $(\mathbf{C}_0, \mathbf{D}_0)$. The contents of these registers are shifted one or two positions to the left according to the shift schedule (see Table 3.2). These 56 key bits $(\mathbf{C}_i, \mathbf{D}_i)$, $1 \le i \le 16$, are concatenated in the ordered set and reduced down to 48 key bits through the permuted choice 2 (PC−2). Thus, these 48-bit keys $\mathbf{K}_1, \mathbf{K}_2, \ldots, \mathbf{K}_{16}$ are created and executed for encipherment at each round in the order $\mathbf{K}_1$ through $\mathbf{K}_{16}$.

The 64-bit input key is expressed in binary notation as

$$\mathbf{K} = (\ 0101\ 1000\ 0001\ 1111\ 1011\ 1100\ 1001\ 0100$$
$$1101\ 0011\ 1010\ 0100\ 0101\ 0010\ 1110\ 1010\ ) \quad (3.1)$$

The register contents $\mathbf{C}_0$ (left) and $\mathbf{D}_0$ (right) are determined by considering the key bits located at the positions given in Table 3.1 (PC−1).

Table 3.1 Permuted Choice 1 (PC–1)

57	49	41	33	25	17	9	1	58	50	42	34	26	18
10	2	59	51	43	35	27	19	11	3	60	52	44	36
63	55	47	39	31	23	15	7	62	54	46	38	30	22
14	6	61	53	45	37	29	21	13	5	28	20	12	4

Table 3.2 Shifted Schedule for Encipherment

Round Number	1	2	3	4	5	6	7	8	9	10	11	12	13	14	15	16
Number of Left Shifts	1	1	2	2	2	2	2	2	1	2	2	2	2	2	2	1

Using Table 3.1, the blocks $\mathbf{C}_0$ and $\mathbf{D}_0$ are immediately obtained as shown below.

$$\mathbf{C}_0 = (1\,0\,1\,1\,1\,1\,0\,0\,1\,1\,0\,1\,0\,0$$

$$0\,1\,1\,0\,1\,0\,0\,1\,0\,0\,0\,1\,0\,1) \tag{3.2}$$

$$\mathbf{D}_0 = (1\,1\,0\,1\,0\,0\,1\,0\,0\,0\,1\,0\,1\,1$$

$$1\,0\,1\,0\,0\,0\,0\,1\,1\,1\,1\,1\,1\,1) \tag{3.3}$$

Using Table 3.2, the blocks $\mathbf{C}_1$ and $\mathbf{D}_1$ are obtained from the blocks $\mathbf{C}_0$ and $\mathbf{D}_0$, respectively, by shifting one place to the left as shown in the following.

$$\mathbf{C}_1 = (\ 0111\ \ 1001\ \ 1010\ \ 0011\ \ 0100\ \ 1000\ \ 1011\ ) \tag{3.4}$$

$$\mathbf{D}_1 = (\ 1010\ \ 0100\ \ 0101\ \ 1101\ \ 0000\ \ 1111\ \ 1111\ ) \tag{3.5}$$

Permuted choice 2 (PC–2) of Table 3.3 is the rule that defines how the 48-bit key vectors $\mathbf{K}_1, \mathbf{K}_2, \ldots, \mathbf{K}_{16}$ are derived from the concatenated blocks $(\mathbf{C}_1, \mathbf{D}_1), (\mathbf{C}_2, \mathbf{D}_2), \ldots, (\mathbf{C}_{16}, \mathbf{D}_{16})$, respectively.

Table 3.3 Permuted Choice 2 (PC–2)

14	17	11	24	1	5	3	28	15	6	21	10
23	19	12	4	26	8	16	7	27	20	13	2
41	52	31	37	47	55	30	40	51	45	33	48
44	49	39	56	34	53	46	42	50	36	29	32

The 48-bit key vector $\mathbf{K}_1$ is derived from $(\mathbf{C}_1, \mathbf{D}_1)$ by taking the key bits located in Table 3.3.

$$\mathbf{K}_1 = (\ 001001\ \ 111010\ \ 000101\ \ 101001\ \ 111001\ \ 011000\ \ 110111\ \ 011010\ ) \tag{3.6}$$

Since the number of left shifts is 1 at round 2, the concatenated block $(\mathbf{C}_2, \mathbf{D}_2)$ is created from the block $(\mathbf{C}_1, \mathbf{D}_1)$ by shifting one place to the left as shown below.

$$\mathbf{C}_2 = (\ 1111\ \ 0011\ \ 0100\ \ 0110\ \ 1001\ \ 0001\ \ 0110\ ) \tag{3.7}$$

$$\mathbf{D}_2 = (\ 0100\ \ 1000\ \ 1011\ \ 1010\ \ 0001\ \ 1111\ \ 1111\ ) \tag{3.8}$$

Using PC–2, $\mathbf{K}_2$ is easily obtained as

$$\mathbf{K}_2 = (\ 110110\ \ 101001\ \ 000111\ \ 011101\ \ 110101\ \ 111011\ \ 011101\ \ 001000\ ) \tag{3.9}$$

These two internal keys $\mathbf{K}_1$ and $\mathbf{K}_2$ obtained in Eqs. 3.6 and 3.9 are used in rounds 1 and 2, respectively, for the purpose of encipherment. Thus, we see that these 48-bit internal keys are generated through a series of permutations and left shifts of the 56 key bits selected from the 64-bit external key.

■ **Example 3.1** Find the internal key $\mathbf{K}_3$ from the key block $(\mathbf{C}_2, \mathbf{D}_2)$ shown in Eqs. 3.7 and 3.8. The concatenated block $(\mathbf{C}_3, \mathbf{D}_3)$ is generated from shifting $(\mathbf{C}_2, \mathbf{D}_2)$ two places to the left as follows:

$$\mathbf{C}_3 = (\ 1100\ \ 1101\ \ 0001\ \ 1010\ \ 0100\ \ 0101\ \ 1011\ )$$

$$\mathbf{D}_3 = (\ 0010\ \ 0010\ \ 1110\ \ 1000\ \ 0111\ \ 1111\ \ 1101\ )$$

Using Table 3.3,

$$\mathbf{K}_3 = (\ 000111\ \ 011100\ \ 001001\ \ 001011\ \ 111110\ \ 001001\ \ 011101\ \ 101000\ )$$

It is known that the DES strength will be reduced if the internal keys are all the same, i.e. if $\mathbf{K}_1 = \mathbf{K}_2 = \ldots = \mathbf{K}_{16}$. There is a set of weak keys within DES whenever the bits in $(\mathbf{C}_0, \mathbf{D}_0)$ are all ones or zeros. There exist four weak keys altogether, represented by the external keys as follows:

01 01 01 01 01 01 01 01
1F 1F 1F 1F 0E 0E 0E 0E
E0 E0 E0 E0 F1 F1 F1 F1
FE FE FE FE FE FE FE FE

■ **Example 3.2** Consider the 64-bit weak key of **K**= (01 01 01 01 01 01 01 01). Then **K** = (0000 0001 0000 0001 0000 0001 0000 0001 0000 0001 0000 0001 0000 0001 0000 0001). After removing the 8-bit parity vector from **K**, the register contents ($\mathbf{C}_0, \mathbf{D}_0$) are determined from Table 3.1 as follows:

$$\mathbf{C}_0 = (\,0000\ \ 0000\ \ 0000\ \ 0000\ \ 0000\ \ 0000\ \ 0000\,)$$

$$\mathbf{D}_0 = (\,0000\ \ 0000\ \ 0000\ \ 0000\ \ 0000\ \ 0000\ \ 0000\,)$$

The key blocks ($\mathbf{C}_i$, $\mathbf{D}_i$), $i = 1, 2, \ldots, 16$ are consecutively computed from the block ($\mathbf{C}_0$, $\mathbf{D}_0$) by shifting one or two places to the left according to Table 3.2. However, since the register contents ($\mathbf{C}_0$, $\mathbf{D}_0$) are all zeros, no matter how many times ($\mathbf{C}_0$, $\mathbf{D}_0$) is shifted to the left, ($\mathbf{C}_i$, $\mathbf{D}_i$), $1 \le i \le 16$ turns out to be all zeros. Therefore, the internal keys $\mathbf{K}_i$, $1 \le i \le 16$ are all zeroes, i.e., $\mathbf{K}_1 = \mathbf{K}_2 = \ldots = \mathbf{K}_{16}$ = (000000 000000 000000 000000 000000 000000 000000 000000). Since all the internal keys are identical, there is no distinction between the operations of encipherment and decipherment. Even though the number of such weak keys is samll in comparison to the key space 2^{56} which is why there is no significant threat to DES security, these keys should be avoided during key generation.

There is another key group comprising what are known as semiweak keys. For example, a semiweak key occurs whenever the repeating bit patterns in the registers $\mathbf{C}_i$ and $\mathbf{D}_i$ are $\mathbf{C}_i$ = (0101 . . . 0101) and $\mathbf{D}_i$ = (1010 . . . 1010) or vice versa.

■ **Example 3.3** Consider the registers $\mathbf{C}_1$ and $\mathbf{D}_1$ that are represented by the 28 bits of $\mathbf{C}_1$ = (0101 . . . 0101) and $\mathbf{D}_1$ = (1010 . . . 1010), respectively. From the key block ($\mathbf{C}_1$, $\mathbf{D}_1$), the bits of registers $\mathbf{C}_0$ and $\mathbf{D}_0$ are immediately determined as $\mathbf{C}_0$ = (1010. . . 1010) and $\mathbf{D}_0$ = (0101 . . . 0101), respectively. Using Table 3.1 and reinstating the 8-bit parity vector such that each byte is of odd parity results in the following external key.

$$\mathbf{K} = (\,1110\ \ 0000\ \ 0001\ \ 1111\ \ 1110\ \ 0000\ \ 0001\ \ 1111$$
$$1111\ \ 0001\ \ 0000\ \ 1110\ \ 1111\ \ 0001\ \ 0000\ \ 1110\,)$$
$$= (\,E\ \ 0\ \ 1\ \ F\ \ E\ \ 0\ \ 1\ \ F\ \ F\ \ 1\ \ 0\ \ E\ \ F\ \ 1\ \ 0\ \ E\,)$$

This is the semiweak key.

There are altogether 12 semiweak keys as shown below.

E0	FE	E0	FE	F1	FE	F1	FE
FE	E0	FE	E0	FE	F1	FE	F1
1F	FE	1F	FE	0E	FE	0E	FE
01	FE	01	FE	01	FE	01	FE
1F	E0	F1	E0	0E	F1	0E	F1
01	E0	01	E0	01	F1	01	F1
FE	1F	FE	1F	FE	0E	FE	0E
E0	F1	E0	F1	F1	0E	F1	0E
FE	01	FE	01	FE	01	FE	01
E0	01	E0	01	F1	01	F1	01
01	1F	01	1F	01	0E	01	0E
1F	01	1F	01	0E	01	0E	01

The relation $E_K E_K(\mathbf{X}) = \mathbf{X}$ holds good for any weak key $\mathbf{K}$ and any given plaintext $\mathbf{X}$. For any semiweak key $\mathbf{K}_\alpha$ there is another semiweak key $\mathbf{K}_\beta$ such that $E_{K\alpha} E_{K\beta}(\mathbf{X}) = \mathbf{X}$ and $E_{K\beta} E_{K\alpha}(\mathbf{X}) = \mathbf{X}$ for any plaintext $\mathbf{X}$. These problems related to encipherment will be considered in the following section.

3.3 ENCIPHERMENT

The numerical computation is given first, along with a detailed explanation of how the algorithm is used for encipherment. The basic scheme for encipherment applied to DES is shown in Fig. 3.1. As assumed in Sec. 3.1, the 64-bit plaintext to be enciphered is

$$\begin{aligned}\mathbf{X} &= (x_1, x_2, \ldots, x_{64}) \\ &= (0011\ 0101\ 0111\ 0000\ 1110\ 0010\ 1111\ 0001 \\ &\quad\ 1011\ 1010\ 0100\ 0110\ 1000\ 0010\ 1100\ 0111)\end{aligned} \tag{3.10}$$

This plaintext $\mathbf{X}$ is first subjected to an initial permutation (IP) to make it split into two blocks $\mathbf{L}_0$ (left) and $\mathbf{R}_0$ (right) where each of them consists of $X/2 = 32$ bits as indicated in Table 3.4, where the indices have been instated only for convenience of representation, e.g. $x_{58} \rightarrow$ 58. This permuted plaintext has bit 58 of the input as its first bit, bit 50 as its second bit, and so on with bit 7 as the last bit. This 64-bit permuted plaintext consists of a 32-bit block $\mathbf{L}_0$ followed by another 32-bit block $\mathbf{R}_0$. Thus, $(\mathbf{L}_0, \mathbf{R}_0)$ denotes a concatenation consisting of the bits of $\mathbf{L}_0$ followed by those of $\mathbf{R}_0$. Thus, using Table 3.4, we can construct the 32-bit vectors $\mathbf{L}_0$ and $\mathbf{R}_0$ as follows:

Table 3.4 Initial Permutation (IP)

	58	50	42	34	26	18	10	2
$\mathbf{L}_0$	60	52	44	36	28	20	12	4
	62	54	46	38	30	22	14	6
	64	56	48	40	32	24	16	8
	57	49	41	33	25	17	9	1
$\mathbf{R}_0$	59	51	43	35	27	19	11	3
	61	53	45	37	29	21	13	5
	63	55	47	39	31	23	15	7

Table 3.5 *E* Bit-Selection Table

32	1	2	3	4	5
4	5	6	7	8	9
8	9	10	11	12	13
12	13	14	15	16	17
16	17	18	19	20	21
20	21	22	23	24	25
24	25	26	27	28	29
28	29	30	31	32	1

$$\mathbf{L}_0 = (\,1010\;\;1110\;\;0001\;\;1011\;\;1010\;\;0001\;\;1000\;\;1001\,) \tag{3.11}$$
A E 1 B A 1 8 9

$$\mathbf{R}_0 = (\,1101\;\;1100\;\;0001\;\;1111\;\;0001\;\;0000\;\;1111\;\;0100\,) \tag{3.12}$$
D C 1 F 1 0 F 4

The right half of the plaintext to round 0, $\mathbf{R}_0$, is expanded from 32 bits to 48 bits according to Table 3.5.

The symbol E of $E\,(\mathbf{R}_0)$ denotes a function which takes a block of 32 bits as its input and yields one of 48 bits as its output. Note that Table 3.5 consists of eight blocks of 6 bits each, but the central portion (set in the box) represents the data (plaintext) and the first and last columns denote appendices for expansion. Hence, we have

$$E(\mathbf{R}_0) = (\,011011\;\;111000\;\;000011\;\;111110$$
$$100010\;\;100001\;\;011110\;\;101001\,) \tag{3.13}$$

Thus, the 32-bit $\mathbf{R}_0$ can be spread out and scrambled into 48 bits with the E-table.

Table 3.6 Primitive S-Box Functions

							S_1								
14	4	13	1	2	15	11	8	3	10	6	12	5	9	0	7
0	15	7	4	14	2	13	1	10	6	12	11	9	5	3	8
4	1	14	8	13	6	2	11	15	12	9	7	3	10	5	0
15	12	8	2	4	9	1	7	5	11	3	14	10	0	6	13
							S_2								
15	1	8	14	6	11	3	4	9	7	2	13	12	0	5	10
3	13	4	7	15	2	8	14	12	0	1	10	6	9	11	5
0	14	7	11	10	4	13	1	5	8	12	6	9	3	2	15
13	8	10	1	3	15	4	2	11	6	7	12	0	5	14	9
							S_3								
10	0	9	14	6	3	15	5	1	13	12	7	11	4	2	8
13	7	0	9	3	4	6	10	2	8	5	14	12	11	15	1
13	6	4	9	8	15	3	0	11	1	2	12	5	10	14	7
1	10	13	0	6	9	8	7	4	15	14	3	11	5	2	12
							S_4								
7	13	14	3	0	6	9	10	1	2	8	5	11	12	4	15
13	8	11	5	6	15	0	3	4	7	2	12	1	10	14	9
10	6	9	0	12	11	7	13	15	1	3	14	5	2	8	4
3	15	0	6	10	1	13	8	9	4	5	11	12	7	2	14
							S_5								
2	12	4	1	7	10	11	6	8	5	3	15	13	0	14	9
14	11	2	12	4	7	13	1	5	0	15	10	3	9	8	6
4	2	1	11	10	13	7	8	15	9	12	5	6	3	0	14
11	8	12	7	1	14	2	13	6	15	0	9	10	4	5	3
							S_6								
12	1	10	15	9	2	6	8	0	13	3	4	14	7	5	11
10	15	4	2	7	12	9	5	6	1	13	14	0	11	3	8
9	14	15	5	2	8	12	3	7	0	4	10	1	13	11	6
4	3	2	12	9	5	15	10	11	14	1	7	6	0	8	13
							S_7								
4	11	2	14	15	0	8	13	3	12	9	7	5	10	6	1
13	0	11	7	4	9	1	10	14	3	5	12	2	15	8	6
1	4	11	13	12	3	7	14	10	15	6	8	0	5	9	2
6	11	13	8	1	4	10	7	9	5	0	15	14	2	3	12
							S_8								
13	2	8	4	6	15	11	1	10	9	3	14	5	0	12	7
1	15	13	8	10	3	7	4	12	5	6	11	0	14	9	2
7	11	4	1	9	12	14	2	0	6	10	13	15	3	5	8
2	1	14	7	4	10	8	13	15	12	9	0	3	5	6	11

The key-dependent function, $\mathbf{\Gamma}_j = E(\mathbf{R}_i) \oplus \mathbf{K}_j$, $0 \le i \le 15$, $1 \le j \le 16$ can be computed in terms of the E bit-selection $E(\mathbf{R}_i)$, $0 \le i \le 15$ and the key schedule $\mathbf{K}_j$, $1 \le j \le 16$. The cipher function f_i, $1 \le i \le 16$, is defined in terms of $\mathbf{\Gamma}_j$ and the permutation function $P(\mathbf{B}_j)$.

Once $E(\mathbf{R}_0)$ is generated, it is added bit-by-bit to $\mathbf{K}_1$. Using Eqs. 3.6 and 3.13, a 48-bit vector $\mathbf{\Gamma}_1$ is resulted in

$$\begin{aligned}\mathbf{\Gamma}_1 &= E(\mathbf{R}_0) \oplus \mathbf{K}_1 \\ &= (\ 010010\quad 000010\quad 000110\quad 010111 \\ &\quad\ \ 011011\quad 111001\quad 101001\quad 110011\ )\end{aligned} \tag{3.14}$$

where $\oplus$ denotes bit-by-bit addition modulo-2. This 48-bit input Γ_1 to the S-boxes is passed through a nonlinear S-box transformation to form the 32-bit output.

The elements of vector $\mathbf{\Gamma}_j$, $1 \le j \le 16$ are used as arguments in the substitution operations (S-boxes) S_1 through S_8. Each S-box is described as a matrix of four rows and 16 columns as shown in Table 3.6. If S_i, $1 \le i \le 8$, is a matrix box defined in Table 3.6 and $\mathbf{A}$ an input block of 6 bits, then $S_i(\mathbf{A})$ is defined as follows:

The first and last bits of $\mathbf{A}$ represent the row of the matrix S_i (labeled either 00, or 01, or 10, or 11), while the middle 4 bits of $\mathbf{A}$ represent a column number in the range 0 to 15 (labeled either 0000, or 0001, . . . , or 1111). For example, for the input (010011) to S_1, denoted as S_1^{01} (1001), the row is 01, i.e. row 1, and the column is determined by 1001, i.e. column 9. Since the number in row 1 column 9 is 6, the output of S_1 is (0110). Thus, the choice of the primitive functions $\mathbf{K}_j$ for $1 \le j \le 16$, S_i for $1 \le i \le 8$, and P (permutation) is critical to the strength of an encipherment resulting from the data encryption algorithm. In fact, the expansion from 32 bits to 48 bits performed by the E-table followed by compression back to 32 bits by the S-boxes is the crucial part of the whole algorithm.

Grouping the 48-bit $\mathbf{\Gamma}_1$ into sets of 6 bits, as expressed in Eq. 3.14, leads to easy computation of the substitution operations for S_1 through S_8 as follows:

$$\begin{aligned}
S_1^{00}(1001) &= S_1^{0}(9) &= 10 &= 1010 \\
S_2^{00}(0001) &= S_2^{0}(1) &= 1 &= 0001 \\
S_3^{00}(0011) &= S_3^{0}(3) &= 14 &= 1110 \\
S_4^{01}(1011) &= S_4^{1}(11) &= 12 &= 1100
\end{aligned}$$

$$S_5^{01}(1101) = S_5^1(13) = 9 = 1001 \qquad (3.15)$$

$$S_6^{11}(1100) = S_6^3(12) = 6 = 0110$$

$$S_7^{11}(0100) = S_7^3(4) = 1 = 0001$$

$$S_8^{11}(1001) = S_8^3(9) = 12 = 1100$$

Each member in Eq. 3.15 represents the 4-bit output of an individual S-box, and concatenating all of these outputs yields the 32 bits represented by vector $\mathbf{B}_1$.

$$\mathbf{B}_1 = (\,1010 \;\; 0001 \;\; 1110 \;\; 1100 \;\; 1001 \;\; 0110 \;\; 0001 \;\; 1100\,) \qquad (3.16)$$

The permutation function $P(\mathbf{B}_1)$ yields a 32-bit output from a 32-bit input by permuting the bits of Eq. 3.16. Such a function is defined by Table 3.7.

The output $P(\mathbf{B}_1)$ defined by Table 3.7 is obtained from the input $\mathbf{B}_1$ by taking the 16th bit of $\mathbf{B}_1$ as the first bit of $P(\mathbf{B}_1)$, the seventh bit as the second bit of $P(\mathbf{B}_1)$, and so on until the 25th bit of $\mathbf{B}_1$ is taken as the 32nd bit of $P(\mathbf{B}_1)$. Thus the result can be represented as

$$P(\mathbf{B}_1) = (\,0010 \;\; 1011 \;\; 1010 \;\; 0001 \;\; 0101 \;\; 0011 \;\; 0110 \;\; 1100\,) \qquad (3.17)$$

Modulo-2 addition of $P(\mathbf{B}_1)$ with $\mathbf{L}_0$ may be expressed as

$$\mathbf{R}_1 = P(\mathbf{B}_1) \oplus \mathbf{L}_0$$

$$= (\,1000 \;\; 0101 \;\; 1011 \;\; 1010 \;\; 1111 \;\; 0010 \;\; 1110 \;\; 0101\,) \qquad (3.18)$$

8 5 B A F 2 E 5

This is the result representing the right-half output after round one. Since $\mathbf{L}_1 = \mathbf{R}_0$, the left half output after round one is immediately obtained from Eq. 3.12 such that

Table 3.7 Permutation Function P

16	7	20	21
29	12	28	17
1	15	23	26
5	18	31	10
2	8	24	14
32	27	3	9
19	13	30	6
22	11	4	25

$$\mathbf{L}_1 = (\,1101\ \ 1100\ \ 0001\ \ 1111\ \ 0001\ \ 0000\ \ 1111\ \ 0100\,) \qquad (3.19)$$
$$\quad\ \mathrm{D}\quad\ \mathrm{C}\quad\ 1\quad\ \mathrm{F}\quad\ 1\quad\ 0\quad\ \mathrm{F}\quad\ 4$$

Thus, computation of $\mathbf{R}_1$ and $\mathbf{L}_1$ completes the first-round encipherment.

Let us now consider the second-round encipherment. Expanding $\mathbf{R}_1$ of Eq. 3.18 with the aid of Table 3.5, we have

$$E\,(\mathbf{R}_1) = (\,110000\ \ 001011\ \ 110111\ \ 110101 \qquad (3.20)$$
$$011110\ \ 100101\ \ 011100\ \ 001011\,)$$

Modulo-2 addition of $E\,(\mathbf{R}_1)$ with $\mathbf{K}_2$ yields

$$\Gamma_2 = E\,(\mathbf{R}_1) \oplus \mathbf{K}_2$$
$$= (\,000110\ \ 100010\ \ 110000\ \ 101000 \qquad (3.21)$$
$$101011\ \ 011110\ \ 000001\ \ 000011\,)$$

The substitution operations for S-boxes are followed by

$$S_1^{00}\,(0011) = S_1^0\,(3) = 1 = 0001$$
$$S_2^{10}\,(0001) = S_2^2\,(1) = 14 = 1110$$
$$S_3^{10}\,(1000) = S_3^2\,(8) = 11 = 1011$$
$$S_4^{10}\,(0100) = S_4^2\,(4) = 12 = 1100$$
$$S_5^{11}\,(0101) = S_5^3\,(5) = 14 = 1110 \qquad (3.22)$$
$$S_6^{00}\,(1111) = S_6^0\,(15) = 11 = 1011$$
$$S_7^{01}\,(0000) = S_7^1\,(0) = 13 = 1101$$
$$S_8^{01}\,(0001) = S_8^1\,(1) = 15 = 1111$$

Concatenating all these results of Eq. 3.22 yields

$$\mathbf{B}_2 = (\,0001\ \ 1110\ \ 1011\ \ 1100\ \ 1110\ \ 1011\ \ 1101\ \ 1111\,) \qquad (3.23)$$

Using Table 3.7, the permutation $P\,(\mathbf{B}_2)$ becomes

$$P\,(\mathbf{B}_2) = (\,0101\ \ 1111\ \ 0011\ \ 1110\ \ 0011\ \ 1001\ \ 1111\ \ 0111\,) \qquad (3.24)$$

Table 3.8 Inverse of Initial Permutation, IP^{-1}

40	8	48	16	56	24	64	32
39	7	47	15	55	23	63	31
38	6	46	14	54	22	62	30
37	5	45	13	53	21	61	29
36	4	44	12	52	20	60	28
35	3	43	11	51	19	59	27
34	2	42	10	50	18	58	26
33	1	41	9	49	17	57	25

Thus, the right-half output after round two is obtained by modulo-2 addition of $P\ (\mathbf{B}_2)$ with $\mathbf{L}_1$ such that

$$\mathbf{R}_2 = P\ (\mathbf{B}_2) \oplus \mathbf{L}_1$$

$$= (\,1000\ \ 0011\ \ 0010\ \ 0001\ \ 0010\ \ 1001\ \ 0000\ \ 0011\,) \quad (3.25)$$
$$\ \ 8\qquad 3\qquad 2\qquad 1\qquad 2\qquad 9\qquad 0\qquad 3$$

The left-half output after round two becomes

$$\mathbf{L}_2 = \mathbf{R}_1 = (\,1000\ \ 0101\ \ 1011\ \ 1010\ \ 1111\ \ 0010\ \ 1110\ \ 0101\,) \quad (3.26)$$
$$\ \ 8\qquad 5\qquad B\qquad A\qquad F\qquad 2\qquad E\qquad 5$$

Concatenation of $\mathbf{R}_2$ with $\mathbf{L}_2$ is called the preoutput block in our two-round cipher system.

The permutation IP^{-1} applied to the preoutput block is the inverse of the initial permutation IP applied to the input (plaintext). Therefore, the preoutput is then subjected to the permutation IP^{-1} according to Table 3.8.

The top numbers of the odd columns in IP^{-1} are expressed by $8\,(5+i)$, $0 \le i \le 3$, while the top numbers of the even columns are expressed by $8i$, $1 \le i \le 4$. Thus, the entries of the odd number columns consist of $40-j$, $48-j$, $56-j$, and $64-j$ where $0 \le j \le 7$. The entries of the even number columns consist of $8-j$, $16-j$, $24-j$ and $32-j$ where $0 \le j \le 7$. The output $\mathbf{Y}$ of the algorithm has bit 40 of the preoutput block as its first bit, bit 8 as its second bit, and so on, until bit 25 of the preoutput is the last bit of the output (ciphertext) $\mathbf{Y}$. Thus, the output of the DES algorithm at the end of the second round is the ciphertext $\mathbf{Y}=IP^{-1}$. That is,

$$\mathbf{Y} = (\,y_1, y_2, y_3, \ldots, y_{64})$$
$$= (\,1101\ \ 0111\ \ 0110\ \ 1001\ \ 1000\ \ 0010\ \ 0010\ \ 0100$$
$$0010\ \ 1000\ \ 0011\ \ 1110\ \ 0000\ \ 1010\ \ 1110\ \ 1010\,) \quad (3.27)$$
$$= (D\ \ 7\ \ 6\ \ 9\ \ 8\ \ 2\ \ 2\ \ 4\ \ 2\ \ 8\ \ 3\ \ E\ \ 0\ \ A\ \ E\ \ A)$$

which completes the two-round ciphertext computation.

■ **Example 3.4** Consider the case where the plaintext **X**= (35 70 E2 F1 BA 46 82 C7) and the external semiweak key **K** = (01 01 01 01 01 01 01 01) are given. Let us show that $E_K E_K(\mathbf{X}) = \mathbf{X}$. As seen from Example 3.2, the 28-bit register contents are all zeroes, such that

$$\mathbf{C}_0 = \mathbf{C}_1 = \mathbf{C}_2 = (0000 \quad 0000 \quad 0000 \quad \ldots \quad 0000 \quad 0000)$$

$$\mathbf{D}_0 = \mathbf{D}_1 = \mathbf{D}_2 = (0000 \quad 0000 \quad 0000 \quad \ldots \quad 0000 \quad 0000)$$

Thus, the 48-bit internal keys are, respectively,

$$\begin{aligned}\mathbf{K}_1 = \mathbf{K}_2 = (&000000 \quad 000000 \quad 000000 \quad 000000 \\ &000000 \quad 000000 \quad 000000 \quad 000000)\end{aligned}$$

From the given plaintext **X**, we have

$$\mathbf{L}_0 = (1010 \quad 1110 \quad 0001 \quad 1011 \quad 1010 \quad 0001 \quad 1000 \quad 1001)$$

$$\mathbf{R}_0 = (1101 \quad 1100 \quad 0001 \quad 1111 \quad 0001 \quad 0000 \quad 1111 \quad 0100)$$

Using Table 3.5, we compute

$$\begin{aligned}E(\mathbf{R}_0) = (&011011 \quad 111000 \quad 000011 \quad 111110 \\ &100010 \quad 100001 \quad 011110 \quad 101001)\end{aligned}$$

Since the input to the S-boxes is $\Gamma_1 = E(\mathbf{R}_0) \oplus \mathbf{K}_1 = E(\mathbf{R}_0)$, each S-box function can be computed as follows:

$$S_1^{01}(1101) = 5 = 0101 \qquad S_5^{10}(0001) = 2 = 0010$$

$$S_2^{10}(1100) = 9 = 1001 \qquad S_6^{11}(0000) = 4 = 0100$$

$$S_3^{01}(0001) = 7 = 0111 \qquad S_7^{00}(1111) = 1 = 0001$$

$$S_4^{10}(1111) = 4 = 0100 \qquad S_8^{11}(0100) = 4 = 0100$$

Hence, the output of the S-boxes is obtained by concatenating all of these results. That is,

$$\mathbf{B}_1 = (0101 \quad 1001 \quad 0111 \quad 0100 \quad 0010 \quad 0100 \quad 0001 \quad 0100)$$

Applying the permutation to $\mathbf{B}_1$ yields

$$P(\mathbf{B}_1) = (0000 \quad 0110 \quad 0000 \quad 1001 \quad 1101 \quad 0000 \quad 1010 \quad 1110)$$

Thus, the right-half output after round one is computed by modulo-2 addition of $P(\mathbf{B}_1)$ with $\mathbf{L}_0$ such that

$$\mathbf{R}_1 = \mathbf{L}_0 \oplus P(\mathbf{B}_1) = (1010 \quad 1000 \quad 0001 \quad 0010 \quad 0111 \quad 0001 \quad 0010 \quad 0111)$$

and

$$\mathbf{L}_1 = \mathbf{R}_0 = (\,1101\;\;1100\;\;0001\;\;1111\;\;0001\;\;0000\;\;1111\;\;0100\,)$$

The preoutput block $(\mathbf{R}_1, \mathbf{L}_1)$ is then subjected to $\mathbf{Y} = \mathrm{IP}^{-1}$ (Table 3.8), and thus the ciphertext is computed as

$$\mathbf{Y} = (\,0010\;\;0101\;\;0011\;\;0001\;\;1010\;\;0011\;\;1110\;\;0000\;\;1011\;\;1110\;\;0100\;\;0111\;\;1000\;\;0110\;\;1100\;\;0010\,)$$

This is the ciphertext after round one.

Consider next the encipherment of $\mathbf{Y} = E_K(\mathbf{X})$ with the 48-bit all zero key $\mathbf{K}_1$ or $\mathbf{K}_2$. The initial permuted blocks $\mathbf{L}_0$ and $\mathbf{R}_0$ are, respectively,

$$\mathbf{L}_0 = (\,1010\;\;1000\;\;0001\;\;0010\;\;0111\;\;0001\;\;0010\;\;0111\,)$$

$$\mathbf{R}_0 = (\,1101\;\;1100\;\;0001\;\;1111\;\;0001\;\;0000\;\;1111\;\;0100\,)$$

Expanding $\mathbf{R}_0$ with the aid of Table 3.5 yields

$$E(\mathbf{R}_0) = (\,011011\;\;111000\;\;000011\;\;111110\;\;100010\;\;100001\;\;011110\;\;101001\,) = \Gamma_1$$

This is the input to the S-boxes. The output of the S-boxes, $\mathbf{B}_1$, can be obtained by the substitution operation as

$$\mathbf{B}_1 = (\,0101\;\;1001\;\;0111\;\;0100\;\;0010\;\;0100\;\;0001\;\;0100\,)$$

Applying the permutation P to $\mathbf{B}_1$, we have

$$P(\mathbf{B}_1) = (\,0000\;\;0110\;\;0000\;1001\;\;1101\;\;0000\;1010\;\;1110\,)$$

Thus, the right-half output $\mathbf{R}_1$ after round one becomes

$$\mathbf{R}_1 = P(\mathbf{B}_1) \oplus \mathbf{L}_0 = (\,1010\;\;1110\;\;0001\;\;1011\;\;1010\;\;0001\;\;1000\;\;1001\,)$$

and the left-half output $\mathbf{L}_1$ after round one is

$$\mathbf{L}_1 = \mathbf{R}_0 = (\,1101\;\;1100\;\;0001\;\;1111\;\;0001\;\;0000\;\;1111\;\;0100\,)$$

Applying the permutation IP^{-1} to the preoutput $(\mathbf{R}_1, \mathbf{L}_1)$ yields

$$\mathbf{X} = E_K(\mathbf{Y}) = (\,0011\;\;0101\;\;0111\;\;0000\;\;1110\;\;0010\;\;1111\;\;0001\;\;1011\;\;1010\;\;0100\;\;0110\;\;1000\;\;0010\;\;1100\;\;0111\,) = (\,35\;\;70\;\;\mathrm{E2}\;\;\mathrm{F1}\;\;\mathrm{BA}\;\;46\;\;82\;\;\mathrm{C7}\,)$$

Thus, it is proved that $E_K E_K(\mathbf{X}) = \mathbf{X}$.

■ **Example 3.5** Consider the enciphering operations with two semiweak keys, $\mathbf{K}_\alpha$ = (1F FE 1F FE 0E FE 0E FE) and $\mathbf{K}_\beta$ = (FE 1F FE 1F FE 0E FE 0E). Let us show the relation $E_{K\beta} \cdot E_{K\alpha}(\mathbf{X}) = \mathbf{X}$ where **X** = (35 70 E2 F1 BA 46 82 C7) is the plaintext.

Enciphering the plaintext **X** under the semiweak key $\mathbf{K}_\alpha$, we can obtain the ciphertext **Y** after 16 rounds as

$$\begin{aligned}\mathbf{Y} &= E_{K\alpha}(\mathbf{X}) \\ &= (1001\ 1100\ 1110\ 0000\ 0000\ 1101\ 1100\ 0010 \\ &\quad\ 0111\ 1110\ 0011\ 0001\ 1011\ 0101\ 1101\ 0100) \\ &= (9\ C\ E\ 0\ 0\ D\ C\ 2\ 7\ E\ 3\ 1\ B\ 5\ D\ 4)\end{aligned}$$

Next, let us encipher **Y** with the semiweak key $\mathbf{K}_\beta$, i.e. $\mathbf{E}_{K\beta}(\mathbf{Y})$. Considering **Y** as the ciphertext input, encipher **Y** with $\mathbf{K}_\beta$ into DES. Then, after 16 rounds of encipherment, the original plaintext is recreated as

$$\begin{aligned}\mathbf{X} &= E_{K\beta}(\mathbf{Y}) \\ &= (0011\ 0101\ 0111\ 0000\ 1110\ 0010\ 1111\ 0001 \\ &\quad\ 1011\ 1010\ 0100\ 0110\ 1000\ 0010\ 1100\ 0111) \\ &= (3\ 5\ 7\ 0\ E\ 2\ F\ 1\ B\ A\ 4\ 6\ 8\ 2\ C\ 7)\end{aligned}$$

Thus it is proved that $E_{K\beta} E_{K\alpha}(\mathbf{X}) = \mathbf{X}$.

■ **Example 3.6** Consider the encryption of plaintext **X**= (7 8 5 A C 3 A 4 B D 0 F E 1 2 D) by the external key **K** = (3 8 A 8 4 F F 8 9 8 B 9 0 B 8 F). Using Table 3.1 (PC–1), 56 key bits, after stripping off eight parity bits from the 64 external key bits, are loaded into two 28-bit shift registers ($\mathbf{C}_0$, $\mathbf{D}_0$). They are

$$\mathbf{C}_0 = (B\ A\ 0\ C\ 2\ B\ 3)$$

$$\mathbf{D}_0 = (C\ 4\ 8\ 4\ F\ F\ 9)$$

The contents of these two registers are shifted one position to the left by Table 3.2. Then the shifted concatenation becomes

$$(\mathbf{C}_1, \mathbf{D}_1) = (7\ 4\ 1\ 8\ 5\ 6\ 7\ 8\ 9\ 0\ 9\ F\ F\ 3)$$

The 48-bit internal key $\mathbf{K}_1$ is derived from ($\mathbf{C}_1$, $\mathbf{D}_1$) by taking the key bits located in Table 3.3 (PC–2).

$$\mathbf{K}_1 = (0\ 3\ 4\ B\ 8\ F\ C\ C\ F\ D\ 2\ E)$$

Table 3.3 (PC–2) is the rule that defines how the 48-bit key vectors $\mathbf{K}_1$, $\mathbf{K}_2, \ldots, \mathbf{K}_{16}$ are derived from the concatenated blocks $(\mathbf{C}_1, \mathbf{D}_1)$, $(\mathbf{C}_2, \mathbf{D}_2)$, $\ldots, (\mathbf{C}_{16}, \mathbf{D}_{16})$, respectively. Thus, $\mathbf{K}_2, \mathbf{K}_3, \ldots, \mathbf{K}_{16}$ can be computed as follows:

$$
\begin{aligned}
\mathbf{K}_2 &= (6\ \ E\,2\,6\,8\,9\ \ 0\,D\ \ D\,D\,2\,9\,)\\
\mathbf{K}_3 &= (5\ \ B\,9\,C\,0\,C\ \ C\,A\ \ 7\,C\,7\,0\,)\\
\mathbf{K}_4 &= (4\ \ 8\,A\,8\,D\,A\ \ E\,9\ \ C\,B\,3\,C\,)\\
\mathbf{K}_5 &= (3\ \ 4\,E\,C\,2\,E\ \ 9\,1\ \ 5\,E\,9\,A\,)\\
\mathbf{K}_6 &= (E\ \ 2\,2\,D\,0\,2\ \ D\,D\ \ 1\,2\,3\,5\,)\\
\mathbf{K}_7 &= (6\ \ 8\,A\,E\,3\,5\ \ 9\,3\ \ 6\,A\,E\,C\,)\\
\mathbf{K}_8 &= (C\ \ 5\,B\,4\,1\,A\ \ 3\,0\ \ B\,B\,9\,5\,)\\
\mathbf{K}_9 &= (C\ \ 0\,4\,3\,E\,E\ \ B\,E\ \ 2\,0\,9\,D\,)\\
\mathbf{K}_{10} &= (B\ \ 0\,D\,3\,3\,1\ \ A\,3\ \ 7\,3\,C\,7\,)\\
\mathbf{K}_{11} &= (8\ \ 5\,1\,B\,6\,3\ \ 3\,6\ \ A\,3\,A\,3\,)\\
\mathbf{K}_{12} &= (A\ \ 3\,7\,2\,D\,5\ \ F\,6\ \ 0\,D\,4\,7\,)\\
\mathbf{K}_{13} &= (1\ \ D\,5\,7\,C\,0\ \ 4\,E\ \ A\,3\,D\,A\,)\\
\mathbf{K}_{14} &= (5\ \ 2\,5\,1\,F\,9\ \ 7\,5\ \ F\,5\,4\,9\,)\\
\mathbf{K}_{15} &= (9\ \ D\,C\,1\,4\,5\ \ 6\,A\ \ 9\,4\,6\,A\,)\\
\mathbf{K}_{16} &= (9\ \ F\,2\,D\,1\,A\ \ 5\,A\ \ D\,5\,F\,A\,)
\end{aligned}
$$

Thus, these 48-bit internal keys $\mathbf{K}_1$ through $\mathbf{K}_{16}$ are generated through a series of permutations and left shifts with the 56-bit key blocks $(\mathbf{C}_i, \mathbf{D}_i)$, $i = 0, 1, 2, \ldots, 15$ as shown above.

The 64-bit plaintext $\mathbf{X}$ to be enciphered is first subjected to an initial permutation (Table 3.4) in order for $\mathbf{X}$ to split into two blocks $\mathbf{L}_0$ (left) and $\mathbf{R}_0$ (right).

Using Table 3.4, we have

$$\mathbf{L}_0 = (4\ \ 7\,1\,3\,B\,8\,F\,4\,)$$

and

$$\mathbf{R}_0 = (5\ \ C\,D\,9\,B\,3\,2\,6\,)$$

According to Table 3.5, $E(\mathbf{R}_0)$ becomes

$$E(\mathbf{R}_0) = (\,2F96F3DA690C\,)$$

The key-dependent function $\mathbf{\Gamma}_1 = E(\mathbf{R}_0) \oplus \mathbf{K}_1$ is computed as

$$\Gamma_1 = (\,2CDD7C169422\,)$$

which is actually the input to the S-boxes. After passing through a nonlinear S-box transformation, it forms a 32-bit output as follows:

$$\mathbf{B}_1 = (2\,8\,E\,8\,2\,9\,3\,B)$$

Using Table 3.7, $P(\mathbf{B}_1)$ becomes

$$P(\mathbf{B}_1) = (1\,A\,0\,B\,2\,F\,C\,4)$$

Modulo-2 addition of $P(\mathbf{B}_1)$ with $\mathbf{L}_0$ becomes

$$\begin{aligned}\mathbf{R}_1 &= P(\mathbf{B}_1) \oplus \mathbf{L}_0 \\ &= (5\,D\,1\,8\,9\,7\,3\,0)\end{aligned}$$

which is the right-half output $\mathbf{R}_1$ after round one. Since $\mathbf{L}_1 = \mathbf{R}_0$, the left-half output $\mathbf{L}_1$ after round one is

$$\begin{aligned}\mathbf{L}_1 &= \mathbf{R}_0 \\ &= (5\,C\,D\,9\,B\,3\,2\,6)\end{aligned}$$

We have thus completed the first round of encipherment.

In similar fashion, we can easily compute the output $(\mathbf{L}_i, \mathbf{R}_i)$, $2 \le i \le 16$, as follows:

$$\begin{aligned}
\mathbf{L}_2 &= (5\ D\ 1\ 8\ 9\ 7\ 3\ 0) & \mathbf{R}_2 &= (E\ 0\ E\ 7\ A\ 0\ 3\ 9)\\
\mathbf{L}_3 &= (E\ 0\ E\ 7\ A\ 0\ 3\ 9) & \mathbf{R}_3 &= (6\ 1\ 1\ 2\ 3\ D\ 5\ D)\\
\mathbf{L}_4 &= (6\ 1\ 1\ 2\ 3\ D\ 5\ D) & \mathbf{R}_4 &= (A\ 6\ F\ 2\ 9\ 5\ 8\ 1)\\
\mathbf{L}_5 &= (A\ 6\ F\ 2\ 9\ 5\ 8\ 1) & \mathbf{R}_5 &= (C\ 1\ F\ E\ 0\ F\ 0\ 5)\\
\mathbf{L}_6 &= (C\ 1\ F\ E\ 0\ F\ 0\ 5) & \mathbf{R}_6 &= (8\ E\ 6\ F\ 6\ 7\ 9\ 8)\\
\mathbf{L}_7 &= (8\ E\ 6\ F\ 6\ 7\ 9\ 8) & \mathbf{R}_7 &= (6\ B\ C\ 3\ 4\ 4\ 5\ 5)\\
\mathbf{L}_8 &= (6\ B\ C\ 3\ 4\ 4\ 5\ 5) & \mathbf{R}_8 &= (E\ C\ 6\ D\ 1\ A\ B\ 8)\\
\mathbf{L}_9 &= (E\ C\ 6\ D\ 1\ A\ B\ 8) & \mathbf{R}_9 &= (D\ 0\ D\ 1\ 0\ 4\ 2\ 3)\\
\mathbf{L}_{10} &= (D\ 0\ D\ 1\ 0\ 4\ 2\ 3) & \mathbf{R}_{10} &= (5\ 6\ A\ 0\ E\ 2\ 0\ 1)\\
\mathbf{L}_{11} &= (5\ 6\ A\ 0\ E\ 2\ 0\ 1) & \mathbf{R}_{11} &= (B\ 6\ C\ 7\ 3\ 7\ 2\ 6)\\
\mathbf{L}_{12} &= (B\ 6\ C\ 7\ 3\ 7\ 2\ 6) & \mathbf{R}_{12} &= (6\ F\ F\ 2\ E\ F\ 6\ 0)\\
\mathbf{L}_{13} &= (6\ F\ F\ 2\ E\ F\ 6\ 0) & \mathbf{R}_{13} &= (F\ 0\ 4\ B\ F\ 1\ A\ D)\\
\mathbf{L}_{14} &= (F\ 0\ 4\ B\ F\ 1\ A\ D) & \mathbf{R}_{14} &= (F\ 0\ D\ 3\ 5\ 5\ 3\ 0)\\
\mathbf{L}_{15} &= (F\ 0\ D\ 3\ 5\ 5\ 3\ 0) & \mathbf{R}_{15} &= (0\ 7\ B\ 5\ C\ F\ 7\ 4)\\
\mathbf{L}_{16} &= (0\ 7\ B\ 5\ C\ F\ 7\ 4) & \mathbf{R}_{16} &= (0\ 9\ E\ F\ 5\ B\ 6\ 9)
\end{aligned}$$

The preoutput block $(\mathbf{R}_{16}, \mathbf{L}_{16})$ is the concatenation of $\mathbf{R}_{16}$ with $\mathbf{L}_{16}$. Using Table 3.8, the inverse permutation IP^{-1} applied to the preoutput block $(\mathbf{R}_{16}, \mathbf{L}_{16})$ yields the output of the DES algorithm, which produces the ciphertext **Y**.

$$\mathbf{Y} = (\mathrm{F\,D\,9\,C\,B\,A\,5\,D\,2\,6\,3\,3\,1\,F\,3\,8})$$

This completes encipherment of the plaintext **X** = (7 8 5 A C 3 A 4 B D 0 F 1 2 D) by DES.

3.4 DECIPHERMENT

For the purpose of deciphering, it is necessary to apply the same DES algorithm as used for encipherment, to an enciphered data block. In each round of computation, the same key bits $\mathbf{K}_i$ are used during decipherment. During a deciphering operation, $\mathbf{K}_{16}$ must be used in round one, $\mathbf{K}_{15}$ in round two, and so forth. But care must be taken that the key vector $\mathbf{K}_{16}$ at round one omits the first shift operation and that K_{15} at round two shifts $\mathbf{C}_0$ $(\mathbf{C}_{16})$ and $\mathbf{D}_0$ $(\mathbf{D}_{16})$ one bit to the right. And the rest of the internal keys must be created in the same manner as done while enciphering according to the shift schedule in Table 3.2, except that left shifts are altered to right shifts.

The 64 bits of the ciphertext **Y** to be deciphered are first subjected to the initial permutation IP of Table 3.4. This results in

$$\begin{aligned} \mathbf{L}_0 &= (\,1000\ \ 0011\ \ 0010\ \ 0001\ \ 0010\ \ 1001\ \ 0000\ \ 0011\,) \quad (3.28)\\ &\qquad\ 8 \qquad\ 3 \qquad\ 2 \qquad\ 1 \qquad\ 2 \qquad\ 9 \qquad\ 0 \qquad\ 3 \\ \mathbf{R}_0 &= (\,1000\ \ 0101\ \ 1011\ \ 1010\ \ 1111\ \ 0010\ \ 1110\ \ 0101\,) \quad (3.29)\\ &\qquad\ 8 \qquad\ 5 \qquad\ \mathrm{B} \qquad\ \mathrm{A} \qquad\ \mathrm{F} \qquad\ 2 \qquad\ \mathrm{E} \qquad\ 5 \end{aligned}$$

Using Table 3.5, $\mathbf{R}_0$ is expanded from 32 bits to 48 bits as follows:

$$\begin{aligned} E(\mathbf{R}_0) = (\,&110000\ \ 001011\ \ 110111\ \ 110101\\ &011110\ \ 100101\ \ 011100\ \ 001011\,) \end{aligned} \tag{3.30}$$

Once $E(\mathbf{R}_0)$ is generated, it is added module 2 to $\mathbf{K}_2$. This results in a 48-bit vector $\boldsymbol{\Gamma}_1$.

$$\begin{aligned} \boldsymbol{\Gamma}_1 &= E(\mathbf{R}_0) \oplus \mathbf{K}_2\\ &= (\,000110\ \ 100010\ \ 110000\ \ 101000\\ &\qquad 101011\ \ 011110\ \ 000001\ \ 000011\,) \end{aligned} \tag{3.31}$$

We recognize that the 48 bits of Γ_1 are grouped into sets of 6 bits for S-boxes. Now, each S-box can be expressed in terms of four substitution functions $S_i^{00}, S_i^{01}, S_i^{10}$, and S_i^{11} for $1 \le i \le 8$, where the superscript identifies the row of the matrix. Thus, using Eq. 3.31, if follows that

$$S_1^{00}(0011) = S_1^0(3) = 1 = 0001$$

$$S_2^{10}(0001) = S_2^2(1) = 14 = 1110$$

$$S_3^{10}(1000) = S_3^2(8) = 11 = 1011$$

$$S_4^{10}(0100) = S_4^2(4) = 12 = 1100 \qquad (3.32)$$

$$S_5^{11}(0101) = S_5^3(5) = 14 = 1110$$

$$S_6^{00}(1111) = S_6^0(15) = 11 = 1011$$

$$S_7^{01}(0000) = S_7^1(0) = 13 = 1101$$

$$S_8^{01}(0001) = S_8^1(1) = 15 = 1111$$

Concatenating all these substitution functions results in

$$\begin{array}{lllllllll} \mathbf{B}_1 = & (0001 & 1110 & 1011 & 1100 & 1110 & 1011 & 1101 & 1111) \\ & 1 & E & B & C & E & B & D & F \end{array} \qquad (3.33)$$

which is the output of S-boxes. Using Table 3.7, the permutation of $\mathbf{B}_1$ gives

$$P(\mathbf{B}_1) = (0101\ \ 1111\ \ 0011\ \ 1110\ \ 0011\ \ 1001\ \ 1111\ \ 0111) \qquad (3.34)$$

Thus, the right-half output after round one is obtained by module-2 addition of $P(\mathbf{B}_1)$ with $\mathbf{L}_0$ as follows:

$$\begin{array}{llllllllll} \mathbf{R}_1 & = P(\mathbf{B}_1) \oplus \mathbf{L}_0 \\ & = (1101 & 1100 & 0001 & 1111 & 0001 & 0000 & 1111 & 0100) \\ & \quad D & C & 1 & F & 1 & 0 & F & 4 \end{array} \qquad (3.35)$$

Since $\mathbf{L}_1 = \mathbf{R}_0$, from Eq. 3.29 we have

$$\begin{array}{lllllllll} \mathbf{L}_1 = & (1000 & 0101 & 1011 & 1010 & 1111 & 0010 & 1110 & 0101) \\ & 8 & 5 & B & A & F & 2 & E & 5 \end{array} \qquad (3.36)$$

Applying Table 3.5 for E bit-selection, to $\mathbf{R}_1$ yields

$$\begin{array}{ll} E(\mathbf{R}_1) = & (011011\ \ 111000\ \ 000011\ \ 111110 \\ & 100010\ \ 100001\ \ 011110\ \ 101001) \end{array} \qquad (3.37)$$

Modulo-2 addition of $E(\mathbf{R}_1)$ with $\mathbf{K}_1$ produces

$$\begin{array}{ll} \Gamma_2 & = E(\mathbf{R}_1) \oplus \mathbf{K}_1 \\ & = (010010\ \ 000010\ \ 000110\ \ 010111 \\ & \quad 011011\ \ 111001\ \ 101001\ \ 110011) \end{array} \qquad (3.38)$$

Thus, the substitution operations on S-boxes will give the following results:

$$
\begin{aligned}
S_1^{00}(1001) &= S_1^0(9) &&= 10 = 1010 \\
S_2^{00}(0001) &= S_2^0(1) &&= 1 = 0001 \\
S_3^{00}(0011) &= S_3^0(3) &&= 14 = 1110 \\
S_4^{01}(1011) &= S_4^1(11) &&= 12 = 1100 \\
S_5^{01}(1101) &= S_5^1(13) &&= 9 = 1001 \\
S_6^{11}(1100) &= S_6^3(12) &&= 6 = 0110 \\
S_7^{11}(0100) &= S_7^3(4) &&= 1 = 0001 \\
S_8^{11}(1001) &= S_8^3(9) &&= 12 = 1100
\end{aligned}
\tag{3.39}
$$

Concatenating the results of Eq. 3.39 yields

$$\mathbf{B}_2 = (\,1010\;\;0001\;\;1110\;\;1100\;\;1001\;\;0110\;\;0001\;\;1100\,) \tag{3.40}$$

Using Table 3.7, the permutation P of vector $\mathbf{B}_2$ results in

$$P(\mathbf{B}_2) = (\,0010\;\;1011\;\;1010\;\;0001\;\;0101\;\;0011\;\;0110\;\;1100\,) \tag{3.41}$$

Modulo-2 addition of $P(\mathbf{B}_2)$ with $\mathbf{L}_1$ gives the right-half output after round two.

$$
\begin{aligned}
\mathbf{R}_2 &= P(\mathbf{B}_2) \oplus \mathbf{L}_1 \\
&= (\,1010\;\;1110\;\;0001\;\;1011\;\;1010\;\;0001\;\;1000\;\;1001\,) \qquad (3.42) \\
&\qquad\;\; \mathrm{A}\qquad\;\; \mathrm{E}\qquad\;\; 1\qquad\;\; \mathrm{B}\qquad\;\; \mathrm{A}\qquad\;\; 1\qquad\;\; 8\qquad\;\; 9 \\
\mathbf{L}_2 = \mathbf{R}_1 &= (\,1101\;\;1100\;\;0001\;\;1111\;\;0001\;\;0000\;\;1111\;\;0100\,) \qquad (3.43) \\
&\qquad\;\; \mathrm{D}\qquad\;\; \mathrm{C}\qquad\;\; 1\qquad\;\; \mathrm{F}\qquad\;\; 1\qquad\;\; 0\qquad\;\; \mathrm{F}\qquad\;\; 4
\end{aligned}
$$

Hence, the preoutput block is

$$
\begin{aligned}
(\mathbf{R}_2, \mathbf{L}_2) = (\,&1010\;\;1110\;\;0001\;\;1011\;\;1010\;\;0001\;\;1000\;\;1001 \\
&1101\;\;1100\;\;0001\;\;1111\;\;0001\;\;0000\;\;1111\;\;0100\,)
\end{aligned}
\tag{3.44}
$$

This preoutput is then subjected to the inverse of the initial permutation (see Table 3.8), and thus we can recover the plaintext $\mathbf{X} = \mathrm{IP}^{-1}$. That is,

$$
\begin{aligned}
\mathbf{X} = (\,&0011\;\;0101\;\;0111\;\;0000\;\;1110\;\;0010\;\;1111\;\;0001 \\
&1011\;\;1010\;\;0100\;\;0110\;\;1000\;\;0010\;\;1100\;\;0111\,)
\end{aligned}
\tag{3.45}
$$

$= (3\ 5\ 7\ 0\ E\ 2\ F\ 1\ B\ A\ 4\ 6\ 8\ 2\ C\ 7)$

which is the deciphered plaintext, as expected.

■ **Example 3.7** Consider the decryption of ciphertext $\mathbf{Y} = (F\ D\ 9\ C\ B\ A\ 5\ D\ 2\ 6\ 3\ 3\ 1\ F\ 3\ 8)$, which was obtained in Example 3.6, back into the plaintext $\mathbf{X} = (7\ 8\ 5\ A\ C\ 3\ A\ 4\ B\ D\ 0\ F\ E\ 1\ 2\ D)$. Using the initial permutation (IP) of Table 3.4, the 64-bit ciphertext $\mathbf{Y}$ is grouped into two blocks such that

$$\mathbf{L}_0 = (0\ 9\ E\ F\ 5\ B\ 6\ 9)$$

and

$$\mathbf{R}_0 = (0\ 7\ B\ 5\ C\ F\ 7\ 4)$$

$\mathbf{R}_0$ (the right-half of $\mathbf{Y}$) is expanded into 48 bits:

$$E(\mathbf{R}_0) = (0\ 0\ F\ D\ A\ B\ E\ 5\ E\ B\ A\ 8)$$

The input Γ_1 to the S-boxes is computed by modulo-2 addition of $E(\mathbf{R}_0)$ with $\mathbf{K}_{16}$ such that

$$\Gamma_1 = (9\ F\ D\ 0\ B\ 1\ B\ F\ 3\ E\ 5\ 2)$$

The substitution operations on S-boxes with Γ_1 yields the output of S-boxes:

$$\mathbf{B}_1 = (2\ E\ 0\ 9\ E\ E\ 9)$$

Using Table 3.7, the permutation of $\mathbf{B}_1$ gives

$$P(\mathbf{B}_1) = (F\ 9\ 3\ C\ 0\ E\ 5\ 9)$$

Thus, the right-half output $\mathbf{R}_1$ after round one becomes

$$\mathbf{R}_1 = \mathbf{L}_0 \oplus P(\mathbf{B}_1)$$

$$= (F\ 0\ D\ 3\ 5\ 5\ 3\ 0)$$

Since $\mathbf{L}_1 = \mathbf{R}_0$, the left-half output $\mathbf{L}_1$ after round one is

$$\mathbf{L}_1 = \mathbf{R}_0 = (0\ 7\ B\ 5\ C\ F\ 7\ 4)$$

Thus, we have accomplished the first round encipherment. The encipherments of the second through the 16th rounds will be shown in the following.

Round 2

$$E(\mathbf{R}_1) = (7\ 4\ 1\ 6\ A\ 6\ A\ A\ A\ 9\ A\ 1)$$
$$\Gamma_2 = E(\mathbf{R}_1) \oplus \mathbf{K}_{15}$$
$$= (E\ 7\ D\ 7\ E\ 3\ C\ 0\ 3\ D\ C\ B)$$

Round 3

$$E(\mathbf{R}_2) = (F\ A\ 0\ 2\ 5\ 7\ F\ A\ 3\ D\ 5\ 8)$$
$$\Gamma_3 = E(\mathbf{R}_2) \oplus \mathbf{K}_{14}$$
$$= (A\ 8\ 5\ 3\ A\ E\ 8\ F\ C\ 8\ 1\ 2)$$

$$\begin{aligned}
\mathbf{B}_2 &= (\mathrm{AE1FFFF3}) \\
P(\mathbf{B}_2) &= (\mathrm{F7FE3ED9}) \\
\mathbf{R}_2 &= \mathbf{L}_1 \oplus P(\mathbf{B}_2) \\
&= (\mathrm{F04BF1AD}) \\
\mathbf{L}_2 &= \mathbf{R}_1 \\
&= (\mathrm{F0D35530})
\end{aligned}$$

$$\begin{aligned}
\mathbf{B}_3 &= (\mathrm{645D8B19}) \\
\mathrm{P}(\mathbf{B}_3) &= (\mathrm{9F21DA50}) \\
\mathbf{R}_3 &= \mathbf{L}_2 \oplus P(\mathbf{B}_3) \\
&= (\mathrm{6FF2EF60}) \\
\mathbf{L}_3 &= \mathbf{R}_2 \\
&= (\mathrm{F04BF1AD})
\end{aligned}$$

Round 4

$$\begin{aligned}
E(\mathbf{R}_3) &= (\mathrm{35FFA575EB00}) \\
\Gamma_4 &= E(\mathbf{R}_3) \oplus \mathbf{K}_{13} \\
&= (\mathrm{28A8653B48DA}) \\
\mathbf{B}_4 &= (\mathrm{FB1064B0}) \\
P(\mathbf{B}_4) &= (\mathrm{468CC68B}) \\
\mathbf{R}_4 &= \mathbf{L}_3 \oplus P(\mathbf{B}_4) \\
&= (\mathrm{B6C73726}) \\
\mathbf{L}_4 &= \mathbf{R}_3 \\
&= (\mathrm{6FF2EF60})
\end{aligned}$$

Round 5

$$\begin{aligned}
E(\mathbf{R}_4) &= (\mathrm{5AD60E9AE90D}) \\
\Gamma_5 &= E(\mathbf{R}_4) \oplus \mathbf{K}_{12} \\
&= (\mathrm{F5A4DB6CE44A}) \\
\mathbf{B}_5 &= (\mathrm{008A98EF}) \\
P(\mathbf{B}_5) &= (\mathrm{39520D61}) \\
\mathbf{R}_5 &= \mathbf{L}_4 \oplus P(\mathbf{B}_5) \\
&= (\mathrm{56A0E201}) \\
\mathbf{L}_5 &= \mathbf{R}_4 \\
&= (\mathrm{B6C73726})
\end{aligned}$$

Round 6

$$\begin{aligned}
E(\mathbf{R}_5) &= (\mathrm{AAD501704002}) \\
\Gamma_6 &= E(\mathbf{R}_5) \oplus \mathbf{K}_{11} \\
&= (\mathrm{2FCE6246E3A1}) \\
\mathbf{B}_6 &= (\mathrm{22B653D2}) \\
P(\mathbf{B}_6) &= (\mathrm{66763305}) \\
\mathbf{R}_6 &= \mathbf{L}_5 \oplus P(\mathbf{B}_6) \\
&= (\mathrm{D0B10423}) \\
\mathbf{L}_6 &= \mathbf{R}_5 \\
&= (\mathrm{56A0E201})
\end{aligned}$$

Round 7

$$\begin{aligned}
E(\mathbf{R}_6) &= (\mathrm{EA15A2808107}) \\
\Gamma_7 &= E(\mathbf{R}_6) \oplus \mathbf{K}_{10} \\
&= (\mathrm{5AC69323F2C0}) \\
\mathbf{B}_7 &= (\mathrm{CD477D9D}) \\
P(\mathbf{B}_7) &= (\mathrm{BACDF8B9}) \\
\mathbf{R}_7 &= \mathbf{L}_6 \oplus P(\mathbf{B}_7) \\
&= (\mathrm{EC6D1AB8}) \\
\mathbf{L}_7 &= \mathbf{R}_6 \\
&= (\mathrm{D0B10423})
\end{aligned}$$

Round 8

$$\begin{aligned}
E(\mathbf{R}_7) &= (\mathrm{75835A8F55F1}) \\
\Gamma_8 &= (\mathrm{B5C0B431756C}) \\
\mathbf{B}_8 &= (\mathrm{1503BE5E}) \\
P(\mathbf{B}_8) &= (\mathrm{BB7240BA}) \\
\mathbf{R}_8 &= \mathbf{L}_7 \oplus P(\mathbf{B}_8) \\
&= (\mathrm{6BC34499}) \\
\mathbf{L}_8 &= \mathbf{R}_7 \\
&= (\mathrm{EC6D1AB8})
\end{aligned}$$

Round 9

$$\begin{aligned}
E(\mathbf{R}_8) &= (\mathrm{B57E06A094F2}) \\
\Gamma_9 &= (\mathrm{70CA1C902F67}) \\
\mathbf{B}_9 &= (\mathrm{03841137}) \\
P(\mathbf{B}_9) &= (\mathrm{62027D20}) \\
\mathbf{R}_9 &= \mathbf{L}_8 \oplus P(\mathbf{B}_9) \\
&= (\mathrm{8E6F6798}) \\
\mathbf{L}_9 &= \mathbf{R}_8 \\
&= (\mathrm{6BC34499})
\end{aligned}$$

Round 10

$$E(\mathbf{R}_9) = (67C35EB0FCF1)$$
$$\Gamma_{10} = (2D6D6B23961D)$$
$$\mathbf{B}_{10} = (2DE17659)$$
$$P(\mathbf{B}_{10}) = (AA3D4B9C)$$
$$\mathbf{R}_{10} = \mathbf{L}_9 \oplus P(\mathbf{B}_{10}) = (C1FE0F05)$$
$$\mathbf{L}_{10} = \mathbf{R}_9 = (8E6F6798)$$

Round 11

$$E(\mathbf{R}_{10}) = (E03FFC05E80B)$$
$$\Gamma_{11} = (0212FED8FA3E)$$
$$\mathbf{B}_{11} = (ED4455C8)$$
$$P(\mathbf{B}_{11}) = (289DF219)$$
$$\mathbf{R}_{11} = \mathbf{L}_{10} \oplus P(\mathbf{B}_{11}) = (A6F29581)$$
$$\mathbf{L}_{11} = \mathbf{R}_{10} = (C1FE0F05)$$

Round 12

$$E(\mathbf{R}_{11}) = (D0D7A54ABC03)$$
$$\Gamma_{12} = (E43B8BDBE299)$$
$$\mathbf{B}_{12} = (AD0F5600)$$
$$P(\mathbf{B}_{12}) = (A0EC5258)$$
$$\mathbf{R}_{12} = \mathbf{L}_{11} \oplus P(\mathbf{B}_{12}) = (61125D5D)$$
$$\mathbf{L}_{12} = \mathbf{R}_{11} = (A6F29581)$$

Round 13

$$E(\mathbf{R}_{12}) = (B028A42FAAFA)$$
$$\Gamma_{13} = (F8807EC661C6)$$
$$\mathbf{B}_{13} = (06D46574)$$
$$P(\mathbf{B}_{13}) = (461535B8)$$
$$\mathbf{R}_{13} = \mathbf{L}_{12} \oplus P(\mathbf{B}_{13}) = (E0E7A039)$$
$$\mathbf{L}_{13} = \mathbf{R}_{12} = (61125D5D)$$

Round 14

$$E(\mathbf{R}_{13}) = (F0170FD001F3)$$
$$\Gamma_{14} = (AB8B031A7D83)$$
$$\mathbf{B}_{14} = (69381C8F)$$
$$P(\mathbf{B}_{14}) = (3C0ACA6D)$$
$$\mathbf{R}_{14} = \mathbf{L}_{13} \oplus P(\mathbf{B}_{14}) = (5D189730)$$
$$\mathbf{L}_{14} = \mathbf{R}_{13} = (E0E7A039)$$

Round 15

$$E(\mathbf{R}_{14}) = (2FA8F14AE9A0)$$
$$\Gamma_{15} = (418E78473489)$$
$$\mathbf{B}_{15} = (3CB55ECA)$$
$$P(\mathbf{B}_{15} = (BC3E131F)$$
$$\mathbf{R}_{15} = \mathbf{L}_{14} \oplus P(\mathbf{B}_{15}) = (5CD9B326)$$
$$\mathbf{L}_{15} = \mathbf{R}_{14} = (5D189730)$$

Round 16

$$E(\mathbf{R}_{15}) = (2F96F3DA690C)$$
$$\Gamma_{16} = (2CDD7C169422)$$
$$\mathbf{B}_{16} = (28E8293B)$$
$$P(\mathbf{B}_{16}) = (1A0B2FC4)$$
$$\mathbf{R}_{16} = \mathbf{L}_{15} \oplus P(\mathbf{B}_{16}) = (4713B8F4)$$
$$\mathbf{L}_{16} = \mathbf{R}_{15} = (5CD9B326)$$

Thus, the preoutput block becomes

$$(\mathbf{R}_{16}, \mathbf{L}_{16}) = (0100\ 0111\ 0001\ 0011\ 1011\ 1000\ 1111\ 0100$$
$$0101\ 1100\ 1101\ 1001\ 1011\ 0011\ 0010\ 0110)$$

Applying this preoutput to Table 3.8 (IP^{-1}), the plaintext can be computed as

$$\mathbf{X} = (0111\ 1000\ 0101\ 1010\ 1100\ 0011\ 1010\ 0100$$
$$1011\ 1101\ 0000\ 1111\ 1110\ 0001\ 0010\ 1101)$$
$$= (7\,8\,5\,A\,C\,3\,A\,4\,B\,D\,0\,F\,E\,1\,2\,D)$$

which is the original plaintext as expected.

■ **Example 3.8** Consider the substitution operations on S-boxes at round 9, discussed in Example 3.7. Modulo-2 addition of $E(\mathbf{R}_8)$ with $\mathbf{K}_9$ yields the input, $\mathbf{\Gamma}_9 = E(\mathbf{R}_8) \oplus \mathbf{K}_9$, to the S-boxes.

$$\mathbf{\Gamma}_9 = (7\,0\,C\,A\,1\,C\,9\,0\,2\,F\,6\,7)$$
$$= (011100\ 001100\ 101000\ 011100$$
$$100100\ 000010\ 111101\ 100111)$$

The substitution operations on S-boxes are shown below:

$$S_1^{00}(1110) = S_1^0(14) = 0 = 0000$$
$$S_2^{00}(0110) = S_2^0(6) = 3 = 0011$$
$$S_3^{10}(0100) = S_3^2(4) = 8 = 1000$$
$$S_4^{00}(1110) = S_4^0(14) = 4 = 0100$$
$$S_5^{10}(0010) = S_5^2(2) = 1 = 0001$$
$$S_6^{00}(0001) = S_6^0(1) = 1 = 0001$$
$$S_7^{11}(1110) = S_7^3(14) = 3 = 0011$$
$$S_8^{11}(0011) = S_8^3(3) = 7 = 0111$$

Each operation above represents the four-bit output of individual S-boxes. Thus, concatenating all of these outputs yields the 32-bit output of S-boxes.

$$\mathbf{B}_9 = (0000\ 0011\ 1000\ 0100\ 0001\ 0001\ 0011\ 0111)$$
$$= (0\ 3\ 8\ 4\ 1\ 1\ 3\ 7)$$

3.5 *S*-BOX ANALYSIS AND DESIGN

Several cryptographers (Hellman [8] and others in 1979) have deliberated on whether the *S*-boxes are highly secure. Also, the analysis of *S*-box design has not yet been revealed by IBM and is currently classified by NBS. The *S*-boxes are actually a set of eight nonlinear transformations, each of which transforms 6 bits of input into 4 bits of output. Carefully selected *S*-box functions will produce a much stronger algorithm and lead to easy implementation. Therefore, the design of *S*-box structure is a subject to be studied as part of an independent analysis of DES. The following analysis relating to the number of logic circuits describing an *S*-box will give the reader some insight into the design of DES's *S*-box functions.

A circuit with multiple outputs, such as an *S*-box function, is described by a set of Boolean functions, one for each output variable. An *S*-box is a Boolean function that maps six input bits $\mathbf{\Gamma} = (x_1, x_2, x_3, x_4, x_5, x_6)$ into four output bits $\mathbf{B} = (y_1, y_2, y_3, y_4)$. Each output bit y_j can be expressed as a sum of minterms utilizing a logical OR operation. Since each of the six input bits is either 0 or 1, these are $2^6 = 64$ minterms. To see how to determine the Boolean expression for a given *S*-box function, the map method would seem to be preferable to the tabulation method. However, for more than six variables, one cannot be certain that the best simplified expression has been found. In most applications, the function to be simplified comes from a truth table, from which the minterm list is readily available. The Karnaugh map provides a simple procedure for minimizing minterms for an *S*-box function.

Consider an S_1-box which has six inputs and four outputs. The primitive S_1-box function is tabulated in the top block of Table 3.6. The output $\mathbf{B} = (y_4, y_3, y_2, y_1)$ can be expressed in terms of the input $\mathbf{\Gamma} = (x_6, x_5, x_4, x_3, x_2, x_1)$ as indicated in the following truth table.

Table 3.9 Truth Table for S_1-box Function

x_6	x_5	x_4	x_3	x_2	x_1	y_4	y_3	y_2	y_1
0	0	0	0	0	0	1	1	1	0
0	0	0	0	0	1	0	1	0	0
0	0	0	0	1	0	1	1	0	1
0	0	0	0	1	1	0	0	0	1
0	0	0	1	0	0	0	0	1	0
0	0	0	1	0	1	1	1	1	1
0	0	0	1	1	0	1	0	1	1
0	0	0	1	1	1	1	0	0	0
0	0	1	0	0	0	0	0	1	1
0	0	1	0	0	1	1	0	1	0

Table 3.9 (Contd.)

x_6	x_5	x_4	x_3	x_2	x_1	y_4	y_3	y_2	y_1
0	0	1	0	1	0	0	1	1	0
0	0	1	0	1	1	1	1	0	0
0	0	1	1	0	0	0	1	0	1
0	0	1	1	0	1	1	0	0	1
0	0	1	1	1	0	0	0	0	0
0	0	1	1	1	1	0	1	1	1
0	1	0	0	0	0	0	0	0	0
0	1	0	0	0	1	1	1	1	1
0	1	0	0	1	0	0	1	1	1
0	1	0	0	1	1	0	1	0	0
0	1	0	1	0	0	1	1	1	0
0	1	0	1	0	1	0	0	1	0
0	1	0	1	1	0	1	1	0	1
0	1	0	1	1	1	0	0	0	1
0	1	1	0	0	0	1	0	1	0
0	1	1	0	0	1	0	1	1	0
0	1	1	0	1	0	1	1	0	0
0	1	1	0	1	1	1	0	1	1
0	1	1	1	0	0	1	0	0	1
0	1	1	1	0	1	0	1	0	1
0	1	1	1	1	0	0	0	1	1
0	1	1	1	1	1	1	0	0	0
1	0	0	0	0	0	0	1	0	0
1	0	0	0	0	1	0	0	0	1
1	0	0	0	1	0	1	1	1	0
1	0	0	0	1	1	1	0	0	0
1	0	0	1	0	0	1	1	0	1
1	0	0	1	0	1	0	1	1	0
1	0	0	1	1	0	0	0	1	0
1	0	0	1	1	1	1	0	1	1
1	0	1	0	0	0	1	1	1	1
1	0	1	0	0	1	1	1	0	0
1	0	1	0	1	0	1	0	0	1
1	0	1	0	1	1	0	1	1	1
1	0	1	1	0	0	0	0	1	1
1	0	1	1	0	1	1	0	1	0
1	0	1	1	1	0	0	1	0	1
1	0	1	1	1	1	0	0	0	0
1	1	0	0	0	0	1	1	1	1
1	1	0	0	0	1	1	1	0	0
1	1	0	0	1	0	1	0	0	0

Table 3.9 (Contd.)

x_6	x_5	x_4	x_3	x_2	x_1	y_4	y_3	y_2	y_1
1	1	0	0	1	1	0	0	1	0
1	1	0	1	0	0	0	1	0	0
1	1	0	1	0	1	1	0	0	1
1	1	0	1	1	0	0	0	0	1
1	1	0	1	1	1	0	1	1	1
1	1	1	0	0	0	0	1	0	1
1	1	1	0	0	1	1	0	1	1
1	1	1	0	1	0	0	0	1	1
1	1	1	0	1	1	1	1	1	0
1	1	1	1	0	0	1	0	1	0
1	1	1	1	0	1	0	0	0	0
1	1	1	1	1	0	0	1	1	0
1	1	1	1	1	1	1	1	0	1

Thus, the Boolean expression for y_1 is

$$\begin{aligned}
y_1 = {} & \bar{x}_6\bar{x}_5\bar{x}_4\bar{x}_3x_2\bar{x}_1 + \bar{x}_6\bar{x}_5\bar{x}_4\bar{x}_3x_2x_1 + \bar{x}_6\bar{x}_5\bar{x}_4x_3\bar{x}_2x_1 + \bar{x}_6\bar{x}_5\bar{x}_4x_3x_2\bar{x}_1 \\
& + \bar{x}_6\bar{x}_5\bar{x}_4\bar{x}_3\bar{x}_2\bar{x}_1 + \bar{x}_6\bar{x}_5x_4x_3\bar{x}_2\bar{x}_1 + \bar{x}_6\bar{x}_5x_4x_3\bar{x}_2x_1 + \bar{x}_6\bar{x}_5x_4x_3x_2x_1 \\
& + \bar{x}_6\bar{x}_5x_4\bar{x}_3\bar{x}_2x_1 + \bar{x}_6x_5\bar{x}_4\bar{x}_3x_2\bar{x}_1 + \bar{x}_6x_5\bar{x}_4x_3x_2\bar{x}_1 + \bar{x}_6x_5\bar{x}_4x_3x_2x_1 \\
& + \bar{x}_6x_5x_4\bar{x}_3x_2x_1 + \bar{x}_6x_5x_4x_3\bar{x}_2\bar{x}_1 + \bar{x}_6x_5x_4x_3\bar{x}_2x_1 + \bar{x}_6x_5x_4x_3x_2\bar{x}_1 \qquad (3.46) \\
& + x_6\bar{x}_5\bar{x}_4\bar{x}_3\bar{x}_2x_1 + x_6\bar{x}_5\bar{x}_4x_3\bar{x}_2\bar{x}_1 + x_6\bar{x}_5\bar{x}_4x_3x_2x_1 + x_6\bar{x}_5x_4\bar{x}_3\bar{x}_2\bar{x}_1 \\
& + x_6\bar{x}_5x_4\bar{x}_3x_2\bar{x}_1 + x_6\bar{x}_5x_4\bar{x}_3x_2x_1 + x_6\bar{x}_5x_4x_3\bar{x}_2\bar{x}_1 + x_6\bar{x}_5x_4x_3x_2\bar{x}_1 \\
& + x_6x_5\bar{x}_4\bar{x}_3\bar{x}_2\bar{x}_1 + x_6x_5\bar{x}_4x_3\bar{x}_2x_1 + x_6x_5\bar{x}_4x_3x_2\bar{x}_1 + x_6x_5\bar{x}_4x_3x_2x_1 \\
& + x_6x_5x_4\bar{x}_3\bar{x}_2\bar{x}_1 + x_6x_5x_4\bar{x}_3\bar{x}_2x_1 + x_6x_5x_4\bar{x}_3x_2\bar{x}_1 + x_6x_5x_4x_3x_2x_1
\end{aligned}$$

A minterm is included in Eq. 3.46 if the corresponding output bit y_1 is equal to 1 in the truth table. Therefore, the Boolean expression for y_1 consists of 32 minterms. The input-output logical circuit for an S-box is expressed in four Boolean functions, one for each output variable. Each output Boolean function requires a Karnaugh map for its simplification. A map assigns a binary reflected code sequence to the rows and columns. Each map must have 64 squares, since each output is a function of six input variables. Figure 3.2 is used for simplifying the four-output function. The 1s in the square for the map of y_1 are determined directly from the truth table. It is desirable that a derived Boolean expression be normally reduced to find an equivalent expression so that the number of logic circuits needed to implement the S-box functions may be reduced. Therefore, the output y_1 can be simplified to a 23 literal expression as follows:

$$
\begin{aligned}
y_1 = {} & \bar{x}_6\bar{x}_5\bar{x}_4\bar{x}_3x_2 + \bar{x}_6\bar{x}_5\bar{x}_4x_2\bar{x}_1 + \bar{x}_6\bar{x}_5x_3\bar{x}_2x_1 + \bar{x}_6\bar{x}_5x_4\bar{x}_2\bar{x}_1 \\
& + \bar{x}_6\bar{x}_5x_4x_3x_1 + \bar{x}_6x_5x_4\bar{x}_3x_2x_1 + \bar{x}_6x_5x_3x_2\bar{x}_1 + \bar{x}_6x_5x_4x_3\bar{x}_2 \\
& + \bar{x}_6x_5\bar{x}_4\bar{x}_3\bar{x}_2x_1 + \bar{x}_6\bar{x}_5x_4\bar{x}_2x_1 + \bar{x}_6x_5\bar{x}_4x_3x_2 + x_6x_5\bar{x}_3\bar{x}_2\bar{x}_1 \\
& + x_6x_5\bar{x}_4x_3x_2 + x_6x_5\bar{x}_4x_3x_1 + x_6x_5x_4\bar{x}_3\bar{x}_2 + x_6x_4\bar{x}_3x_2\bar{x}_1 \\
& + x_6x_5x_3x_2x_1 + x_6\bar{x}_5x_4\bar{x}_2\bar{x}_1 + x_6\bar{x}_5x_4\bar{x}_3x_2 + x_6\bar{x}_5x_4x_2\bar{x}_1 \\
& + x_6\bar{x}_5\bar{x}_4\bar{x}_3\bar{x}_2x_1 + x_6\bar{x}_5\bar{x}_4x_3x_2x_1 + x_6\bar{x}_5x_3\bar{x}_2\bar{x}_1
\end{aligned}
\tag{3.47}
$$

For example, we can see that $y_1 = 0$ when $x_6 = 0$, $x_5 = 0$, $x_4 = 1$, $x_3 = 0$, $x_2 = 0$, and $x_1 = 1$ (see row 10 in Table 3.9)

Similarly, the rest of the S_1-box outputs y_2, y_3 and y_4 are also derived by plotting their respective minterms on a Karnaugh map. In addition, the output bits y_j, $1 \le j \le 4$ for boxes S_2 through S_8 are also computed without difficulty. Maps of more than six variables are not as simple to use, because the number of squares becomes excessively large and the combination of adjacent squares more involved.

■ **Example 3.9** Compute the output bit y_3 of an S_1-box. Using Table 3.9, the Boolean function for y_3 can be computed from the truth table for an S_1-box. The Boolean expression for y_3 consists of 32 minterms as shown below.

$$
\begin{aligned}
y_3 = {} & \bar{x}_6\bar{x}_5\bar{x}_4\bar{x}_3\bar{x}_2\bar{x}_1 + \bar{x}_6\bar{x}_5\bar{x}_4\bar{x}_3\bar{x}_2x_1 + \bar{x}_6\bar{x}_5\bar{x}_4\bar{x}_3x_2\bar{x}_1 + \bar{x}_6\bar{x}_5\bar{x}_4x_3\bar{x}_2x_1 \\
& + \bar{x}_6\bar{x}_5x_4\bar{x}_3x_2\bar{x}_1 + \bar{x}_6\bar{x}_5x_4\bar{x}_3x_2x_1 + \bar{x}_6\bar{x}_5x_4x_3\bar{x}_2\bar{x}_1 + \bar{x}_6\bar{x}_5x_4x_3x_2x_1 \\
& + \bar{x}_6x_5\bar{x}_4\bar{x}_3\bar{x}_2x_1 + \bar{x}_6x_5\bar{x}_4\bar{x}_3x_2\bar{x}_1 + \bar{x}_6x_5\bar{x}_4\bar{x}_3x_2x_1 + \bar{x}_6x_5\bar{x}_4x_3\bar{x}_2\bar{x}_1 \\
& + \bar{x}_6x_5\bar{x}_4x_3x_2\bar{x}_1 + \bar{x}_6x_5x_4\bar{x}_3\bar{x}_2x_1 + \bar{x}_6x_5x_4\bar{x}_3x_2\bar{x}_1 + \bar{x}_6x_5x_4x_3\bar{x}_2x_1 \\
& + x_6\bar{x}_5\bar{x}_4\bar{x}_3\bar{x}_2\bar{x}_1 + x_6\bar{x}_5\bar{x}_4\bar{x}_3x_2\bar{x}_1 + x_6\bar{x}_5\bar{x}_4x_3\bar{x}_2\bar{x}_1 + x_6\bar{x}_5\bar{x}_4x_3\bar{x}_2x_1 \\
& + x_6\bar{x}_5x_4\bar{x}_3\bar{x}_2\bar{x}_1 + x_6\bar{x}_5x_4\bar{x}_3\bar{x}_2x_1 + x_6\bar{x}_5x_4\bar{x}_3x_2x_1 + x_6\bar{x}_5x_4x_3x_2\bar{x}_1 \\
& + x_6x_5\bar{x}_4\bar{x}_3\bar{x}_2\bar{x}_1 + x_6x_5\bar{x}_4\bar{x}_3\bar{x}_2x_1 + x_6x_5\bar{x}_4x_3\bar{x}_2\bar{x}_1 + x_6x_5\bar{x}_4x_3x_2x_1 \\
& + x_6x_5x_4\bar{x}_3\bar{x}_2\bar{x}_1 + x_6x_5x_4\bar{x}_3x_2x_1 + x_6x_5x_4x_3x_2\bar{x}_1 + x_6x_5x_4x_3x_2x_1
\end{aligned}
$$

$x_6x_5x_4$ \ $x_3x_2x_1$	0 0 0	0 0 1	0 1 1	0 1 0	1 1 0	1 1 1	1 0 1	1 0 0
0 0 0			1	1	1		1	
0 0 1	1					1	1	1
0 1 1			1		1		1	1
0 1 0		1		1	1	1		
1 1 0	1				1	1	1	
1 1 1	1	1		1		1		
1 0 1	1		1	1	1			1
1 0 0		1				1		1

Fig. 3.2 Map for the output bit y_1 of S_1-box function

The plot on the map for a bit y_3 of an S_1-box output is shown in Fig. 3.3. This Karnaugh map required for the simplification of y_3 will be reduced down to the literal 16 terms as follows:

$$y_3 = \bar{x}_6\bar{x}_3x_2\bar{x}_1 + x_6\bar{x}_3\bar{x}_2\bar{x}_1 + \bar{x}_6\bar{x}_5\bar{x}_4\bar{x}_3\bar{x}_2 + \bar{x}_6\bar{x}_5x_4x_2x_1$$

$$+ \bar{x}_6x_5x_4\bar{x}_2x_1 + \bar{x}_6x_5\bar{x}_4\bar{x}_3x_1 + \bar{x}_5\bar{x}_4x_3\bar{x}_2x_1 + x_6\bar{x}_5\bar{x}_4\bar{x}_3\bar{x}_1$$

$$+ x_6x_5\bar{x}_4\bar{x}_3\bar{x}_2 + x_6x_5x_4x_2x_1 + \bar{x}_6x_5\bar{x}_4x_3\bar{x}_1 + x_6\bar{x}_5x_4\bar{x}_3x_1$$

$$+ x_6x_4x_3x_2\bar{x}_1 + x_6x_5x_3x_2x_1 + x_6\bar{x}_4x_3\bar{x}_2x_1 + \bar{x}_6\bar{x}_5x_4x_3\bar{x}_2\bar{x}_1$$

3.6 INTERSYMBOL DEPENDENCIES [13]

With the 16-round cipher operation of DES, the 64 bits of plaintext are transformed into 64 bits of ciphertext under the control of a 56-bit key. Each bit of ciphertext produced by DES is a complex function of all plaintext bits and all key bits. The strength of DES will depend upon the permutation (*P*-box), substitutions (*S*-boxes), and the number of rounds. The analysis of intersymbol dependence is undertaken to evaluate how fast this dependence builds up as a function of the number of

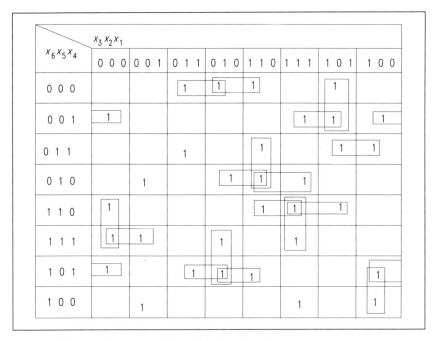

$x_6x_5x_4$ \ $x_3x_2x_1$	0 0 0	0 0 1	0 1 1	0 1 0	1 1 0	1 1 1	1 0 1	1 0 0
0 0 0	1	1		1			1	
0 0 1			1	1		1		1
0 1 1		1		1			1	
0 1 0		1	1	1	1			1
1 1 0	1	1				1		1
1 1 1	1		1		1	1		
1 0 1	1	1	1		1			
1 0 0	1			1			1	1

Fig. 3.3 Map for the S_1-box output bit y_3

rounds. Therefore, for a good cipher system, an output ciphertext bit depends more and more on input plaintext bits as the number of rounds increases.

To investigate the intersymbol dependence between the input $(\mathbf{L}_0, \mathbf{R}_0)$ and the output $(\mathbf{L}_i, \mathbf{R}_i)$ in round i, $i = 1, 2, \ldots, 16$, let us introduce a matrix $\mathbf{M}_i^j$ such that

$$\mathbf{M}_i^j = \begin{bmatrix} \mathbf{M}_{L_i}^{L_j} & \mathbf{M}_{R_i}^{L_j} \\ \mathbf{M}_{L_i}^{R_j} & \mathbf{M}_{R_i}^{R_j} \end{bmatrix} \quad \text{for} \quad 0 \le i \le 15, \quad 1 \le j \le 16 \tag{3.48}$$

The matrix $\mathbf{M}_i^j$ consists of 64 rows and 64 columns. As observed from Fig. 3.1, the output and the input of round each are expressed as

$$\mathbf{L}_{i+1} = \mathbf{R}_i \tag{3.49}$$

$$\mathbf{R}_{i+1} = P(\mathbf{B}_{i+1}) \oplus \mathbf{L}_i \quad \text{for} \quad 0 \le i \le 15 \tag{3.50}$$

Therefore, it is needed to partition the matrix $\mathbf{M}_i^j$ into four submatrices of 32 rows and 32 columns each, as shown in Eq. 3.48.

The dependence of the output bits $\mathbf{B}_1$ from the S-boxes on the input bits $\mathbf{R}_0$ is evaluated first. Since the first and sixth input bits to S_1 select the substitution S-function, all output bits from S_1 depend on bits 32 and 5 of the expanded version of $\mathbf{R}_0$, that is, $E(\mathbf{R}_0)$ or the key-dependent function $\mathbf{\Gamma}_1 = E(\mathbf{R}_0) \oplus \mathbf{K}_1$. In fact, since Γ_1 is derived from the 32 input bits as well as key bits due to the modulo-2 addition of $E(\mathbf{R}_0)$ and $\mathbf{K}_1$, the selection of substitution functions not only depends on the key but also on the input data. This E expansion characteristic introduces an autoclave or a self-keying feature [14]. Therefore, the dependencies of output $\mathbf{R}_i$ on the plaintext $\mathbf{R}_0$ and on the key can be treated separately because the rule of superposition does hold good.

The dependence of ith output $(\mathbf{L}_i, \mathbf{R}_i)$ on the key block $(\mathbf{C}_1, \mathbf{D}_1)$ can also be evaluated by the following 64 × 56 matrix $\mathbf{N}_i$ which is partitioned into two submatrices of 32 rows and 56 columns such that

$$\mathbf{N}_i = \begin{bmatrix} \mathbf{N}_i^L \\ \mathbf{N}_i^R \end{bmatrix} \qquad \text{for} \quad 1 \le i \le 16 \tag{3.51}$$

The matrices represented by Eqs. 3.48 and 3.51 are the key equations for analyzing intersymbol dependencies.

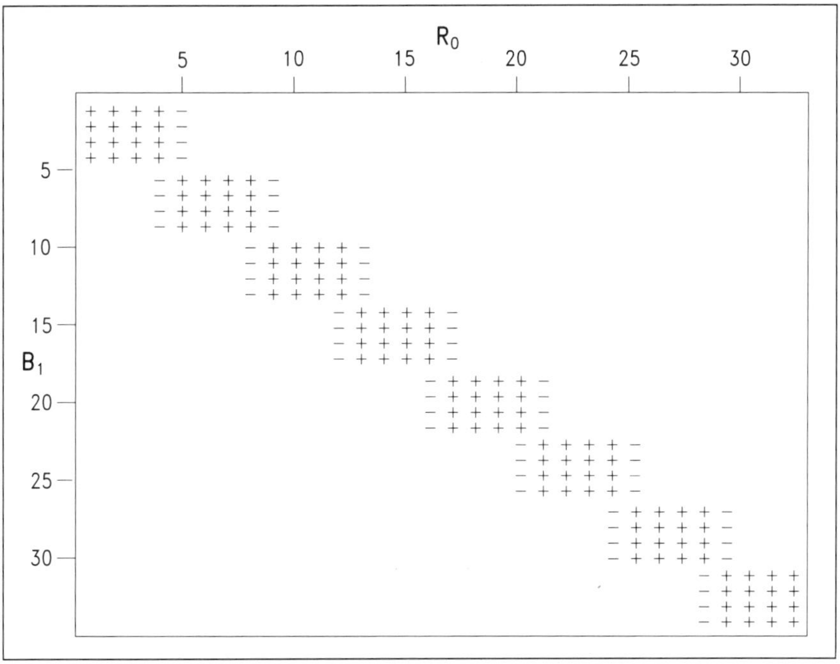

Fig. 3.4 Data dependence of $\mathbf{B}_1$ on $\mathbf{R}_0$ without permutation

3.6.1 Data Dependence

Let us first consider the case of data dependence. Since $\mathbf{R}_0$ is the right-half 32 bits of input data, the functional dependence of $\mathbf{B}_1$ on $\mathbf{R}_0$ prior to permutation $P(\mathbf{B}_1)$ can be plotted as shown in Fig. 3.4. In this figure, the bits are blank if a dependency does not exist between the input and output bits. But if a dependency exists on data bits only, the mark is set as (+). If the dependency is via self-keying, the bit is set as (−). If data bits as well as self-keying bits influence the output, set the mark (∗) for them. With this convention, entries at positions where rows 1 through 4 intersect columns 1 through 4 are marked (+). Among the entries in rows 1 through 4 only columns 32 and 5 are set as (−). All other entries of rows 1 through 4 are blank because four output bits of the S_1-box depend only on six input bits. This completes the analysis for S_1-box. Applying the same method for analyses of the S_2-box through the S_8-box will result in the submatrix $\mathbf{M}_{R_0}^{B_1}$ without the permutation $P(\mathbf{B}_1)$.

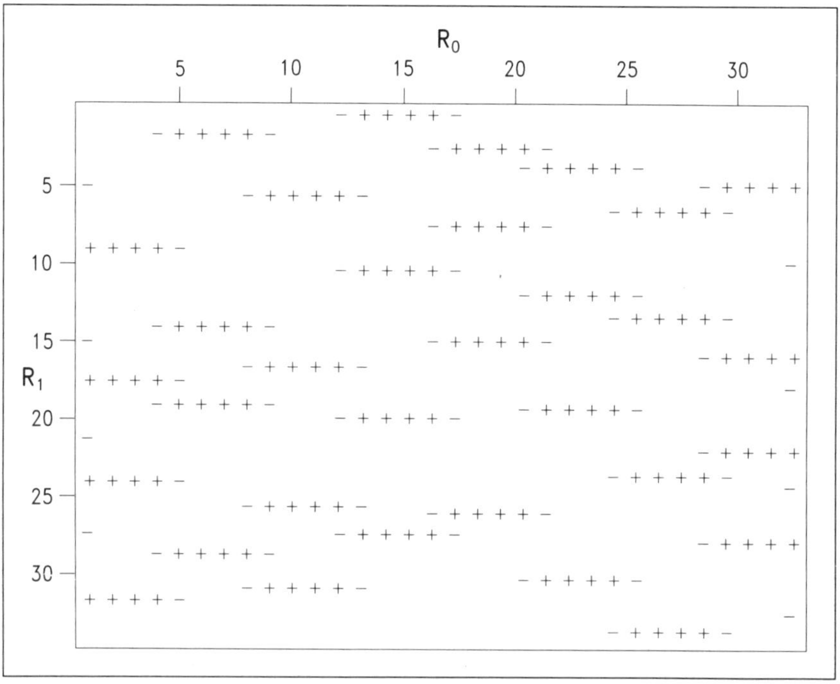

Fig. 3.5 Data dependence of $\mathbf{R}_1$ on $\mathbf{R}_0$, represented by the submatrix $\mathbf{M}_{R_0}^{R_1}$

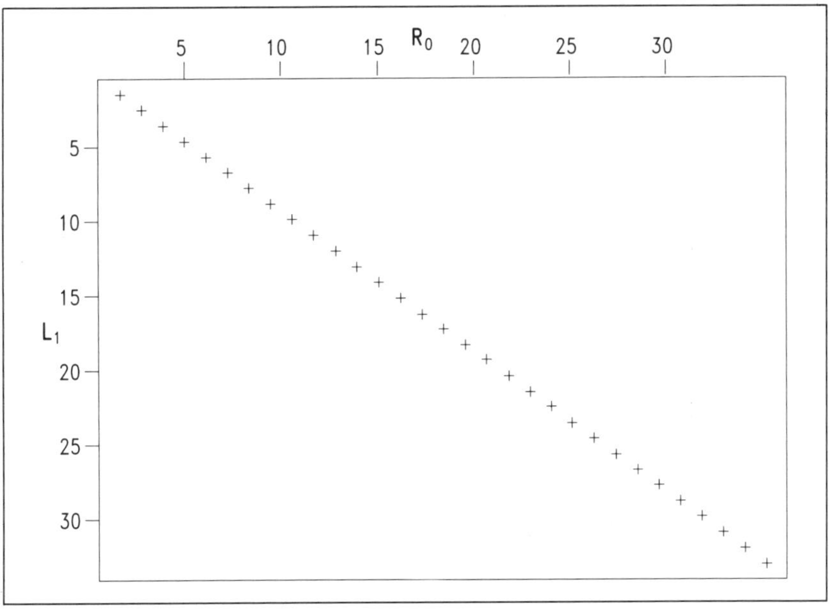

Fig. 3.6 Functional dependence of $\mathbf{L}_1$ on $\mathbf{R}_0$ for the submatrix $\mathbf{M}_{R_0}^{L_1}$

Taking permutation into account, the submatrix rows must be rearranged according to the permutation schedule $P(\mathbf{B}_1)$ shown in Table 3.7. Figure 3.5 shows this rearranged plot and represents the relationship that exists between $P(\mathbf{B}_1)$ and $\mathbf{R}_0$ or $\mathbf{R}_1$ and $\mathbf{R}_0$.

Referring to Fig. 3.1, $\mathbf{L}_1$ does not depend on $\mathbf{L}_0$. Therefore, the elements of submatrix $\mathbf{M}_{L_0}^{L_1}$ are all blank. Since $\mathbf{L}_1 = \mathbf{R}_0$, the functional relationship between $\mathbf{L}_1$ and $\mathbf{R}_0$ is expressed by the elements of $\mathbf{M}_{R_0}^{L_1}$. Since the relationship between $\mathbf{L}_1$ and $\mathbf{R}_0$ is strictly linear, the elements are located only on the diagonal and marked (+) as shown in Fig. 3.6. We also see that the remaining elements are all blank.

Lastly, let us find the functional relationship between $\mathbf{R}_1$ and $\mathbf{L}_0$. Using Eq. 3.50, we have $\mathbf{R}_1 = P(\mathbf{B}_1) \oplus \mathbf{L}_0$ which shows the relationship among $\mathbf{R}_1$, $\mathbf{L}_0$, $\mathbf{K}_1$ and $\mathbf{R}_0$. But, since dependence on $\mathbf{K}_1$ is not of interest here, $\mathbf{R}_1 = \mathbf{L}_0 \oplus g(\mathbf{R}_0)$. Thus, we see that $\mathbf{R}_1$ has a linear dependence on $\mathbf{L}_0$. Therefore the diagonal elements of $\mathbf{M}_{L_0}^{R_1}$ are set as (+), whereas the remaining elelments are all blank as shown in Fig. 3.7. Thus, the first-

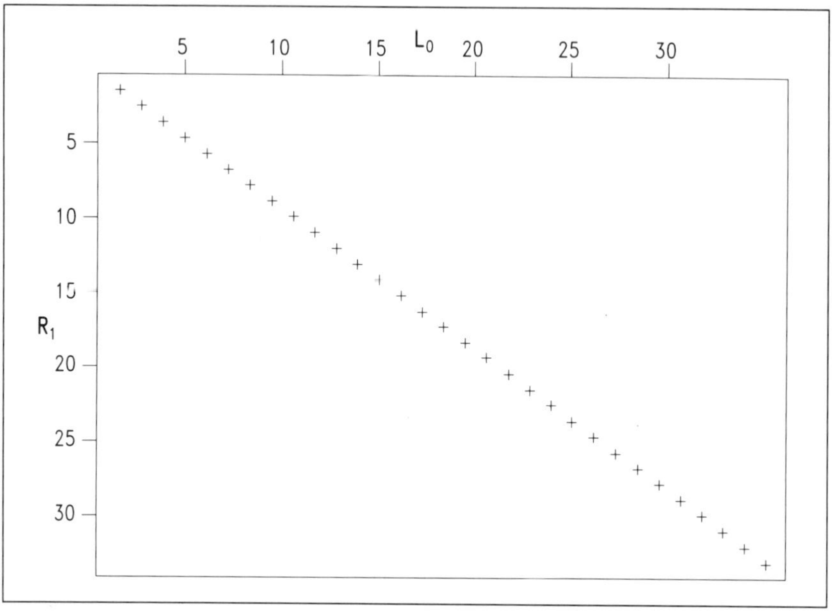

Fig. 3.7 Functional dependence of $\mathbf{R}_1$ on $\mathbf{L}_0$ for the submatrix $\mathbf{M}_{L_0}^{R_1}$

round data dependency is completely analyzed. In fact, combining the submatrices $\mathbf{M}_{R_0}^{R_1}$ (Fig. 3.5), $\mathbf{M}_{R_0}^{L_1}$ (Fig. 3.6), $\mathbf{M}_{L_0}^{R_1}$ (Fig. 3.7), and the blank submatrix $\mathbf{M}_{L_0}^{L_1}$ yields the functional dependency matrix $\mathbf{M}_0^1$ which shows the data dependency for round one. It is shown in Fig. 3.8.

Consider next the data dependence for two rounds. Let the matrix $\mathbf{M}_0^2$ be expressed in terms of the matrix $\mathbf{M}_0^1$. From Eq. 3.49, the functional dependence of $\mathbf{L}_2$ on the data block $(\mathbf{L}_0, \mathbf{R}_0)$ is identical to that of $\mathbf{R}_1$ on $(\mathbf{L}_0, \mathbf{R}_0)$. Since the dependence of $\mathbf{L}_2$ on $(\mathbf{L}_0, \mathbf{R}_0)$ is actually given by $(\mathbf{M}_{L_0}^{L_2}, \mathbf{M}_{R_0}^{L_2})$ and that of $\mathbf{R}_1$ on $(\mathbf{L}_0, \mathbf{R}_0)$ by $(\mathbf{M}_{L_0}^{R_1}, \mathbf{M}_{R_0}^{R_1})$, it follows that

$$\mathbf{M}_{L_0}^{L_2} = \mathbf{M}_{L_0}^{R_1} \tag{3.52}$$

$$\mathbf{M}_{R_0}^{L_2} = \mathbf{M}_{R_0}^{R_1} \tag{3.53}$$

From Eq. 3.52, we see that the functional dependence of $\mathbf{L}_2$ on $\mathbf{L}_0$ is identical to that of $\mathbf{R}_1$ on $\mathbf{L}_0$. Therefore, the submatrix $\mathbf{M}_{L_0}^{L_2}$ has the same plot as shown in Fig. 3.7. From Eq. 3.53, since the functional dependence of $\mathbf{L}_2$ on $\mathbf{R}_0$ is identical to that of $\mathbf{R}_1$ on $\mathbf{R}_0$, the plot representing $\mathbf{M}_{R_0}^{L_2}$ is exactly the same as shown in Fig. 3.5.

The elements of row ν of $\mathbf{M}_{L_0}^{R_2}$ give the relationship between bit ν of $\mathbf{R}_2$ and $\mathbf{L}_0$, which is equivalent to the relationship between bit ν of $\mathbf{R}_1$ and $\mathbf{R}_0$ (see Fig. 3.5). Finally, the elements of row ν of $\mathbf{M}_{R_0}^{R_2}$ give the relationship between bit ν of $\mathbf{R}_2$ and $\mathbf{R}_0$. As seen from Fig. 3.1, bit ν of $\mathbf{R}_2$ will linearly depend on $\mathbf{L}_1$. From Fig. 3.5, it may be observed that bit ν of $\mathbf{R}_1$ depends on $\mathbf{R}_0$ such that bit ν depends on 2 bits of $\mathbf{R}_0$ through self-keying and on 4 bits of $\mathbf{R}_0$ through a data relationship. Let the columns of these entries (– + + + + –) in $\mathbf{M}_{R_0}^{R_1}$ be designated d_1 (ν), d_2 (ν), . . . , d_6 (ν). Now, the submatrix $\mathbf{M}_{L_0}^{R_2}$ can be computed through the following steps. The elements of row ν of $\mathbf{M}_{L_0}^{L_1}$ and those of rows d_1 (ν), d_2 (ν), . . . , d_6 (ν) of $\mathbf{M}_{L_0}^{R_1}$ must be combined. But the elements of $\mathbf{M}_{L_0}^{L_1}$ do not contribute in our computation because they are all blank. Therefore, the elements of rows d_1 (ν) through d_6 (ν) at $\mathbf{M}_{L_0}^{R_1}$ may be marked (+) at columns d_1 (ν) through d_6 (ν). But care must be taken that the entries at columns d_1 (ν) and d_6 (ν) are changed to (–) for self-keying before all entries are combined to obtain the elements of row ν in $\mathbf{M}_{L_0}^{R_2}$. These entries are then equal to (– + + + + –) at columns d_1 (ν) through d_6 (ν), i.e. identical to the ones in $\mathbf{M}_{R_0}^{R_1}$. Therefore, it may be concluded that

$$\mathbf{M}_{L_0}^{R_2} = \mathbf{M}_{R_0}^{R_1} \tag{3.54}$$

Combining Eqs. 3.54 and 3.53 gives the following identities:

$$\mathbf{M}_{L_0}^{R_2} = \mathbf{M}_{R_0}^{L_2} = \mathbf{M}_{R_0}^{R_1} \tag{3.55}$$

At the same time, it may also be seen that Eq. 3.52 permits the evaluation of the matrix $\mathbf{M}_0^2$ in terms of $\mathbf{M}_0^1$.

Consider next the submatrix $\mathbf{M}_{R_0}^{R_2}$ which can be evaluated as follows: The elements in row 1 of $\mathbf{M}_{R_0}^{R_2}$ may be obtained by combining row 1 of $\mathbf{M}_{R_0}^{L_1}$ with rows d_1 (ν) through d_6 (ν) of $\mathbf{M}_{R_0}^{R_1}$. To provide more insight into the influence of self-keying, the following rules should be set for entries to be combined.

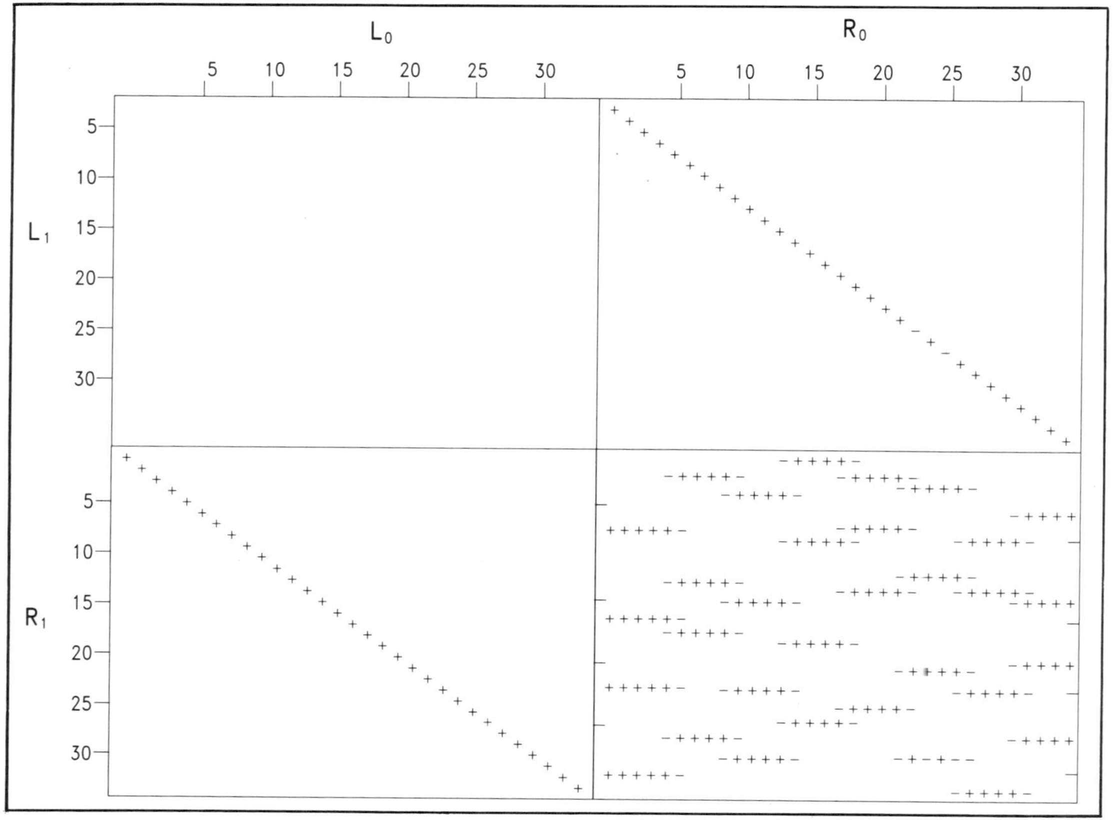

Fig. 3.8 The one-round data dependence, represented by $\mathbf{M}_0^1$

1. All elements of $\mathbf{M}_{R_0}^{R_1}$ for rows d_1 (v) and d_6 (v) should be set to (–).
2. When the proper rows of $\mathbf{M}_{R_0}^{R_1}$ and $\mathbf{M}_{R_0}^{L_1}$ are combined, the combination of mixed entries (+ and –) must be set to (∗).

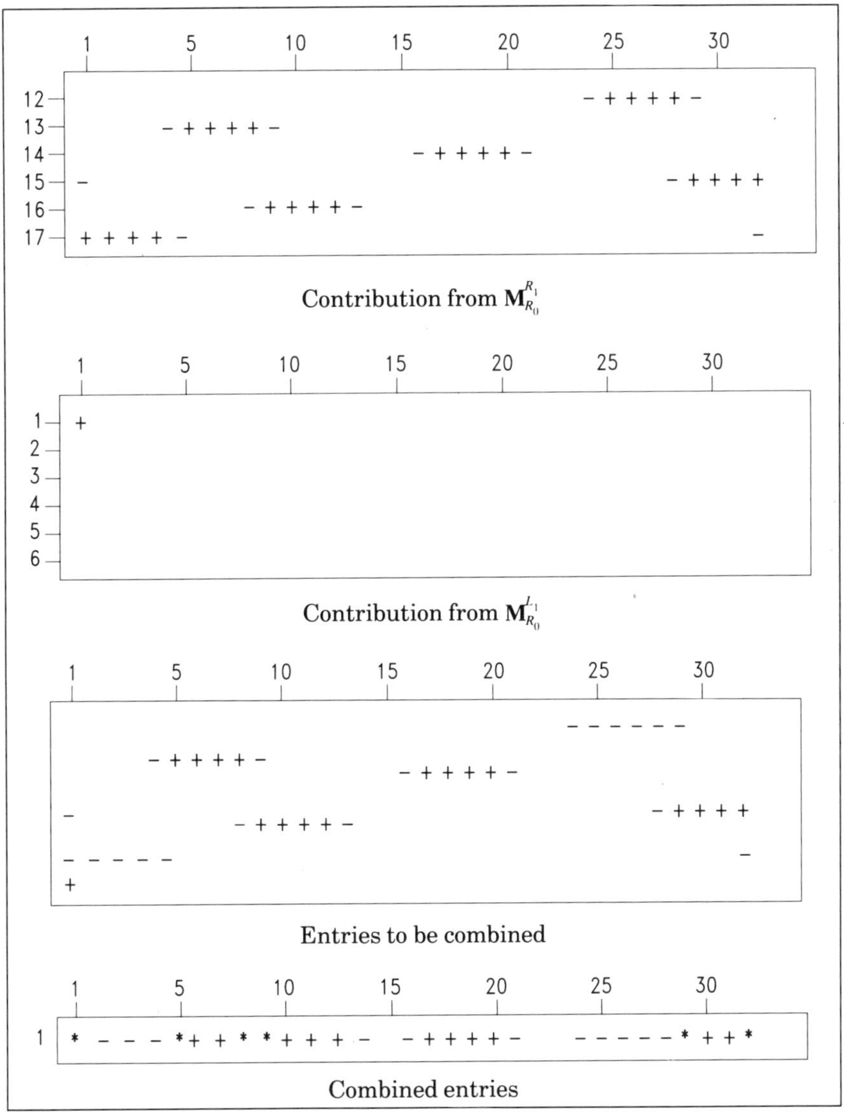

Fig. 3.9 Functional dependence of 1st bit of $\mathbf{R}_2$ on $\mathbf{R}_0$

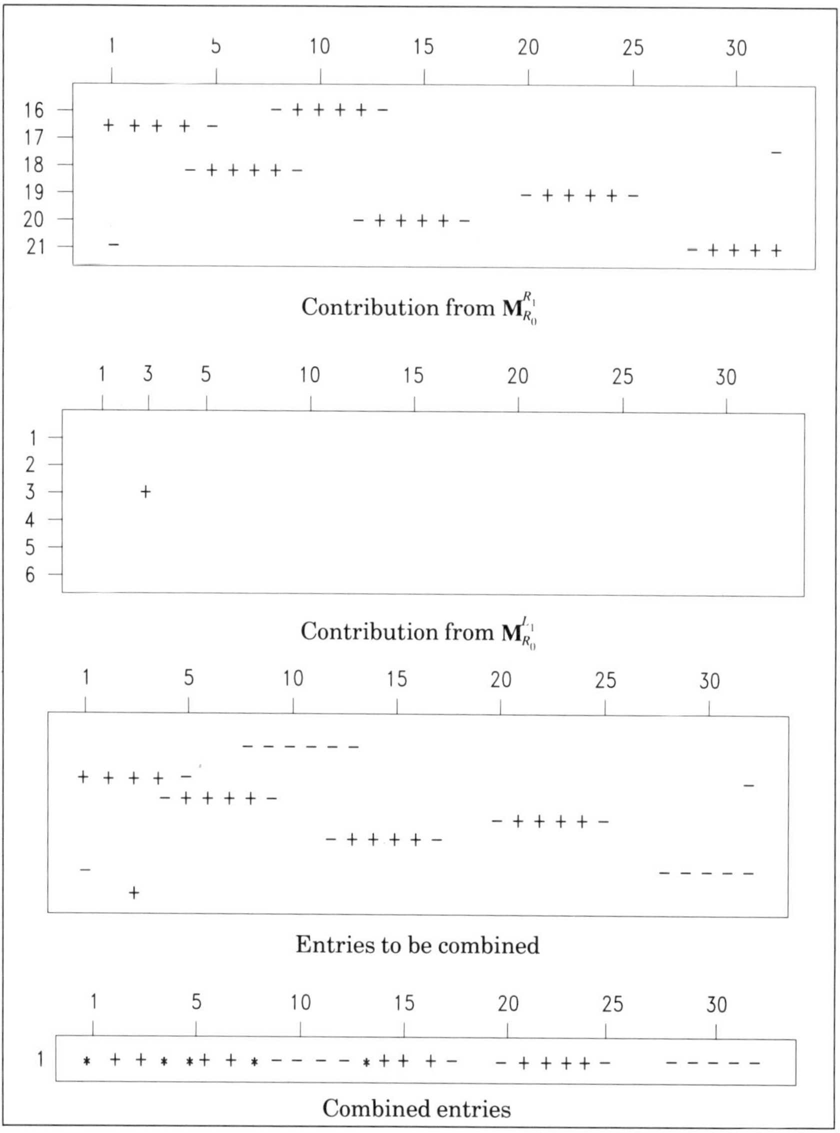

Fig. 3.10 Functional dependence of 3rd bit, of $\mathbf{R}_2$ on $\mathbf{R}_0$

For ease of understanding, the detailed steps for computing the elements of row ν (for example, ν = 1, 3) of $\mathbf{M}_{R_0}^{R_2}$ from the matrix $\mathbf{M}_0^1$ are illustrated in the following examples.

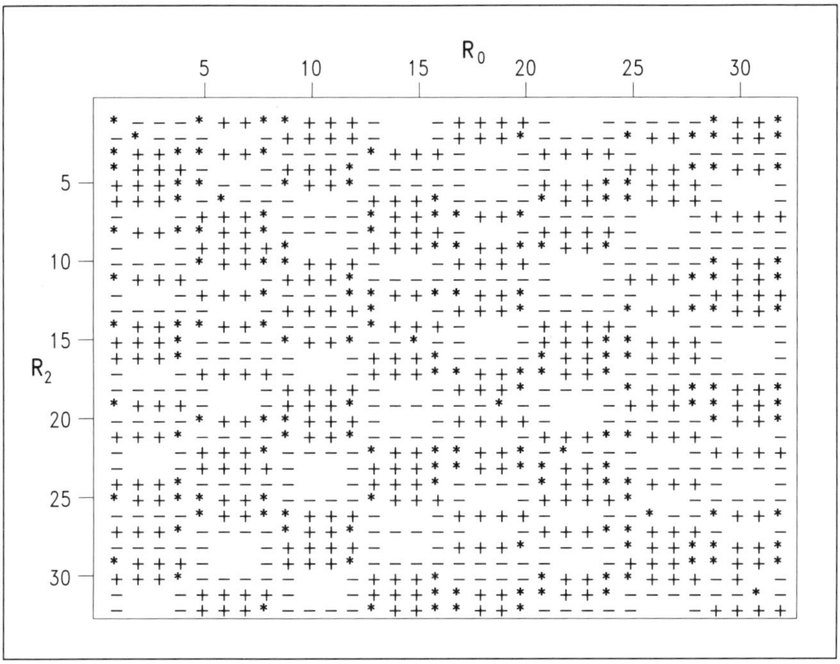

Fig. 3.11 Data dependence of $\mathbf{R}_2$ on $\mathbf{R}_0$, representing the matrix $\mathbf{M}_{R_0}^{R_2}$

■ **Example 3.10** For $\nu = 1$, we obtain (from Fig. 3.5) $d_1(\nu) = 12$, $d_2(\nu) = 13$, $d_3(\nu) = 14$, $d_4(\nu) = 15$, $d_5(\nu) = 16$, and $d_6(\nu) = 17$. They are actually the columns in which the nonblank elements in row 1 of $\mathbf{M}_{R_0}^{R_1}$ are located. The elements in row 1 of $\mathbf{M}_{R_0}^{R_2}$ are computed by combining row 1 of $\mathbf{M}_{R_0}^{L_1}$ with rows $d_1(\nu) = 12, d_2(\nu) = 13, \ldots, d_6(\nu) = 17$ of $\mathbf{M}_{R_0}^{R_1}$. The process of combined entries resulting in row 1 of $\mathbf{M}_{R_0}^{R_2}$ is illustrated in Fig. 3.9.

■ **Example 3.11** For $\nu = 3$, we obtain $d_1(\nu) = 16$, $d_2(\nu) = 17$, $d_3(\nu) = 18$, $d_4(\nu) = 19$, $d_5(\nu) = 20$, and $d_6(\nu) = 21$. As in Example 3.10, the elements in row 3 of $\mathbf{M}_{R_0}^{R_2}$ are evaluated by combining row 3 of $\mathbf{M}_{R_0}^{L_1}$ (Fig. 3.6) with rows $d_1(\nu) = 16, d_2(\nu) = 17, \ldots, d_6(\nu) = 21$ of $\mathbf{M}_{R_0}^{R_1}$ (Fig. 3.5). The detailed steps for obtaining the entries of row 3 of $\mathbf{M}_{R_0}^{R_2}$ are shown in Fig. 3.10.

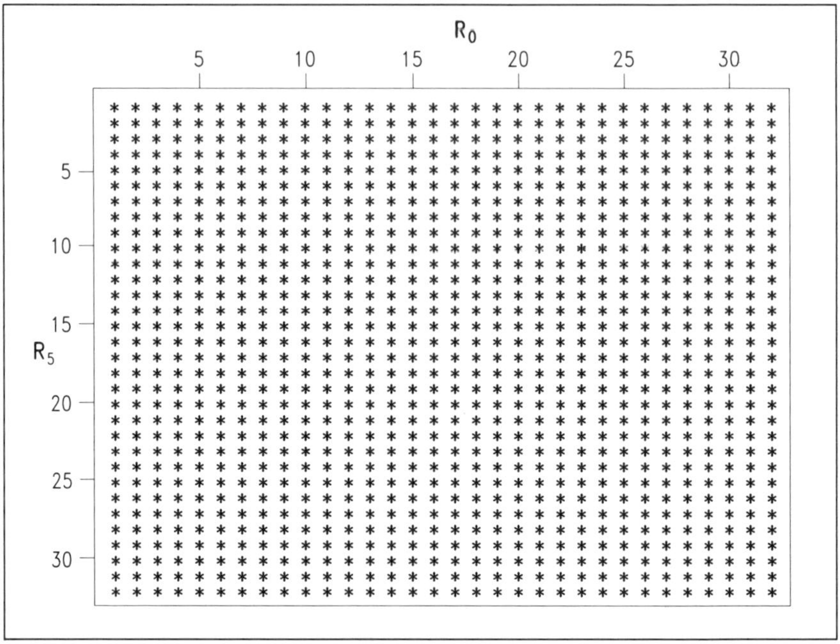

Fig. 3.12 Intersymbol dependence between ciphertext and plaintext data after five rounds

In similar fashion, all elements in rows (for $v = 2, 4, 5, 6, \ldots, 31, 32$) of $\mathbf{M}_{R_0}^{R_2}$ can be computed. The data dependence of $\mathbf{R}_2$ on $\mathbf{R}_0$ may be readily plotted as shown in Fig. 3.11.

The intersymbol dependence between ciphertext and plaintext data after three, four and five rounds can be similarly analyzed as above by evaluating how fast the intersymbol dependence of $\mathbf{R}_i$, $i = 3, 4, 5$ on $\mathbf{R}_0$ can be achieved. This analysis has revealed that each ciphertext bit depends on all plaintext bits after five rounds. The degree of intersymbol dependence after five rounds is illustrated by the plot shown in Fig. 3.12. It can be seen from Fig. 3.12 that complete dependence has been achieved after five rounds, because all entries of the matrix $\mathbf{M}_0^5$ are occupied by the symbol $(*)$.

3.6.2 Key Dependence

We have so far discussed how, after two rounds, each ciphertext bit has to depend on all plaintext bits, through data dependence as well as self-keying dependence. A similar analysis will be undertaken in this section to illustrate that each ciphertext bit also depends on all key bits.

Our aim is to investigate the functional relationship between the input to the ith round, for $i = 1, 2$ only, and the key. Recall that the input plaintext consists of 64 bits and that the key block $(\mathbf{C}_1, \mathbf{D}_1)$ prior to PC–2 contains 56 bits. The block $(\mathbf{C}_1, \mathbf{D}_1)$ represents the key obtained by loading the 64-bit external key into two 28-bit shift registers after the parity bits $\mathbf{K}_8, \mathbf{K}_{16}, \mathbf{K}_{24}, \mathbf{K}_{32}, \mathbf{K}_{40}, \mathbf{K}_{48}, \mathbf{K}_{56}$, and $\mathbf{K}_{64}$ have been systematically removed. Thus, we can consider a 64 × 56 matrix $\mathbf{N}_i$ which is partitioned into two submatrices of 32 rows and 56 columns such that

$$\mathbf{N}_i = \begin{bmatrix} \mathbf{N}_i^L \\ \mathbf{N}_i^R \end{bmatrix} \qquad \text{for} \quad 1 \le i \le 16 \tag{3.56}$$

where the submatrix $\mathbf{N}_i^L$ represents the relation for $\mathbf{L}_i$ versus $(\mathbf{C}_1, \mathbf{D}_1)$ and $\mathbf{N}_i^R$ that for $\mathbf{R}_i$ versus $(\mathbf{C}_1, \mathbf{D}_1)$.

Consider the matrix $\mathbf{N}_1$ for $i = 1$. Since $\mathbf{L}_1 = \mathbf{R}_0$, $\mathbf{L}_1$ does not depend on any key bits. Hence the elements of the submatrix $\mathbf{N}_1^L$ are blank. Similarly, from $\mathbf{R}_1 = \mathbf{L}_0 \oplus f(\Gamma_1) = \mathbf{L}_0 \oplus f(\mathbf{R}_0, \mathbf{K}_1)$, it can be observed that $\mathbf{R}_1$ depends on $(\mathbf{C}_1, \mathbf{D}_1)$ via $\mathbf{K}_1$ because $\mathbf{L}_0$ and $\mathbf{R}_0$ do not depend on $(\mathbf{C}_1, \mathbf{D}_1)$. Compute the submatrix $\mathbf{N}_1^R$ next. The dependence of the output bits $\mathbf{B}_1$ from S-boxes on key bits $\mathbf{K}_1$ may be considered as follows: The selection of the substitution function in the S_1-box depends on the first and sixth bits of $\mathbf{K}_1$. Therefore, key bits 1 and 6 of $\mathbf{K}_1$ affect the output four bits from the S_1-box by influencing the selection of an S-function. This functional relationship is represented by (–). The other four bits of $\mathbf{K}_1$ affect the output four bits by influencing the arguments of the S-function. This kind of dependence is indicated by (+). If a bit from the key affects the output by selecting an S-function as well as an argument, the symbol (∗) is used. Of course, if the output does not depend on the key, a blank is employed. The functional dependence of $\mathbf{B}_1$ on $\mathbf{K}_1$ is shown in Fig. 3.13.

Because of the permutation given by $P(\mathbf{B}_1)$ (see Table 3.7), the rows of Fig. 3.13 must be rearranged accordingly, and the result is plotted in Fig. 3. 14. Figure 3.14 represents the functional dependence of $\mathbf{R}_1$ on $\mathbf{K}_1$. Next, the dependence of $\mathbf{R}_1$ on $(\mathbf{C}_1, \mathbf{D}_1)$ can be determined by relating each bit of $\mathbf{K}_1$ to each bit of $(\mathbf{C}_1, \mathbf{D}_1)$. Figure 3.15 is constructed by replacing each bit of $\mathbf{K}_1$ by an appropriate bit of $(\mathbf{C}_1, \mathbf{D}_1)$. The block $(\mathbf{C}_1, \mathbf{D}_1)$ represents the 56-bit key obtained by loading the 64-bit external key, $\mathbf{K} = (k_1, k_2, \ldots, k_{64})$, into two 28-bit registers $\mathbf{C}_1$ and $\mathbf{D}_1$ after

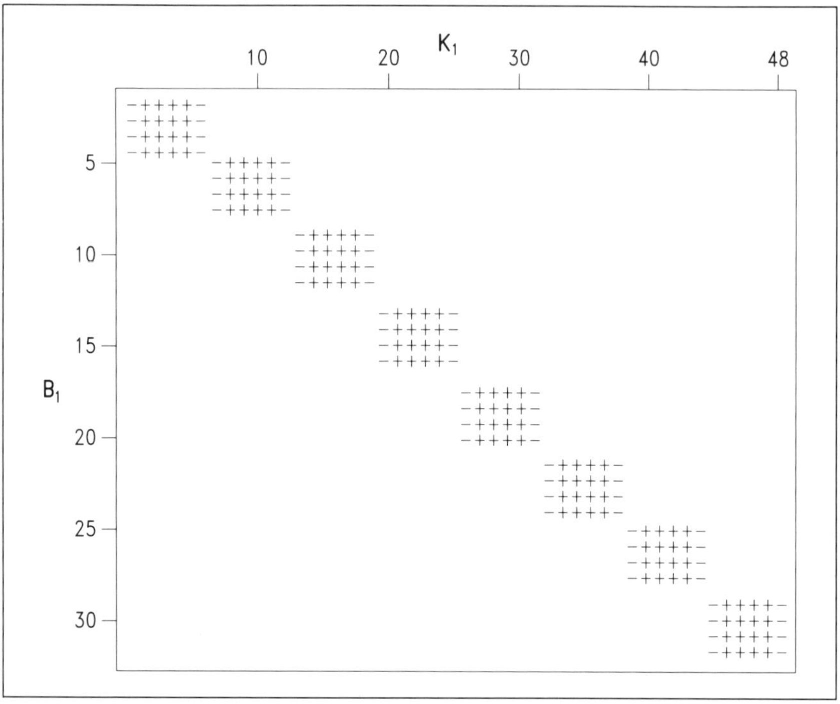

Fig. 3.13 Functional dependence of the output bits $\mathbf{B}_1$ from S-boxes on key bits $\mathbf{K}_1$

removing the 8-bit parity bits and shifting 1 bit to the left. Thus, the elements of $(\mathbf{C}_1, \mathbf{D}_1)$ are related to $\mathbf{K}_i$, $1 \le i \le 3$, as follows:

$$\begin{aligned}(\mathbf{C}_1, \mathbf{D}_1) = (\ & 49, 41, 33, 25, 17, 9, 1, 58, 50, 42, 34, 26, 18, 10,\\ & 2, 59, 51, 43, 35, 27, 19, 11, 3, 60, 52, 44, 36, 57,\\ & 55, 47, 39, 31, 23, 15, 7, 64, 54, 46, 38, 30, 22, 14,\\ & 6, 61, 53, 45, 37, 29, 21, 13, 5, 28, 20, 12, 4, 63\ )\end{aligned} \tag{3.57}$$

Referring to Table 3.3 (PC–2), the internal key $\mathbf{K}_1$ is related to $(\mathbf{C}_1, \mathbf{D}_1)$ as follows:

$$\begin{aligned}\mathbf{K}_1 = (\ & 14, 17, 11, 24, 1, 5, 3, 28, 15, 6, 21, 10,\\ & 23, 19, 12, 4, 26, 8, 16, 7, 27, 20, 13, 2,\\ & 41, 52, 31, 37, 47, 55, 30, 40, 51, 45, 33, 48,\\ & 44, 49, 39, 56, 34, 53, 46, 42, 50, 36, 29, 32\ )\end{aligned} \tag{3.58}$$

In fact, $\mathbf{K}_2$ is obtained by shifting $\mathbf{K}_1$ 1 bit to the left, and $\mathbf{K}_3$ is computed by a 3-bit shift of $\mathbf{K}_1$ to the left. Hence, with $\mathbf{K}_1$ specified

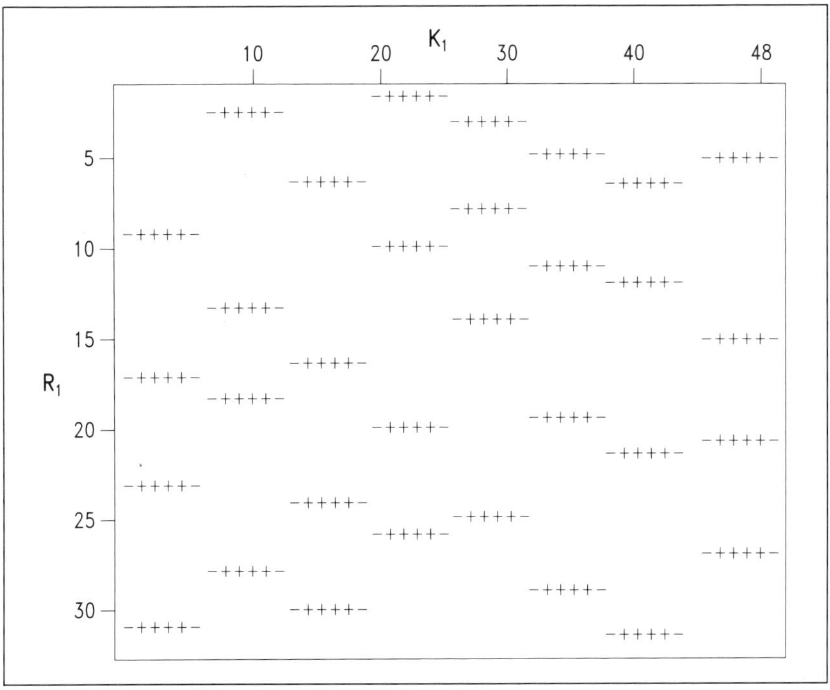

Fig. 3.14 Functional dependence of $\mathbf{R}_1$ on $\mathbf{K}_1$ after permutation $P(\mathbf{B}_1)$

in Eq. 3.58, the internal keys $\mathbf{K}_2$ and $\mathbf{K}_3$ are related to $(\mathbf{C}_1, \mathbf{D}_1)$ as shown below:

$$\begin{aligned}\mathbf{K}_2 = (\ & 15, 18, 12, 25, 2, 6, 4, 1, 16, 7, 22, 11,\\ & 24, 20, 13, 5, 27, 9, 17, 8, 28, 21, 14, 3,\\ & 42, 53, 32, 38, 48, 56, 31, 41, 52, 46, 34, 49,\\ & 45, 50, 40, 29, 35, 54, 47, 43, 51, 37, 30, 33\ )\end{aligned} \tag{3.59}$$

$$\begin{aligned}\mathbf{K}_3 = (\ & 17, 20, 14, 27, 4, 8\ 6, 3, 18, 9, 24, 13,\\ & 26, 22, 15, 7, 1, 11, 19, 10, 2, 23, 16, 5,\\ & 44, 55, 34, 40, 50, 30, 33, 43, 54, 48, 36, 51,\\ & 47, 52, 42, 31, 37, 56, 49, 45, 53, 39, 32, 35\ )\end{aligned} \tag{3.60}$$

■ **Example 3.12** Transforming Fig. 3.14 to Fig. 3.15, we must replace each bit of $\mathbf{K}_1$ with an appropriate bit of $(\mathbf{C}_1, \mathbf{D}_1)$ on the basis of Eq. 3.58. Considering the first row of $\mathbf{R}_1$, $\mathbf{K}_1$=(19, 20, 21, 22, 23, 24) = (− + + + −) corresponds to $(\mathbf{C}_1, \mathbf{D}_1)$ = (16, 7, 27, 20, 13, 2) = (− + + + + −), or $(\mathbf{C}_1, \mathbf{D}_1) = (2, 7, 13, 16, 20, 27) = (- + + - + +)$. For the seventh row of $\mathbf{R}_1$, we have $(\mathbf{C}_1, \mathbf{D}_1) = (34, 39, 44, 49, 53, 56) = (+ + - + - +)$ corresponding to $\mathbf{K}_1 = (37, 38, 39, 40, 41, 42) = (- + + + + -)$. Similarly, by evaluating all 32 rows of $\mathbf{R}_1$ with respect to the different set of $(\mathbf{C}_1, \mathbf{D}_1)$, we can plot the functional dependence of $\mathbf{R}_1$ on $(\mathbf{C}_1, \mathbf{D}_1)$ as shown in Fig. 3.15.

Evaluate the matrix $\mathbf{N}_2$ for $i = 2$. Referring to Fig. 3.1, we have $\mathbf{L}_2 = \mathbf{R}_1$. Therefore, $\mathbf{L}_2$ also depends on $(\mathbf{C}_1, \mathbf{D}_1)$ because $\mathbf{R}_1$ depends on $(\mathbf{C}_1, \mathbf{D}_1)$. Since the dependence of $\mathbf{L}_2$ on $(\mathbf{C}_1, \mathbf{D}_1)$ is denoted by $\mathbf{N}_2^L$, and that of $\mathbf{R}_1$ on $(\mathbf{C}_1, \mathbf{D}_1)$ by $\mathbf{N}_1^R$, it follows that

$$\mathbf{N}_2^L = \mathbf{N}_1^R \tag{3.61}$$

Using Eq. 3.21, we have

$$\begin{aligned}\mathbf{R}_2 &= \mathbf{L}_1 \oplus f(\Gamma_2)\\ &= \mathbf{L}_1 \oplus f(\mathbf{R}_1, \mathbf{K}_2)\end{aligned} \tag{3.62}$$

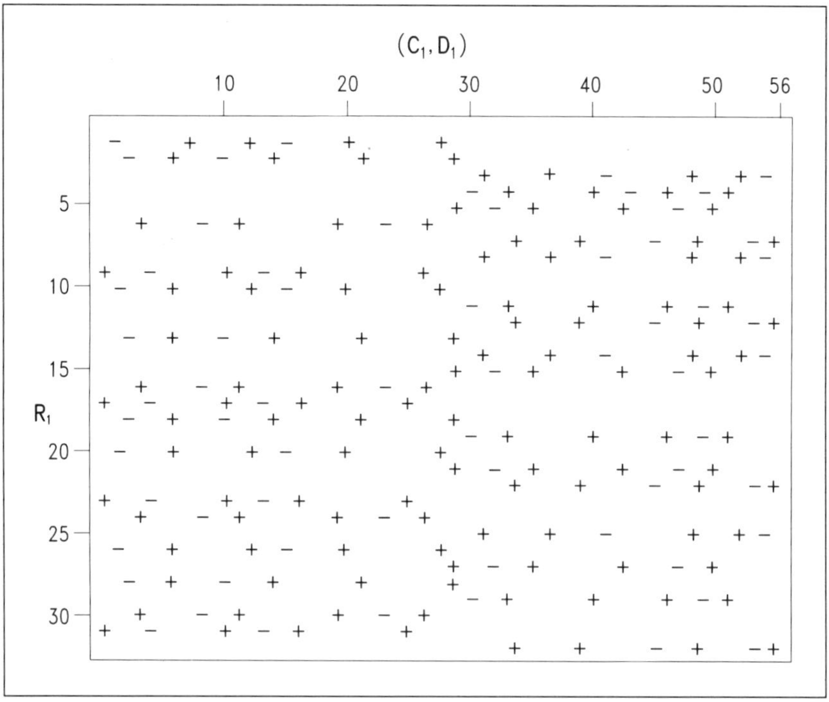

Fig. 3.15 Functional dependence of $\mathbf{R}_1$ on $(\mathbf{C}_1, \mathbf{D}_1)$

The relationship between $\mathbf{R}_2$ and $\mathbf{R}_1$ was already established with $\mathbf{M}_{R_1}^{R_2}$ for $i = 2$ (see Fig. 3.5). The relationship between $\mathbf{R}_1$ and $(\mathbf{C}_1, \mathbf{D}_1)$ is given by $\mathbf{N}_1^R$ (see Fig. 3.15). Also, the relationship between $\mathbf{R}_2$ and $\mathbf{L}_1$ has been already established during the evaluation of $\mathbf{M}_{L_1}^{R_2}$. But since $\mathbf{L}_1$ does not depend on $(\mathbf{C}_1, \mathbf{D}_1)$, it can be ignored for this part. The functional dependence of $\mathbf{R}_2$ on $(\mathbf{C}_1, \mathbf{D}_1)$ can be obtained by computing the submatrices $\mathbf{N}_2^L = \mathbf{N}_1^R$ and $\mathbf{N}_2^R$. In fact, the rows ν of $\mathbf{N}_2^R$ can be constructed from the matrix $\mathbf{N}_1$. The construction of the kth row of $\mathbf{R}_2$ with respect to $(\mathbf{C}_1, \mathbf{D}_1)$ is best explained by the following example.

■ **Example 3.13** Show the method for construction of the second row (for $k = 2$) of $\mathbf{N}_2^R$. To begin with, the translation of $\mathbf{K}_2$ elements into $(\mathbf{C}_1, \mathbf{D}_1)$ elements through Eq. 3.59 is considered to be important. From Fig. 3.14, the dependence of $\mathbf{R}_2$ on $\mathbf{K}_2$ is also marked by (− + + + + −) for bits 7, 8, 9, 10, 11, 12 of $\mathbf{K}_2$. These bits correspond to $(\mathbf{C}_1, \mathbf{D}_1) = (4, 1, 16, 7, 22, 11)$ via Eq. 3.59. Thus, the entries of $(\mathbf{C}_1, \mathbf{D}_1)$ corresponding to row 2 of $\mathbf{R}_2$ are shown in Fig. 3.16(a).

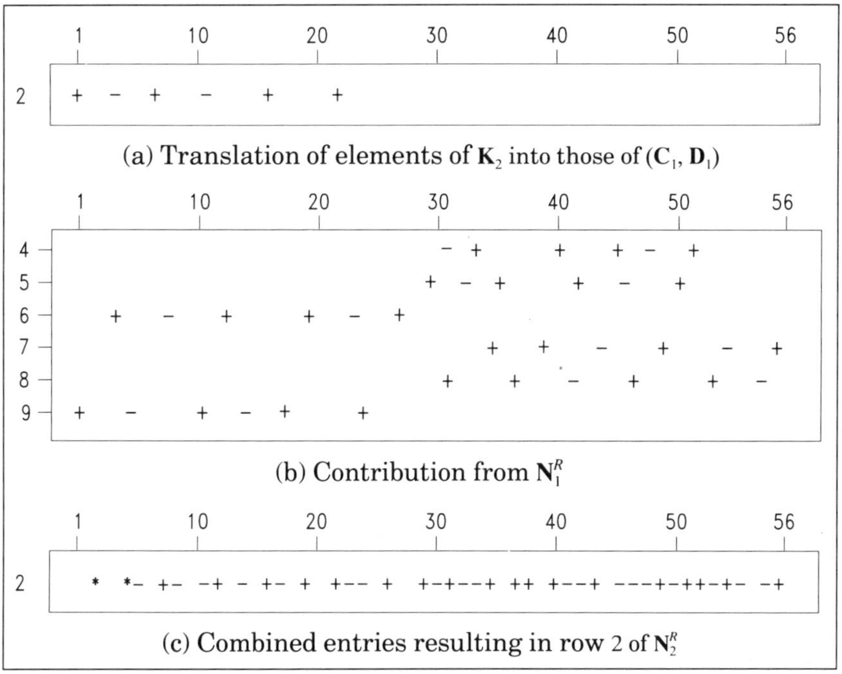

Fig. 3.16 Functional dependence of second bit of $\mathbf{R}_2$ on $(\mathbf{C}_1, \mathbf{D}_1)$

From Fig. 3.5, we observe that, for $\nu = 2$, $d_1(\nu) = 4$, $d_2(\nu) = 5$, $d_3(\nu) = 6$, $d_4(\nu) = 7$, $d_5(\nu) = 8$, and $d_6(\nu) = 9$, respectively. Next, rows 4 through 9 of $\mathbf{N}_1^R$ shown in Fig. 3.15 are also used for the construction of $\mathbf{R}_2$ with respect to $(\mathbf{C}_1, \mathbf{D}_1)$. The details are shown in Fig. 3.16 (b).

In order to apply the same rules as established previously for data dependence, entries in rows $d_1(\nu) = 4$ and $d_6(\nu) = 9$ of $\mathbf{N}_1^R$ in Fig. 3.16 (b) must be set as (–) after which all the elements in Figs. 3.16 (a) and (b) should be combined column by column in order to evaluate the functional dependence of the second bit of $\mathbf{R}_2$ on $(\mathbf{C}_1, \mathbf{D}_1)$. Thus, the final result of the dependency plot for the second bit of $\mathbf{R}_2$ versus $(\mathbf{C}_1, \mathbf{D}_1)$ is obtained as shown in Fig. 3.16 (c).

A repetition of this procedure for $1 \le \nu \le 32$ yields Fig. 3.17 and hence $\mathbf{N}_2^R$ is completely obtained. Since $\mathbf{N}_2^L = \mathbf{N}_1^R$, the matrix $\mathbf{N}_2$ is computed as

$$\mathbf{N}_2 = \begin{bmatrix} \mathbf{N}_1^R \\ --- \\ \mathbf{N}_2^R \end{bmatrix} = \begin{bmatrix} \text{Fig.3.15} \\ ------ \\ \text{Fig.3.17} \end{bmatrix} \tag{3.63}$$

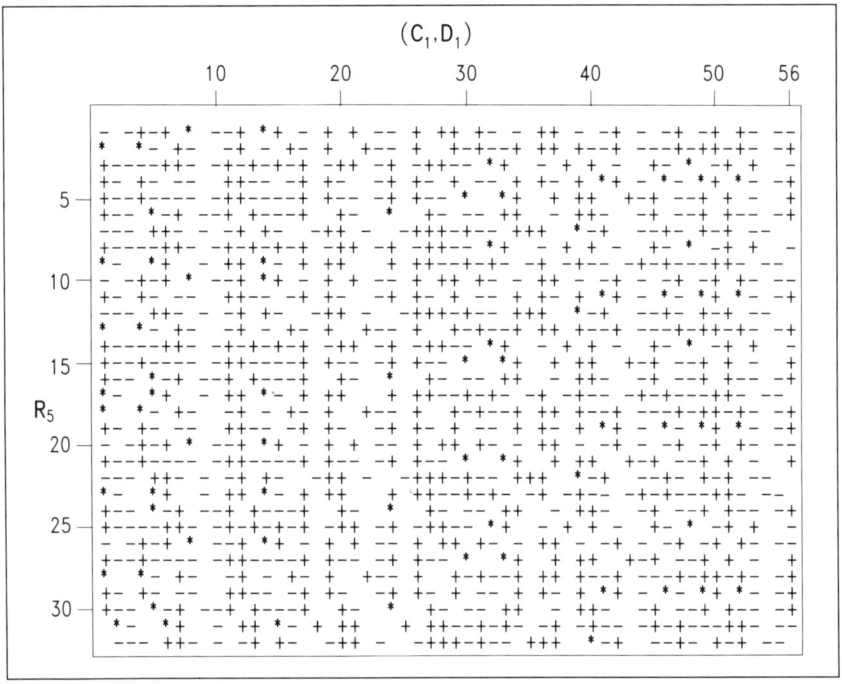

Fig. 3.17 Complete plot of key dependence for $\mathbf{N}_2^R$

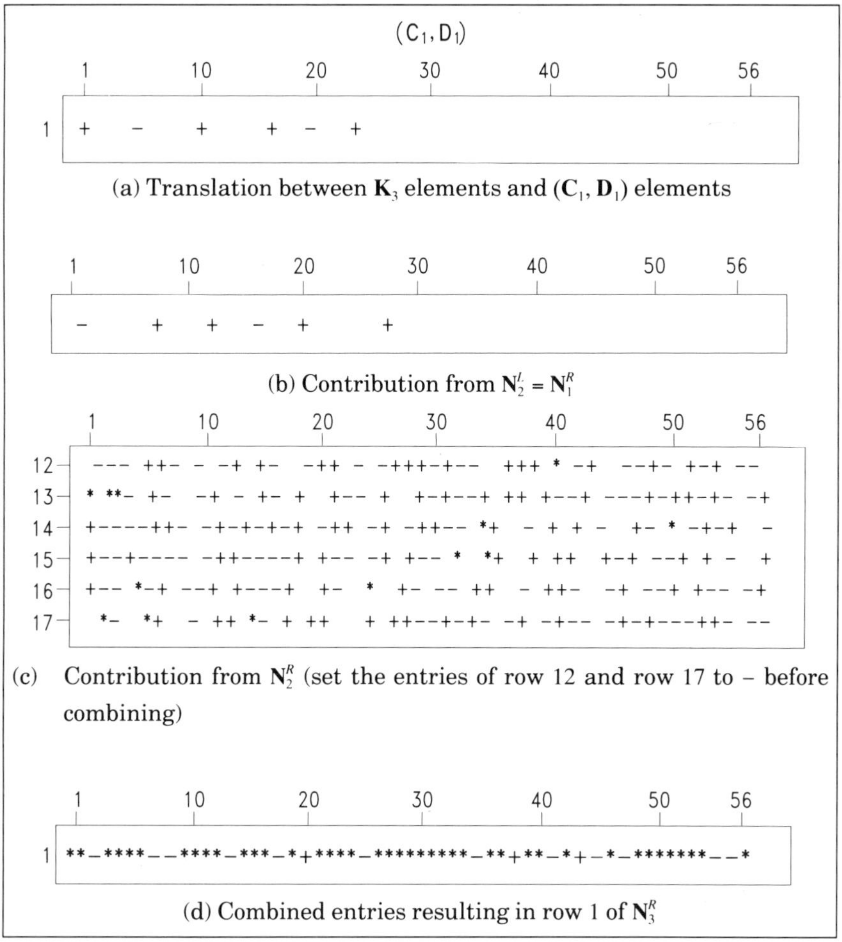

Fig. 3.18 Functional dependence of 1st bit of $\mathbf{R}_3$ on $(\mathbf{C}_1, \mathbf{D}_1)$

■ **Example 3.14** Consider the matrix $\mathbf{N}_3$. Let us evaluate the functional dependence of the first bit of $\mathbf{R}_3$ on $(\mathbf{C}_1, \mathbf{D}_1)$. The bit positions 19, 20, 21, 22, 23, 24 of $\mathbf{K}_3$ correspond to the entries 19, 10, 2, 23, 16, 5 of $(\mathbf{C}_1, \mathbf{D}_1)$ via Eq. 3.60. The corresponding entries of $(\mathbf{C}_1, \mathbf{D}_1)$ with respect to the first bit of $\mathbf{R}_3$ are illustrated in Fig. 3.18 (a). Since $\mathbf{N}_2^L = \mathbf{N}_1^R$, it can be plotted as Fig. 3.18 (b), because the first row of $\mathbf{N}_2^L$ is identical to the first row of $\mathbf{N}_1^R$ of Fig. 3.15. From Fig. 3.5, it follows that bit ν of $\mathbf{R}_2$ depends on $\mathbf{R}_1$ via − + + + + −. Let the columns of these entries be

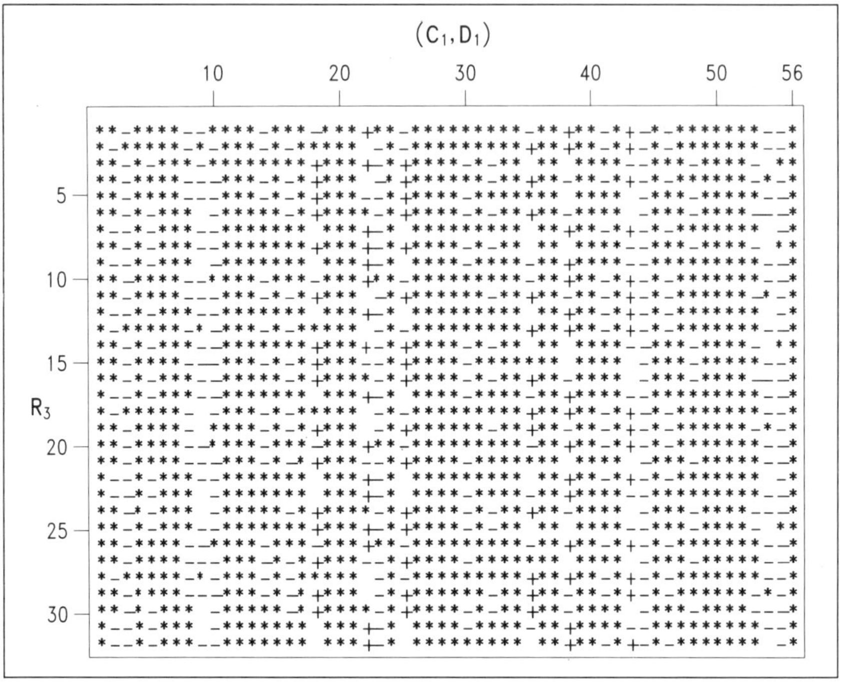

Fig. 3.19 Functional dependence of $\mathbf{R}_3$ on $(\mathbf{C}_1, \mathbf{D}_1)$, matrix $\mathbf{N}_3^R$

designated $d_1(\nu)$ through $d_6(\nu)$. Then, for $\nu = 1$, $d_1(\nu) = 12$, $d_2(\nu) = 13$, $d_3(\nu) = 14$, $d_4(\nu) = 15$, $d_5(\nu) = 16$, and $d_6(\nu) = 17$. Thus, the rows 12 through 17 of Fig. 3.17 must be used to obtain the construction of $\mathbf{R}_3$ with respect to $(\mathbf{C}_1, \mathbf{D}_1)$, as shown in Fig. 3.18 (c). The entries in rows 12 and 17 must be set equal to (–) before combining. Combining the several elements indicated in Fig. 3.18 (a), (b) and (c) column by column, the final result of the functional dependence of the first bit of $\mathbf{R}_3$ on $(\mathbf{C}_1, \mathbf{D}_1)$ is obtained as shown in Fig. 3.18 (d).

Repeating this procedure for $1 \le \nu \le 32$, all rows of $\mathbf{N}_3^R$ can be plotted as shown in Fig. 3.19. Thus, using $\mathbf{N}_3^L = \mathbf{N}_2^R$, the matrix $\mathbf{N}_3$ is then computed by combining $\mathbf{N}_2^R$ of Fig. 3.17 and $\mathbf{N}_3^R$ of Fig. 3.19 in Eq. 3.56 for $i = 3$ as shown below.

$$\mathbf{N}_3 = \begin{bmatrix} \mathbf{N}_2^R \\ --- \\ \mathbf{N}_3^R \end{bmatrix} = \begin{bmatrix} \text{Fig.3.17} \\ ------ \\ \text{Fig.3.19} \end{bmatrix} \tag{3.64}$$

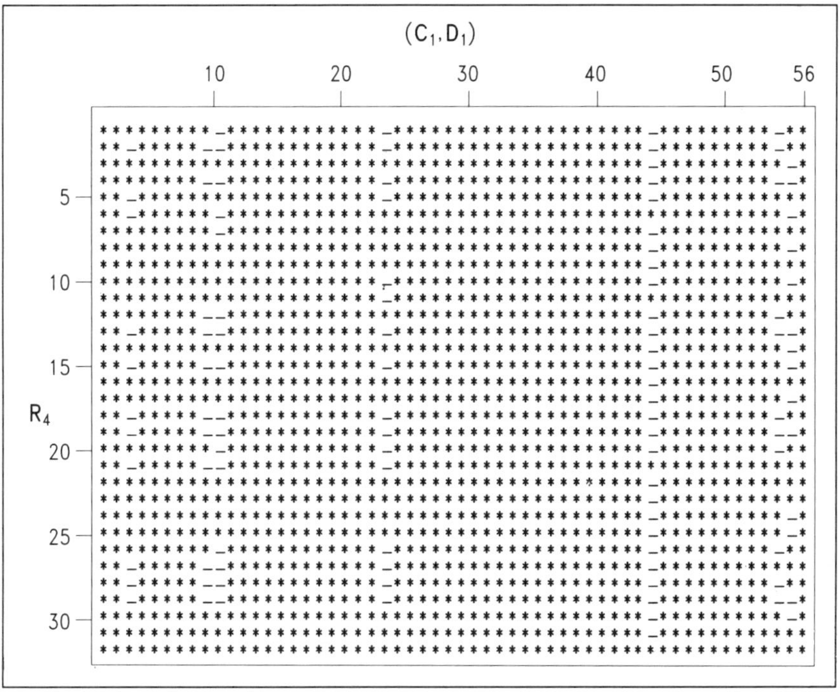

Fig. 3.20 Functional dependence of $\mathbf{R}_4$ on $(\mathbf{C}_1, \mathbf{D}_1)$, matrix $\mathbf{N}_4^R$

■ **Example 3.15** Let $\mathbf{N}_4$ and $\mathbf{N}_5$ be computed. The steps to obtain the functional dependence of each bit of $\mathbf{R}_4$ or $\mathbf{R}_5$ on $(\mathbf{C}_1, \mathbf{D}_1)$ can be computed by following the same rules as done in the two preceding examples. Hence, by using all rows $\mathbf{N}_i^R$ for $i = 4, 5$ and the relation of $\mathbf{N}_i^L = \mathbf{N}_{i-1}^R$ for $i = 4, 5$, the plots of the final results for the matrices $\mathbf{N}_4^R$ and $\mathbf{N}_5^R$ may be shown in Figs. 3.20 and 3.21, respectively. Observing Fig. 3.21, the functional dependence of $\mathbf{R}_5$ on $(\mathbf{C}_1, \mathbf{D}_1)$ not only indicates all nonblank entries, but is filled almost entirely by $(*)$.

Data protection by cryptography is indeed revolutionary. A cryptographic algorithm provides effective data security between two users within a communication network. The DES was designed for use in many commercial applications, such as banking systems and modem communications, to provide cryptographic protection for information data. The DES is the sole algorithm ever published in the USA, and it has been a challenge to break it. Many cryptographers have probably tried to uncover the details of the DES algorithm. However, Diffie and

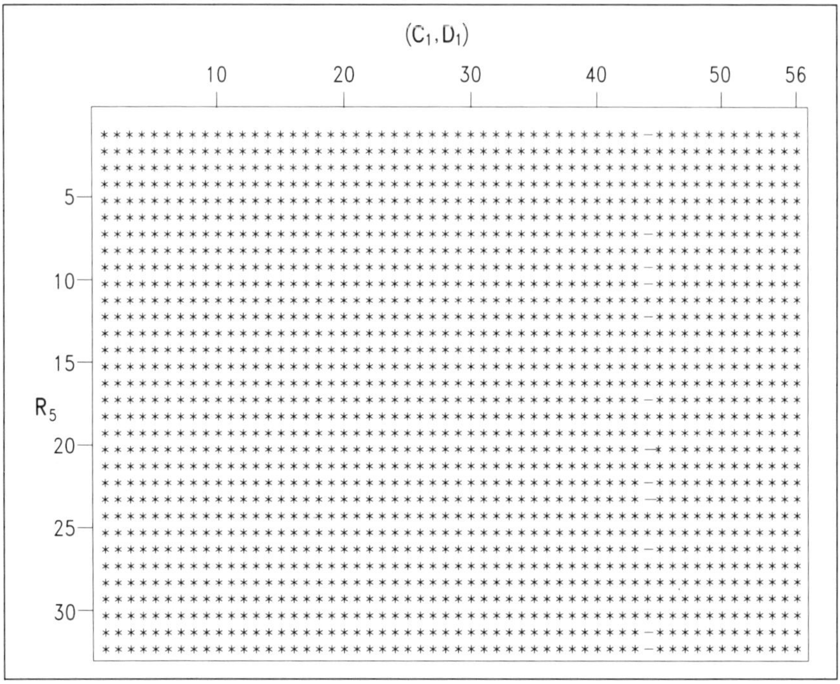

Fig. 3.21 Functional dependence of $\mathbf{R}_5$ on $(\mathbf{C}_1, \mathbf{D}_1)$, matrix $\mathbf{N}_5^R$

Hellman [11], and others were concerned about the possible weakness that, with 56-bit keys, the DES could be broken by an exhaustive key search. In [11] they claimed that an appropriate machine consisting of a million LSI chips could try all $2^{56} \cong 10^{17}$ keys in one day for the entire search. The cost of such a machine would be about $20 million. It is also reported that: (i) a key of 56 bits for DES allows no real safety margin and (ii) the *S*-box design is often criticized. But we do not intend here to make any judgement on these criticisms.

The purpose of detailed DES analysis is to provide the reader with a greater insight and better understanding of DES's operation. The analysis and design of a two-round DES system have been presented in detail in this chapter because the DES system represents one of the best known examples of a secret key system. The DES can be employed within a cryptography system with considerable flexibility. There are several modes in which the DES can be used. These modes are the electronic code book (ECB), cipher block chaining (CBC), output feedback (OFB), and cipher feedback (CFB) modes. The schematic

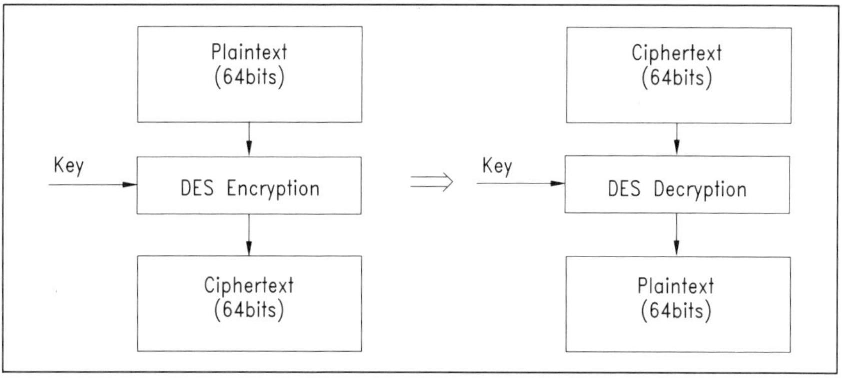

Fig. 3.22 Electronic code book (ECB) mode (DES algorithm)

illustrations for these modes are shown in Figs. 3.22, 3.23, 3.24, and 3.25. In addition, the DES can also be used for authentication in either CBC or CFB modes.

In 1986, NTT in Japan developed the DES-like secret-key cipher called the Fast Data Encipherment Algorithm (FEAL-8). The FEAL-8 cipher was designed to be a high-speed software cipher and is being used in many commercial applications, such as facsimile terminals, modem equipment, and IC or telephone cards, due to its compactness.

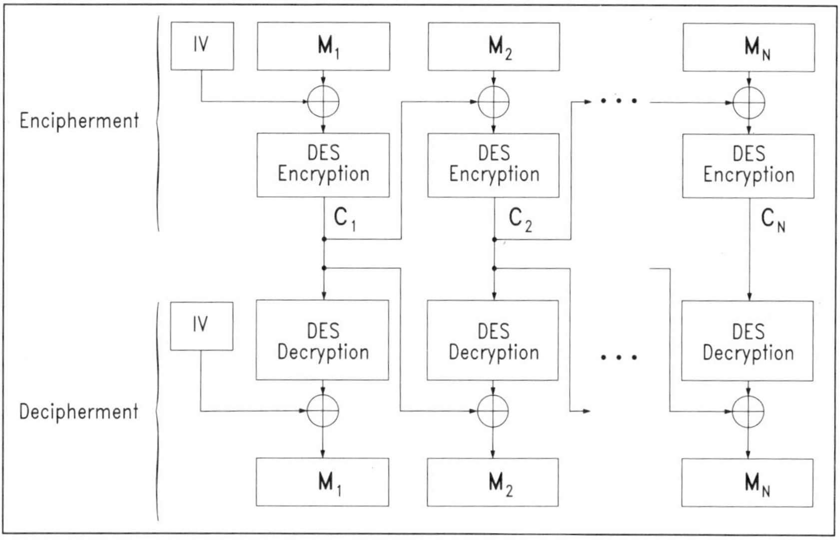

Fig. 3.23 Cipher block chaining (CBC) mode (Block chaining using ciphertext feedback)

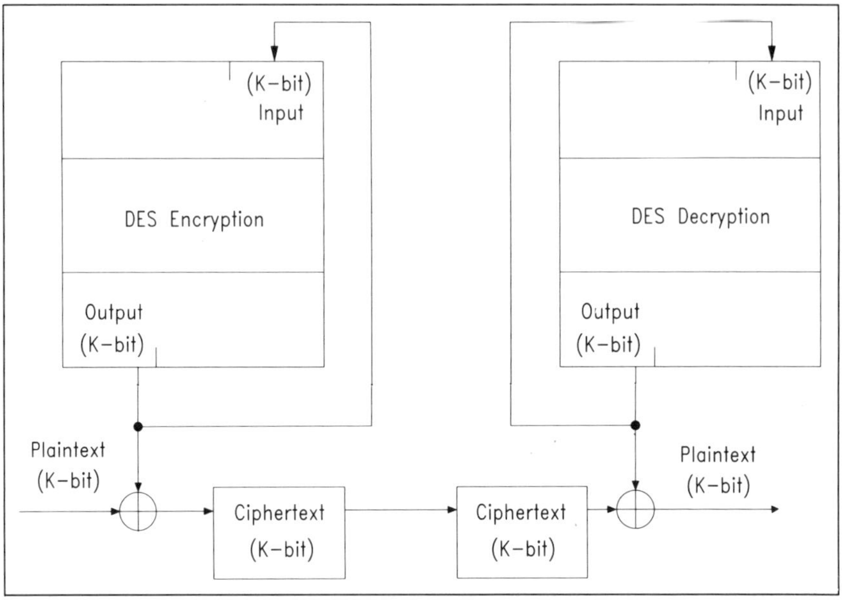

Fig. 3.24 Output feedback (OFB) mode (Key-autokey synchronous cipher system)

However, some users want to use upgraded versions to counter chosen plaintext attacks or exhaustive key search. In response to these demands, FEAL-8 has been expanded to FEAL-*N* (FEAL cipher family), where $N = 2^x$ for $x \geq 2$ denotes *N*-round FEAL with 64-bit keys. It is also reported that FEAL-*N* has been expanded to FEAL-NX, i.e. an *N*-round FEAL with 128-bit keys. For instance, when the chosen plaintext attack is still a threat for the round number $N = 8$ selected, the user can opt for an increased value of *N*.

In 1990, Brown, Piepzyk, and Seberry at UNSW in Australia proposed a new DES-like cipher LOKI, which encrypts and decrypts a 64-bit block of data using a 64-bit key. The structure of LOKI is very much like that of DES. But the main difference between DES and LOKI is in the *S*-boxes. All the four LOKI *S*-boxes take a 12-bit input and produce an 8-bit output, and they are all equal.

In the 1990s, the concept of differential cryptanalysis proposed by Biham and Shamir (1990) will be extremely important as a topic of research. Biham and Shamir demonstrated that many symmetric cryptosystems can be broken by their method. Therefore, the differential cryptanalysis introduced by them will be one of the most powerful modes of attack on DES-like cryptosystems.

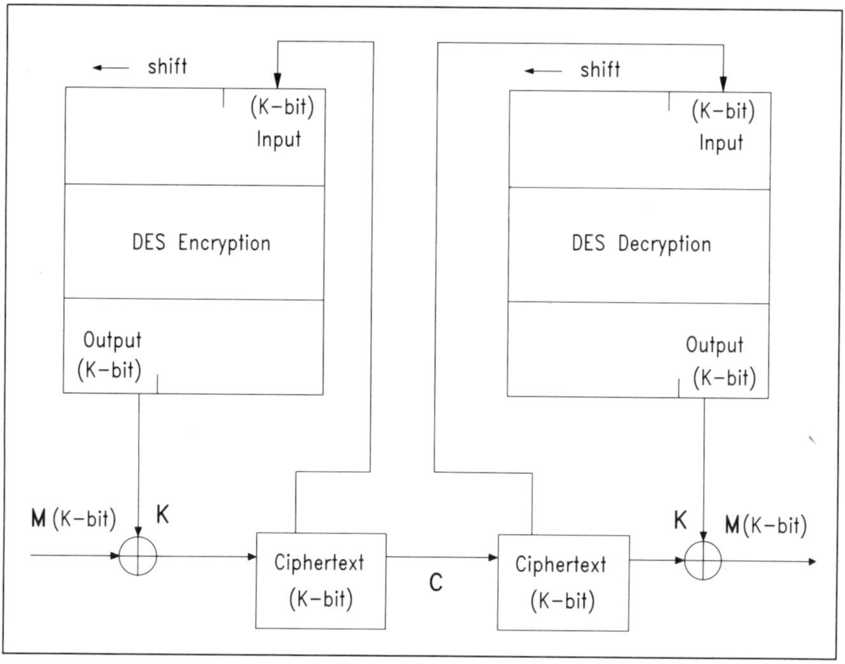

Fig. 3.25 Cipher feedback (CFB) mode (self-synchronizing stream cipher with ciphertext feedback)

REFERENCES

1. Biham, E. and A. Shamir : "Differential Cryptanalysis of DES-Like cryptosystems", *Proc. Crypto 90*, pp –17, Santa Barbara, CA, Aug. 1990.
2. Biham, E. and A. Shamir : "Differential Cryptanalysis of FEAL and N-ltash", in *Eurocrypt 91 Abstracts*, A. J. Clark, ed., IACR, Brighton, UK, pp 8–11, Apr. 1991.
3. Biham, E. and A. Shamir : "Differential Cryptanalysis—Snefru, Kharfe, REDOC-II, LOKI, and Lucifer", *Proc. Crypto 91*, IACR, Santa Barbara, Aug. 1991.
4. Brickell, E. F., J.H. Moore, and M.R. Purtill : "Structures in the *S*-boxes of the DES", *Proc. of Crypto 86*, Springer-Verlag, New York, LNCS 435, pp 3–8, 1986.
5. Brown, L : "A Proposed Design for an Extended DES", in *Proc. 5th Int. Conf. and Exhib. Computer Security*, IFIP, Gold Coast, Queensland, Australia, May 1988.
6. Brown, L., J. Pieprzyk, and J. Seberry : "LOKI–A Cryptographic Primitive for Authentication and Secrecy Applications", *Advances in Cryptology–Auscrypt 90*, Sydney, Springer-Verlag, Berlin, *Lecture Notes 453*, pp 229–236, 1990.

7. Data Encryption Standard, Federal Information Processing Standard (FIPS) Publication 46, National Bureau of Standards, US Department of Commerce, Washington, DC, Jan. 1977.
8. Davies, D.W. : "Some Regular Properties of the Data Encryption Standard", in *Advances in Cryptology–Proc. Crypto 82*, Plenum Press, New York, pp 89–96, 1982.
9. Davis, M., Y. Desmedt, M. Fosseprez, R. Goraerts, J. Hulsbosch, P. Neutjens, P. Piret, J. Quisquater, J. Vanderwalle, and P. Wouters : "Analytical Characteristics of the DES", in *Advances in Cryptology–Proc. Crypto 83*, Plenum Press, New York, pp 171–202, 1983.
10. Davis, R.L. "The Data Encryption Standard in Prespective," *IEEE Communications Society Magazine*, vol. 16, no. 6, pp 5–9, November 1978.
11. Deffie, W. and M. Hellman : "Exhaustive Cryptanalysis of the NBS Data Encryption Standard," *Computer*, vol. 10, no. 6, June 1977.
12. *DES Modes of Operation*, National Bureau of Standard, US Department of Commerce, Federal Information Standard (FIPS) Publication no. 81, Dec. 1980.
13. Federal Standard 1027, *Telecommunications : General Security Requirments for Equipment Using the Data Encryption Standard*, General Service Administration, Washington, DC, Apr. 14, 1982.
14. Feistel, H. : "Block Cipher Cryptographic System," *US Patent no. 3,798,359*, March 1974.
15. Hellman, M.E. : "DES will be totally insecure within ten years", *SPECTRUM*, vol. 16, no. 7, pp 31–41, July 1979.
16. Kam, J.B. and G.I. Davida : "Structured Design of Substitution–Permutation Encryption Networks", *IEEE Trans. on Computers*, vol. C–28, no. 10, pp 747–753, Oct. 1979.
17. Kim, K. : "Construction of DES-Like *S*-boxes based on Boolean Functions Satisfying the SAC", *Proc. Asiacrypt 91*, pp 35–40, 1991.
18. Matyas, S.M., C.H. Meyer, and L.B. Tuckerman, "Method and Apparatus for Enciphering Blocks which Succeed Short Blocks in a Key-Controlled Block-Cipher Cryptographic System," *US Patent no. 4,229,818*, Oct. 1980.
19. Meyer, C.H. : "Ciphertext/Plaintext and Ciphertext/Key Dependence vs. Number of Rounds for the Data Encryption Standard," *Proc. of AFIPS Conf.* vol. 47, pp 1119–1126, June 1978.
20. Meyer, C.H. and S.M. Matyas : *Cryptography : A New Dimension in Computer Data Security*, Wiley, New York, 1982.
21. Miyaguchi, S., A. Shiraishi, and A. Shimizu : "Fast Data Encipherment Algorithm FEAL–8", *Review of Electrical Communication Lab.*, Tokyo vol. 36, no. 4, 1988.
22. Shimizu, A. and S. Miyaguchi : "Fast Data Encipherment Algorithm FEAL", *Proc. of Eurocrypt 87*, Apr. 1987.
23. Tuchman, W.L. and C.H. Meyer : "Efficiency of the Data Encryption Standard in Data Processing", *Proc. COMPCON 78*, pp 340–347, Sep. 1978.
24. "United States Senate Select Committee on Intelligence", *Unclassified Summary : Involvement of the NSA in the Development of the Data Encryption Standard*, reprinted in the *IEEE Com. Soc. Magazine*, vol. 16, no. 6, pp 53–55, Nov. 1978.

Chapter

4

Stream Cipher Systems

There are two types of stream ciphers—one for which the key-bit stream is independent of the plaintext and the other for which the key-bit stream is a function of either the plaintext or the ciphertext, depending on the feedback connection. The former is often called a synchronous cipher because it requires synchronization between the key-bit stream and the ciphertext for successful decipherment. The latter is often referred to as a self-synchronizing cipher or auto-key cipher with ciphertext feedback because an erroneously added or deleted bit causes only a fixed number of errors in the deciphered plaintext, after which the correct plaintext is again restored.

Almost all past cipher systems, those used not only in military applications but which are commercially available as well, are based on stream ciphers. The key-bit stream which is a coded sequence from an m-stage shift register with linear feedback is modulo-2 added to the plaintext to produce the ciphertext. A linear feedback shift register (LFSR) is often used as the cryptographic key encoder for a stream cipher system. One of the main reasons for this is that LFSR is easily obtainable and comparatively inexpensive. The encoder that generates the key-bit stream must be deterministic so that the key-bit stream may be reproduced for decipherment. A key encoder which produces at least a pseudorandom sequence must be implemented as the algorithm so that the key-bit stream is cryptographically strong. The pseudo-randomness should make it difficult for an opponent (eavesdropper) to use statistical attacks against the cryptographic algorithm.

Gilbert Vernam was the first to recognize the merit of encipherment and decipherment to combine the key-bit stream either with the plaintext to produce the ciphertext, or with the ciphertext to recover the plaintext. The Vernam cipher over the binary alphabet {0, 1} is similar to a Vigenère cipher modulo 26. The Vigenère cipher is a form of periodic substitution cipher invented by the French cryptologist Vigenère in the 16th century. In 1918, Vernam designed a cryptographic device for telegraphic communications based on the 32-character code for the American Telephone and Telegraph Company (AT&T). Each character is represented as a combination of mark (labelled "on(1)") and space (labelled "off(0)"), converting it into five binary digits over GF (2).

The message plaintext normally employs a large alphabet. For transmitting the plaintext, each character has to be converted by a set of bits. In order to transmit the English-alphabet plaintext, we would need a character set of 26 elements plus six more characters, such as letters, figures, space, null, and two more. Since a character set consists of 32 elements, each character has the same size of $\log_2 32$ bits each, i.e. five bits per character.

Stream encipherment is rather preferred to block encipherment when the transmission channel is noisy. Unlike in the block cipher version of DES, a single error in transmission results in only a single error upon decipherment in the synchronous cipher system.

After World War II, the most significant factors in cipher-system development were the advent of the computer, VLSI technology, and mathematical rigour. Some of the differences between block and stream ciphers are:

1. The block cipher enciphers a single data block at one time, but the stream cipher requires to encipher or decipher on a bit-by-bit basis;
2. In the block cipher, every ciphertext bit is a complex function of plaintext and key bits via intersymbol dependence, but in the stream cipher every cipher bit is produced by $\mathbf{Y} = E_Z(\mathbf{X}) = (y_1, y_2, \cdots)$ where $y_i = (x_i + z_i) \bmod 2,\ i = 1, 2, \cdots$.
3. The block cipher may not require an initial seed vector, but the stream cipher does; and
4. Block ciphers like DES are used in the commercial sector, but stream ciphers are used for military purposes.

4.1 SYNCHRONOUS STREAM CIPHERS

A stream cipher is a system in which the actual external key is fed to the keystream generator, referred to as an encoder, which generates an infinite key-bit sequence. Figure 4.1 illustrates a stream cipher for which the key-bit sequence is independent of the plaintext for encipherment and of the ciphertext for decipherment. Any cryptosystem which can resist any cryptanalytic attack, no matter how much computation is allowed, is said to be unconditionally secure. The one-time pad is the only unconditionally secure system in common use. One of the most remarkable ciphers is the one-time pad (Vernam cipher type) where the ciphertext is the bit-by-bit modulo-2 sum of the plaintext and a nonrepeating keystream of the same length. However, the one-time pad is inappropriate to use because the large amount of key makes it impractical for most applications. One of the major advantages of a stream cipher over a block cipher is that there is no error propagation.

Both the plaintext and the infinite key-bit sequence generally use a character set of GF(2). For example, International Telegraph Alphabet No. 2 (ITA2) utilizes 5 bits per character. ITA2, shown in Table 4.1, is a common code converting teletypewriter characters to binary.

■ **Example 4.1** Using ITA2, show first that the plaintext (message) **X** "START WITH 1990" can be represented by

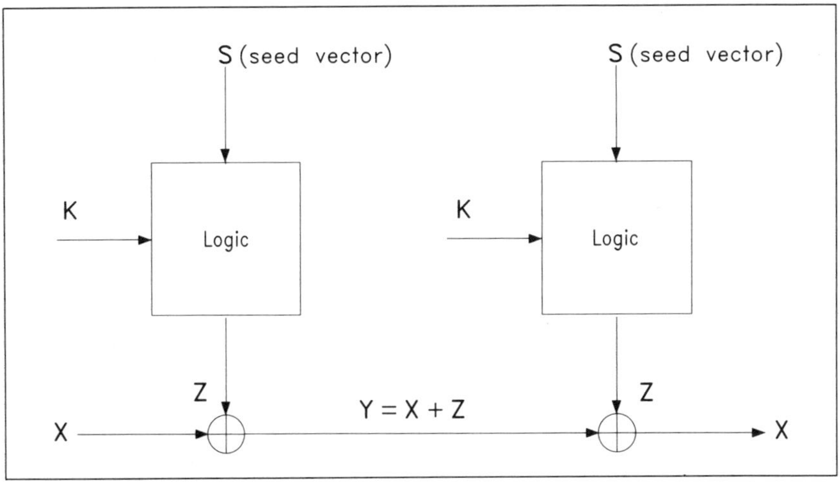

Fig. 4.1 Generic form of a stream cipher

$$
\begin{aligned}
\mathbf{X} &= \text{Letter, START, Space, Letter, WITH, Space, Figure, 1990} \\
&= 11111\ 10100\ 00001\ 11000\ 01010\ 00001\ 00100\ 11111\ 11001 \\
&\quad\ 01100\ 00001\ 00101\ 00100\ 11011\ 11101\ 00011\ 00011\ 01101
\end{aligned}
$$

If the key-bit sequence (coded sequence) **Z** is assumed as

$$
\begin{aligned}
\mathbf{Z} &= \text{R W B 0 Z V G M D H A X Q Y B I F J} \\
&= 01010\ 11001\ 10011\ 00011\ 10001\ 01111\ 01011\ 00111\ 10010 \\
&\quad\ 00101\ 11000\ 11001\ 11101\ 10101\ 10011\ 01100\ 10110\ 11010
\end{aligned}
$$

then the ciphertext (cryptogram) **Y** becomes

$$
\begin{aligned}
\mathbf{Y} &= \mathbf{X} + \mathbf{Z} \\
&= \text{Y P D Figure Figure C V A G L W U W C C V Y X} \\
&= 10101\ 01101\ 10010\ 11011\ 11011\ 01110\ 01111\ 11000\ 01011 \\
&\quad\ 01001\ 11001\ 11100\ 11001\ 01110\ 01110\ 01111\ 10101\ 10111
\end{aligned}
$$

Thus, the plaintext (message) **X** can be recovered as

$$
\begin{aligned}
\mathbf{X} &= \mathbf{Y} + \mathbf{Z} \\
&= 11111\ 10100\ 00001\ 11000\ 01010\ 00001\ 00100\ 11111\ 11001 \\
&\quad\ 01100\ 00001\ 00101\ 00100\ 11011\ 11101\ 00011\ 00011\ 01101
\end{aligned}
$$

as expected.

For keeping the stream cipher system secure, the key-bit stream (or running key) must be unpredictable. A necessary requirement for unpredictability is a long period of the key-bit stream. For the running key sequence to be unpredictable, it is necessary that its linear complexity be large. Thus, a major factor contributing towards establishing the unpredictability of a key-bit sequence is linear complexity. Since the period of the sequence is always at least as large as its linear complexity, a large linear complexity implies a large period.

Injection or deletion of digits in the ciphertext (i.e. digits are added or lost during transmission) will cause immediate loss of synchronization. To reestablish synchronization at the receiver usually involves searching over all possible offsets either by reinitialization of the keystream at the sender end or by error correction at the receiver end prior to decipherment. The difficulty of reestablishing synchronization is considered to be the major drawback of synchronous stream ciphers. Therefore, it is important to strike an acceptable balance between security and difficulty of synchronization.

Table 4.1 International Telegraph Alphabet No. 2 [1]

Character no.	Code bits	British teleprinter keyboard		Character no.	Code bits	British teleprinter keyboard	
1	11000	A	–	17	11101	Q	1
2	10011	B	?	18	01010	R	4
3	01110	C	:	19	10100	S	,
4	10010	D	WRU	20	00001	T	5
5	10000	E	3	21	11100	U	7
6	10110	F	%	22	01111	V	=
7	01011	G	@	23	11001	W	2
8	00101	H	£	24	10111	X	/
9	01100	I	8	25	10101	Y	6
10	11010	J	BELL	26	10001	Z	+
11	11110	K	(	27	00010	CARRIAGE RETURN	
12	01001	L	)	28	01000	LINE FEED	
13	00111	M	.	29	11111	LETTER	
14	00110	N	,	30	11011	FIGURE	
15	00011	O	9	31	00100	SPACE	
16	01101	P	0	32	00000	NULL	

4.1.1 Key Encoding by LFSR

Consider an m-stage LFSR with taps (i.e. feedback coefficients) g_1 to g_m and m flip-flops, as illustrated in either Fig. 4.2 or 4.3. Even if the key-bit stream (encoded sequence) from the LFSR shows the statistical property of randomness, a linear relationship exists between the original key and the corresponding key-bit stream. Therefore, a key stream generated from the LFSR is not appropriate for use as a cryptographic key because it does not ensure security of plaintext. In fact, only $2m$ bits of known plaintext and ciphertext are sufficient to break the key-bit stream by determining both the taps and the initial contents of the shift register. The period of the key stream depends on the choice of taps in the register. Since the primitive generating polynomial $p(x)$ of GF (2^m) for every integer m is given, we can devise an m-stage LFSR with period $2^m - 1$. Consequently, taps are easily found from any value of m. Therefore, the encoded keystream generated from this LFSR encoder is provably insecure and can be broken in a few seconds on a minicomputer for smaller value of m.

As depicted in Figs 4.2 and 4.3, consider now the LFSR whose initial contents are designated by $s_1, s_2, \ldots, s_m$ where $s_i \in GF(2)$ and whose taps are $g_1, g_2, \ldots, g_m$ where g_i is either 1 or 0 depending on whether the tap is closed or open. An LFSR arrangement of this kind is called a shift register encoding scheme, and can be represented by the matrix **T**. If the external key vector is $\mathbf{K} = (k_0, k_1, \cdots, k_{2m-1})$, the encoded key-stream **Z** becomes

$$\mathbf{Z} = \mathbf{T} \cdot \mathbf{K} \tag{4.1}$$

where **T** is called the transfer matrix.

Since LFSR encoding is demonstrably linear, Eq. 4.1 can be represented analytically by the delay operator D such that

$$z(D) = T(D)k(D) \tag{4.2}$$

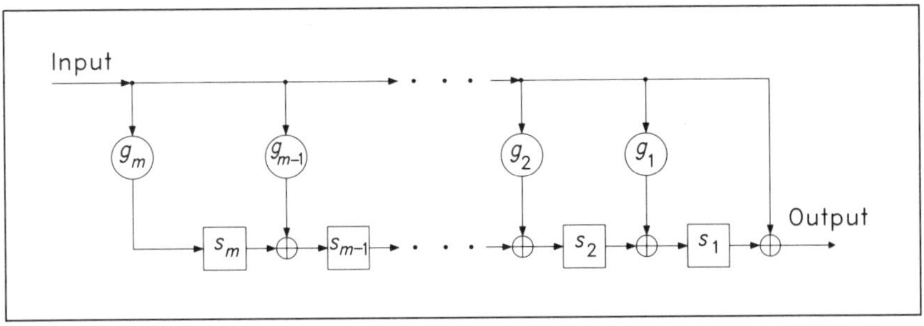

Fig. 4.2 An m- stage LFSR with taps g_1 to g_m and m flip-flops. This configuration can be used for the key encoder

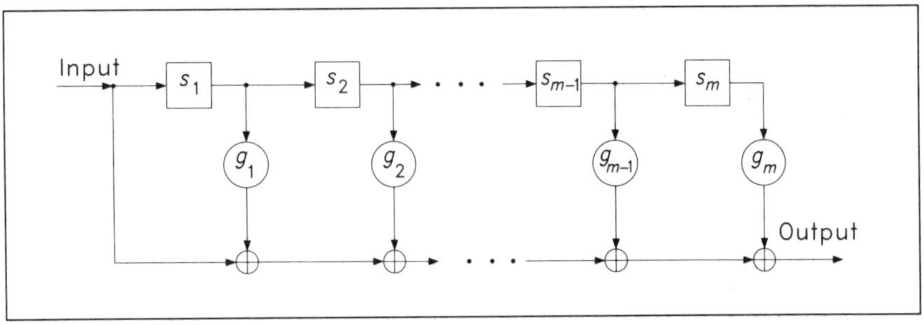

Fig. 4.3 An alternate scheme of m- stage LFSR with taps g_1 to g_m and m flip-flops

$$\text{where} \quad k(D) = \sum_{i=0}^{2m-1} k_i D^i \qquad \text{(key input)}$$

$$\text{and} \quad z(D) = \sum_{j=1}^{m} (k(D)D^j)\, g_j \qquad \text{(encoded key output)}$$

Let $\mathbf{K} = (k_0, k_1, \cdots, k_{2m-1})$ be the original input key and $\mathbf{Z} = (z_0, z_1, \cdots, z_{2m-1})$ the corresponding encoded key. Then the LFSR encoder consists of the taps $g_1, g_2, \ldots, g_m$ and the m register stages where the initial contents (seed vector) $\mathbf{S} = (s_1, s_2, \ldots, s_m)$ will reside temporarily. It is of interest to show that only $2m$ bits of known key sequence and corresponding encoded sequence are needed in order to rapidly determine both the tap settings and the initial contents of the LFSR encoder. Once these conditions are known, the key-bit stream from the m-stage LFSR can be broken and hence the complete original key can be deciphered. The following examples should suffice to illustrate this.

Example 4.2 Consider the four-stage LFSR encoder shown in Fig. 4.4. As is obvious from the figure itself, the tap settings of the encoder are g_1, g_2, g_3 and g_4. If the initial contents of the encoder are s_1, s_2, s_3 and s_4, then, for $2m = 8$, the input key sequence can be set as $\mathbf{K} = (k_0, k_1, \ldots, k_7)$ and the encoded keystream as $\mathbf{Z} = (z_0, z_1, \ldots, z_7)$. Since, in modulo-2 arithmetic, $k_j + s_j = z_j$ is expressible as $z_j + k_j = s_j$, a careful analysis of this four-stage encoder will lead to the following set of equations.

$$z_0 + k_0 = s_1$$

$$z_1 + k_1 = g_1 k_0 + s_2$$

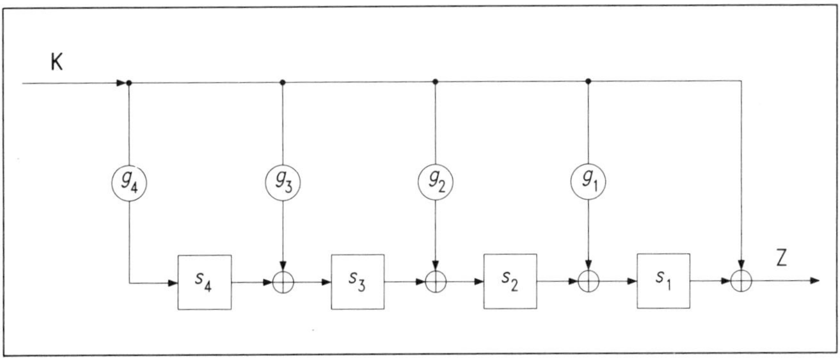

Fig. 4.4 The four-stage LFSR key encoder

$$
\begin{aligned}
z_2 + k_2 &= g_1 k_1 + g_2 k_0 + s_3 \\
z_3 + k_3 &= g_1 k_2 + g_2 k_1 + g_3 K_0 + s_4 \\
z_4 + k_4 &= g_1 k_3 + g_2 k_2 + g_3 k_1 + g_4 k_0 \\
z_5 + k_5 &= g_1 k_4 + g_2 k_3 + g_3 k_2 + g_4 k_1 \\
z_6 + k_6 &= g_1 k_5 + g_2 k_4 + g_3 k_3 + g_4 k_2 \\
z_7 + k_7 &= g_1 k_6 + g_2 k_5 + g_3 k_4 + g_4 k_3
\end{aligned}
\tag{4.3}
$$

Equation 4.3 can also be expressed in matrix form as follows:

$$
\begin{bmatrix} z_0 + k_0 \\ z_1 + k_1 \\ z_2 + k_2 \\ z_3 + k_3 \\ z_4 + k_4 \\ z_5 + k_5 \\ z_6 + k_6 \\ z_7 + k_7 \end{bmatrix}
=
\begin{bmatrix}
0 & 0 & 0 & 0 & 1 & 0 & 0 & 0 \\
k_0 & 0 & 0 & 0 & 0 & 1 & 0 & 0 \\
k_1 & k_0 & 0 & 0 & 0 & 0 & 1 & 0 \\
k_2 & k_1 & k_0 & 0 & 0 & 0 & 0 & 1 \\
k_3 & k_2 & k_1 & k_0 & 0 & 0 & 0 & 0 \\
k_4 & k_3 & k_2 & k_1 & 0 & 0 & 0 & 0 \\
k_5 & k_4 & k_3 & k_2 & 0 & 0 & 0 & 0 \\
k_6 & k_5 & k_4 & k_3 & 0 & 0 & 0 & 0
\end{bmatrix}
\begin{bmatrix} g_1 \\ g_2 \\ g_3 \\ g_4 \\ s_1 \\ s_2 \\ s_3 \\ s_4 \end{bmatrix}
\tag{4.4}
$$

Assuming that all initial seeds in the register stages are equal to zero, i.e. that all register stages are initially reset, $s_i = 0$ for $1 \le i \le 4$. In that case, Eq. 4.4 reduces to

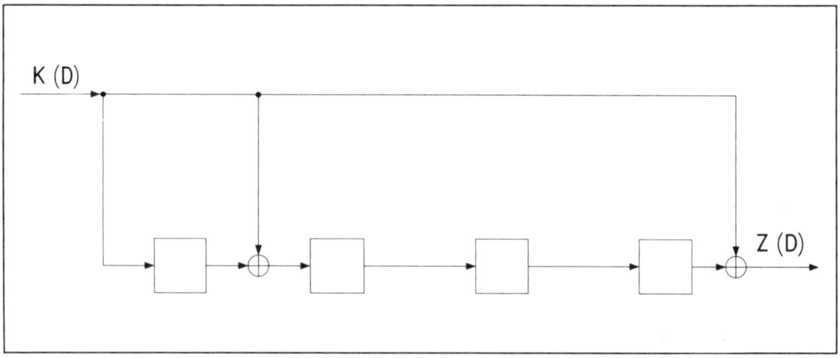

Fig. 4.5 The four-stage LFSR key encoder for $T(D) = 1 + D^3 + D^4$

$$\begin{bmatrix} z_4+k_4 \\ z_5+k_5 \\ z_6+k_6 \\ z_7+k_7 \end{bmatrix} = \begin{bmatrix} k_3 & k_2 & k_1 & k_0 \\ k_4 & k_3 & k_2 & k_1 \\ k_5 & k_4 & k_3 & k_2 \\ k_6 & k_5 & k_4 & k_3 \end{bmatrix} \begin{bmatrix} g_1 \\ g_2 \\ g_3 \\ g_4 \end{bmatrix} \tag{4.5}$$

As a specific example, let us provide the four-stage encoder as shown in Fig. 4.5. It now remains to prove a linear relationship between the input key **K** and the encoded output key **Z**. Since the generator feedback coefficients are $g_1 = g_2 = 0$ and $g_3 = g_4 = 1$, the transfer function of the encoding circuit is derived as $T(D) = D^4 + D^3 + 1$. Assuming that the input key vector is **K** = (1 1 0 1 0 0 0 1), we then have $k(D) = 1 + D + D^3 + D^7$. Since the encoder of Fig. 4.5 is a modulo-2 polynomial multiplier, the output keystream in polynomial form becomes

$$\begin{aligned} z(D) &= T(D)k(D) \\ &= (D^4 + D^3 + 1)(1 + D + D^3 + D^7) \\ &= 1 + D + D^5 + D^6 + D^{10} + D^{11} \end{aligned}$$

Ignoring the term D^i for $i > 7$, $z(D) = 1 + D + D^5 + D^6$ or **Z** = (1 1 0 0 0 1 1 0). Combining **Z** and **K** on a bit-by-bit basis, we have

$$\mathbf{Z} + \mathbf{K} = (0\,0\,0\,1\,0\,1\,1\,1)$$

from which

$$\begin{aligned} z_4 + k_4 &= 0 \\ z_5 + k_5 &= 1 \\ z_6 + k_6 &= 1 \\ z_7 + k_7 &= 1 \end{aligned}$$

Substituting these values in Eq. 4.5, we can determine the feedback coefficients g_1 through g_4 as follows:

$$\begin{bmatrix} 0 \\ 1 \\ 1 \\ 1 \end{bmatrix} = \begin{bmatrix} 1 & 0 & 1 & 1 \\ 0 & 1 & 0 & 1 \\ 0 & 0 & 1 & 0 \\ 0 & 0 & 0 & 1 \end{bmatrix} \begin{bmatrix} g_1 \\ g_2 \\ g_3 \\ g_4 \end{bmatrix}$$

from which we have

$$g_1 + g_3 + g_4 = 0$$

$$g_2 + g_4 = 1$$

$$g_3 = 1$$

$$g_4 = 1$$

The solutions for g_i, $1 \le i \le 4$, from the above simultaneous equations are

$$g_1 = 0, g_2 = 0, g_3 = 1 \text{ and } g_4 = 1$$

However, given the same input key **K** = (1 1 0 1 0 0 0 1) and the output key **Z** = (1 1 0 0 0 1 1 0), Eq. 4.5 is not the only matrix system for determining the tap coefficients g_i, $1 \le i \le 4$. Besides Eq. 4.5, there are three more matrix systems for obtaining identical solutions for g_i, $1 \le i \le 4$. They are:

$$\begin{bmatrix} z_1 + k_1 \\ z_2 + k_2 \\ z_3 + k_3 \\ z_4 + k_4 \end{bmatrix} = \begin{bmatrix} k_0 & 0 & 0 & 0 \\ k_1 & k_0 & 0 & 0 \\ k_2 & k_1 & k_0 & 0 \\ k_3 & k_2 & k_1 & k_0 \end{bmatrix} \begin{bmatrix} g_1 \\ g_2 \\ g_3 \\ g_4 \end{bmatrix}$$

$$\begin{bmatrix} z_2 + k_2 \\ z_3 + k_3 \\ z_4 + k_4 \\ z_5 + k_5 \end{bmatrix} = \begin{bmatrix} k_1 & k_0 & 0 & 0 \\ k_2 & k_1 & k_0 & 0 \\ k_3 & k_2 & k_1 & k_0 \\ k_4 & k_3 & k_2 & k_1 \end{bmatrix} \begin{bmatrix} g_1 \\ g_2 \\ g_3 \\ g_4 \end{bmatrix}$$

and

$$\begin{bmatrix} z_3 + k_3 \\ z_4 + k_4 \\ z_5 + k_5 \\ z_6 + k_6 \end{bmatrix} = \begin{bmatrix} k_2 & k_1 & k_0 & 0 \\ k_3 & k_2 & k_1 & k_0 \\ k_4 & k_3 & k_2 & k_1 \\ k_5 & k_4 & k_3 & k_2 \end{bmatrix} \begin{bmatrix} g_1 \\ g_2 \\ g_3 \\ g_4 \end{bmatrix}$$

The tap coefficients can be determined as $g_1 = g_2 = 0$ and $g_3 = g_4 = 1$ from any of these matrix sets, under the condition that the initial contents of LFSR are all zeroes, i.e. $s_i = 0$ for $1 \le i \le 4$.

The procedure just described applies only to the configuration type of Fig. 4.2. The alternate circuit of Fig. 4.3 will be discussed in the following example. However, it is not difficult to see that the multipliers

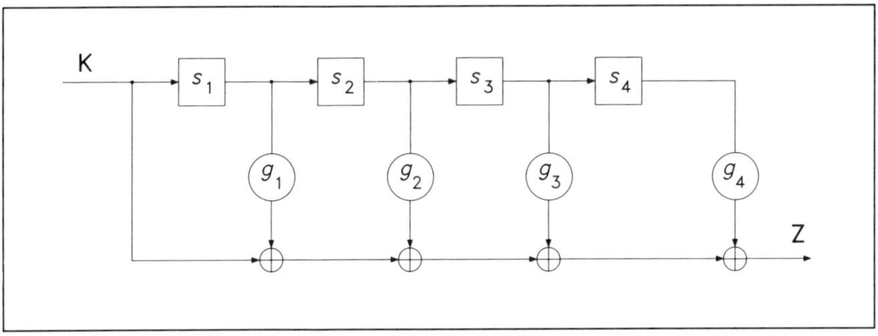

Fig. 4.6 An alternate scheme for the four-stage key encoder

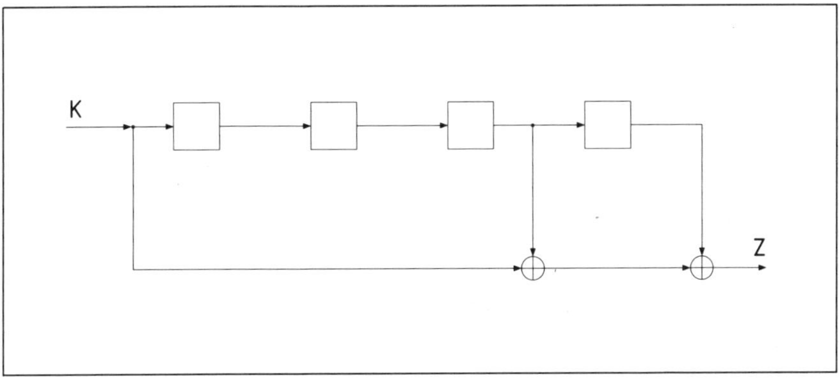

Fig. 4.7 The four-stage key encoder with feedback coefficients $g_1 = 0$, $g_2 = 0$, $g_3 = 1$ and $g_4 = 1$

of Figs 4.4 and 4.6 are identical. In fact, the configuration of Fig. 4.2 can function at higher speeds than that of Fig. 4.3 because there is less propagation delay in the feedback path.

■ **Example 4.3** Consider the alternate scheme for the four-stage key encoder as illustrated in Fig. 4.6. As before, the initial contents of the LFSR encoder are designated by s_1, s_2, s_3 and s_4, where $s_i \in \mathrm{GF}(2)$. The analysis of this four-stage key encoder is represented by the following set of equations:

$$z_0 + k_0 = g_1 s_1 + g_2 s_2 + g_3 s_3 + g_4 s_4$$

$$z_1 + k_1 = g_1 k_0 + g_2 s_1 + g_3 s_2 + g_4 s_3$$

$$z_2 + k_2 = g_1 k_1 + g_2 k_0 + g_3 s_1 + g_4 s_2$$

$$\begin{aligned}
z_3 + k_3 &= g_1 k_2 + g_2 k_1 + g_3 k_0 + g_4 s_1 \\
z_4 + k_4 &= g_1 k_3 + g_2 k_2 + g_3 k_1 + g_4 k_0 \\
z_5 + k_5 &= g_1 k_4 + g_2 k_3 + g_3 k_2 + g_4 k_1 \\
z_6 + k_6 &= g_1 k_5 + g_2 k_4 + g_3 k_3 + g_4 k_2 \\
z_7 + k_7 &= g_1 k_6 + g_2 k_5 + g_3 k_4 + g_4 k_3
\end{aligned} \tag{4.6}$$

The set of these linear equations may be expressed in matrix form as follows:

$$\begin{bmatrix} z_0 + k_0 \\ z_1 + k_1 \\ z_2 + k_2 \\ z_3 + k_3 \\ z_4 + k_4 \\ z_5 + k_5 \\ z_6 + k_6 \\ z_7 + k_7 \end{bmatrix} = \begin{bmatrix} s_1 & s_2 & s_3 & s_4 \\ k_0 & s_1 & s_2 & s_3 \\ k_1 & k_0 & s_1 & s_2 \\ k_2 & k_1 & k_0 & s_1 \\ k_3 & k_2 & k_1 & k_0 \\ k_4 & k_3 & k_2 & k_1 \\ k_5 & k_4 & k_3 & k_2 \\ k_6 & k_5 & k_4 & k_3 \end{bmatrix} \begin{bmatrix} g_1 \\ g_2 \\ g_3 \\ g_4 \end{bmatrix} \tag{4.7}$$

If it is assumed that all register stages are initially reset, then the initial seeds s_i for $1 \le i \le 4$ become zero and Eq. 4.7 may then be expressed in the following simplified matrix form:

$$\begin{bmatrix} z_4 + k_4 \\ z_5 + k_5 \\ z_6 + k_6 \\ z_7 + k_7 \end{bmatrix} = \begin{bmatrix} k_3 & k_2 & k_1 & k_0 \\ k_4 & k_3 & k_2 & k_1 \\ k_5 & k_4 & k_3 & k_2 \\ k_6 & k_5 & k_4 & k_3 \end{bmatrix} \begin{bmatrix} g_1 \\ g_2 \\ g_3 \\ g_4 \end{bmatrix} \tag{4.8}$$

which is identical to Eq. 4.5.

With the feedback coefficients of $g_1 = g_2 = 0$ and $g_3 = g_4 = 1$, Fig. 4.6 can be drawn as Fig. 4.7. Since $z(t) = k(t)[(D^3 + 1) + D^4]$ from Fig. 4.7, the transfer function of the encoder is derived as $T(D) = D^4 + D^3 + 1$, which is exactly the same expression as the one obtained in Example 4.2. Under the same assumption of $k(D) = 1 + D + D^3 + D^7$ as in the previous example, the output function becomes $z(D) = T(D)\,k(D) = 1 + D + D^5 + D^6 + D^{10} + D^{11}$. Thus, combining **Z** and **K** and utilizing Eq. 4.8, the feedback coefficients g_i for $1 \le i \le 4$ can be determined as $g_1 = g_2 = 0$ and

$g_3 = g_4 = 1$ as obtained before. Through these two examples, we have seen that only $2m = 8$ bits of known keytext and corresponding coded keystream can determine the tap settings (feedback coefficients) of the LFSR encoder.

At this point, it is worth commenting on the LFSR encoder of Fig. 4.2. If the input key $\mathbf{K} = (k_0, k_1, \cdots, k_{2m-1}, \cdots)$ is replaced by the plaintext $\mathbf{X} = (x_0, x_1, \cdots, x_{2m-1}, \cdots)$, the output encoded key $\mathbf{Z} = (z_0, z_1, \cdots, z_{2m-1}, \cdots)$ by the ciphertext $\mathbf{Y} = (y_0, y_1, \cdots, y_{2m-1}, \cdots)$, and the feedback coefficients of the LFSR by the key settings, the key encoder of Fig. 4.2 then becomes a complete enciphering circuit. However, the configuration of Fig. 4.2 appears to be a weak cipher system because only $2m$ bits of the known plaintext $\mathbf{X}$ and the corresponding ciphertext $\mathbf{Y}$ are needed to determine the key settings and hence an opponent (eavesdropper) can decipher with the estimated keystream to obtain the complete plaintext. Thus, this kind of synchronous cipher system is weak and can be easily broken.

4.1.2 Encipherment and Decipherment

A synchronous stream cipher is a system in which the key-bit stream $\mathbf{Z} = (z_0, z_1, \ldots)$ is generated independently of the plaintext. We have observed in the previous subsection that tap settings of the m-stage LFSR can be easily determined using just $2m$ bits of the key-encoded-key pairs (or plaintext-ciphertext pairs). Let $\mathbf{Y} = (y_0, y_1, \cdots, y_{2m-1})$ be the ciphertext corresponding to the plaintext $\mathbf{X} = (x_0, x_1, \cdots, x_{2m-1})$. Then the key bits $\mathbf{K} = (k_0, k_1, \cdots, k_{2m-1})$ can be determined by computing $x_i + y_i = x_i + (x_i + k_i) = k_i$ for $0 \le i \le 2m - 1$. Therefore, a synchronous stream cipher is often breakable if the key-bit sequence repeats itself with a period of $2^m - 1$. In order to be unbreakable, the key stream must be a random sequence as long as the plaintext. However, the LFSR is not always suitable for key generation because an opponent can easily derive the entire key stream from $2m$ bits of plaintext-ciphertext pairs. Nevertheless, the m-stage LFSR that generates the key-bit stream must be deterministic so that the key-bit stream can be reproduced for decipherment. Let us consider the encipherment and decipherment of the synchronous stream cipher through the following illustrative examples.

■ **Example 4.4** Using the key encoder of Fig. 4.5 in Example 4.2, let us construct the encipher-decipher pair as shown in Fig. 4.8. Suppose the original key sequence is $\mathbf{K}$ = (1 1 0 1 0 0 0 1). Then the corresponding coded key becomes **Z** = (1 1 0 0 0 1 1 0). When the plaintext is assumed as **X** = (0 1 0 0 1 0 0 1), the ciphertext is **Y** = **X** + **Z** = (1 0 0 0 1 1 1 1). Thus, the deciphered sequence **X** = **Y** + **Z** = (0 1 0 0 1 0 0 1) is a recovered plaintext.

■ **Example 4.5** Consider the encipher-decipher pair of Fig. 4.9, arranged in a configuration different from the one in Fig. 4.8. With the A–A′ pair switch position, Fig. 4.9 becomes the enciphering device where the input designates the plaintext $x\,(t)$ and the output indicates the ciphertext $y\,(t)$. Whereas, with the B–B′ switch pair, Fig. 4.9 becomes the deciphering device where the input becomes the ciphertext $y\,(t)$ and the output $u\,(t)$ will be the recovered plaintext $x\,(t)$.

With the A–A′ switch pair, enciphering with the LFSR is represented as

$$y(t) = [(D+1)D^3 + 1]x(t)$$

$$= (D^4 + D^3 + 1)x(t) \tag{4.9}$$

where the LFSR is analyzed by the delay operator D.

Similarly, with the B–B′ switch pair, deciphering with the same LFSR can be analyzed by

$$u\,(t) = [(D+1)D^2u(t) + y(t)]D$$

or

$$Dy\,(t) = (D^4 + D^3 + 1)u(t) \tag{4.10}$$

Multiplying Eq. 4.9 by D and comparing with Eq. 4.10 results in

$$u\,(t) = Dx\,(t) \tag{4.11}$$

Thus the deciphered output $u\,(t)$ is identical to the plaintext $x\,(t)$ delayed by 1 bit. Thus, we can see that the original plaintext $x\,(t)$ is correctly recovered as $u\,(t)$ delayed by 1 bit.

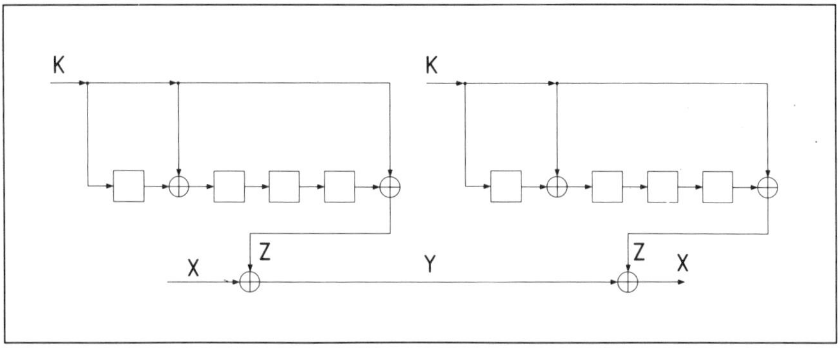

Fig. 4.8 Encipher-decipher pair by using key encoding

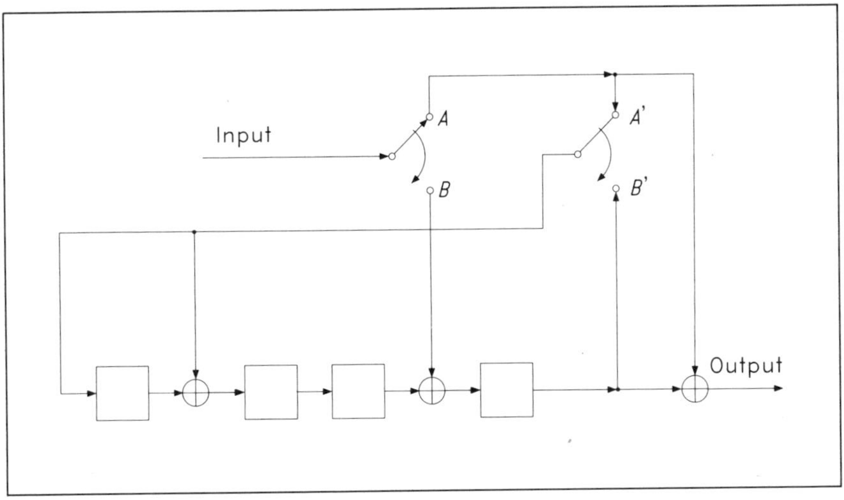

Fig. 4.9 Encipher-decipher pair using LFSR

Comparing the two synchronous ciphers discussed in Examples 4.4 and 4.5 reveals that the cipher system of Fig. 4.8 performs two levels of ciphering processes, whereas Fig. 4.9 shows a single level of ciphering process. Therefore, it seems that the cipher system of Fig. 4.9 is simpler than that of Fig. 4.8, but will be cryptographically weaker.

As discussed so far, we have seen that just $2m$ bits of the plaintext-ciphertext pair available to the cryptanalyst are actually sufficient to determine the feedback taps (key bits) of the m-stage LFSR. Therefore, a linear or affine device produces a readily predictable keystream and is thus cryptanalytically weak. Building a synchronous stream cipher involves generation of a pseudorandom key sequence (whose period must be very long), which is combined with the bits of the plaintext. Such a synchronous cipher with very long period may be made more complex by introducing the DES of the block cipher. A secure block cipher (DES) can play an important role in the construction of a stronger synchronous cipher system, as shown in Fig. 4.10.

Stream ciphers utilize deterministically encoded random sequences to encipher the bits of the plaintext. Since the key encoder (LFSR) is a finite-state machine, the encoded keystream is periodic. The LFSR outputs bits of zero (0) or one (1), both being equally likely, making the operation similar to a coin-tossing experiment. One method for achieving high unpredictability of the encoded keystream, is cascading the LFSR with a nonlinear device like the DES of a block cipher, as depicted in Fig. 4.10. Such an arrangement may render the

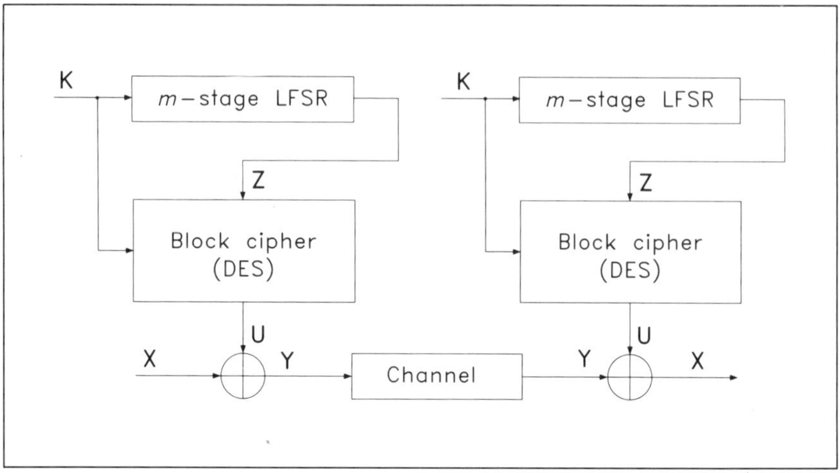

Fig. 4.10 A synchronous stream cipher derived from concatenation of LFSR and DES

cryptosystem secure because it is too complex to be analyzed. However, since there are practical limits to the number of shift register stages, one or more shift registers are required to produce secure keystreams by employing nonlinear operations at their outputs. Therefore, nonlinear operations with relatively few stages of LFSR can produce an unpredictable keystream; this would require an enormous number of stages in the linear equivalent. We shall discuss such nonlinear transformation of periodic sequences later in this chapter.

■ **Example 4.6** Consider the synchronous stream cipher system of Fig. 4.10 which consists of an LFSR of $m = 32$ stages and a 16-round DES. If the external key is assumed to be

$$\mathbf{K} = (5\,8\,1\,F\,B\,C\,9\,4\,D\,3\,A\,4\,5\,2\,E\,A) \quad \text{(hexadecimal)}$$

$$= (0101\ 1000\ 0001\ 1111\ 1011\ 1100\ 1001\ 0100$$

$$1101\ 0011\ 1010\ 0100\ 0101\ 0010\ 1110\ 1010) \quad \text{(binary)} \quad (4.12)$$

then the key polynomial can be expressed as

$$K(x) = x + x^3 + x^4 + x^{11} + x^{12} + x^{13} + x^{14} + x^{15} + x^{16} + x^{18} + x^{19}$$
$$+ x^{20} + x^{21} + x^{24} + x^{27} + x^{29} + x^{32} + x^{33} + x^{35} + x^{38} + x^{39} + x^{40}$$
$$+ x^{42} + x^{45} + x^{49} + x^{51} + x^{54} + x^{56} + x^{57} + x^{58} + x^{60} + x^{62} \quad (4.13)$$

Since the primitive polynomial of degree 32 in either octal or binary representation is given by

$$\mathbf{T} = (4\,0\,0\,2\,0\,0\,0\,0\,0\,0\,7) \qquad \text{(octal)}$$

$$= (100\;000\;000\;010\;000\;000\;000\;000\;000\;000\;111) \qquad \text{(binary)}$$

the corresponding polynomial becomes

$$T(x) = x^{32} + x^{22} + x^{2} + x + 1 \tag{4.14}$$

This is the characteristic equation representing the tap settings in LFSR. The output key polynomial $Z(x)$ from LFSR is obtained as

$$Z(x) = K(x)\,T(x) \tag{4.15}$$

Using Eq. 4.14, if the output key polynomial $Z(x)$ is represented by the powers of its nonzero terms,

$$\mathbf{Z} = (94\ 92\ 90\ 89\ 88\ 86\ 84\ 83\ 82\ 81\ 80\ 79\ 78\ 77\ 76\ 74\ 73\ 72\ 70\ 65\ 64\ 63\ 62\ 61\ 60\ 59\ 58\ 57\ 56\ 48\ 46\ 43\ 42\ 41\ 36\ 34\ 32\ 31\ 30\ 28\ 27\ 24\ 21\ 20\ 16\ 15\ 14\ 13\ 11\ 6\ 2\ 1)$$

Ignoring the terms x^i for $i > 63$,

$$\mathbf{Z} = (63\ 62\ 61\ 60\ 59\ 58\ 57\ 56\ 48\ 46\ 43\ 42\ 41\ 36\ 34\ 32\ 31\ 30\ 28\ 27\ 24\ 21\ 20\ 16\ 15\ 14\ 13\ 11\ 6\ 2\ 1) \tag{4.16}$$

or

$$Z(x) = x + x^{2} + x^{6} + x^{11} + x^{13} + x^{14} + x^{15} + x^{16} + x^{20} + x^{21} + x^{24} + x^{27} + x^{28} + x^{30} + x^{31} + x^{32} + x^{34} + x^{36} + x^{41} + x^{42} + x^{43} + x^{46} + x^{48} + x^{56} + x^{57} + x^{58} + x^{59} + x^{60} + x^{61} + x^{62} + x^{63} \tag{4.17}$$

The binary notation of $Z(x)$ is then

$$\mathbf{Z} = (0110\ 0010\ 0001\ 0111\ 1000\ 1100\ 1001\ 1011\ 1010\ 1000\ 0111\ 0010\ 1000\ 0000\ 1111\ 1111) \tag{4.18}$$

and its hexadecimal representation is

$$\mathbf{Z} = (6\ 2\ 1\ 7\ 8\ C\ 9\ B\ A\ 8\ 7\ 2\ 8\ 0\ F\ F)$$

The 64-bit external key $\mathbf{K}$ of Eq. 4.12 for the DES key schedule is split into two parts $\mathbf{C}_0$ (left content) and $\mathbf{D}_0$ (right content) according to

Table 3.1 and the register contents $\mathbf{C}_1$ and $\mathbf{D}_1$ are obtained from the blocks $\mathbf{C}_0$ and $\mathbf{D}_0$ by shifting one place to the left. Table 3.3 (PC–2) is the rule defining how to derive the 48-bit internal key vectors $\mathbf{K}_1$, $\mathbf{K}_2, \ldots, \mathbf{K}_{16}$ from the concatenated blocks $(\mathbf{C}_1, \mathbf{D}_1), (\mathbf{C}_2, \mathbf{D}_2), \ldots, (\mathbf{C}_{16}, \mathbf{D}_{16})$. Actually, the 48-bit internal keys of DES are generated through a series of permutations and left shifts of the 56 key bits from the 64-bit external key.

Thus, the 16 internal keys of DES are computed as follows:

$\mathbf{K}_1$ = (0010 0111 1010 0001 0110 1001 1110 0101 1000 1101 1101 1010)

$\mathbf{K}_2$ = (1101 1010 1001 0001 1101 1101 1101 0111 1011 0111 0100 1000)

$\mathbf{K}_3$ = (0001 1101 1100 0010 0100 1011 1111 1000 1001 0111 0110 1000)

$\mathbf{K}_4$ = (0010 0011 0101 1001 1010 1110 0101 1000 1111 1110 0010 1110)

$\mathbf{K}_5$ = (1011 1000 0010 1001 1100 0101 0111 1100 0111 1100 1011 1000)

$\mathbf{K}_6$ = (0001 0001 0110 1110 0011 1001 1010 1001 0111 1000 0111 1011)

$\mathbf{K}_7$ = (1100 0101 0011 0101 1011 0100 1010 0111 1111 1010 0011 0010)

$\mathbf{K}_8$ = (1101 0110 1000 1110 1100 0101 1011 0101 0000 1111 0111 0110)

$\mathbf{K}_9$ = (1110 1000 0000 1101 0011 0011 1101 0111 0101 0011 0001 0100)

$\mathbf{K}_{10}$ = (1110 0101 1010 1010 0010 1101 1101 0001 0010 0011 1110 1100)

$\mathbf{K}_{11}$ = (1000 0011 1011 0110 1001 0010 1111 0000 1011 1010 1000 1101)

$\mathbf{K}_{12}$ = (0111 1100 0001 1110 1111 0010 0111 0010 0011 0110 1011 1111)

$\mathbf{K}_{13}$ = (1111 0110 1111 0000 0100 1000 0011 1111 0011 1001 1010 1011)

$\mathbf{K}_{14}$ = (0000 1010 1100 0111 0101 0110 0010 0110 0111 1001 0111 0011)

$\mathbf{K}_{15}$ = (0110 1100 0101 1001 0001 1111 0110 0111 1010 1001 0111 0110)

$\mathbf{K}_{16}$ = (0100 1111 0101 0111 1010 0000 1100 0110 1100 0011 0101 1011)

The key output **Z** from LFSR, indicated by Eq. 4.18, becomes the input to DES in the cipher system. The DES input **Z** is then split into two 32-bit blocks $\mathbf{L}_0$ (left) and $\mathbf{R}_0$ (right). The 32-bit $\mathbf{R}_0$ is expanded and scrambled in 48 bits with *E*-table of Table 3.5. $E(\mathbf{R}_0)$ is thus added bit-by-bit to $\mathbf{K}_1$; and this resulting 48-bit $E(\mathbf{R}_0) \oplus \mathbf{K}_1$ becomes the input to the *S*-boxes to form the 32-bit output $\mathbf{B}_1$ through a nonlinear *S*-box transformation. Permuting the bits of $\mathbf{B}_1$ first and adding $P(\mathbf{B}_1)$ and $\mathbf{L}_0$ results in the right-half output $\mathbf{R}_1$ after round one. Since $\mathbf{L}_1 = \mathbf{R}_0$, the left-half output after round one is immediately obtained. Let $\mathbf{U}_i$ be the output of each round. It is expressed as

$$\mathbf{U}_i = \mathbf{L}_i * \mathbf{R}_i, \qquad 1 \le i \le 16 \tag{4.19}$$

where $\mathbf{L}_i = \mathbf{R}_{i-1}$ and $*$ denotes the symbol for concatenation.

Hence, the round-one output for $i = 1$ is

$\mathbf{U}_1$ = (1101 1100 1011 0001 1001 1100 1010 1011 1010 0000 0111 0000 0101 1111 0011 0010)

Similarly, the enciphered outputs $\mathbf{U}_2$ through $\mathbf{U}_{16}$ after each separate round are easily obtained as follows:

$\mathbf{U}_2$ = (1010 0000 0111 0000 0101 1111 0011 0010 1001 0001 1111 0101 1101 1000 0010 0101)

$\mathbf{U}_3$ = (1001 0001 1111 0101 1101 1000 0010 0101 1010 0100 0001 1000 0001 0001 1111 1100)

$\mathbf{U}_4$ = (1010 0100 0001 1000 0001 0001 1111 1100 0110 1111 1010 1110 1100 0101 1111 1101)

$\mathbf{U}_5$ = (0110 1111 1010 1110 1100 0101 1111 1101 0110 0011 1111 0111 1101 0010 1011 0110)

U_6 = (0110 0011 1111 0111 1101 0010 1011 0110 1110 0100 1011
0101 1101 1010 1110 1000)

U_7 = (1110 0100 1011 0101 1101 1010 1110 1000 1100 0011 1101
0011 1101 1011 1111 0000)

U_8 = (1100 0011 1101 0011 1101 1011 1111 0000 1001 1001
1111 0010 1100 0011 0110 0010)

U_9 = (1001 1001 1111 0010 1100 0011 0110 0010 0001 1101
1111 0011 0100 1011 0100 1100)

U_{10} = (0001 1101 1111 0011 0100 1011 0100 1100 0000 0110 0000
1001 1001 0001 0011 0111)

U_{11} = (0000 0110 0000 1001 1001 0001 0011 0111 1000 1001 0111
1111 1111 0000 1001 1001)

U_{12} = (1000 1001 0111 1111 1111 0000 1001 1001 0000 1110 1001
1010 1011 1010 1011 0101)

U_{13} = (0000 1110 1001 1010 1011 1010 1011 0101 1011 1100 0001
0010 1101 1101 1001 0000)

U_{14} = (1011 1100 0001 0010 1101 1101 1001 0000 0110 0010 0000
1110 0000 0010 1011 1100)

U_{15} = (0110 0010 0000 1110 0000 0010 1011 1100 1100 1010 1000
0011 1011 0010 0101 1011)

However, the 64-bit block of preoutput is computed as

$U_{16} = \mathbf{R}_{16} * \mathbf{L}_{16}$

= (1100 1010 1000 0011 1011 0010 0101 1011 0111 1111 0101
1001 1011 0100 1001 1101)

This preoutput data block is now subjected to an inverse initial permutation (Table 3.8) and the final key-bit stream is obtained as

$$\mathbf{U} = (\,0111\ 0011\ 1110\ 1010\ 0100\ 0101\ 1101\ 0011\ 0101\ 1111\ 0100$$

$$1100\ 1101\ 0010\ 1010\ 1101\,) \tag{4.20}$$

$$= (\,7\ 3\ E\ A\ 4\ 5\ D\ 3\ 5\ F\ 4\ C\ D\ 2\ A\ D\,) \qquad (\text{ hexadecimal })$$

Assume that the 64-bit plaintext

$$\mathbf{X} = (\,9\ A\ 2\ 6\ F\ 4\ 6\ 5\ D\ C\ 2\ 6\ B\ E\ 1\ 8\,)$$

$$= (\,1001\ 1010\ 0010\ 0110\ 1111\ 0100\ 0101\ 0011\ 1101\ 1100$$

$$0010\ 0110\ 1011\ 1110\ 0001\ 1000\,)$$

enciphers into the 64-bit ciphertext **Y** under the control of a 64-bit keystream **U**, derived previously in Eq. 4.20. Then the ciphertext **Y** is obtained by bit-by-bit addition of **X** and **U** in the following manner.

$$\mathbf{Y} = \mathbf{X} + \mathbf{U}$$

$$= (\,1110\ 1001\ 1100\ 1100\ 1011\ 0001\ 1011\ 0110\ 1000\ 0011$$

$$0110\ 1110\ 0110\ 1100\ 1011\ 0101\,) \tag{4.21}$$

$$= (\,E\ 9\ C\ C\ B\ 1\ B\ 6\ 8\ 3\ 6\ E\ 6\ C\ B\ 5\,)$$

The deciphering procedure using modulo-2 addition is extremely simple. The plaintext **X** can be recovered by adding the same key-bit stream **U** to the ciphertext **Y** such that $\mathbf{X} = \mathbf{Y} + \mathbf{U}$.

4.1.3 Key Autokey Synchronous Ciphers

A special type of synchronous stream cipher is the key autokey cipher where the feedback is obtained continuously from the key-bit stream as shown in Fig. 4.11. In the key autokey cipher, there is no error propagation due to the deciphering process, because an error in the ciphertext **Y** produces an error only in the corresponding bit positions of the recovered plaintext **X**. In Fig. 4.11, $\mathbf{S} = (s_1, s_2, \cdots, s_m)$ is the register's initial contents and $\mathbf{T} = (g_1, g_2, \cdots, g_m)$ the tap coefficients.

Suppose the plaintext sequence is $\mathbf{X} = (x_0, x_1, \cdots, x_i, \cdots)$, the key-bit stream $\mathbf{K} = (k_0, k_1, \cdots, k_i, \cdots)$ and the ciphertext sequence $\mathbf{Y} = (y_0, y_1, \cdots, y_i, \cdots)$. The enciphering and deciphering operations under key **K**

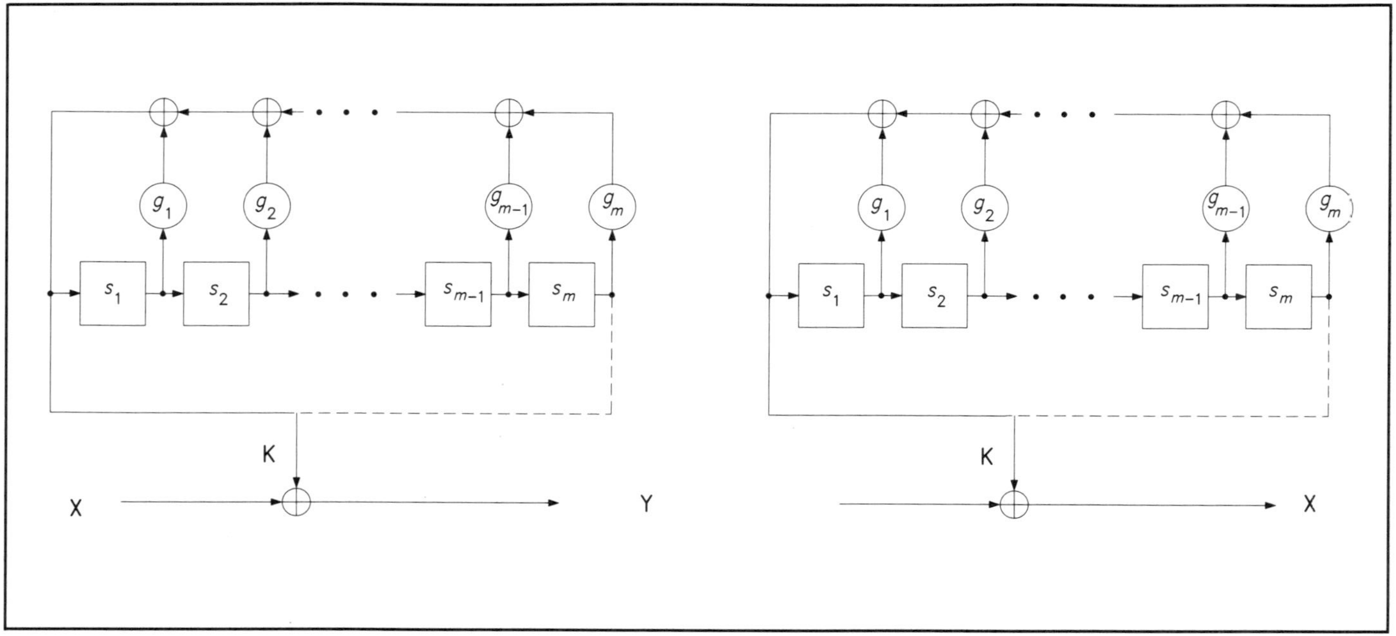

Fig. 4.11 Key autokey cipher system composed of an m-stage LFSR

are thus defined as

$$\begin{aligned} y_i &= x_i + k_i \\ & \qquad\qquad i = 0, 1, 2 \cdots \\ x_i &= y_i + k_i \end{aligned} \tag{4.22}$$

where x_i and y_i denote the ith plaintext and ciphertext bits, respectively. Referring to Fig. 4.11, the key bits k_i, $0 \le i \le m$, from the key stream **K** are represented as

$$\begin{array}{llllll} k_0 & = g_m s_m & + g_{m-1} s_{m-1} & + \ldots + & g_2 s_2 & + g_1 s_1 \\ k_1 & = g_m s_{m-1} & + g_{m-1} s_{m-2} & + \ldots + & g_2 s_1 & + g_1 k_0 \\ \cdots & \cdots & \cdots & \cdots & \cdots & \cdots \\ k_{m-1} & = g_m s_1 & + g_{m-1} k_0 & + \ldots + & g_2 k_{m-3} & + g_1 k_{m-2} \\ k_m & = g_m k_0 & + g_{m-1} k_1 & + \ldots + & g_2 k_{m-2} & + g_1 k_{m-1} \end{array} \tag{4.23}$$

The matrix expression for the key bits of Eq. 4.23 is

$$\begin{bmatrix} k_0 \\ k_1 \\ \cdot \\ \cdot \\ \cdot \\ k_{m-1} \\ k_m \end{bmatrix} = \begin{bmatrix} s_m & s_{m-1} & \cdots & s_2 & s_1 \\ s_{m-1} & s_{m-2} & \cdots & s_1 & k_0 \\ \cdot & & & & \cdot \\ \cdot & & & & \cdot \\ \cdot & & & & \cdot \\ s_1 & k_0 & \cdots & k_{m-3} & k_{m-2} \\ k_0 & k_1 & \cdots & k_{m-2} & k_{m-1} \end{bmatrix} \begin{bmatrix} g_m \\ g_{m-1} \\ \cdot \\ \cdot \\ \cdot \\ g_2 \\ g_1 \end{bmatrix} \tag{4.24}$$

Equation 4.23 can be also expressed in the following compact form:

$$k_i = \begin{cases} \sum_{\lambda=1}^{i} g_\lambda k_{i-\lambda} + \sum_{\lambda=i+1}^{m} g_\lambda s_{\lambda-i} & 0 \le i \le m-1 \\ \sum_{\lambda=1}^{m} g_\lambda k_{i-\lambda} & m \le i \end{cases} \tag{4.25}$$

Once the key bits k_i are determined, the enciphering and deciphering transformations can be easily obtained by substituting Eq. 4.25 into Eq. 4.22.

■ **Example 4.7** Use the generator polynomial $g(x) = 1 + x + x^3$ of the (7, 4) Hamming code as the tap polynomial $T(x)$ of LFSR as shown in Fig. 4.12 and determine the key bits $\mathbf{K} = (k_0, k_1, k_2, k_3)$ under the initial seed vector $\mathbf{S} = (1\ 0\ 0)$.

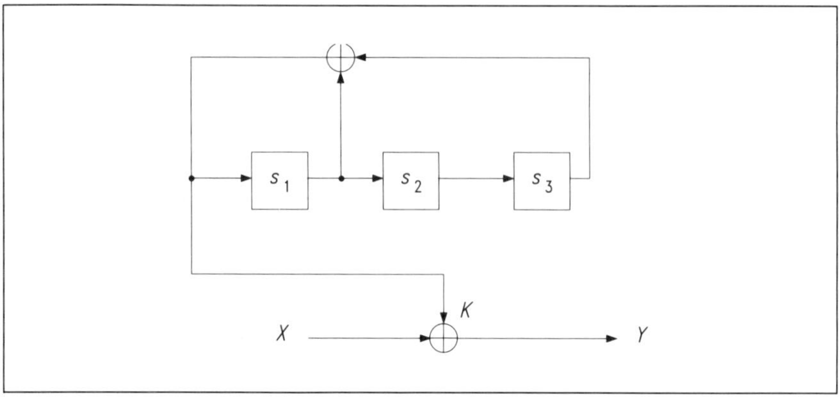

Fig. 4.12 Key autokey encipher using the three-stage LFSR

Applying Eq. 4.24 to this problem, we have

$$\begin{bmatrix} k_0 \\ k_1 \\ k_2 \\ k_3 \end{bmatrix} = \begin{bmatrix} s_3 & s_2 & s_1 \\ s_2 & s_1 & k_0 \\ s_1 & k_0 & k_1 \\ k_0 & k_1 & k_2 \end{bmatrix} \begin{bmatrix} g_3 \\ g_2 \\ g_1 \end{bmatrix} \tag{4.26}$$

Substituting the initial seeds and tap coefficients in Eq. 4.26 yields

$$\begin{bmatrix} k_0 \\ k_1 \\ k_2 \\ k_3 \end{bmatrix} = \begin{bmatrix} 0 & 0 & 1 \\ 0 & 1 & k_0 \\ 1 & k_0 & k_1 \\ k_0 & k_1 & k_2 \end{bmatrix} \begin{bmatrix} 1 \\ 0 \\ 1 \end{bmatrix}$$

from which we have

$$k_0 = 1$$

$$k_1 = k_0$$

$$k_2 = 1 + k_1$$

$$k_3 = k_0 + k_2$$

Thus, we can determine the key bits $k_0 = 1$, $k_1 = 1$, $k_2 = 0$, and $k_3 = 1$, i.e. $\mathbf{K} = (1\ 1\ 0\ 1)$. Since the key bits **K** are derived, the enciphering and deciphering operations can be easily undertaken by using Eq. 4.22 if the plaintext sequence **X** is given.

Let us try another approach towards generating the key-bit stream **K**. Consider the LFSR implemented in Fig. 4.11. The tap generating polynomial (sometimes called the characteristic polynomial) is expressed as $T(x) = 1 + g_1 x + \ldots + g_{m-1}x^{m-1} + g_m x^m$, where $g_i \in \mathrm{GF}(2)$ are the tap coefficients (or the feedback coefficients). If $s_i(t)$ denotes the ith content of LFSR after the pulsing time t, then it holds $s_i(t+1) = s_{i-1}(t)$ for $i = 1, 2, \ldots, m$. Looking at the LFSR in Fig. 4.11, the following relations are found:

$$\begin{aligned}
s_m(t+1) &= s_{m-1}(t) \\
s_{m-1}(t+1) &= s_{m-2}(t) \\
&\cdots\cdots \\
s_2(t+1) &= s_1(t) \\
s_1(t+1) &= g_m s_m(t) + g_{m-1}s_{m-1}(t) + \cdots + g_2 s_2(t) + g_1 s_1(t)
\end{aligned} \tag{4.27}$$

where $s_i(t)$ is the ith content of LFSR at pulsing time t.
Expressing Eq. 4.27 in matrix form,

$$\begin{bmatrix} s_m(t+1) \\ s_{m-1}(t+1) \\ \cdot \\ \cdot \\ \cdot \\ s_2(t+1) \\ s_1(t+1) \end{bmatrix} = \begin{bmatrix} 0 & 1 & 0 & 0 & \cdots & 0 & 0 \\ 0 & 0 & 1 & 0 & \cdots & 0 & 0 \\ & & \cdot & & & & \\ & & \cdot & & & & \\ & & \cdot & & & & \\ 0 & 0 & 0 & 0 & \cdots & 0 & 1 \\ g_m & g_{m-1} & g_{m-2} & g_{m-3} & \cdots & g_2 & g_1 \end{bmatrix} \begin{bmatrix} s_m(t) \\ s_{m-1}(t) \\ \cdot \\ \cdot \\ \cdot \\ s_2(t) \\ s_1(t) \end{bmatrix} \tag{4.28}$$

or $$\mathbf{S}_{t+1} = \mathbf{T}\,\mathbf{S}_t \tag{4.29}$$

where the $m \times m$ matrix **T** is called the tap generating matrix or characteristic matrix.

■ **Example 4.8** Consider again Fig. 4.12 shown in Example 4.7. Assume the initial seed vector is $\mathbf{S} = (s_1, s_2, s_3) = (1\,0\,0)$ which will become the excitation to the LFSR. Then the shifting operations, by clocking, to the right produce register contents as shown in Table 4.2.

The leftmost column (i.e., s_1-column) of the register contents in Table 4.2 represents the key bits over one period. Note that the period of the shift register is $p = 2^m - 1 = 7$ for $m = 3$. Thus, the diagram representing the state transitions can be drawn as shown in Fig. 4.13.

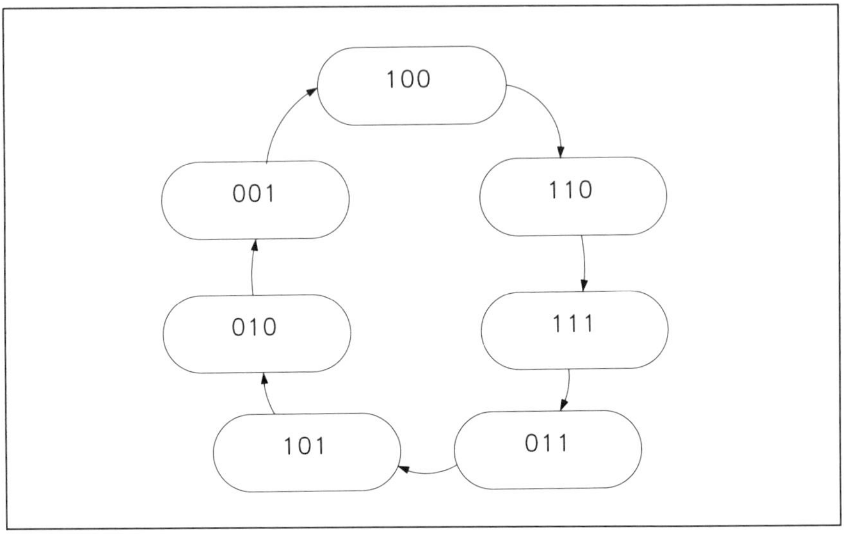

Fig. 4.13 Stage transition diagram created by the shifting operations of LFSR

Table 4.2 Register Contents Obtained by Shifting to the Right

Shift number i	Register contents s_1	s_2	s_3	
0	1	0	0	(initial seeds)
1	1	1	0	
2	1	1	1	
3	0	1	1	
4	1	0	1	
5	0	1	0	
6	0	0	1	

■ **Example 4.9** Let us consider a different approach to Example 4.8, utilizing Eq. 4.28. The 3×3 tap matrix in Eq. 4.28 is

$$\mathbf{T} = \begin{bmatrix} 0 & 1 & 0 \\ 0 & 0 & 1 \\ 1 & 0 & 1 \end{bmatrix}$$

Using Eq. 4.29, since we have

$$\mathbf{S}_1 = \begin{bmatrix} s_3 \\ s_2 \\ s_1 \end{bmatrix} = \begin{bmatrix} 0 \\ 0 \\ 1 \end{bmatrix}$$

$$\mathbf{S}_2 = \mathbf{T} \cdot \mathbf{S}_1 = \begin{bmatrix} 0 & 1 & 0 \\ 0 & 0 & 1 \\ 1 & 0 & 1 \end{bmatrix} \begin{bmatrix} 0 \\ 0 \\ 1 \end{bmatrix} = \begin{bmatrix} 0 \\ 1 \\ 1 \end{bmatrix} = \begin{bmatrix} s_3 \\ s_2 \\ s_1 \end{bmatrix}$$

Executing the recursive operations,

$$\mathbf{S}_3 = \mathbf{T} \cdot \mathbf{S}_2 = \begin{bmatrix} 0 & 1 & 0 \\ 0 & 0 & 1 \\ 1 & 0 & 1 \end{bmatrix} \begin{bmatrix} 0 \\ 1 \\ 1 \end{bmatrix} = \begin{bmatrix} 1 \\ 1 \\ 1 \end{bmatrix}$$

$$\mathbf{S}_4 = \mathbf{T} \cdot \mathbf{S}_3 = \begin{bmatrix} 0 & 1 & 0 \\ 0 & 0 & 1 \\ 1 & 0 & 1 \end{bmatrix} \begin{bmatrix} 1 \\ 1 \\ 1 \end{bmatrix} = \begin{bmatrix} 1 \\ 1 \\ 0 \end{bmatrix}$$

$$\mathbf{S}_5 = \mathbf{T} \cdot \mathbf{S}_4 = \begin{bmatrix} 0 & 1 & 0 \\ 0 & 0 & 1 \\ 1 & 0 & 1 \end{bmatrix} \begin{bmatrix} 1 \\ 1 \\ 0 \end{bmatrix} = \begin{bmatrix} 1 \\ 0 \\ 1 \end{bmatrix}$$

$$\mathbf{S}_6 = \mathbf{T} \cdot \mathbf{S}_5 = \begin{bmatrix} 0 & 1 & 0 \\ 0 & 0 & 1 \\ 1 & 0 & 1 \end{bmatrix} \begin{bmatrix} 1 \\ 0 \\ 1 \end{bmatrix} = \begin{bmatrix} 0 \\ 1 \\ 0 \end{bmatrix}$$

$$\mathbf{S}_7 = \mathbf{T} \cdot \mathbf{S}_6 = \begin{bmatrix} 0 & 1 & 0 \\ 0 & 0 & 1 \\ 1 & 0 & 1 \end{bmatrix} \begin{bmatrix} 0 \\ 1 \\ 0 \end{bmatrix} = \begin{bmatrix} 1 \\ 0 \\ 0 \end{bmatrix}$$

← End of a period

$$\mathbf{S}_8 = \mathbf{T} \cdot \mathbf{S}_7 = \begin{bmatrix} 0 & 1 & 0 \\ 0 & 0 & 1 \\ 1 & 0 & 1 \end{bmatrix} \begin{bmatrix} 1 \\ 0 \\ 0 \end{bmatrix} = \begin{bmatrix} 0 \\ 0 \\ 1 \end{bmatrix} = \mathbf{S}_1$$

$$\mathbf{S}_9 = \mathbf{T} \cdot \mathbf{S}_8 = \begin{bmatrix} 0 & 1 & 0 \\ 0 & 0 & 1 \\ 1 & 0 & 1 \end{bmatrix} \begin{bmatrix} 0 \\ 0 \\ 1 \end{bmatrix} = \begin{bmatrix} 0 \\ 1 \\ 1 \end{bmatrix} = \mathbf{S}_2$$

. . . .

Now we can see that after $\mathbf{S}_7$ the register states (or contents) repeat themselves periodically. We may therefore summarize the results as follows:

t	1	2	3	4	5	6	7	8	9	10	$\cdots$
s_3	0	0	1	1	1	0	1	0	0	1	$\cdots$
s_2	0	1	1	1	0	1	0	0	1	1	$\cdots$
s_1	1	1	1	0	1	0	0	1	1	1	$\cdots$

$\longleftarrow$ one period $\longrightarrow| \longleftarrow$ repetition $\longrightarrow$

The key-bit stream **K** represents the entity of the bottom row above, that is,

$$\mathbf{K} = (\,1110100 \quad 1110100 \quad 1110100 \quad \cdots)$$

If $T(x) = g_0 + g_1 x + g_2 x^2 + \cdots + g_m x^m$ be the tap polynomial of degree m, then $T^{-1}(x)$ will be a sequence generated by the LFSR. We shall justify this proposition through the following example.

■ **Example 4.10** Let $T(x) = 1 + x + x^3$ be the tap polynomial. Then $T^{-1}(x) = 1/T(x)$ may be evaluated as

$$T^{-1}(x) = 1 + x + x^2 + x^4 + x^7 + x^8 + x^9 + x^{11} + x^{14} + x^{15} + x^{16} + x^{18} + x^{21} + \cdots$$

by dividing 1 by $T(x)$ using long division.

$$\mathbf{T}^{-1} = \mathbf{K} = (\,1110100 \quad 1110100 \quad 1110100 \quad 1110100 \quad \cdots)$$

which is also the key-bit stream with a 7-bit period, representing the entity in the bottom row (s_1-row).

Consider Fig. 4.11 where the key-bit stream flows out of LFSR from the right end, as indicated by the dotted line. Assume $T(x) = g_0 + g_1 x + \cdots + g_{m-1} x^{m-1} + g_m x^m$ is the tap polynomial, $A(x) = a_0 + a_1 x + \cdots + a_{m-1} x^{m-1}$ is a polynomial which is functionally related to the initial contents of LFSR, and that the output key polynomial is $K(x) = k_0 + k_1 x + \cdots + k_{m-1} x^{m-1} + k_m x^m + \cdots$.

Then, as we can see from Example 4.10, the following relation holds good:

$$A(x) = K(x)\,T(x) \tag{4.30}$$

where

$$K(x)\,T(x) = k_0 g_0 + (k_0 g_1 + k_1 g_0)\,x + (k_0 g_2 + k_1 g_1 + k_2 g_0)\,x^2 + \cdots$$

$$+ (k_0 g_{m-1} + k_1 g_{m-2} + \cdots + k_{m-1} g_0)\,x^{m-1} \tag{4.31}$$

From Eqs 4.30 and 4.31, the coefficients of these polynomials are found to be

$$a_0 = k_0 g_0$$

$$a_1 = k_0 g_1 + k_1 g_0$$

$$a_2 = k_0 g_2 + k_1 g_1 + k_2 g_0 \tag{4.32}$$

$$\cdots\cdots\cdots\cdots\cdots\cdots$$

$$a_{m-1} = k_0 g_{m-1} + k_1 g_{m-2} + \cdots + k_{m-1} g_0$$

or

$$a_\lambda = \sum_{i=0}^{\lambda} k_i g_{\lambda-i}, \qquad 0 \le i \le m-1 \tag{4.33}$$

Equation 4.32 can also be expressed in matrix form as

$$\begin{bmatrix} a_0 \\ a_1 \\ a_2 \\ \cdot \\ \cdot \\ \cdot \\ a_{m-1} \end{bmatrix} = \begin{bmatrix} g_0 & 0 & 0 & \cdots & 0 & 0 \\ g_1 & g_0 & 0 & \cdots & 0 & 0 \\ g_2 & g_1 & g_0 & \cdots & 0 & 0 \\ & \cdot & & & \cdot & \\ & \cdot & & & \cdot & \\ & \cdot & & & \cdot & \\ g_{m-1} & g_{m-2} & g_{m-3} & \cdots & g_1 & g_0 \end{bmatrix} \begin{bmatrix} k_0 \\ k_1 \\ k_2 \\ \cdot \\ \cdot \\ \cdot \\ k_{m-1} \end{bmatrix} \tag{4.34}$$

We can thus see that if $\mathbf{T} = (g_0, g_1, \cdots, g_{m-1})$ and $\mathbf{K} = (k_0, k_1, \cdots, k_{m-1})$ are known, the third vector $\mathbf{A} = (a_0, a_1, \cdots, a_{m-1})$ can be easily determined from Eq. 4.34.

■ **Example 4.11** Assume that the tap polynomial $T(x) = 1 + x^2 + x^5$ and the truncated output sequence $\mathbf{K} = (1\ 0\ 0\ 0\ 0)$ are given. Then we can determine $\mathbf{A}$ by virtue of Eq. 4.34. Since the tap coefficients are $g_0 = 1$, $g_1 = 0$, $g_2 = 1$, $g_3 = 0$, $g_4 = 0$ and $g_5 = 1$, Eq. 4.34 yields

$$\begin{bmatrix} a_0 \\ a_1 \\ a_2 \\ a_3 \\ a_4 \end{bmatrix} = \begin{bmatrix} 1 & 0 & 0 & 0 & 0 \\ 0 & 1 & 0 & 0 & 0 \\ 1 & 0 & 1 & 0 & 0 \\ 0 & 1 & 0 & 1 & 0 \\ 0 & 0 & 1 & 0 & 1 \end{bmatrix} \begin{bmatrix} 1 \\ 0 \\ 0 \\ 0 \\ 0 \end{bmatrix} = \begin{bmatrix} 1 \\ 0 \\ 1 \\ 0 \\ 0 \end{bmatrix}$$

from which the output is found as $A(x) = 1 + x^2$, or $\mathbf{A} = (1\ 0\ 1\ 0\ 0)$.

Let $A(x)$ denote the characterizing polynomial representing the start of sequence, truncated by m bits of $K(x)$. Then the register contents of LFSR can be obtained as

$$K(x) = A(x)\,T^{-1}(x) \tag{4.35}$$

Since $A(x) = 1 + x^2$ and $T(x) = 1 + x^2 + x^5$, $K(x)$ in Eq. 4.35 becomes $K(x) = 1 + x^5 + x^7 + x^9 + x^{10} + \cdots$ or $\mathbf{K} = (\underline{1\,0\,0\,0\,0}\,1\,0\,1\,0\,1\,1\cdots) = (k_0, k_1, k_2, k_3, k_4, k_5, k_6, k_7, \cdots)$. The underlined first five digits in **K** represent the initial seeds, that is, $\mathbf{K} = (1\,0\,0\,0\,0)$ as expected. Since the polynomial corresponding to initial seeds is $A(x) = 1 + x^2$, $x^kA(x)$ (modulo $1 + x^2 + x^5$) represents the cyclic shift k digits of $A(x)$ to the right. For $k = 2$, we have $x^2A(x) = x^2 + x^4$. Then the shifted contents give $A^{(2)}(x) = (x^2 + x^4) / (1 + x^2 + x^5) = x^2 + x^7 + x^9 + x^{11} + \cdots$. Hence, the register contents after two shifts become $\mathbf{A}^{(2)} = (0\,0\,1\,0\,0)$. The shifted contents for $k = 17$ is $x^{17}A(x) = x^{17} + x^{19}$. Applying two field elements $x^{17} = 1 + x + x^4$ and $x^{19} = x + x^2$ from GF (2^5) to $x^{17}A(x)$, we have $x^{17}A(x) = 1 + x^2 + x^4$. Thus,

$$A^{(17)}(x) = 1 + x^2 + x^4 / 1 + x^2 + x^5 = 1 + x^4 + x^5 + x^6 + \cdots.$$

Therefore, we see that the register contents at the 17th shift yield $\mathbf{A}^{(17)} = (1\,0\,0\,0\,1)$.

In this section, we have discussed synchronous stream ciphers in which the key-bit stream is generated independently of the plaintext. Therefore, in the loss of a ciphertext bit during transmission, the key generator at both ends must resynchronize before proceeding further. Hence, the loss of a bit causes loss of synchronization, and all ciphertext following the loss will be decrypted incorrectly. We also saw that synchronous stream ciphers could be broken when the key-bit stream was repeated periodically. For this reason, synchronous stream ciphers have limited applicability to file and database encryption. However, they do protect the ciphertext to some extent from search by opponents because identical blocks in the plaintext are enciphered in different parts of the key stream. They also ensure protecting against injection of false ciphertext, replay, and ciphertext deletion, because insertion or deletion in the ciphertext causes loss of synchronization.

Synchronous stream ciphers have the advantage of no error propagation. In fact, a transmission error affecting one bit will not affect subsequent bits. But this fact may also be a disadvantage because it is easier for an opponent to modify a single bit of ciphertext than a block of bits.

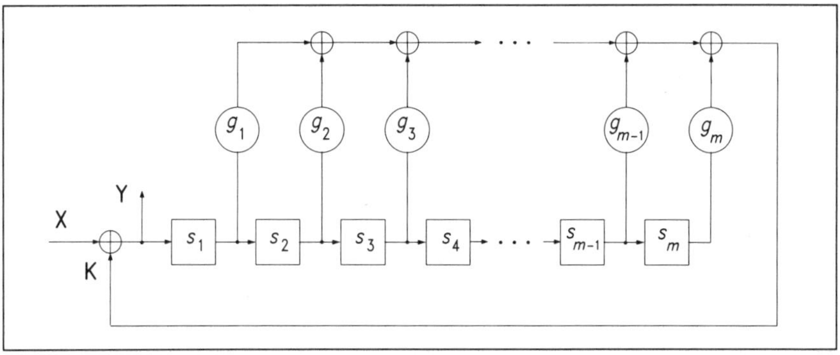

Fig. 4.14 Autokey enciphering system with ciphertext feedback

4.2 SELF-SYNCHRONIZING CIPHERS

Self-synchronizing cipher systems are another class of stream ciphers and are categorized as ciphertext autokey ciphers and plaintext autokey ciphers. A ciphertext autokey cipher is one in which the key is derived from the ciphertext, and is called a self-synchronizing stream cipher with ciphertext feedback. Since each key bit is computed from the preceding ciphertext bit, it is functionally dependent on all preceding bits in the plaintext plus the priming key. This makes cryptanalysis more difficult, because the statistical properties of the plaintext are diffused across the ciphertext. Another kind of autokey cipher is any self-synchronizing system with plaintext feedback. A plaintext autokey cipher is one in which the key is derived from the plaintext to be encrypted. These two autokey ciphers will be analyzed in detail in the following subsections.

4.2.1 Ciphertext Autokey Ciphers

Ciphertext autokey ciphers are cipher systems with ciphertext feedback, as shown in Fig. 4.14.

Let us consider the simple case when $m = 4$ in Fig. 4.14. Then we have a cipher system with a four-stage LFSR as devised in Fig. 4.15.

Let $T(x)$ be the transfer polynomial and $S(x)$ the seed polynomial, respectively. They may be expressed in terms of the delay operator D as follows:

$$T(D) = g_1 + g_2D + g_3D^2 + g_4D^3 \tag{4.36}$$

and

$$S(D) = s_1 + s_2D^{-1} + s_3D^{-2} + s_4D^{-3} \tag{4.37}$$

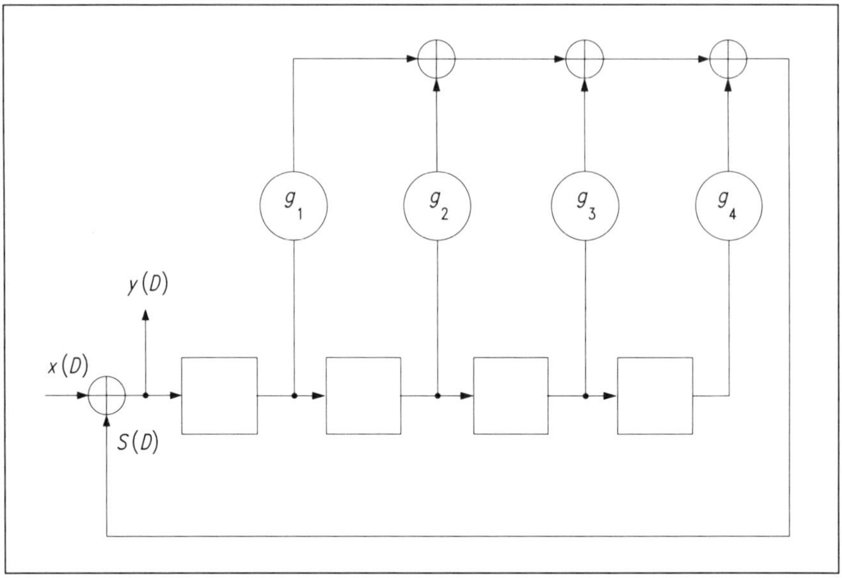

Fig. 4.15 A ciphertext feedback enciphering system with the four-stage LFSR

The ciphertext polynomial $y(x)$ then becomes

$$y(D) = x(D) + T(D)Dy(D) + T(D)S(D)$$

$$= x(D) + g_1 Dy(D) + g_2 D^2 y(D) + g_3 D^3 y(D) + g_4 D^4 y(D)$$

$$+ (g_1 + g_2 D + g_3 D^2 + g_4 D^3)(s_1 + s_2 D^{-1} + s_3 D^{-2} + s_4 D^{-3}) \quad (4.38)$$

where $x(D) = x_0 + x_1 D + x_2 D^2 + \cdots$ represents the plaintext polynomial and $y(D) = y_0 + y_1 D + y_2 D^2 + \cdots$ the ciphertext polynomial. Expanding Eq. 4.38 and rearranging it in ascending order with respect to D, we get the ciphertext bits y_i, $0 \le i \le 4$, and $4 \le i$ as follows:

$$y_0 = x_0 + g_1 s_1 + g_2 s_2 + g_3 s_3 + g_4 s_4 = x_0 + \sum_{\lambda=1}^{4} g_\lambda s_\lambda$$

$$y_1 = x_1 + g_1 y_0 + g_2 s_1 + g_3 s_2 + g_4 s_3 = x_1 + g_1 y_0 + \sum_{\lambda=2}^{4} g_\lambda s_{\lambda-1}$$

$$y_2 = x_2 + g_1 y_1 + g_2 y_0 + g_3 s_1 + g_4 s_2 = x_2 + \sum_{\lambda=1}^{2} g_\lambda y_{2-\lambda} + \sum_{\lambda=3}^{4} g_\lambda s_{\lambda-2}$$

$$y_3 = x_3 + g_1 y_2 + g_2 y_1 + g_3 y_0 + g_4 s_1 = x_3 + \sum_{\lambda=1}^{3} g_\lambda y_{3-\lambda} + g_4 s_1 \tag{4.39}$$

$$y_4 = x_4 + g_1 y_3 + g_2 y_2 + g_3 y_1 + g_4 y_0 = x_4 + \sum_{\lambda=1}^{4} g_\lambda y_{4-\lambda}$$

$$y_5 = x_5 + g_1 y_4 + g_2 y_3 + g_3 y_2 + g_4 y_1 = x_5 + \sum_{\lambda=1}^{4} g_\lambda y_{5-\lambda}$$

$$y_6 = x_6 + g_1 y_5 + g_2 y_4 + g_3 y_3 + g_4 y_2 = x_6 + \sum_{\lambda=1}^{4} g_\lambda y_{6-\lambda}$$

$$y_7 = x_7 + g_1 y_6 + g_2 y_5 + g_3 y_4 + g_4 y_3 = x_7 + \sum_{\lambda=1}^{4} g_\lambda y_{7-\lambda}$$

Hence, the general expression of Eq. 4.39 for the ciphertext bit at an arbitrary time unit i is as follows:

$$y_i = \begin{cases} x_1 + \sum_{\lambda=1}^{i} g_\lambda y_{i-\lambda} + \sum_{\lambda=i+1}^{m} g_\lambda s_{\lambda-i} & 0 \le i \le m-1 \\ x_i + \sum_{\lambda=1}^{m} g_\lambda y_{i-\lambda} & i \le m \end{cases} \tag{4.40}$$

where m denotes the number of stages in LFSR.

Equation 4.39 may be expressed in matrix form as

$$\begin{bmatrix} y_0 \\ y_1 \\ y_2 \\ y_3 \\ y_4 \\ y_5 \\ y_6 \\ y_7 \end{bmatrix} = \begin{bmatrix} x_0 \\ x_1 \\ x_2 \\ x_3 \\ x_4 \\ x_5 \\ x_6 \\ x_7 \end{bmatrix} + \begin{bmatrix} 0 & 0 & 0 & 0 \\ y_0 & 0 & 0 & 0 \\ y_1 & y_0 & 0 & 0 \\ y_2 & y_1 & y_0 & 0 \\ y_3 & y_2 & y_1 & y_0 \\ y_4 & y_3 & y_2 & y_1 \\ y_5 & y_4 & y_3 & y_2 \\ y_6 & y_5 & y_4 & y_3 \end{bmatrix} \begin{bmatrix} g_1 \\ g_2 \\ g_3 \\ g_4 \end{bmatrix} + \begin{bmatrix} s_1 & s_2 & s_3 & s_4 \\ 0 & s_1 & s_2 & s_3 \\ 0 & 0 & s_1 & s_2 \\ 0 & 0 & 0 & s_1 \\ 0 & 0 & 0 & 0 \\ 0 & 0 & 0 & 0 \\ 0 & 0 & 0 & 0 \\ 0 & 0 & 0 & 0 \end{bmatrix} \begin{bmatrix} g_1 \\ g_2 \\ g_3 \\ g_4 \end{bmatrix} \tag{4.41}$$

In Eq. 4.41, we can observe that the ciphertext consists of three terms—the plaintext term, and contributions from the ciphertext feedback and the initializing seed vector. As we know, Eq. 4.41 is equivalent to Eq. 4.40. It may be further reduced to

$$\begin{bmatrix} y_0 \\ y_1 \\ y_2 \\ y_3 \\ y_4 \\ y_5 \\ y_6 \\ y_7 \end{bmatrix} = \begin{bmatrix} x_0 \\ x_1 \\ x_2 \\ x_3 \\ x_4 \\ x_5 \\ x_6 \\ x_7 \end{bmatrix} + \begin{bmatrix} s_1 & s_2 & s_3 & s_4 \\ y_0 & s_1 & s_2 & s_3 \\ y_1 & y_0 & s_1 & s_2 \\ y_2 & y_1 & y_0 & s_1 \\ y_3 & y_2 & y_1 & y_0 \\ y_4 & y_3 & y_2 & y_1 \\ y_5 & y_4 & y_3 & y_2 \\ y_6 & y_5 & y_4 & y_3 \end{bmatrix} \begin{bmatrix} g_1 \\ g_2 \\ g_3 \\ g_4 \end{bmatrix} \tag{4.42}$$

This is the matrix system for encipherment.

■ **Example 4.12** Consider the ciphertext feedback enciphering system for $m = 4$ with the tap coefficients $\mathbf{T} = (g_1, g_2, g_3, g_4) = (0\ 1\ 0\ 1)$, as shown in Fig. 4.16.

Suppose the 8-bit plaintext vector for $2m = 8$ is $\mathbf{X} = (1\ 1\ 1\ 0\ 1\ 0\ 0\ 1)$ and the initial seed vector stored in the LFSR is $\mathbf{S} = (s_1, s_2, s_3, s_4) = (0\ 0\ 1\ 1)$. Then the 8-bit ciphertext bits can be computed from Eq. 4.40 as follows:

$$y_0 = x_0 + \sum_{\lambda=1}^{4} g_\lambda s_\lambda = x_0 + g_2 s_2 + g_4 s_4 = x_0 + s_2 + s_4 = 1 + 0 + 1 = 0$$

$$y_1 = x_1 + g_1 y_0 + \sum_{\lambda=2}^{4} g_\lambda s_{\lambda-1} = x_1 + g_2 s_1 + g_4 s_3 = x_1 + s_1 + s_3 = 1 + 0 + 1 = 0$$

$$y_2 = x_2 + \sum_{\lambda=1}^{2} g_\lambda y_{2-\lambda} + \sum_{\lambda=3}^{4} g_\lambda s_{\lambda-2} = x_2 + y_0 + s_2 = 1 + 0 + 0 = 1$$

$$y_3 = x_3 + \sum_{\lambda=1}^{3} g_\lambda y_{3-\lambda} + g_4 s_1 = x_3 + y_1 + s_1 = 0 + 0 + 0 = 0$$

$$y_4 = x_4 + \sum_{\lambda=1}^{4} g_\lambda y_{4-\lambda} = x_4 + y_2 + y_0 = 1 + 1 + 0 = 0$$

$$y_5 = x_5 + \sum_{\lambda=1}^{4} g_\lambda y_{5-\lambda} = x_5 + y_3 + y_1 = 0 + 0 + 0 = 0$$

$$y_6 = x_6 + \sum_{\lambda=1}^{4} g_\lambda y_{6-\lambda} = x_6 + y_4 + y_2 = 0 + 0 + 1 = 1$$

$$y_7 = x_7 + \sum_{\lambda=1}^{4} g_\lambda s_{7-\lambda} = x_7 + y_5 + y_3 = 1 + 0 + 0 = 1$$

Thus, the 8-bit ciphertext gives

$$\mathbf{Y} = (y_0, y_1, y_2, y_3, y_4, y_5, y_6, y_7) = (0\,0\,1\,0\,0\,0\,1\,1) \qquad (4.43)$$

If we use Eq. 4.42 rather than Eq. 4.40, the ciphertext bits with ciphertext feedback are easily obtained as shown in the following example.

■ **Example 4.13** Repeat Example 4.12 by using the matrix representation of Eq. 4.42. Since we assumed the $2m$ plaintext sequence $\mathbf{X} = (1\,1\,1\,0\,1\,0\,0\,1)$, the initial seed vector $\mathbf{S} = (0\,0\,1\,1)$, and the transfer coefficient $\mathbf{T} = (0\,1\,0\,1)$, we can immediately form the matrix system for computing the ciphertext bits as follows:

$$\begin{bmatrix} y_0 \\ y_1 \\ y_2 \\ y_3 \\ y_4 \\ y_5 \\ y_6 \\ y_7 \end{bmatrix} = \begin{bmatrix} 1 \\ 1 \\ 1 \\ 0 \\ 1 \\ 0 \\ 0 \\ 1 \end{bmatrix} + \begin{bmatrix} 0 & 0 & 1 & 1 \\ y_0 & 0 & 0 & 1 \\ y_1 & y_0 & 0 & 0 \\ y_2 & y_1 & y_0 & 0 \\ y_3 & y_2 & y_1 & y_0 \\ y_4 & y_3 & y_2 & y_1 \\ y_5 & y_4 & y_3 & y_2 \\ y_6 & y_5 & y_4 & y_3 \end{bmatrix} \begin{bmatrix} 0 \\ 1 \\ 0 \\ 1 \end{bmatrix} = \begin{bmatrix} 1+1 \\ 1+1 \\ 1+y_0 \\ 0+y_1 \\ 1+y_2+y_0 \\ 0+y_3+y_1 \\ 0+y_4+y_2 \\ 1+y_5+y_3 \end{bmatrix}$$

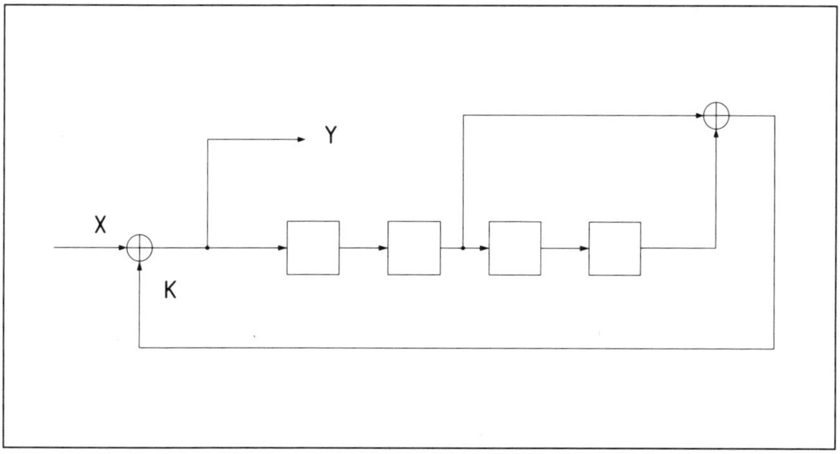

Fig. 4.16 The enciphering system with ciphertext feedback for $m = 4$ and $T = (0\,1\,0\,1)$

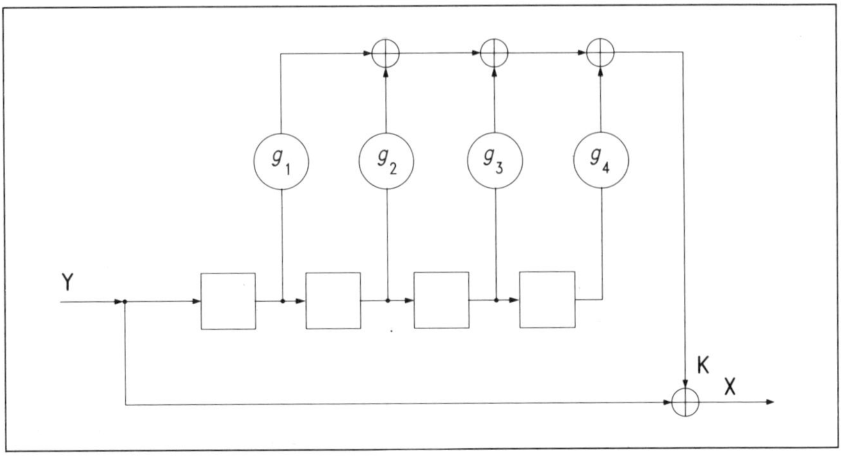

Fig. 4.17 A ciphertext autokey deciphering system with a four-stage LFSR

Thus,

$$y_0 = 1 + 1 = 0 \qquad y_4 = 1 + y_2 + y_0 = 1 + 1 + 0 = 0$$

$$y_1 = 1 + 1 = 0 \qquad y_5 = 0 + y_3 + y_1 = 0 + 0 + 0 = 0$$

$$y_2 = 1 + y_0 = 1 + 0 = 1 \qquad y_6 = 0 + y_4 + y_2 = 0 + 0 + 1 = 1$$

$$y_3 = 0 + y_1 = 0 + 0 = 0 \qquad y_7 = 1 + y_5 + y_3 = 1 + 0 + 0 = 1$$

Therefore, the ciphertext bits are produced as

$$\mathbf{Y} = (0\,0\,1\,0\,0\,0\,1\,1) \tag{4.44}$$

which is identical to Eq. 4.43.

As seen from Examples 4.12 and 4.13, Eq. 4.42 can be generally expressed as

$$\begin{bmatrix} y_0 \\ y_1 \\ y_2 \\ \cdot \\ \cdot \\ \cdot \\ y_{2m-2} \\ y_{2m-1} \end{bmatrix} = \begin{bmatrix} x_0 \\ x_1 \\ x_2 \\ \cdot \\ \cdot \\ \cdot \\ x_{2m-2} \\ x_{2m-1} \end{bmatrix} + \begin{bmatrix} s_1 & s_2 & s_3 & \cdots & s_{m-1} & s_m \\ y_0 & s_1 & s_2 & \cdots & s_{m-2} & s_{m-1} \\ y_1 & y_0 & s_1 & \cdots & s_{m-3} & s_{m-2} \\ & \cdot & & & \cdot & \\ & \cdot & & & \cdot & \\ & \cdot & & & \cdot & \\ y_{2m-3} & y_{2m-4} & y_{2m-5} & \cdots & y_{m-1} & y_{m-2} \\ y_{2m-2} & y_{2m-3} & y_{2m-4} & \cdots & y_m & y_{m-1} \end{bmatrix} \begin{bmatrix} g_1 \\ g_2 \\ g_3 \\ \cdot \\ \cdot \\ \cdot \\ g_{m-1} \\ g_m \end{bmatrix} \tag{4.45}$$

Let $\mathbf{X}_i$ be the plaintext sequence at an arbitrary time unit i and $\mathbf{Y}_i$ the corresponding ciphertext sequence. Then, they are expressed as $\mathbf{X}_i = (x_i, x_{i+1}, \cdots, x_{i+m-1})$ and $\mathbf{Y}_i = (y_i, y_{i+1}, \cdots, y_{i+m-1})$, respectively. The initial contents of LFSR in autokey ciphers become irrelevant after the first m clock pulses shift the initial seeds out. Therefore, Eq. 4.45 can be modified as

$$\mathbf{Y}_{i+m} = \mathbf{X}_{i+m} + \mathbf{T}\,\mathbf{Y}(i), \qquad 0 \le i \tag{4.46}$$

where

$$\mathbf{Y}(i) = \begin{bmatrix} y_{i+m-1} & y_{i+m} & \cdots & y_{i+2m-3} & y_{i+2m-2} \\ y_{i+m-2} & y_{i+m-1} & \cdots & y_{i+2m-4} & y_{i+2m-3} \\ \cdot & & & \cdot & \\ \cdot & & & \cdot & \\ \cdot & & & \cdot & \\ y_{i+1} & y_{i+2} & \cdots & y_{i+m-1} & y_{i+m} \\ y_i & y_{i+1} & \cdots & y_{i+m-2} & y_{i+m-1} \end{bmatrix} \tag{4.47}$$

From Eq. 4.46, the tap coefficients $\mathbf{T} = (g_1, g_2, \cdots, g_m)$ can be determined in the following manner.

$$\mathbf{T} = (\mathbf{Y}_{i+m} + \mathbf{X}_{i+m})\mathbf{Y}^{-1}(i) \tag{4.48}$$

For $i = 0$,

$$\mathbf{T} = (\mathbf{Y}_m + \mathbf{X}_m)\mathbf{Y}^{-1}(0) \tag{4.49}$$

■ **Example 4.14** Consider again Fig. 4.16 where the plaintext is $\mathbf{X} = (1\,1\,1\,0\,1\,0\,0\,1)$ and the corresponding ciphertext is $\mathbf{Y} = (0\,0\,1\,0\,0\,0\,1\,1)$. Let us determine the transfer coefficients **T** and the initial seeds **S**.

For $i = 0$ and $m = 4$, Eq. 4.47 becomes

$$\mathbf{Y}(0) = \begin{bmatrix} y_3 & y_4 & y_5 & y_6 \\ y_2 & y_3 & y_4 & y_5 \\ y_1 & y_2 & y_3 & y_4 \\ y_0 & y_1 & y_2 & y_3 \end{bmatrix} = \begin{bmatrix} 0 & 0 & 0 & 1 \\ 1 & 0 & 0 & 0 \\ 0 & 1 & 0 & 0 \\ 0 & 0 & 1 & 0 \end{bmatrix}$$

Using Eq. 4.49 for $m = 4$, we have

$$\mathbf{T} = (\mathbf{Y}_4 + \mathbf{X}_4)\mathbf{Y}^{-1}(0) = (0\,0\,1\,1 + 1\,0\,0\,1)\begin{bmatrix} 0 & 1 & 0 & 0 \\ 0 & 0 & 1 & 0 \\ 0 & 0 & 0 & 1 \\ 1 & 0 & 0 & 0 \end{bmatrix}^{-1} = (0\,1\,0\,1)$$

Thus, the transfer coefficients (feedback coefficients or taps of LFSR) have been completely determined. Under the condition that the sequence begin at $i = 0$, Eq. 4.40 can be used to determine the initial seeds. That is,

$$\begin{aligned} y_0 &= x_0 + s_2 + s_4 \\ y_1 &= x_1 + s_1 + s_3 \\ y_2 &= x_2 + y_0 + s_2 \\ y_3 &= x_3 + y_1 + s_1 \end{aligned}$$

from which

$$\begin{aligned} s_1 &= y_3 + x_3 + y_1 = 0 + 0 + 0 = 0 \\ s_2 &= y_2 + x_2 + y_0 = 1 + 1 + 0 = 0 \\ s_3 &= y_1 + x_1 + s_1 = 0 + 1 + 0 = 1 \\ s_4 &= y_0 + x_0 + s_2 = 0 + 1 + 0 = 1 \end{aligned}$$

Thus, the initial seed vector is

$$\mathbf{S} = (s_1, s_2, s_3, s_4) = (0\,0\,1\,1)$$

Finally, consider a deciphering system with ciphertext feedback as illustrated in Fig. 4.17. Using the same **T** and **S** as the enciphering system, the plaintext is reproduced by the following relations, that is,

$$x_i = \begin{cases} y_1 + \sum\limits_{\lambda=1}^{i} g_\lambda\, y_{i-\lambda} + \sum\limits_{\lambda=i+1}^{m} g_\lambda\, s_{\lambda-i} & 0 \le i \le m-1 \\ y_i + \sum\limits_{\lambda=1}^{m} g_\lambda\, y_{i-\lambda} & i \le m \end{cases} \tag{4.50}$$

■ **Example 4.15** Consider Fig. 4.17 for the decipherment to reproduce plaintext **X** corresponding to ciphertext $\mathbf{Y} = (0\,0\,1\,0\,0\,0\,1\,1)$, with tap coefficients $\mathbf{T} = (0\,1\,0\,1)$ and initial seed vector $\mathbf{S} = (0\,0\,1\,1)$, as assumed before.

Using Eq. 4.50, let us determine the plaintext bits to be recovered.

$$x_0 = y_0 + \sum_{\lambda=1}^{4} g_\lambda s_\lambda = y_0 + s_2 + s_4 = 0 + 0 + 1 = 1$$

$$x_1 = y_1 + g_1 y_0 + \sum_{\lambda=2}^{4} g_\lambda s_{\lambda-1} = y_1 + s_2 + s_3 = 0 + 0 + 1 = 1$$

$$x_2 = y_2 + \sum_{\lambda=1}^{2} g_\lambda y_{2-\lambda} + \sum_{\lambda=3}^{4} g_\lambda s_{\lambda-2} = y_2 + y_0 + s_2 = 1 + 0 + 0 = 1$$

$$x_3 = y_3 + \sum_{\lambda=1}^{3} g_\lambda y_{3-\lambda} + g_4 s_1 = y_3 + y_1 + s_1 = 0 + 0 + 0 = 0$$

$$x_4 = y_4 + \sum_{\lambda=1}^{4} g_\lambda y_{4-\lambda} = y_4 + y_2 + y_0 = 0 + 1 + 0 = 1$$

$$x_5 = y_5 + \sum_{\lambda=1}^{4} g_\lambda y_{5-\lambda} = y_5 + y_3 + y_1 = 0 + 0 + 0 = 0$$

$$x_6 = y_6 + \sum_{\lambda=1}^{4} g_\lambda y_{6-\lambda} = y_6 + y_4 + y_2 = 1 + 0 + 1 = 0$$

$$x_7 = y_7 + \sum_{\lambda=1}^{4} g_\lambda y_{7-\lambda} = y_7 + y_5 + y_3 = 1 + 0 + 0 = 1$$

Thus, the recovered plaintext bits are

$$\mathbf{X} = (1\,1\,1\,0\,1\,0\,0\,1)$$

as expected.

4.2.2 Plaintext Autokey Ciphers

Plaintext autokey ciphers are often called self-synchronizing ciphers with plaintext input to the shift register.

Let $\mathbf{X}_i = (x_i, x_{i+1}, \cdots, x_{i+m-1})$ be the plaintext sequence at the i time unit and $\mathbf{Y}_i = (y_i, y_{i+1}, \cdots, y_{i+m-1})$ the corresponding ciphertext sequence. Then we have

$$\mathbf{Y}_{i+m} = \mathbf{X}_{i+m} + \mathbf{X}(i)\,\mathbf{T} \qquad 0 \le i \tag{4.51}$$

where

$$\mathbf{X}(i) = \begin{bmatrix} x_{i+m-1} & x_{i+m} & \cdots & x_{i+2m-2} \\ x_{i+m-2} & x_{i+m-1} & \cdots & x_{i+2m-3} \\ \cdot & & & \cdot \\ \cdot & & & \cdot \\ x_i & x_{i+1} & \cdots & x_{i+m-1} \end{bmatrix}$$

from which the tap coefficients $\mathbf{T}$ are obtained as

$$\mathbf{T} = \mathbf{X}^{-1}(i)\,(\mathbf{Y}_{i+m} + \mathbf{X}_{i+m}) \tag{4.52}$$

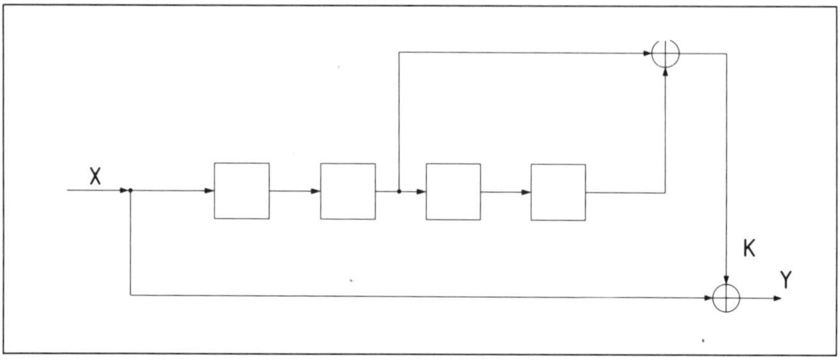

Fig. 4.18 A self-synchronizing encipher with plaintext excitation

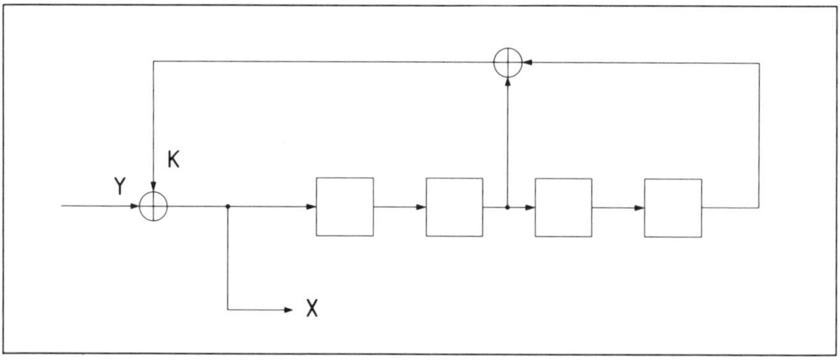

Fig. 4.19 An autokey decipher system with plaintext feedback

■ **Example 4.16** Consider the self-synchronizing encipher with plaintext excitation as shown in Fig. 4.18. Assume that we have the tap settings $\mathbf{T} = (g_1, g_2, g_3, g_4) = (0\ 1\ 0\ 1)$, the initial seeds $\mathbf{S} = (s_1, s_2, s_3, s_4) = (0\ 0\ 1\ 1)$, and the plaintext sequence $\mathbf{X} = (1\ 1\ 1\ 0\ 1\ 0\ 0\ 1)$. Since $m = 4$, the ciphertext bits y_0 to y_7 can be found from Eq. 4.40, but replacing $y_{i-\lambda}$ with $x_{i-\lambda}$, as follows:

$$y_0 = x_0 + \sum_{\lambda=1}^{4} g_\lambda s_\lambda = x_0 + s_2 + s_4 = 1 + 0 + 1 = 0$$

$$y_1 = x_1 + g_1 x_0 + \sum_{\lambda=2}^{4} g_\lambda s_{\lambda-1} = x_1 + s_1 + s_3 = 1 + 0 + 1 = 0$$

$$y_2 = x_2 + \sum_{\lambda=1}^{2} g_\lambda x_{2-\lambda} + \sum_{\lambda=3}^{4} g_\lambda s_{\lambda-2} = x_2 + x_0 + s_2 = 1 + 1 + 0 = 0$$

$$y_3 = x_3 + \sum_{\lambda=1}^{3} g_\lambda x_{3-\lambda} + g_4 s_1 = x_3 + x_1 + s_1 = 0 + 1 + 0 = 1$$

$$y_4 = x_4 + \sum_{\lambda=1}^{4} g_\lambda x_{4-\lambda} = x_4 + x_2 + x_0 = 1 + 1 + 1 = 1$$

$$y_5 = x_5 + \sum_{\lambda=1}^{4} g_\lambda x_{5-\lambda} = x_5 + x_3 + x_1 = 0 + 0 + 1 = 1$$

$$y_6 = x_6 + \sum_{\lambda=1}^{4} g_\lambda x_{6-\lambda} = x_6 + x_4 + x_2 = 0 + 1 + 1 = 0$$

$$y_7 = x_7 + \sum_{\lambda=1}^{4} g_\lambda x_{7-\lambda} = x_7 + x_5 + x_3 = 1 + 0 + 0 = 1$$

Thus, the ciphertext sequence is **Y** = (0 0 0 1 1 1 0 1).

■ **Example 4.17** Consider Fig. 4.18 again in order to determine the tap vector **T** and the initial seed vector **S**. The ciphertext **Y** = (0 0 0 1 1 1 0 1) corresponding to plaintext **X** = (1 1 1 0 1 0 0 1) was obtained in Example 4.16. For $i = 0$ and $m = 4$, Eq. 4.52 becomes

$$\mathbf{T} = \mathbf{X}^{-1}(0)\,(\mathbf{Y}_4 + \mathbf{X}_4)$$

where

$$\mathbf{X}(0) = \begin{bmatrix} x_3 & x_4 & x_5 & x_6 \\ x_2 & x_3 & x_4 & x_5 \\ x_1 & x_2 & x_3 & x_4 \\ x_0 & x_1 & x_2 & x_3 \end{bmatrix} = \begin{bmatrix} 0 & 1 & 0 & 0 \\ 1 & 0 & 1 & 0 \\ 1 & 1 & 0 & 1 \\ 1 & 1 & 1 & 0 \end{bmatrix}$$

Since the determinant of **X** (0) is $|\mathbf{X}(0)| = 0$, the matrix **X** (0) is singular. Therefore, $\mathbf{X}^{-1}(0)$ is undefined. Consequently, the tap coefficients **T** are impossible to determine for this case. The reason for this is that no feedback path is available for the plaintext.

■ **Example 4.18** Consider an autokey decipher with plaintext feedback as shown in Fig. 4.19. As analyzed in Example 4.16, we have the tap settings **T** = (0 1 0 1), the initial seeds **S** = (0 0 1 1), and the ciphertext sequence **Y** = (0 0 0 1 1 1 0 1).

Using Eq. 4.50 by replacing $y_{i-\lambda}$ with $x_{i-\lambda}$, the plaintext bits to be recovered can be found as follows:

$$x_0 = y_0 + \sum_{\lambda=1}^{4} g_\lambda s_\lambda = y_0 + s_2 + s_4 = 0 + 0 + 1 = 1$$

$$x_1 = y_1 + g_1 x_0 + \sum_{\lambda=2}^{4} g_\lambda s_{\lambda-1} = y_1 + s_1 + s_3 = 0 + 0 + 1 = 1$$

$$x_2 = y_2 + \sum_{\lambda=1}^{2} g_\lambda x_{2-\lambda} + \sum_{\lambda=3}^{4} g_\lambda s_{\lambda-2} = y_2 + x_0 + s_2 = 0 + 1 + 0 = 1$$

$$x_3 = y_3 + \sum_{\lambda=1}^{3} g_\lambda x_{3-\lambda} + g_4 s_1 = y_3 + x_1 + s_1 = 1 + 1 + 0 = 0$$

$$x_4 = y_4 + \sum_{\lambda=1}^{4} g_\lambda x_{4-\lambda} = y_4 + x_2 + x_0 = 1 + 1 + 1 = 1$$

$$x_5 = y_5 + \sum_{\lambda=1}^{4} g_\lambda x_{5-\lambda} = y_5 + x_3 + x_1 = 1 + 0 + 1 = 0$$

$$x_6 = y_6 + \sum_{\lambda=1}^{4} g_\lambda x_{6-\lambda} = y_6 + x_4 + x_2 = 0 + 1 + 1 = 0$$

$$x_7 = y_7 + \sum_{\lambda=1}^{4} g_\lambda x_{7-\lambda} = y_7 + x_5 + x_3 = 1 + 0 + 0 = 1$$

Thus, the recovered plaintext is $\mathbf{X} = (1\ 1\ 1\ 0\ 1\ 0\ 0\ 1)$.

4.3 ERROR PROPAGATION

As shown in the examples in Chapter 3, block ciphers divide the plaintext into blocks of the same size and encipher or decipher each block with the same key independently. Since each bit of ciphertext is a complex function of all bits of the plaintext and the key due to the intersymbol dependence, no bit of the plaintext appears directly in the ciphertext. Due to the fact that block encryption is not inherently faster than stream encryption, stream ciphers are adequate for applications requiring high speed. However, such ciphers may be more susceptible to cryptanalysis than block ciphers such as DES.

In block encryption, transmission errors in one ciphertext block have no effect on other blocks. In fact, block encryption is not vulnerable to insertion and deletion of blocks, because changes to the ciphertext in case of such encryption do not affect surrounding blocks. The purpose of authentication is to prevent an opponent from injecting false data into the channel or altering encrypted data. In this respect, the error propagation in a block cipher system is useful in authentication.

The stream cipher enciphers the message into the ciphertext in a manner which depends on the internal state of the encipher device. In fact, two encipherments of the same plaintext will usually not result in the same ciphertext. In a synchronous stream cipher, the key-bit stream is generated independently of plaintext bits. Therefore synchronous stream ciphers do not propagate errors because each ciphertext block is independently enciphered and deciphered. Thus, each block corrupted in transmission noise will result in precisely one erroneous deciphered block. But, self-synchronous stream ciphers propagate errors because each key character is functionally dependent on the entire preceding ciphertext or plaintext block. Particularly, in a ciphertext autokey system, an erroneous or lost ciphertext character causes only a fixed number of errors in the deciphered plaintext, after which correct plaintext is again produced. However, in a plaintext autokey system, an erroneous ciphertext block causes indefinite error propagation in the deciphered plaintext blocks. In the key autokey system, each block of ciphertext corrupted in transmission noise (false bits) produces only one erroneous deciphered block.

The results of error propagation will be illustrated in the following examples.

■ **Example 4.19** Consider again the self-synchronizing cipher with ciphertext feedback mode, discussed in Examples 4.12 and 4.15. The ciphertext is $\mathbf{Y} = (0\ 0\ 1\ 0\ 0\ 0\ 1\ 1)$ corresponding to the plaintext $\mathbf{X} = (1\ 1\ 1\ 0\ 1\ 0\ 0\ 1)$. We utilize Fig. 4.17 with the tap coefficients $\mathbf{T} = (g_1, g_2, g_3, g_4) = (0\ 1\ 0\ 1)$ and initial seeds $\mathbf{S} = (s_1, s_2, s_3, s_4) = (0\ 0\ 1\ 1)$. Let us assume that one error occurs in the ciphertext input to Fig. 4.17 like $\hat{\mathbf{Y}} = (0\ 1\ 1\ 0\ 0\ 0\ 1\ 1)$. It is of interest to observe the error propagation in the recovered plaintext $\hat{\mathbf{X}}$ by deciphering this erroneous ciphertext $\hat{\mathbf{Y}}$. Our analysis for erroneous plaintext may be shown as follows:

$$x_0 = y_0 + s_2 + s_4 = 0 + 0 + 1 = 1$$

$$x_1 = y_1 + s_1 + s_3 = 1 + 0 + 1 = 0$$

$$x_2 = y_2 + y_0 + s_2 = 1 + 0 + 0 = 1$$

$$x_3 = y_3 + y_1 + s_1 = 0 + 1 + 0 = 1$$

$$x_4 = y_4 + y_2 + y_0 = 0 + 1 + 0 = 1$$

$$x_5 = y_5 + y_3 + y_1 = 0 + 0 + 1 = 1$$

$$x_6 = y_6 + y_4 + y_2 = 1 + 0 + 1 = 0$$

$$x_7 = y_7 + y_5 + y_3 = 1 + 0 + 0 = 1$$

Thus, the erroneous plaintext is recovered as $\hat{\mathbf{X}} = (1\ 0\ 1\ 1\ 1\ 1\ 0\ 1)$. Comparing the original plaintext $\mathbf{X} = (1\ 1\ 1\ 0\ 1\ 0\ 0\ 1)$ with $\hat{\mathbf{X}} = (1\ 0\ 1\ 1\ 1\ 1\ 0\ 1)$, the triple error is found, which is caused by one bit error in $\hat{\mathbf{Y}}$.

It is worthwhile to observe the error propagation patterns in the recovered plaintext $\hat{\mathbf{X}}$ corresponding to the erroneous ciphertext input $\hat{\mathbf{Y}}$. Table 4.3 shows the error distribution pattern of the ciphertext feedback mode.

■ **Example 4.20** Consider the error propagation problem of the self-synchronizing cipher with plaintext feedback as discussed in Examples 4.16 and 4.18. Referring to Fig. 4.19, the LFSR contains tap settings $\mathbf{T} = (0\ 1\ 0\ 1)$ and initial seeds $\mathbf{S} = (0\ 0\ 1\ 1)$. Let us explore the error propagation pattern in recovered plaintext corresponding to the erroneous ciphertext input $\hat{\mathbf{Y}}$ to Fig. 4.19. Referring to Fig. 4.18, the

Table 4.3 Error Distribution Pattern in $\hat{\mathbf{X}}$ with respect to a Single Error in $\hat{\mathbf{Y}}$ for Ciphertext Feedback Mode

Ciphertext input $\mathbf{Y}$	Ciphertext with single error $\hat{\mathbf{Y}}$	Error distribution in recovered plaintext $\hat{\mathbf{X}}$	Genuine plaintext $\mathbf{X}$
	*	* * *	
00100011	10100011	01000001	11101001
	*	* * *	
00100011	01100011	10111101	11101001
	*	* * *	
00100011	00000011	11000011	11101001
	*	* * *	
00100011	00110011	11111100	11101001
	*	* *	
00100011	00101011	11100011	11101001
	*	* *	
00100011	00100111	11101100	11101001
	*	*	
00100011	00100001	11101011	11101001
	*	*	
00100011	00100010	11101000	11101001

* indicates the error positions

Table 4.4 Error Propagation Pattern in $\hat{\mathbf{X}}$ corresponding to a Single Error in $\hat{\mathbf{Y}}$ for Plaintext Feedback Mode

Ciphertext input **Y**	Ciphertext with single error $\hat{\mathbf{Y}}$	Error distribution in recovered plaintext $\hat{\mathbf{X}}$	Genuine plaintext **X**
	*	* * *	
00011101	10011101	01001011	11101001
	*	* * *	
00011101	01011101	10111000	11101001
	*	* *	
00011101	00111101	11000001	11101001
	*	* *	
00011101	00001101	11111101	11101001
	*	* *	
00011101	00010101	11100011	11101001
	*	* *	
00011101	00011001	11101100	11101001
	*	*	
00011101	00011111	11101011	11101001
	*	*	
00011101	00011100	11101000	11101001

* denotes the error positions

ciphertext corresponding to plaintext **X** = (1 1 1 0 1 0 0 1) is **Y** = (0 0 0 1 1 1 0 1). Assuming that the second bit of **Y** is in error, that is, $\hat{\mathbf{Y}}$ = (0 1 0 1 1 1 0 1), the recovered plaintext bits can be found as follows:

$$
\begin{aligned}
x_0 &= y_0 + s_2 + s_4 = 0+0+1 = 1 \\
x_1 &= y_1 + s_1 + s_3 = 1+0+1 = 0 \qquad \text{(error)} \\
x_2 &= y_2 + x_0 + s_2 = 0+1+0 = 1 \\
x_3 &= y_3 + x_1 + s_1 = 1+0+0 = 1 \qquad \text{(error)} \\
x_4 &= y_4 + x_2 + x_0 = 1+1+1 = 1 \\
x_5 &= y_5 + x_3 + x_1 = 1+1+0 = 0 \\
x_6 &= y_6 + x_4 + x_2 = 0+1+1 = 0 \\
x_7 &= y_7 + x_5 + x_3 = 1+0+1 = 0 \qquad \text{(error)}
\end{aligned}
$$

Thus, the erroneous plaintext sequence is recovered as $\hat{\mathbf{X}}$ = (1 0 1 1 1 0 0 0), where a triple error occurs in $\hat{\mathbf{X}}$ at positions 2, 4 and 8.

The error propagation pattern in $\hat{\mathbf{X}}$ corresponding to the single-error ciphertext input $\hat{\mathbf{Y}}$ is tabulated in Table 4.4.

We are now in a position to illustrate that (i) in ciphertext autokey systems there is no error propagation beyond the corresponding block of recovered plaintext, and (ii) in plaintext autokey systems erroneous

Table 4.5 Error Propagation in $\hat{\mathbf{X}}$ for Plaintext Feedback Mode

Single error in first symbol (00011101) of **Y**	Error propagation in $\hat{\mathbf{X}}$						Number of errors in 48 bits
*	* * *	* * *	* *	* * *	* *	* *	
10011101	01001011	00100100	11000011	00011001	00111101	00010010	15
*	* * *	* * *	* *	* * *	* * *	* *	
01011101	10111000	11101011	11111111	11101010	11110010	00101110	16
*	* *	* * *	* * *	* *	* * *	* * *	
00111101	11000001	00001100	01100001	10010011	00010101	10110000	16
*	* *	* * *	* * *	* *	* * *	* * *	
00001101	11111101	11111111	10101110	10101111	11100110	01111111	16
*	* *	* *	* * *	* * *	* *	* * *	
00010101	11100011	10000110	01001001	00110001	10011111	10011000	15
*	* *	* *	* * *	* * *	* *	* * *	
00011001	11101100	10111010	10111010	11111110	10100011	01101011	15
*	*	* * *	* *	* * *	* * *	* *	
00011111	11101011	00100100	11000011	00011001	00111101	00010010	14
*	*	* * *	* *	* * *	* * *	* *	
00011100	11101000	11101011	11111111	11101010	11110010	00101110	14

* denotes the error position

bits in a ciphertext block will cause error propagation indefinitely in the recovered plaintext as can be seen in Example 4.21.

■ **Example 4.21** Consider the plaintext autokey cipher whose plaintext input is **X** = (11101001 10101110 11101011 10111011 10110111 00111010). The encipherment of **X** produces the ciphertext as **Y** = (00011101 01011111 10111111 11101110 11100001 10000111). The decipherment of **Y** without any error in it will be the legitimate plaintext **X** recovered. However, if a single error occurs in any 8-bit symbol of **Y**, then errors in the recovered **X** will propagate indefinitely starting from the corresponding symbol as shown in Table 4.5.

■ **Example 4.22** Consider the ciphertext autokey cipher whose plaintext input is **X** = (11101001 10101110 11101011 10111011 10110111 00111010). Enciphering **X** with the keystream produced from the ciphertext feedback, the ciphertext becomes **Y** = (00100011 01001000 01110000 10010111 00000110 11101111). Suppose a single error occurs in any 8-bit symbol of **Y**. Then the recovered plaintext **X** will contain the errors, but the error propagation is limited to only within a single 8-bit symbol block as shown in Table 4.6.

To conclude, autokey ciphers with ciphertext feedback have the advantage of no propagation of errors. A transmission error affecting one symbol block of **Y** does not affect subsequent symbol blocks in the

Table 4.6 Error Propagation in $\hat{\mathbf{X}}$ for Ciphertext Feedback Mode

Single error in first symbol (00100011) of **Y**	Error propagation in $\hat{\mathbf{X}}$					
*	* * *					
10100011	01000001	10101110	11101011	10111011	10110111	00111010
*	* * *					
01100011	10111101	10101110	11101011	10111011	10110111	00111010
*	* * *					
00000011	11000011	10101110	11101011	10111011	10110111	00111010
*	* * *					
00110011	11111100	10101110	11101011	10111011	10110111	00111010
*	* *					
00101011	11100011	10101110	11101011	10111011	10110111	00111010
*	* *					
00100111	11101100	10101110	11101011	10111011	10110111	00111010
*	*					
00100001	11101011	10101110	11101011	10111011	10110111	00111010
*	*					
00100010	11101000	10101110	11101011	10111011	10110111	00111010

* denotes the error positions

recovered plaintext **X**; whereas autokey ciphers with plaintext feedback have the disadvantage of indefinite error propagation in **X**.

4.4 NONLINEAR COMBINATIONS OF LFSR SEQUENCES

As the running key generators in stream ciphers, PN-sequences generated from LFSRs combined by some nonlinear function have been proposed by several cryptologists for crypto-applications. PN-sequences exhibit certain statistical properties and linear complexity. These properties are largely governed by the number of memory cells and the feedback connections in the shift register. Many proposed keystream generators consist of a number of maximum-length shift registers combined by a nonlinear function. The nonlinear function should destroy the linearity in such a manner that it gives the output sequence a large linear complexity. In fact, a single LFSR device has low linear complexity because it is easily analyzed. Therefore, many cryptologists have striven to find nonlinear combination techniques of LFSR sequences that will produce the output sequence with both good pseudo-random properties and high linear complexity. The purpose of nonlinear combinations is to produce an equivalent system which can withstand any cryptanalytic attack. In order to avoid correlation attacks, the combining function must be correlation-immune and the output sequence from the nonlinear combiner should also be statistically independent of the input sequences.

From among the many papers on nonlinear transformations of LFSR sequences, we shall introduce one typical method in the following.

4.4.1 Rueppel's Nonlinear Combiners

Many proposed keystream generators consist of a number of maximum-length shift registers combined in a linearly interconnected configuration. Consider an m-stage LFSR generating a binary sequence which is applied to a nonlinear filtering function f, as shown in Fig. 4.20. An m-stage LFSR with period $p = 2^m - 1$ is said to be a maximum-length shift register if it generates a PN-sequence. The nonlinear function is arbitrary but known. However, for purposes of filtering or combining, the nonlinear function must be used in order to avoid a cryptanalytic attack. Therefore, such a nonlinear function should be devised as to destroy linearity, so that the output sequence provides a large linear complexity.

Let s_0 denote the initial seed of LFSR and $\mathbf{Z} = (z_0, z_1, \ldots, z_{2^m-2})$ be the f-output vector during the first period of LFSR. There is then a unique correspondence between $\mathbf{Z}$ and the function f with respect to the m-stage LFSR's state vector $\mathbf{S} = (s_0, s_1, \ldots, s_{2^m-2})$ such that $z_0 = f(s_0)$, $z_1 = f(s_1), \ldots, z_{2^m-2} = f(s_{2^m-2})$ where all $2^m - 1$ consecutive states s_i for $0 \leq i \leq 2^m - 2$ are distinct and nonzero. Since there are 2^{2^m-1} different sequences of period $p = 2^m - 1$, the nonlinear function f may generate all those periodic sequences which have a linear complexity close to the period length.

■ **Example 4.23** Consider a five-stage LFSR and choose the primitive polynomial $G(D) = 1 + D^2 + D^5$ as its generator polynomial. Let the initial state be (1 1 1 1 0) which corresponds to the characteristic phase of the LFSR. Then a simple nonlinear keystream generator can be devised as shown in Fig. 4.20.

A nonlinear keystream generator must be secure cryptanalytically; it should be too complex to be analyzed. For achieving high unpredictability of the generated keystream, we develop a nonlinear theory of binary sequences which reflects directly the sum of k variable products in a Boolean function.

Let $f(x)$ be an arbitrary nonlinear function of the components of $\mathbf{X}$ such that

$$f(x) = a_0 + a_1x_1 + \cdots + a_nx_n + a_{12}x_1x_2 + \cdots + a_{n-1,n}x_{n-1}x_n$$

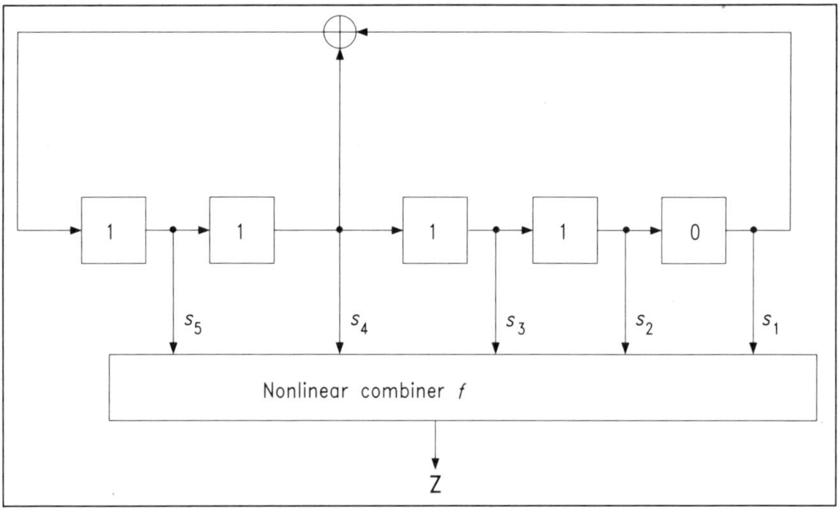

Fig. 4.20 A simple nonlinear generator (key output **Z** filtered by the nonlinear combiner)

$$+ a_{123}x_1x_2x_3 + \cdots + a_{n-2,n-1,n}x_{n-2}x_{n-1}x_n$$

$$\cdots\cdots\cdots\cdots\cdots\cdots\cdots\cdots\cdots\cdots\cdots\cdots$$

$$+ a_{12\cdots n}\, x_1x_2 \cdots x_n \tag{4.53}$$

where a product of k variables is called a kth order product. Thus, the order of $f(x)$ will be the maximum among the orders of its product terms.

■ **Example 4.24** Consider again the nonlinear keystream generator as devised in Fig. 4.20. Under the initial state vector (1 1 1 1 0), the five-stage LFSR with the tap (or generator) polynomial $G(D) = 1 + D^2 + D^5$ produces sequences corresponding to the individual terms s_i for $1 \le i \le 5$ over the period $p = 31$. According to Eq. 4.53, the output sequence **Z** of the nonlinear combiner is the sum of individual terms at each stage of the LFSR and their product terms over the first period as shown below:

$$Z = a_1s_1 + a_2s_2 + \cdots + a_5s_5 + a_{12}s_1s_2 + \cdots + a_{23}s_2s_3 + a_{34}s_3s_4 + a_{35}s_3s_5$$

$$+ a_{45}s_4s_5 + a_{123}s_1s_2s_3 + \cdots + a_{234}s_2s_3s_4 + \cdots + a_{345}s_3s_4s_5$$

$$+ a_{1234}s_1s_2s_3s_4 + \cdots + a_{2345}s_2s_3s_4s_5 + a_{12345}s_1s_2s_3s_4s_5 \tag{4.54}$$

There are exactly $2^m - 1$ coefficients (a_i's) and $2^m - 1$ vectors in Z which are arranged lexicographically. Equation 4.54 may be expressed in matrix form as

$$\mathbf{Z} = \mathbf{P}^T \cdot \mathbf{A} \tag{4.55}$$

where **P** denotes the matrix whose rows are formed by all the isolated product vectors and **A** the coefficient matrix. By shifting the five-stage LFSR of Fig. 4.20 cyclically to the right, the sequences $s_1, s_2, \ldots, s_5$ generated at each stage of the LFSR and their distinct product sequence are listed in Table 4.7.

Since the period is $p = 2^m - 1 = 31$ for $m = 5$, we factor $1 + D^{31}$ into irreducible polynomials such that

$$1 + D^{31} = (1 + D)(1 + D^2 + D^5)(1 + D^3 + D^5)(1 + D + D^2 + D^3 + D^5) \tag{4.56}$$

$$(1 + D + D^2 + D^4 + D^5)(1 + D + D^3 + D^4 + D^5)(1 + D^2 + D^3 + D^4 + D^5)$$

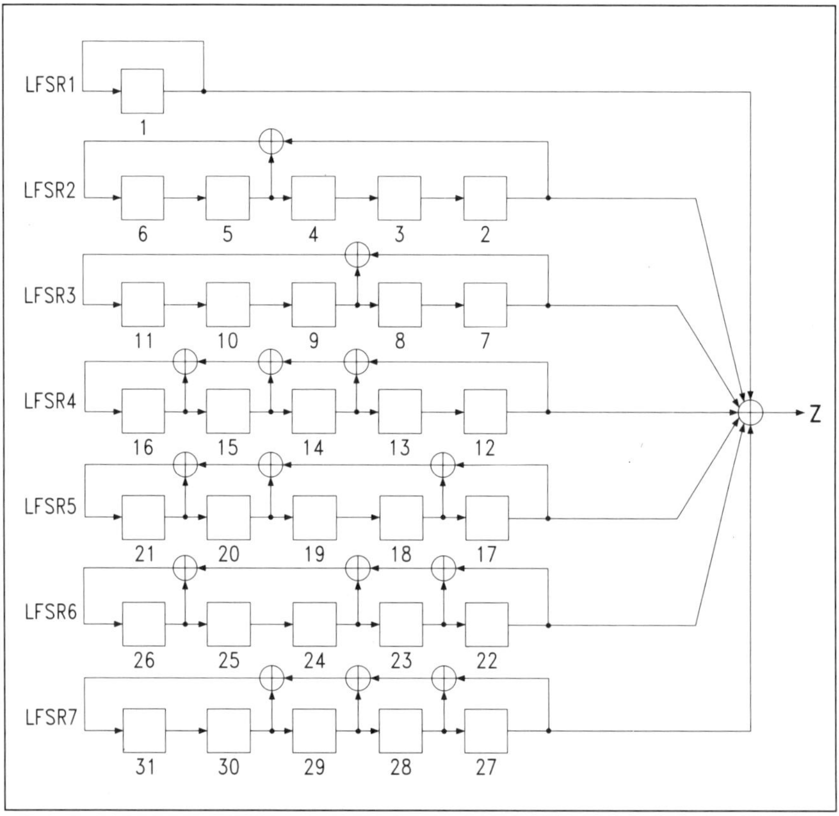

Fig. 4.21 The decomposed register bank sketched according to the factored generator polynomials

Consider the case where the 31-stage shift register is decomposed into seven distinct LFSRs having the seven different generator polynomials obtained in Eq. 4.56.

Consider next the structural properties of sequences having the period $p = 31$. Utilizing the factored polynomial in Eq. 4.56, the decomposed linear equivalent of the shift register of length 31 is sketched in Fig. 4.21. The 31 state locations in Fig. 4.21 are marked by consecutive numerals from LFSR1 through LFSR7. Consider each LFSR in the decomposed register bank. When any LFSR in the bank is derived by a single state bit $s_i = 1$ (for example, $i = 2, 3, 4, 5, 6$ for LFSR2), the register output will be five distinct and linearly independent sequences. For example,

State output					Register output
s_6	s_5	s_4	s_3	s_2	$\mathbf{u}_i$
0	0	0	0	1	$\mathbf{u}_2 = (1\,0\,0\,0\,0\,1 \cdots)$
1	0	0	0	0	
0	1	0	0	0	
1	0	1	0	0	
0	1	0	1	0	
1	0	1	0	1	
		⋅			
		⋅			
		⋅			
0	0	0	1	0	$\mathbf{u}_3 = (0\,1\,0\,0\,0\,0\,1 \cdots)$
0	0	0	0	1	
1	0	0	0	0	
0	1	0	0	0	
1	0	1	0	0	
0	1	0	1	0	
1	0	1	0	1	
		⋅			
		⋅			
		⋅			
		etc.			

Thus, the 31 distinct and linearly independent sequences can be produced by a single state s_i at any of the 31 possible state locations. Therefore, any 31-dimensional output vector can be expressed as

$$\mathbf{Z} = s_1\mathbf{u}_1 + s_2\mathbf{u}_2 + \cdots + s_{31}\mathbf{u}_{31} \tag{4.57}$$

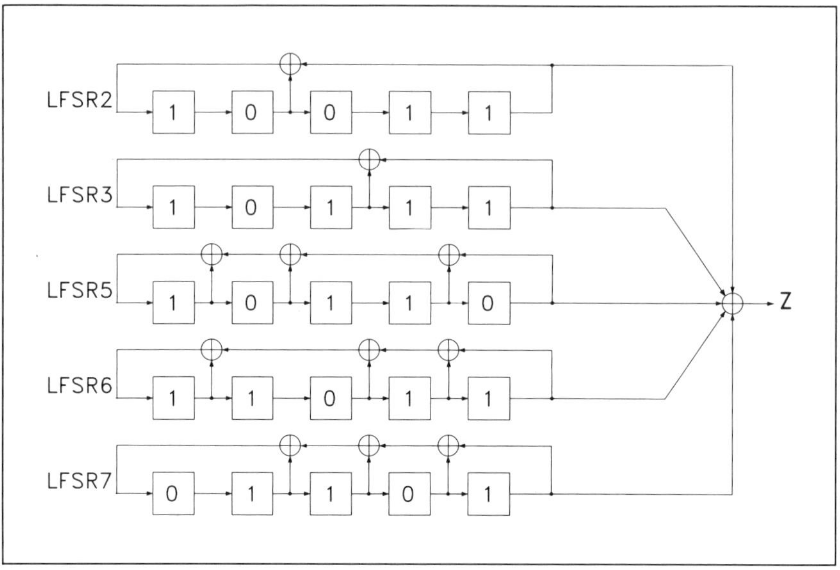

Fig. 4.22 The decomposed register bank based on the coin sequence **Z** of Eq. 4.59

Also, Eq. 4.57 may be expressed in matrix form as

$$\mathbf{Z} = \mathbf{U}^T \cdot \mathbf{S} \tag{4.58}$$

where $\mathbf{U}^T$ denotes the 31 × 31 transposed matrix whose row vectors are $\mathbf{u}_1, \mathbf{u}_2, \cdots, \mathbf{u}_{31}$ and **S** the initial loading of the 31 memory cells in the decomposed register bank. The $\mathbf{u}_i$ vectors corresponding to the state bit $s_i = 1$ are listed in Table 4.8.

The nonlinear combiner forms the specific nonlinear function which produces an output sequence **Z** of period $p = 2^m - 1$. The decomposed linear equivalent determines not only the linear complexity of **Z**, but finds which of the factored polynomials contribute to the production of **Z**. Consider 31 trials of coin tossing. Then one possible outcome may result in the following sequence of period 31.

$$\mathbf{Z} = (0\,0\,1\,0\,0\,1\,1\,1\,0\,0\,1\,0\,1\,1\,1\,1\,0\,0\,1\,1\,1\,0\,1\,0\,0\,0\,1\,0\,1\,0\,1) \tag{4.59}$$

We use Eq. 4.58 to determine the initial state vector as follows.

$$\mathbf{S} = (\mathbf{U}^T)^{-1} \cdot \mathbf{Z} \tag{4.60}$$

Using Eq. 4.59 and the 31 × 31 matrix **U** in Table 4.8, we can easily compute the initial state vector as

$$\mathbf{S} = (\underline{0}\,1\,1\,0\,0\,1\,1\,1\,1\,0\,1\,\underline{0\,0\,0\,0\,0}\,0\,1\,1\,0\,1\,1\,1\,0\,1\,1\,1\,0\,1\,1\,0) \tag{4.61}$$

Table 4.7 Individual Stage Sequences from LFSR and their Product Sequences for the 31-Dimensional Vector **Z**

Individual output sequence of **Z**	First period vector corresponding to output sequences
s_1	0111110011010010000101011101100
s_2	1111100110100100001010111011000
s_3	1111001101001000010101110110001
s_4	1110011010010000101011101100011
s_5	1100110100100001010111011000111
s_{12}	0111100010000000000000011001000
s_{13}	0111000001000000000101010100000
s_{14}	0110010010010000000001001100000
s_{15}	0100110000000000000101011000100
s_{23}	1111000100000000000000110010000
s_{24}	1110000010000000001010101000000
s_{25}	1100100100100000000010011000000
s_{34}	1110001000000000000001100100001
s_{35}	1100000100000000000101010000001
s_{45}	1100010000000000000011001000011
s_{123}	0111000000000000000000010000000
s_{124}	0110000010000000000000001000000
s_{125}	0100100000000000000000011000000
s_{134}	0110000000000000000001000100000
s_{135}	0100000000000000000101010000000
s_{145}	0100010000000000000001001000000
s_{234}	1110000000000000000000100000000
s_{235}	1100000100000000000000010000000
s_{245}	1100000000000000000010001000000
s_{345}	1100000000000000000001000000001
s_{1234}	0110000000000000000000000000000
s_{1235}	0100000000000000000000010000000
s_{1245}	0100000000000000000000001000000
s_{1345}	0100000000000000000001000000000
s_{2345}	1100000000000000000000000000000
s_{12345}	0100000000000000000000000000000

Note: s_{ijk} denotes the product $s_i\, s_j\, s_k$

Observing Eq. 4.61, the underlined digits represent $s_1 = 0$ and $s_{12} = s_{13} = \cdots = s_{16} = 0$. Therefore, we see that LFSR1 and LFSR4 in the decomposed register bank contribute nothing to the generation of the output sequence **Z**. As a result, the linear complexity of the coin-tossing sequence **Z** becomes only 25; and the decomposed register bank of Fig. 4.21 is reduced to Fig. 4.22.

Table 4.8 $\mathbf{u}_i$ Vector Corresponding to State Bit $s_i = 1$

State bit s_i	$\mathbf{u}_i$ vector corresponding to s_i
s_1	1 1 1 1 1 1 1 1 1 1 1 1 1 1 1 1 1 1 1 1 1 1 1 1 1 1 1 1 1 1 1
s_2	1 0 0 0 0 1 0 1 0 1 1 1 0 1 1 0 0 0 1 1 1 1 1 0 0 1 1 0 1 0,0
s_3	0 1 0 0 0 0 1 0 1 0 1 1 1 0 1 1 0 0 0 1 1 1 1 1 0 0 1 1 0 1 0
s_4	0 0 1 0 0 0 0 1 0 1 0 1 1 1 0 1 1 0 0 0 1 1 1 1 1 0 0 1 1 0 1
s_5	0 0 0 1 0 1 0 1 1 1 0 1 1 0 0 0 1 1 1 1 1 0 0 1 1 0 1 0 0 1 0
s_6	0 0 0 0 1 0 1 0 1 1 1 0 1 1 0 0 0 1 1 1 1 1 0 0 1 1 0 1 0 0 1
s_7	1 0 0 0 0 1 0 0 1 0 1 1 0 0 1 1 1 1 1 0 0 0 1 1 0 1 1 1 0 1 0
s_8	0 1 0 0 0 0 1 0 0 1 0 1 1 0 0 1 1 1 1 1 0 0 0 1 1 0 1 1 1 0 1
s_9	0 0 1 0 0 1 0 1 1 0 0 1 1 1 1 1 0 0 0 1 1 0 1 1 1 0 1 0 1 0 0
s_{10}	0 0 0 1 0 0 1 0 1 1 0 0 1 1 1 1 1 0 0 0 1 1 0 1 1 1 0 1 0 1 0
s_{11}	0 0 0 0 1 0 0 1 0 1 1 0 0 1 1 1 1 1 0 0 0 1 1 0 1 1 1 0 1 0 1
s_{12}	1 0 0 0 0 1 1 0 0 1 0 0 1 1 1 1 1 0 1 1 1 0 0 0 1 0 1 0 1 1 0
s_{13}	0 1 0 0 0 0 1 1 0 0 1 0 0 1 1 1 1 1 0 1 1 1 0 0 0 1 0 1 0 1 1
s_{14}	0 0 1 0 0 1 1 1 1 1 0 1 1 1 0 0 0 1 0 1 0 1 1 0 1 0 0 0 0 1 1
s_{15}	0 0 0 1 0 1 0 1 1 0 1 0 0 0 0 1 1 0 0 1 0 0 1 1 1 1 1 0 1 1 1
s_{16}	0 0 0 0 1 1 0 0 1 0 0 1 1 1 1 1 0 1 1 1 0 0 0 1 0 1 0 1 1 0 1
s_{17}	1 0 0 0 0 1 1 0 1 0 1 0 0 1 0 0 0 1 0 1 1 1 1 1 0 1 1 0 0 1 1
s_{18}	0 1 0 0 0 1 0 1 1 1 1 1 0 1 1 0 0 1 1 1 0 0 0 0 1 1 0 1 0 1 0
s_{19}	0 0 1 0 0 0 1 0 1 1 1 1 1 0 1 1 0 0 1 1 1 0 0 0 0 1 1 0 1 0 1
s_{20}	0 0 0 1 0 1 1 1 1 1 0 1 1 0 0 1 1 1 0 0 0 0 1 1 0 1 0 1 0 0 1
s_{21}	0 0 0 0 1 1 0 1 0 1 0 0 1 0 0 0 1 0 1 1 1 1 1 0 1 1 0 0 1 1 1
s_{22}	1 0 0 0 0 1 1 1 0 0 1 1 0 1 1 1 1 1 0 1 0 0 0 1 0 0 1 0 1 0 1
s_{23}	0 1 0 0 0 1 0 0 1 0 1 0 1 1 0 0 0 0 1 1 1 0 0 1 1 0 1 1 1 1 1
s_{24}	0 0 1 0 0 1 0 1 0 1 1 0 0 0 0 1 1 1 0 0 1 1 0 1 1 1 1 1 0 1 0
s_{25}	0 0 0 1 0 0 1 0 1 0 1 1 0 0 0 0 1 1 1 0 0 1 1 0 1 1 1 1 1 0 1
s_{26}	0 0 0 0 1 1 1 0 0 1 1 0 1 1 1 1 1 0 1 0 0 0 1 0 0 1 0 1 0 1 1
s_{27}	1 0 0 0 0 1 0 1 1 0 1 0 1 0 0 0 1 1 1 0 1 1 1 1 1 0 0 1 0 0 1
s_{28}	0 1 0 0 0 1 1 1 0 1 1 1 1 1 0 0 1 0 0 1 1 0 0 0 0 1 0 1 1 0 1
s_{29}	0 0 1 0 0 1 1 0 0 0 0 1 0 1 1 0 1 0 1 0 0 0 1 1 1 0 1 1 1 1 1
s_{30}	0 0 0 1 0 1 1 0 1 0 1 0 0 0 1 1 1 0 1 1 1 1 1 0 0 1 0 0 1 1 0
s_{31}	0 0 0 0 1 0 1 1 0 1 0 1 0 0 0 1 1 1 0 1 1 1 1 1 0 0 1 0 0 1 1

Deleting the tap polynomials $G_1(D) = 1 + D$ for LFSR1 and $G_4(D) = 1 + D + D^2 + D^4 + D^5$ for LFSR4 from Eq. 4.56 yields the equivalent generator polynomial representing the decomposed register bank illustrated in Fig. 4.22. That is

$$G(D) = (1 + D^2 + D^5)(1 + D^3 + D^5)(1 + D + D^2 + D^4 + D^5)$$
$$(1 + D + D^3 + D^4 + D^5)(1 + D^2 + D^3 + D^4 + D^5)$$
$$= 1 + D^4 + D^5 + D^6 + D^8 + D^{10} + D^{13} + D^{15} + D^{16} + D^{17} + D^{18}$$
$$+ D^{21} + D^{22} + D^{24} + D^{25} \tag{4.62}$$

By loading initially the coin sequence **Z** into a 25-stage shift register having the tap generator $G(D)$ of Eq. 4.62, we can obtain the linear equivalent as shown in Fig. 4.23.

Now the problem is reduced to that of determining a nonlinear function f which can produce the coin sequence of Eq. 4.59. In order to compute the coefficient vector **A** of a nonlinear function f, we use Eq. 4.55 such that

$$\mathbf{A} = (\mathbf{P}^T)^{-1} \cdot \mathbf{Z} \tag{4.63}$$

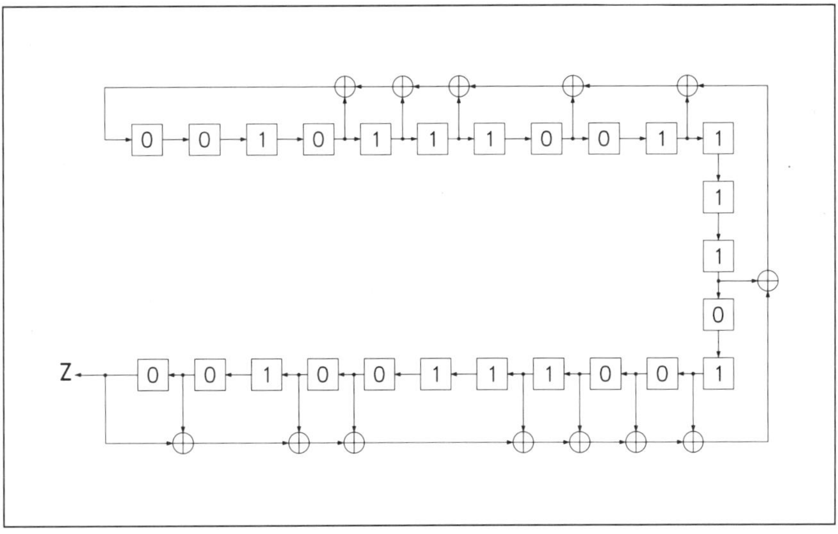

Fig. 4.23 The linear equivalent register associated with the coin sequence **Z**

Using Eq. 4.59 and the 31 × 31 matrix **P** in Table 4.7, the coefficient vector can be computed as

$$\mathbf{A} = (1\,1\,1\,0\,1\,0\,0\,1\,1\,1\,0\,1\,0\,0\,1\,0\,1\,1\,1\,1\,0\,0\,0\,1\,0\,0\,1\,0\,0\,1\,0) \tag{4.64}$$

which allows us to write the algebraic form of f such that

$$\begin{aligned} f(s_1, s_2, s_3, s_4, s_5) &= s_1 + s_2 + s_3 + s_5 + s_1s_4 + s_1s_5 + s_2s_3 \\ &\quad + s_2s_5 + s_4s_5 + s_1s_2s_4 + s_1s_2s_5 + s_1s_3s_4 \\ &\quad + s_1s_3s_5 + s_2s_4s_5 + s_1s_2s_3s_5 + s_2s_3s_4s_5 \end{aligned} \tag{4.65}$$

Thus, combining Eq. 4.65 with the stages of the driving LFSR, we can devise the nonlinear generator associated with the coin sequence of Eq. 4.59 as shown in Fig. 4.24.

So far, we have had some limitations in driving the decomposed register bank and the nonlinear generator because an arbitrary (coin) sequence **Z** was selected prior to the analysis. What the cryptanalysist wants to do is to find a method which can specify the linear complexity of a sequence and then obtain a nonlinear function that produces a sequence of the specified linear complexity.

Coupling Eqs 4.58 and 4.63 yields

$$\mathbf{A} = (\mathbf{P}^T)^{-1}\,\mathbf{U}^T\,\mathbf{S} = (\mathbf{UP}^{-1})^T\,\mathbf{S} \tag{4.66}$$

where $\mathbf{UP}^{-1}$ is a 31 × 31 matrix whose rows correspond to coefficient (or tap) vectors $\mathbf{a}_i$ of nonlinear functions f associated with the state bits s_i = 1. Using matrix **P** in Table 4.7 and matrix **U** in Table 4.8, Eq. 4.66 can be calculated by a computer as shown in Table 4.9. Multiplying $(\mathbf{UP}^{-1})^T$ by the initial state vector **S**, we obtain the coefficient vector **A** which defines the nonlinear function f. If this function is connected to the driving LFSR's stages, we can obtain the desired nonlinear LFSR. The activating polynomial $G_i(D)$ is the tap polynomial of the decomposed linear equivalent of the sequence produced by $\mathbf{a}_i$ coupled with the driving LFSR. For example, if we select row 17 of $\mathbf{UP}^{-1}$ in Table 4.9, then the nonlinear generator defined by the driving LFSR and the nonlinear coefficient vector $\mathbf{a}_{17}$ exhibits the behavior of the LFSR with the tap polynomial $G_{17} = 1 + D + D^2 + D^4 + D^5$ and the initial state (0 0 0 0 1), as shown in Fig. 4.25. Thus, we see that the components s_2, $s_1\,s_2$, $s_2\,s_4$, $s_3\,s_4$, $s_3\,s_5$ and $s_4\,s_5$, contribute only to the nonlinear coefficient vector $\mathbf{a}_{17}$. Similarly, any member register in the decomposed register bank can be easily transformed into the nonlinear generator as discussed above.

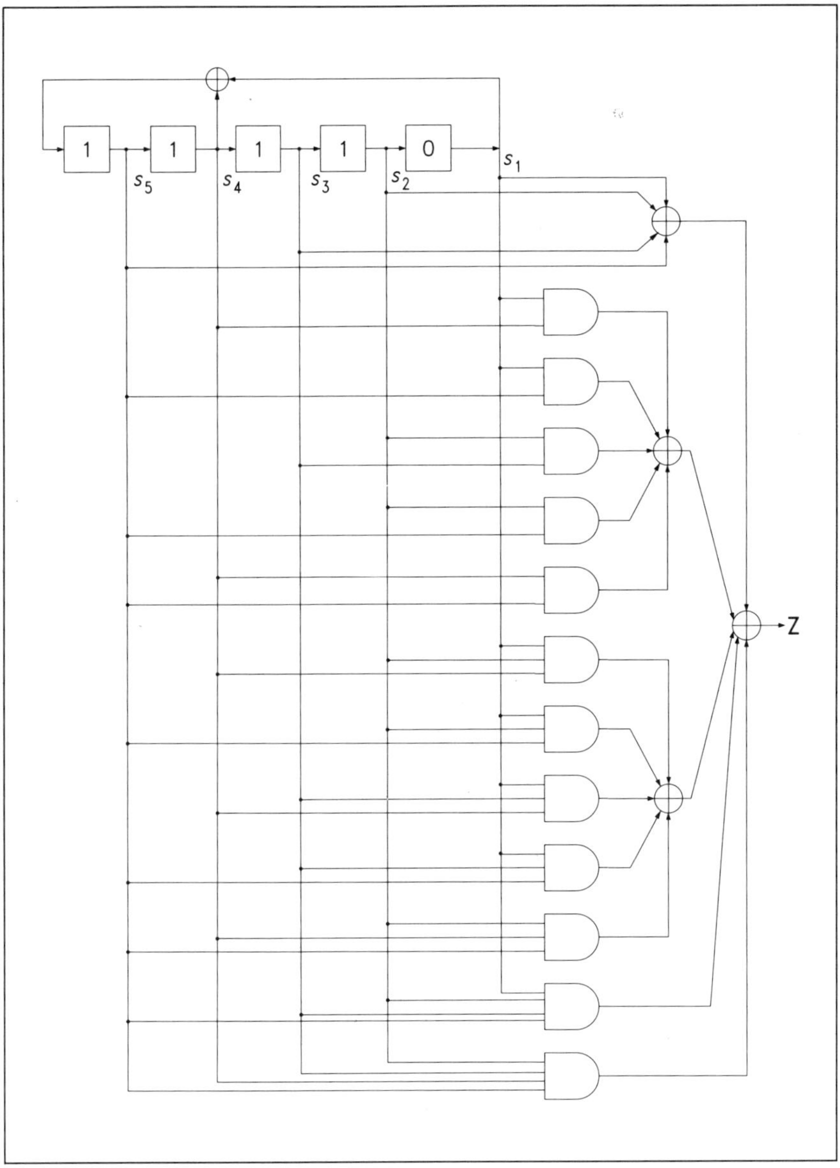

Fig. 4.24 The nonlinear key generator associated with the coin sequence **Z**

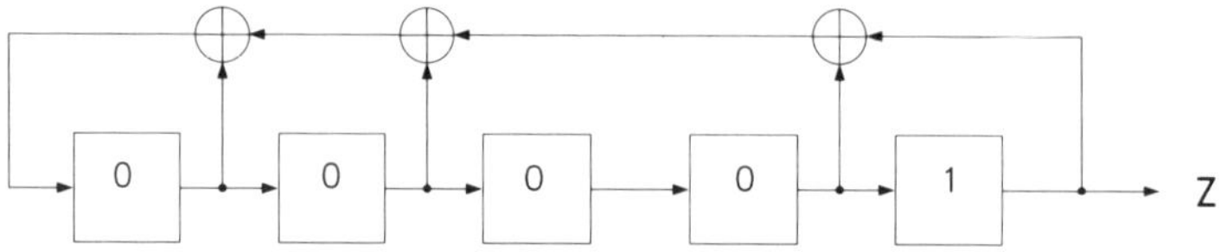

(a) LSFR with the activating tap polynomial $G_{17} = 1 + D + D^2 + D^4 + D^5$ and the initial contents $\mathbf{S} = (0\,0\,0\,0\,1)$

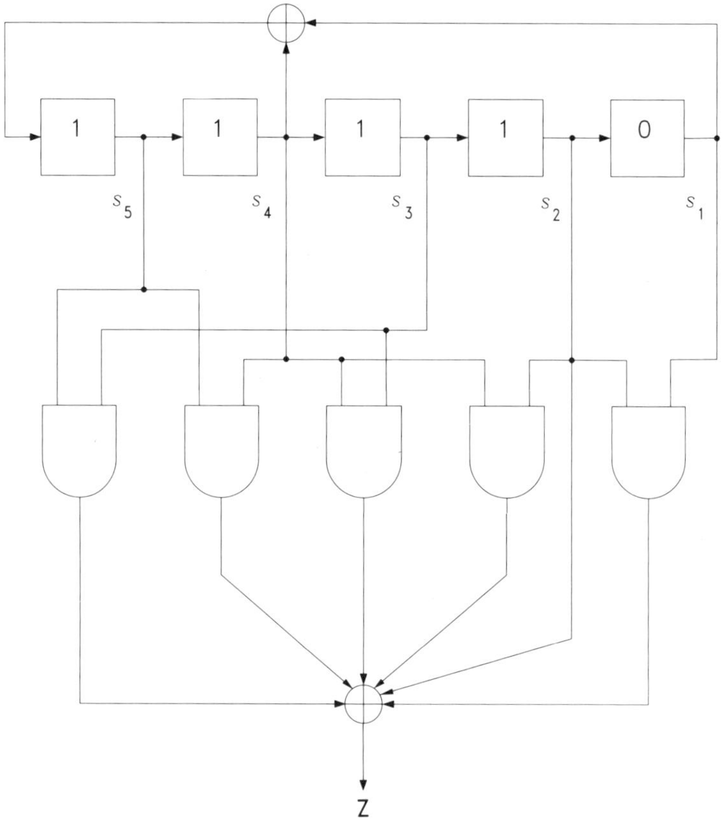

(b) Nonlinear generator devised by the driving LSFR and the coefficient vector $\mathbf{G}_{17}$

Fig. 4.25 Nonlinear generator equivalent to LFSR with $G_{17} = 1 + D + D^2 + D^4 + D^5$

Table 4.9 Coefficient Vector $\mathbf{a}_i$ in the 31 × 31 Matrix $\mathbf{UP}^{-1}$

Activating polynomial $G_i(D)$	State bit s_i	Matrix $\mathbf{UP}^{-1}$, each row of which represents coefficient vector $\mathbf{a}_i$ corresponding to state bit s_i
$1+D$	1	11111 1111111111 1111111111 11111 1
$1+D^2+D^5$	2	11000 0000000000 0000000000 00000 0
	3	10101 0000000000 0000000000 00000 0
	4	01111 0000000000 0000000000 00000 0
	5	00110 0000000000 0000000000 00000 0
	6	01100 0000000000 0000000000 00000 0
$1+D^3+D^5$	7	10011 0110100101 1000100010 11001 0
	8	00111 1000001110 0011001010 01100 0
	9	11101 0001110101 0001110110 01111 0
	10	11111 1100000101 0100000111 00111 0
	11	11011 0001001100 0100100000 10011 0
$1+D+D^2+D^3+D^5$	12	11111 0101110101 1001000001 00000 0
	13	11011 1100101001 1010001100 00000 0
	14	01100 1010011001 1110010001 00000 0
	15	00011 0010110111 0010111000 00000 0
	16	11101 1001000111 0000011010 00000 0
$1+D+D^2+D^4+D^5$	17	01000 1000010111 0000000000 00000 0
	18	11000 1001100011 0000000000 00000 0
	19	10101 1101010001 0000000000 00000 0
	20	00111 1001111110 0000000000 00000 0
	21	00110 0011100010 0000000000 00000 0
$1+D+D^3+D^4+D^5$	22	11011 0111001000 1010100001 00000 0
	23	01100 0101100111 0001110011 00000 0
	24	00011 1111110101 1011100110 00000 0
	25	00010 1001101011 1110011110 00000 0
	26	11111 1100011101 1100010000 00000 0
$1+D^2+D^3+D^4+D^5$	27	00110 1110101001 0000000000 00000 0
	28	01110 0001000111 0000000000 00000 0
	29	11010 1110011000 0000000000 00000 0
	30	10011 1101000011 0000000000 00000 0
	31	00011 0101111001 0000000000 00000 0

Observing matrix $\mathbf{UP}^{-1}$ in Table 4.9, the right entries with respect to the dashed line are all zeros, but correspond to a higher order nonlinearity than the left entries. Therefore, the dashed line indicates how much nonlinearity contributes towards activating any of the LFSRs in the decomposed register bank. With the driving LFSR with $G(D) = 1 + D^2 + D^5$, we only need linear logic to activate $G_2(D) = 1 + D^2 + D^5$, second-order logic to activate $G_5(D) = 1 + D + D^2 + D^4 + D^5$ and $G_7(D) = 1 + D^2 + D^3 + D^4 + D^5$, third-order logic to activate $G_4(D) = 1 + D + D^2 + D^3 + D^5$ and $G_6(D) = 1 + D + D^3 + D^4 + D^5$, fourth-order logic to activate $G_3(D) = 1 + D^3 + D^5$, and finally $G_1(D) = 1 + D$ can only be activated by fifth-order logic. Referring to Table 4.9 again, if the second-order function f is applied to the driving LFSR with $G(D) = 1 + D^2 + D^5$, then we know certainly that $G_1(D)$, $G_3(D)$, $G_4(D)$, and $G_6(D)$ do not contribute to the linear complexity of the produced sequence **Z**. But $G_2(D)$, $G_5(D)$ and $G_7(D)$ surely contribute to the linear complexity of the produced sequence.

Since the factored polynomials of $1 + D^{2^m - 1}$ have degree either m or 1, as seen from Eq. 4.56, it is possible to represent any linear complexity between 0 and $2^m - 1$ as the degree of a product of three polynomials. For example, with the aid of Table 4.9, it can be shown that the produced sequence **Z** has a linear complexity between 0 and 31. The linear complexities for a nonlinear combiner filtering a maximum-length LFSR of prime length m have the form of μm or $\mu m + 1$ where $0 \le \mu \le (2^m - 2)/m$. The problem is to find the nonlinear functions f which produce sequences having legitimate linear complexity. However, it must be borne in mind that the order of the nonlinear function f is correlated with the linear complexity of the produced sequence **Z**. But the uncertainty about actual linear complexity needs to be studied further, and can only be resolved by acquiring additional structural information about f or the generated sequence **Z**.

4.4.2 Tutorial Reviews on PN Property and Linear Complexity

Pseudonoise sequences generated by combinations of linear feedback shift registers (LFSR) with some nonlinear function have been proposed for cryptographic applications as running-key generators. A running-key generator consists of n driving linear feedback shift registers and a nonlinear function f operating on the n input sequences in order to produce the running key **Z**. Some of the generating polynomials specifying the feedback connection of the register yield maximum-length sequences. Maximum-length sequences exhibit good statistical pseudorandom properties. These noise-like sequences have been used in various stream cipher crypto-applications. The drawback with a linear shift register sequence is that it can be easily analyzed by solving a system of $2m$ linear equations, where m is the length of the shift register. In fact, the number of unknown variables in the system of linear equations can be uniquely determined by solving $2m$ linear equations. In order to rectify such a drawback, considerable research on nonlinear arrangements of linear shift register sequences has been done employing certain methodologies such that the output sequences exhibit both good pseudorandom properties and high linear complexity. Linear complexity is the degree of the generating polynomial for the shortest linear feedback shift register that can generate that sequence.

For the stream cipher system to be secure, the key stream must be unpredictable. A necessary requirement for unpredictability is a long period of the key stream. For the key stream to be unpredictable, it is necessary that its linear complexity be large. The most fundamental basis for estimating the unpredictability of a key stream is linear complexity. Since the period of a key sequence is always at least as large as its linear complexity, a large complexity implies a large period.

Geffe [6] introduced the concept of a nonlinear combination of shift registers whose model is a multiplexer arrangement using three registers. This configuration seems to be a rather nice arrangement and results in a sequence with good statistical properties and high linear complexity. Hurd [12] presented the linear interconnection of several short shift registers in a linear manner in such a way that different widely spaced phase shifts of the same pseudorandom sequence appeared in the stages of the several registers. He also discussed some algorithms for efficiently generating pseudorandom sequences in both software and hardware implementations. Maritsas, Arvillias, and Bounas [19] proposed a systematic method for the analysis and synthesis of pseudorandom number generators based on linearly interconnected shift registers; this is similar to Hurd's structure. They proposed various configurations of the phase-shifted pseudorandom sequence generator, and presented a case study to demonstrate the procedure for proper algorithm operation. Brüer [3] presented new models for nonlinear combinations of linear shift register sequences, and analyzed the linear complexity and statistical pseudorandomness of the proposed combination. In a sequel, he proved that the linear complexity of the proposed system was higher than that of Geffe's system. The linear complexity profile of binary sequences has become a widely accepted tool for the assessment of keystream sequences in the context of stream ciphers. The linear complexity of a sequence is defined by the shortest LFSR that generates it. If a sequence has small linear complexity, then the synthesis of a linear equivalent of the sequence generator becomes computationally feasible. Jennings [13] introduced the multiplexed sequence for many practical key stream generators. The periodicity and minimum polynomial of the multiplexed sequence were analyzed. He also derived some results obtained from the autocorrelation function of the multiplexed sequence. Lempel and Eastman [16] proposed a construction employing at the most k linear shift registers of degree n or less, operated at a given rate R, which makes possible the generation of any given maximal length sequence at the rate kR. The proposed construction is of special significance for such fast rates where the cost of a single shift register capable of operating at the rate kR is much higher than just k times the cost of one operable rate R. Lai [15] established the necessary and sufficient condition for a feedback shift register over a general finite field to be nonsingular.

Siegenthaler [34] presented the correlation attack to break nonlinear feedback shift registers and demonstrated the validity of his analysis by comparison of computer and theoretical results based on statistical models for Geffe's and Brüer's systems and Pless's nonlinear system. The number of trials to find the key sequences can be reduced significantly in these cases where a cross-correlation exists between the input and output of the combining function f in the pseudonoise (PN) generator. The PN-generator should be constructed using nonlinear functions f which have the property that the output $\mathbf{Z}$ is uncorrelated to all input $\mathbf{X}_i$ to the nonlinear function f. The mth order correlation-immunity means that there is no statistical dependency between the output and any of the m inputs. Thus, the concept of mth order correlation-immunity for combining functions was introduced as a means to counter such correlation attack. Therefore, to withstand a correlation attack, the output sequence of the PN-generator and the sequences generated by the LFSRs should be uncorrelated. Of course, the input sequences should be assumed to be independent of each other. Siegenthaler showed that several running-key generators employing nonlinear functions which had statistical dependency between simple input and output streams were vulnerable to the so-called "divide-and-conquer" attacks using the correlation technique. He also proposed a method which ensured that divide-and-conquer attacks on such PN-generators were prevented. His method stimulated some interest in the nonlinear functions which could resist the correlation attack. He also proposed the concept of the mth order correlation-immunity of nonlinear combining functions for cryptographic application. If a Boolean function is found to be mth order correlation-immune, it means that there is no statistical dependency between the output sequence and any subset of m input sequences of a nonlinear function, provided the input sequences are independent of each other and uniformly distributed. Unfortunately for such memoryless combining functions, there exists a tradeoff between the attainable nonlinear order and the attainable level of correlation-immunity. In fact, the greater the correlation-immunity, the smaller is the nonlinear order of the function f and consequently the smaller is the linear complexity of the running-key. Rueppel [30] showed that this inconvenient tradeoff can be avoided by a proper use of memory in the nonlinear combining function, and demonstrated that integer addition, which is an extremely nonlinear operation when considered over GF (2), defines inherently a maximally correlation-immune combiner. Moreover, he proposed that a key stream generator employing integer addition in random-sequence generation attains high linear complexity and avoids correlation attacks.

Linear shift registers are clocked regularly, while some clock-controlled shift registers are clocked in an irregular manner under the control of the other registers for achieving higher linear complexity and good pseudorandom characteristics. An obvious arrangement of clock-controlled shift registers is cascade, where all registers except the first are clock-controlled by their predecessors. Early results on the linear complexity of the clock-controlled shift registers were given by Nyffeler [23]. In about 1984 several cryptanalysts realized simultaneously how easy it is to obtain huge linear complexity from clock-controlled shift registers. The algebraic foundations of the underlying theory have been traced back by Smeets. Smeets [35] dealt with two types of clock-controlled shift registers, as suggested by P. Nyffeler. For one of these types, sufficient conditions for maximal linear complexity are given. Gollman [8] presented a cascade connection of clock-controlled shift registers which was used as a generator of pseudorandom sequence, and proved that any output sequence of the cascade connection has a period p^n, where p is the length of the shift register, and that linear recursion can be computed directly from the initial state of the shift register. Vogel [36] presented two types of cascaded coupled sequence generators, to achieve large linear complexity. Letting one linear feedback shift register clock a second LFSR is an implicit method of generating nonlinear effects. Sequence generators of the first type work as follows: The shift register 1 (SR1) is shifted with every clock. If the output of SR1 is "1", the shift register 2 (SR2) is shifted and the output bit is derived from the first stage of SR2. If the output of SR1 is "0", SR2 is not shifted and the output sequence is "0". Sequence generators of the second type work in the following manner: If the output of SR1 is "1", SR2 is shifted and the output of SR2 is used for that of the sequence generator. Otherwise, SR2 is not shifted and the previously generated bit of SR2 is used as the output bit. For the second type of sequence generator, if the cascade sequence generators consist of n registers of length m, then the linear complexity is greater than $m(2^m - 1)^{n-1}$ and the period of this sequence is $2^m - 1$. For the first type, the lower bound for the linear complexity is $m(2^m - 1)$. The linear complexity for cascaded configurations using three or five LFSRs, was also analyzed in Vogel's work.

REFERENCES

1. Arvillias, A.C. and D.G. Martisas: "Combinational logic-free realization for high-speed m-sequence generation", *Electronic Letters*, vol. 13, No. 17, pp. 500–502, 1977.
2. Beker, H. and F. Piper: *Cipher Systems: The Protection of Communications*, Wiley, New York, 1982.
3. Brüer, J.O.: "On nonlinear combinations of linear shift register sequences", *Proc. IEEE Int. Symp. Inform. Theory*, Les Ares, France, June 21–25, 1982.
4. Chambers, W.G. and D. Gollmann: "Lock-in effect in cascades of clock-controlled shift-registers", *Proc. Eurocrypt' 88*, Springer LNCS 330, pp 331–342, 1988.
5. Chambers, W.G. and S.M. Jennings: "Linear equivalence of certain BRM shift-register sequences", *Electronic Letters*, vol. 20, pp 1018–1019, Nov. 1984.
6. Geffe, P.R.: "How to protect data with ciphers that are really hard to break", *Electronics*, pp 99–101, Jan. 4, 1973.
7. Golic, J.D.: "On the linear complexity of functions of periodic GF (q) sequences", *IEEE Trans. Inform Theory*, vol. 35, no. 1, Jan. 1989.
8. Gollman, D.: "Pseudorandom properties of cascade connections of clock controlled shift registers", *Proc. Eurocrypt' 84*, pp 93–98, 1984.
9. Golomb, S.W.: *Shift Register Sequences*, Holden-Day, San Francisco, CA, 1967.
10. Groth, E.J.: "Generation of binary sequences with controllable complexity", *IEEE Trans. Inform. Theory*, vol. IT–17, 1971.
11. Herlestam, T.: "On the complexity of functions of linear shift register sequences", *Proc. IEEE Int. Symp. Inform. Theory*, Les Ares, France, June 21–25, 1982.
12. Hurd, W.J.: "Efficient generation of statistically good pseudonoise by linearly interconnected shift registers", *IEEE Trans. Computers*, vol. C–23, pp 146–152, Feb. 1974.
13. Jennings, S.M.: "Autocorrelation function of the multiplexed sequence", *IEEE Proc.*, vol. 131, Part F, No. 2, Apr. 1984.

14. Key, E.L.: "An analysis of the structure and complexity of nonlinear binary sequence generators", *IEEE Trans. Inform. Theory*, vol. IT–22, pp 732–736, 1976.
15. Lai, X.: "Condition for the nonsingularity of a feedback shift register over a general finite field", *IEEE Trans. Inform. Theory*, Correspondence, vol. IT–33, no. 5, pp 747–749, 1987.
16. Lempel, A. and W.L. Eastman: "High-speed generation of maximal length sequences", *IEEE Trans. Computers*, Short Notes, vol. C–20, pp 227–229, 1971.
17. Lempel, A. and J. Ziv: "On the complexity of finite sequences", *IEEE Trans. Inform. Theory*, vol. IT–22, no. 1, pp 75–81, Jan. 1976.
18. Maritsas, D.G.: "The autocorrelation function of the two feedback shift register pseudorandom source", *IEEE Trans. Computers*, vol. C–22, pp 962–964, Oct. 1973.
19. Maritsas, D., A. Arvillias, and A. Bounas: "Phase-shift analysis of linear feedback shift register structures generating pseudorandom sequences", *IEEE Trans. Computers*, vol. C–27, No. 7, July 1978.
20. Massey, J.L. and R.A. Rueppel: "Linear ciphers and random sequence generators with multiple clocks", *Eurocrypt' 84*, Paris, pp 74–87, 1984.
21. Meir, W. and O. Staffelback: "Fast correlation attacks on certain stream ciphers", *J. of Cryptology*, vol. 1, pp 159–176, 1989.
22. Niederreiter, H.: "Sequences with almost perfect linear complexity profile", *Proc. Eurocrypt' 87*, pp 37–51, 1988.
23. Nyffeler, P.: "Binäre automaten und ihre linearen rekursionen", *Ph.D. Dissertation*, Universität Bern, Switzerland, 1975.
24. Payne, W.H. and T.G. Lewis: "Generalized feedback shift register pseudorandom number algorithms", *J. Assoc. Comput. Mach.*, vol. 20, pp 456–468, July, 1973.
25. Piper, F.C. and T. Beth: "The stop-and-go generator", *Proc. Eurocrypt' 84*, Paris, 1984.
26. Pless, V.S.: "Encryption schemes for computer confidentiality", *IEEE Trans. Computers*, vol. C–26, pp 1133–1136, Nov. 1977.
27. Reeds, J.: "Cracking a random number generator", *Cryptologia*, vol. 1, pp 20–26, Jan, 1977.
28. Rubin, F.: "Decrypting a stream cipher based on J-K Flip-Flops", *IEEE Trans. Computers*, vol. C–28, No. 7, July 1979.
29. Rueppel, R.A.: *Analysis and Design of Stream Ciphers*, Springer-Verlag, Berlin, 1986.
30. Rueppel, R.A.: "Linear complexity and random sequences", *Proc. Eurocrypt' 85*, pp 167–188, 1986.
31. Sarwate, D.V. and M.B. Pursley: "Crosscorrelation properties of pseudorandom and related sequences", *Proc. IEEE*, vol. 68, No. 5, May 1980.
32. Siegenthaler, T.: "Cryptanalysts representation of nonlinearly filtered ML-sequences", *Advances in Cryptology, Eurocrypt' 85*, Linz, Springer-Verlag, LNCS vol. 219, pp 103–110, 1986.
33. Siegenthaler, T.: "Decrypting a class of stream ciphers using ciphertext only", *IEEE Trans. Computers*, vol. C–34, no. 1, Jan. 1985.

34. Siegenthaler, T.: "Correlation immunity of nonlinear combining functions for cryptographic applications", *IEEE Trans. Inform. Theory*, vol. IT–30, no. 5, Sep. 1984.
35. Smeets, B.: "A note on sequence generated by clock controlled shift registers", *Advances in Cryptology, Eurocrypt' 85*, Linz, pp 142–148, 1985.
36. Vogel, R.: "On the Linear Complexity of Cascaded Sequences", *Proc. Eurocrypt' 84*, pp 99–109, 1984.
37. Xiao, G.Z. and J.L. Massey: "A spectral characterization of correlation-immune combining functions", *IEEE Trans. Inform. Theory*, vol. IT–34, pp 569–571, 1988.
38. Zierler, N. and W.H. Mills: "Products of Linear Recurring Sequences", *J. Algebra*, vol. 27, 1973.

Chapter

5

Public Key Cryptosystems

In the early part of the seventies, only classical block ciphersystems were known. But they were found to be of not much use for commercial encryption. However, the situation changed drastically in the later part of that decade. Public-key cryptosystems invented by Diffie, Merkle, and Hellman, as well as Rivest, Shamir, and Adleman provided provable security even with insecure public channels avoiding a major disadvantage of classical cryptography. Since then, a large set of mathematical tools useful for cryptanalysis has been developed. Thus, an avenue with scope for considerable growth has been opened up in the field of cryptography, presenting the exciting prospect of new cryptosystems along with various tools for computational feasibility being developed.

Public-key cryptosystems generally use a public key K_p for encipherment and a secret key K_s for decipherment. But either encipherment followed by decipherment or decipherment followed by encipherment can recover the original plaintext X such that

$$D_{K_s}(E_{K_p}(X)) = E_{K_p}(D_{K_s}(X)) = X$$

In public-key algorithms, unlike in the DES algorithm, the decipher must ensure that the enciphering steps are not revealed or retraced, to prevent determination of the deciphering process. A conventional symmetrical algorithm like DES is so complex that the solution for the mathematical expressions describing its operation is almost impossible to arrive at analytically; whereas public-key asymmetrical algorithms can be easily described in mathematical equations, but they should also be difficult to solve. However, it is reported that most cryptosystems thought to be secure have actually been broken. Another difference between private-key and public-key algorithms is the manner in which keys are generated. In a public-key algorithm, the secret key is intentionally made obscure so that a special procedure is required to conceal and authenticate the real messages. However, in a conventional private-key algorithm the enciphering key is equivalent to the deciphering key.

This chapter outlines a selection of the attacks that have been used and, in particular, considers some of the earliest public-key algorithms, namely the public-key distribution systems proposed by Diffie and Hellman (1976), the RSA cryptosystem invented by Rivest, Shamir, and Adleman (1978), the Knapsack cryptosystem designed by Merkle and Hellman (1978), the McEliece algebraic codes cryptosystem (1978), and others.

5.1 PUBLIC KEY DISTRIBUTION SYSTEMS

A cryptographic system is said to be secure if and only if computing logarithms over GF(q) is infeasible. The public key distribution algorithm proposed by Diffie and Hellman [16] appears to be difficult for computing logarithms over GF(q) with q elements $\{0, 1, 2, \ldots, q-1\}$.

Consider a pair of inverse functions

$$Y \equiv \alpha^X \pmod{q} \tag{5.1}$$

$$X \equiv \log_\alpha Y \quad \text{over} \quad \mathrm{GF}(q) \tag{5.2}$$

where $1 \le X, Y \le q - 1$, respectively, q is prime, and α is a primitive element of GF(q). Calculation of Y from X is easy, but computation of X from Y is more difficult, because computing logarithms over GF(q) is believed to be much harder. Hence, in the Diffie-Hellman key exchange protocol, security is based on the difficulty of taking discrete logarithms which reverse the process of exponentiation in the finite field GF(q). In fact, the security of most cryptosystems resides in the domains of computational complexity and analysis of algorithms. A cursory introduction to the theory of complexity will be found in most introductory texts. In public-key distribution systems, two users who wish to exchange a key communicate back and forth until they arrive at a key in common. A possible solution to a public-key distribution problem is given in the following [16].

Each user generates an independent random number X_i chosen uniformly from the set of integers {1, 2, . . . , $q-1$}. The user keeps X_i secret, but places

$$Y_i \equiv \alpha^{X_i} \pmod{q} \tag{5.3}$$

in a public file. When users i and j wish to communicate privately, they use their common key as

$$K_{ij} \equiv \alpha^{X_i X_j} \pmod{q} \tag{5.4}$$

User i computes K_{ij} by obtaining Y_j from the public file and letting

$$\begin{aligned} K_{ij} &\equiv Y_j^{X_i} \pmod{q} \\ &\equiv (\alpha^{X_j})^{X_i} \pmod{q} \\ &\equiv \alpha^{X_j X_i} \pmod{q} \equiv \alpha^{X_i X_j} \pmod{q} \end{aligned} \tag{5.5}$$

User j obtains the common key K_{ij} in a similar fashion as

$$K_{ji} \equiv Y_i^{X_j} \pmod{q} \equiv \alpha^{X_i X_j} \pmod{q} \tag{5.6}$$

Consequently the other user must compute the key K_{ij} from Y_i and Y_j by computing

$$K_{ij} = K_{ji} \equiv Y_i^{(\log_\alpha Y_j)} \pmod{q} \tag{5.7}$$

Therefore we see that if logarithms over GF(q) are easily computed, the system can be broken; whereas the system will be secure if logarithms over GF(q) are difficult to compute. Thus computing the key K_{ij} from Y_i and Y_j is almost infeasible without obtaining first either X_i or X_j.

The arithmetic of exponential key exchange is not restricted to prime fields GF(q), where q is a prime. It can also be done in Galois fields with 2^m elements, i.e. GF (2^m).

Key exchange problems in GF(q) (prime field), as well as in the Galois field GF (2^m) are illustrated in the following examples.

■ **Example 5.1** (I) Consider a prime field GF(q) with a prime number q. Let α be a fixed primitive element of GF(q) such that the powers of α produce all nonzero elements 1, 2, . . . , $q-1$ of GF(q). Let us pick $\alpha = 2$ and $q = 11$. The powers of $\alpha = 2$ (mod 11) produce the following table.

$\alpha^\lambda, 0 \le \lambda \le q-2$	2^0	2^1	2^2	2^3	2^4	2^5	2^6	2^7	2^8	2^9
$\alpha^\lambda \pmod{11}$	1	2	4	8	5	10	9	7	3	6

To initiate communication, user i chooses a random number $X_i = 5$ from the integer set 2^{λ} (mod 11) = {1, 2, 3, . . ., 10} in the above table and keeps it secret. He sends $Y_i \equiv \alpha^{X_i}$ (mod q) to user j. Similarly, user j chooses a random number $X_j = 7$ and sends the corresponding Y_j to user i. Now, the two users can compute $K_{ij} \equiv \alpha^{X_i X_j}$ (mod q). Thus, $Y_i \equiv 2^5$ (mod 11) = 10 and $Y_j \equiv 2^7$ (mod 11) = 7. Finally, we compute their common key K_{ij} as follows: $K_{ij} = Y_j^{X_i}$ (mod 11) $\equiv 7^5$ (mod 11) $\equiv 2^{35}$ (mod 11) = 10 and $K_{ji} = Y_i^{X_j}$ (mod 11) $\equiv 10^7$ (mod 11) $\equiv (2^5)^7$ (mod 11) $\equiv 2^{35}$ (mod 11) = 10. Thus, each user completes computation of the common key.

(II) Consider the key exchange problem in GF (2^m) for $m = 3$. A primitive polynomial $p(x)$ of degree $m = 3$ over GF (2) is $p(x) = 1 + x + x^3$. If α be a root of $p(x)$ over GF (2), then the field elements of GF (2^3) generated by $p(\alpha) = 1 + \alpha + \alpha^3 = 0$ are shown in Table 5.1.

Suppose users i and j select $X_i = 2$ and $X_j = 5$, respectively. Both X_i and X_j are kept secret, but

$$Y_i \equiv \alpha^{X_i} \pmod 7 \equiv \alpha^2 \pmod 7 = 0\,0\,1$$

and

$$Y_j \equiv \alpha^{X_j} \pmod 7 \equiv \alpha^5 \pmod 7 = 1\,1\,1$$

are placed in the public file. User i can communicate with user j by taking $Y_j = 1\,1\,1$ from the public file and computing their common key K_{ij} as follows:

$$K_{ij} \equiv (Y_j)^{X_i} \pmod 7 \equiv (\alpha^5)^2 \pmod 7 \equiv \alpha^{10} \pmod 7 \equiv \alpha^3 = 1\,1\,0$$

Table 5.1 Field Elements of GF (2^3) for $q = 7$

Power	Polynomial			Vector
1	1			100
α		α		010
α^2			α^2	001
α^3	1 +	α		110
α^4		α +	α^2	011
α^5	1 +	α +	α^2	111
α^6	1	+	α^2	101

User j obtains K_{ij} in a similar fashion:

$$K_{ij} \equiv (Y_i)^{X_j} \pmod 7 \equiv (\alpha^2)^5 \pmod 7 \equiv \alpha^{10} \pmod 7 \equiv \alpha^3 = 1\,1\,0$$

Thus two users i and j arrive at a key K_{ij} in common. The example just given is extremely small in size and was intended only to illustrate the technique.

A cryptosystem is considered to be a collection of enciphering and deciphering systems and the key generator coupled with the protocols of key distribution. A block ciphersystem like DES is sometimes called a symmetric cryptosystem, because both the enciphering and deciphering processes usually execute with the same cryptographic key; whereas a public key cryptosystem is sometimes said to involve asymmetric algorithms because it uses two different keys when cryptographic transformations are processed. Therefore, the asymmetric cryptosystem uses two different keys, namely the public and secret keys. The characteristic feature of asymmetric cryptosystems is that both the public key and the ciphertext may be sent via insecure communication channels so that the opponent may know both the cryptogram and the public key.

5.2 MERKLE-HELLMAN KNAPSACK CRYPTOSYSTEMS

The knapsack problem is a mathematically attractive proposition for cryptography. The Merkle-Hellman scheme [32] based on the trapdoor knapsack problem is a public-key asymmetric cryptosystem.

Assume a key $\mathbf{K} = (k_1, k_2 \ldots, k_n)$ where k_i are integers for $1 \le i \le n$, and the n-bit plaintext is $\mathbf{X} = (x_1, x_2, \ldots, x_n)$ where $x_i \in GF(2)$ for $1 \le i \le n$. Then the knapsack cryptosystem enciphers the n-bit plaintext into the m-bit ciphertext, $n < m$, according to the following formula:

$$\mathbf{Y} = \mathbf{K} \cdot \mathbf{X} = k_1x_1 + k_2x_2 + \ldots + k_nx_n = \sum_{i=1}^{n} k_ix_i \tag{5.8}$$

Calculation of $\mathbf{Y}$ is as simple as seen from Eq. 5.8, but recovery of $\mathbf{X}$ from $\mathbf{Y}$ and $\mathbf{K}$ involves solving a knapsack problem and is generally difficult when n is large and $\mathbf{K}$ is randomly chosen.

If the key $\mathbf{K}$ is chosen such that each element of $\mathbf{K}$ is larger than the sum of the preceding elements, the corresponding knapsack problem becomes very simple. That is,

$$k_i > k_1 + k_2 + \ldots + k_{i-1} = \sum_{j=1}^{i-1} k_j \qquad 1 \le i \le n \tag{5.9}$$

Letting

$$\begin{aligned} y_1 &= k_1x_1 \\ y_2 &= k_1x_1 + k_2x_2 \\ &\cdots\cdots \\ y_n &= k_1x_1 + k_2x_2 + \ldots + k_nx_n \end{aligned}$$

where y_n represents the ciphertext **Y** i.e. **Y** $= y_n$. Now, the plaintext **X** can be recovered from y_i for $1 \le i \le n$ and the key **K** according to the following procedure. If $y_n < k_n$, then set $x_n = 0$ and $y_{n-1} = y_n$. If $y_n > k_n$, then set $x_n = 1$ and $y_{n-1} = y_n - k_n$. Using the computed value of y_{n-1}, we can find x_{n-1} and y_{n-2} in a similar fashion. The recovery procedure continues until $\mathbf{X} = (x_1, x_2, \ldots, x_n)$ has been completely recreated. The knapsack problem will be illustrated by the following simple example.

■ **Example 5.2** Letting the plaintext block **X** = (1 1 0 0 1) and the key **K** = (151, 187, 426, 1091, 2412), the ciphertext **Y** becomes

$$\mathbf{Y} = \mathbf{K} \cdot \mathbf{X} = 151 + 187 + 2412 = 2750$$

Since $\mathbf{Y} = y_5 = 2750$ is the ciphertext, the recovery of x_5 from y_5 and k_5 is $x_5 = 1$ because $y_5 = 2750 > k_5 = 2412$. Hence the procedure for recovery of x_i for $1 \le i \le 5$ will continue as shown below.

Since $y_5 = 2750 > k_5 = 2412, x_5 = 1$
Since $y_4 = y_5 - k_5 = 338 < k_4 = 1091, x_4 = 0$
Since $y_3 = 338 < k_3 = 426, x_3 = 0$
Since $y_2 = 338 > k_2 = 187, x_2 = 1$
Since $y_1 = y_2 - k_2 = 151 = k_1 , x_1 = 1$

Thus the recovered plaintext is **X** = (1 1 0 0 1) as expected. However, this simple knapsack vector **K** cannot be used as a public enciphering key because someone can easily recover **X** from **Y**.

The generation of a public key is nothing but the selection of a random knapsack vector $\mathbf{K}_p$ which may have several hundred components. Anyone who desires to communicate a message **X** to a user enciphers **X** first by using the knapsack vector $\mathbf{K}_p$ such that $\mathbf{Y} = \mathbf{K}_p \cdot \mathbf{X}$. The designer chooses two large secret integers m and w such that $m > w$. They must be relatively prime, i.e. gcd $(w, m) = 1$. Moreover, m has to be larger than Σk_i, i.e. $m > \Sigma k_i$ for $1 \le i \le n$, where k_i is an element of superincreasing knapsack vector.

Recovering the original plaintext **X** from the ciphertext **Y** sometimes requires the transformation of **Y** into **Y**$'$ via v which is the multiplicative inverse of w modulo m. That is,

$$\mathbf{Y}' \equiv v\mathbf{Y} \pmod{m} \tag{5.10}$$

where a secret quantity $v = w^{-1}$ is calculated from m and w such that

$$wv \equiv 1 \pmod{m}$$

or

$$ww^{-1} \equiv 1 \pmod{m} \tag{5.11}$$

Using Eq. 5.11, Eq. 5.10 can also be written as

$$\mathbf{Y} \equiv w\mathbf{Y}' \pmod{m} \tag{5.12}$$

A trapdoor knapsack vector $\mathbf{K}_p = w\,\mathbf{K}_p'$ is also published by the user as his public key, while the parameters $v = w^{-1}$ and m are kept secret as his private keys. $\mathbf{K}_p$ is generated by multiplying each component of the knapsack $\mathbf{K}_p' = (k_1', k_2', \ldots, k_n')$ by w modulo m such that

$$k_i \equiv wk_i' \pmod{m}, \quad 1 \le i \le n \tag{5.13}$$

Hence, using Eq. 5.12, the designer can easily compute the transformed ciphertext $\mathbf{Y}'$ as

$$\mathbf{Y}' \equiv w^{-1}\mathbf{Y} \pmod{m}$$

$$\equiv w^{-1} \sum_{i=1}^{n} k_i x_i \pmod{m}$$

Substituting Eq. 5.13 into this equation yields

$$\mathbf{Y}' \equiv w^{-1} \sum_{i=1}^{n} wk_i'x_i \pmod{m} \equiv (ww^{-1}) \sum_{i=1}^{n} k_i'x_i \pmod{m}$$

$$\equiv \sum_{i=1}^{n} k_i'x_i \pmod{m} = \mathbf{K}_p' \cdot \mathbf{X} \tag{5.14}$$

On the other hand, since $\mathbf{Y} = \mathbf{K}_p \cdot \mathbf{X} = \sum_{i=1}^{n} k_i x_i$, it follows that

$$\mathbf{Y} \equiv \sum_{i=1}^{n} [wk_i' \pmod{m}]x_i$$

$$\equiv \sum_{i=1}^{n} ww^{-1}k_i x_i \pmod{m}$$

$$\equiv \sum_{i=1}^{n} k_i x_i \pmod{m} = \mathbf{K}_p \cdot \mathbf{X} \tag{5.15}$$

The knapsack problem of Eq. 5.14 is easily solved for $\mathbf{X}$ with $\mathbf{K}_p'$, even though it is apparently difficult to compute. The solution is the same as the one for the trapdoor knapsack problem of Eq. 5.15.

We shall now present a simple example in order to make these ideas clearer to the reader.

■ **Example 5.3** Let the simple knapsack vector $\mathbf{K}_p'$ be a sequence of superincreasing integers such as $\mathbf{K}_p' = (151, 187, 426, 1091, 2412)$.

Then we have

$$\sum_{i=1}^{5} k_i' = 151 + 187 + 426 + 1091 + 2412 = 4267$$

Choose the secret integers as $m = 4617$ and $w = 1175$ such that $m > w$ and gcd $(w, m) = 1$. Let us show that gcd $(1175, 4617) = 1$ by using the following Euclidean algorithm.

$$\begin{aligned}
4617 &= (1175)\,3 + 1092 \\
1175 &= (1092)\,1 + 83 \\
1092 &= (83)\,13 + 13 \\
83 &= (13)\,6 + 5 \\
13 &= (5)\,2 + 3 \\
5 &= (3)\,1 + 2 \\
3 &= (2)\,1 + 1 \\
2 &= (1)\,2
\end{aligned}$$

where the process stops when a remainder of zero is obtained. The last nonzero remainder is the greatest common divisor, i.e. gcd (1175, 4617) = 1. Hence $w = 1175$ and $m = 4617$ are relatively prime. From Eq. 5.13, i.e. $k_i \equiv 1175\ k_i' \bmod 4617$, we have

$$\begin{aligned}
k_1 &= (151)\,(1175) - (38)\,(4617) = 1979 \\
k_2 &= (187)\,(1175) - (47)\,(4617) = 2726 \\
k_3 &= (426)\,(1175) - (108)\,(4617) = 1914 \\
k_4 &= (1091)\,(1175) - (277)\,(4617) = 3016 \\
k_5 &= (2412)\,(1175) - (613)\,(4617) = 3879
\end{aligned}$$

Thus the trapdoor knapsack vector can be computed to be

$$\mathbf{K}_p = (1979, 2726, 1914, 3016, 3879)$$

■ **Example 5.4** Compute the value of $v = w^{-1}$ by rewriting the iterative equations obtained with Euclidean algorithm in Example 5.3. For any integers w and m there exist two integers v and u such that gcd $(w, m) = vw + um$. Since gcd (w, m) = gcd $(1175, 4617) = 1$, we have $1 = 1175\ v + 4617\ u$. This equation can be expressed by the congruence as $1 \equiv 1175\ v \bmod 4617$. By making use of this relation, one may proceed as follows:

$$\begin{aligned}
1 &= 3 - (2)\,1 \\
1 &= (3)\,2 - 5 \\
1 &= (13)\,2 - (5)\,5 \\
1 &= (13)\,32 - (83)\,5 \\
1 &= (1092)\,32 - (83)\,421 \\
1 &= (1092)\,453 - (1175)\,421 \\
1 &= (4617)\,453 - (1175)\,1780
\end{aligned}$$

This last equation designates $1 \equiv -(1175)(1780) \bmod 4617$. Thus $v \equiv -1780 \pmod{4617} = 2837$ is the multiplicative inverse of $w \equiv 1175$ modulo m (= 4617).

Utilizing the transformed ciphertext $\mathbf{Y}' \equiv v\mathbf{Y}$ modulo m and $\mathbf{Y}' = \mathbf{K}_p' \cdot \mathbf{X}$, we shall illustrate the use of the trapdoor knapsack public-key algorithm for recovering plaintext **X** in the following example.

■ **Example 5.5** Assume that the plaintext **X** = (11001) is given. Following the same procedure as in Examples 5.3 and 5.4, the trapdoor knapsack vector $\mathbf{K}_p$ = (1979, 2726, 1914, 3016, 3879) may be found and the secret integer $v = 2837$ derived under the condition that $\mathbf{K}_p'$ = (151, 187, 426, 1091, 2412) and two chosen secret integers $w = 1175$ and $m = 4617$ given. The ciphertext then becomes $\mathbf{Y} = \mathbf{K}_p \cdot \mathbf{X} = 1979 + 2726 + 3879 = 8584$ and the transformed ciphertext $\mathbf{Y}' \equiv vY \bmod m \equiv (2837)(8584) \bmod 4617 \equiv 24,352,808 \bmod 4617 = 2750$. **X** can be recovered as follows:

i	y_i'	k_i'	x_i
5	2750	> 2412	1
4	338	< 1091	0
3	338	< 426	0
2	338	> 187	1
1	151	= 151	1

and the value of **X** is (11001) as assumed.

The examples given here are extremely small in scope and are meant only to illustrate the technique to be followed. Of course, it is found that it succeeds in recovering the exact plaintext **X** with one trial. Exhaustive trial and error search over all possible **X**s is computationally required without using v and w. Thus the knapsack problem becomes extremely difficult as n becomes large, depending entirely on the choice of v, w and K_p'.

■ **Example 5.6** Choose first w and m such that gcd $(w, m) = 1$. Taking $w = 2550$, $m = 8443$, and K_p' = (171, 196, 457, 1191, 2410), the trapdoor knapsack problem will be analyzed as shown below.

$$
\begin{aligned}
8443 &= (2550)\,3 + 793 \\
2550 &= (793)\,3 + 171 \\
793 &= (171)\,4 + 109 \\
171 &= (109)\,1 + 62 \\
109 &= (62)\,1 + 47
\end{aligned}
$$

$$62 = (47)1 + 15$$
$$47 = (15)3 + 2$$
$$15 = 2(7) + 1$$
$$2 = (1)2$$

Thus, gcd (2550, 8443) = 1 (relatively prime). Using $k_i \equiv 2550\ k_i'$ mod 8443, $1 \le i \le 5$, we have

$$k_1 = (2550)\,171 - (8443)\,51 = 5457$$
$$k_2 = (2550)\,196 - (8443)\,59 = 1663$$
$$k_3 = (2550)\,457 - (8443)\,138 = 216$$
$$k_4 = (2550)\,1191 - (8443)\,359 = 6013$$
$$k_5 = (2550)\,2410 - (8443)\,727 = 7439$$

Hence, we have $\mathbf{K}_p$ = (5457, 1663, 216, 6013, 7439). Since $m = 8443$ and $\sum_{i=1}^{5} k_i' = 171 + 196 + 457 + 1191 + 2410 = 4425$, it meets the requirements of $m > \sum_{i=1}^{5} k_i'$ because 8443 > 4425.

Compute $v = w^{-1}$ by the Euclidean algorithm:

$$1 = 15 - (2)\,7$$
$$1 = (15)\,22 - (47)\,7$$
$$1 = (62)\,22 - (47)\,29$$
$$1 = (62)\,51 - (109)\,29$$
$$1 = (171)\,51 - (109)\,80$$
$$1 = (171)\,371 - (793)\,80$$
$$1 = (2550)\,371 - (793)\,1193$$
$$1 = (2550)\,3950 - (8443)\,1193$$

Since the last equation can be expressed as $1 \equiv (2550)\,(3950)$ mod 8443, we can determine $v = 3950$. If the plaintext is assumed as $\mathbf{X}$ = (01011), then the ciphertext becomes $\mathbf{Y} = \mathbf{K}_p \cdot \mathbf{X} = 1663 + 6013 + 7439 = 15,115$. Subsequently, $\mathbf{Y}' \equiv v\mathbf{Y} \bmod m \equiv (3950)\,(15{,}115) \bmod 8443 = 3797$. Thus, the recovery of $\mathbf{X}$ proceeds as follows:

i	y_i'	k_i'	x_i
5	3900	> 2410	1
4	1387	> 1191	1
3	196	< 457	0
2	196	= 196	1
1	0	< 171	0

and the recovered plaintext is $\mathbf{X}$ = (01011) as expected.

5.2.1 Multiplicative Trapdoor Knapsacks

Another type of Merkle-Hellman cryptosystem is a multiplicative knapsack algorithm. A multiplicative knapsack is transformed into an additive knapsack by taking logarithms. The designer selects a knapsack vector $K_p' = (k_1', k_2', \ldots, k_n')$ whose entries are relatively prime and chooses a prime number q such that

$$q > \prod_{i=1}^{n} k'_i \tag{5.16}$$

Let β be the primitive element of the finite field GF (q). It is then required to determine the public key k_i from the discrete logarithms of k_i' to base β such that

$$k_i' \equiv \beta^{k_i} \pmod{q} \tag{5.17}$$

where q, β, and k_i' for $1 \le i \le n$ constitute the trapdoor information.

The ciphertext to be transmitted is now computed by

$$\mathbf{Y} = \sum_{i=1}^{n} k_i x_i \tag{5.18}$$

Knowing q, β, and k_i', we are able to compute

$$Y' \equiv \beta^{\mathrm{Y}} \pmod{q} \tag{5.19}$$

where

$$\begin{aligned} \beta^{\mathrm{Y}} &= \beta^{(\Sigma k_i x_i)} \\ &= \beta^{k_1 x_1} \cdot \beta^{k_2 x_2} \ldots \beta^{k_n x_n} \\ &= \prod_{i=1}^{n} \beta^{k_i x_i} = \prod_{i=1}^{n} (\beta^{k_i})^{x_i} \\ &= \prod_{i=1}^{n} (k_i')^{x_i} \pmod{q} \end{aligned} \tag{5.20}$$

and q must satisfy Eq. 5.16.

In order to determine the public key k_i, we employ the Chinese remainder theorem which is represented as the vector congruences:

$$k_i \equiv [\beta_1 \pmod{q_1}, \beta_2 \pmod{q_2}, \ldots, \beta_n \pmod{q_n}] \tag{5.21}$$

Thus, the calculations of k_i are accomplished by computing β_i for $i = 1, 2, \ldots, n$. For evaluating β_i, we first calculate

$$z_i = k_i'^{(q-1)/q_i} = (\beta^{k_i})^{(q-1)/q_i} = \left[\beta^{(q-1)/q_i}\right]^{k_i} \tag{5.22}$$

If we put $\gamma_i = \beta^{(q-1)/q_i}$, z_i is an element of sequence $\gamma_i^0 = 1, \gamma_i^1, \gamma_i^2, \ldots, \gamma_i^{q_i - 1}$, and we obtain $k_i = \beta_i$. Thus, we are now searching for β_i such that $z_i = \gamma_i^{\beta_i}$, $0 \le \beta_i \le q_i - 1$. This technique will be used in Example 5.7.

The following example illustrates a small multiplicative knapsack problem.

Example 5.7 Take $n = 3$, $\mathbf{K}_p' = (2, 3, 5)$, GF (q) where q is so chosen that $q = 31 > \prod_{i=1}^{3} k'_{pi} = (2)(3)(5) = 30$, and the base of the logarithm $\beta = 24$. Under these given conditions, let us solve the multiplicative trapdoor knapsack problem for a binary n-vector $\mathbf{X} = (x_1, x_2, x_3) = (1\ 1\ 1)$ where $n = 3$.

Using an algorithm published by Pohlig and Hellman [41], we compute discrete algorithms over GF (q), where q is a prime. Let $q - 1 = q_1 q_2 \ldots q_k$, $q_i < q_{i+1}$ for $i = 1, 2, \ldots, k$ be the prime factorization of $q - 1$, where q_is are distinct primes. Knowing the trapdoor information $q = 31$, $\beta = 24$, and $k_1' = 2$, the public key k_1 is determined according to the equation

$$2 \equiv 24^{k_1} \pmod{31}$$

Note that $q - 1 = q_1 q_2 q_3 = 30 = (2)(3)(5)$, and so factorization gives $q_1 = 2$, $q_2 = 3$, and $q_3 = 5$. β_i is calculated according to the following steps.

For $q_1 = 2$, we calculate

$$\gamma_1 \equiv \beta^{(q-1)/q_1} \equiv 24^{15} \pmod{31}$$

Since $24^2 = 576 \pmod{31} \equiv 18$, we have $24^4 \equiv 324 \pmod{31} \equiv 14$ and $24^8 \equiv 14^2 \pmod{31} \equiv 196 \pmod{31} \equiv 10$. Thus, it follows that $24^{15} = (24)^8 (24)^4 (24)^2 (24) \equiv 10 \cdot 14 \cdot 18 \cdot 24 \pmod{31} \equiv 30 \pmod{31} \equiv -1$. This yields $\gamma_1 \equiv -1 \pmod{31}$, whence $\gamma_1^0 = 1$ and $\gamma_1^1 = -1$. On the other hand, from $z_1 = k_1'^{(q-1)/q_1}$, we have $z_1 = 2^{15} \equiv 1 \pmod{31}$. From the sequence $(\gamma_1^0, \gamma_1^1) = (1, -1)$, we select one element which is identical to z_1. This is $\gamma_1^0 = 1 = z_1$, and therefore $\beta_1 = 0$.

For $q_2 = 3$, we have

$$\gamma_2 \equiv \beta^{(q-1)/q_2} \equiv 24^{10} \pmod{31}$$

Using $24^2 \equiv 18 \pmod{31}$ and $24^8 \equiv 10 \pmod{31}$, $\gamma_2 = (24)^8 (24)^2 \equiv 180 \pmod{31} \equiv 25$. Therefore, $\gamma_2^0 = 1$, $\gamma_2^1 = 25$, and $\gamma_2^2 = (25)^2 \pmod{31} \equiv 5$.

Comparing $z_2 = k_1'^{(q-1)/q_2} = 2^{10} \equiv 1024 \pmod{31} \equiv 1$ with the sequence $(\gamma_2^0, \gamma_2^1, \gamma_2^2) = (1, 25, 5)$, we obtain $\beta_2 = 0$.

For $q_3 = 5$, we compute

$$\gamma_3 = \beta^{(q-1)/q_3} = 24^6 = (24)^4(24)^2 \equiv (14)(18) \pmod{31} \equiv 4$$

This gives the sequence $\gamma_3^0 = 1, \gamma_3^1 = 4, \gamma_3^2 = 16, \gamma_3^3 = 2$, and $\gamma_3^4 = 8 \pmod{31}$. Next, we obtain $z_3 = 2^6 = 64 \equiv 2 \pmod{31}$. Comparing z_3 with the element γ_3^i, we have $z_3 = 2 = \gamma_3^3$, whence $\beta_3 = 3$.

Finally, the public key k_1 can be determined by

$$k_1 \equiv [0 \pmod 2, 0 \pmod 3, 3 \pmod 5]$$

$$\equiv 18 \pmod{30}$$

It is easily checked that $k_1 = 18$ is accurate from $2 \equiv 24^{k_1} \pmod{31}$ as follows:

$$24^{18} = (24)^8(24)^8(24)^2 \equiv (10)(10)(18) \pmod{31}$$

$$\equiv 1800 \pmod{31} \equiv 2$$

Let us determine the public key k_2 from $3 \equiv 24^{k_2} \pmod{31}$.

For $q_1 = 2$, $\beta = 24$, and $k_2' = 3$, we have

$$\gamma_1 = \beta^{(q-1)/q_1} = 24^{15} \equiv -1 \pmod{31}$$

Hence, $\gamma_1^0 = 1, \gamma_1^1 = -1$. Using $z_1 = (k_2')^{(q-1)/q_1} = 3^{15}$, we have

$$z_1 = (3)^8(3)^4(3)^3 = (20)(19)(-4) \pmod{31} \equiv -1520 \pmod{31} \equiv -1$$

Since $z_1 \equiv -1 \pmod{31}$, $z_1 = -1 = \gamma_1^1$ whence $\beta_1 = 1$.

For $q_2 = 3$, $\gamma_2 = (24)^{10} \pmod{31} \equiv 25$ as before. Therefore, $\gamma_2^0 = 1, \gamma_2^1 = 25$, and $\gamma_2^2 = 5 \pmod{31}$. Since $3^4 = 81 \equiv 19 \pmod{31}$, we have

$$z_2 = (k_2')^{(q-1)/q_2} = 3^{10} \pmod{31} \equiv (9)(19)(19) \pmod{31} \equiv 25$$

Comparing z_2 with the elements γ_2^i, we have $z_2 = 25 = \gamma_2^1$ from which $\beta_2 = 1$.

For $q_3 = 5$, $\gamma_3 = 4 \pmod{31}$ so that the sequence is

$$(\gamma_3^0, \gamma_3^1, \gamma_3^2, \gamma_3^3, \gamma_3^4) = (1, 4, 16, 2, 8)$$

Since $z_3 = (k_2')^{(q-1)/q_3} = 3^6 = 729 \equiv 16 \pmod{31}$, $z_3 = 16 = \gamma_3^2$. Hence we determine $\beta_3 = 2$. Thus, the public key k_2 is found as

$$k_2 \equiv [1 \pmod 2, 1 \pmod 3, 2 \pmod 5] \equiv 7 \pmod{30}$$

Finally, let us determine the public key k_3 from $5 \equiv 24^{k_3} \pmod{31}$.

For $q_1 = 2$, $\gamma_1 \equiv -1 \pmod{31}$ so that $\gamma_1^{\,0} = 1$, $\gamma_1^{\,1} = -1$. Since $5^4 \pmod{31} \equiv 5$, $5^8 \pmod{31} \equiv 25$, and $5^3 \pmod{31} \equiv 1$,

$$z_1 \equiv 5^{15} \pmod{31} \equiv (5^8)(5^4)(5^3) \pmod{31} \equiv (25)(5)(1) \pmod{31}$$

$$\equiv 125 \pmod{31} \equiv 1.$$

Thus, $z_1 = 1 = \gamma_1^{\,0}$, whence $\beta_1 = 0$.

For $q_2 = 3$, since $\gamma_2 \equiv 25 \pmod{31}$, we have $\gamma_2^{\,0} = 1$, $\gamma_2^{\,1} = 25$, and $\gamma_2^{\,2} = 5$. Knowing $5^2 = 25 \equiv -6 \pmod{31}$, we have $5^4 \equiv 36 \pmod{31} \equiv 5$. Hence $z_2 = 5^{10} \pmod{31} \equiv (5)(5)(25) \pmod{31} \equiv 625 \pmod{31} \equiv 5$. Comparing z_2 with the elements $\gamma_2^{\,i}$ for $i = 0, 1, 2$, it gives $z_2 = 5 = \gamma_2^{\,2}$, whence $\beta_2 = 2$.

For $q_3 = 5$, $\gamma_3 \equiv 4 \pmod{31}$ and $\gamma_3^{\,0} = 1$, $\gamma_3^{\,1} = 4$, $\gamma_3^{\,2} = 16$, $\gamma_3^{\,3} = 2$, $\gamma_3^{\,4} = 8$ as evaluated before. Since $z_3 = 5^6 = (5^4)(5^2) = 125 \equiv 1 \pmod{31}$, $z_3 = 1 = \gamma_3^{\,0}$ whence $\beta_3 = 0$. Finally, the public key k_3 is found as

$$k_3 \equiv [0 \pmod 2), 2 \pmod 3), 0 \pmod 5)] \equiv 20 \pmod{30}$$

Thus, the public key vector is obtained as

$$\mathbf{K}_p = (k_1, k_2, k_3) = (18, 7, 20)$$

Using Eq. 5.18, the ciphertext to be transmitted is

$$\mathbf{Y} = k_1x_1 + k_2x_2 + k_3x_3$$

But, since $\mathbf{X} = (x_1, x_2, x_3) = (1\ 1\ 1)$,

$$\mathbf{Y} = k_1 + k_2 + k_3 = 18 + 7 + 20 = 45$$

Using Eq. 5.19, we have

$$\mathbf{Y}' \equiv \beta^{\mathbf{Y}} \equiv 24^{45} \pmod{31}$$

where $\beta = 24$ and $\mathbf{Y} = 45$. As found before, $24^{15} \pmod{31} \equiv 30 \pmod{31} \equiv -1$. Thus, it follows that

$$\mathbf{Y}' \equiv (24)^{15}(24)^{15}(24)^{15} \pmod{31}$$

$$\equiv (-1)(-1)(-1) \pmod{31} \equiv 30$$

$$\equiv (2^1)(3^1)(5^1)$$

which implies that $\mathbf{X} = (1\ \ 1\ \ 1)$ as expected.

5.2.2 Multiple Iterative Knapsacks

The third type of Merkle-Hellman knapsack algorithm is an iterative knapsack method based on modular multiplications.

Let the public enciphering key be

$$\mathbf{K}_p = (k_1, k_2, \ldots, k_n)$$

The secret deciphering key $\mathbf{K}_s$ is obtained by a method for transforming K_p into an easy knapsack, and $\mathbf{K}_s$ is a vector of n positive integers

$$\mathbf{K}_s = (k'_1, k_2', \ldots, k_n')$$

which is a superincreasing sequence such that $k_i' > \sum_{j=1}^{i-1} k_j'$ for $1 \leq i \leq n$. Encryption is a sum $Y = \sum_{i=1}^{n} k_i x_i$ and decryption consists in solving the knapsack problem with a knapsack $k_1, k_2, \ldots, k_n$ and a specified sum Y.

Let the secret key $\mathbf{K}_s$ be defined as $\mathbf{K}_s^k$ for $0 \leq k \leq j$ for iterative key generation such that

$$\mathbf{K}_s^0 = (k_0^1, k_0^2, \ldots, k_0^n)$$

$$\mathbf{K}_s^1 = (k_1^1, k_1^2, \ldots k_1^n)$$

$$\mathbf{K}_s^2 = (k_2^1, k_2^2, \ldots, k_2^n) \tag{5.23}$$

$$\cdots\cdots\cdots$$

$$\mathbf{K}_s^j = (k_j^1, k_j^2, \ldots, k_j^n) = \mathbf{K}_p$$

where $k_m^i > \sum_{\lambda=1}^{i-1} k_m^\lambda$ for $1 \leq i \leq n$ and $0 \leq m \leq j$.

The designer must select two large secret integers m_i and w_i such that $m_i > \sum_{\lambda=1}^{n} k_i^\lambda$ and gcd $(w_i, m_i) = 1$ for $0 \leq i \leq j - 1$. The following steps should be taken for computing K_s^j.

For $i = 0$, $m_0 > \sum_{\lambda=1}^{n} k_0^\lambda$ and gcd $(w_0, m_0) = 1$

$$k_1^1 \equiv w_0 k_0^1 \pmod{m_0}$$

$$k_1^2 \equiv w_0 k_0^2 \pmod{m_0}$$

$$\cdots\cdots\cdots$$

$$k_1^n \equiv w_0 k_0^n \pmod{m_0} \tag{5.24}$$

For $i = 1, m_1 > \sum_{\lambda=1}^{n} k_1^{\lambda}$ and gcd $(w_1, m_1) = 1$

$$
\begin{aligned}
k_2^1 &\equiv w_1 k_1^1 \pmod{m_1} \\
k_2^2 &\equiv w_1 k_1^2 \pmod{m_1} \\
&\cdots\cdots \\
k_2^n &\equiv w_1 k_1^n \pmod{m_1}
\end{aligned}
\tag{5.25}
$$

Similarly, for $i = j - 1$, we have $m_{j-1} > \sum_{\lambda=1}^{n} k_{j-1}^{\lambda}$ and gcd $(w_{j-1}, m_{j-1}) = 1$

$$
\begin{aligned}
k_j^1 &\equiv w_{j-1} k_{j-1}^1 \pmod{m_{j-1}} \\
k_j^2 &\equiv w_{j-1} k_{j-1}^2 \pmod{m_{j-1}} \\
&\cdots\cdots \\
k_j^n &\equiv w_{j-1} k_{j-1}^n \pmod{m_{j-1}}
\end{aligned}
\tag{5.26}
$$

The secret key and public key are determined as follows:

$$\mathbf{K}_s^0 = (k_0^1, k_0^2, \ldots, k_0^n) \qquad \text{(secret deciphering key)}$$

$$\mathbf{K}_p = \mathbf{K}_s^j = (k_j^1, k_j^2, \ldots, k_j^n) \qquad \text{(public enciphering key)}$$

$$\{(w_0, m_0), (w_1, m_1), \ldots, (w_{j-1}, m_{j-1})\} \qquad \text{(secret key variant)}$$

By enciphering the plaintext $\mathbf{X}$ with the public key $\mathbf{K}_p$, the ciphertext is obtained as $\mathbf{Y} = \mathbf{K}_p \cdot \mathbf{X}$. Recovering $\mathbf{X}$ from $\mathbf{Y}$ it requires one step to transform $\mathbf{Y}$ into $\mathbf{Y}'$ via v which is the multiplicative inverse to w modulo m such that $\mathbf{Y}' \equiv v\mathbf{Y} \pmod{m}$, where $v = w^{-1}$ and $ww^{-1} = 1$. Thus, we have

$$
\begin{aligned}
w_0 w_0^{-1} &\equiv 1 \pmod{m_0} \\
w_1 w_1^{-1} &\equiv 1 \pmod{m_1} \\
&\cdots\cdots \\
w_{j-1} w_{j-1}^{-1} &\equiv 1 \pmod{m_{j-1}}
\end{aligned}
\tag{5.27}
$$

Suppose the plaintext vector is $\mathbf{X} = (x_0, x_1, \ldots, x_n)$ and the public key is $\mathbf{K}_p = (k_0, k_1, \ldots, k_n)$. Then the ciphertext is obtained from

$$\mathbf{Y} = \mathbf{K}_p \cdot \mathbf{X} = \sum_{i=1}^{n} k_i x_i$$

$$= k_1 x_1 + k_2 x_2 + \ldots + k_n x_n$$

The iterative transformations for the deciphering process will be shown below. After receiving the ciphertext $\mathbf{Y}$, we compute $\mathbf{Y}^{(1)}$ by multiplying $\mathbf{Y}$ by w_{j-1}^{-1} modulo m_{j-1} as follows:

$$\mathbf{Y}^{(1)} \equiv w_{j-1}^{-1} \mathbf{Y} \pmod{m_{j-1}} \tag{5.28}$$

Since $\mathbf{Y} = \sum_{i=1}^{n} k_j^i x_i$ from $k_i = k_j^i$, by referrring to Eq. 5.26

$$\mathbf{Y}^{(1)} \equiv w_{j-1}^{-1} \sum_{i=1}^{n} w_{j-1} k_{j-1}^i x_i \pmod{m_{j-1}}$$

$$\equiv \sum_{i=1}^{n} k_{j-1}^i x_i \pmod{m_{j-1}} \tag{5.29}$$

Similarly, the second transformation becomes

$$\mathbf{Y}^{(2)} \equiv w_{j-2}^{-1} \mathbf{Y}^{(1)} \pmod{m_{j-2}} \tag{5.30}$$

Since $k_{j-1}^i = w_{j-2} k_{j-2}^i$ from Eq. 5.26,

$$\mathbf{Y}^{(2)} \equiv w_{j-2}^{-1} \sum_{i=1}^{n} w_{j-2} k_{j-2}^i x_i \pmod{m_{j-2}}$$

$$\equiv \sum_{i=1}^{n} k_{j-2}^i x_i \pmod{m_{j-2}} \tag{5.31}$$

where $w_{j-2}^{-1} w_{j-2} = 1$. Since we have done the transformation twice, there is no problem in doing it j times. Thus it is clear that this process can be repeated as many times as desired. With each successive transformation, the structure in the public key $\mathbf{K}_p$ will become more and more obscure.

Thus the jth transformation of $\mathbf{Y}$ can be computed as

$$\mathbf{Y}^{(j)} \equiv w_0^{-1} \mathbf{Y}^{(j-1)} \pmod{m_0}$$

$$\equiv w_0^{-1} \sum_{i=1}^{n} k_1^i x_i \pmod{m_0}$$

$$\equiv w_0^{-1} \sum_{i=1}^{n} (w_0 k_0^i)\, x_i \pmod{m_0}$$

Using Eq. 5.27 the above becomes

$$\mathbf{Y}^{(j)} \equiv \sum_{i=1}^{n} k_0^i x_i \pmod{m_0} \qquad (5.32)$$

The following example should help understand the iterative method.

■ **Example 5.8** Assume that the secret key $\mathbf{K}_s^0 = (k_0^1, k_0^2, k_0^3) = (5, 10, 20)$ is chosen such that $k_0^i > \sum_{j=1}^{n-1} k_0^j$. Let us compute the iterative keys $\mathbf{K}_s^1$ and $\mathbf{K}_s^2 = \mathbf{K}_p$ (public key). Two numbers w and m are chosen such that w is invertible modulo m and gcd $(w, m) = 1$. Taking $w_0 = 17$ and $m_0 = 47 > \sum_{\lambda=1}^{3} k_0^\lambda = 5 + 10 + 20 = 35$, gcd $(w_0, m_0) =$ gcd $(17, 47) = 1$. Compute the first iterative key $\mathbf{K}_s^1 = (k_1^1, k_1^2, k_1^3)$, where

$$k_1^1 \equiv w_0 k_0^1 \pmod{m_0}$$

$$\equiv 17 \cdot 5 \pmod{47} \equiv 38$$

$$k_1^2 \equiv w_0 k_0^2 \pmod{m_0}$$

$$\equiv 17 \cdot 10 \pmod{47} \equiv 29$$

$$k_1^3 \equiv w_0 k_0^3 \pmod{m_0}$$

$$\equiv 17 \cdot 20 \pmod{47} \equiv 11$$

Thus, $\mathbf{K}_s^1 = (38, 29, 11)$.

Taking w_1 and m_1 such that $w_1 = 3$ and $m_1 = 89 > \sum_{\lambda=1}^{3} k_1^\lambda = 38 + 29 + 11 = 78$, gcd $(w_1, m_1) =$ gcd $(3, 89) = 1$. Compute the second iterative key $\mathbf{K}_s^2 = (k_2^1, k_2^2, k_2^3)$ which is exactly identical to the public key $\mathbf{K}_p = (k_1, k_2, k_3)$. Thus, the components of $\mathbf{K}_p$ are

$$k_1 \equiv w_1 k_1^1 \pmod{m_1}$$

$$\equiv 3 \cdot 38 \pmod{89} \equiv 25$$

$$k_2 \equiv w_1 k_1^2 \pmod{m_1}$$

$$\equiv 3 \cdot 29 \pmod{89} \equiv 87$$

$$k_3 \equiv w_1 k_1^3 \pmod{m_1}$$

$$\equiv 3 \cdot 11 \pmod{89} \equiv 33$$

Hence, the public key is

$$\mathbf{K}_p = (25, 87, 33)$$

Using the Euclideans algorithm, w_0^{-1} is determined from the parameters $w_0 = 17$ and $m_0 = 47$ as follows:

$$47 = (17)\,2 + 13$$

$$17 = (13)\,1 + 4$$

$$13 = (4)\,3 + 1$$

$$4 = (4)\,1$$

Thus, gcd (17, 47) = 1. Now, we can find the inverse of w_0 modulo m_0 such that

$$13 = 47 - (17)\,2$$

$$4 = 17 - (13)\,1 = (17)\,3 - 47$$

$$1 = 13 - (4)\,3 = (47)\,4 - (17)\,11$$

Since the last equation can be expressed as $1 \equiv (-11)\,17 \pmod{47}$, we have $w_0^{-1} \equiv -11 \pmod{47} \equiv (-11 + 47) \pmod{47} \equiv 36$. Similarly, w_1^{-1} can be computed using $w_1 = 3$ and $m_1 = 89$.

$$89 = (3)\,29 + 2$$

$$3 = (2)\,1 + 1$$

$$2 = (2)\,1$$

which shows that gcd (3, 89) = 1. From the above equations, it follows that

$$2 = 89 - (3)\,29$$

$$1 = 3 - (2)\,1 = 3 - (89 - 3 \times 29)$$

$$= (3)\,30 - 89$$

The last equation is modularly expressed as $1 \equiv (3)\,30 \pmod{89}$. Hence, the multiplicative inverse of $w_1 = 3$ is $w_1^{-1} = 30$.

Assume that the plaintext to be enciphered is $\mathbf{X} = (1\ \ 0\ \ 1)$. Then the ciphertext $\mathbf{Y}$ is obtained as

$$\mathbf{Y} = \mathbf{X} \cdot \mathbf{K}_p = \sum_{i=1}^{3} k_i x_i = 25 + 33 = 58$$

Consider next the decryption procedure. Upon receiving the ciphertext $\mathbf{Y} = 58$, we need to recreate the plaintext $\mathbf{X}$ with the secret key $\mathbf{K}_s^0 = (5, 10, 20)$ under the multiplicative inverses $w_0^{-1} = 36$ and $w_1^{-1} = 30$; moduli $m_0 = 47$ and $m_1 = 89$.

If $\mathbf{Y}$ is multiplied by w_1^{-1}, $\mathbf{Y}^{(1)}$ is obtained as

$$\mathbf{Y}^{(1)} \equiv w_1^{-1}\mathbf{Y} \pmod{m_1}$$

$$\equiv (30)(58) \pmod{89} \equiv 49$$

Multiplying $\mathbf{Y}^{(1)}$ by w_0^{-1} modulo m_0 results in

$$\mathbf{Y}^{(2)} \equiv w_0^{-1}\mathbf{Y}^{(1)} \pmod{m_0}$$

$$\equiv (36)(49) \pmod{47} = 25$$

Since $\mathbf{Y}^{(2)} = 25 = 5 + 20$, the recovered plaintext is $\mathbf{X} = (1\ \ 0\ \ 1)$.

The Merkle-Hellman systems are based on the knapsack problems, and involve a multiplicative method as well as an iterated method. The iterated method was originally introduced for improving the security and utility of the basic additive and mutiplicative method in order to disguise an easy knapsack. However, Shamir (1984) presented a paper in which the basic knapsack cryptosystem was insecure [46]. In addition, Adleman (1983) and Brickell (1985) demonstrated the insecurity of iterated cryptosystems [2] [6]. For more detail on this subject, the interested reader should study the papers presented by Brickell, Lagarias, and Odlyzko [4], and more extensively the one by Lagarias [25].

5.3 THE RSA CRYPTOSYSTEM

Shortly after Diffie and Hellman [16] introduced the idea of a public-key cryptosystem, Rivest, Shamir, and Adleman (RSA) proposed the most promising cryptosystem of this kind. We shall present a complete description of the RSA scheme in this section, but the interested reader should consult [43] for more original details.

The cryptosystem is made up of a collection of users, each having his own enciphering and deciphering keys. The enciphering key (non-secret) consists of integers r and K_p, and the deciphering key (secret) is an integer K_s. In this scheme, r is an integer which is the product of two carefully selected large primes p and q, i.e. $r = pq$; K_p denotes the public key and K_s the private key. The keys K_s and K_p must be selected in such a way that each is relatively prime to $\phi(r)$ where $\phi(r) = (p-1)(q-1)$ is called the Euler totient function.

The ciphertext Y can be obtained by raising the plaintext X, $0 \le X \le r-1$, to the power of K_p modulo r, whereas decipherment is performed by raising the ciphertext Y to the power of K_s modulo r as shown below.

$$E_{k_p}(X) = Y \equiv X^{K_p} \pmod{r} \tag{5.33}$$

$$D_{K_s}(Y) = Y^{K_s} \pmod{r} \equiv X^{K_p K_s} \pmod{r} \equiv X \pmod{r} \tag{5.34}$$

where $0 \le X \le r-1$ and $\gcd(X, r) = 1$.

Referring to Theorem 2.6, Euler's formula is $a^{\phi(r)} \equiv 1 \pmod{r}$ for $\gcd(a, r) = 1$. Let a be the plaintext X. Then Euler's formula becomes

$$X^{\phi(r)} \equiv 1 \pmod{r} \tag{5.35}$$

where $\gcd(X, r) = 1$, i.e. the plaintext X is relatively prime to r. Utilizing Theorem 2.3, i.e. $a^\lambda \equiv b^\lambda \pmod{r}$ for any positive integer λ if $a \equiv b \pmod{r}$, Eq. 5.35 can be written as

$$X^{\lambda\phi(r)} \equiv 1 \pmod{r} \tag{5.36}$$

Since $a\,\mu \equiv b\,\mu \pmod{r}$ for any integer μ if $a \equiv b \pmod{r}$, Eq. 5.36 becomes

$$X^{\lambda\phi(r)}X \equiv X \pmod{r}$$

or

$$X^{\lambda\phi(r)+1} \equiv X \pmod{r} \tag{5.37}$$

If we choose something like $\lambda\phi(r) + 1 = K_pK_s$, the public key K_p and secret key K_s can be selected so that they satisfy

$$K_pK_s \equiv 1 \pmod{\phi(r)} \tag{5.38}$$

Thus Eq. 5.37 can be rewritten as

$$X^{K_pK_s} \equiv X \pmod{r} \tag{5.39}$$

which is true for any plaintext X if $\gcd(X, r) = 1$. Equation 5.39 may also be expressed as $Y^{K_s} \equiv X \pmod{r} \equiv D_{K_s}(Y)$ which represents the deciphering transformation, where the ciphertext is $Y \equiv X^{K_p} \pmod{r}$.

■ **Example 5.9** Find Euler's totient function of the composite number 21 which has two prime factors, 3 and 7. Because $\phi(21) = (3-1)(7-1) = 12$ integers must be relatively prime to 21, they are 1, 2, 4, 5, 8, 10, 11, 13, 16, 17, 19, 20.

Consider the following procedure for creating a pair of keys, i.e. K_p (public key) and K_s (secret key).

1. Select two secret primes, p and q, where $p \neq q$.
2. Compute the product $r = pq$ which is the public modulus, where p and q are randomly selected.
3. Calculate Euler's ϕ –function, $\phi(r) = (p-1)(q-1)$, which gives the secret numbers.
4. Select the keys, K_p and K_s, which are relatively prime to $\phi(r)$, such that $K_pK_s \equiv 1 \pmod{\phi(r)}$ holds good.
5. Calculate the multiplicative inverse of either K_p or K_s modulo r by using the Euclidean algorithm.

All that remains to be seen is that K_p and K_s be so chosen as to satisfy these requirements.

According to Theorem 2.8, the linear congruence $az \equiv b \pmod{n}$ has exactly d solutions only if $d \mid b$ where $d = \gcd(a, n)$. But, letting $a = K_s$, $b = 1$, and $n = \phi(r)$, then K_s is relatively prime to $\phi(r)$ if and only if gcd $(K_s, \phi(r)) = 1$ and consequently gcd $(K_s, \phi(r)) = 1$ divides 1. Thus, the congruence $K_sz \equiv 1 \pmod{\phi(r)}$ becomes $K_sK_p \equiv 1 \pmod{\phi(r)}$ when choosing $z = K_p$, which is Eq. 5.38. This congruence provides an efficient means of finding K_p and K_s. A method of finding K_p and K_s satisfying $K_sK_p \equiv 1 \pmod{\phi(r)}$ is discussed in Example 5.11.

It is recommended that the readers not only choose the secret primes from a sufficiently large set, but ensure that they are computationally efficient. As large a table of prime numbers as possible is required for choosing p and q in order to provide adequate security. For illustrative purposes, we list primes from 1 to 100 below, but of course they are too few to be of any use. The number of primes below 100 is 25, as shown in the following.

2	3	5	7	11
13	17	19	23	29
31	37	41	43	47
53	59	61	67	71
73	79	83	89	97

■ **Example 5.10** Choose the primes $p = 41$ and $q = 59$. Then $r = pq = 2419$ and $\phi(r) = (p-1)(q-1) = 2320$. Let $K_s = 151$ be the secret key.

Find the multiplicative inverse of 151 modulo 2320 which will be the public key K_p corresponding to $K_s = 151$. gcd $(K_s, \phi(r))$ = gcd (151, 2320) = 1 can be proved with Euclid's algorithm. The value of K_p is computed as follows:

$$
\begin{aligned}
2320 &= (151)15 + 55 \\
151 &= (55)2 + 41 \\
55 &= (41)1 + 14 \\
41 &= (14)2 + 13 \\
14 &= (13)1 + 1 \quad \text{last nonzero remainder} \\
13 &= (1)13
\end{aligned}
$$

Since the last nonzero remainder is 1, gcd (151, 2320) = 1. Therefore, the two integers 151 and 2320 are relatively prime. Now we can express 1 as a linear combination of 2320 and 151 by the relation gcd $(K_s, \phi(r)) = aK_s + b\phi(r)$.

$$1 = 14 - (13)1$$

$$1 = 14 - (41 - 14 \times 2) = (14)3 - 41$$

$$1 = (55 - 41)3 - 41 = (55)3 - (41)4$$

$$1 = (55)3 - (151 - 55 \times 2)4 = (55)11 - (151)4$$

$$1 = (2320 - 151 \times 15)11 - (151)4$$

$$1 = (2320)11 - (151)169 \tag{5.40}$$

where $a = 169 = K_p$ and $b = 11$. Equation 5.40 can be rewritten as $1 \equiv -(151)(169) \pmod{2320}$. Hence we can see that the public key K_p = 2151 is the multiplicative inverse of the secret key $K_s = 151$ modulo $\phi(r) = 2320$.

■ **Example 5.11** Show that $\alpha^{\phi(r)+1} = \alpha \pmod{r}$ holds good for any integer α where $r = pq$ and α is restricted to the set $\{0, 1, 2, \ldots, r-1\}$. By Euler's theorem, $\alpha^{\phi(r)} \equiv 1 \pmod{r}$ holds true for the values of α in the set $\{0, 1, 2, \ldots, r-1\}$. Consider the case of $p = 3$ and $q = 5$. Then $r = pq = 15$. Euler's totient function of r is $\phi(r) = (p-1)(q-1) = 8$, which designates eight numbers relatively prime to $r = 15$. Consider the set (0, 1, 2, 3, 4, 5, 6, 7, 8, 9, 10, 11, 12, 13, 14}. Then the set of αs relatively prime to $r = 15$ is {1, 2, 4, 7, 8, 11, 13, 14}. The evaluation of $\alpha^{\phi(r)+1} = \alpha \pmod{r}$ for all values of α in the set {0, 1, 2, . . . , 12, 13, 14} is done below. Since $r = 15$ and $\phi(r) = 8$, $\phi(15) + 1 = 9$.

α	$\alpha^{\phi(15)+1} (\text{mod}\ 15)$
1	1
2	2^9 (mod 15) = 512 (mod 15) = 2
3	3^9 (mod 15) = 19,683 (mod 15) = 3
4	4^9 (mod 15) = 262, 144 (mod 15) = 4
5	5^9 (mod 15) = 1, 953, 125 (mod 15) = 5
.	.
.	.
.	.
13	13^9 (mod 15) = 10, 604, 499, 373 (mod 15) = 13
14	14^9 (mod 15) = 20, 661, 046, 784 (mod 15) = 14

Thus we have seen that $\alpha^{\phi(r)+1} \equiv \alpha \pmod r$ holds true for any value of α which is restricted to the set $\{1, 2, \ldots, r-1\}$ where $r = pq$.

Given K_p and K_s satisfying $K_pK_s \equiv 1 \pmod{\phi(r)}$ and a plaintext X in the set $(0, 1, 2, \ldots, r-1)$ such that gcd $(X, r) = 1$, we have shown that $X^{K_pK_s} \equiv X \pmod r$. Now $K_pK_s \equiv 1 \pmod{\phi(r)}$ implies that $K_pK_s = m\,\phi(r) + 1$ for some integer m. Thus, $X^{K_pK_s} \equiv X^{m\phi(r)+1} \equiv X \cdot X^{m\phi(r)} \equiv X(X^{\phi(r)})^m \equiv X(1)^m \pmod r$, i.e. $X^{K_pK_s} \equiv X \pmod r$. Since $K_pK_s = K_sK_p$, encipherment and decipherment are commutative by symmetry. Due to this symmetry the RSA scheme can also be used for digital signature and authenticity in a public-key system.

To encipher the message plaintext X, we break it into a series of n digits each such that $1 < n < r - 1$. Characters are usually represented by their 8-bit ASCII Codes, but for simplicity we use here a two-digit number for each character of the plaintext as shown below.

Bank	00	E	05	J	10	O	15	T	20	Y	25
A	01	F	06	K	11	P	16	U	21	Z	26
B	02	G	07	L	12	Q	17	V	22		
C	03	H	08	M	13	R	18	W	23		
D	04	I	09	N	14	S	19	X	24		

■ **Example 5.12** Choose $p = 41$ and $q = 59$, whence $r = (41)(59) = 2419$ and $\phi(r) = (40)(58) = 2320$. Choosing $K_s = 151$ gives $K_p = 169$. Express the plaintext "PUBLIC KEY CRYPTOGRAPHY" in blocks of four digits each, as

1621 0212 0903 0011 0525 0003
1825 1620 1507 1801 1608 2500

The first block, 1621, is enciphered by raising it to the power $K_p = 169$, dividing by $r = 2419$ and taking the remainder 1757 as the first block of ciphertext Y, i.e. $1621^{169} \pmod{2419} = 1757$. Thus the whole plaintext X is enciphered as

1757 0874 1272 1447 0241 1315
1843 2376 1931 1842 0788 1393

Similarly, the first block of ciphertext Y, 1757, is deciphered by raising it to the power $K_s = 151$, dividing by $r = 2419$, and taking the remainder 1258 as the first block of recovered plaintext X. Thus, the recovered plaintext is computed as

1258 1974 1026 0220 2055 1613
1519 0330 0496 2282 2246 1762

which turns out to be entirely different from the original plaintext due to the improper relationship $K_pK_s = -1 \pmod{\phi(r)}$. Thus, in fact, the decryption has not been proper. To overcome this difficulty, we must therefore seek another technique.

Equation 5.40 has the form

$$1 = c\phi(r) - K_sK_p \tag{5.41}$$

where $c = 11$, $\phi(r) = 2320$, $K_s = 151$, and $K_p = 169$.

If K_s in Eq. 5.41 is replaced by $\phi(r) - K_s$, then

$$1 = (c - K_p)\,\phi(r) + K_sK_p \tag{5.42}$$

where $c - K_p$ is an integer. Hence Eq. 5.42 can be expressed as

$$1 \equiv K_sK_p \pmod{\phi(r)}$$

by replacing K_s in Eq. 5.41 by $\phi(r) - K_s$.

Since the new secret key is $K_s' = \phi(r) - K_s = 2169$, the recovered plaintext blocks x_i, $1 \le i \le 12$, are obtained as $1757^{2169} \pmod{2419} \equiv 1621$, $0874^{2169} \pmod{2419} \equiv 0121$, and so on. Thus the recreated plaintext of this example is as follows:

1621 0212 0903 0011 0525 0003
1825 1620 1507 1801 1608 2500

■ **Example 5.13** Use again the secret primes $p = 41$ and $q = 59$. Then $r = pq = 2419$ and $\phi(r) = (p - 1)(q - 1) = 2320$ as before, but choose the secret key as $K_s = 157$. With the aid of the Euclidean algorithm, we check whether K_s is relatively prime to $\phi(r)$, i.e. $\gcd(K_s, \phi(r)) = \gcd(157, 2320) = 1$ as follows:

$$2320 = (157)14 + 122$$

$$157 = (122)1 + 35$$

$$122 = (35)3 + 17$$

$$35 = (17)2 + 1$$

$$17 = (1)17$$

Thus it is proved that gcd (157, 2320) = 1.
Next, compute the public key K_p which is the multiplicative inverse of $K_s = 157$ such that

$$1 = 35 - (17)2$$

$$1 = (35)7 - (122)2$$

$$1 = (157)7 - (122)9$$

$$1 = (157)133 - (2320)9$$

which represents $1 \equiv (157)\ (133) \pmod{2320} = K_s K_p \pmod{\phi\,(r)}$ where $K_s = 157$ and $K_p = 133$.

Using the public key $K_p = 133$, the plaintext "PUBLIC KEY CRYPTOGRAPHY" is enciphered into the ciphertext in blocks:

2362 0299 0821 0663 0555 1022
1153 0251 1460 0823 2100 1229

Using the secret key $K_s = 157$, the first block of the ciphertext Y can be deciphered as $2363^{157} \pmod{2419} \equiv 1621$ which is the first block of recovered plaintext. Similarly, we can decipher all the blocks of ciphertext and obtain the total recovered plaintext by means of block-by-block decipherment.

5.4 RSA AUTHENTICATION SCHEME

The RSA system is the only public-key cryptosystem which can be used for both secrecy and authentication. The aspect of secrecy of the RSA cryptosystem was considered in the previous section. Authentication problems related to various cryptosystems will be discussed in detail in Chapter 10. But we shall cover the RSA authentication method in this chapter because we feel it is necessary to discuss secrecy and authentication on the RSA system at the same time.

The ciphertext Y is obtained by raising the plaintext X, $0 < X \leq r - 1$, to the power of the secret key K_s modulo r ; and the plaintext X is recreated by raising the ciphertext Y to the power of the public key K_p modulo r such that

$$(X^{K_s} \bmod r)^{K_p} \bmod r \equiv X \tag{5.43}$$

where $K_s \cdot K_p \equiv 1 \pmod{\phi(r)}$ and $0 < X \le r - 1$. In the RSA algorithm, Eq. 5.43 can also be written as

$$\left(X^{K_p} \bmod r\right)^{K_s} \bmod r \equiv X \tag{5.44}$$

User A selects an appropriate modulo $r = p \cdot q$ where p and q are primes. The sender A computes the multiple $\phi(r)$ of $p - 1$ and $q - 1$ such that $\phi(r) = \text{lcm}(p - 1, q - 1)$ where lcm stands for 'least common multiple'. Now sender A chooses his secret and public keys, K_{sa} and K_{pa} such that $K_{sa} \cdot K_{pa} \equiv 1 \pmod{\phi(r)}$. The modulo r and the key K_{pa} are published. A enciphers the message X to the cryptogram Y under his own secret key K_{sa} such that

$$Y \equiv X^{K_{sa}} \pmod r \tag{5.45}$$

and sends it to the receiver B, along with the pair (K_{pa}, r). Receiver B recreates the message X using (Y, K_{pa}, r) such that

$$\begin{aligned} X &\equiv Y^{K_{pa}} \pmod r \\ &\equiv (X^{K_{sa}})^{K_{pa}} \pmod r \\ &\equiv X^{K_{sa}K_{pa}} \pmod r \equiv X \end{aligned} \tag{5.46}$$

where $K_{sa} K_{pa} \equiv 1 \pmod{\phi(r)}$ from the sender's pair of keys and $0 \le X \le r - 1$.

Example 5.14 Let $p = 11$ and $q = 17$, whence $r = pq = 187$. $\phi(r)$ stands for $\text{lcm}(p - 1, q - 1)$ such that $\phi(r) = \text{lcm}(p - 1, q - 1) = \text{lcm}(10, 16) = 80$. Pick $K_{pa} = 27$. Then

$$\begin{aligned} K_{pa}K_{sa} &\equiv 1 \quad \pmod{\phi(r)} \\ 27K_{sa} &\equiv 1 \quad \pmod{80} \end{aligned}$$

Since $(27)(3) \equiv 81 \pmod{80} \equiv 1$, K_{sa} is determined as $K_{sa} = 3$. Suppose $X = 55$. Then

$$\begin{aligned} Y &\equiv X^{K_{sa}} \quad \pmod{187} \\ &\equiv 55^3 \quad \pmod{187} \equiv 132 \end{aligned}$$

At the receiving end, the message is recreated as

$$X \equiv Y^{K_{pa}} \pmod{r} \equiv (132)^{27} \pmod{187} \equiv 55$$

Thus, the message X is accepted as authentic.

5.5 McELIECE'S ALGEBRAIC CODES CRYPTOSYSTEM

In 1978 McEliece proposed a public-key cryptosystem based on error correcting codes [31]. His cryptosystem is based on the Goppa codes with the generator matrix **G** and then transforming this matrix into **G**′ which is the public key of this system. A message **m** is encrypted by multiplying it with **G**′ and adding the error pattern **e** of length n and weight t to the code word **c**. The legitimate message is then recovered by using a decoding algorithm applicable to the original Goppa code.

Before describing the McEliece scheme, we shall briefly discuss the error correction method. Let a k-bit message be $\mathbf{m} = (m_0, m_1, \ldots, m_{k-1})$. Multiplying **m** onto a $(k \times n)$ generator matrix $\mathbf{G} = [\mathbf{P}_{k \times (n-k)} \mathbf{I}_k]$ to form the code word $\mathbf{c} = (c_0, c_1, \ldots, c_{n-1})$ results in

$$\mathbf{c} = \mathbf{m} \cdot \mathbf{G} \tag{5.47}$$

where $\mathbf{c} = (\gamma_0, \gamma_1, \ldots, \gamma_{n-k-1}, m_0, m_1, \ldots, m_{k-1})$ is called the code word for an (n, k) linear systematic code. The component $(\gamma_0, \gamma_1, \ldots, \gamma_{n-k-1})$ in **c** represents the parity-check bits. The code word **c** is transmitted via an insecure channel and usually corrupted by the error pattern $\mathbf{e} = (e_0, e_1, \ldots, e_{n-1})$. The received word $\mathbf{r} = (r_0, r_1, \ldots, r_{n-1})$ is then created as a vector sum of **c** and **e** such that

$$\mathbf{r} = \mathbf{c} + \mathbf{e} \tag{5.48}$$

Upon receiving **r**, the decoder first starts to compute the syndrome. The decoder attempts to determine the corresponding error pattern **e**. Once this error pattern is found, the vector **r** + **e** is used as the legitimate code word. That is,

$$\mathbf{c} = \mathbf{r} + \mathbf{e} \tag{5.49}$$

Thus, the received word **r** at the decoder must be corrected, after which the message may be recovered.

McEliece's public-key scheme can be briefly described as shown below. Let **G** denote a t-error correcting $(k \times n)$ generator matrix of a linear code. McEliece scrambles **G** by selecting a random $(k \times k)$ non-singular matrix **S** and a random $(n \times n)$ permutation matrix **P**. Then the matrix **G** is transformed into

$$\mathbf{G}' = \mathbf{S\,G\,P} \tag{5.50}$$

which generates a linear code with the same rate k/n and minimum distance $d_{\min}$ as the code generated by **G**. **G**′ is called the $(k \times n)$ public generator matrix. **G**′ is published as the encryption key, but its component matrices **G**, **S**, and **P** are all secret. From $\mathbf{G}' = \mathbf{S\,G\,P}$, we can obtain $\mathbf{G} = \mathbf{S}^{-1}\mathbf{G}'\mathbf{P}^{-1}$. Now, the sender encrypts a k-bit plaintext **m** into an n-bit ciphertext **c** by

$$\mathbf{c} = \mathbf{mG}' + \mathbf{e}$$

$$= \mathbf{mSGP} + \mathbf{e} \tag{5.51}$$

On receipt of **c**, the received ciphertext becomes

$$\mathbf{c}' = \mathbf{cP}^{-1} = (\mathbf{mS})\,\mathbf{G} + \mathbf{e}' \tag{5.52}$$

where $\mathbf{e}' = \mathbf{eP}^{-1}$. A decoding algorithm for the original code shows how to remove the error vector **e**′ and recover the vector **mS**. Thus, the message plaintext **m** is easily found according to the equation

$$\mathbf{m} = (\mathbf{mS})\,\mathbf{S}^{-1} \tag{5.53}$$

Depending on the choice of k and t, computational complexity can be maximized and can strengthen the algorithm against cryptographic attack. An obvious attack on this system is to pick k columns of the matrix **G**′. Since **m** is a k-bit message, Eq. 5.51 can be reduced to [1]

$$\mathbf{c}_k = \mathbf{mG}_k' + \mathbf{e}_k \tag{5.54}$$

where $\mathbf{c}_k$, $\mathbf{G}_k'$, and $\mathbf{e}_k$ are restrictions on these k columns. From Eq. 5.54, it follows that

$$\mathbf{c}_k + \mathbf{e}_k = \mathbf{mG}_k'$$

or

$$\mathbf{m} = (\mathbf{c}_k + \mathbf{e}_k)(\mathbf{G}_k')^{-1} \tag{5.55}$$

If $e_k = 0$, then Eq. 5.55 is reduced to

$$\mathbf{m} = \mathbf{c}_k(\mathbf{G}_k')^{-1} \tag{5.56}$$

and **m** can be found without decoding.

McEliece suggests a Goppa code with block length $n = 2^m = 2^{10} = 1024$ and $t = 50$. Then the plaintext block is $k = n - mt = 524$ and the rate $k/n \cong 0.5$. For $n = 1024$ and $t = 50$, the expected number of operations before a success is about $2^{80.7}$. However, Adams and Meijer [1] showed that $t = 37$ along with $n = 1024$ is the optimum value based on this attack and the expected number of operations is about $2^{84.1}$ at $t = 37$.

The following example illustrates McEliece's work by taking a simple linear code.

■ **Example 5.15** Consider the single-error-correcting (7, 4) BCH code with minimum distance $d_{min} = 3$. Suppose the generator matrix **G**, the scramble matrix **S**, and the permutation matrix **P** are given, respectively, as

$$\mathbf{G} = \begin{bmatrix} 1101000 \\ 0110100 \\ 1110010 \\ 1010001 \end{bmatrix} \qquad \mathbf{S} = \begin{bmatrix} 1110 \\ 1010 \\ 0110 \\ 1011 \end{bmatrix}$$

$$\mathbf{P} = \begin{bmatrix} 0010000 \\ 1000000 \\ 0000100 \\ 0100000 \\ 0000001 \\ 0000010 \\ 0001000 \end{bmatrix}$$

Using Eq. 5.50, compute the public encryption key G' as follows:

$$\mathbf{S\,G} = \begin{bmatrix} 0101110 \\ 0011010 \\ 1000110 \\ 1001011 \end{bmatrix}$$

from which

$$\mathbf{G}' = \mathbf{S\,G\,P} = \begin{bmatrix} 1100011 \\ 0100110 \\ 0010011 \\ 0111010 \end{bmatrix}$$

Assume the message plaintext $\mathbf{m} = (0\ 1\ 0\ 0)$ and the error pattern $\mathbf{e} = (0\,0\,0\,0\,1\,0\,0)$ occurred during transmission. Then, from Eq. 5.51, the encrypted ciphertext can be found as

$$\mathbf{c} = \mathbf{m}\mathbf{G}' + \mathbf{e}$$

$$= (0\,1\,0\,0) \begin{bmatrix} 1100011 \\ 0100110 \\ 0010011 \\ 0111010 \end{bmatrix} + (0\,0\,0\,0\,1\,0\,0)$$

$$= (0\,1\,0\,0\,1\,1\,0) + (0\,0\,0\,0\,1\,0\,0)$$

$$= (0\,1\,0\,0\,0\,1\,0)$$

Using Eq. 5.52, the received ciphertext $\mathbf{c}' = \mathbf{c}\ \mathbf{P}^{-1}$ can be computed as follows: Determinant is computed from the permutation matrix **P** as 1. After calculating the cofactors of the square matrix **P**, the inverse of matrix **P** is the adjoint matrix divided by the determinant of **P**.
We can now compute $\mathbf{P}^{-1}$ as

$$\mathbf{P}^{-1} = \frac{[\text{cofactors } P_{ij}]^T}{|\mathbf{P}|} = \begin{bmatrix} 0100000 \\ 0001000 \\ 1000000 \\ 0000001 \\ 0010000 \\ 0000010 \\ 0000100 \end{bmatrix}$$

Thus, the received ciphertext is calculated as $\mathbf{c}' = \mathbf{c} \cdot \mathbf{P}^{-1} = (0\,0\,0\,1\,0\,1\,0)$.
Similarly we can calculate the inverse matrix $\mathbf{S}^{-1}$ of the scramble matrix **S**. Since the determinant $|\ \mathbf{S}\ | = 1$, we obtain it as

$$\mathbf{S}^{-1} = \begin{bmatrix} 1010 \\ 1100 \\ 1110 \\ 0101 \end{bmatrix}$$

The syndrome, denoted by **s**, of $\mathbf{c}'$ is defined to be the following three-tuple row vector such that

$$\mathbf{s} = \mathbf{c}'\mathrm{H}^{\mathrm{T}} = (s_0, s_1, s_2)$$

where $\mathbf{H}^T$ is the transposed matrix of the parity-check matrix **H** which is easily derived from **G**. Since we compute

$$\mathbf{H} = \begin{bmatrix} 1001011 \\ 0101110 \\ 0010111 \end{bmatrix}$$

its transposed matrix is

$$\mathbf{H}^T = \begin{bmatrix} 1\,0\,0 \\ 0\,1\,0 \\ 0\,0\,1 \\ 1\,1\,0 \\ 0\,1\,1 \\ 1\,1\,1 \\ 1\,0\,1 \end{bmatrix}$$

Hence the syndrome is

$$\mathbf{s} = (0\,0\,0\,1\,0\,1\,0) \begin{bmatrix} 1\,0\,0 \\ 0\,1\,0 \\ 0\,0\,1 \\ 1\,1\,0 \\ 0\,1\,1 \\ 1\,1\,1 \\ 1\,0\,1 \end{bmatrix} = (0\,0\,1)$$

The error vector $\mathbf{e}'$ can then be computed as

$$\mathbf{e}' = \mathbf{e} \cdot \mathbf{P}^{-1} = (0\,0\,0\,0\,1\,0\,0) \begin{bmatrix} 0\,1\,0\,0\,0\,0\,0 \\ 0\,0\,0\,1\,0\,0\,0 \\ 1\,0\,0\,0\,0\,0\,0 \\ 0\,0\,0\,0\,0\,0\,1 \\ 0\,0\,1\,0\,0\,0\,0 \\ 0\,0\,0\,0\,0\,1\,0 \\ 0\,0\,0\,0\,1\,0\,0 \end{bmatrix}$$

$$= (0\,0\,1\,0\,0\,0\,0)$$

Combining $\mathbf{c}'$ and $\mathbf{e}'$, we obtain

$$\mathbf{c}' + \mathbf{e}' = (0\,0\,1\,1\,0\,1\,0)$$

in which the four digits on the right represent $\mathbf{m}' = \mathbf{mS} = (1\,0\,1\,0)$. Using Eq. 5.53, we can finally recover the plaintext as

$$(\mathbf{mS})\mathbf{S}^{-1} = (1\,0\,1\,0) \begin{bmatrix} 1\,0\,1\,0 \\ 1\,1\,0\,0 \\ 1\,1\,1\,0 \\ 0\,1\,0\,1 \end{bmatrix} = (0\,1\,0\,0)$$

This cryptoscheme has one major drawback, that is, the key could have 2^{19} bits as suggested by McEliece. Because the key is quite large, the bandwidth increases. Consequently, the ciphertext would be twice as long as the corresponding plaintext. This cryptosystem is also not suitable for producing signatures as the algorithm is truly asymmetric and not one-to-one.

5.6 BIBLIOGRAPHICAL AND HISTORICAL REVIEW

With the advent of modern computer and communication technologies, the need for cryptographic protection was widely recognized and the direction of researches changed drastically. At the beginning of the seventies, only symmetrical (single-key) cryptography was known. Moreover, classified researches in cryptography discouraged cryptologists who sought to discover new cryptosystems. Nevertheless the explosive growth in unclassified research in all aspects of cryptology has progressed since the second half of the seventies. Since 1980, cryptanalysis has been one of the most active areas of research and a large set of mathematical tools useful for such analysis has been developed with progress in research on computational complexity. In fact, there is no doubt that the extensive research on cryptography and computational complexity has helped cryptologists understand better what makes a system insecure. However, unfortunately, no rigorous proofs of effectiveness exist for justifying many cryptanalytic attacks.

Historically, research related to public-key cryptosystems began with the classic paper by Diffie and Hellman (1976). Since then, Rivest, Shamir, and Adleman (1978) discovered the RSA asymmetric cryptosystem which depends on the difficulty of factoring large integers; Merkle and Hellman (1978) produced another two-key cryptosystem which is based on the knapsack problem.

It was known till 1982 that the public-key algorithms for solving the knapsack problem are of exponential computational complexity because this problem is NP-complete. Particularly the iterated Merkle-Hellman scheme was claimed to be secure. However, the basic Merkle-Hellman additive knapsack system was shown by Shamir (1982) to be easy to crack [46]. Subsequently, Adleman (1983) proposed attacks on the iterated Merkle-Hellman cryptosystem [2] by cracking the enciphering key obtained using the Graham-Shamir knapsack [45], but Adleman's attack on the multiple iterated knapsack systems does not quite succeed. Brickell, Lagarias, and Odlyzko (1984) evaluated the Adleman attacks on the multiple iterated knapsack system [4]. In addition, Desmedt, Vandewalle, and Govaerts (1982, 1984) claimed that the iterated Merkle-Hellman systems are insecure, since an enciphering key can be cracked [14]. A multiple iterated knapsack scheme is a cryptosystem relying on modular multiplications which are used for disguising an easy knapsack. Lagarias (1984) and Brickell (1985) have intensively studied these systems by using simultaneous diophantine approximation [25, 6]. Goodman and McAuley (1985) proposed another knapsack cryptosystem using modular multiplication to disguise an easy knapsack, but that system is substantially different from those mentioned above [21]. However, this cryptosystem can still be broken using lattice basis reduction. Pieprzyk (1985) designed a knapsack system similar to that of Goodman and McAuley knapsack except that the integers were replaced by polynomials over GF (2) [40].

Brickell (1984), and Lagarias and Odlyzko (1985), proposed the algorithms for solving knapsacks of low density [5, 26]. Schnorr (1988) developed the more efficient lattice basis reduction algorithm which could be successful on knapsacks of much higher density [47]. Other knapsack cryptosystems that have been proposed are the Lu-Lee scheme [29], the Niederreiter cryptosystem [33], and the Chor-Rivest knapsack system [11]. Lu and Lee (1977) proposed a cryptosystem, but several authors, namely Goethals and Couvrcur (1980), Kochauski (1980), Adiga and Shankar (1985), and Adleman and Rivest (1979), criticized their system and came up with several cryptanalytic attacks. Niederreiter (1986) proposed a knapsack cryptosystem using algebraic coding theory. Chor and Rivest (1985) designed a knapsack cryptosystem that does not use any form of modular multiplication to disguise an easy knapsack.

A few two-key cryptosystems which rely on the composition of a polynomial over a finite field have been proposed. But it is reported that all such schemes may be vulnerable to certain specific attacks. Matsumoto and Imai (1983) proposed a cryptosystem which uses a polynomial over GF (2^m) [30]. But Delsarte et al. (1984) expressed reservations about this system [12]. Yagisawa (1985) introduced a cryptosystem which combined exponentiation mod p with arithmetic mod $p - 1$ [51]. But Brickell (1986) showed that it could be broken without finding the private key [7]. Cade (1985, 86) devised public-key cryptosystems which also use polynomials over GF (2^m) [9, 10].

The RSA scheme is the best known two-key cryptosystem. A message plaintext is encrypted as $Y \equiv X^e \pmod r$, where $e = K_p$ is the public key and is relatively prime to $\phi(r) = (p-1)(q-1)$; and r is a composite integer which consists of only two primes such that $r = pq$. Both r and K_p are public, while p and q are secret integers. If the cryptanalysis can factor r, then the message plaintext can be decrypted. However, it is not known how to break the RSA system without factoring r. The techniques for integer factorization has advanced significantly in the last decade and the largest hard integer up to almost 90 decimal integers in length had been factored. If a machine capable of factoring 150-digit integers is built, it can break the RSA cryptosystem. There are several integer factoring algorithms proposed by Lenstra and Lenstra (1989), Pomerance (1987), and Gordon (1985). Even though the original RSA cryptosystem is capable of strongly resisting all attacks, this is not true for all variants of it. Kravity and Reed (1982) have proposed using an irreducible polynomial over GF (2) in place of the primes p and q. That is, the public modulus is the polynomial $r(z) = p(z)\, q(z)$ which indicates the product of polynomials of degree t and s and the public key exponent $e = K_p$ is chosen to be relatively prime to $(2^t - 1)(2^s - 1)$ [24]. This system can be broken by factoring $r(z)$. The weakness of this system has been extensively studied by Delsarte and Piret (1982) and Gait (1982) [13, 19].

McEliece (1978) introduced a two-key cryptosystem based on error correcting codes. It has two major drawbacks: the key is quite large and increases the bandwidth, and the ciphertext would be twice as long as the corresponding plaintext. Adams and Meijer (1987) showed that for $n = 1024$ (code length), $t = 37$ (error correcting capability) is the optimum value and the expected number of operations is about $2^{84.1}$. Later, Lee and Brickell (1989) modified this attack [3]. Rao and Nam (1986) have proposed a variant scheme of the McEliece cryptosystem as a single-key cryptosystem. Struik and Tilburg (1987) showed how to break the Rao-Nam system [49].

Ong, Schnorr and Shamir (1984) proposed a signature scheme based on polynomial equations modulo n [36]. The first such scheme used a polynomial P of degree 2 [37], and was cracked by Pollard (1987). The Ong-Schnorr-Shamir signature scheme of a cubic version was also broken by Pollard [42]. Subsequently, the authors published a quadratic version, but this version was also broken by Estes *et al.* (1986), and independently by Schnorr (1987). Since this scheme was broken so often by cryptanalysts, it implies that there are no secure signature schemes of this type. Okamoto and Schiraishi (1985) proposed a signature scheme which is based on the difficulty of finding approximate kth roots and n [39]. Their original scheme was for $k = 2$. Not only the $k = 2$ case, but the $k = 3$ case also was quickly broken by Brickell and DeLaurentis (1986). For $k \geq 4$, these schemes can be broken by another attack recently discussed by Vallec, Girault, and Toffin (1988).

The eighties were the first full decade of public key cryptography. Many systems were proposed and many broken. Brickell and Odlyzko provide a well documented historical overview in the proceedings of the IEEE in 1988. Since 1976, more than 200 papers have appeared in professional journals, conference proceedings, and research reports. It is impossible to introduce all of them in this section. Therefore, this historical review on public key cryptosystems is neither exhaustive nor complete.

REFERENCES

1. Adams, C.M. and H. Meijer: "Security-related comments regarding McEliece's public-key cryptosystem", *Advances in Cryptology-Crypto '87*, pp 224–228, Springer-Verlag, New York, 1987.
2. Adleman, L.M.: "On breaking the iterated Merkle-Hellman public key cryptosystem", *Advances in Cryptology: Proc. Crypto '82*, Plenum Press, New York, 1983.
3. Brickell, E.F. and A.M. Odlyzko: "Cryptanalysis: A survey of recent results", *Proc. IEEE*, vol. 76, no. 5, 1988.
4. Brickell, E.F., J.C. Lagarias, and A.M. Odlyzko: "Evaluation of the Adleman attack on multiply iterated knapsack cryptosystems", *Proc. Crypto '83*, Plenum Press, New York, 1984.
5. Brickell, E.F.: "Solving low density knapsacks", *Advances in Cryptology, Proc. Crypto '83*, Plenum Press, New York, 1984.
6. ------,: "Breaking iterated knapsacks", in *Advances in Crytology, Proc. Crypto '84*, Springer-Verlag, New York, LNCS vol. 218, 1985.
7. ------,: "Cryptanalysis of the Yagisawa public key cryptosystem", *Abstract at Eurocrypt '86*, Linkoping, May 20–22, 1986.
8. Brickell, E.F. and J.M. DeLaurentis: "An attack on a signature scheme proposed by Okamoto and Schiraishi", *Advances in Cryptology–Crypto '85*, Springer-Verlag, New York, LNCS, vol. 263, pp 28–32, 1986.
9. Cade, J.J.: "A public key cipher which allows signatures", *2nd SIAM Conf. Applied Linear Algebra*, Raleigh, NC, 1985.
10. ------,: "A modification of a broken public-key cipher", *Advances in Cryptology–Crypto '86*, pp 64–83, Springer-Verlag, New York.
11. Chor, B. and R. Rivest: "A knapsack type public key cryptosystem based on arithmetic in finite fields", *Advances in Cryptology–Crypto '84*, Springer-Verlag, New York, LNCS 263, pp 54–65, 1985.
12. Delsarte, P., Y. Desmedt, A. Odlyzko, and P. Piret: "Fast cryptanalysis of the Matsumoto-Imai public key scheme", *Advances in Cryptology–Eurocrypt '84*, Springer-Verlag, Berlin, LNCS 209, pp 142–149, 1985.
13. Delsarte, P. and P. Piret: "Comment on extension of RSA cryptostructure: A Galois approach," *Electronics Letters*, vol. 18, pp 582–583, 1982.
14. Desmedt, Y., J. Vandewalle, and R. Govaerts: "How iterative transformations can help to crack the Merkle-Hellman cryptographic scheme", *Electronic Letters*, vol. 18, pp 910–911, 1982.
15. ------,: "A critical analysis of the security of knapsack public-key algorithm", *IEEE Trans. Inform. Theory*, vol. IT-30, no. 4, pp 601–611, 1984.
16. Diffie, W. and M.E. Hellman: "New directions in cryptography", *IEEE Trans. Inform. Theory*, vol. IT-22, no. 6, pp 644–654, 1976.
17. ------,: "Privacy and authentication: An introduction to cryptography",

Proc. IEEE, vol. 67, no. 3, pp 397–427, 1979.

18. Estes, D., L.M. Adleman, K. Kompella, K.S. McCurley, and G.L. Miller: "Breaking the Ong-Schnorr-Shamir signature scheme for quadratic number fields", *Advances in Cryptology–Crypto '85*, Springer-Verlag, New York, LNCS 263, pp 3–13, 1986.
19. Gait, J.: "Short cycling in the Kravity-Reed public-key encryption system", *Electronic Letters*, vol. 18, pp 706–707, 1982.
20. Gordon, J.A.: "Strong primes are easy to find", *Advances in Cryptology–Eurocrypt '84*, Paris, Springer-Verlag, Berlin, LNCS 209, pp 216–223, 1985.
21. Goodman, R.M. and A.J. McAuley: "A new trapdoor knapsack public-key cryptosystem", *Advances in Cryptology–Proc. Eurocrypt '84*, Springer-Verlag, Berlin, LNCS 209, 1985.
22. Herlestam, H.: "On the complexity of functions of linear shift register sequences", *Int. Symp. Inf. Theory*, Les Arc, France, 1982.
23. Key, E.L.: "An analysis of the structure and complexity of nonlinear binary sequence generators", *IEEE Trans. Inform. Theory*, vol. IT-22, Nov. 1976.
24. Kravity, D. and I. Reed: "Extension of RSA cryptostructure: A Galois approach", *Electronic Letters*, vol. 18, pp 255–256, 1982.
25. Lagarias, J.C.: "Knapsack public-key cryptosystems and diophantine approximation", *Advances in Cryptology–Proc. Crypto '83*, Plenum Press, New York, 1984.
26. Lagarias, J.C. and A.M. Odlyzko: "Solving low density subset sum problems", *J. Assoc. Comp. Mach.*, vol. 23, 1985.
27. Lenstra, A.K. and H.W. Lenstra: "Algorithms in number theory", *Handbook of Theoretical Computer Science*, to appear.
28. Lenstra, A.K.: "Factoring multivariate polynomials over finite fields", *J. Computer and System Sci.*, vol. 30, no. 2, pp 235–248, 1985.
29. Lu, S.C. and L.N. Lee: "A simple and effective public-key cryptosystem", *COMSAT Tech. Rev.*, pp 15–24, 1979.
30. Matsumoto, T. and H. Imai: "A class of asymmetric cryptosystems based on polynomials over finite rings", *IEEE Intern. Symp. Inform. Theory*, St. Jovite, Quebec, pp 131–132, 1983.
31. McEliece, R.J.: "A public-key cryptosystem based on algebraic coding theory", *DSN Progress Rep.*, Jet Propulsion Laboratory, Pasadena, CA, pp 114–116, Jan.-Feb. 1978.
32. Merkle, R.C., and M.E. Hellman: "Hiding information and signatures in trapdoor knapsacks", *IEEE Trans. Inform. Theory*. vol. IT-24, no. 5, pp 525–530, 1978.
33. Niederreiter, H.: "Knapsack-type cryptosystem and algebraic coding theory", *Problems of Control and Information Theory*, vol. 15, pp 159–166, 1986.
34. Odlyzko A.M.: Discrete logarithms in finite fields and their cryptographic significance", *Advances in Cryptography–Proc. Eurocrypt '84*, pp 224–314, 1984.
35. Odlyzko, A.M.: "Cryptanalytic attacks on the multiplicative knapsack cryptosystem and on Shamir's fast signature system", *IEEE Trans. Inform. Theory*, vol. IT-30, no. 4, pp 594–601, 1984.

36. Ong, H., C.P. Schnorr, and A. Shamir: "An efficient signature scheme based on quadratic equations", *Proc. 16th ACM Symp. Theory of Computing*, Washington, pp 208–216, 1984.
37. Ong, H. and C.P. Schnorr: "Signatures through approximate representations by quadratic forms", *Advances in Cryptology–Proc. Crypto '83*, Plenum Press, New York, pp 117–132, 1984.
38. ------,: "Efficient signature schemes based on polynomial equations", *Advances in Cryptology–Crypto '84*, Springer-Verlag, New York, pp 37–46, 1985.
39. Okamoto, T. and A. Schiraishi: "A fast signature scheme based on quadratic inequalities", *Proc. IEEE Symp. Security and Privacy*, pp 123–132, 1985.
40. Picprzyk, J.P.: "On public-key cryptosystems built using polynomial rings", *Advances in Cryptology–Eurocrypt '85*, Linz, Springer-Verlag, Berlin, pp 73–80, 1985.
41. Pohlig, S.C. and M.E. Hellman: "An improved algorithm for computing logarithms over GF (p) and its cryptographic significance", *IEEE Trans. Inform. Theory*, vol. IT-24, no. 1, 1978.
42. Pollard, J.M. and C.P. Schnorr: "An efficient solution of the congruence $x^2 + ky^2 = m \pmod{n}$", *IEEE Trans. Inform. Theory*, vol. IT-33, no. 5, pp 702–709, 1987.
43. Rivest, R.L., A. Shamir, and L. Adleman: "A method for obtaining digital signatures and public-key cryptosystems", *Comm. ACM*, vol. 21, no. 2, pp 120–126, 1978.
44. Rao, T.R.N. and K.H. Nam: "Private-key algebraic-code encryptions", IEEE *Trans. Inform. Theory*, IT–35, vol. 35, no. 4, pp 829–833, 1989.
45. Shamir, A. and R.E. Zippel: "On the security of the Merkle-Hellman cryptographic scheme", *IEEE Trans. Inform. Theory*, vol. IT-26, no. 3, pp 339–340, 1980.
46. Shamir, A: "A polynomial time algorithm for breaking the basic Merkle-Hellman cryptosystem", *IEEE Trans. Inform. Theory*, vol. IT-30, no. 5, 1984.
47. Schnorr C.P.: "A more efficient algorithm for a lattice basis reduction", *J. Algorithms*, vol. 9, pp 47–62, 1988.
48. ------,: "A hierarchy of polynomial time lattice basis reduction algorithms", *Theoretical Computer Science*, vol. 53, pp 201–224, 1987.
49. Struik, R. and J. Van Tilburg: "The Rao-Nam scheme is insecure against a chosen-plaintext attack", *Advances in Cryptology–Proc. Crypto '87*, Springer-Verlag, New York, pp 445–457, 1988.
50. Vallec, B., M. Girault, and P. Toffin: "How to guess l-th roots modulo n when reducing lattice basis", Preprint, Univ. Caen, Jan. 1988.
51. Yagisawa, M.: "A new method for realizing a public-key cryptosystem", *Cryptologia*, vol. 9, no. 4, pp 360–380, 1985.
52. Zierler, N. and W.H. Mills: "Products of linear recurring sequences", *J. Algebra*, vol. 27, 1973.

Chapter

6

Galois Field Arithmetic for Logic Devices

Arithmetic operations in GF (2^m) play an important role in encoding and decoding certain error-correcting codes. This chapter describes arithmetic operations that compute addition, multiplication, division and square roots in GF (2^m). A number of additions, multiplications, and multiplicative inversions in GF (2^m) are required to implement logical devices such as decoders for BCH codes as well as Reed-Solomon codes. VLSI fabrication makes possible some arrays of logical devices to perform such functions. Any reduction in either the cost or the computation time of the logical devices required to perform these operations may result in considerable improvement of the design of decoders. Recent developments in VLSI technology are becoming increasingly attractive because of their easy fabrication. The work described in this chapter presents mainly a number of circuits for computing the product of two arbitrary elements of GF (2^m) because an error-control decoder deals with multipliers to a considerable extent.

To improve the performance of a cryptographic communication system or data file system, an error-correcting code can be concatenated between the enciphering and the deciphering, as discussed in Chapter 9.

Table 6.1 Field Elements of GF (2^5) for $p(x) = 1 + x^2 + x^5$

Power form	Polynomial form	5-tuple vector form
0	0	00000
1	1	10000
α	α	01000
α^2	α^2	00100
α^3	α^3	00010
α^4	α^4	00001
α^5	$1 + \alpha^2$	10100
α^6	$\alpha \quad \alpha^3$	01010
α^7	$\alpha^2 + \alpha^4$	00101
α^8	$1 + \alpha^2 + \alpha^3$	10110
α^9	$\alpha \quad \alpha^3 + \alpha^4$	01011
α^{10}	$1 + \alpha^4$	10001
α^{11}	$1 + \alpha + \alpha^2$	11100
α^{12}	$\alpha + \alpha^2 + \alpha^3$	01110
α^{13}	$\alpha^2 + \alpha^3 + \alpha^4$	00111
α^{14}	$1 + \alpha^2 + \alpha^3 + \alpha^4$	10111
α^{15}	$1 + \alpha + \alpha^2 + \alpha^3 + \alpha^4$	11111
α^{16}	$1 + \alpha + \alpha^3 + \alpha^4$	11011
α^{17}	$1 + \alpha + \alpha^4$	11001
α^{18}	$1 + \alpha$	11000
α^{19}	$\alpha + \alpha^2$	01100
α^{20}	$\alpha^2 + \alpha^3$	00110
α^{21}	$\alpha^3 + \alpha^4$	00011
α^{22}	$1 + \alpha^2 + \alpha^4$	10101
α^{23}	$1 + \alpha + \alpha^2 + \alpha^3$	11110
α^{24}	$\alpha + \alpha^2 + \alpha^3 + \alpha^4$	01111
α^{25}	$1 + \alpha^3 + \alpha^4$	10011
α^{26}	$1 + \alpha + \alpha^2 + \alpha^4$	11101
α^{27}	$1 + \alpha + \alpha^3$	11010
α^{28}	$\alpha + \alpha^2 + \alpha^4$	01101
α^{29}	$1 + \alpha^3$	10010
α^{30}	$\alpha + \alpha^4$	01001

6.1 GALOIS FIELD ADDER

In this section we consider the operating circuit that performs over the finite field GF (2^m). GF (2^m) is called an extension field of the ground field GF (2) of 2 elements and contains 2^m elements. The 2^m-1 nonzero elements of GF (2^m) are represented as the powers of primitive element α, where α is a root of a primitive irreducible polynomial $p(x) = p_0 + p_1x + \ldots + p_{m-1}x^{m-1} + x^m$ over GF (2). Since $p(\alpha) = 0$, $\alpha^m = p_0 + p_1 \alpha + \ldots + p_{m-1}\alpha^{m-1}$. Therefore, any element of GF (2^m) can be expressed as a polynomial of α with degree $m-1$ or less. The field elements in GF (2^m) can also be represented by an ordered sequence of m components, called an m-tuple vector, $\boldsymbol{\alpha}^m = (p_0, p_1, \ldots, p_{m-1})$. These m components are simply the m coefficients of the polynomial of α^m. Thus any field element can then be represented as either a vector or a polynomial. For example, the field elements of GF (2^5) generated by $p(x) = 1 + x^2 + x^5$ are given in Table 6.1.

In general, power representation is convenient for multiplication and polynomial representation for addition. Let $A(\alpha)$ and $B(\alpha)$ denote two elements in GF (2^m) in a polynomial form or a vector form such that

$$A(\alpha) = a_0 + a_1\alpha + \cdots + a_{m-1}\alpha^{m-1} \tag{6.1}$$

or

$$\mathbf{A} = (a_0, a_1, \cdots, a_{m-1}) \tag{6.2}$$

$$B(\alpha) = b_0 + b_1\alpha + \cdots + b_{m-1}\alpha^{m-1} \tag{6.3}$$

or

$$\mathbf{B} = (b_0, b_1, \cdots, b_{m-1}) \tag{6.4}$$

Adding $A(\alpha)$ and $B(\alpha)$, the polynomial representation for $A(\alpha) + B(\alpha)$ becomes

$$A(\alpha) + B(\alpha) = (a_0 + b_0) + (a_1 + b_1)\alpha + \cdots + (a_{m-1} + b_{m-1})\alpha^{m-1} \tag{6.5}$$

or

$$\mathbf{A} + \mathbf{B} = (a_0 + b_0, a_1 + b_1, \cdots, a_{m-1} + b_{m-1}) \tag{6.6}$$

Thus, if two field elements are added, then the resultant vector is simply the vector representation of the sum of these two field elements, as shown in Fig. 6.1. Therefore, addition in GF (2^m) is straightforward.

6.2 COMBINATIONAL LOGIC MULTIPLIERS

We consider here combinational logic circuits for the multiplication of two arbitrary elements in GF (2^m). Let $A(\alpha) = a_0 + a_1\alpha + \ldots + a_{m-1}\alpha^{m-1}$

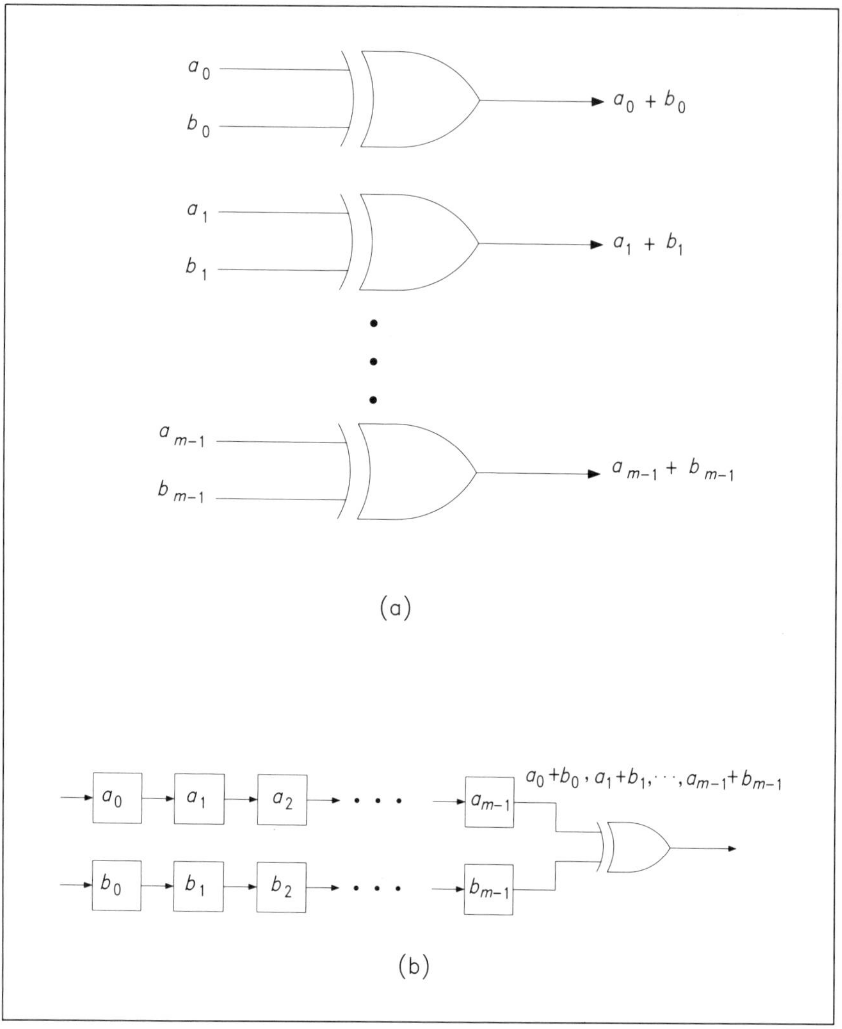

Fig. 6.1 Galois field adder: (a) parallel type, and (b) serial type.

and $B(\alpha) = b_0 + b_1 \alpha + \ldots + b_{m-1} \alpha^{m-1}$ be two field elements, expressed in polynomial form. The product $Z(\alpha) = A(\alpha) B(\alpha)$ can be expressed as follows:

$$Z(\alpha) = A(\alpha) B(\alpha)$$

$$= A(\alpha) \sum_{i=0}^{m-1} b_i \alpha^i = \sum_{i=0}^{m-1} b_i (\alpha^i A(\alpha)) \tag{6.7}$$

or in matrix form, as

$$(z_0, z_1, \ldots, z_{m-1}) = (b_0, b_1, \ldots, b_{m-1}) \begin{bmatrix} A(\alpha) \\ \alpha A(\alpha) \\ \alpha^2 A(\alpha) \\ \cdot \\ \cdot \\ \cdot \\ \alpha^{m-1} A(\alpha) \end{bmatrix} \tag{6.8}$$

■ **Example 6.1** Consider GF (2^5) for $m = 5$. The polynomial $p(x) = 1 + x^2 + x^5$ is a primitive polynomial over GF (2). If α is a root of $p(x)$, then $p(\alpha) = 0$, i.e. $\alpha^5 = 1 + \alpha^2$. Using this α^5, $\alpha^i A(\alpha)$ in Eq. 6.8 for $0 \le i \le 4$ becomes

$$A(\alpha) = a_0 + a_1\alpha + a_2\alpha^2 + a_3\alpha^3 + a_4\alpha^4$$

$$\alpha A(\alpha) = a_4 + a_0\alpha + (a_1 + a_4)\alpha^2 + a_2\alpha^3 + a_3\alpha^4$$

$$\alpha^2 A(\alpha) = a_3 + a_4\alpha + (a_0 + a_3)\alpha^2 + (a_1 + a_4)\alpha^3 + a_2\alpha^4$$

$$\alpha^3 A(\alpha) = a_2 + a_3\alpha + (a_2 + a_4)\alpha^2 + (a_0 + a_3)\alpha^3 + (a_1 + a_4)\alpha^4$$

$$\alpha^4 A(\alpha) = (a_1 + a_4) + a_2\alpha + (a_1 + a_3 + a_4)\alpha^2 + (a_2 + a_4)\alpha^3 + (a_0 + a_3)\alpha^4$$

Substituting these $\alpha^i A(\alpha)$s, $0 \le i \le 4$, in Eq. 6.8 yields

$$z_0 = a_0b_0 + a_4b_1 + a_3b_2 + a_2b_3 + (a_1 + a_4)\,b_4$$

$$z_1 = a_1b_0 + a_0b_1 + a_4b_2 + a_3b_3 + a_2b_4$$

$$z_2 = a_2b_0 + (a_1 + a_4)\,b_1 + (a_0 + a_3)\,b_2 + (a_2 + a_4)\,b_3 + (a_1 + a_3 + a_4)\,b_4$$

$$z_3 = a_3b_0 + a_2b_1 + (a_1 + a_4)\,b_2 + (a_0 + a_3)\,b_3 + (a_2 + a_4)\,b_4$$

$$z_4 = a_4b_0 + a_3b_1 + a_2b_2 + (a_1 + a_4)\,b_3 + (a_0 + a_3)\,b_4$$

Based on these expressions for z_i, we obtain combinational logic circuits (as shown in Fig. 6.2) which are capable of multiplying any element $A(\alpha)$ in GF (2^5) by another element $B(\alpha)$. Thus, multiplication of two elements in GF (2^m) can be implemented by a combinational logic circuit with $2m$ inputs and m outputs. However, as m increases, it becomes prohibitively complex and costly. But the advantage of a combinational multiplier is its speed.

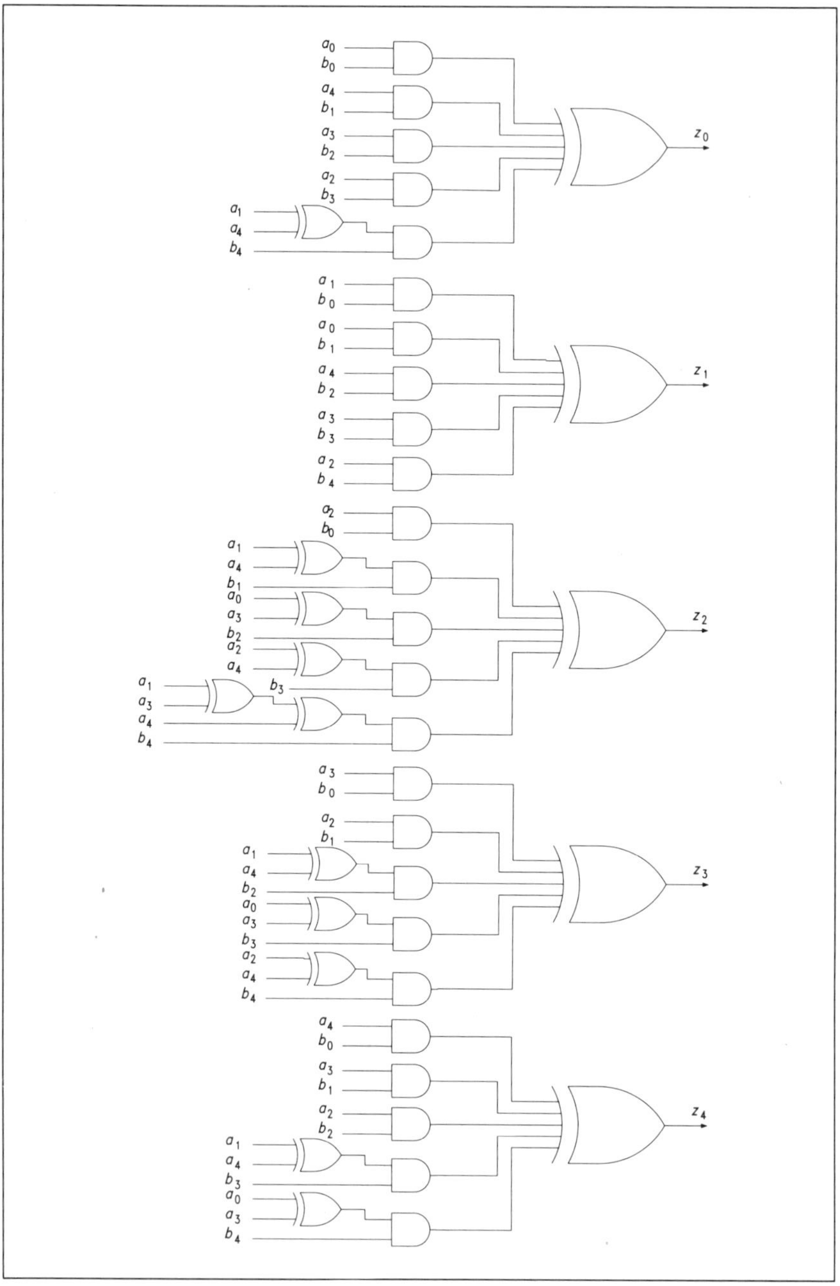

Fig. 6.2 Combinational circuit for multiplying two elements of GF (2^5) based on a primitive polynomial $p(x) = 1 + x^2 + x^5$

6.3 SEQUENTIAL LOGIC MULTIPLIERS

Multipliers can also be implemented in a sequential manner. Let $A(\alpha)$ and $B(\alpha)$ be two elements in GF (2^m), as assumed in Sec. 6.2. If the product of $Z(\alpha) = A(\alpha)B(\alpha)$ is expressed in the form

$$Z(\alpha) = \sum_{i=0}^{m-1} b_i(\alpha^i A(\alpha)) \tag{6.9}$$

then we have

$$Z(\alpha) = (\cdots(((b_0A(\alpha)) + b_1A(\alpha)\alpha) + b_2A(\alpha)\alpha^2) + \cdots) + b_{m-1}A(\alpha)\alpha^{m-1} \tag{6.10}$$

We first consider multiplying a field element $A(\alpha) = a_0 + a_1\alpha + \cdots + a_{m-1}\alpha^{m-1}$ in GF (2^m) by the primitive element α which is a root of the polynomial $p(x) = p_0 + p_1x + \cdots + p_{m-1}x^{m-1} + x^m$. Since $p(\alpha) = 0$, $\alpha^m = p_0 + p_1\alpha + \cdots + p_{m-1}\alpha^{m-1}$.

Using this α^m in $A(\alpha)\alpha$, we have

$$A(\alpha)\alpha = a_0\alpha + a_1\alpha^2 + \cdots + a_{m-1}(p_0 + p_1\alpha + \cdots + p_{m-1}\alpha^{m-1})$$

$$= a_{m-1}p_0 + (a_0 + a_{m-1}p_1)\alpha + (a_1 + a_{m-1}p_2)\alpha^2 + \cdots + (a_{m-2} + a_{m-1}p_{m-1})\alpha^{m-1} \tag{6.11}$$

Thus, the multiplying operation of Eq. 6.11 can be carried out by the feedback shift register shown in Fig. 6.3.

Now, we want to devise a multiplying circuit of $Z(\alpha) = A(\alpha)B(\alpha)$, given in Eq. 6.10, by making use of Fig. 6.3. The resultant circuit is shown in Fig. 6.4.

■ **Example 6.2** Let $m = 5$. The primitive polynomial over GF (2) is $p(x) = 1 + x^2 + x^5$. Since $p(\alpha) = 0$, $\alpha^5 = 1 + \alpha^2$. For multiplying two elements $A(\alpha)$ and $B(\alpha)$ in GF (2^5), Eq. 6.10 becomes

$$Z(\alpha) = ((((b_0A(\alpha)) + b_1A(\alpha)\alpha) + b_2A(\alpha)\alpha^2) + b_3A(\alpha)\alpha^3) + b_4A(\alpha)\alpha^4 \tag{6.12}$$

The circuit representing Eq. 6.12 can be drawn as Fig. 6.5.

If the product $Z(\alpha) = A(\alpha)B(\alpha)$ is expressed in the following form

$$Z(\alpha) = \sum_{i=0}^{m-1} (b_iA(\alpha))\alpha^i$$

$$= (\cdots(A(\alpha)b_{m-1})\alpha + A(\alpha)b_{m-2})\alpha + \cdots)\alpha + A(\alpha)b_0 \tag{6.13}$$

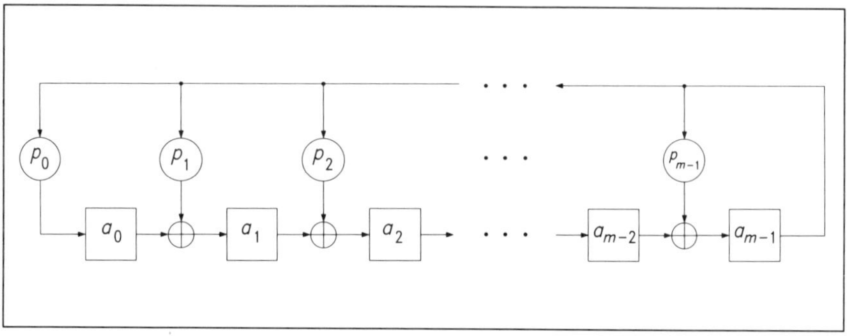

Fig. 6.3 *A* (α) α–multiplying circuit of GF (2^m)

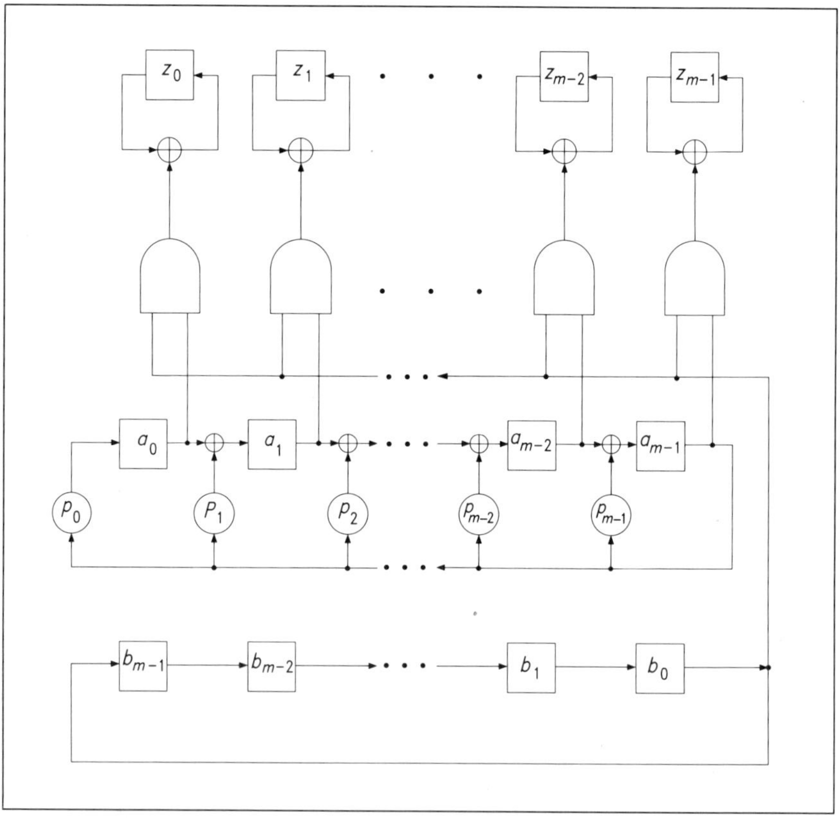

Fig. 6.4 Circuit for multiplying two arbitrary elements in GF (2^m)

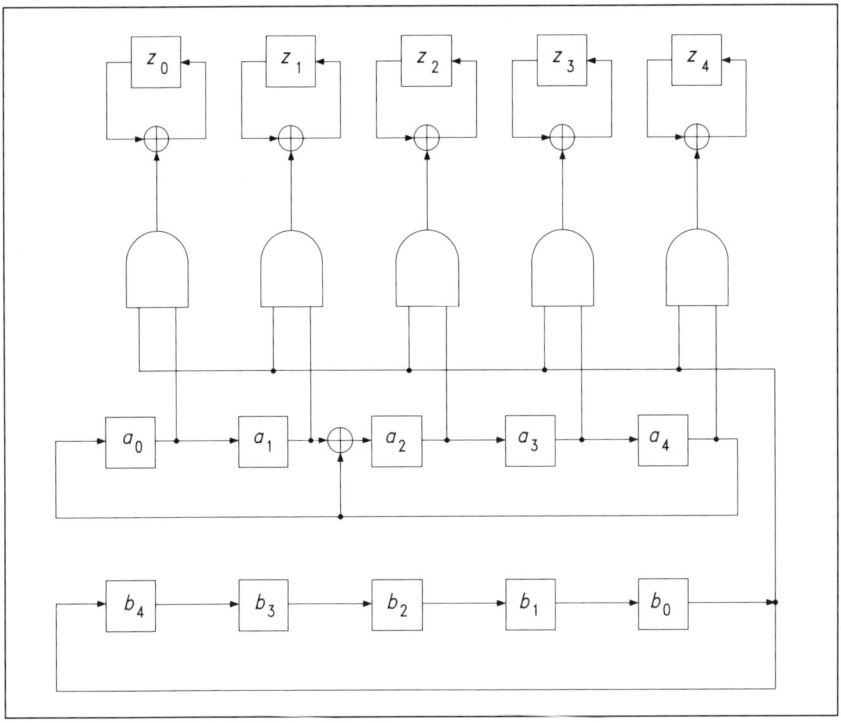

Fig. 6.5 Multiplier for two elements in GF (2^5)

we will obtain a different multiplier, as shown in Fig. 6.6. In operating this circuit, we have to (i) multiply $b_{m-1} A(\alpha)$ by α and add it to $b_{m-2}A(\alpha)$, (ii) multiply $b_{m-1} A(\alpha) + b_{m-2} A(\alpha)$ by α and add it to $b_{m-3} A(\alpha)$ and (iii) proceed with this operation m times. Then we can obtain $Z(\alpha) = A(\alpha) B(\alpha)$.

■ **Example 6.3** Consider again $Z(\alpha) = A(\alpha)\ B(\alpha)$ for GF (2^5). Using $\alpha^5 = 1 + \alpha^2$, Eq. 6.13 reduces to

$$Z(\alpha) = A(\alpha) B(\alpha)$$
$$= ((((A(\alpha) b_4) \alpha + A(\alpha) b_3) \alpha + A(\alpha) b_2) \alpha + A(\alpha) b_1) \alpha + A(\alpha) b_0 \quad (6.14)$$

The multiplier carrying out the computation given by Eq. 6.14 is shown in Fig. 6.7.

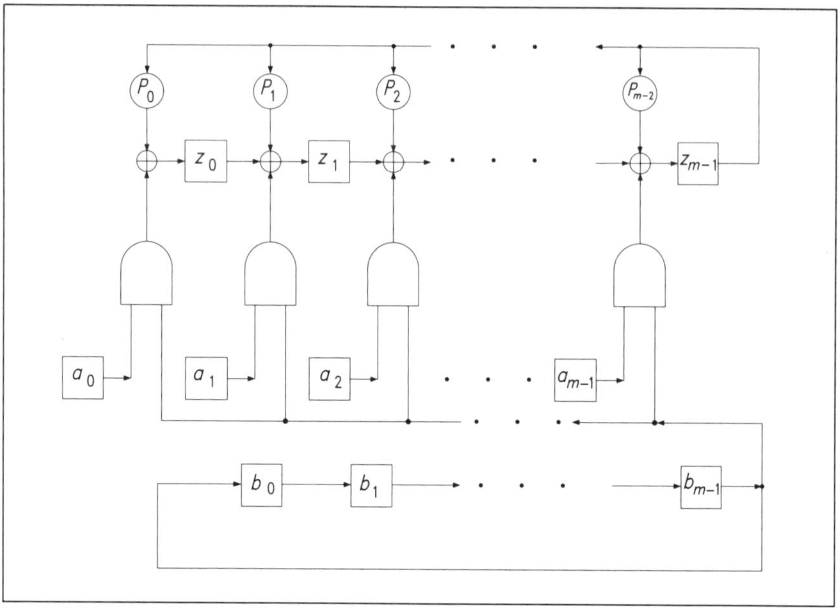

Fig. 6.6 Another kind of circuit for multiplying two elements in GF (2^m)

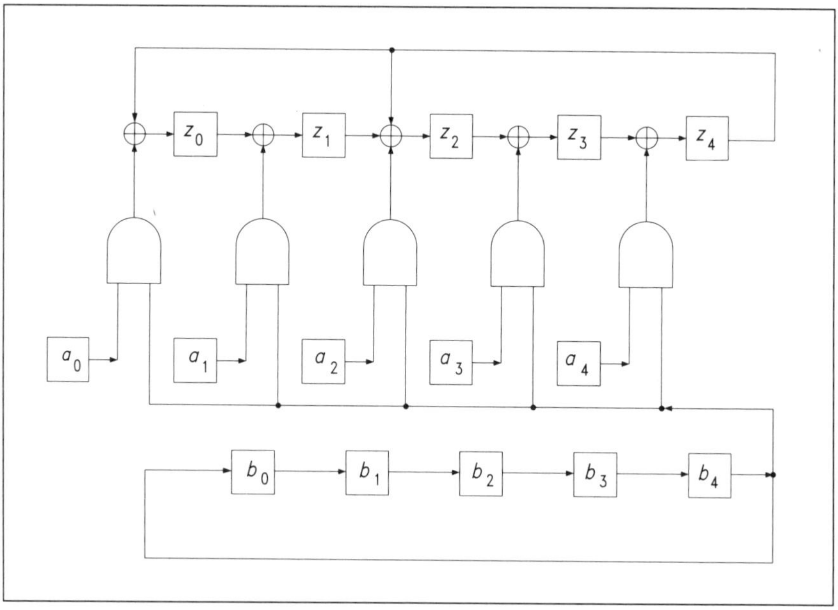

Fig. 6.7 Multiplier for two elements in GF (2^5)

The most common circuit uses a linear feedback shift register (LFSR) to perform desired multiplication or division sequentially in m clock pulses. This sequential circuit is simple and relatively economical. However, the sequential shift-register multiplier operates rather slower than the fastest combinational multiplier because of the m flip-flop delays incurred.

6.4 CELLULAR-ARRAY MULTIPLIER

This section describes a combinational cellular array that computes the product of two arbitrary elements in GF (2^m). Gate-array fabrications resulting from VLSI technology have become increasingly popular for the design of devices for encoding, decoding and cryptographic data ciphering due to the effective performance of their logical operations. Such cellular arrays exhibit a high degree of regularity and ease of generalization. But they use more gates and are slower than the fastest combinational multiplier. Of course, they are faster than conventional shift-register multipliers. Laws and Rushforth presented a paper relating to a cellular-array multiplier for GF (2^m) in 1971 [1].

A combinational cellular array consists of m^2 identical cells as shown in Fig. 6.8. Fig. 6.9 shows an individual cell in the array. Rewriting Eq. 6.13, the product $Z(\alpha) = A(\alpha) B(\alpha)$ is

$$Z(\alpha) = (\cdots((A(\alpha) b_{m-1}) \alpha + A(\alpha) b_{m-2}) \alpha + \cdots) \alpha + A(\alpha) b_0 \qquad (6.15)$$

The first row of the cellular array produces its output polynomial as $b_{m-1}A(\alpha)$. These output coefficients then move one column to the right and one row down, appearing in the second row as the polynomial $b_{m-1} \alpha A(\alpha)$. The output of the rightmost cell in the first row is placed on the feedback line to reduce the term α^m, where $\alpha^m = p_0 + p_1 \alpha + \cdots + p_{m-1} \alpha^{m-1}$. The polynomial $b_{m-2} A(\alpha)$ is added in the second row so that it produces the net output $b_{m-1}(\alpha) A(\alpha) + b_{m-2} A(\alpha)$. This process continues row-by-row until the product $Z(\alpha) = A(\alpha) B(\alpha)$ appears as the final output after all signals have passed through the array.

■ **Example 6.4** Consider GF (2^5) with $p(x) = 1 + x^2 + x^5$. Based on the array principle discussed above, a cellular-array multiplier for GF (2^5) can be shown as in Fig. 6.10. Since the product polynomial

$Z(\alpha) = A(\alpha) B(\alpha)$ for GF (2^5) is

$$Z(\alpha) = ((((A(\alpha) b_4) \alpha + A(\alpha) b_3) \alpha + A(\alpha) b_2) \alpha + A(\alpha) b_1) \alpha + A(\alpha) b_0 \qquad (6.16)$$

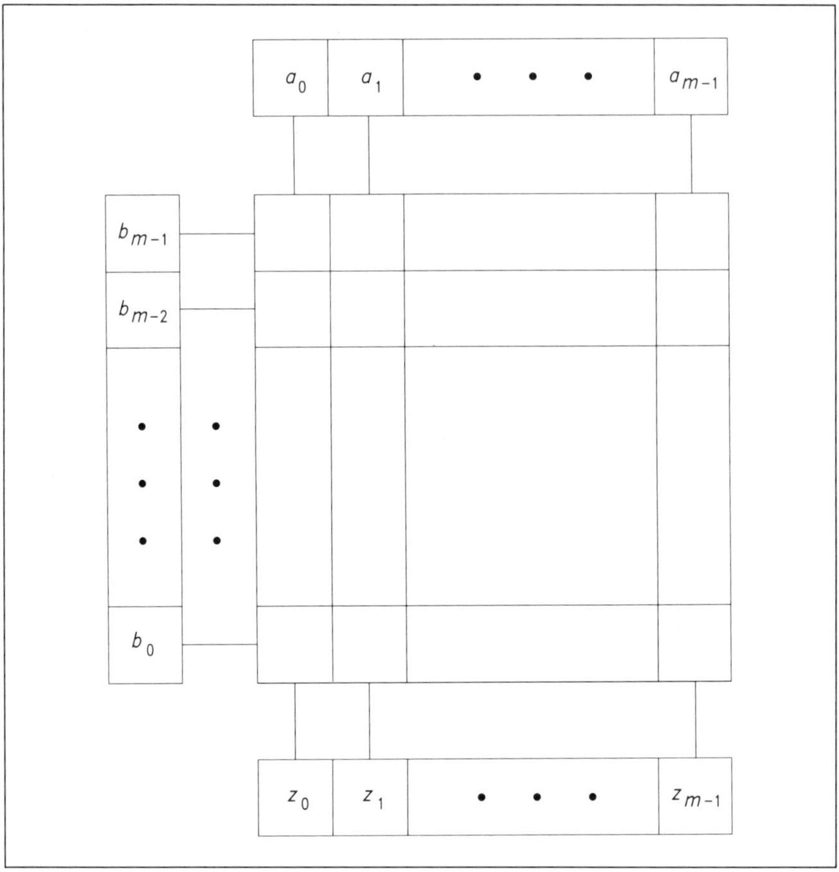

Fig. 6.8 Combinational cellular-array multiplier

the output of the first row in Fig. 6.10 is $b_4 A(\alpha)$. This output $b_4 A(\alpha)$ is then shifted one column to the right and one row down, resulting in $b_4 A(\alpha)\alpha$. The polynomial $b_3 A(\alpha)$ is added in the second row, producing the result of $b_4 A(\alpha)\alpha + b_3 A(\alpha)$. If we continue this process row-by-row three times more, then we get the final output $Z(\alpha)$ as expressed by Eq. 6.16. Refer to Fig. 6.9 (b). From the primitive polynomial $p(x) = 1 + x^2 + x^5$, we have $p_0 = 1$, $p_1 = 0$, $p_2 = 1$, and $p_3 = p_4 = 0$. Therefore, the individual cells in the first and third columns are sketched for $p_0 = p_2 = 1$, whereas the individual cells in the second, fourth, and fifth columns correspond to $p_1 = p_3 = p_4 = 0$.

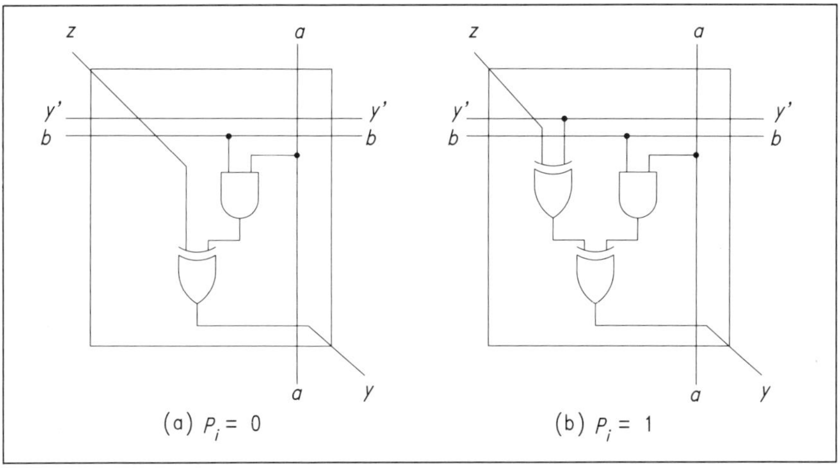

Fig. 6.9 Individual cells in the cellular array

6.5 CIRCUITS FOR SQUARES AND SQUARE ROOTS

Let $A(\alpha) = a_0 + a_1\alpha + \cdots + a_{m-1}\alpha^{m-1}$ be a field element of GF (2^m). It is worthwhile to consider the multiplication of any element in the field by itself. That is,

$$Z(\alpha) = (a_0 + a_1\alpha + \cdots + a_{m-1}\alpha^{m-1})^2$$

$$= a_0 + a_1(\alpha)^2 + \cdots + a_{m-1}(\alpha^{m-1})^2 \tag{6.17}$$

Thus, the vector $\mathbf{Z} = (z_0, z_1, \cdots, z_{m-1})$ in Eq. 6.17 can be expressed as the multiplication of a row vector $\mathbf{A} = (a_0, a_1, \cdots, a_{m-1})$ by a matrix $\mathbf{M}$ as follows:

$$(z_0, z_1, \cdots, z_{m-1}) = (a_0, a_1, \cdots, a_{m-1}) \begin{bmatrix} (\alpha^0)^2 \\ (\alpha^1)^2 \\ (\alpha^2)^2 \\ \cdot \\ \cdot \\ \cdot \\ (\alpha^{m-1})^2 \end{bmatrix} \tag{6.18}$$

or

$$\mathbf{Z} = \mathbf{A} \cdot \mathbf{M} \tag{6.19}$$

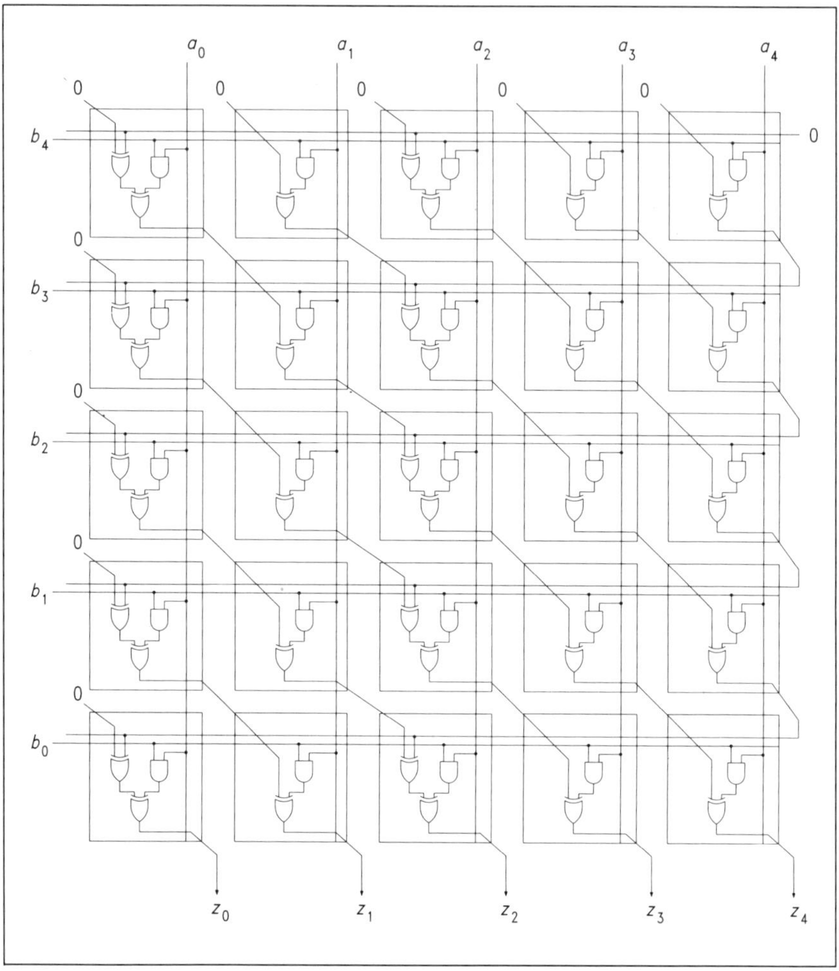

Fig. 6.10 Cellular-array multiplier for GF (2^5)

■ **Example 6.5** Consider again the finite field GF (2^5) with the primitive polynomial $p(x) = 1 + x^2 + x^5$. If α is a root of $p(x)$, then $\alpha^5 = 1 + \alpha^2$, and α is called the primitive element of GF (2^5). Using $\alpha^5 = 1 + \alpha^2$, the components of the matrix **M** can be found as

$$(\alpha^0)^2 = 1$$

$$(\alpha^1)^2 = \alpha^2$$

$$(\alpha^2)^2 = \alpha^4$$

$$(\alpha^3)^2 = \alpha^6 = \alpha(1 + \alpha^2) = \alpha + \alpha^3$$

$$(\alpha^4)^2 = \alpha^8 = \alpha^3(1 + \alpha^2) = 1 + \alpha^2 + \alpha^3$$

Thus, Eq. 6.18 can be expressed as

$$(z_0, z_1, z_2, z_3, z_4) = (a_0, a_1, a_2, a_3, a_4) \begin{bmatrix} 1\,0\,0\,0\,0 \\ 0\,0\,1\,0\,0 \\ 0\,0\,0\,0\,1 \\ 0\,1\,0\,1\,0 \\ 1\,0\,1\,1\,0 \end{bmatrix} \tag{6.20}$$

from which we obtain

$$z_0 = a_0 + a_4$$

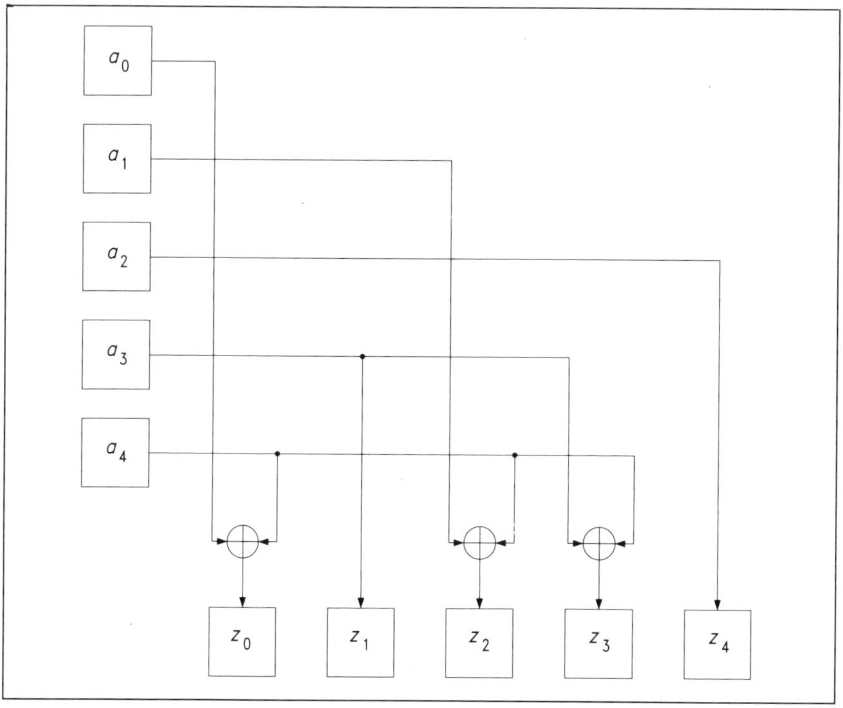

Fig. 6.11 Computation circuit for $Z = A^2$ over GF (2^5)

$$z_1 = a_3$$

$$z_2 = a_1 + a_4$$

$$z_3 = a_3 + a_4$$

$$z_4 = a_2$$

Hence, the matrix multiplication of Eq. 6.20 can be implemented by the circuit shown in Fig. 6.11.

Let $Z = A^{1/2}$ be the square root of a field element A of GF (2^m). Then it follows that

$$\begin{aligned} Z(\alpha) &= [A(\alpha)]^{1/2} = (a_0 + a_1\alpha + \cdots + a_{m-1}\alpha^{m-1})^{1/2} \\ &= a_0(\alpha^0)^{1/2} + a_1(\alpha^1)^{1/2} + a_2(\alpha^2)^{1/2} + \cdots + a_{m-1}(\alpha^{m-1})^{1/2} \end{aligned} \tag{6.21}$$

If $Z(\alpha)$ is expressed in matrix form, we get

$$(z_0, z_1, \cdots, z_{m-1}) = (a_0, a_1, \cdots, a_{m-1}) \begin{bmatrix} (\alpha^0)^{1/2} \\ (\alpha^1)^{1/2} \\ (\alpha^2)^{1/2} \\ \cdot \\ \cdot \\ \cdot \\ (\alpha^{m-1})^{1/2} \end{bmatrix} \tag{6.22}$$

or

$$\mathbf{Z} = \mathbf{A} \cdot \mathbf{M}' \tag{6.23}$$

Evidently the square root of a field element $A(\alpha)$ of GF (2^m) can be found by multiplying **A** by **M**′.

■ **Example 6.6** Applying $\alpha^5 = 1 + \alpha^2$ to the elements in GF (2^5), we obtain

$$(\alpha^0)^{1/2} = 1$$

$$(\alpha^1)^{1/2} = \alpha^{(31+1)/2} = \alpha^{16} = 1 + \alpha + \alpha^3 + \alpha^4$$

$$(\alpha^2)^{1/2} = \alpha$$

$$(\alpha^3)^{1/2} = \alpha^{(31+13)/2} = \alpha^{17} = 1 + \alpha + \alpha^4$$

$$(\alpha^4)^{1/2} = \alpha^2$$

Substituting these components into the **M**′ matrix in Eq. 6.22, we have

$$(z_0, z_1, z_2, z_3, z_4) = (a_0, a_1, a_2, a_3, a_4)\begin{bmatrix} 1\,0\,0\,0\,0 \\ 1\,1\,0\,1\,1 \\ 0\,1\,0\,0\,0 \\ 1\,1\,0\,0\,1 \\ 0\,0\,1\,0\,0 \end{bmatrix} \tag{6.24}$$

from which we get

$$z_0 = a_0 + a_1 + a_3$$

$$z_1 = a_1 + a_2 + a_3$$

$$z_2 = a_4$$

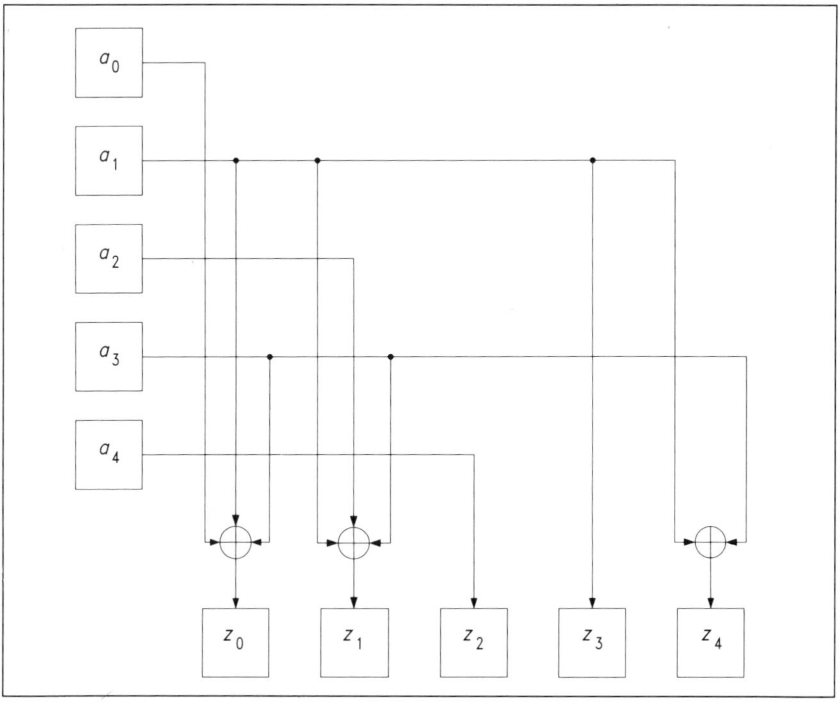

Fig. 6.12 Computation circuit for $Z = A^2$ over $GF(2^5)$

$$z_3 = a_1$$

$$z_4 = a_1 + a_3$$

Thus, $Z = \sqrt{A}$ or $\mathbf{Z} = \mathbf{A} \cdot \mathbf{M}'$ can be implemented by the circuit as shown in Fig. 6.12.

6.6 DIVISION CIRCUITS OVER GF (2^m)

Let A and B be any two elements in GF (2^m). Consider the arithmetic operation for division over GF (2^m). Dividing A by B, we simply multiply A by the multiplicative inverse B^{-1} of divisor B such that

$$D = A/B = A \cdot B^{-1} \tag{6.25}$$

Since $B^{2^m-1} = 1$, the multiplicative inverse B^{-1} can be found as

$$B^{-1} = B^{2^m-2} \tag{6.26}$$

where $2^m - 2 = 2 + 2^2 + 2^3 + \cdots + 2^{m-1}$

Thus, Eq. 6.26 becomes [3]

$$B^{-1} = B^{(2+2^2+2^3+\cdots+2^{m-1})}$$

$$= (B^2)(B^{2^2})(B^{2^3})\cdots(B^{2^{m-1}}) \tag{6.27}$$

Once B^{-1} is found, a division circuit for A/B can be easily implemented by $D = A \cdot B^{-1}$, where A is a dividend.

■ **Example 6.7** Let B be an arbitrary element of GF (2^5). From Eq. 6.27, with $m = 5$, the multiplicative inverse B^{-1} can be found as

$$B^{-1} = (B^2)(B^4)(B^8)(B^{16}) = B^{30} \tag{6.28}$$

Table 6.2 Division Table for GF (2^5)

Step	Switch position SW1	SW2	SW3	SQ input	SQ output	MUT input X	Y	MUT output
1	1	1	1	B	B^2	B^2	1	B^2
2	2	1	2	B^2	B^4	B^4	B^2	B^6
3	2	1	2	B^4	B^8	B^8	B^6	B^{14}
4	2	1	2	B^8	B^{16}	B^{16}	B^{14}	B^{30}
5	X	2	2	X	X	A	B^{30}	$AB^{30} = AB^{-1}$

SQ : Squaring device MUT : Multiplier X : Don't care

To perform the operation of division in GF (2^5), it is useful to construct a table, illustrated on the previous page.

Using Table 6.2, the division circuit can be implemented directly as shown in Fig. 6.13.

So far, we have discussed the arithmetic operations in GF (2^m) according to conventional basis representation. In the next two sections, we shall present analyses based on exponent as well as normal basis of GF (2^m).

6.7 GF (2^m)-ARITHMETIC BASED ON EXPONENT REPRESENTATION

2^m-1 elements of GF (2^m) can be represented as a polynomial over GF (2) modulo $p(x)$ which is called a primitive polynomial of degree m. If α is a root of $p(x)$, then α is called the primitive element of GF (2^m). Any nonzero element in GF (2^m) can be expressed in terms of the coefficients of a polynomial of degree $m-1$; this is called vector representation. Up to Sec. 6.6, the GF (2^m)-arithmetic we considered was based on either polynomial or vector representation. From now on, we shall construct logic circuits by using exponent representation, in which any nonzero element in GF (2^m) can be expressed as a power of α. For example, a power of α in GF (2^4) can be expressed as a 8421-weight code. Calculations based on such representation are convenient because all multiplications and divisions of field elements are reduced to addition and subtraction (modulo 2^m-1) of the exponents of α.

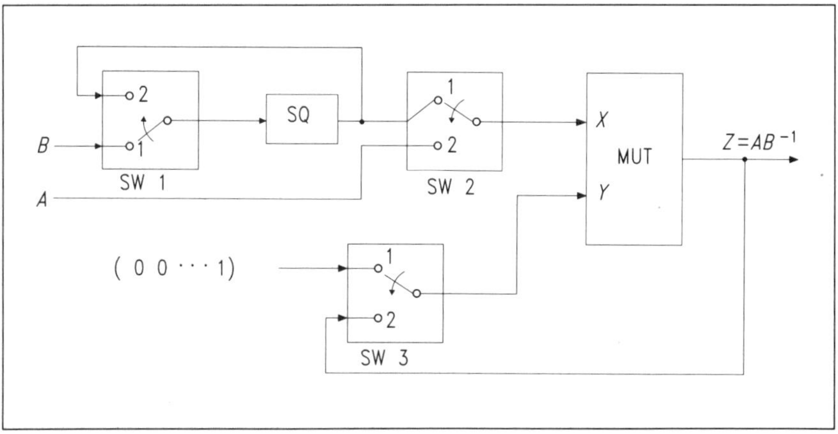

Fig. 6.13 A division circuit for two arbitrary elements A and B from GF (2^5)

■ **Example 6.8** Consider GF (2^5) with the primitive polynomial $p(x) = 1 + x^2 + x^5$. If $p(\alpha) = 0$, then $\alpha^5 = 1 + \alpha^2$. For example, three different representations each for α^{10} and α^{23} can be shown as follows:

Element	Polynomial representation	Vector representation	Exponent representation
α^{10}	$1 + \alpha^4$	1 0 0 0 1	0 1 0 1 0
α^{23}	$1 + \alpha + \alpha^2 + \alpha^3$	1 1 1 1 0	1 0 1 1 1

6.7.1 Multiplication Circuit

The zero element and α^0 element in GF (2^m) are assumed to represent, with m bits, either Case 1 or Case 2 shown below.

Case 1

0	$111 \cdots 1$
α^0	$000 \cdots 0$

Case 2

0	$000 \cdots 0$
α^0	$111 \cdots 1$

Table 6.3 Exponent Representation of the Elements in GF (2^5)

Elements	Exponent representation	Elements	Exponent representation
0	1 1 1 1 1 (C1)	α^{14}	0 1 1 1 0
	0 0 0 0 0 (C2)	α^{15}	0 1 1 1 1
α^0	0 0 0 0 0 (C1)	α^{16}	1 0 0 0 0
	1 1 1 1 1 (C2)	α^{17}	1 0 0 0 1
α^1	0 0 0 0 1	α^{18}	1 0 0 1 0
α^2	0 0 0 1 0	α^{19}	1 0 0 1 1
α^3	0 0 0 1 1	α^{20}	1 0 1 0 0
α^4	0 0 1 0 0	α^{21}	1 0 1 0 1
α^5	0 0 1 0 1	α^{22}	1 0 1 1 0
α^6	0 0 1 1 0	α^{23}	1 0 1 1 1
α^7	0 0 1 1 1	α^{24}	1 1 0 0 0
α^8	0 1 0 0 0	α^{25}	1 1 0 0 1
α^9	0 1 0 0 1	α^{26}	1 1 0 1 0
α^{10}	0 1 0 1 0	α^{27}	1 1 0 1 1
α^{11}	0 1 0 1 1	α^{28}	1 1 1 0 0
α^{12}	0 1 1 0 0	α^{29}	1 1 1 0 1
α^{13}	0 1 1 0 1	α^{30}	1 1 1 1 0

C1 : Case 1, C2 : Case 2

Exponent representation for the elements of GF (2^5) generated by $p(x) = 1 + x^2 + x^5$ is shown in Table 6.3.

If $A = \alpha^i$ and $B = \alpha^j$ are two nonzero elements of GF (2^m), then their product is

$$Z = A \cdot B = \alpha^{i + j \pmod{2^m - 1}} \tag{6.29}$$

Thus, we see that the product of two elements is reduced to conventional addition (mod 2^m-1) of the exponents of α.

■ **Example 6.9** Consider the two field elements $A = \alpha^5$ and $B = \alpha^{10}$ in GF (2^5). The exponent representations of A and B are, respectively,

$$A = \alpha^5 \rightarrow (0\,0\,1\,0\,1) \quad \text{for} \quad i = 5$$
$$B = \alpha^{10} \rightarrow (0\,1\,0\,1\,0) \quad \text{for} \quad j = 10$$

The product of A and B is

$$Z = A \cdot B = \alpha^{15} \rightarrow (0\,1\,1\,1\,1) \quad \text{for} \quad i + j = 15$$

■ **Example 6.10** Consider the two field elements $A = \alpha^{15}$ and $B = \alpha^{20}$ in GF (2^5). Hence $i = 15$ and $j = 20$. The product of these two elements simply indicates conventional addition (mod 31) of the exponent of α. That is,

$$\alpha^{15} \,.\, \alpha^{20} = \alpha^4 \rightarrow i + j = 4 \pmod{31}.$$

$$\begin{array}{llll}
\alpha^{15}: & & 01\,1\,1\,1 & \text{for } i = 15 \\
\alpha^{20}: & + & 10\,1\,0\,0 & \text{for } j = 20 \\
\hline
 & & 10\,0\,0\,1\,1 & \\
 & + & 1 \rightarrow \text{carry} & \\
\hline
 & & 0\,0\,1\,0\,0 & \text{for } i + j = 4 \pmod{31}
\end{array}$$

Thus, the exponent representation of α^4 or $i + j = 4$ is obtained as (0 0 1 0 0) by shifting a carry to the rightmost position and adding up, as shown above.

Next, consider $\alpha^{15} \cdot \alpha^{16} = \alpha^0$.

$$\begin{array}{llll}
\alpha^{15}: & & 0\,1\,1\,1\,1 & \text{for } i = 15 \\
\alpha^{16}: & + & 1\,0\,0\,0\,0 & \text{for } j = 16 \\
\hline
 & & 1\,1\,1\,1\,1 & \text{for } i + j = 0 \pmod{31}
\end{array}$$

This is the exponent representation of α^0 for Case 2.

$$\begin{array}{r} 11111 \\ + \quad\quad 1 \\ \hline 00000 \end{array}$$

This additive operation indicates that addition of 0 0 0 0 1 to 1 1 1 1 1 produces 0 0 0 0 0 which is the exponent representation of α^0 for Case 1.

With exponent representation, a multiplier is used to compute the product of two elements in GF (2^m) and can be implemented by addition (modulo 2^m-1). The block diagram and its symbol for the multiplication circuit are shown in Fig. 6.14 [5].

In this figure, corresponding to Case 1, FA1 is a full adder of m bits which processes addition of two exponent representations, $i + j$. If FA1 produces a carry, then 1 (one) is added to FA2 which is also a full adder, to perform modulo 2^m-1. A1Ds are all 1 detectors which detect either i or j or $i + j$ as $0 = (1\ 1\ 1 \ldots 1)$. Hence A1D is a zero-element detecting circuit. A1O is the all 1 output circuit which produces a zero element, $0 = (1\ 1\ 1 \ldots 1)$.

For Case 2 with $0 = (0\ 0\ 0 \ldots 0)$ and $\alpha^0 = (1\ 1\ 1 \ldots 1)$, Fig. 6.14 will be modified as Fig. 6.15, in which AZD is an all zero detector for detecting $0 = (0\ 0\ 0 \ldots 0)$ and is implemented by an m-input NOR gate. AZO is a device which produces the allzero output $0 = (0\ 0\ 0 \ldots 0)$. One of the advantages of Fig. 6.15 is the elimination of A1D circuit in Fig. 6.14 which is connected between FA1 and FA2 to perform modulo $2^m - 1$.

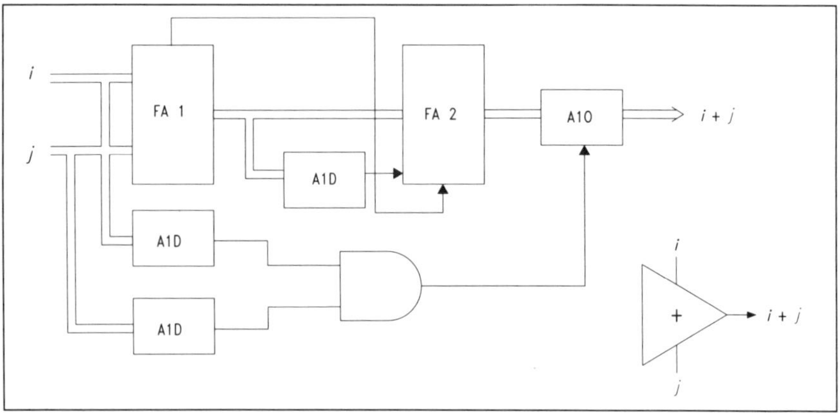

Fig. 6.14 Block diagram and symbol for an exponent multiplier for Case 1

6.7.2 Division Circuit

The purpose of a division circuit is to perform division of elements in GF (2^m). Let $A = \alpha^i$ and $B = \alpha^j$ be any two elements of GF (2^m). If A is divided by B, then

$$Z = A/B = \alpha^{i-j \pmod{2^m - 1}} \tag{6.30}$$

Thus, a division circuit can be implemented in such a manner as to subtract the exponent of a divisor from that of a dividend. This operation can be accomplished by adding an inversion circuit to the multiplier, so as to obtain the 1's complements for m bits. The block diagram for Case 2 and its symbol representing this division circuit are shown

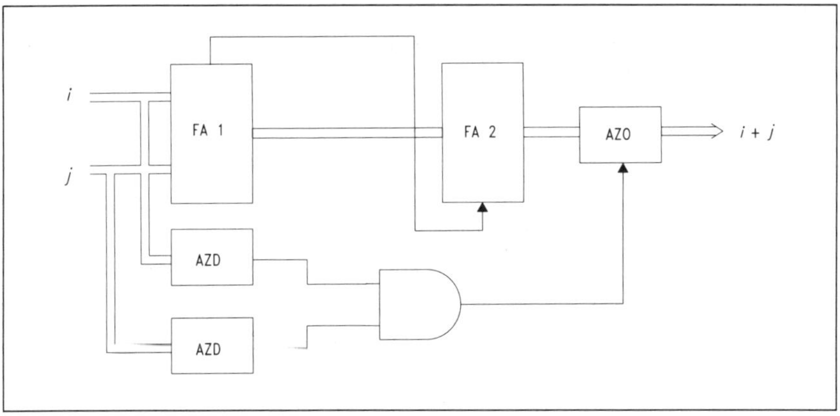

Fig. 6.15 Block diagram for an exponent multiplier for Case 2

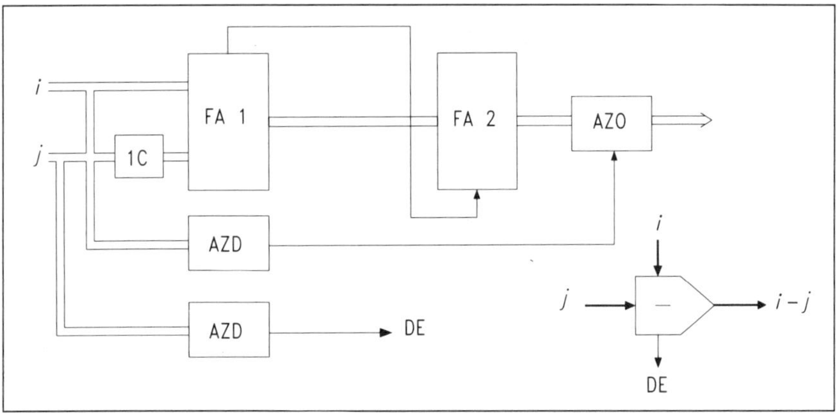

Fig. 6.16 A division circuit based on the exponent representation for Case 2

in Fig. 6.16. 1C is a device for the 1's complement. DE is the output when a divisor is a zero element.

6.7.3 Addition Circuit

Let $A = \alpha^i$ and $B = \alpha^j$ be two nonzero elements of GF (2^m).
Then this sum can be expressed as

$$Z = A + B = \alpha^i + \alpha^j = \alpha^i (1 + \alpha^{j-i}) \tag{6.31}$$

If we set $j-i = k$, then $1 + \alpha^{j-i}$ becomes $1 + \alpha^k = \alpha^\rho$. Therefore, it follows that

$$Z = \alpha^i + \alpha^j = \alpha^i \alpha^\rho = \alpha^{i+\rho} \tag{6.32}$$

Thus, we see that the addition of two elements can be transformed into the multiplication of two elements. The block diagram representing an addition circuit can be drawn by the combination of multiplication and division circuits, as shown in Fig. 6.17.

■ **Example 6.11** Consider a Galois field GF (2^5) with $p(\alpha) = 1 + \alpha^2 + \alpha^5 = 0$. Addition of two nonzero elements α^5 and α^{10} is $\alpha^5 + \alpha^{10} = \alpha^5 (1 + \alpha^5) = \alpha^5\alpha^2$. Thus, it follows that $\rho = 2$.

In Fig. 6.17, ROM takes the difference $j - i$ of the exponents of two elements as its input, and its output is the exponent of $1 + \alpha^{j-i}$. If $\alpha^i = 0$, DE becomes $1 = (0\ 0\ 0 \ldots 0\ 0\ 0)$ and α^j is only selected by the output selector. If $\alpha^i \neq 0$, it becomes the division circuit. Hence, α^k, $k = j - i$, is the input to ROM and $1 + \alpha^k$ is its output. Thus, α^i and α^ρ are the inputs to the multiplication circuit, and addition of α^i and α^j is accomplished.

6.7.4 Circuits for Square and Square Root

Let $A = \alpha^i$ be an arbitrary element of GF (2^m). If the exponent representation of $A = \alpha^i$ for $0 \le i \le 2^m - 1$ is assumed as $(a_0, a_1, \ldots, a_{m-1})$, then we have

$$i = a_0 + a_1 2 + a_2 2^2 + \cdots + a_{m-1} 2^{m-1} \tag{6.33}$$

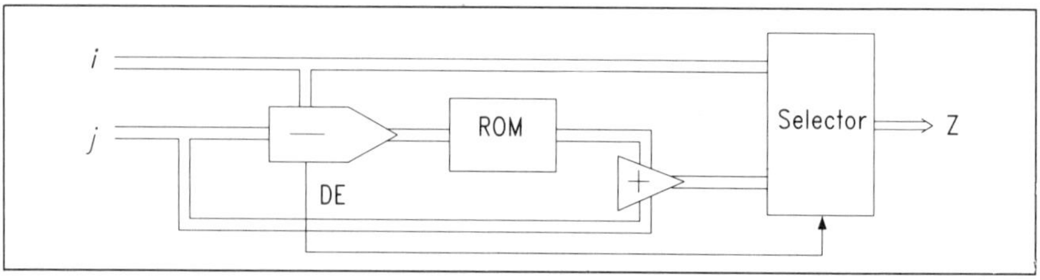

Fig. 6.17 Addition circuit using exponent representation

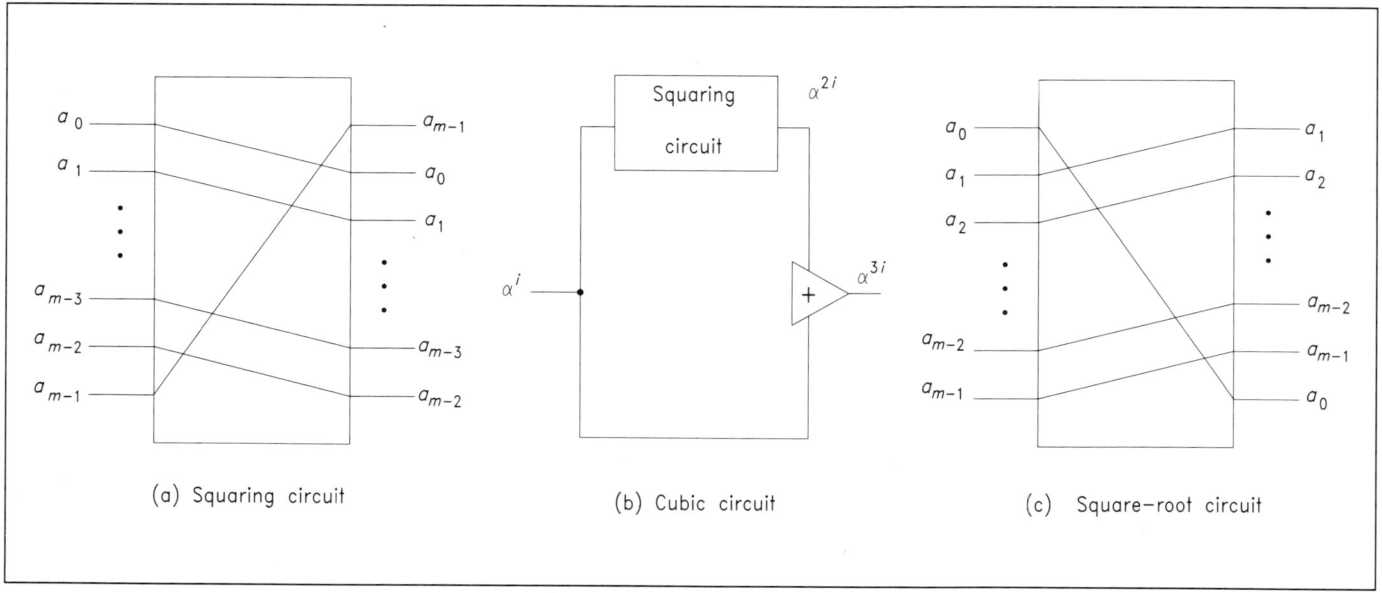

Fig. 6.18 Circuits for computing square, cube, and square root

The square of A becomes

$$Z = A^2 = \alpha^{2i \,(\mathrm{mod}\ 2^m - 1)} \tag{6.34}$$

Using Eq. 6.33, it follows that

$$2i = a_0 2 + a_1 2^2 + \cdots + a_{m-2} 2^{m-1} + a_{m-1} 2^m \tag{6.35}$$

where $2^m = 1$ because $\alpha^{2^m - 1} = 1$. Knowing that $2^m = 1$, Eq. 6.35 becomes

$$2i = a_{m-1} + a_0 2 + a_1 2^2 + \cdots + a_{m-2} 2^{m-1} \tag{6.36}$$

Therefore, the exponent representation of $Z = \alpha^{2i}$ becomes $(a_{m-1}, a_0, a_1, \ldots, a_{m-2})$. Thus, we know that squaring A results in shifting one bit to the right cyclically. Figure 6.18(a) shows this squaring circuit.

Next, considering $Z^2 = A^4 = \alpha^{4i}$ for raising to the fourth power, we have

$$4i = a_{m-1} 2 + a_0 2^2 + a_1 2^3 + \cdots + a_{m-2} 2^m$$

$$= a_{m-2} + a_{m-1} 2 + a_0 2^2 + a_1 2^3 + \cdots + a_{m-3} 2^{m-1} \tag{6.37}$$

Therefore, the exponent representation of $Z^2 = \alpha^{4i}$ becomes $(a_{m-2}, a_{m-1}, a_0, a_1, \cdots, a_{m-3})$. Thus, we generally see that raising an element to the 2^jth power ($j = 1, 2, \ldots$) means shifting that element cyclically j bits to the right. Figure 6.18(b) shows the cubic circuit resulting from combining the square circuit with a multiplication circuit.

Finally, consider the circuit for the square root of A. It may be represented as

$$A^{1/2} = \alpha^{i/2 \,(\mathrm{mod}\ 2^m - 1)} \tag{6.38}$$

Using Eq. 6.33, this becomes

$$i/2 = a_1 + a_2 2 + \cdots + a_{m-1} 2^{m-2} + a_0 2^{m-1} \tag{6.39}$$

where $2^{m-1} = 1/2$. Therefore, the exponent representation of $\alpha^{i/2}$ is $(a_1, a_2, \ldots, a_{m-1}, a_0)$. Thus, the square root of α^i can be obtained by shifting cyclically one bit to the left. Figure 6.18(c) illustrates the circuit for the square root.

■ **Example 6.12** Consider an element α^5 of GF (2^5). The square of α^5 is α^{10}. The exponent representation of α^5 is (10100) and that of α^{10} is (01010). If we shift α^5 = (10100) cyclically one bit to the right, then we obtain the exponent representation (01010) of α^{10}. Consider the square root of α^5. Since $\alpha^5 = \alpha^5 \cdot 1 = \alpha^5 \cdot \alpha^{31} = \alpha^{36}$, the square root of α^5 becomes

α^{18}. The exponent representation of α^{18} is (01001). It is certainly true that sifting α^5 = (10100) cyclically one bit to the left produces α^{18} = (01001). Finally, consider the circuit for the cube of α^5.

Since α^5 = (10100), we have α^{10} = (01010) by shifting α^5 by one bit to the right. The exponent representation of α^{15} is computed as $(\alpha^{10}) \cdot (\alpha^5)$ = (01010) + (10100) = (11110). Thus, the circuit for the cube α^{15} is simply implemented by combining the square circuit with a multiplication circuit as shown in Fig. 6.18(b).

6.8 GF (2^m)-ARITHMETIC ON NORMAL BASIS

In this section, a new multiplication and inversion algorithm for GF (2^m) will be presented based on a normal basis representation. The simple squaring property of such representation can be applied to multipliers, as well as for the design of inverse elements in GF (2^m) [3] [4].

Some other previous work on the multiplier in GF (2^m) is based on the conventional standard basis of GF (2^m). But their GF (2^m)-arithmetic is not suitable for VLSI implementation due to irregular wire routing and nonmodular structure [1].

6.8.1 Normal Basis Representation

The elements in the finite field GF (2^m) are represented by a standard basis $\{1, \alpha, \alpha^2, \alpha^3, \cdots, \alpha^{m-1}\}$, where α is a root of a primitive polynomial $p(x)$ of degree m over GF (2). If α is a primitive element of GF (2^m), the powers $\alpha, \alpha^2, \alpha^{2^2}, \cdots \alpha^{2^{m-1}}$ are linearly independent. A basis set $\{\alpha, \alpha^2, \alpha^{2^2}, \cdots, \alpha^{2^{m-1}}\}$ is called the normal basis of GF (2^m). Each element in this basis is also represented by m bits. In normal basis representation, squaring the sum of any elements in GF (2^m) may be expressed as $(\alpha + \beta + \cdots + \gamma)^2 = \alpha^2 + \beta^2 + \cdots + \gamma^2$.

■ **Example 6.13** Consider the finite field GF (2^5) generated by the primitive polynomial $p(x) = 1 + x^2 + x^5$ over GF (2). Since $\alpha^8 = 1 + \alpha^2 + \alpha^3$ in polynomial form, it follows that $\alpha^{16} = (\alpha^8)^2 = 1 + \alpha^4 + \alpha^6 = 1 + \alpha^4 + \alpha + \alpha^3$ by the squaring property. Using this result, we have

$$\alpha + \alpha^2 + \alpha^4 + \alpha^8 + \alpha^{16} = \alpha + \alpha^2 + \alpha^4 + (1 + \alpha^2 + \alpha^3) + (1 + \alpha + \alpha^3 + \alpha^4) = 0 \qquad (6.40)$$

which indicates that the basis is not linearly independent, which is why the set $\{\alpha, \alpha^2, \alpha^4, \alpha^8, \alpha^{16}\}$ does not constitute the normal basis of GF (2^5).

On the other hand, over the field GF (2^m) with $p(x) = 1 + x^2 + x^3 + x^4 + x^5$, we have

$$\alpha + \alpha^2 + \alpha^4 + \alpha^8 + \alpha^{16} = \alpha + \alpha^2 + \alpha^4 + (\alpha^2 + \alpha^3 + \alpha^4) + (1 + \alpha + \alpha^3) = 1 \tag{6.41}$$

This indicates that the basis set $\{\alpha, \alpha^2, \alpha^4, \alpha^8, \alpha^{16}\}$ is linearly independent and therefore constitutes the normal basis of GF (2^5). Equation 6.41 also implies the normal basis representation of $\alpha^0 = (11111)$.

6.8.2 Transformation to the Normal Basis

Transformation from the standard basis to the normal basis is considered in this section. If A represents an arbitrary element of GF (2^5), then

$$A = a_0 + a_1 \alpha + a_2 \alpha^2 + a_3 \alpha^3 + a_4 \alpha^4 \tag{6.42}$$

The standard basis representation of Eq. 6.42 is as follows.

$$\mathbf{A} = \{\alpha^0, \alpha^1, \alpha^2, \alpha^3, \alpha^4\} \tag{6.43}$$

Using the irreducible polynomial $p(x) = 1 + x^2 + x^3 + x^4 + x^5$, the basis elements in Eq. 6.43 can be computed as

$$\alpha^0 = \alpha + \alpha^2 + \alpha^4 + \alpha^8 + \alpha^{16}$$

$$\alpha^1 = \alpha$$

$$\alpha^2 = \alpha^2$$

$$\alpha^3 = \alpha^2 + \alpha^4 + \alpha^8$$

$$\alpha^4 = \alpha^4$$

Substituting these α^is, $0 \le i \le 4$, in Eq. 6.42 yields the following equation for normal basis representation:

$$\begin{aligned} A &= a_0 (\alpha + \alpha^2 + \alpha^4 + \alpha^8 + \alpha^{16}) + a_1 \alpha + a_2 \alpha^2 + a_3 (\alpha^2 + \alpha^4 + \alpha^8) + a_4 \alpha^4 \\ &= (a_0 + a_1) \alpha + (a_0 + a_2 + a_3) \alpha^2 + (a_0 + a_3 + a_4) \alpha^4 + (a_0 + a_3) \alpha^8 + a_0 \alpha^{16} \end{aligned} \tag{6.44}$$

Using Eq. 6.44, the normal basis representation of the field elements in GF (2^5) is tabulated in Table 6.4.

Table 6.4 Normal Basis Representation of GF (2^5) Generated by $p(x) = 1 + x^2 + x^3 + x^4 + x^5$

Power	Standard basis representation	Normal basis representation	Power	Standard basis representation	Normal basis representation
0	00000	00000	α^{15}	11011	00101
α^0	10000	11111	α^{16}	11010	00001
α^1	01000	10000	α^{17}	01101	11100
α^2	00100	01000	α^{18}	10001	11011
α^3	00010	01110	α^{19}	11111	01101
α^4	00001	00100	α^{20}	11000	01111
α^5	10111	11101	α^{21}	01100	11000
α^6	11100	00111	α^{22}	00110	00110
α^7	01110	10110	α^{23}	00011	01010
α^8	00111	00010	α^{24}	10110	11001
α^9	10100	10111	α^{25}	01011	11010
α^{10}	01010	11110	α^{26}	10010	10001
α^{11}	00101	01100	α^{27}	01001	10100
α^{12}	10101	10011	α^{28}	10011	10101
α^{13}	11101	00011	α^{29}	11110	01001
α^{14}	11001	01011	α^{30}	01111	10010

6.8.3 Circuits for Squaring and Square Root

As seen in Table 6.3, there always exists a normal basis $\{\alpha, \alpha^2, \alpha^4, \ldots, \alpha^{2^{(m-1)}}\}$ in GF (2^m) for all positive integers m. Hence, every field element A in GF (2^m) for the normal basis can be expressed as

$$A = a_0 \alpha + a_1 \alpha^2 + a_2 \alpha^{2^2} + \cdots + a_{m-1} \alpha^{2^{(m-1)}} \tag{6.45}$$

or in vector form as

$$\mathbf{A} = (a_0, a_1, a_2, \cdots, a_{m-1}) \tag{6.46}$$

In normal basis representation, the squaring of an element A in GF (2^m) is readily shown to be a simple cyclic shift of its binary digits. Using $\alpha^{2^m} = \alpha$, the square of Eq. 6.45 becomes

$$A^2 = \left(a_0 \alpha + a_1 \alpha^2 + \cdots + a_{m-1} \alpha^{2^{(m-1)}}\right)^2$$

$$= a_{m-1} \alpha + a_0 \alpha^2 + a_1 \alpha^4 + \cdots + a_{m-2} \alpha^{2^{(m-1)}} \tag{6.47}$$

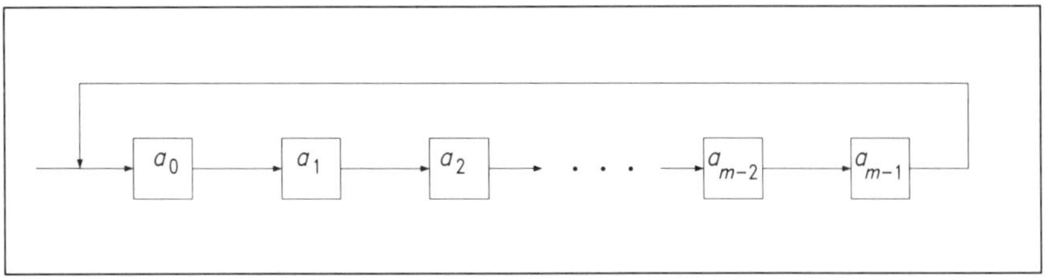

Fig. 6.19 Squaring register for normal basis representation over GF (2^m)

If the coefficients of A^2 are represented in vector form, the normal basis components of A^2 may be expressed as

$$\mathbf{A}^2 = (a_{m-1}, a_0, a_1, \cdots, a_{m-2}) \tag{6.48}$$

which indicates a cyclic shift of **A** to the right. Thus, squaring in GF (2^m) can be implemented by logic circuitry which accomplishes cyclic shifts in a shift register. The block diagram for such a squaring circuit is shown in Fig. 6.19.

Next, consider the square-root circuitry for $A^{1/2}$, where $A = a_0\alpha + a_1\alpha^2 + a_2\alpha^{2^2} + \ldots + a_{m-1}\alpha^{2^{m-1}}$.

$$A^{1/2} = \left(a_0\alpha + a_1\alpha^2 + \ldots + a_{m-1}\alpha^{2^{(m-1)}}\right)^{1/2}$$

$$= a_1\alpha + a_2\alpha^2 + \ldots + a_{m-1}\alpha^{2^{m-2}} + a_0\alpha^{2^{m-1}} \tag{6.49}$$

If $A^{1/2}$ is expressed in vector form with its coefficients, then we get

$$\mathbf{A}^{1/2} = (a_1, a_2, \ldots, a_{m-1}, a_0) \tag{6.50}$$

which is also the normal basis representation in GF (2^m). Comparing Eq. 6.50 with Eq. 6.46, we see that the vector of $A^{1/2}$ is a cyclic shift of **A** once to the left. Therefore, the circuitry for $A^{1/2}$ can also be devised by a shift register.

6.8.4 Normal Base Multiplier

Let $\mathbf{A} = (a_0, a_1, \cdots, a_{m-1})$ and $\mathbf{B} = (b_0, b_1 \cdots, b_{m-1})$ be two field elements of GF (2^m) in a normal basis representation. The product **C** of these two elements can be written as

$$\mathbf{C} = \mathbf{A} \cdot \mathbf{B} = (c_0, c_1, \cdots, c_{m-1}) \tag{6.51}$$

The last component c_{m-1} is expressed by a logic function of the components of **A** and **B** such that

$$c_{m-1} = f(a_0, a_1, \cdots, a_{m-1} : b_0, b_1, \cdots, b_{m-1}) \tag{6.52}$$

Since squaring **C** of Eq. 6.51 results in a cyclic shift of **C** to the right, it follows that

$$\mathbf{C}^2 = \mathbf{A}^2 \cdot \mathbf{B}^2 = (c_{m-1}, c_0, c_1, \cdots, c_{m-2}) \tag{6.53}$$

Thus, the last component c_{m-2} of $\mathbf{C}^2$ can be obtained by the same logic function of Eq. 6.52 in terms of the components of $\mathbf{A}^2 = (a_{m-1}, a_0, a_1, \cdots, a_{m-2})$ and $\mathbf{B}^2 = (b_{m-1}, b_0, b_1, \cdots, b_{m-2})$.
By squaring **C** repeatedly, it is evident that

$$\begin{aligned} c_{m-2} &= f(a_{m-1}, a_0, a_1, \cdots, a_{m-2} : b_{m-1}, b_0, b_1, \cdots b_{m-2}) \\ &\cdots\cdots\cdots\cdots\cdots\cdots \\ c_0 &= f(a_1, a_2, \cdots, a_{m-1}, a_0 : b_1, b_2, \cdots, b_{m-1}, b_0) \end{aligned} \tag{6.54}$$

Using Eqs 6.52 and 6.54, the Massey-Omura type multiplier over GF (2^m) [4] can be implemented as shown in Fig. 6.20 for the sequential type. The multiplier structures for both the sequential type and the parallel type will be best explained by the following example.

■ **Example 6.14** Consider a device for the GF (2^m)-multiplier generated by $p(x) = 1 + x + x^2 + x^4 + x^5$. If α is a root of $p(x)$, the conjugates of α are α^2, α^4, α^8, and α^{16}. The set of these roots $(\alpha, \alpha^2, \alpha^4, \alpha^8, \alpha^{16})$ constitutes a normal basis of GF (2^m). Based on the polynomial $p(x) = 1 + x + x^2 + x^4 + x^5$, the normal basis representation of GF (2^5) is shown in Table 6.5.

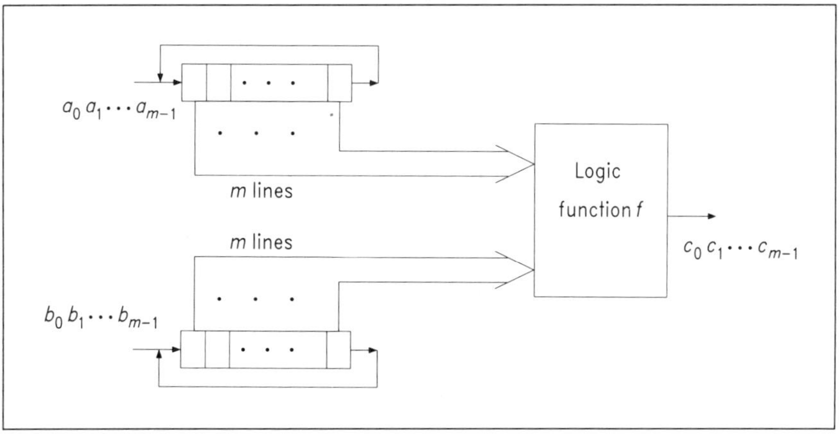

Fig. 6.20 Block diagram of sequential-type multiplier over GF (2^m)

Table 6.5 Normal Basis Representation of GF (2^5) Generated by $p(x) = 1 + x + x^2 + x^4 + x^5$

Power	Standard basis representation	Normal basis representation	Power	Standard basis representation	Normal basis representation
0	00000	00000	α^{15}	10101	10011
α^0	10000	11111	α^{16}	10111	00001
α^1	01000	10000	α^{17}	10110	00101
α^2	00100	01000	α^{18}	01011	00110
α^3	00010	10010	α^{19}	11000	01111
α^4	00001	00100	α^{20}	01100	11000
α^5	11101	00011	α^{21}	00110	11010
α^6	10011	01001	α^{22}	00011	10110
α^7	10100	10111	α^{23}	11100	00111
α^8	01010	00010	α^{24}	01110	01010
α^9	00101	01100	α^{25}	00111	11110
α^{10}	11111	10001	α^{26}	11110	10101
α^{11}	10010	01101	α^{27}	01111	01110
α^{12}	01001	10100	α^{28}	11010	11101
α^{13}	11001	01011	α^{29}	01101	11100
α^{14}	10001	11011	α^{30}	11011	11001

The product of any elements A and B in GF (2^5) is

$$C = A \cdot B = (a_0\alpha + a_1\alpha^2 + a_2\alpha^4 + a_3\alpha^8 + a_4\alpha^{16})(b_0\alpha + b_1\alpha^2 + b_2\alpha^4 + b_3\alpha^8 + b_4\alpha^{16}) = c_0\alpha + c_1\alpha^2 + c_2\alpha^4 + c_3\alpha^8 + c_4\alpha^{16} \tag{6.55}$$

Multiplying throughout the right-hand side of Eq. 6.55, combining like terms, and using Table 6.5, we get the coefficients c_i, $0 \le i \le 4$, as follows :

$$\begin{aligned}
c_4 &= a_3b_3 + a_2b_0 + a_0b_2 + a_2b_1 + a_1b_2 + a_3b_1 + a_1b_3 + a_4b_0 + a_0b_4 \\
c_3 &= a_2b_2 + a_1b_0 + a_0b_1 + a_2b_0 + a_0b_2 + a_4b_1 + a_1b_4 + a_4b_3 + a_3b_4 \\
c_2 &= a_1b_1 + a_3b_0 + a_0b_3 + a_3b_2 + a_2b_3 + a_4b_0 + a_0b_4 + a_4b_1 + a_1b_4 \\
c_1 &= a_0b_0 + a_2b_1 + a_1b_2 + a_3b_0 + a_0b_3 + a_4b_2 + a_2b_4 + a_4b_3 + a_3b_4 \\
c_0 &= a_4b_4 + a_1b_0 + a_0b_1 + a_3b_1 + a_1b_3 + a_3b_2 + a_2b_3 + a_4b_2 + a_2b_4
\end{aligned} \tag{6.56}$$

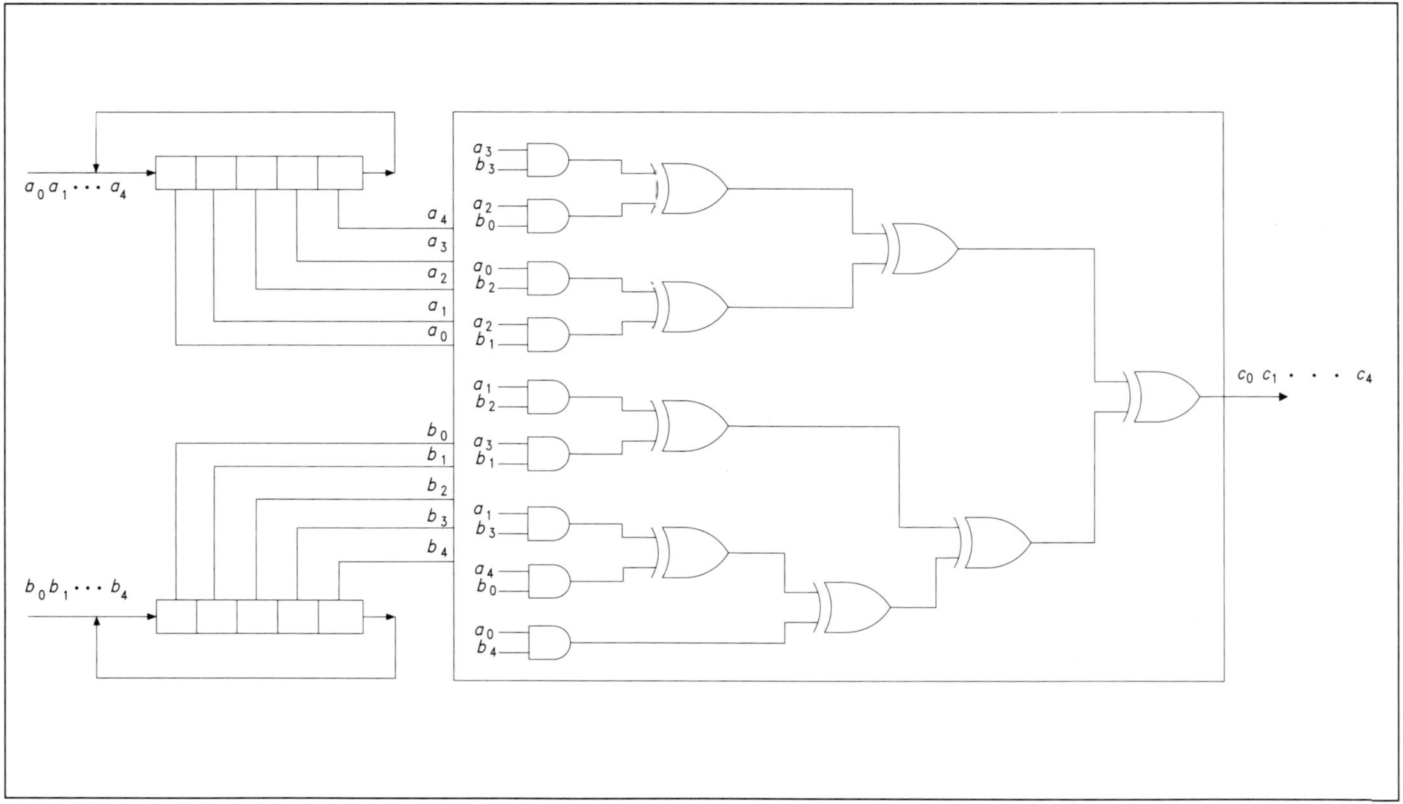

Fig. 6.21 Logic diagram of sequential-type multiplier over GF (2^5)

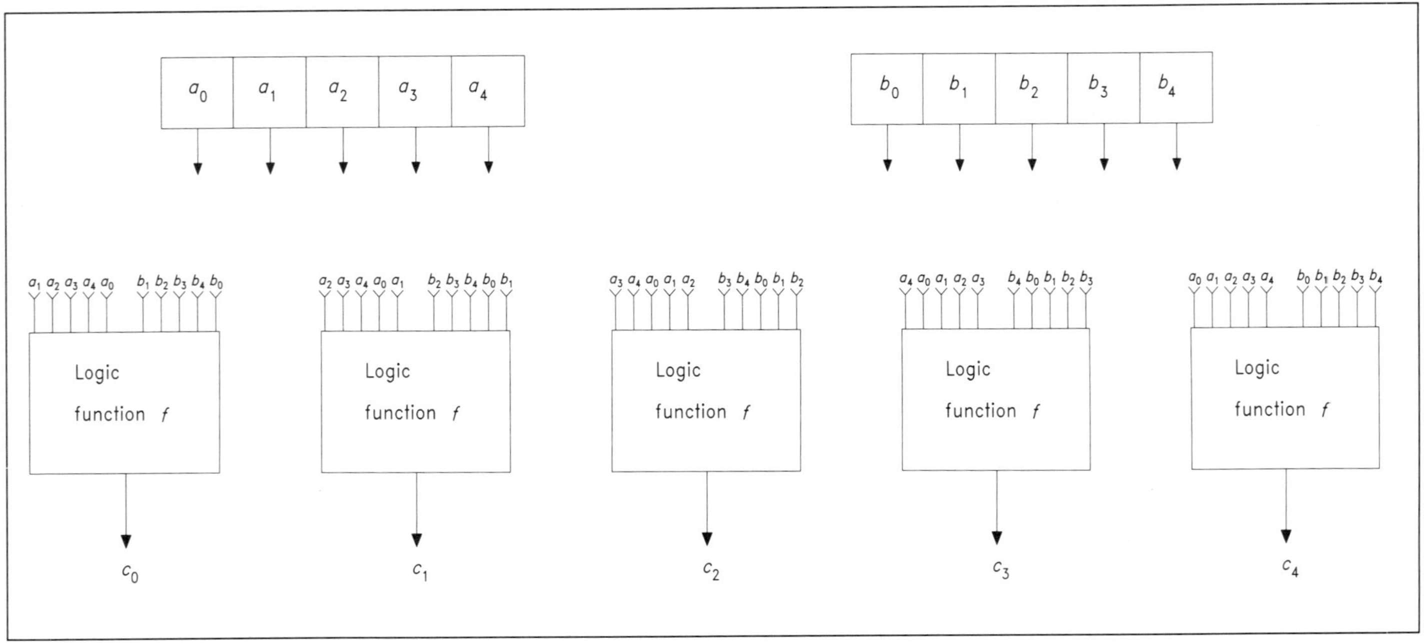

Fig. 6.22 Logic diagram of parallel-type multiplier over GF (2^5)

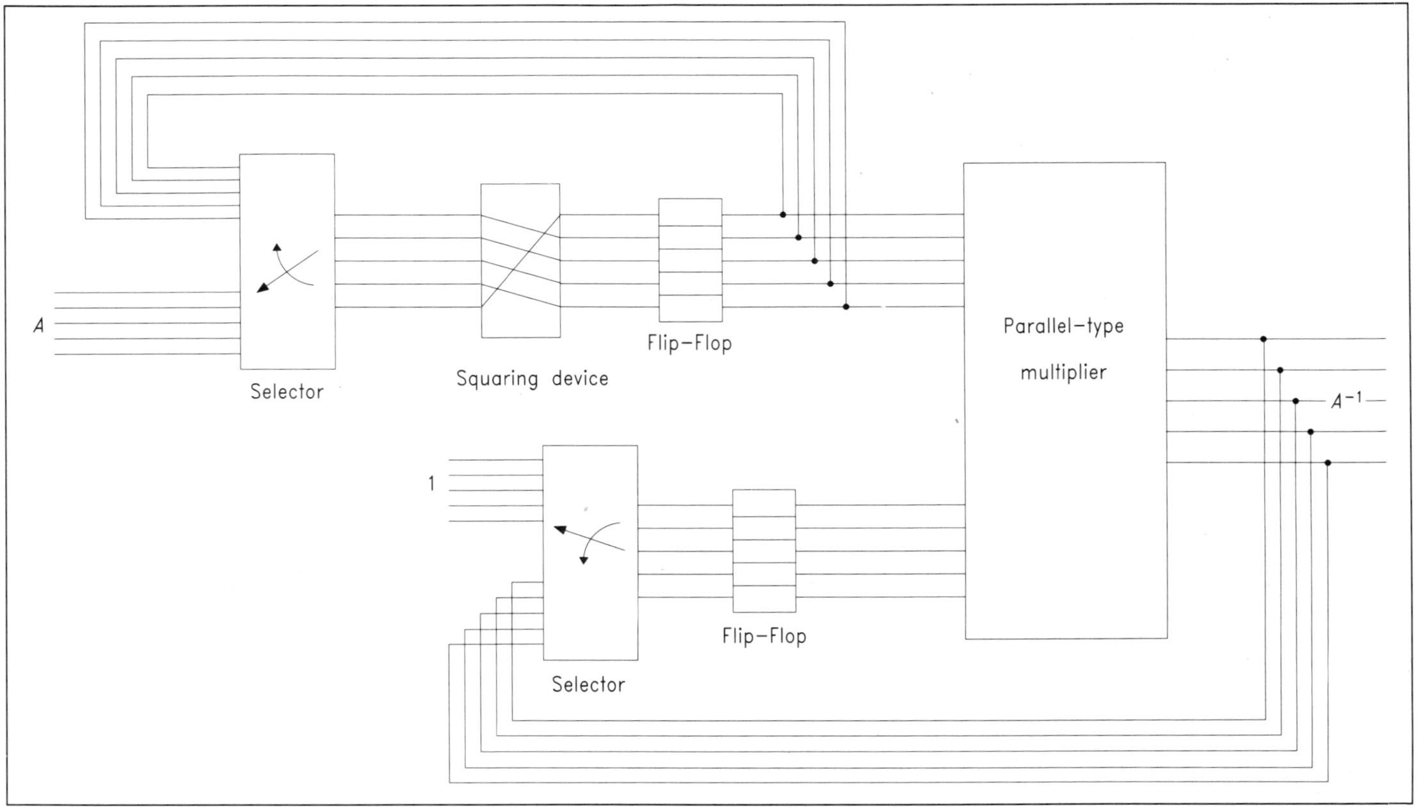

Fig. 6.23 Circuit for computing the inverse element in $GF(2^5)$

As explained in Eq. 6.52, the logic function f is the last component c_4 of the product C and is also used to find sequentially the remaining components c_3, c_2, c_1 and c_0 of this product. Only one logic function f of the $2m = 10$ components of A and B is required to compute sequentially the five components of C. Thus, the logic function f consists of nine AND gates and eight EX–ORs. The block diagram for this sequential-type multiplier is illustrated in Fig. 6.21.

Alternatively, the parallel-type multiplier requires $m = 5$ identical logic functions f (but cyclically shifted versions) for computing simultaneously all components of the product C. Figure 6.22 shows the structure of this parallel-type multiplier of GF (2^5), illustrating the connections of the components of A and B with the five logic functions f directly.

6.8.5 Inverse Element Implementation

For any element A in GF (2^m), the inverse is expressed as $A^{-1} = A^{2^m - 2}$, as discussed in Sec. 6.6. From Eq. 6.27, we have

$$A^{-1} = (A^2)(A^{2^2})(A^{2^3}) \cdots (A^{2^{m-1}}) \tag{6.57}$$

where A is a normal basis representation. A squaring of A in Eq. 6.57 results in a cyclic shift. Therefore, A^{2^i} designates the ith cyclic shift of A. Thus, the inverse element A^{-1} can be implemented by using repeated operations of cyclic shift coupled with the parallel-type multiplier, as shown in Fig. 6.23.

REFERENCES

1. Laws, B.A. and C.K. Rushforth: "A cellular-array multiplier for finite field GF (2^m)", *IEEE Trans. Comput.*, vol. C–20, pp 1573–1578, Dec. 1971.
2. Okano, H. and H. Imai: "A construction method of high-speed decoding using ROMs for Bose-Chaudhuri-Hocquenghem and Reed-Solomon codes", *IEEE Trans. Comput.*, C–36, pp 1165–1171, 1987.
3. Rhee, M.Y.: *BCH Codes and Reed-Solomon Codes*, Minum Sha, Seoul, 1990.
4. Wang, C.C., T.K. Troung, H. Shao, L. Deutch, J. Omura, and I. Reed: "VLSI architecture for computing multiplications and inverses in GF (2^m)", *IEEE Trans. Comput.*, vol. C–34, pp 709–716, Aug. 1985.
5. Yamagishi, A. and H. Imai: "A construction method for decoders of BCH codes using ROMs", *Trans. IEICE Japan*, vol. J63–D, pp 1034–1041, Dec. 1980.

Chapter

7

Bose-Chaudhuri-Hocquenghem Codes

Error-correction BCH codes are widely used for various communication and data processing systems, such as computers, satellite or space communication, optical disks, cryptographic communication, mobile telephones, etc. Several efficient decoding algorithms for double-, triple-, quadruple-, and multiple-error-correcting BCH codes have been developed. This chapter presents many such algorithms and techniques proposed by several coding theorists.

7.1 EXPRESSION OF CYCLIC CODES

Suppose $g(x) = 1 + g_1x + \cdots + g_{n-k-1}x^{n-k-1} + x^{n-k}$ is a generator polynomial of an (n, k) cyclic code. If $d(x) = d_0 + d_1x + \cdots + d_{k-1}x^{k-1}$ is the information polynomial to be encoded, then the corresponding code polynomial $c(x)$ is expressed by the following nonsystematic form

$$
\begin{aligned}
c(x) &= d(x)\,g(x) \\
&= c_0 + c_1x + c_2x^2 + \cdots + c_{n-1}x^{n-1} \qquad (7.1)
\end{aligned}
$$

The encoding of an (n, k) cyclic code in systematic form can be achieved by multiplying $d(x)$ by x^{n-k} and dividing $x^{n-k}d(x)$ by $g(x)$ such that

$$x^{n-k}d(x) = q(x)g(x) + p(x) \tag{7.2}$$

where $q(x)$ is the quotient polynomial and the remainder $p(x)$ is the parity-check polynomial of degree $n - k - 1$ or less. Thus, the code polynomial can be expressed in systematic form as

$$\begin{aligned} c(x) &= p(x) + x^{n-k}d(x) \\ &= p_0 + p_1 x + \cdots + p_{n-k-1}x^{n-k-1} + d_0 x^{n-k} \\ &\quad + d_1 x^{n-k+1} + \cdots + d_{k-1}x^{n-1} \end{aligned} \tag{7.3}$$

which corresponds to the code word

$$\mathbf{c} = (p_0, p_1, \cdots, p_{n-k-1}, d_0, d_1, \cdots, d_{k-1}) \tag{7.4}$$

From Eq. 7.4, we see that the code word consists of k unaltered information digits followed by $n - k$ parity-check digits.

The generator matrix $\mathbf{G}$ can be obtained in systematic form by dividing x^{n-k+i} by $g(x)$ such that

$$x^{n-k+i} = q_i(x)g(x) + p_i(x) \qquad 0 \le i \le k-1 \tag{7.5}$$

or

$$c_i(x) = p_i(x) + x^{n-k+i} \qquad 0 \le i \le k-1 \tag{7.6}$$

because $p_i(x) + x^{n-k+i}$, $0 \le i \le k-1$ are multiples of $g(x)$. If we arrange these k code polynomials as rows of a $k \times n$ matrix, we obtain the generator matrix $\mathbf{G}$ in systematic form as follows:

$$\mathbf{G} = \begin{bmatrix} \mathbf{g}_0 \\ \mathbf{g}_1 \\ \cdot \\ \cdot \\ \cdot \\ \mathbf{g}_{k-1} \end{bmatrix} = \begin{bmatrix} p_{00} & p_{01} & \cdots & p_{0,n-k-1} & 1 & 0 & 0 & \cdots & 0 \\ p_{10} & p_{11} & \cdots & p_{1,n-k-1} & 0 & 1 & 0 & \cdots & 0 \\ & \cdot & & \cdot & & & & & \\ & \cdot & & \cdot & & & & & \\ & \cdot & & \cdot & & & & & \\ p_{k-1,0} & p_{k-1,1} & \cdots & p_{k-1,n-k-1} & 0 & 0 & 0 & \cdots & 1 \end{bmatrix} \tag{7.7}$$

Therefore, the code word is found as

$$\begin{aligned} \mathbf{C} &= (c_0, c_1, c_2, \cdots, c_{n-1}) \\ &= (d_0, d_1, d_2, \cdots, d_{k-1})[\mathbf{g}_0, \mathbf{g}_1, \mathbf{g}_2, \cdots, \mathbf{g}_{k-1}]^T \end{aligned} \tag{7.8}$$

7.2 BCH CODE STRUCTURE AND ENCODING

The generator polynomial of a binary t-error-correcting BCH code of block length $n = 2^m - 1$ is the product of distinct minimal polynomials

$m_i(x)$, $1 \le i \le 2t$, of $\alpha, \alpha^2, \cdots, \alpha^{2t}$, where $\alpha \in GF(2^m)$ is a root of the primitive polynomial $p(x)$. Let $c(x) = c_0 + c_1x + c_2x^2 + \cdots + c_{n-1}x^{n-1}$ be a code polynomial with coefficients c_i, $0 \le i \le n-1$, from GF (2). If $c(x)$ has roots $\alpha, \alpha^2, \cdots, \alpha^{2t}$, then $c(x)$ is divisible by the minimal polynomials $m_1(x)$, $m_2(x), \cdots, m_{2t}(x)$ of $\alpha, \alpha^2, \cdots, \alpha^{2t}$. Thus, the generator polynomial $g(x)$ of the t-error-correcting BCH code is found as the least common multiple of these minimal polynomials such that

$$g(x) = \text{LCM}\{m_1(x), m_2(x), \cdots, m_{2t}(x)\} \tag{7.9}$$

However, since every even power of α has the same minimal polynomial, Eq. 7.9 can be reduced to

$$g(x) = \text{LCM}\{m_1(x), m_3(x), \cdots, m_{2t-1}(x)\} \tag{7.10}$$

which implies that $c(x)$ is a code word if and only if $\alpha, \alpha^3, \cdots, \alpha^{2t-1}$ are roots of $c(x)$. Since the degree of each minimal polynomial is m or less, the degree of $g(x)$ will be at the most mt. Therefore, the code has a maximum of mt parity-check digits, namely, $n - k \le mt$.

■ **Example 7.1** Consider the triple-error-correcting (31, 16) BCH code with the generator polynomial

$$g(x) = m_1(x)\, m_3(x)\, m_5(x) \tag{7.11}$$

Let α be a primitive element of GF (2^5) given by Table 6.1. The minimal polynomials of α, α^3, and α^5 are easily found with the aid of this table, as follows:

$$m_1(x) = (x+\alpha)(x+\alpha^2)(x+\alpha^4)(x+\alpha^8)(x+\alpha^{16})$$

$$= 1 + x^2 + x^5$$

Similarly, $$m_3(x) = 1 + x^2 + x^3 + x^4 + x^5$$

and $$m_5(x) = 1 + x + x^2 + x^4 + x^5$$

Substituting $m_i(x)$s, $i = 1, 3, 5$, in Eq. (7.11) yields the generator polynomial

$$g(x) = 1 + x + x^2 + x^3 + x^5 + x^7 + x^8 + x^9 + x^{10} + x^{11} + x^{15}$$

Dividing x^{15+i} by $g(x)$ in order to determine the generator matrix **G**

$$x^{15+i} = q_i(x)\, g(x) + p_i(x)$$

or $$c_i(x) = p_i(x) + x^{15+i} \qquad 0 \le i \le 15 \tag{7.12}$$

If these 16 code polynomials are arranged in rows of a 16 × 31 matrix, the generator matrix can be obtained in systematic form as

$$
\mathbf{G} = \begin{bmatrix} \mathbf{g}_0 \\ \mathbf{g}_1 \\ \mathbf{g}_2 \\ \mathbf{g}_3 \\ \mathbf{g}_4 \\ \mathbf{g}_5 \\ \mathbf{g}_6 \\ \mathbf{g}_7 \\ \mathbf{g}_8 \\ \mathbf{g}_9 \\ \mathbf{g}_{10} \\ \mathbf{g}_{11} \\ \mathbf{g}_{12} \\ \mathbf{g}_{13} \\ \mathbf{g}_{14} \\ \mathbf{g}_{15} \end{bmatrix} = \begin{bmatrix}
1111010111110001000000000000000 \\
0111101011111000100000000000000 \\
0011110101111100010000000000000 \\
0001111010111110001000000000000 \\
1111101010101110000100000000000 \\
1000100010100110000010000000000 \\
1011000110100010000001000000000 \\
1010110100100000000000100000000 \\
0101011010010000000000010000000 \\
0010101101001000000000001000000 \\
0001010110100100000000000100000 \\
0000101011010010000000000010000 \\
1111000010011000000000000001000 \\
0111100001001100000000000000100 \\
0011110000100110000000000000010 \\
1110101111100010000000000000001
\end{bmatrix} \tag{7.13}
$$

Thus, if the information vector $\mathbf{d} = (d_0, d_1, d_2, \cdots, d_{15})$ is given, then the code words are found as

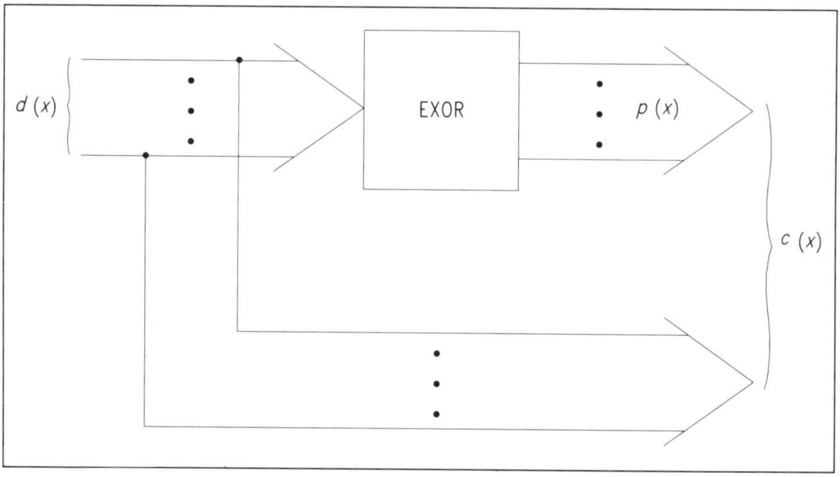

Fig. 7.1 Block diagram for triple-error-correcting (31, 16) BCH encoder with parallel connection

$$\mathbf{c} = (c_0, c_1, c_2, c_3, \cdots, c_{30})$$
$$= (d_0, d_1, d_2, d_3, \cdots, d_{15}) \cdot \mathbf{G} \tag{7.14}$$

where **G** is the generator matrix given in Eq. 7.13. For example, for $d(x) = 1$, the code word becomes $c(x) = 1 + x + x^2 + x^3 + x^5 + x^7 + x^8 + x^9 + x^{10} + x^{11}$. Using Eq. 7.14, an encoder for the triple-error-correcting (31, 16) BCH code with parallel connection can be devised as shown in Fig. 7.1.

If α^i, $1 \le i \le 2t$, are the roots of $c(x)$, then $c(\alpha^i) = c_0 + c_1(\alpha^i)^1 + c_2(\alpha^i)^2 + \cdots + c_{n-1}(\alpha^i)^{n-1} = 0$ which can also be expressed in the following matrix form.

$$(c_0, c_1, c_2, \cdots, c_{n-1}) \cdot \begin{bmatrix} (\alpha^i)^0 \\ (\alpha^i)^1 \\ (\alpha^i)^2 \\ \cdot \\ \cdot \\ \cdot \\ (\alpha^i)^{n-1} \end{bmatrix} = 0 \qquad 1 \le i \le 2t \tag{7.15}$$

Equation 7.15 denotes $\mathbf{c} \cdot \mathbf{H}^T = 0$ because $\mathbf{c} = (c_0, c_1, c_2, \cdots, c_{n-1})$ is a code word of the t-error-correcting BCH code. Thus, the parity-check matrix of this code is

$$\mathbf{H} = [(\alpha^i)^0\,(\alpha^i)^1\,(\alpha^i)^2 \cdots (\alpha^i)^{n-1}] \qquad 1 \le i \le 2t \tag{7.16}$$

where the entries of **H** are elements of GF (2^m). The powers of α in Eq. 7.16 represent $2t$-tuple column vectors and every nonzero column of length $2t$ (or $d_0 - 1$) appears as a column of **H** as shown below.

$$\mathbf{H} = \begin{bmatrix} 1 & \alpha & \alpha^2 & \cdots & \alpha^{n-1} \\ 1 & \alpha^2 & (\alpha^2)^2 & \cdots & (\alpha^2)^{n-1} \\ 1 & \alpha^3 & (\alpha^3)^2 & \cdots & (\alpha^3)^{n-1} \\ \cdot & \cdot & \cdot & & \cdot \\ \cdot & \cdot & \cdot & & \cdot \\ \cdot & \cdot & \cdot & & \cdot \\ 1 & \alpha^{2t} & (\alpha^{2t})^2 & \cdots & (\alpha^{2t})^{n-1} \end{bmatrix} \tag{7.17}$$

If each entry of **H** is replaced by its corresponding m tuples over GF (2) arranged in column form, we shall have a binary parity-check matrix

$\mathbf{H}$ for the code. However, it should be borne in mind that any set of $2t$ columns of $\mathbf{H}$ cannot be linearly dependent. Therefore, the t-error-correcting BCH code has a minimum distance of at least $2t + 1$. Thus, no $2t$ or fewer columns of $\mathbf{H}$ given by Eq. 7.17 sum to zero. Let α^j, $j = 2i, 4i, \cdots$ be conjugates of α^i for some i. Then, $c(\alpha^i) = 0$ because α^i is the root of $c(x)$. So are $c(\alpha^j) = 0$. Hence, we may conclude that the even-number rows of $\mathbf{H}$ can be omitted from Eq. 7.17.

■ **Example 7.2** Consider again the triple-error-correcting (31, 16) BCH code with the minimum distance $d_{\min} = 7$. Using Eq. 7.17 and Table 6.1, the parity-check matrix of this code is found as

$$\mathbf{H} = \left[\begin{matrix} \alpha^0 & \alpha^1 & \alpha^2 & \alpha^3 & \alpha^4 & \alpha^5 & \alpha^6 & \alpha^7 & \alpha^8 & \alpha^9 & \alpha^{10} & \alpha^{11} & \alpha^{12} & \alpha^{13} & \alpha^{14} \\ \alpha^0 & \alpha^3 & \alpha^6 & \alpha^9 & \alpha^{12} & \alpha^{15} & \alpha^{18} & \alpha^{21} & \alpha^{24} & \alpha^{27} & \alpha^{30} & \alpha^2 & \alpha^5 & \alpha^8 & \alpha^{11} \\ \alpha^0 & \alpha^5 & \alpha^{10} & \alpha^{15} & \alpha^{20} & \alpha^{25} & \alpha^{30} & \alpha^4 & \alpha^9 & \alpha^{14} & \alpha^{19} & \alpha^{24} & \alpha^{29} & \alpha^3 & \alpha^8 \end{matrix}\right.$$
$$\left.\begin{matrix} \alpha^{15} & \alpha^{16} & \alpha^{17} & \alpha^{18} & \alpha^{19} & \alpha^{20} & \alpha^{21} & \alpha^{22} & \alpha^{23} & \alpha^{24} & \alpha^{25} & \alpha^{26} & \alpha^{27} & \alpha^{28} & \alpha^{29} & \alpha^{30} \\ \alpha^{14} & \alpha^{17} & \alpha^{20} & \alpha^{23} & \alpha^{26} & \alpha^{29} & \alpha^1 & \alpha^4 & \alpha^7 & \alpha^{10} & \alpha^{13} & \alpha^{16} & \alpha^{19} & \alpha^{22} & \alpha^{25} & \alpha^{28} \\ \alpha^{13} & \alpha^{18} & \alpha^{23} & \alpha^{28} & \alpha^2 & \alpha^7 & \alpha^{12} & \alpha^{17} & \alpha^{22} & \alpha^{27} & \alpha^1 & \alpha^6 & \alpha^{11} & \alpha^{16} & \alpha^{21} & \alpha^{26} \end{matrix}\right] \tag{7.18}$$

All the entries of Eq. 7.18 are elements of GF (2^5). With the aid of Table 6.1, each entry of $\mathbf{H}$ is replaced by its corresponding 5 bits arranged in column form. Thus, the parity-check matrix of this code is obtained as the following 15×31 matrix.

$$\mathbf{H} = \left[\begin{array}{c}
1\,0\,0\,0\,0\,1\,0\,0\,1\,0\,1\,1\,0\,0\,1\,1\,1\,1\,1\,0\,0\,0\,1\,1\,0\,1\,1\,1\,0\,1\,0 \\
0\,1\,0\,0\,0\,0\,1\,0\,0\,0\,0\,1\,1\,0\,0\,1\,1\,1\,1\,1\,0\,0\,0\,1\,1\,0\,1\,1\,1\,0\,1 \\
0\,0\,1\,0\,0\,1\,0\,1\,1\,0\,0\,1\,1\,1\,1\,1\,0\,0\,0\,1\,1\,0\,1\,1\,1\,0\,1\,0\,1\,0\,0 \\
0\,0\,0\,1\,0\,0\,1\,0\,1\,1\,0\,0\,1\,1\,1\,1\,1\,0\,0\,0\,1\,1\,0\,1\,1\,1\,0\,1\,0\,1\,0 \\
0\,0\,0\,0\,1\,0\,0\,1\,0\,1\,1\,0\,0\,1\,1\,1\,1\,1\,0\,0\,0\,1\,1\,0\,1\,1\,1\,0\,1\,0\,1 \\
\hdashline
1\,0\,0\,0\,0\,1\,1\,0\,0\,1\,0\,0\,1\,1\,1\,1\,1\,0\,1\,1\,1\,0\,0\,0\,1\,0\,1\,0\,1\,1\,0 \\
0\,0\,1\,1\,1\,1\,1\,0\,1\,1\,1\,0\,0\,0\,1\,0\,1\,0\,1\,1\,0\,1\,0\,0\,0\,0\,1\,1\,0\,0\,1 \\
0\,0\,0\,0\,1\,1\,0\,0\,1\,0\,0\,1\,1\,1\,1\,1\,0\,1\,1\,1\,0\,0\,0\,1\,0\,1\,0\,1\,1\,0\,1 \\
0\,1\,1\,1\,1\,1\,0\,1\,1\,1\,0\,0\,0\,1\,0\,1\,0\,1\,1\,0\,1\,0\,0\,0\,0\,1\,1\,0\,0\,1\,0 \\
0\,0\,0\,1\,0\,1\,0\,1\,1\,0\,1\,0\,0\,0\,0\,1\,1\,0\,0\,1\,0\,0\,1\,1\,1\,1\,1\,0\,1\,1\,1 \\
\hdashline
1\,1\,1\,1\,0\,1\,0\,0\,0\,1\,0\,0\,1\,0\,1\,0\,1\,1\,0\,0\,0\,0\,1\,1\,1\,0\,0\,1\,1\,0\,1 \\
0\,0\,0\,1\,0\,0\,1\,0\,1\,0\,1\,1\,0\,0\,0\,0\,1\,1\,1\,0\,0\,1\,1\,0\,1\,1\,1\,1\,1\,0\,1 \\
0\,1\,0\,1\,1\,0\,0\,0\,0\,1\,1\,1\,0\,0\,1\,1\,0\,1\,1\,1\,1\,1\,0\,1\,0\,0\,0\,1\,0\,0\,1 \\
0\,0\,0\,1\,1\,1\,0\,0\,0\,1\,0\,1\,1\,1\,1\,1\,0\,1\,0\,0\,0\,1\,0\,0\,1\,0\,1\,0\,1\,1\,0 \\
0\,0\,1\,1\,0\,1\,1\,1\,1\,1\,0\,1\,0\,0\,0\,1\,0\,0\,1\,0\,1\,0\,1\,1\,0\,0\,0\,0\,1\,1\,1
\end{array}\right] \tag{7.19}$$

7.3 SYNDROME COMPUTATION

The first step in decoding a code word is to compute the syndrome $s(x)$ from the received word $r(x)$. For decoding a t-error-correcting BCH code, the $2t$-tuple syndrome is given by

$$\mathbf{s} = (s_1, s_2, \cdots, s_{2t}) = \mathbf{r} \cdot \mathbf{H}^T \tag{7.20}$$

where the parity-check matrix **H** is given by Eq. 7.17.

If a code word $c(x)$ is transmitted, then the received word becomes

$$r(x) = c(x) + e(x) \tag{7.21}$$

caused by the channel noise $e(x) = e_0 + e_1 x + \cdots + e_{n-1} x^{n-1}$.

Suppose ν errors actually occur in random locations j_λ, $1 \le \lambda \le \nu$ such that

$$e(x) = \sum_{\lambda=1}^{\nu} x^{j_\lambda} \qquad 0 \le j_\lambda \le n-1 \tag{7.22}$$

Since $\alpha, \alpha^2, \cdots, \alpha^{2t}$ are roots of each polynomial in the code, $c(\alpha^i) = 0$ for $1 \le i \le 2t$. Therefore, Eq. 7.21 becomes

$$r(\alpha^i) = e(\alpha^i) \qquad i = 1, 2, \cdots, 2t \tag{7.23}$$

On the other hand, the syndrome components are computed from dividing $r(x)$ by the minimal polynomial $m_k(x)$, $1 \le k \le 2t$, of α^k such that

$$r(x) = q_k(x)\, m_k(x) + \gamma_k(x) \tag{7.24}$$

where the remainder $\gamma_k(x)$ with $x = \alpha^k$ is the syndrome component s_k due to the fact that $m_k(\alpha^k) = 0$. Thus, in general, computing $r(\alpha^i)$ is equivalent to computing $\gamma_k(\alpha^i)$. Hence, coupled with Eq. 7.23, the syndrome component may also be expressed as

$$s_k = \gamma_k(\alpha^k) = r(\alpha^k) = e(\alpha^k) \quad 1 \le k \le 2t \tag{7.25}$$

From Eq. 7.25, we see that the syndrome **s** also depends on error pattern **e**.

■ **Example 7.3** Consider the triple-error-correcting (31, 16) BCH code with designed distance $d_0 = 7$. Suppose that an allzero code word $\mathbf{c} = (0\,0\,0 \cdots 0)$ is transmitted and $r(x) = x^2 + x^{11} + x^{20}$ is received. Clearly, there are three errors at the locations x^2, x^{11}, and x^{20}. Since $2t = 6$, the syndrome consists of six tuples, and each tuple contains five digits as follows:

$$\mathbf{s} = (s_1, s_2, s_3, s_4, s_5, s_6)$$

The minimal polynomials $m_i(x)$ for α^i, $i = 1, 3, 5$ are

$$m_1(x) = 1 + x^2 + x^5$$

$$m_3(x) = 1 + x + x^2 + x^3 + x^4 + x^5$$

and $$m_5(x) = 1 + x + x^2 + x^4 + x^5$$

Dividing $r(x)$ by $m(x)$ gives the remainder

$$\gamma(x) = \gamma_0 + \gamma_1 x + \gamma_2 x^2 + \gamma_3 x^3 + \gamma_4 x^4$$

Using Table 6.1 for GF (2^5), the syndrome digits can be obtained as

$$s_1 = \gamma(\alpha) = \gamma_0 + \gamma_1 \alpha + \gamma_2 \alpha^2 + \gamma_3 \alpha^3 + \gamma_4 \alpha^4$$

$$s_2 = \gamma(\alpha^2) = (\gamma_0 + \gamma_4) + \gamma_3 \alpha + (\gamma_1 + \gamma_4)\alpha^2 + (\gamma_3 + \gamma_4)\alpha^3 + \gamma_2 \alpha^4$$

$$s_4 = \gamma(\alpha^4) = (\gamma_0 + \gamma_2 + \gamma_4) + (\gamma_3 + \gamma_4)\alpha + (\gamma_2 + \gamma_3)\alpha^2 + (\gamma_2 + \gamma_3 + \gamma_4)\alpha^3 + (\gamma_1 + \gamma_4)\alpha^4$$

$$s_3 = \gamma(\alpha^3) = \gamma_0 + (\gamma_2 + \gamma_3 + \gamma_4)\alpha + \gamma_4 \alpha^2 + (\gamma_1 + \gamma_2 + \gamma_3 + \gamma_4)\alpha^3 + \gamma_3 \alpha^4$$

$$s_6 = \gamma(\alpha^6) = (\gamma_0 + \gamma_3) + (\gamma_1 + \gamma_2 + \gamma_3 + \gamma_4)\alpha + (\gamma_2 + \gamma_4)\alpha^2 + (\gamma_1 + \gamma_2 + \gamma_4)\alpha^3 + \gamma_4 \alpha^4$$

$$s_5 = \gamma(\alpha^5) = (\gamma_0 + \gamma_1 + \gamma_2 + \gamma_3) + \gamma_3 \alpha + (\gamma_1 + \gamma_3 + \gamma_4)\alpha^2 + (\gamma_3 + \gamma_4)\alpha^3 + (\gamma_2 + \gamma_3)\alpha^4$$

Thus, the syndrome generator for the (31, 16) BCH code can be devised as shown in Fig. 7.2.

Since the received word is $r(x) = x^2 + x^{11} + x^{20}$ when the allzero code word $\mathbf{c} = 0$ is transmitted, division of $r(x) = x^2 + x^{11} + x^{20}$ by $m_1(x) = 1 + x^2 + x^5$ yields the remainder $\gamma_1(x) = 1 + x + x^2 + x^3$.

The syndrome digits are obtained by substituting $x = \alpha$, α^2, and α^4, respectively, into $\gamma_1(x)$. Hence, with the aid of Table 6.1, we have

$$s_1 = \gamma_1(\alpha) = 1 + \alpha + \alpha^2 + \alpha^3 = \alpha^{23}$$

$$s_2 = \gamma_1(\alpha^2) = 1 + \alpha + \alpha^2 + \alpha^3 + \alpha^4 = \alpha^{15}$$

$$s_4 = \gamma_1(\alpha^4) = \alpha + \alpha^4 = \alpha^{30}$$

Similarly, dividing $r(x) = x^2 + x^{11} + x^{20}$ by $m_3(x) = 1 + x^2 + x^3 + x^4 + x^5$ gives the remainder $\gamma_3(x) = 1 + x + x^4$. Thus, the syndrome digits for $x = \alpha^3$ and α^6 become

$$s_3 = \gamma_3(\alpha^3) = 1 + \alpha + \alpha^2 = \alpha^{11}$$

$$s_6 = \gamma_3(\alpha^6) = 1 + \alpha^2 + \alpha^4 = \alpha^{22}$$

Finally, dividing $r(x) = x^2 + x^{11} + x^{20}$ by $m_5(x) = 1 + x + x^2 + x^4 + x^5$ yields the remainder $\gamma_5(x) = 1 + x + x^3$. Substituting α^5 into this $\gamma_5(x)$,

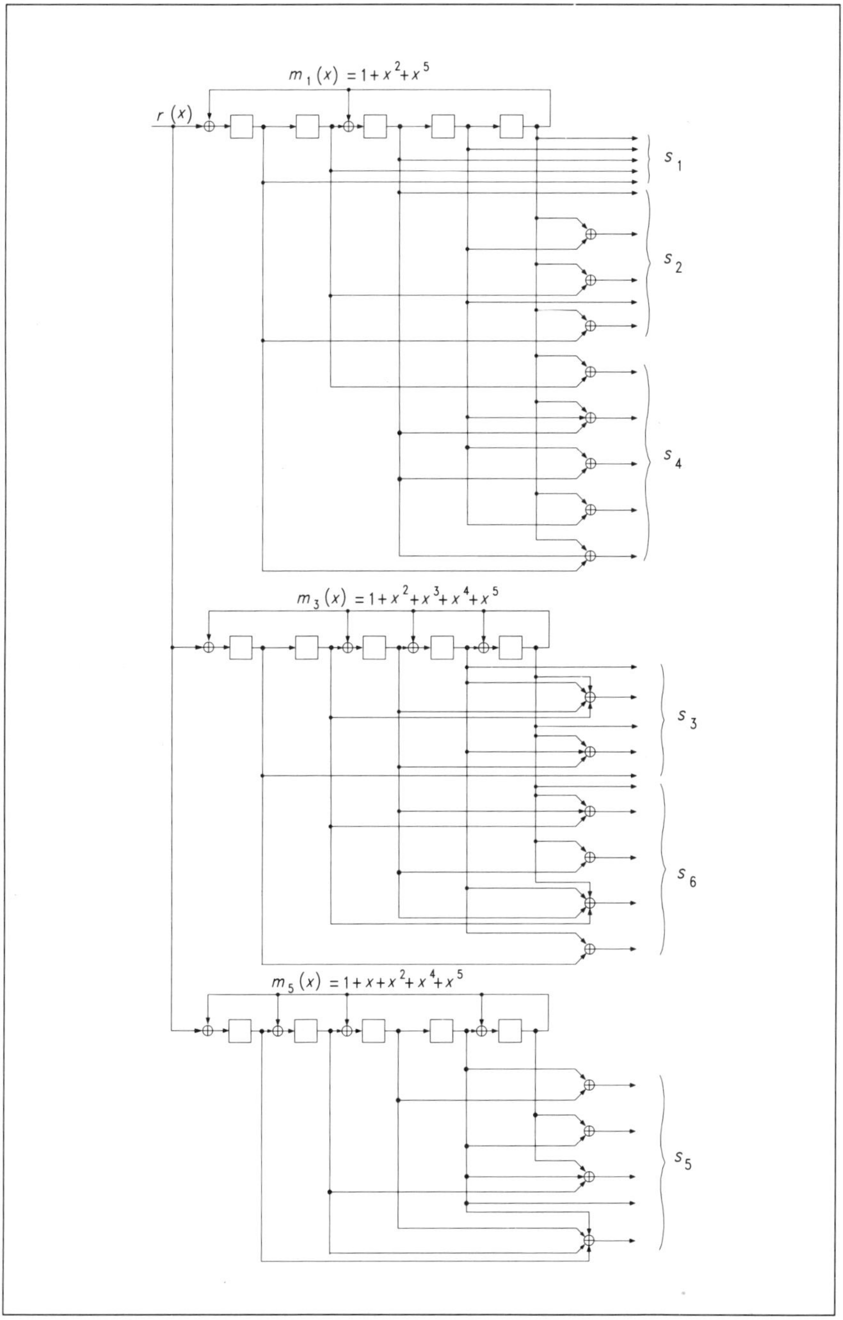

Fig. 7.2 Syndrome computation circuit for (31, 16) BCH code

we obtain the syndrome digit

$$s_5 = \gamma_5(\alpha^5) = 1 + \alpha + \alpha^3 + \alpha^4 = \alpha^{16}$$

Thus, the six-tuple syndrome is obtained as

$$\mathbf{s} = (\alpha^{23}, \alpha^{15}, \alpha^{11}, \alpha^{30}, \alpha^{16}, \alpha^{22})$$

7.4 BCH DECODING

The algorithms and techniques for decoding a BCH code have been appeared in several papers since 1964, but each has relative advantages and disadvantages, depending upon the number of errors to be corrected.

As seen from Eq. 7.25, each syndrome component s_k is simply the error pattern $e(x)$ evaluated at $x = \alpha^k$ and thus is represented as some field element of GF (2^m). Suppose ν $(1 \le \nu \le t)$ errors actually occur and that they do so in unknown locations $j_1, j_2, \cdots, j_\nu$. We can then write the error pattern as

$$e(x) = \sum_{\lambda=1}^{\nu} x^{j_\lambda} \qquad 0 \le j_\lambda \le n-1 \tag{7.26}$$

Coupled Eq. 7.26 with Eq. 7.25, the syndrome components may be expressed as

$$s_k = \sum_{\lambda=1}^{\nu} (\alpha^k)^{j_\lambda} = \sum_{\lambda=1}^{\nu} \left(\alpha^{j_\lambda}\right)^k = \sum_{\lambda=1}^{\nu} (\beta_\lambda)^k \qquad 1 \le k \le 2t \tag{7.27}$$

where $\beta_\lambda = \alpha^{j_\lambda}$, $1 \le \lambda \le \nu$, are called the error-location numbers. Thus, Eq. 7.27 will generate a set of equations relating to between the syndrome components s_k, $1 \le k \le 2t$, and the error-location numbers α^{j_λ}, $1 \le \lambda \le \nu$. They are

$$\begin{aligned} s_1 &= \sum_{\lambda=1}^{\nu} \beta_\lambda \\ s_2 &= \sum_{\lambda=1}^{\nu} (\beta_\lambda)^2 \\ &\cdots\cdots\cdots \\ s_{2t} &= \sum_{\lambda=1}^{\nu} (\beta_\lambda)^{2t} \end{aligned} \tag{7.28}$$

These $2t$ equations are known as syndrome equations or power-sum symmetric functions. Decoding BCH codes involves solving these syndrome equations and finding the error-location number α^{j_λ}, $\lambda = 1, 2, \cdots, \nu$ from the syndrome components.

Suppose that $\nu \le t$ errors actually occur. Let the error-locator polynomial be

$$\sigma(x) = \sigma_0 + \sigma_1 x + \sigma_2 x^2 + \cdots + \sigma_\nu x^\nu$$
$$= (1 + \beta_1 x)(1 + \beta_2 x) \cdots (1 + \beta_\nu x) \qquad (7.29)$$

which has the inverse of the error-location numbers as roots. The coefficients σ_i, $0 \le i \le \nu$ in Eq. 7.29 are seen to be given by the elementary symmetric functions of the error-location numbers such that

$$\sigma_0 = 1$$
$$\sigma_1 = \sum_{i=1}^{\nu} \beta_i$$
$$\sigma_2 = \sum_{i=1}^{\nu-1} \beta_i \beta_{i+1}$$
$$\cdots\cdots\cdots\cdots \qquad (7.30)$$
$$\sigma_\nu = \beta_1 \beta_2 \cdots \beta_\nu$$

where $\beta_\lambda = \alpha^{j_\lambda}$, $0 \le \lambda \le \nu$ whose reciprocals β_λ^{-1} are the roots of $\sigma(x)$.

At this point, it is worthwhile to outline the major steps for BCH decoding. The procedure involves (i) computing the syndrome **s** from the received word $r(x)$, (ii) determining the coefficients σ_i of the error-locator polynomial $\sigma(x)$ from the syndrome **s**, (iii) working out the error-location numbers β_λ, $0 \le \lambda \le \nu$, by finding the roots of $\sigma(x)$, and (iv) correcting the errors in $r(x)$ in the position indicated by error-location numbers.

Starting from the next section, six different decoding methods of BCH codes will be discussed, and illustrated in appropriate examples.

7.5 DIRECT SOLUTION METHOD BY PETERSON, GORENSTEIN, AND ZIERLER

Peterson's algorithm (1960) for binary BCH codes was extended by Gorenstein and Zierler (1961) for nonbinary BCH codes. We will present here the general case which can be applied to the decoding of BCH as well as Reed-Solomon codes.

Let the error polynomial $e(x) = e_0 + e_1x + \cdots + e_{n-1}x^{n-1}$, where $\nu \le t$ coefficients are nonzero. Therefore, the errors occur in random locations at j_λ, $1 \le \lambda \le \nu$ such that

$$e(x) = e_{j_1}x^{j_1} + e_{j_2}x^{j_2} + \cdots + e_{j_\nu}x^{j_\nu} \tag{7.31}$$

where e_{j_λ} is called the error value at the location j_λ. In fact, for binary codes $e_{j_\lambda} = 1$. For nonbinary cases such as Reed-Solomon codes, the error values at the error locations should be evaluated, and will be covered in detail in Chapter 8.

As usual, the syndrome s_k can be computed from the received polynomial $r(x)$. For $k = 1$,

$$\begin{aligned} s_1 &= r(\alpha) = e(\alpha) \\ &= e_{j_1}\alpha^{j_1} + e_{j_2}\alpha^{j_2} + \cdots + e_{j_\nu}\alpha^{j_\nu} \\ &= Y_1\beta_1 + Y_2\beta_2 + \cdots + Y_\nu\beta_\nu \end{aligned} \tag{7.32}$$

where $\beta_\lambda = \alpha^{j_\lambda}$, $1 \le \lambda \le \nu$, are the error-location numbers and $Y_\lambda = e_{j_\lambda}$, $1 \le \lambda \le \nu$, represents the error values. In general, the syndromes s_k, $1 \le k \le 2t$, can be computed as

$$\begin{aligned} s_k &= r(\alpha^k) = e(\alpha^k) \\ &= Y_1\beta_1^k + Y_2\beta_2^k + \cdots + Y_\nu\beta_\nu^k \qquad 1 \le k \le 2t \end{aligned} \tag{7.33}$$

From Eq. 7.33, the following set of $2t$ simultaneous equations with the unknowns β_ν and Y_ν for $1 \le \lambda \le \nu$ can be formed as

$$\begin{aligned} s_1 &= Y_1\beta_1 + Y_2\beta_2 + \cdots + Y_\nu\beta_\nu \\ s_2 &= Y_1\beta_1^2 + Y_2\beta_2^2 + \cdots + Y_\nu\beta_\nu^2 \\ s_3 &= Y_1\beta_1^3 + Y_2\beta_2^3 + \cdots + Y_\nu\beta_\nu^3 \\ &\cdots\cdots\cdots\cdots\cdots\cdots \\ s_{2t} &= Y_1\beta_1^{2t} + Y_2\beta_2^{2t} + \cdots + Y_\nu\beta_\nu^{2t} \end{aligned} \tag{7.34}$$

Equation 7.34 has to be observed, and at least one unique solution has to be found.

Consider the error-locator polynomial $\sigma(x)$,

$$\sigma(x) = 1 + \sigma_1 x + \sigma_2 x^2 + \cdots + \sigma_\nu x^\nu$$

$$= (1 + \beta_1 x)(1 + \beta_2 x) \cdots (1 + \beta_\nu x) \tag{7.35}$$

Multiplying both sides of Eq. 7.35 by $Y_\gamma \beta_\gamma^{k+\nu}$ and setting $x = \beta_\gamma^{-1}$, it yields $\sigma(\beta_\gamma^{-1}) = 0$. But the right sides of Eq. 7.35 become

$$Y_\gamma (\beta_\gamma^{k+\nu} + \sigma_1 \beta_\gamma^{k+\nu-1} + \sigma_2 \beta_\gamma^{k+\nu-2} + \cdots + \sigma_\nu \beta_\gamma^{k}) = 0 \tag{7.36}$$

Summing on γ for $1 \le \gamma \le \nu$, for each k, we have

$$\sum_{\gamma=1}^{\nu} Y_\gamma \beta_\gamma^{k+\nu} + \sigma_1 \sum_{\gamma=1}^{\nu} Y_\gamma \beta_\gamma^{k+\nu-1} + \cdots + \sigma_\nu \sum_{\gamma=1}^{\nu} Y_\gamma \beta_\gamma^{k} = 0 \tag{7.37}$$

Referring to Eq. 7.33, each sum in Eq. 7.37 is recognized as the syndrome. Therefore, Eq. 7.37 can be also expressed as

$$s_{k+\nu} + \sigma_1 s_{k+\nu-1} + \sigma_2 s_{k+\nu-2} + \cdots + \sigma_\nu s_k = 0 \tag{7.38}$$

or $\quad \sigma_\nu s_k + \sigma_{\nu-1} s_{k+1} + \sigma_{\nu-2} s_{k+2} + \cdots + \sigma_2 s_{k+\nu-2} + \sigma_1 s_{k+\nu-1} = -s_{k+\nu} \tag{7.39}$

Since $\nu \le t$, for $1 \le k \le \nu$ Eq. 7.39 generates the following set of equations:

$$\sigma_\nu s_1 + \sigma_{\nu-1} s_2 + \nu_{\nu-2} s_3 + \cdots + \sigma_2 s_{\nu-1} + \sigma_1 s_\nu = -s_{\nu-1}$$

$$\sigma_\nu s_2 + \sigma_{\nu-1} s_3 + \sigma_{\nu-2} s_4 + \cdots + \sigma_2 s_\nu + \sigma_1 s_{\nu+1} = -s_{\nu+2}$$

$$\cdots\cdots\cdots\cdots\cdots\cdots\cdots\cdots\cdots\cdots\cdots\cdots\cdots\cdots \tag{7.40}$$

$$\sigma_\nu s_{\nu-1} + \sigma_{\nu-1} s_\nu + \sigma_{\nu-2} s_{\nu+1} + \cdots + \sigma_2 s_{2\nu-3} + \sigma_1 s_{2\nu-2} = -s_{2\nu-1}$$

$$\sigma_\nu s_\nu + \sigma_{\nu-1} s_{\nu+1} + \sigma_{\nu-2} s_{\nu+2} + \cdots + \sigma_2 s_{2\nu-2} + \sigma_1 s_{2\nu-1} = -s_{2\nu}$$

This is the set of linear equations coupling the syndrome with the coefficients of $\sigma(x)$. Equation 7.40 is sometimes called Newton's identities. Another method of deriving Eq. 7.40 is given in [12]. If expressed in matrix form, Eq. 7.40 gives

$$\begin{bmatrix} s_1 & s_2 & s_3 & \cdots & s_{\nu-1} & s_\nu \\ s_2 & s_3 & s_4 & \cdots & s_\nu & s_{\nu+1} \\ \cdot & \cdot & \cdot & & \cdot & \cdot \\ \cdot & \cdot & \cdot & & \cdot & \cdot \\ \cdot & \cdot & \cdot & & \cdot & \cdot \\ s_{\nu-1} & s_\nu & s_{\nu+1} & \cdots & s_{2\nu-3} & s_{2\nu-2} \\ s_\nu & s_{\nu+1} & s_{\nu+2} & \cdots & s_{2\nu-2} & s_{2\nu-1} \end{bmatrix} \begin{bmatrix} \sigma_\nu \\ \sigma_{\nu-1} \\ \cdot \\ \cdot \\ \cdot \\ \sigma_2 \\ \sigma_1 \end{bmatrix} = \begin{bmatrix} -s_{\nu+1} \\ -s_{\nu+2} \\ \cdot \\ \cdot \\ \cdot \\ -s_{2\nu-1} \\ -s_{2\nu} \end{bmatrix} \tag{7.41}$$

or

$$\begin{bmatrix} \sigma_\nu \\ \sigma_{\nu-1} \\ \cdot \\ \cdot \\ \cdot \\ \sigma_2 \\ \sigma_1 \end{bmatrix} = \mathbf{M}^{-1} \begin{bmatrix} -S_{\nu+1} \\ -S_{\nu+2} \\ \cdot \\ \cdot \\ \cdot \\ -S_{2\nu-1} \\ -S_{2\nu} \end{bmatrix} \tag{7.42}$$

where

$$\mathbf{M}^{-1} = \begin{bmatrix} S_1 & S_2 & S_3 & \cdots & S_{\nu-1} & S_\nu \\ S_2 & S_3 & S_4 & \cdots & S_\nu & S_{\nu+1} \\ \cdot & \cdot & \cdot & & \cdot & \cdot \\ \cdot & \cdot & \cdot & & \cdot & \cdot \\ \cdot & \cdot & \cdot & & \cdot & \cdot \\ S_{\nu-1} & S_\nu & S_{\nu+1} & \cdots & S_{2\nu-3} & S_{2\nu-2} \\ S_\nu & S_{\nu+1} & S_{\nu+2} & \cdots & S_{2\nu-2} & S_{2\nu-1} \end{bmatrix}^{-1} \tag{7.43}$$

Thus, the coefficients σ_i, $1 \le i \le \nu$, of $\sigma(x)$ can be obtained by inverting the matrix **M** if it is nonsingular and substituting it into Eq. 7.42.

The first step of the decoding algorithm is to find a condition that can examine $\nu \le t$ in Eq. 7.41, where ν is the number of errors that actually occurred. The syndrome matrix **M** is nonsingular if $t = \nu$. But the matrix **M** is singular if $\nu < t$. Consequently, when $\nu < t$, the determinant of **M** is zero, i.e. det $[\mathbf{M}] = |\mathbf{M}| = 0$. Thus, if $|\mathbf{M}| \neq 0$ for $\nu = t$, ν is the correct value. But if $|\mathbf{M}| = 0$, set $\nu = t - 1$ by reducing the trial value of ν by 1 and repeat. Continuing in this way, we must find the value of ν until $|\mathbf{M}| \neq 0$ is obtained.

As shown in Eq. 7.42, we first invert **M** and determine σ_i, $1 \le i \le \nu$. After that, we can compute the error-locator polynomial $\sigma(x)$ and find the roots of $\sigma(x)$ in order to determine the error location numbers.

■ **Example 7.4** Consider the triple-error-correcting (31, 16) BCH code, given in Example 7.3, with the generator polynomial $g(x) = 1 + x + x^2 + x^3 + x^5 + x^7 + x^8 + x^9 + x^{10} + x^{11} + x^{15}$. For proceeding through the steps of the decoding algorithm, first the syndrome components should be computed as follows. Suppose the received polynomial is $r(x) = x + x^{12} + x^{25}$ when $c(x) = 0$ is transmitted. $r(x)$ then represents nothing but the error polynomial $e(x)$. Referring to Example 7.1, the minimal polynomial corresponding to α, α^3, and α^5 are, respectively,

$$m_1(x) = 1 + x^2 + x^5$$

$$m_3(x) = 1 + x^2 + x^3 + x^4 + x^5$$

$$m_5(x) = 1 + x + x^2 + x^4 + x^5$$

The syndrome components are computed from the remainders resulting from the division of $r(x)$ by $m_k(x)$, $k = 1, 3, 5$. Therefore, they may be easily found as

$$s_1 = 1 + \alpha^2 + \alpha^4 = \alpha^{22}$$

$$s_2 = 1 + \alpha^4 + \alpha^8 = \alpha^{13}$$

$$s_3 = 1 + \alpha^5 + \alpha^9 = \alpha^{10}$$

$$s_4 = 1 + \alpha^8 + \alpha^{16} = \alpha^{26}$$

$$s_5 = \alpha^{10} + \alpha^{15} = \alpha^{12}$$

$$s_6 = 1 + \alpha^{12} + \alpha^{18} = \alpha^{20}$$

Thus, the syndrome of $r(x)$ is

$$\mathbf{s} = (\alpha^{22}, \alpha^{13}, \alpha^{10}, \alpha^{26}, \alpha^{12}, \alpha^{20})$$

Now we have to find the error-locator polynomial $\sigma(x)$ by applying the Peterson algorithm described above. Set $\nu = 3$ because a triple error has occurred. Using Eq. 7.43, the matrix becomes

$$\mathbf{M} = \begin{bmatrix} s_1 & s_2 & s_3 \\ s_2 & s_3 & s_4 \\ s_3 & s_4 & s_5 \end{bmatrix} = \begin{bmatrix} \alpha^{22} & \alpha^{13} & \alpha^{10} \\ \alpha^{13} & \alpha^{10} & \alpha^{26} \\ \alpha^{10} & \alpha^{26} & \alpha^{12} \end{bmatrix}$$

$$|\mathbf{M}| = \begin{vmatrix} \alpha^{22} & \alpha^{13} & \alpha^{10} \\ \alpha^{13} & \alpha^{10} & \alpha^{26} \\ \alpha^{10} & \alpha^{26} & \alpha^{12} \end{vmatrix} = \alpha^{13} + \alpha^{12} + \alpha^7 + \alpha^{30} = \alpha^7$$

which is not zero. Since $|\mathbf{M}| \neq 0$, $\nu = 3$ is the correct value of ν. Next, let us compute the inverse matrix of $\mathbf{M}$.

$$\mathbf{M}^{-1} = \alpha^{-7} \begin{bmatrix} \alpha^8 & \alpha^{13} & 1 \\ \alpha^{13} & \alpha^2 & \alpha^{13} \\ 1 & \alpha^{13} & \alpha^{22} \end{bmatrix} = \begin{bmatrix} \alpha & \alpha^6 & \alpha^{24} \\ \alpha^6 & \alpha^{26} & \alpha^6 \\ \alpha^{24} & \alpha^6 & \alpha^{15} \end{bmatrix}$$

From Eq. 7.42, we have

$$\begin{bmatrix}\sigma_3\\ \sigma_2\\ \sigma_1\end{bmatrix} = \mathbf{M}^{-1}\begin{bmatrix}s_4\\ s_5\\ s_6\end{bmatrix}$$

$$= \begin{bmatrix}\alpha^{27}+\alpha^{18}+\alpha^{44}\\ \alpha^{32}+\alpha^{38}+\alpha^{26}\\ \alpha^{50}+\alpha^{18}+\alpha^{35}\end{bmatrix} = \begin{bmatrix}\alpha^{7}\\ 1\\ \alpha^{22}\end{bmatrix}$$

Hence the error-locator polynomial $\sigma(x)$ can be found as

$$\sigma(x) = 1 + \alpha^{22}x + x^2 + \alpha^7 x^3 \tag{7.44}$$

There are two ways of finding the roots of $\sigma(x)$. One method involves substituting all the elements α^i, $0 \le i \le 30$, of GF (2^5) into Eq. 7.44; the other is Chien search. Hence, the roots of $\sigma(x)$ are α^{30}, α^{19}, and α^6, and the error location numbers are at the reciprocals of these roots, i.e. $1/\alpha^{30} = \alpha$, $1/\alpha^{19} = \alpha^{12}$, and $1/\alpha^6 = \alpha^{25}$. Thus, the error pattern is $e(x) = x + x^{12} + x^{25}$ because the error values are 1s due to the fact that the code is binary.

■ **Example 7.5** Consider this time the correction of a double error using the binary (31, 16) BCH code. If $r(x) = x^5 + x^{28}$ is received when the allzero code word, $c(x) = 0$, is transmitted, then we know that a double error has occurred at the positions x^5 and x^{28}. Using Eq. 7.33, the syndrome can be computed as follows:

$$s_1 = r(\alpha) = \alpha^5 + \alpha^{28} = \alpha^{17}$$

$$s_2 = r(\alpha^2) = \alpha^3$$

$$s_3 = r(\alpha^3) = \alpha^{15} + \alpha^{22} = \alpha^6$$

$$s_4 = r(\alpha^4) = \alpha^6$$

$$s_5 = r(\alpha^5) = \alpha^{25} + \alpha^{11} = \alpha$$

$$s_6 = r(\alpha^6) = \alpha^{12}$$

Set $\nu = 2$. Thus Eq. 7.43 becomes

$$\mathbf{M} = \begin{bmatrix}s_1 & s_2\\ s_2 & s_3\end{bmatrix} = \begin{bmatrix}\alpha^{17} & \alpha^3\\ \alpha^3 & \alpha^6\end{bmatrix}$$

Since $|\mathbf{M}| = \alpha^{23} + \alpha^{6} = \alpha^{5}$, the inverse matrix of **M** is

$$\mathbf{M}^{-1} = 1/\alpha^{5}\begin{bmatrix}\alpha^{6} & \alpha^{3}\\ \alpha^{3} & \alpha^{17}\end{bmatrix} = \begin{bmatrix}\alpha & \alpha^{29}\\ \alpha^{29} & \alpha^{12}\end{bmatrix}$$

Using Eq. 7.42, the coefficients of the error-locator polynomial $\sigma(x)$ are obtained as

$$\begin{bmatrix}\sigma_2\\ \sigma_1\end{bmatrix} = \begin{bmatrix}\alpha & \alpha^{29}\\ \alpha^{29} & \alpha^{12}\end{bmatrix}\begin{bmatrix}\alpha^{6}\\ \alpha^{6}\end{bmatrix} = \begin{bmatrix}\alpha^{2}\\ \alpha^{17}\end{bmatrix}$$

Thus, the error-locator polynomial is

$$\sigma(x) = 1 + \alpha^{17}x + \alpha^{2}x^{2} \tag{7.45}$$

Since $\sigma(\alpha^{3}) = \sigma(\alpha^{26}) = 0$, the roots of $\sigma(x)$ are α^{3} and α^{26}. Their inverses are α^{28} and α^{5} which designate the error-location numbers. Therefore, the error pattern is $e(x) = x^{5} + x^{28}$. Adding $e(x)$ to $r(x)$, we obtain the allzero code word $c(x) = 0$, as expected.

Chien [2] has given a rough estimate of the processing time required for finding the roots of $\sigma(x)$, that is, approximately $3tn$ clock periods. For the triple-error-correcting (31, 16) BCH code, $3tn$ = (3) (3) (31) = 279 clock periods will be taken as the processing time. A search for finding the roots of $\sigma(x)$ will be presented in the following.

Let us denote the error-locator polynomial as

$$\sigma(x) = \sigma_0 + \sigma_1 x + \sigma_2 x^2 + \cdots + \sigma_t x^t$$

$$= \sum_{j=0}^{t} \sigma_j x^j \tag{7.46}$$

where $\sigma_0 = 1$.

Finding the roots of $\sigma(x)$ is important because the error-location numbers α^{n-j_λ}, $0 \le j_\lambda \le n-1$, are the reciprocals of roots α^{j_λ} of $\sigma(x)$. Hardware implementation for error location is shown in Fig. 7.3. The α^{k}-multipliers are to multiply the contents of the σ_k-register by α^{k} and subsequently store the product in the σ_k-register. The circuit for detecting the condition $\sum_{j=0}^{t} \sigma_j \alpha^{j\lambda} = 0$ is a simple adder with an OR gate followed by an inverter at the output. Thus, the inverter output is one (1) if and only if the output of the detector circuit is zero (0). More specifically, $\sigma_1, \sigma_2, \cdots, \sigma_t$ are initially loaded into the σ_k-registers and the α^{k}-multipliers are shifted n times. At the end of the λth shift, the σ_k-registers contain $\sigma_1\alpha^{\lambda}, \sigma_2\alpha^{2\lambda}, \cdots, \sigma_t\alpha^{t\lambda}$. Thus, the sum $1 + \sigma_1\alpha^{\lambda} + \sigma_2\alpha^{2\lambda} + \cdots + \sigma_t\alpha^{t\lambda}$ is tested. If it is zero, α^{n-1} is an error-location number;

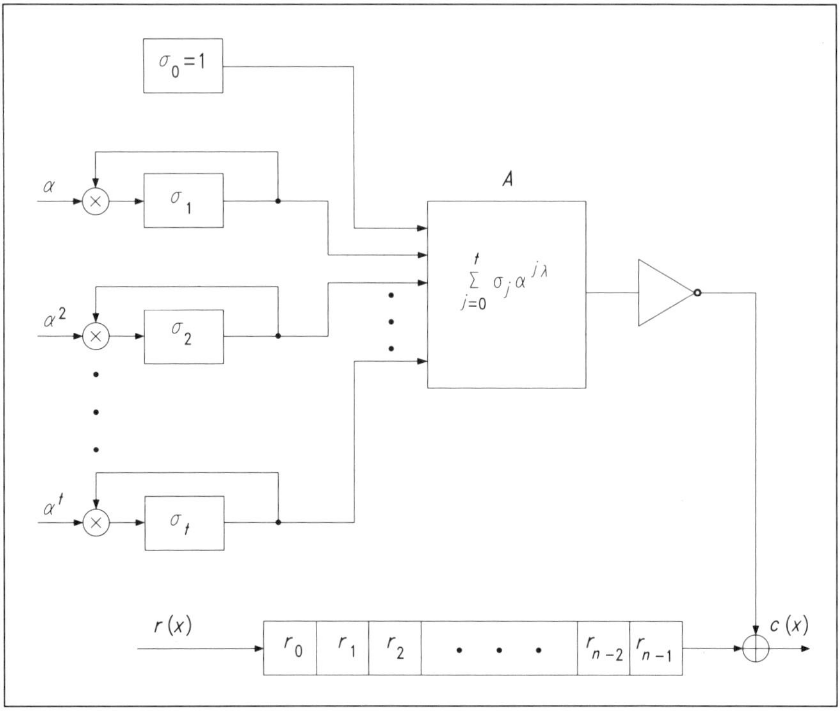

Fig. 7.3 Chien's search unit

otherwise α^λ is not a root of $\sigma(x)$.

Assume that the highest-order bit r_{n-1} is erroneous. To correct the digit r_{n-1}, the output of the logic circuit is tested, i.e. it is checked if the sum is zero. The output of the inverter then becomes 1 and hence corrects the digit r_{n-1} emerging from the buffer register. Having decoded r_{n-1}, the α^k-multipliers are pulses again. And the sum is tested for 0. If the sum is 0, r_{n-2} is read out of the buffer register and corrected by the output of the inverter. Thus, the searching unit decodes $r(x)$ on a bit-by-bit basis in this manner until the entire received word is read out of the buffer register.

■ **Example 7.6** Consider again the triple-error-correcting (31, 16) BCH code having $r(x) = x + x^{12} + x^{25}$ when $c(x) = 0$. In Example 7.4, the error-locator polynomial was found as $\sigma(x) = 1 + \alpha^{22}x + x^2 + \alpha^7x^3$. Devise Chien' searching circuit for finding the roots of $\sigma(x)$.

From $n = 2^m - 1$, we have $2^m = 32$ from which $m = 5$. Therefore, an arbitrary element of GF (2^5) can be written as $\beta = b_0 + b_1\,\alpha + b_2\,\alpha^2 + b_3\,\alpha^3 + b_4\,\alpha^4$. Since $t = 3$, we will require three multipliers for multiplying α, α^2, and α^3 as follows:

$$\alpha\,\beta = b_4 + b_0\,\alpha + (b_1 + b_4)\,\alpha^2 + b_2\alpha^3 + b_3\,\alpha^4$$

$$\alpha^2\,\beta = b_3 + b_4\,\alpha + (b_0 + b_3)\,\alpha^2 + (b_1 + b_4)\,\alpha^3 + b_2\,\alpha^4$$

$$\alpha^3\,\beta = b_2 + b_3\,\alpha + (b_2 + b_4)\,\alpha^2 + (b_2 + b_3)\,\alpha^3 + (b_1 + b_4)\,\alpha^4$$

Using these three multiplications, a Chien's searching circuit for the triple-error-correcting (31, 16) BCH code can be plotted as shown in Fig. 7.4.

On the other hand, once $\sigma(x) = 1 + \alpha^{22}x + x^2 + \alpha^7x^3$ has been found, there is a substitution method for computing the roots of $\sigma(x)$. By substituting the field elements α^k, $1 \le k \le 31$, of GF (2^5) in $\sigma(x)$, the roots of

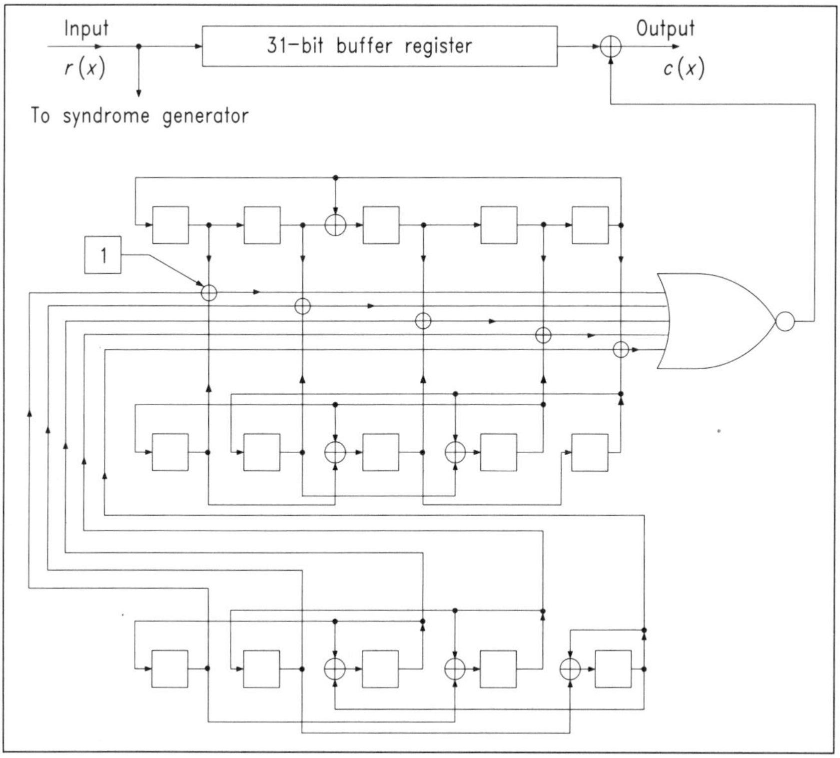

Fig. 7.4 Chien's searching circuit for the triple-error-correcting (31, 16) BCH code

$\sigma(x)$ satisfying $\sigma(\alpha^k) = 0$ are α^6, α^{19}, and α^{20}. Thus, the error-location numbers are easily found by taking the reciprocals of these roots. They are easily found by taking the reciprocals of these roots. They are α^{25}, α^{12}, and α, respectively. Therefore, the error pattern is $e(x) = x + x^{12} + x^{25}$. Adding this error pattern $e(x)$ to the received polynomial $r(x)$ definitely yields the allzero transmitted code word $c(x)$.

7.6 DIRECT DECODING BY CHIEN'S METHOD

Another direct decoding method proposed by Chien [2], although a little different from Peterson's method which we had discussed in Sec. 7.5, is similar to it in many ways.

Let $r(x) = r_0 + r_1 x + r_2 x^2 + \cdots + r_{n-1} x^{n-1}$ be the received sequence. The syndrome elements (or power sums) s_i from $r(x)$ are given by

$$s_i = r(\alpha^i) \qquad i = 1, 3, 5, \cdots, 2t-1 \tag{7.47}$$

The coefficients (or elementary symmetric functions) σ_k, $k = 1, 2, \cdots, t$ of the error-locator polynomial $\sigma(x)$ can be computed from the syndrome s_i. To obtain the σ_ks from the s_is, one must employ Newton's identities for the binary BCH code as shown below [12].

$$\begin{aligned} &s_1 + \sigma_1 = 0 \\ &s_3 + \sigma_1 s_2 + \sigma_2 s_1 + \sigma_3 = 0 \\ &s_5 + \sigma_1 s_4 + \sigma_2 s_3 + \sigma_3 s_2 + \sigma_4 s + \sigma_5 = 0 \\ &\cdot \\ &\cdot \\ &\cdot \end{aligned} \tag{7.48}$$

where the values of σ_k, $k = 1, 2, \cdots, t$ are known. Newton's identities of Eq. 7.48 can also be expressed in matrix form as follows:

$$\mathbf{A} \cdot \sigma = \mathbf{B} \tag{7.49}$$

where

$$\mathbf{A} = \begin{bmatrix} 1 & 0 & 0 & \cdots & 0 \\ s_2 & s_1 & 1 & \cdots & 0 \\ s_4 & s_3 & s_2 & \cdots & 0 \\ \cdot & & \cdot & & \cdot \\ \cdot & & \cdot & & \cdot \\ \cdot & & \cdot & & \cdot \\ s_{2t-2} & s_{2t-3} & s_{2t-4} & \cdots & s_{t-1} \end{bmatrix} \tag{7.50}$$

$$\sigma = \begin{bmatrix} \sigma_1 \\ \sigma_2 \\ \sigma_3 \\ \cdot \\ \cdot \\ \cdot \\ \sigma_t \end{bmatrix} \quad \text{and} \quad \mathbf{B} = \begin{bmatrix} s_1 \\ s_3 \\ s_5 \\ \cdot \\ \cdot \\ \cdot \\ s_{2t-1} \end{bmatrix}$$

If the determinant $|\mathbf{A}|$ is not zero, Eq. 7.49 becomes

$$\sigma = \mathbf{A}^{-1} \cdot \mathbf{B} \tag{7.51}$$

or

$$\begin{bmatrix} \sigma_1 \\ \sigma_2 \\ \sigma_3 \\ \cdot \\ \cdot \\ \cdot \\ \sigma_t \end{bmatrix} = \frac{1}{|\mathbf{A}|} \begin{bmatrix} A_{11} & A_{21} & \cdots & A_{t1} \\ A_{12} & A_{22} & \cdots & A_{t2} \\ A_{13} & A_{23} & \cdots & A_{t3} \\ \cdot & \cdot & & \cdot \\ \cdot & \cdot & & \cdot \\ \cdot & \cdot & & \cdot \\ A_{1t} & A_{2t} & \cdots & A_{tt} \end{bmatrix} \begin{bmatrix} s_1 \\ s_3 \\ s_5 \\ \cdot \\ \cdot \\ \cdot \\ s_{2t-1} \end{bmatrix} \tag{7.52}$$

where $A_{i,k}$ denote the cofactors of $|\mathbf{A}|$. Thus, from Eq. 7.52, σ_k, $k = 1, 2, \cdots, t$ can be obtained as

$$\sigma_1 = \frac{1}{|\mathbf{A}|}(A_{11}s_1 + A_{21}s_3 + A_{31}s_5 + \cdots + A_{t1}s_{2t-1})$$

$$\sigma_2 = \frac{1}{|\mathbf{A}|}(A_{12}s_1 + A_{22}s_3 + A_{32}s_5 + \cdots + A_{t2}s_{2t-1})$$

$$\sigma_3 = \frac{1}{|\mathbf{A}|}(A_{13}s_1 + A_{23}s_3 + A_{33}s_5 + \cdots + A_{t3}s_{2t-1})$$

$$\cdots\cdots\cdots\cdots\cdots\cdots\cdots\cdots\cdots\cdots\cdots\cdots$$

$$\sigma_t = \frac{1}{|\mathbf{A}|}(A_{1t}s_1 + A_{2t}s_3 + A_{3t}s_5 + \cdots + A_{tt}s_{2t-1})$$

Hence, σ_k, $k = 1, 2, \cdots, t$ can be expressed as

$$\sigma_k = \frac{1}{|\mathbf{A}|} \sum_{i=1}^{t} A_{i,k}\, s_{2i-1} \qquad k = 1, 2, \cdots, t \tag{7.53}$$

where $A_{i,k}$, $1 \le k \le t$, represents the cofactors of $|\mathbf{A}|$.

Let $\sigma(x)$ be the error-locator polynomial

$$\sigma(x) = 1 + \sigma_1 x + \sigma_2 x^2 + \cdots + \sigma_t x^t$$

$$= (1 + \beta_1 x)(1 + \beta_2 x) \cdots (1 + \beta_t x) \tag{7.54}$$

One method of finding the roots of $\sigma(x)$ is to substitute all the field elements α_k into $\sigma(x)$ for $\sigma(\alpha^k) = 0$. This can be accomplished by checking whether $\sigma(\alpha^k) = 0$ among the following equations.

$$\sigma(1) = 1 + \sigma_1 + \sigma_2 + \cdots + \sigma_t$$

$$\sigma(\alpha) = 1 + \sigma_1 \alpha + \sigma_2 \alpha^2 + \cdots + \sigma_t \alpha^t$$

$$\sigma(\alpha^2) = 1 + \sigma_1 \alpha^2 + \sigma_2 (\alpha^2)^2 + \cdots + \sigma_t (\alpha^2)^t$$

$$\cdots\cdots\cdots\cdots\cdots\cdots\cdots\cdots\cdots\cdots\cdots\cdots$$

$$\alpha(\alpha^{2^m-1}) = 1 + \sigma_1 \alpha^{2^m-1} + \sigma_2 (\alpha^{2^m-1})^2 + \cdots + \sigma_t (\alpha^{2^m-1})^t$$

If 1 is a root of $\sigma(x)$, then we have

$$1 + \sum_{k=1}^{t} \sigma_k = 0$$

or

$$\sum_{k=1}^{t} \sigma_k = 1 \tag{7.55}$$

Substituting Eq. 7.53 into Eq. (7.55), we obtain

$$\sum_{k=1}^{t} \sigma_k = \sum_{k=1}^{t} \frac{1}{|\mathbf{A}|} \sum_{i=1}^{t} A_{i,k} s_{2i-1} = 1$$

which yields

$$\sum_{k=1}^{t} \sum_{i=1}^{t} A_{i,k} s_{2i-1} - |\mathbf{A}| = 0 \tag{7.56}$$

For the binary field GF (2), Eq. 7.56 becomes

$$\sum_{k=1}^{t} \sum_{i=1}^{t} A_{i,k} s_{2i-1} + |\mathbf{A}| = 0 \tag{7.57}$$

Expanding Eq. 7.57,

$$(A_{1,1} + A_{1,2} + \cdots + A_{1,t}) s_1 + (A_{2,1} + A_{2,2} + \cdots + A_{2,t}) s_3$$

$$+ \cdots + (A_{t,1} + A_{t,2} + \cdots + A_{t,t}) s_{2t-1} = |\mathbf{A}| \tag{7.58}$$

Thus, we have

$$\sum_{k=1}^{t}\sum_{i=1}^{t} A_{i,k}\, s_{2i-1} + |\mathbf{A}| = |\mathbf{A}| + (A_{1,1} + A_{1,2} + \cdots + A_{1,t})\, s_1 + (A_{2,1} + A_{2,2} + \cdots + A_{2,t})\, s_3 + \cdots + (A_{t,1} + A_{t,2} + \cdots + A_{t,t})\, s_{2t-1} = 0 \tag{7.59}$$

Now, it remains to show that Eq. 7.59 is exactly equivalent to setting the determinant Δ to zero [2]. That is,

$$\Delta = \begin{vmatrix} 1 & 1 & 1 & \cdots & 1 \\ s_1 & 1 & 0 & \cdots & 0 \\ s_3 & s_2 & s_1 & \cdots & 0 \\ s_5 & s_4 & s_3 & \cdots & 0 \\ \cdot & \cdot & & & \cdot \\ \cdot & \cdot & & & \cdot \\ \cdot & \cdot & & & \cdot \\ s_{2t-1} & s_{2t-2} & s_{2t-3} & \cdots & s_{t-1} \end{vmatrix}$$

$$= \Delta_0 + s_1\Delta_1 + s_3\Delta_3 + \cdots + s_{2t-1}\Delta_{2t-1} = 0 \tag{7.60}$$

where

$$\Delta_0 = |\mathbf{A}|$$

$$\Delta_1 = \begin{vmatrix} 1 & 1 & 1 & 1 & \cdots & 1 \\ s_2 & s_1 & 1 & 0 & \cdots & 0 \\ s_4 & s_3 & s_2 & s_1 & \cdots & 0 \\ \cdot & & \cdot & & \cdot & \\ \cdot & & \cdot & & \cdot & \\ \cdot & & \cdot & & \cdot & \\ s_{2t-2} & s_{2t-3} & s_{2t-4} & s_{2t-5} & \cdots & s_{t-1} \end{vmatrix}$$

$$= \begin{vmatrix} s_1 & 1 & 0 & \cdots & 0 \\ s_3 & s_2 & s_1 & \cdots & 0 \\ \cdot & & \cdot & & \cdot \\ \cdot & & \cdot & & \cdot \\ \cdot & & \cdot & & \cdot \\ s_{2t-3} & s_{2t-4} & s_{2t-5} & \cdots & s_{t-1} \end{vmatrix} + \begin{vmatrix} s_2 & 1 & 0 & \cdots & 0 \\ s_4 & s_2 & s_1 & \cdots & 0 \\ \cdot & & \cdot & & \cdot \\ \cdot & & \cdot & & \cdot \\ \cdot & & \cdot & & \cdot \\ s_{2t-2} & s_{2t-4} & s_{2t-5} & \cdots & s_{t-1} \end{vmatrix} +$$

$$\cdots + \begin{vmatrix} s_2 & s_1 & 1 & \cdots & 0 \\ s_4 & s_3 & s_2 & \cdots & 0 \\ \cdot & & \cdot & & \cdot \\ \cdot & & \cdot & & \cdot \\ \cdot & & \cdot & & \cdot \\ s_{2t-2} & s_{2t-3} & s_{2t-4} & \cdots & s_t \end{vmatrix} = (A_{1,1} + A_{1,2} + \cdots + A_{1,t})$$

$$\Delta_3 = (A_{2,1} + A_{2,2} + \cdots + A_{2,t})$$

$$\cdot$$
$$\cdot$$
$$\cdot$$

$$\Delta_{2t-1} = (A_{t,1} + A_{t,2} + \cdots + A_{t,t})$$

Substituting Δ_i, $i = 0, 1, 3, \cdots, 2t - 1$, into Eq. 7.60 and using Eq. 7.58, we obtain

$$\Delta = |\mathbf{A}| + (A_{1,1} + A_{1,2} + \cdots + A_{1,t})\, s_1 + (A_{2,1} + A_{2,2} + \cdots + A_{2,t})\, s_3$$
$$+ \cdots + (A_{t,1} + A_{t,2} + \cdots + A_{t,t})\, s_{2t-1} = 0 \tag{7.61}$$

Comparing Eq. 7.59 with Eq. 7.61, it is proved to be

$$\Delta = \sum_{k=1}^{t} \sum_{i=1}^{t} A_{i,k}\, s_{2i-1} + |\mathbf{A}| = 0 \tag{7.62}$$

We shall now illustrate this error-correcting procedure and its implementation through the following example.

■ **Example 7.7** Devise the (31, 16) BCH decoder for $t = 3$ by using the direct decoding procedure described in this section.

Referring to Eq. 7.60, Δ for $t = 3$ is obtained as

$$\Delta = \begin{vmatrix} 1 & 1 & 1 & 1 \\ s_1 & 1 & 0 & 0 \\ s_3 & s_2 & s_1 & 1 \\ s_5 & s_4 & s_3 & s_2 \end{vmatrix}$$

$$= s_1 s_2 + s_3 + s_1^2 s_2 + s_1 s_3 + s_1 s_2^2 + s_1 s_4 + s_2 s_3$$
$$+ s_5 + s_1 s_2 s_3 + s_1^2 s_4 + s_3^2 + s_1 s_5$$

Since $s_2 = s_1^{\,2}$ and $s_4 = s_1^{\,4}$ in view of Eq. 7.28, Δ becomes

$$\Delta = (1 + s_1 + s_1^3)\, s_1^3 + (1 + s_1 + s_1^2 + s_1^3 + s_3)\, s_3 + (1 + s_1)\, s_5$$

For the case of $r(x) = x + x^{12} + x^{25}$, the syndrome components $s_1, s_2, \cdots, s_{2t}$ are, respectively,

$$\begin{aligned}
s_1 &= r(\alpha) = \alpha + \alpha^{12} + \alpha^{25} = 1 + \alpha^2 + \alpha^4 = \alpha^{22} \\
s_2 &= r(\alpha^2) = s_1^2 = \alpha^{13} \\
s_3 &= r(\alpha^3) = \alpha^3 + \alpha^5 + \alpha^{13} = 1 + \alpha^4 = \alpha^{10} \\
s_4 &= r(\alpha^4) = s_2^2 = \alpha^{26} \\
s_5 &= r(\alpha^5) = \alpha^5 + \alpha^{29} + \alpha = \alpha + \alpha^2 + \alpha^3 = \alpha^{12} \\
s_6 &= r(\alpha^6) = s_3^2 = \alpha^{20}
\end{aligned} \tag{7.63}$$

We now need to check whether the condition $\Delta = 0$ is true. Let us construct a table (Table 7.1) for checking if $\Delta = 0$ at the error positions x, x^{12}, and x^{25}.

Table 7.1 Checking Table for $\Delta = 0$ at Error Positions

PN SC	31	30	29	28	27	26	25	24	...	13	12	11	...	2	1	0
s_1	α^{22}	α^{23}	α^{24}	α^{25}	α^{26}	α^{27}	α^{28}	α^{29}	...	α^{9}	α^{10}	α^{11}	...	α^{20}	α^{21}	α^{22}
s_3	α^{10}	α^{13}	α^{16}	α^{19}	α^{22}	α^{25}	α^{28}	α^{31}	...	α^{2}	α^{5}	α^{8}	...	α^{4}	α^{7}	α^{10}
s_5	α^{12}	α^{17}	α^{22}	α^{27}	α	α^{6}	α^{11}	α^{16}	...	α^{9}	α^{14}	α^{19}	...	α^{2}	α^{7}	α^{12}

PN: Position Number; SC: Syndrome Component

Since the power sums $s_1 = \alpha^{28}$, $s_3 = \alpha^{28}$, and $s_5 = \alpha^{11}$ at position number 25,

$$\begin{aligned}
\Delta &= (1 + s_1 + s_1^3)\, s_1^3 + (1 + s_1 + s_1^2 + s_1^3 + s_3)\, s_3 + (1 + s_1)\, s_5 \\
&= (1 + \alpha^{28} + \alpha^{22})\, \alpha^{22} + (1 + \alpha^{28} + \alpha^{25} + \alpha^{22} + \alpha^{28})\, \alpha^{28} + (1 + \alpha^{28})\, \alpha^{11} \\
&= (\alpha)\, \alpha^{22} + (1 + \alpha^2 + \alpha^3)\, \alpha^{28} + (\alpha^2 + \alpha^4)\, \alpha^{11} \\
&= \alpha^{23} + \alpha^5 + \alpha^6 = 0
\end{aligned}$$

Since $\Delta = 0$, we know that x^{25} is an error position. Similarly, the value of Δ with $s_1 = \alpha^{10}$, $s_3 = \alpha^5$, and $s_5 = \alpha^{14}$ is

$$\Delta = (1 + \alpha^{10} + \alpha^{30})\,\alpha^{30} + (1 + \alpha^{10} + \alpha^{20} + \alpha^{30} + \alpha^{5})\,\alpha^{5} + (1 + \alpha^{10})\,\alpha^{14}$$

$$= 1 + \alpha + \alpha^{18} = 0$$

Therefore, x^{12} is also proved to be an error position. Lastly, when $s_1 = \alpha^{21}$, $s_3 = \alpha^7$, and $s_5 = \alpha^7$, at position number 1, yields

$$\Delta = (1 + \alpha^{21} + \alpha^{63})\,\alpha^{63} + (1 + \alpha^{21} + \alpha^{42} + \alpha^{63} + \alpha^{7})\,\alpha^{7} + (1 + \alpha^{21})\,\alpha^{7}$$

$$= \alpha^{17} + \alpha^{10} + \alpha = 0$$

Hence, x indicates another error position. Thus, we conclude that the error pattern is $e\,(x) = x + x^{12} + x^{25}$ as expected.

Next, consider the implementation of the decoding device for the current (31, 16) BCH code. Using Eq. 7.50, for $t = 3$ or 2,

$$|\mathbf{A}| = \begin{vmatrix} 1 & 0 & 0 \\ s_2 & s_1 & 1 \\ s_4 & s_3 & s_2 \end{vmatrix}$$

$$= s_1 s_2 + s_3 = s_1^3 + s_3$$

If $|\mathbf{A}| \neq 0$, two or three errors have occurred, because the s_is are power sums of $t = 3$ or 2 distinct roots. In this case, we must check whether $\Delta = 0$ for decoding, i.e. whether

$$\Delta = \begin{vmatrix} 1 & 1 & 1 & 1 \\ s_1 & 1 & 0 & 0 \\ s_3 & s_2 & s_1 & 1 \\ s_5 & s_4 & s_3 & s_2 \end{vmatrix} = 0$$

If $|\mathbf{A}| = 0$, we know that a single error has occurred, because s_i is the power sum of $t - 2 = 1$. In this case, where $|\mathbf{A}| \neq 0$, we must check whether

$$\Delta = \begin{vmatrix} 1 & 1 \\ s_1 & 1 \end{vmatrix} = s_1 + 1 = 0$$

A system for decoding such a code is shown in Fig. 7.5.

7.7 BCH DECODING BY THE BERLEKAMP ALGORITHM

The direct decoding methods of Peterson (Sec. 7.5) and Chien (Sec. 7.6) are ideal for error patterns where $t < 5$. These techniques are designed

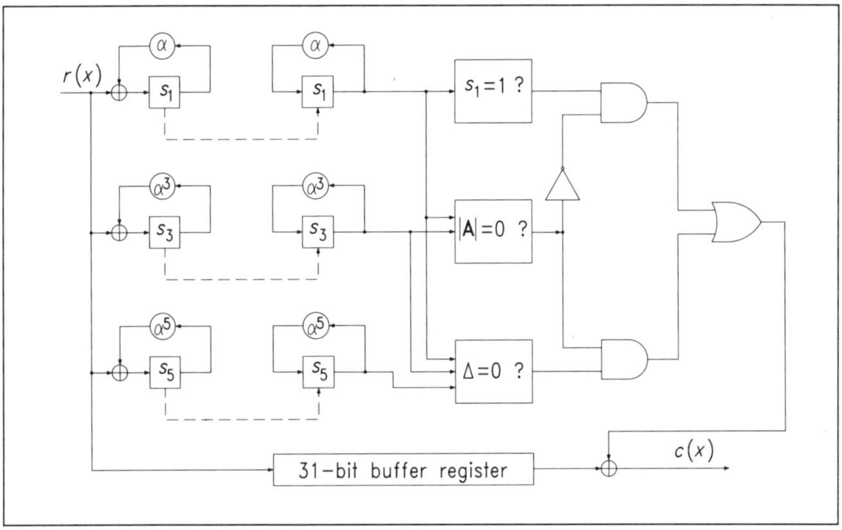

Fig. 7.5 A direct decoding circuit for (31, 16) BCH code

for finding error-location numbers directly from the syndrome without using Berlekamp's iterative algorithm to determine the error-locator polynomial. However, for the correction of a large number of errors, these direct methods would be cumbersome and inefficient because too many multiplications and divisions that would need to be performed. The conventional iterative algorithm proposed by Berlekamp [1] and also by Massey [7] and Peterson [10] will be presented in this section.

7.7.1 Berlekamp's Iterative Algorithm

We present Berlekamp's iterative algorithm for finding the error-locator polynomial. As stated before, as the error pattern in a binary BCH code word becomes larger, the direct method of solving for the coefficients of $\sigma(x)$ from the syndrome elements becomes impractical. In such a case, it is preferable to employ an iterative algorithm developed by Berlekamp. This algorithm also has a computational complexity that grows with the number of errors to be corrected. However, it has a strong feature acceptable for any kind of error pattern. The problem of finding the minimal-degree solution to the error-locator polynomial $\sigma(x)$ is best explained by the iterative operation. At each step of iteration, this algorithm must retain both a minimal-degree polynomial whose coefficients satisfy Newton's identity and a possible correction term associated with the discrepancy.

The reader interested in details of this algorithm is referred to Berlekamp [1], Peterson and Weldon [10], Lin and Costello [6], and Rhee [12]. The Berlekamp algorithm, promoted by Peterson, may now be stated formally as follows:

1. Start at $n = 0$ with the initial conditions

$$\sigma^{(-1)}(x) = 1,\ l_{-1} = 0,\ d_{-1} = 1$$

$$\sigma^{(0)}(x) = 1,\ l_0 = 0,\ d_0 = s_1$$

2. If $d_n = 0$, then $\sigma^{(n+1)}(x) = \sigma^{(n)}(x)$ and $l_{n+1} = l_n$.
3. If $d_n \neq 0$, find $\sigma^{(m)}(x)$ prior to $\sigma^{(n)}(x)$ such that $d_m \neq 0$, $1 \leq m \leq n$, and the number $m - l_m$ has the largest value. Then

$$\sigma^{(n+1)}(x) = \sigma^{(n)}(x) - d_n d_m^{-1} x^{n-m} \sigma^{(m)}(x)$$

$$l_{n+1} = \max\,[l_n,\ l_m + n - m]$$

4. With either $d_n = 0$ or $d_n \neq 0$, the next discrepancy is

$$d_{n+1} = s_{n+2} + s_{n+1}\sigma_1^{(n+1)} + \cdots + s_{n+2-l_{n+1}}\sigma_{l_{n+1}}^{(n+1)}$$

where $\sigma_i^{(n+1)}$, $1 \leq i \leq l_{n+1}$ are the coefficients of $\sigma^{(n+1)}(x)$.

Note that, in this iterative algorithm, $\sigma^{(n)}(x)$ denotes a minimal-solution polynomial of degree l_n determined at the nth step of iteration; and d_n represents the nth discrepancy. The detailed steps for obtaining the error-locator polynomial $\sigma(x)$ are illustrated in the following example.

Example 7.8 Consider the triple-error-correcting (31, 16) BCH code given in previous several examples. If the received polynomial is $r(x) = x + x^{12} + x^{25}$ when the code polynomials $c(x) = 0$ is transmitted, then $r(x)$ is identical to the error pattern $e(x)$. The syndrome components s_k, $k = 1, 2, \cdots, 6$ are computed either from the remainders resulting from the division of $r(x)$ by the minimal polynomial $m_k(x)$, $k = 1, 3, 5$ or from the received polynomial $r(x)$ evaluated at $x = \alpha^k$, $1 \leq k \leq 6$. As we can see from Eq. 7.63, they are

$$s_1 = \alpha^{22} \qquad s_2 = \alpha^{13} \qquad s_3 = \alpha^{10}$$

$$s_4 = \alpha^{26} \qquad s_5 = \alpha^{12} \qquad s_6 = \alpha^{20}$$

Starting with the initial discrepancy $d_0 = \alpha^{22}$, the following recursive steps are taken.

Step 1 $\sigma^{(1)}(x) = \sigma^{(0)}(x) - d_0 d_{-1}^{-1} x \sigma^{(-1)}(x)$

$= 1 + \alpha^{22} x$

$l_1 = \max[0, 0 + 0 + 1] = 1$

$d_1 = s_2 + s_1 \sigma_1^{(1)} = 0$

$1 - l_1 = 1 - 1 = 0$

Step 2 $\sigma^{(2)}(x) = \sigma^{(1)}(x) = 1 + \alpha^{22} x$

$l_2 = l_1 = 1$

$d_2 = s_3 + s_2 \sigma_1^{(2)} = 1$

$2 - l_2 = 2 - 1 = 1$

Step 3 $\sigma^{(3)}(x) = \sigma^{(2)}(x) - d_2 d_0^{-1} x^2 \sigma^{(0)}(x)$

$= 1 + \alpha^{22} x + \alpha^9 x^2$

$l_3 = \max[1, 0 + 2 - 0] = 2$

$d_3 = s_4 + s_3 \sigma_1^{(3)} + s_2 \sigma_2^{(3)}$

$= \alpha^{26} + \alpha + \alpha^{22} = 0$

$3 - l_3 = 3 - 2 = 1$

Step 4 $\sigma^{(4)}(x) = \sigma^{(3)}(x) = 1 + \alpha^{22} x + \alpha^9 x^2$

$l_4 = l_3 = 2$

$d_4 = s_5 + s_4 \sigma_1^{(4)} + s_3 \sigma_2^{(4)} = 1 + \alpha + \alpha^3 + \alpha^4 = \alpha^{16}$

$4 - l_4 = 4 - 2 = 2$

Step 5 $\sigma^{(5)}(x) = \sigma^{(4)}(x) - d_4 d_2^{-1} x^2 \sigma^{(2)}(x)$

$= 1 + \alpha^{22} x + x^2 + \alpha^7 x^3$

$l_5 = \max[2, 1 + 4 - 2] = 3$

$$d_5 = s_6 + s_5\,\sigma_1^{(5)} + s_4\,\sigma_2^{(5)} + s_3\,\sigma_3^{(5)} = \alpha^{20} + \alpha^{3} + \alpha^{26} + \alpha^{17} = 0$$

$$5 - l_5 = 5 - 3 = 2$$

Step 6 $\quad \sigma^{(6)}(x) = \sigma^{(5)}(x) = 1 + \alpha^{22}x + x^2 + \alpha^7 x^3$

This is the legitimate error-locator polynomial $\sigma(x)$, that is,

$$\sigma(x) = 1 + \alpha^{22}x + x^2 + \alpha^7 x^3$$

Substituting the field elements of GF (2^5), α^k, $1 \le k \le 31$ in $\sigma(x)$, the roots of $\sigma(x)$ satisfying $\sigma(\alpha^k) = 0$ are α^6, α^{19}, and α^{30}. Hence, the error-location numbers are easily found by taking the inverse of these roots. They are α^{25}, α^{12}, and α, respectively. Thus the error pattern is

$$e(x) = x + x^{12} + x^{25}$$

Adding $e(x)$ to the received polynomial $r(x)$, yields the allzero transmitted code word. Since the iterative steps for finding $\sigma(x)$ have been carried out, the result is summarized in Table 7.2 in the compact form, as shown below.

We shall now present another form of the Berlekamp algorithm for finding $\sigma(x)$. Let us define the syndrome **s** as a vector with its components

$$s_i = r(\alpha^{1+i}) \qquad 0 \le i \le 2t - 1 \tag{7.64}$$

where $r(\alpha^{1+i}) = c(\alpha^{1+i}) + e(\alpha^{1+i})$. Since α^{1+i}, $0 \le i \le 2t - 1$ is a root of $c(x)$, Eq. 7.64 becomes

$$s_i = e(\alpha^{1+i}) \qquad 0 \le i \le 2t - 1 \tag{7.65}$$

Table 7.2 Determination of $\sigma(x)$ by the Berlekamp-Peterson Algorithm

n	$\sigma_{(n)}(x)$	d_n	l_n	$n - l_m$
-1	1	1	0	-1
0	1	α^{22}	0	0
1	$1 + \alpha^{22}x$	0	1	0
2	$1 + \alpha^{22}x$	1	1	1
3	$1 + \alpha^{22}x + \alpha^9x^2$	0	2	1
4	$1 + \alpha^{22}x + \alpha^9x^2$	α^{16}	2	2
5	$1 + \alpha^{22}x + x^2 + \alpha^7x^3$	0	3	2
6	$1 + \alpha^{22}x + x^2 + \alpha^7x^3$	–	–	–

Suppose errors of some given number $\nu \le \lfloor (d_{\min} - 1)/2 \rfloor$ have occurred in transmission. Then, the error digits are $e_j = 0$ except for $j = j_1, j_2, \cdots, j_\nu$. Therefore, the error pattern is actually

$$e(x) = x^{j_1} + x^{j_2} + \cdots + x^{j_\nu} \tag{7.66}$$

Thus, the syndrome digits become

$$s_i = (\alpha^{1+i})^{j_1} + (\alpha^{1+i})^{j_2} + \cdots + (\alpha^{1+i})^{j_\nu}$$

$$= \sum_{\lambda=1}^{\nu} (\alpha^{1+i})^{j_\lambda} \qquad 0 \le i \le 2t - 1 \tag{7.67}$$

Let $\sigma^{(n)}(x) = 1 + \sigma_1^{(n)} x + \sigma_2^{(n)} x^2 + \cdots + \sigma_{l_n}^{(n)} x^{l_n}$ be the minimum degree polynomial, determined at the nth step of iteration, whose coefficients satisfy the first n Newton's identities. Also, let the discrepancy at the nth step be

$$d_n = s_n + \sum_{i=1}^{n} \sigma_i^{(n)} s_{n-i} \tag{7.68}$$

where $\sigma_i^{(n)}$, $1 \le i \le l_n$, denotes the coefficients of $\sigma^{(n)}(x)$. If $d_n = 0$, the algorithm increases n by one, but keeps the same register. If $d_n \ne 0$, a correction term is added to $\sigma^{(n)}(x)$ to make it generate the exact value of s_n.

Let us introduce the detailed rules for another algorithm due to Berlekamp in the following.

1. Start at $n = 0$ with the initial conditions

$$\sigma^{(-1)}(x) = 1 \qquad l_{-1} = 0 \qquad d_{-1} = 1$$

$$\sigma^{(0)}(x) = 1 \qquad l_0 = 0 \qquad k_0 = -1$$

2. If $d_n = 0$, then $\sigma^{(n+1)}(x) = \sigma^{(n)}(x)$, $l_{n+1} = l_n$, and $k_{n+1} = k_n$
3. If $d_n \ne 0$, it follows that

$$\sigma^{(n+1)}(x) = \sigma^{(n)}(x) - d_n d_{k_n}^{-1} x^{n-k_n} \sigma^{(k_n)}(x)$$

$$l_{n+1} = \max\,[l_n, n - (k_n - l_{k_n})]$$

and

$$k_{n+1} = \begin{cases} k_n & \text{if } l_{n+1} = l_n \\ n & \text{if } l_{n+1} > l_n \end{cases}$$

4. In either $d_n = 0$ or $d_n \ne 0$, the next discrepancies are

$$d_{k_{n+1}} = s_{k_{n+1}} + \sum_{i=1}^{k_{n+1}} \sigma_i^{(k_{n+1})} s_{k_{n+1}-i}$$

$$d_{n+1} = s_{n+1} + \sum_{i=1}^{n+1} \sigma_i^{(n+1)} s_{n+1-i}$$

We shall illustrate the detailed steps in the following example.

■ **Example 7.9** Consider again the triple-error-correcting (31, 16) BCH code given in Example 7.8. Find the error-locator polynomial $\sigma(x)$ by employing the iterative algorithm listed above.

Using the syndrome components of $s_0 = \alpha^{22}$, $s_1 = \alpha^{13}$, $s_2, = \alpha^{10}$, $s_3 = \alpha^{26}$, $s_4 = \alpha^{12}$, and $s_5 = \alpha^{20}$, let us undertake the recursive operation for finding $\sigma(x)$.

Step 1 For $n = 0$,

$$\sigma^{(1)}(x) = \sigma^{(0)}(x) - d_0 d_{k_0}^{-1} x^{-k_0} \sigma^{(k_0)}(x)$$

where

$$d_0 = s_0 + \sum_{i=1}^{0} \sigma_i^{(k_0)} s_{k_0-i} = \alpha^{22}$$

$$d_{k_0} = d_{-1} = 1$$

Thus

$$\sigma^{(1)}(x) = 1 + \alpha^{22} x$$

$l_1 = \max[0, 0 + 1 + 0] = 1$

Since $l_1 > l_0$, it follows that

$$k_1 = 0$$

$$d_{k_1} = s_{k_1} + \sum_{i=1}^{0} \sigma_i^{(0)} s_{k_0-i} = s_0 = \alpha^{22}$$

$$d_1 = s_1 + \sigma_1^{(1)} s_0 = \alpha^{13} + \alpha^{13} = 0$$

Step 2 For $n = 1$, since $d_1 = 0$, it follows that

$\sigma^{(2)}(x) = \sigma^{(1)}(x) = 1 + \alpha^{22} x$

$l_2 = l_1 = 1$ and $k_2 = k_1 = 0$

$$d_{k_2} = s_{k_2} + \sum_{i=1}^{k_2} \sigma_i^{(k_2)} s_{k_2-i} = s_0 = \alpha^{22}$$

$$d_2 = s_2 + \sum_{i=1}^{2} \sigma_i^{(2)} s_{2-i} = s_2 + \sigma_1^{(2)} s_1 + \sigma_2^{(2)} s_0$$

$$= \alpha^{10} + \alpha^{22} \cdot \alpha^{13} = \alpha^{10} + \alpha^{4} = 1$$

Step 3 For $n = 2$, since $d_2 \neq 0$, we have

$$\sigma^{(3)}(x) = \sigma^{(2)}(x) - d_2 d_{k_2}^{-1} x^{2-k_2} \sigma^{(k_2)}(x)$$

$$= 1 + \alpha^{22} x + (\alpha^{22})^{-1} x_2 = 1 + \alpha^{22} x + \alpha^{9} x^{2}$$

$l_3 = \max [1, 2] = 2$

Since $l_3 > l_2$, $k_3 = 2$

$$d_{k_3} = s_{k_3} + \sum_{i=1}^{k_3} \sigma_i^{(k_3)} s_{k_3 - i} = s_2 + \sum_{i=1}^{2} \sigma_i^{(2)} s_{2-i}$$

$$= s_2 + \sigma_1^{(2)} s_1 = \alpha^{10} + \alpha^{4} = 1$$

$$d_3 = s_3 + \sum_{i=1}^{3} \sigma_i^{(3)} s_{3-i} = s_3 + \sigma_1^{(3)} s_2 + \sigma_2^{(3)} s_1$$

$$= \alpha^{26} + \alpha + \alpha^{22} = 0$$

Step 4 For $n = 3$, because $d_3 = 0$, we have

$$\sigma^{(4)}(x) = \sigma^{(3)}(x) = 1 + \alpha^{22} x + \alpha^{9} x^{2}$$

$$l_4 = l_3 = 2$$

$$k_4 = k_3 = 2$$

$$d_{k_4} = s_{k_4} + \sum_{i=1}^{k_4} \sigma_i^{(k_4)} s_{k_4 - i}$$

$$= s_2 + \sigma_1^{(2)} s_1 = \alpha^{10} + \alpha^{4} = 1$$

$$d_4 = s_4 + \sum_{i=1}^{4} \sigma_i^{(4)} s_{4-i}$$

$$= s_4 + \sigma_1^{(4)} s_3 + \sigma_2^{(4)} s_2$$

$$= \alpha^{12} + \alpha^{17} + \alpha^{19} = \alpha^{16}$$

Step 5 For $n = 4$, since $d_4 \neq 0$, it follows that

$$\sigma^{(5)}(x) = \sigma^{(4)}(x) - d_4 d_{k_4}^{-1} x^{4-k_4} \sigma^{(k_4)}(x)$$

$$= 1 + \alpha^{22} x + \alpha^{9} x^{2} + \alpha^{16} x^{2} (1 + \alpha^{22} x)$$

$$= 1 + \alpha^{22} x + x^2 + \alpha^7 x^3$$

$l_5 = \max\,[l_4, 4 - (2 - l_2)] = \max\,[2, 3] = 3$

Since $l_5 > l_4$, we have $k_5 = 4$.

Thus, it follows that

$$d_{k_5} = s_{k_5} + \sum_{i=1}^{k_5} \sigma_i^{(k_5)} s_{k_5 - i}$$

$$= s_4 + \sum_{i=1}^{4} \sigma_i^{(4)} s_{4-i}$$

$$= \alpha^{12} + \sigma_i^{(4)} s_3 + \sigma_2^{(4)} s_2 = \alpha^{16}$$

$$d_5 = s_5 + \sum_{i=1}^{5} \sigma_i^{(5)} s_{5-i}$$

$$= s_5 + \sigma_1^{(5)} s_4 + \sigma_2^{(5)} s_3 + \sigma_3^{(5)} s_2$$

$$= \alpha^{20} + \alpha^3 + \alpha^{26} + \alpha^{17} = 0$$

Step 6 Take $n = 5$. Since $d_5 = 0$, the minimum-degree polynomial at the sixth step of iteration is finally obtained as

$$\sigma^{(6)}(x) = \sigma^{(5)}(x) = 1 + \alpha^{22} x + x^2 + \alpha^7 x^3$$

This is the required error-locator polynomial $\sigma(x)$ which is exactly identical to the solution arrived at in Example 7.8. Since the roots of $\sigma(x) = \sigma^{(6)}(x)$ are α^6, α^{19}, and α^{30}, the corresponding error-location numbers are α^{25}, α^{12}, and α, respectively.

Therefore, the error pattern is

$$e(x) = x + x^{12} + x^{25}$$

and the resulting decoder output will be $c(x) = r(x) + e(x) = 0$. The detailed steps for finding $\sigma(x)$ of this code are given in Table 7.3.

7.7.2 Decoder Implementation

It is appropriate, at this point, to outline the error-correction procedure for BCH codes. The following is the procedure for decoding.

1. Compute the syndrome $\mathbf{s} = (s_0, s_1, \cdots, s_{2t})$ from the received word $r(x)$.

Table 7.3 Iterative Steps for Finding $\sigma(x)$

n	$\sigma^{(n)}(x)$	l_n	d_n	k_n	d_{k_n}
-1	1	0	1		
0	1	0	α^{22}	-1	1
1	$1+\alpha^{22}x$	1	0	0	α^{22}
2	$1+\alpha^{22}x$	1	1	0	α^{22}
3	$1+\alpha^{22}x+\alpha^{9}x^2$	2	0	2	1
4	$1+\alpha^{22}x+\alpha^{9}x^2$	2	α^{16}	2	1
5	$1+\alpha^{22}x+x^2+\alpha^{7}x^3$	3	0	4	α^{16}
6	$1+\alpha^{22}x+x^2+\alpha^{7}x^3$	–	–	–	–

2. Find the error-locator polynomial $\sigma(x)$ from the syndrome components s_i, $1 \le i \le 2t$, using the iterative algorithm.
3. Determine the error-location numbers by finding the roots of $\sigma(x)$.
4. Determine the error pattern $e(x)$ and correct the errors in $r(x)$ by $c(x) = r(x) + e(x)$.

■ **Example 7.10** Consider the implementation problem for the (31, 16) BCH decoder. As in previous examples, the syndrome is $s = (\alpha^{22}, \alpha^{13}, \alpha^{10}, \alpha^{26}, \alpha^{12}, \alpha^{20})$ and the error-locator polynomial is $\sigma(x) = 1 + \alpha^{22}x + x^2 + \alpha^7 x^3$. By employing the Chien search, the error-location numbers can be determined by the principle explained in Example 7.6. For hardware implementation, the decoding circuit for the triple-error-correcting (31, 16) BCH code is devised as shown in Fig. 7.6.

7.8 DECODING METHOD USING SYMMETRICAL SYNDROME MATRIX

We have so far presented the direct solution methods given by Peterson and independently by Chien, and BCH decoding by the iterative algorithm proposed by Berlekamp. In this section, we discuss one method [4] by which the roots of an error-locator polynomial can be computed from the symmetrical matrix of modified syndrome components.

7.8.1 Symmetrical Syndrome Matrix and Error-locator Polynomial

Referring to Eq. 7.27, the syndrome components are expressed as

$$s_k = \sum_{\lambda=1}^{\nu} (\beta_\lambda)^k \qquad k = 1, 3, \cdots, 2t-1 \tag{7.69}$$

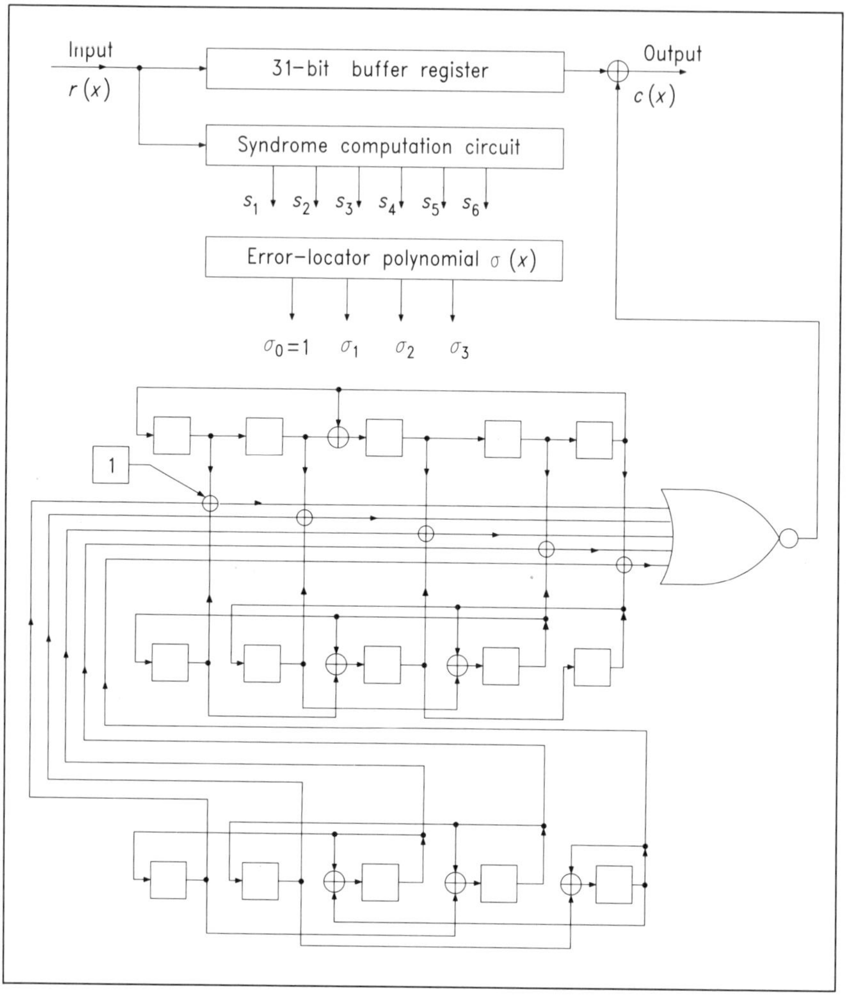

Fig. 7.6 Decoding circuit for triple-error-correcting (31, 16) BCH code

where $\beta_\lambda = \alpha^{j_\lambda}$, $1 \le \lambda \le \nu$, are defined as the error-location numbers, and ν designates the number of errors that actually occurred.

Let the modified syndrome components be defined as

$$S_k = \sum_{k=0}^{\nu} (\beta_\lambda)^k + \beta^k$$

$$= s_k + \beta^k \qquad k = 0, 1, 2, \cdots, 2t \tag{7.70}$$

where $S_0 = s_0 + \beta^0 = 1 + 1 + \cdots + 1$ (1s of $\nu + 1$) and β^k are unknown numbers.

Consider a symmetrical matrix comprising modified syndrome components S_k such that

$$\mathbf{M}_\nu = \begin{bmatrix} S_0 & S_1 & \cdots & S_{\nu-1} & S_\nu \\ S_1 & S_2 & \cdots & S_\nu & S_{\nu+1} \\ \cdot & \cdot & & \cdot & \cdot \\ \cdot & \cdot & & \cdot & \cdot \\ \cdot & \cdot & & \cdot & \cdot \\ S_\nu & S_{\nu+1} & & S_{2\nu-1} & S_{2\nu} \end{bmatrix} \qquad 1 \le \nu \le t \tag{7.71}$$

where $S_0 = \sum_{\lambda=1}^{\nu} (\beta_\lambda)^0 + \beta^0 = 1 + 1 + \cdots + 1 + 1$

$$S_1 = \sum_{\lambda=1}^{\nu} (\beta_\lambda)^1 + \beta^1 = \beta_1 + \beta_2 + \cdots + \beta_\nu + \beta$$

$$\cdots\cdots\cdots\cdots\cdots\cdots\cdots\cdots\cdots\cdots \tag{7.72}$$

$$S_\nu = \sum_{\lambda=1}^{\nu} (\beta_\lambda)^\nu + \beta^\nu = \beta_1{}^\nu + \beta_2{}^\nu + \cdots + \beta_\nu{}^\nu + \beta^\nu$$

Since the product of any matrix and its transpose is symmetrical, Eq. 7.71 can be easily expressed in product form by substituting Eq. 7.72 in Eq. 7.71 as shown below.

$$\mathbf{M}_\nu = \begin{bmatrix} 1 & 1 & \cdots & 1 & 1 \\ \beta_1 & \beta_2 & \cdots & \beta_\nu & \beta \\ \beta_1^2 & \beta_2^2 & \cdots & \beta_\nu^2 & \beta^2 \\ \cdot & & & & \cdot \\ \cdot & & & & \cdot \\ \cdot & & & & \cdot \\ \beta_1^\nu & \beta_2^\nu & \cdots & \beta_\nu^\nu & \beta^\nu \end{bmatrix} \begin{bmatrix} 1 & \beta_1 & \beta_1^2 & \cdots & \beta_1^\nu \\ 1 & \beta_2 & \beta_2^2 & \cdots & \beta_2^\nu \\ & & \cdot & & \cdot \\ & & \cdot & & \cdot \\ & & \cdot & & \cdot \\ 1 & \beta_\nu & \beta_\nu^2 & \cdots & \beta_\nu^\nu \\ 1 & \beta & \beta^2 & \cdots & \beta^\nu \end{bmatrix}$$

$$= \mathbf{D}_\nu \cdot \mathbf{D}_\nu^T \tag{7.73}$$

The determinant of $\mathbf{M}_\nu$ is

$$|\mathbf{M}_\nu| = \begin{vmatrix} 1 & 1 & \cdots & 1 & 1 \\ \beta_1 & \beta_2 & \cdots & \beta_\nu & \beta \\ \cdot & & & \cdot & \\ \cdot & & & \cdot & \\ \cdot & & & \cdot & \\ \beta_1^\nu & \beta_2^\nu & \cdots & \beta_\nu^\nu & \beta^\nu \end{vmatrix} \begin{vmatrix} 1 & \beta_1 & \cdots & \beta_1^\nu \\ 1 & \beta_2 & \cdots & \beta_2^\nu \\ & \cdot & & \cdot \\ & \cdot & & \cdot \\ & \cdot & & \cdot \\ 1 & \beta & \cdots & \beta^\nu \end{vmatrix}$$

$$= |\mathbf{D}_\nu| \cdot |\mathbf{D}_\nu^T| \tag{7.74}$$

In Eq. 7.74, it may be observed that $|\mathbf{D}_\nu|$ can be expressed as a Vandermonde determinant if and only if the elements of the last column are replaced by $\beta = \beta_{\nu+1}$. Thus,

$$|\mathbf{D}_\nu| = \prod_{\substack{i>j \\ j=1}}^{\nu+1} (\beta_i + \beta_j) \tag{7.75}$$

Since the determinant $|\mathbf{D}_\nu|$ has the same value as its transposed determinant $|\mathbf{D}_\nu^T|$, it follows that

$$|\mathbf{M}_\nu| = \begin{vmatrix} 1 & 1 & \cdots & 1 & 1 \\ \beta_1 & \beta_2 & \cdots & \beta_\nu & \beta_{\nu+1} \\ \cdot & & & \cdot & \\ \cdot & & & \cdot & \\ \cdot & & & \cdot & \\ \beta_1^{\nu-1} & \beta_2^{\nu-1} & \cdots & \beta_\nu^{\nu-1} & \beta_{\nu+1}^{\nu-1} \\ \beta_1^\nu & \beta_2^\nu & \cdots & \beta_\nu^\nu & \beta_{\nu+1}^\nu \end{vmatrix} \begin{vmatrix} 1 & \beta_1 & \cdots & \beta_1^{\nu-1} & \beta_1^\nu \\ 1 & \beta_2 & \cdots & \beta_2^{\nu-1} & \beta_2^\nu \\ \cdot & & & \cdot & \\ \cdot & & & \cdot & \\ \cdot & & & \cdot & \\ 1 & \beta_\nu & \cdots & \beta_\nu^{\nu-1} & \beta_\nu^\nu \\ 1 & \beta_{\nu+1} & \cdots & \beta_{\nu+1}^{\nu-1} & \beta_{\nu+1}^\nu \end{vmatrix}$$

$$= \prod_{\substack{i>j \\ j=1}}^{\nu+1} (\beta_i + \beta_j)^2 \tag{7.76}$$

It can be easily shown that Eq. 7.76 becomes

$$|\mathbf{M}_\nu| = \prod_{\substack{i>j \\ j=1}}^{\nu} (\beta_i + \beta_j)^2 \prod_{k=1}^{\nu} (\beta + \beta_k)^2 \tag{7.77}$$

where $\beta = \beta_{\nu+1}$.

Thus, if $\beta \neq \beta_k$ for $k = 1, 2, \cdots, \nu$, then $|\mathbf{M}_\nu| \neq 0$; whereas since $\beta_i \neq \beta_j$, for $i \neq j$, $|\mathbf{M}_\nu| = 0$ if and only if β $(= \beta_{\nu+1})$ is equal to any one of β_k, $k = 1, 2, \cdots, \nu$.

■ **Example 7.11** Prove that $|\mathbf{M}_v| = \prod_{\substack{i>j \\ j=1}}^{v} (\beta_i + \beta_j)^2 \prod_{k=1}^{v} (\beta_{v+1} + \beta_k)^2$ from Eq. 7.76.

$$|\mathbf{M}_v| = \prod_{\substack{i>j \\ j=1}}^{v+1} (\beta_i + \beta_j)^2$$

$$= [(\beta_2 + \beta_1)^2 (\beta_3 + \beta_1)^2 (\beta_3 + \beta_2)^2 \cdots (\beta_v + \beta_1)^2 (\beta_v + \beta_2)^2$$

$$\cdots (\beta_v + \beta_{v-1})^2] \cdot [(\beta_{v+1} + \beta_1)^2 (\beta_{v+1} + \beta_2)^2 \cdots (\beta_{v+1} + \beta_v)^2]$$

$$= \prod_{\substack{i>j \\ j=1}}^{v} (\beta_i + \beta_j)^2 \prod_{k=1}^{v} (\beta_{v+1} + \beta_k)^2$$

Consider the determinant $|\mathbf{D}_v|$ in Eq. 7.76, that is,

$$|\mathbf{D}_v| = \begin{vmatrix} 1 & 1 & \cdots & 1 & 1 \\ \beta_1 & \beta_2 & \cdots & \beta_v & \beta_{v+1} \\ \beta_1^2 & \beta_2^2 & \cdots & \beta_v^2 & \beta_{v+1}^2 \\ \cdot & \cdot & & \cdot & \cdot \\ \cdot & \cdot & & \cdot & \cdot \\ \cdot & \cdot & & \cdot & \cdot \\ \beta_1^v & \beta_2^v & \cdots & \beta_v^v & \beta_{v+1}^v \end{vmatrix}$$

Subtracting all columns (except for the first column) from the first, this determinant becomes

$$|\mathbf{D}_v| = \begin{vmatrix} \beta_2 - \beta_1 & \beta_3 - \beta_1 & \cdots & \beta_v - \beta_1 & \beta_{v+1} - \beta_1 \\ \beta_2^2 - \beta_1^2 & \beta_3^2 - \beta_1^2 & \cdots & \beta_v^2 - \beta_1^2 & \beta_{v+1}^2 - \beta_1^2 \\ \cdot & \cdot & & \cdot & \cdot \\ \cdot & \cdot & & \cdot & \cdot \\ \cdot & \cdot & & \cdot & \cdot \\ \beta_2^v - \beta_1^v & \beta_3^v - \beta_1^v & \cdots & \beta_v^v - \beta_1^v & \beta_{v+1}^v - \beta_1^v \end{vmatrix} \tag{7.78}$$

If we extend Eq. 7.78 into the subdeterminants and delete any such subdeterminant whose two or more columns sum to zero, then all columns of the remaining subdeterminants become distinct and nonzero.

Therefore, Eq. 7.78 can be written as follows:

$$|\mathbf{D}_v| = \begin{vmatrix} \beta_2 & \beta_3 & \cdots & \beta_v & \beta_{v+1} \\ \beta_2^2 & \beta_3^2 & \cdots & \beta_v^2 & \beta_{v+1}^2 \\ \cdot & \cdot & & \cdot & \cdot \\ \cdot & \cdot & & \cdot & \cdot \\ \cdot & \cdot & & \cdot & \cdot \\ \beta_2^v & \beta_3^v & \cdots & \beta_v^v & \beta_{v+1}^v \end{vmatrix} + \begin{vmatrix} \beta_1 & \beta_3 & \cdots & \beta_v & \beta_{v+1} \\ \beta_1^2 & \beta_3^2 & \cdots & \beta_v^2 & \beta_{v+1}^2 \\ \cdot & \cdot & & \cdot & \cdot \\ \cdot & \cdot & & \cdot & \cdot \\ \cdot & \cdot & & \cdot & \cdot \\ \beta_1^v & \beta_3^v & \cdots & \beta_v^v & \beta_{v+1}^v \end{vmatrix}$$

$$+ \begin{vmatrix} \beta_2 & \beta_1 & \cdots & \beta_v & \beta_{v+1} \\ \beta_2^2 & \beta_1^2 & \cdots & \beta_v^2 & \beta_{v+1}^2 \\ \cdot & \cdot & & \cdot & \cdot \\ \cdot & \cdot & & \cdot & \cdot \\ \cdot & \cdot & & \cdot & \cdot \\ \beta_2^v & \beta_1^v & \cdots & \beta_v^v & \beta_{v+1}^v \end{vmatrix} + \cdots + \begin{vmatrix} \beta_2 & \beta_3 & \cdots & \beta_v & \beta_1 \\ \beta_2^2 & \beta_3^2 & \cdots & \beta_v^2 & \beta_1^2 \\ \cdot & \cdot & & \cdot & \cdot \\ \cdot & \cdot & & \cdot & \cdot \\ \cdot & \cdot & & \cdot & \cdot \\ \beta_2^v & \beta_3^v & \cdots & \beta_v^v & \beta_1^v \end{vmatrix} \tag{7.79}$$

Since $|\mathbf{D}_v| = |\mathbf{D}_v^T|$, Eq. 7.76 becomes

$$|\mathbf{M}_v| = |\mathbf{D}_v|^2 = \begin{vmatrix} \beta_2 & \beta_3 & \cdots & \beta_v & \beta_{v+1} \\ \beta_2^2 & \beta_3^2 & \cdots & \beta_v^2 & \beta_{v+1}^2 \\ \cdot & \cdot & & \cdot & \cdot \\ \cdot & \cdot & & \cdot & \cdot \\ \cdot & \cdot & & \cdot & \cdot \\ \beta_2^v & \beta_3^v & \cdots & \beta_v^v & \beta_{v+1}^v \end{vmatrix}^2 + \begin{vmatrix} \beta_1 & \beta_3 & \cdots & \beta_v & \beta_{v+1} \\ \beta_1^2 & \beta_3^2 & \cdots & \beta_v^2 & \beta_{v+1}^2 \\ \cdot & \cdot & & \cdot & \cdot \\ \cdot & \cdot & & \cdot & \cdot \\ \cdot & \cdot & & \cdot & \cdot \\ \beta_1^v & \beta_3^v & \cdots & \beta_v^v & \beta_{v+1}^v \end{vmatrix}^2$$

$$+ \cdots + \begin{vmatrix} \beta_2 & \beta_3 & \cdots & \beta_v & \beta_1 \\ \beta_2^2 & \beta_3^2 & \cdots & \beta_v^2 & \beta_1^2 \\ \cdot & \cdot & & \cdot & \cdot \\ \cdot & \cdot & & \cdot & \cdot \\ \cdot & \cdot & & \cdot & \cdot \\ \beta_2^v & \beta_3^v & \cdots & \beta_v^v & \beta_1^v \end{vmatrix}^2 \tag{7.80}$$

Consider now the case where we have any β_i among $\beta_1, \beta_2, \cdots, \beta_{v+1}$ equal to zero as follows:

$$|\mathbf{D}_{\nu i}|^2 = \begin{vmatrix} \beta_1 & \beta_2 & \cdots & \beta_{i-1} & \beta_{i+1} & \cdots & \beta_{\nu+1} \\ \beta_1^2 & \beta_2^2 & \cdots & \beta_{i-1}^2 & \beta_{i+1}^2 & \cdots & \beta_{\nu+1}^2 \\ \cdot & \cdot & & \cdot & \cdot & & \cdot \\ \cdot & \cdot & & \cdot & \cdot & & \cdot \\ \cdot & \cdot & & \cdot & \cdot & & \cdot \\ \beta_1^\nu & \beta_2^\nu & \cdots & \beta_{i-1}^\nu & \beta_{i+1}^\nu & \cdots & \beta_{\nu+1}^\nu \end{vmatrix}^2$$

$$= \beta_1^2\beta_2^2 \cdots \beta_{i-1}^2\beta_{i+1}^2 \cdots \beta_{\nu+1}^2 \prod_{\substack{\lambda>\mu \\ \lambda\neq i \\ \mu\neq i}}^{\nu+1} (\beta_\lambda + \beta_\mu)^2$$

$$= \prod_{\substack{j\neq i \\ j=1}}^{\nu+1} \beta_j^2 \prod_{\substack{\lambda>\mu \\ \lambda\neq i \\ \mu\neq i}}^{\nu+1} (\beta_\lambda + \beta_\mu)^2 \tag{7.81}$$

which actually represents one of the determinants in Eq. 7.80. Applying Eq. 7.81 to Eq. 7.80, we have

$$|\mathbf{M}_\nu| = \prod_{\substack{j\neq 1 \\ j=1}}^{\nu+1} \beta_j^2 \prod_{\substack{\lambda>\mu \\ \lambda\neq i \\ \mu\neq i}}^{\nu+1} (\beta_\lambda + \beta_\mu)^2 + \prod_{\substack{j\neq 2 \\ j=1}}^{\nu+1} \beta_j^2 \prod_{\substack{\lambda>\mu \\ \lambda\neq i \\ \mu\neq i}}^{\nu+1} (\beta_\lambda + \beta_\mu)^2 + \cdots$$

$$+ \prod_{\substack{j\neq 3 \\ j=1}}^{\nu+1} \beta_j^2 \prod_{\substack{\lambda>\mu \\ \lambda\neq i \\ \mu\neq i}}^{\nu+1} (\beta_\lambda + \beta_\mu)^2 + \cdots + \prod_{\substack{j\neq \nu+1 \\ j=1}}^{\nu+1} \beta_j^2 \prod_{\substack{\lambda>\mu \\ \lambda\neq \nu+1 \\ \mu\neq \nu+1}}^{\nu+1} (\beta_\lambda + \beta_\mu)^2$$

$$= \sum_{i=1}^{\nu+1} \left[\prod_{\substack{j\neq i \\ j=1}}^{\nu+1} \beta_j^2 \prod_{\substack{\lambda>\mu \\ \lambda\neq i \\ \mu\neq i}}^{\nu+1} (\beta_\lambda + \beta_\mu)^2 \right] \tag{7.82}$$

Let $\mathbf{N}_\nu$ be a matrix composed by deleting the first row and first column of the matrix $\mathbf{M}_\nu$. That is, let

$$\mathbf{N}_\nu = \begin{bmatrix} S_2 & S_3 & \cdots & S_{\nu+1} \\ S_3 & S_4 & \cdots & S_{\nu+2} \\ \cdot & \cdot & & \cdot \\ \cdot & \cdot & & \cdot \\ \cdot & \cdot & & \cdot \\ S_{\nu+1} & S_{\nu+2} & \cdots & S_{2\nu} \end{bmatrix} \tag{7.83}$$

where $S_k = \sum_{\lambda=1}^{\nu} (\beta_\lambda)^k + \beta_{\nu+1}^k$, $k = 2, 3, \cdots, 2\nu$.

Substituting these values of S_k for $k = 2, 3, \cdots, 2\nu$ in Eq. 7.83 and then expanding all elements, we have

$$\mathbf{N}_\nu = \begin{bmatrix} \beta_1 & \beta_2 & \cdots & \beta_\nu & \beta_{\nu+1} \\ \beta_1^2 & \beta_2^2 & \cdots & \beta_\nu^2 & \beta_{\nu+1}^2 \\ \cdot & \cdot & & \cdot & \cdot \\ \cdot & \cdot & & \cdot & \cdot \\ \cdot & \cdot & & \cdot & \cdot \\ \beta_1^\nu & \beta_2^\nu & \cdots & \beta_\nu^\nu & \beta_{\nu+1}^\nu \end{bmatrix} \cdot \begin{bmatrix} \beta_1 & \beta_1^2 & \cdots & \beta_1^\nu \\ \beta_2 & \beta_2^2 & \cdots & \beta_2^\nu \\ \cdot & \cdot & & \cdot \\ \cdot & \cdot & & \cdot \\ \cdot & \cdot & & \cdot \\ \beta_{\nu+1} & \beta_{\nu+1}^2 & \cdots & \beta_{\nu+1}^\nu \end{bmatrix} \tag{7.84}$$

Thus, the determinant corresponding to Eq. 7.84 is

$$|\mathbf{N}_\nu| = \begin{vmatrix} \beta_1 & \beta_2 & \cdots & \beta_\nu & \beta_{\nu+1} \\ \beta_1^2 & \beta_2^2 & \cdots & \beta_\nu^2 & \beta_{\nu+1}^2 \\ \cdot & \cdot & & \cdot & \cdot \\ \cdot & \cdot & & \cdot & \cdot \\ \cdot & \cdot & & \cdot & \cdot \\ \beta_1^\nu & \beta_2^\nu & \cdots & \beta_\nu^\nu & \beta_{\nu+1}^\nu \end{vmatrix} \begin{vmatrix} \beta_1 & \beta_1^2 & \cdots & \beta_1^\nu \\ \beta_2 & \beta_2^2 & \cdots & \beta_2^\nu \\ \cdot & \cdot & & \cdot \\ \cdot & \cdot & & \cdot \\ \cdot & \cdot & & \cdot \\ \beta_\nu & \beta_\nu^2 & \cdots & \beta_\nu^\nu \\ \beta_{\nu+1} & \beta_{\nu+1}^2 & \cdots & \beta_{\nu+1}^\nu \end{vmatrix}$$

$$= \begin{vmatrix} \beta_1 & \beta_2 & \cdots & \beta_\nu \\ \beta_1^2 & \beta_2^2 & \cdots & \beta_\nu^2 \\ \cdot & \cdot & & \cdot \\ \cdot & \cdot & & \cdot \\ \cdot & \cdot & & \cdot \\ \beta_1^\nu & \beta_2^\nu & \cdots & \beta_\nu^\nu \end{vmatrix} \begin{vmatrix} \beta_1 & \beta_1^2 & \cdots & \beta_1^\nu \\ \beta_2 & \beta_2^2 & \cdots & \beta_2^\nu \\ \cdot & \cdot & & \cdot \\ \cdot & \cdot & & \cdot \\ \cdot & \cdot & & \cdot \\ \beta_{\nu-1} & \beta_{\nu-1}^2 & \cdots & \beta_{\nu-1}^\nu \\ \beta_\nu & \beta_\nu^2 & \cdots & \beta_\nu^\nu \end{vmatrix}$$

$$+ \begin{vmatrix} \beta_1 & \beta_2 & \cdots & \beta_{\nu-1} & \beta_{\nu+1} \\ \beta_1^2 & \beta_2^2 & \cdots & \beta_{\nu-1}^2 & \beta_{\nu+1}^2 \\ \cdot & \cdot & & \cdot & \cdot \\ \cdot & \cdot & & \cdot & \cdot \\ \cdot & \cdot & & \cdot & \cdot \\ \beta_1^\nu & \beta_2^\nu & \cdots & \beta_{\nu-1}^\nu & \beta_{\nu+1}^\nu \end{vmatrix} \begin{vmatrix} \beta_1 & \beta_1^2 & \cdots & \beta_1^\nu \\ \beta_2 & \beta_2^2 & \cdots & \beta_2^\nu \\ \cdot & \cdot & & \cdot \\ \cdot & \cdot & & \cdot \\ \cdot & \cdot & & \cdot \\ \beta_{\nu-1} & \beta_{\nu-1}^2 & \cdots & \beta_{\nu-1}^\nu \\ \beta_{\nu+1} & \beta_{\nu+1}^2 & \cdots & \beta_{\nu+1}^\nu \end{vmatrix} + \cdots$$

$$+\begin{vmatrix} \beta_1 & \beta_3 & \cdots & \beta_{v+1} \\ \beta_1^2 & \beta_3^2 & \cdots & \beta_{v+1}^2 \\ \cdot & \cdot & & \cdot \\ \cdot & \cdot & & \cdot \\ \cdot & \cdot & & \cdot \\ \beta_1^v & \beta_3^v & \cdots & \beta_{v+1}^v \end{vmatrix} \begin{vmatrix} \beta_1 & \beta_1^2 & \cdots & \beta_1^v \\ \beta_3 & \beta_3^2 & \cdots & \beta_3^v \\ \cdot & \cdot & & \cdot \\ \cdot & \cdot & & \cdot \\ \cdot & \cdot & & \cdot \\ \beta_{v+1} & \beta_{v+1}^2 & \cdots & \beta_{v+1}^v \end{vmatrix}$$

$$+\begin{vmatrix} \beta_2 & \beta_3 & \cdots & \beta_{v+1} \\ \beta_2^2 & \beta_3^2 & \cdots & \beta_{v+1}^2 \\ \cdot & \cdot & & \cdot \\ \cdot & \cdot & & \cdot \\ \cdot & \cdot & & \cdot \\ \beta_2^v & \beta_3^v & \cdots & \beta_{v+1}^v \end{vmatrix} \begin{vmatrix} \beta_2 & \beta_2^2 & \cdots & \beta_2^v \\ \beta_3 & \beta_3^2 & \cdots & \beta_3^v \\ \cdot & \cdot & & \cdot \\ \cdot & \cdot & & \cdot \\ \cdot & \cdot & & \cdot \\ \beta_{v+1} & \beta_{v+1}^2 & \cdots & \beta_{v+1}^v \end{vmatrix} \tag{7.85}$$

The same argument as we have applied in case of Eq. 7.82 is valid for Eq. 7.85 as well. Therefore, Eq. 7.85 becomes

$$|\mathbf{N}_v| = \prod_{\substack{j\neq 1\\ j=1}}^{v+1} \beta_j^2 \prod_{\substack{\lambda>\mu\\ \lambda\neq 1\\ \mu\neq 1}}^{v+1} (\beta_\lambda+\beta_\mu)^2 + \prod_{\substack{j\neq 2\\ j=1}}^{v+1} \beta_j^2 \prod_{\substack{\lambda>\mu\\ \lambda\neq 2\\ \mu\neq 2}}^{v+1} (\beta_\lambda+\beta_\mu)^2 + \cdots$$

$$+ \prod_{\substack{j\neq v\\ j=1}}^{v+1} \beta_j^2 \prod_{\substack{\lambda>\mu\\ \lambda\neq v\\ \mu\neq v}}^{v+1} (\beta_\lambda+\beta_\mu)^2 \prod_{\substack{j\neq v+1\\ j=1}}^{v+1} \beta_j^2 \prod_{\substack{\lambda>\mu\\ \lambda\neq v+1\\ \mu\neq v+1}}^{v+1} (\beta_\lambda+\beta_\mu)^2$$

$$= \sum_{i=1}^{v+1} \left[\prod_{\substack{j\neq i\\ j=1}}^{v+1} \beta_j^2 \prod_{\substack{\lambda>\mu\\ \lambda\neq i\\ \mu\neq i}}^{v+1} (\beta_\lambda+\beta_\mu)^2 \right] \tag{7.86}$$

Now, we can see that Eq. 7.82 is exactly identical to Eq. 7.86, i.e. $|\mathbf{M}_v| = |\mathbf{N}_v|$. The determinant $|\mathbf{N}_v|$ may be used as the error-locator polynomial.

Considering again Eq. 7.83, the determinant of $\mathbf{N}_v$ having elements $S_k = s_k + \beta^k$, $2 \le k \le 2v$, is

$$|\mathbf{N}_v| = \begin{vmatrix} S_2 & S_3 & \cdots & S_{v+1} \\ S_3 & S_4 & \cdots & S_{v+2} \\ \cdot & \cdot & & \cdot \\ \cdot & \cdot & & \cdot \\ \cdot & \cdot & & \cdot \\ S_{v+1} & S_{v+2} & \cdots & S_{2v} \end{vmatrix}$$

$$
= \begin{vmatrix}
s_2 + \beta^2 & s_3 + \beta^3 & \cdots & s_{\nu+1} + \beta^{\nu+1} \\
s_3 + \beta^3 & s_4 + \beta^4 & \cdots & s_{\nu+2} + \beta^{\nu+2} \\
\vdots & \vdots & & \vdots \\
s_{\nu+1} + \beta^{\nu+1} & s_{\nu+2} + \beta^{\nu+2} & \cdots & s_{2\nu} + \beta^{2\nu}
\end{vmatrix}
$$

$$
= \begin{vmatrix}
s_2 & s_3 & s_4 & \cdots & s_{\nu+1} \\
s_3 & s_4 & s_5 & \cdots & s_{\nu+2} \\
\vdots & \vdots & & & \vdots \\
s_{\nu+1} & s_{\nu+2} & s_{\nu+3} & \cdots & s_{2\nu}
\end{vmatrix}
$$

$$
+ \begin{vmatrix}
\beta^2 & s_3 & \cdots & s_{\nu+1} \\
\beta^3 & s_4 & \cdots & s_{\nu+2} \\
\vdots & \vdots & & \vdots \\
\beta^{\nu+1} & s_{\nu+2} & \cdots & s_{2\nu}
\end{vmatrix}
+ \begin{vmatrix}
s_2 & \beta^3 & s_4 & \cdots & s_{\nu+1} \\
s_3 & \beta^4 & s_5 & \cdots & s_{\nu+2} \\
\vdots & \vdots & & & \vdots \\
s_{\nu+1} & \beta^{\nu+2} & s_{\nu+3} & \cdots & s_{2\nu}
\end{vmatrix}
+
$$

$$
\cdots + \begin{vmatrix}
s_2 & s_3 & s_4 & \cdots & s_{\nu+1} & \beta^{\nu+1} \\
s_3 & s_4 & s_5 & \cdots & s_{\nu+2} & \beta^{\nu+2} \\
\vdots & \vdots & & & \vdots & \vdots \\
s_{\nu+1} & s_{\nu+2} & s_{\nu+3} & \cdots & s_{2\nu-1} & \beta^{2\nu}
\end{vmatrix}
+ \sum R_i \qquad (7.87)
$$

where

$$
\Sigma R_i = \begin{vmatrix}
\beta^2 & \beta^3 & \cdots & s_{\nu+1} \\
\beta^3 & \beta^4 & \cdots & s_{\nu+2} \\
\vdots & \vdots & & \vdots \\
\beta^{\nu+1} & \beta^{\nu+2} & \cdots & s_{2\nu}
\end{vmatrix}
+ \cdots +
\begin{vmatrix}
s_2 & s_3 & \cdots & \beta^{\nu} & \beta^{\nu+1} \\
s_3 & s_4 & \cdots & \beta^{\nu+1} & \beta^{\nu+2} \\
\vdots & \vdots & & \vdots & \vdots \\
s_{\nu+1} & s_{\nu+2} & \cdots & \beta^{2\nu-1} & \beta^{2\nu}
\end{vmatrix}
+
$$

$$\cdots + \begin{vmatrix} \beta^2 & \beta^3 & \cdots & \beta^{v+1} \\ \beta^3 & \beta^4 & \cdots & \beta^{v+2} \\ \cdot & \cdot & & \cdot \\ \cdot & \cdot & & \cdot \\ \cdot & \cdot & & \cdot \\ \beta^{v+1} & \beta^{v+2} & \cdots & \beta^{2v} \end{vmatrix}$$

Observing ΣR_i, we see that

$$\begin{vmatrix} \beta^2 & \beta^3 & \cdots & s_{v+1} \\ \beta^3 & \beta^4 & \cdots & s_{v+2} \\ \cdot & \cdot & & \cdot \\ \cdot & \cdot & & \cdot \\ \cdot & \cdot & & \cdot \\ \beta^{v+1} & \beta^{v+2} & \cdots & s_{2v} \end{vmatrix} = \beta^2 \beta^3 \begin{vmatrix} 1 & 1 & \cdots & s_{v+1} \\ \beta & \beta & \cdots & s_{v+2} \\ \cdot & \cdot & & \cdot \\ \cdot & \cdot & & \cdot \\ \cdot & \cdot & & \cdot \\ \beta^{v-1} & \beta^{v-1} & \cdots & s_{2v} \end{vmatrix} = 0$$

and in general

$$\begin{vmatrix} s_2 & \cdots & \beta^i & \beta^{i+1} & \cdots & \beta^{i+l} & \cdots & s_{v+1} \\ s_3 & \cdots & \beta^{i+1} & \beta^{i+2} & \cdots & \beta^{i+(l+1)} & \cdots & s_{v+2} \\ \cdot & & \cdot & \cdot & & \cdot & & \cdot \\ \cdot & & \cdot & \cdot & & \cdot & & \cdot \\ \cdot & & \cdot & \cdot & & \cdot & & \cdot \\ s_{v+1} & \cdots & \beta^{i+(v-1)} & \beta^{i+v} & \cdots & \beta^{i+(v+l-1)} & \cdots & s_{2v} \end{vmatrix}$$

$$= \beta^i \beta^{i+1} \cdots \beta^{i+l} \begin{vmatrix} s_2 & \cdots & 1 & 1 & \cdots & 1 & \cdots & s_{v+1} \\ s_3 & \cdots & \beta & \beta & \cdots & \beta & \cdots & s_{v+2} \\ \cdot & & \cdot & \cdot & & \cdot & & \cdot \\ \cdot & & \cdot & \cdot & & \cdot & & \cdot \\ \cdot & & \cdot & \cdot & & \cdot & & \cdot \\ s_{v+1} & \cdots & \beta^{v-1} & \beta^{v-1} & \cdots & \beta^{v-1} & \cdots & s_{2v} \end{vmatrix} = 0$$

due to the fact that two or more columns in each component determinant in ΣR_i are identical. Thus, it follows that $\Sigma R_i = 0$.

If we expand Eq. 7.87 and cancel like terms, we have

$$|\mathbf{N}_v| = \begin{vmatrix} S_2 & S_3 & S_4 & \cdots & S_{v+1} \\ S_3 & S_4 & S_5 & \cdots & S_{v+2} \\ \cdot & \cdot & & & \cdot \\ \cdot & \cdot & & & \cdot \\ \cdot & \cdot & & & \cdot \\ S_v & S_{v+1} & S_{v+2} & \cdots & S_{2v-1} \\ S_{v+1} & S_{v+2} & S_{v+3} & \cdots & S_{2v} \end{vmatrix} + \beta^2 \begin{vmatrix} S_4 & S_5 & \cdots & S_{v+1} & S_{v+2} \\ S_5 & S_6 & \cdots & S_{v+2} & S_{v+3} \\ \cdot & \cdot & & & \cdot \\ \cdot & \cdot & & & \cdot \\ \cdot & \cdot & & & \cdot \\ S_{v+1} & S_{v+2} & \cdots & S_{2v-2} & S_{2v-1} \\ S_{v+2} & S_{v+3} & \cdots & S_{2v-1} & S_{2v} \end{vmatrix}$$

$$+\beta^4 \begin{vmatrix} S_2 & S_4 & \cdots & S_v & S_{v+1} \\ S_4 & S_6 & \cdots & S_{v+2} & S_{v+3} \\ \cdot & \cdot & & & \cdot \\ \cdot & \cdot & & & \cdot \\ \cdot & \cdot & & & \cdot \\ S_v & S_{v+2} & \cdots & S_{2v-2} & S_{2v-1} \\ S_{v+1} & S_{v+3} & \cdots & S_{2v-1} & S_{2v} \end{vmatrix} + \cdots + \beta^{2v} \begin{vmatrix} S_2 & S_3 & \cdots & S_{v-1} & S_v \\ S_3 & S_4 & \cdots & S_v & S_{v+1} \\ \cdot & \cdot & & & \cdot \\ \cdot & \cdot & & & \cdot \\ \cdot & \cdot & & & \cdot \\ S_{v-1} & S_v & \cdots & S_{2v-4} & S_{2v-3} \\ S_v & S_{v+1} & \cdots & S_{2v-3} & S_{2v-2} \end{vmatrix}$$

$$= A_0 + \beta^2 A_1 + \beta^4 A_2 + \cdots + \beta^{2v} A_v \tag{7.88}$$

where $A_i^{1/2}$, $i = 0, 1, 2, \cdots, v$ represents the coefficients of the error-locator polynomial.

We shall now consider a few examples to determine $|\mathbf{N}_v|$ for finding the error-locator polynomial for $v = 2, 3$, and 4 (double, triple, and quadruple errors) will be shown in the following. The error-locator polynomial is actually given by the relation $\sigma_j(x) = [\mathbf{N}_v(x)]^{1/2}$, $v = 2, 3, \cdots$

■ **Example 7.12** Compute $|\mathbf{N}_v|$, $v = 2, 3$, and 4. Since $S_{2i} = S_i^2$ for $i = 1, 2, \cdots, v$, we have $S_2 = S_1^2$, $S_4 = S_2^2 = S_1^4$, $S_6 = S_3^2$, and $S_8 = S_4^2 = S_1^8$.

For $v = 2$ (double-error correcting codes), we have

$$|\mathbf{N}_2| = \begin{vmatrix} S_2 & S_3 \\ S_3 & S_4 \end{vmatrix} = S_2 S_4 + S_3^2 = S_1^6 + S_3^2 = (S_1^3 + S_3)^2 \tag{7.89}$$

For $v = 3$ (triple-error correcting codes),

$$|\mathbf{N}_3| = \begin{vmatrix} S_2 & S_3 & S_4 \\ S_3 & S_4 & S_5 \\ S_4 & S_5 & S_6 \end{vmatrix}$$

$$= S_1^2 (S_1^4 S_3^2 + S_5^2) + S_3 (S_3^3 + S_1^4 S_5) + S_1^4 (S_3 S_5 + S_1^8)$$

$$= S_1^{12} + S_3^4 + S_1^6 S_3^2 + S_1^2 S_5^2$$

$$= (S_1^6 + S_3^2 + S_1^3 S_3 + S_1 S_5)^2 \tag{7.90}$$

For $\nu = 4$ (quadruple-error correcting codes),

$$|\mathbf{N}_4| = \begin{vmatrix} S_2 & S_3 & S_4 & S_5 \\ S_3 & S_4 & S_5 & S_6 \\ S_4 & S_5 & S_6 & S_7 \\ S_5 & S_6 & S_7 & S_8 \end{vmatrix}$$

$$= S_1^{20} + S_5^4 + S_1^2 S_3^6 + S_1^{14} S_3^2 + S_1^{10} S_5^2 + S_1^6 S_7^2 + S_3^2 S_7^2 + S_1^4 S_3^2 S_5^2$$

$$= (S_1^{10} + S_5^2 + S_1 S_3^3 + S_1^7 S_3 + S_1^5 S_5 + S_1^3 S_7 + S_3 S_7 + S_1^2 S_3 S_5)^2 \tag{7.91}$$

■ **Example 7.13** Compute A_i for $i = 0, 1, 2, \cdots; \nu$.

For $\nu = 2$, we obtain

$$A_0 = \begin{vmatrix} s_2 & s_3 \\ s_3 & s_4 \end{vmatrix} = s_1^6 + s_3^2$$

$$A_1 = s_4 = s_1^4$$

$$A_2 = s_2 = s_1^2$$

Thus, $N_2(x) = (s_1^3 + s_3)^2 + s_1^4 x^2 + s_1^2 x^4 = [(s_1^3 + s_3) + s_1^2 x + s_1 x^2]^2$

Therefore, the error-locator polynomial becomes

$$\sigma_2(x) = (s_1^3 + s_3) + s_1^2 x + s_1 x^2 \tag{7.92}$$

For $\nu = 3$ for the triple-error correcting code, we obtain

$$A_0 = \begin{vmatrix} s_2 & s_3 & s_4 \\ s_3 & s_4 & s_5 \\ s_4 & s_5 & s_6 \end{vmatrix}$$

$$= s_1^2 (s_1^4 s_3^2 + s_5^2) + s_3 (s_3^3 + s_1^4 s_5) + s_1^4 (s_3 s_5 + s_1^8)$$

$$= s_1^{12} + s_3^4 + s_1^6 s_3^2 + s_1^2 s_5^2$$

$$A_1 = \begin{vmatrix} s_4 & s_5 \\ s_5 & s_6 \end{vmatrix} = s_1^4 s_3^2 + s_5^2$$

$$A_2 = \begin{vmatrix} s_2 & s_4 \\ s_4 & s_6 \end{vmatrix} = s_1^2 s_3^2 + s_1^8$$

$$A_3 = \begin{vmatrix} s_2 & s_3 \\ s_3 & s_4 \end{vmatrix} = s_1^6 + s_3^2$$

Thus,

$$N_3(x) = (s_1^{12} + s_3^4 + s_1^6 s_3^2 + s_1^2 s_5^2) + (s_1^4 s_3^2 + s_5^2)x^2 + (s_1^2 s_3^2 + s_1^8)x^4 + (s_1^6 + s_3^2)x^6$$

$$= [(s_1^6 + s_3^2 + s_1^3 s_3 + s_1 s_5) + (s_1^2 s_3 + s_5)x + (s_1 s_3 + s_1^4)x^2 + (s_1^3 + s_3)x^3]^2$$

Therefore, the error-locator polynomial can be written as

$$\sigma_3(x) = [(s_1^6 + s_3^2 + s_1^3 s_3 + s_1 s_5) + (s_1^2 s_3 + s_5)x + (s_1 s_3 + s_1^4)x^2 + (s_1^3 + s_3)x^3] \tag{7.93}$$

Thus, the error-locator polynomial $\sigma_v(x)$ can be easily found once the symmetrical-syndrome determinant $|\mathbf{N}_v|$ is known.

7.8.2 Implementation of BCH Decoder

Based on the theory developed in Subsec. 7.8.1, the practical application of a binary (n, k) v-error-correcting BCH decoder is considered in what follows. Two different types of BCH decoder can be implemented depending on the decoder configurations, one based on the symmetrical-syndrome determinant $|\mathbf{N}_v|$ of Eq. 7.87 and the other on the error-locator polynomial $\sigma_v(x)$ which is generated from Eq. 7.88.

In order to estimate the number of error digits, the matrix of syndrome is used as indicated below.

$$\mathbf{Q}_v = \begin{vmatrix} S_1 & S_2 & \cdots & S_v \\ S_2 & S_3 & \cdots & S_{v+1} \\ \cdot & \cdot & & \cdot \\ \cdot & \cdot & & \cdot \\ \cdot & \cdot & & \cdot \\ S_v & S_{v+1} & \cdots & S_{2v-1} \end{vmatrix} \tag{7.94}$$

where $\mathbf{Q}_1 = s_1$

$$\mathbf{Q}_2 = \begin{vmatrix} s_1 & s_2 \\ s_2 & s_3 \end{vmatrix}$$

$$\mathbf{Q}_3 = \begin{vmatrix} s_1 & s_2 & s_3 \\ s_2 & s_3 & s_4 \\ s_3 & s_4 & s_5 \end{vmatrix}$$

. . . .

$$\mathbf{Q}_{\nu-1} = \begin{vmatrix} s_1 & s_2 & \cdots & s_{\nu-1} \\ s_2 & s_3 & \cdots & s_\nu \\ \cdot & \cdot & & \cdot \\ \cdot & \cdot & & \cdot \\ s_{\nu-1} & s_\nu & \cdots & s_{2\nu-3} \end{vmatrix}$$

If ν errors actually occur, $|\mathbf{Q}_\nu| \neq 0$ (nonsingular), and if fewer than ν errors occur, $|\mathbf{Q}_\nu| = 0$ (singular).

As observed from Examples 7.12 and 7.13, a determinant $|\mathbf{N}_\nu|$ is expressed by the modified syndrome components, and the coefficients of an error-locator polynomial are directly expressed in a determinant form of syndrome components. By incorporating ROMs in a decoder, complex logic circuits are eliminated and then the BCH decoder can be easily constructed by using Eqs. 7.87, 7.88, and 7.94.

Therefore, since $|\mathbf{N}_\nu|$ is expressed by either the determinant of S_i or the polynomial of β, the decoder coupled with $\mathbf{Q}_\nu$ can be implemented by computing either S_i or A_i as shown below.

When the determinant $|\mathbf{N}_\nu|$ has S_i elements, we must first determine each value of S_i corresponding to β^i, and then compute $|\mathbf{N}_\nu|$. If $|\mathbf{N}_\nu| = 0$ at $\beta = \alpha^{n-\lambda}$, $\lambda = 1, 2, \cdots, n$, the λth bit of the received word $\mathbf{r}$ is an erroneous digit and should be corrected. Figure 7.7 shows a type **I** (n, k) BCH decoder based on the determinant $|\mathbf{N}_\nu|$ of S_i elements.

■ **Example 7.14** Consider the TEC (31, 16) BCH code. Suppose the received polynomial is $r(x) = x + x^{12} + x^{25}$ when the allzero code word $c(x)$ is transmitted. This implies that the three errors have occurred at positions x, x^{12}, and x^{25} during transmission. As evaluated in Example 7.4, the syndrome of $r(x)$ is

$$\mathbf{s} = (\alpha^{22}, \alpha^{13}, \alpha^{10}, \alpha^{26}, \alpha^{12}, \alpha^{20})$$

Since $\nu = 3$ for the triple-error-correcting (TEC) code, the coefficients corresponding to β^i, $i = 0, 1, 2, \cdots, \nu$, are

$$A_0 = (s_1^6 + s_1^2 + s_1^3 s_3 + s_1 s_5)^2$$

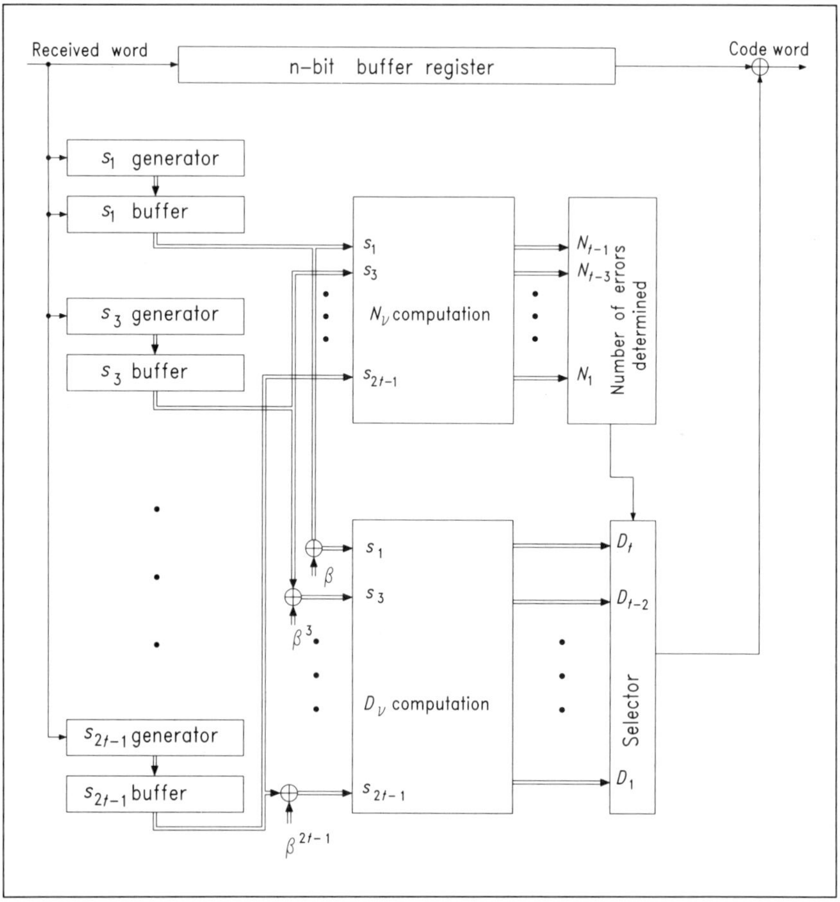

Fig. 7.7 Type I (n, k) BCH decoder based on the determinant $|\mathbf{N}\nu|$ of S_i elements

$$A_1 = (s_1^2 s_3 + s_5)^2$$

$$A_2 = (s_1 s_3 + s_1^4)^2 \qquad (7.95)$$

$$A_3 = (s_1^3 + s_3)^2$$

Using $s_1 = \alpha^{22}$, $s_2 = \alpha^{13}$, $s_3 = \alpha^{10}$, $s_4 = \alpha^{26}$, $s_5 = \alpha^{12}$, and $s_6 = \alpha^{20}$ in Eq. 7.95, $A_i^{1/2}$ for $i = 0, 1, 2$, and 3 becomes $A_0^{1/2} = \alpha^7$, $A_1^{1/2} = 1$, $A_2^{1/2} = \alpha^{22}$, and $A_3^{1/2} = 1$. Thus, the error-locator polynomial can be written as

$$\sigma(x) = \alpha^7 + x + \alpha^{22}x^2 + x^3 \qquad (7.96)$$

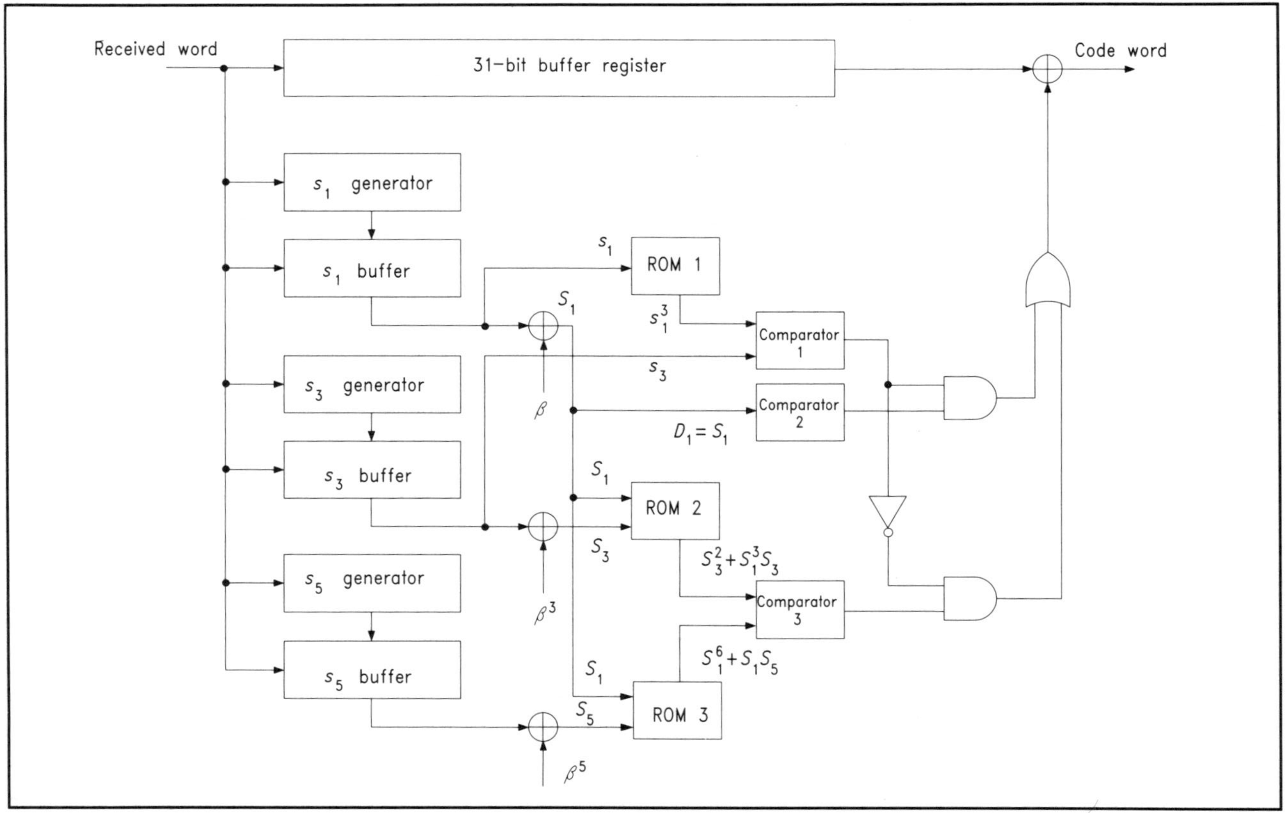

Fig. 7.8 Type I TEC (31, 16) BCH decoder

In order to determine the roots of $\sigma(x)$, we substitute all the elements of GF (2^5) in $\sigma(x)$ and find $\sigma(\alpha^{32-\lambda}) = 0$ where $\lambda = 1, 2, \cdots, 32$. Thus, we can observe that $\sigma(\alpha^{32-\lambda}) = 0$ only for $\lambda = 31, 20$ and 17 as shown below.

$$\sigma(\alpha) = \alpha^7 + \alpha + \alpha^{24} + \alpha^3 = 0$$

$$\sigma(\alpha^{12}) = (\alpha^2 + \alpha^4) + (\alpha + \alpha^2 + \alpha^3) + (1 + \alpha + \alpha^2 + \alpha^3 + \alpha^4)$$
$$+ (1 + \alpha^2) = 0$$

$$\sigma(\alpha^{25}) = (\alpha^2 + \alpha^4) + (1 + \alpha^3 + \alpha^4) + (1 + \alpha^4) + (\alpha^2 + \alpha^3 + \alpha^4) = 0$$

Hence, the error-location numbers are α, α^{12}, and α^{25}.

Thus, the error pattern is given by

$$e(x) = x + x^{12} + x^{25} \tag{7.97}$$

Now we can see that $c(x) = r(x) + e(x) = 0$, which indicates that the all-zero code word was transmitted. Of course, the determination of error-location numbers can also be accomplished by Chein's method which involves searching all elements in GF (2^m). The type I TEC (31, 16) BCH decoder is shown in Fig. 7.8. The number of error digits can be estimated by means of the Q_v circuit. If $s_1^{\,3} = s_3$, the output of comparator 1 becomes one (1), indicating that one error has occurred. If $s_1^{\,3} \neq s_3$, the output of comparator 1 becomes zero (0), meaning that three errors have occurred.

The generation of unknowns β, β^3, and β^5 in Fig. 7.8 may be illustrated in the following way. If an element of GF (2^5) denotes $\lambda = a_0 + a_1 \alpha + a_2 \alpha^2 + a_3 \alpha^3 + a_4 \alpha^4$, then the unknown β can be computed from the following.

$$\beta = \lambda \alpha^{30}$$
$$= a_1 + (a_0 + a_2)\alpha + a_3 \alpha^2 + a_4 \alpha^3 + a_5 \alpha^4$$

which is illustrated in Fig. 7.9. By incorporating ROM, β^3 and β^5 are easily generated.

Based on Eq. 7.88, a type **II** (n, k) BCH decoder can be constructed by computation of A_i. The general block diagram for this type of decoding circuit is shown in Fig. 7.10.

■ **Example 7.15** Consider again the TEC (31, 16) BCH code. The $\mathbf{Q}_v$ circuit for determination of error-location numbers is the same as that drawn for the type **II** TEC (31, 16) BCH decoder. The device for such a decoder is based on the polynomial of β and is shown in Fig. 7.11.

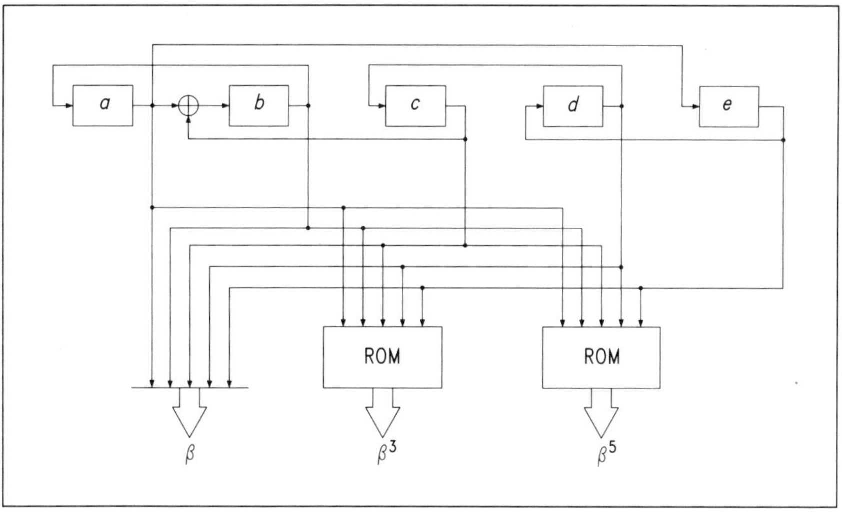

Fig. 7.9 The circuit diagram for generation of unknowns β, β^3, and β^5

7.9 STRAIGHTFORWARD APPROACH FOR BCH DECODING

BCH as well as RS codes are well known for their error-correcting capabilities. Not only digital communication and computer systems but consumer electronic products too , e.g. CD and DAT, are increasingly adapting the error-correcting techniques of BCH or RS codes. In this section, a BCH decoding scheme discussed by [11, 14] is introduced for the case of small error-correcting capabilities.

In coperating with ROMs in a decoder, complex logic circuits can be eliminated, and decoding speed improved. At first, Polkinghorn's method [11] was introduced for solving *n*th order equations, with which some efficient decoders for DEC/TEC BCH codes can be constructed.

7.9.1 Solutions of *n*th-Order Equations

$n = 3$ or lower equations can be effectively solved by using Polkinghorn's techniques, on which our analysis is based.

Let

$$x^n + \sigma_{n,1}x^{n-1} + \sigma_{n,2}x^{n-2} + \cdots + \sigma_{n,n-1}x + \sigma_{n,n} = 0 \tag{7.98}$$

be the *n*th-order equation.

We begin with the first-order equation. For $n = 1$,

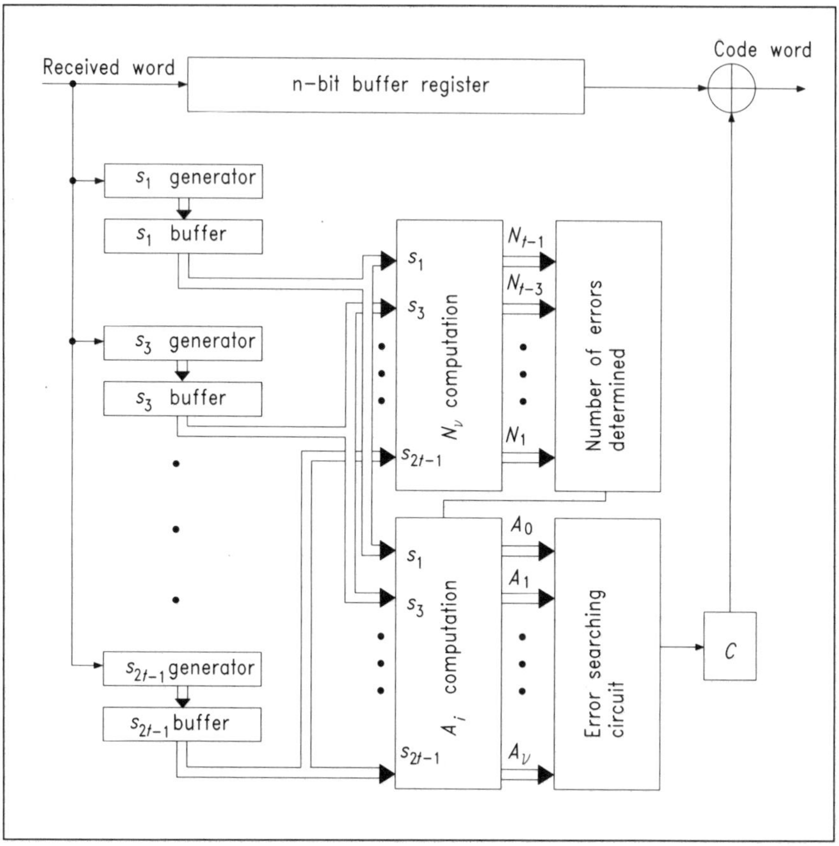

Fig. 7.10 Type **II** (n, k) BCH decoder based on computation of A_i

$$\sigma_{10}x + \sigma_{11} = 0 \tag{7.99}$$

whose root is clearly $x = \sigma_{11}/\sigma_{10}$.

For $n = 2$, the equation is quadratic:

$$x^2 + \sigma_{21}x + \sigma_{22} = 0 \tag{7.100}$$

If $\sigma_{21} = 0$, then $x = \sigma_{22}^{1/2}$. When $\sigma_{21} \neq 0$, Eq. 7.100 can be normalized by substituting $x = \sigma_{21}y$ in Eq. 7.100 such that

$$y^2 + y + C_i = 0 \tag{7.101}$$

where $C_i = \sigma_{22}/\sigma_{21}^2$.

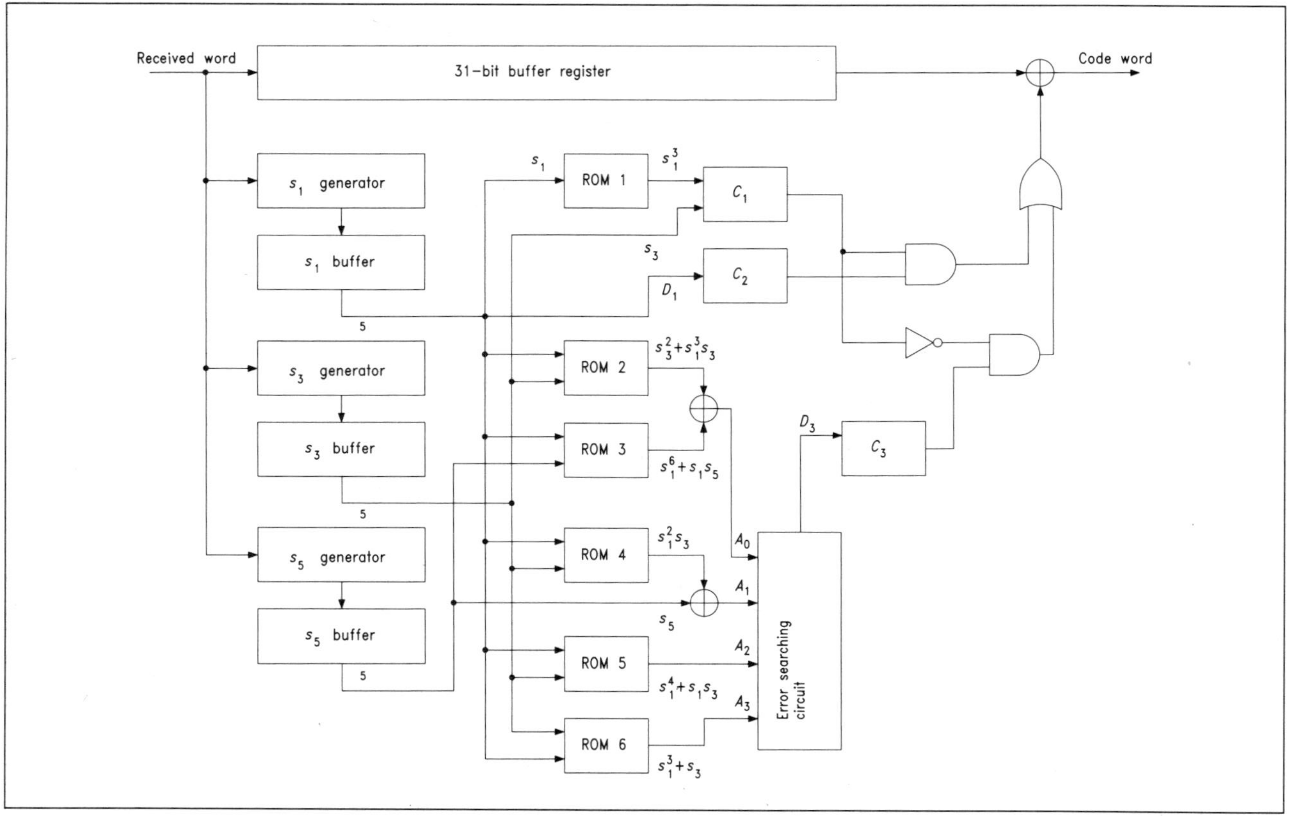

Fig. 7.11 Type **II** TEC (31, 16) BCH decoder

The root of Eq. 7.101, are determined solely depending on C_i. Therefore, if the roots y_1 and y_2 depending on C_is are stored in a memory table, they can easily computed according to C_i. Thus, the roots of Eq. 7.100 are $x_1 = \sigma_{21} y_1$ and $x_2 = \sigma_{21} y_2$, respectively.

Next, for $n = 3$, we have the following cubic equation

$$x^3 + \sigma_{31}x^2 + \sigma_{32}x + \sigma_{33} = 0 \tag{7.102}$$

Substituting $x = y + \sigma_{31}$ in Eq. 7.102 yields

$$y^3 + \lambda y + \mu = 0 \tag{7.103}$$

where $\lambda = \sigma_{31}^2 + \sigma_{32}$ and $\mu = \sigma_{31}\,\sigma_{32} + \sigma_{33}$.

If $\lambda = 0$ in Eq. 7.103, $y = \mu^{1/3}$. If $\lambda \neq 0$, by letting $y = \lambda^{1/2} z$ in Eq. 7.103, we have

$$z^3 + z + C_k = 0 \tag{7.104}$$

where $C_k = \mu/\lambda^{3/2}$.

Thus, the roots of Eq. 7.104 are stored in memory as a table for all possible values of C_k. Then the roots of Eq. 7.102 are

$$x_i = \lambda^{1/2} z_i + \sigma_{31} \qquad i = 1, 2, 3 \tag{7.105}$$

where z_i, $i = 1, 2, 3$ are the roots of Eq. 7.104.

At this point, it is recommended that the reader reviews Sec. 6.7 for understanding the circuit implementation of Eq. 7.103. The block diagram for the circuit to solve the cubic equation $y^3 + \lambda y + \mu = 0$ is shown in Fig. 7.12. Referring to Eq. 7.103, DE becomes 1 when $\lambda = 0$ and switch A is set in the downward position and the solution is three cubic roots. ROM C is a table for these cubic roots. If $\lambda \neq 0$, switch A is set in the upward position. ROM 3 is a table for obtaining the roots of $z^3 + z + C_k = 0$ according to C_k and consists of three ROMs.

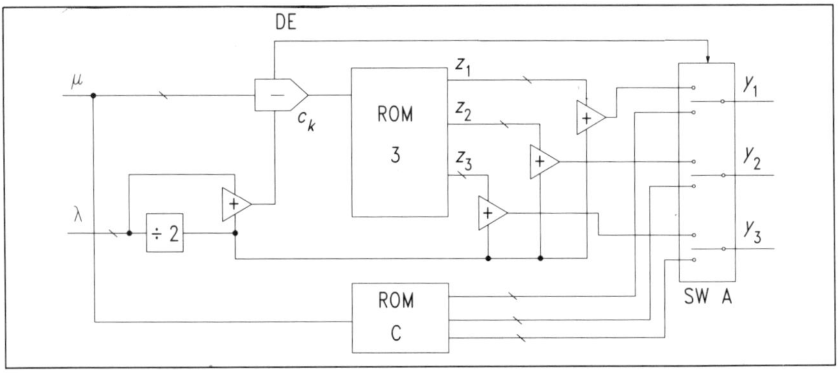

Fig. 7.12 Circuit block diagram for solving $y^3 + \lambda y + \mu = 0$

Table 7.3 Roots of $z^3 + z + C_k = 0$

C_k	z_1	z_2	z_3
0	1		
1			
α	α^{15}		
α^2	α^{30}		
α^3	α^{16}		
α^4	α^{29}		
α^5	α^{20}	α^{22}	α^{25}
α^6	α		
α^7			
α^8	α^{27}		
α^9	α^5	α^{14}	α^{21}
α^{10}	α^9	α^{13}	α^{19}
α^{11}			
α^{12}	α^2		
α^{13}			
α^{14}			
α^{15}	α^{17}		
α^{16}	α^{23}		
α^{17}	α^8		
α^{18}	α^{10}	α^{11}	α^{28}
α^{19}			
α^{20}	α^7	α^{18}	α^{26}
α^{21}			
α^{22}			
α^{23}	α^{24}		
α^{24}	α^4		
α^{25}			
α^{26}			
α^{27}	α^{12}		
α^{28}			
α^{29}	α^6		
α^{30}	α^3		

7.9.2 Coefficients of Error-locator Polynomial

Referring to Eq. 7.41 in Sec. 7.5, the set of linear equations relating the syndromes to the coefficients of the error-locator polynomial $\sigma(x)$ is expressed in matrix from as

$$\begin{bmatrix} s_1 & s_2 & \cdots & s_{v-1} & s_v \\ s_2 & s_3 & \cdots & s_v & s_{v+1} \\ \cdot & \cdot & & \cdot & \cdot \\ \cdot & \cdot & & \cdot & \cdot \\ \cdot & \cdot & & \cdot & \cdot \\ s_{v-1} & s_v & \cdots & s_{2v-3} & s_{2v-2} \\ s_v & s_{v+1} & \cdots & s_{2v-2} & s_{2v-1} \end{bmatrix} \begin{bmatrix} \sigma_v \\ \sigma_{v-1} \\ \cdot \\ \cdot \\ \cdot \\ \sigma_2 \\ \sigma_1 \end{bmatrix} = \begin{bmatrix} -s_{v+1} \\ -s_{v+2} \\ \cdot \\ \cdot \\ \cdot \\ -s_{2v-1} \\ -s_{2v} \end{bmatrix} \tag{7.106}$$

This matrix system can be solved by inverting the syndrome matrix if it is nonsingular.

■ **Example 7.16** Find the roots of $z^3 + z + C_k = 0$ over GF (2^5), as shown in Table 7.3.

Consider the coefficients of the error-locator polynomial for a v-error correcting BCH code. When $v = 3$, Eq. 7.106 becomes

$$\begin{bmatrix} s_1 & s_2 & s_3 \\ s_2 & s_3 & s_4 \\ s_3 & s_4 & s_5 \end{bmatrix} \begin{bmatrix} \sigma_{33} \\ \sigma_{32} \\ \sigma_{31} \end{bmatrix} = \begin{bmatrix} -s_4 \\ -s_5 \\ -s_6 \end{bmatrix} \tag{7.107}$$

which represents the matrix system corresponding to the error-locator polynomial of the triple-error correcting (TEC) BCH code.

Let **S** be the syndrome matrix in Eq. 7.107. That is, let

$$\mathbf{S} = \begin{bmatrix} s_1 & s_2 & s_3 \\ s_2 & s_3 & s_4 \\ s_3 & s_4 & s_5 \end{bmatrix} \tag{7.108}$$

from which the inverse matrix $\mathbf{S}^{-1}$ can be obtained by computing the determinant of $\mathbf{S}$, $|\mathbf{S}|$, and cofactors C_{ij} such that

$$\mathbf{S}^{-1} = [C_{ij}]/|\mathbf{S}| = (-1)^{i+j}\mathbf{M}_{ij}/|\mathbf{S}| \tag{7.109}$$

where $\mathbf{M}_{ij}$ denote the minors. But remember that the ± sign in the binary field is immaterial. Thus,

$$|\mathbf{S}| = s_1 s_3 s_5 + s_1 s_4^2 + s_2^2 s_5 + s_3^3$$

Applying the relations $s_2 = s_1^2$, $s_4 = s_1^4$, and $s_6 = s_3^2$ to the above yields

$$|\mathbf{S}| = s_1s_3s_5 + s_1^9 + s_1^4s_5 + s_3^3 \tag{7.110}$$

Next, let us compute the cofactors C_{ij}:

$$\begin{aligned}
C_{11} &= s_3s_5 - s_4^2 = s_3s_5 + s_1^8 \\
C_{12} &= -s_2s_5 + s_3s_4 = s_1^2s_5 + s_1^4s_3 \\
C_{13} &= s_2s_4 - s_3^2 = s_1^6 + s_3^2 \\
C_{21} &= s_3s_4 - s_2s_5 = s_3s_1^4 + s_1^2s_5 \\
C_{22} &= s_1s_5 - s_3^2 = s_1s_5 + s_3^2 \\
C_{23} &= s_2s_3 - s_1s_4 = s_1^2s_3 + s_1^5 \\
C_{31} &= s_2s_4 - s_3^2 = s_1^6 + s_3^2 \\
C_{32} &= -s_1s_4 + s_2s_3 = s_1^5 + s_1^2s_3 \\
C_{33} &= s_1s_3 - s_2^2 = s_1s_3 + s_1^4
\end{aligned} \tag{7.111}$$

Substituting Eqs 7.110 and 7.111 into Eq. 7.109, we have

$$\mathbf{S}^{-1} = \frac{1}{s_1s_3s_5 + s_1^9 + s_1^4s_5 + s_3^3}\begin{bmatrix} s_3s_5 + s_1^8 & s_1^2s_5 + s_1^4s_3 & s_1^6 + s_3^2 \\ s_1^2s_5 + s_1^4s_3 & s_1s_5 + s_3^2 & s_1^2s_3 + s_1^5 \\ s_1^6 + s_3^2 & s_1^5 + s_1^2s_3 & s_1s_3 + s_1^4 \end{bmatrix} \tag{7.112}$$

Once the inverse matrix of **S** is evaluated, the coefficients of the error-locator polynomial $\sigma(x)$ are easily computed from Eq. 7.107 :

$$\begin{bmatrix} \sigma_{33} \\ \sigma_{32} \\ \sigma_{31} \end{bmatrix} = \mathbf{S}^{-1}\begin{bmatrix} s_1^4 \\ s_5 \\ s_3^2 \end{bmatrix}$$

$$= \frac{1}{s_1s_3s_5 + s_1^9 + s_1^4s_5 + s_3^3}\begin{bmatrix} s_1^{12} + s_1^2s_5^2 + s_1^6s_3^2 + s_3^4 \\ s_1^8s_3 + s_1^6s_5 + s_1s_5^2 + s_3^2s_5 + s_1^2s_3^3 + s_1^5s_3^2 \\ s_1^{10} + s_1^2s_3s_5 + s_1^5s_5 + s_1s_3^3 \end{bmatrix} \tag{7.113}$$

From Eq. 7.113, the coefficients of $\sigma(x)$ become,

$$\sigma_{31} = s_1$$

$$\sigma_{32} = \frac{s_1^2 s_3 + s_5}{s_1^3 + s_3} \tag{7.114}$$

and

$$\sigma_{33} = s_1^3 + s_3 + \frac{s_1(s_1^2 s_3 + s_3)}{s_1^3 + s_3}$$

Thus, the error-locator polynomial $\sigma(x)$ can then be expressed as

$$\sigma(x) = x^3 + \sigma_{31}x^2 + \sigma_{32}x + \sigma_{33}$$

$$= x^3 + s_1 x^2 + \left(\frac{s_1^2 s_3 + s_3}{s_1^3 + s_3}\right) x + s_1^3 + s_3$$

$$+ s_1\left(\frac{s_1^2 s_3 + s_3}{s_1^3 + s_3}\right) \tag{7.115}$$

Based on Subsection 7.9.1, let us compute λ and μ by using Eq. 7.114 :

$$\lambda = \sigma_{31}^2 + \sigma_{32}$$

$$= \frac{s_1^5 + s_5}{s_1^3 + s_3}$$

and

$$\mu = \sigma_{31}\sigma_{32} + \sigma_{33} \tag{7.116}$$

$$= s_1^3 + s_3$$

These values of λ and μ are the inputs to Fig. 7.12.

Thus, a decoder for TEC-BCH codes can be constructed as shown in Fig. 7.13. ROM E converts vector expression to exponential expression. Figure 7.12 is applied to solve $y^3 + \lambda y + \mu = 0$. If $s_1 = s_3 = s_5 = 0$, we conclude that no error exists. If $s_1^3 + s_3 = 0$, switch D moves to the upward position, indicating the occurrence of a single error. If $s_1^3 + s_3 \neq 0$, switch D shifts to the downward position. In this case we conclude that a double or triple error has occurred. This is how the error-correction circuit functions in order to correct erroneous digits corresponding to the error-location numbers.

■ **Example 7.17** Consider DEC-BCH code. If a double error has occurred, at x^{j_1} and x^{j_2}, the error-pattern polynomial is expressed as $e(x) = x^{j_1} + x^{j_2}, 0 < j_1 < j_2$. Therefore, the syndrome bits are

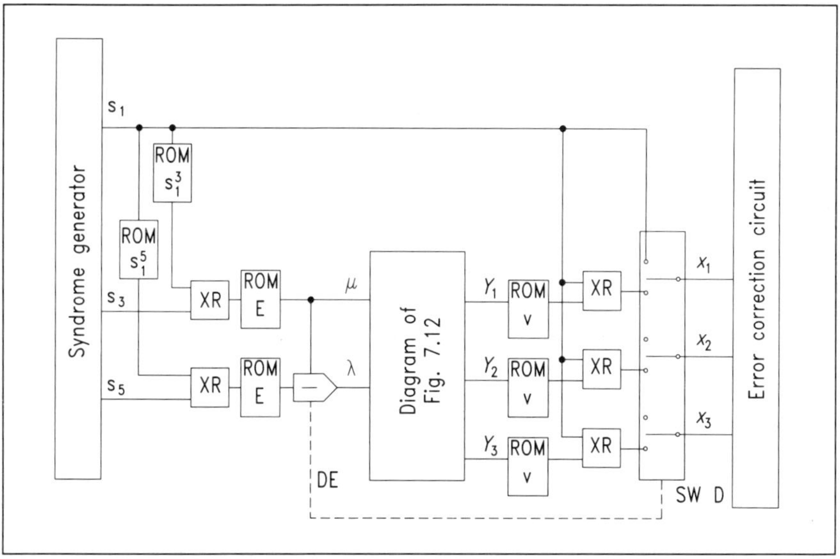

Fig. 7.13 A solution circuit for $x^3 + \sigma_{31}x^2 + \sigma_{32}x + \sigma_{33} = 0$

$$s_1 = e(\alpha) = \alpha^{j_1} + \alpha^{j_2}$$

$$s_3 = e(\alpha^3) = \alpha^{3j_1} + \alpha^{3j_2} \tag{7.117}$$

$$s_5 = e(\alpha^5) = \alpha^{5j_1} + \alpha^{5j_2}$$

Next, by using Eq. 7.100, let us calculate λ and μ for the case of double errors. Multiplying Eq. 7.100 by x yields

$$x^3 + \sigma_{21}x^2 + \sigma_{22}x = 0$$

Letting $x = y + \sigma_{21}$, this equation is reduced to

$$y^3 + (\sigma_{21}{}^2 + \sigma_{22})\,y + \sigma_{21}\sigma_{22} = 0 \tag{7.118}$$

where we can put

$$\lambda = \sigma_{21}^2 + \sigma_{22}$$

$$\mu = \sigma_{21}\sigma_{22} \tag{7.119}$$

Since $\sigma_{21} = s_1$, and $\sigma_{22} = s_1^2 + (s_3 / s_1)$ for the DEC-BCH code, it follows that

$$\lambda = s_1^2 + s_1^2 + \frac{s_3}{s_1} = \frac{s_3}{s_1}.$$

$$\mu = s_1 \left(\frac{s_1^3 + s_3}{s_1} \right) = s_1^3 + s_3 \qquad (7.120)$$

Substituting Eq. 7.117 representing the syndrome into Eq. 7.116 yields

$$\lambda = \frac{s_1^5 + s_5}{s_1^3 + s_3}$$

$$= \frac{(\alpha^{j_1} + \alpha^{j_2})^5 + (\alpha^{5j_1} + \alpha^{5j_2})}{(\alpha^{j_1} + \alpha^{j_2})^3 + (\alpha^{3j_1} + \alpha^{3j_2})} = \frac{s_3}{s_1} \qquad (7.121)$$

$$\mu = s_1^3 + s_3$$

which is identical to Eq. 7.120. This proves that both double and triple errors can be corrected by using Fig. 7.13.

7.9.3 Decoder Implementation for TEC (31, 16) BCH Code

If the received polynomial is $r(x) = x + x^{12} + x^{25}$ when the allzero code word $c(x)$ is transmitted, we know that three errors have occurred at positions x, x^{12} and x^{25} during transmission.

Since the degree of an error-locator polynomial $\sigma(x)$ is identical to the number of error digits, $\sigma(x)$ is a third-order equation, and the inverses of its roots denote the error-location numbers. Moreover, the coefficients of an error-locator polynomial are expressed by some function of syndrome components. Therefore, for solving $\sigma(x)$, the syndrome must be calculated. The syndrome consists of only odd-number components, meaning that $\mathbf{S} = (s_1, s_3, s_5)$ in this case. Since the received polynomial $r(x) = x + x^{12} + x^{25}$ is known, the syndrome components are computed by using Table 6.1.

$$s_1 = r(\alpha) = \alpha + \alpha^{12} + \alpha^{25} = 1 + \alpha^2 + \alpha^4 = \alpha^{22}$$

$$s_3 = r(\alpha^3) = \alpha^3 + \alpha^5 + \alpha^{13} = 1 + \alpha^4 = \alpha^{10} \qquad (7.122)$$

$$s_5 = r(\alpha^5) = \alpha^5 + \alpha^{29} + \alpha = \alpha + \alpha^2 + \alpha^3 = \alpha^{12}$$

Substituting Eq. 7.122 in Eq. 7.116 for a triple error, λ and μ are computed as

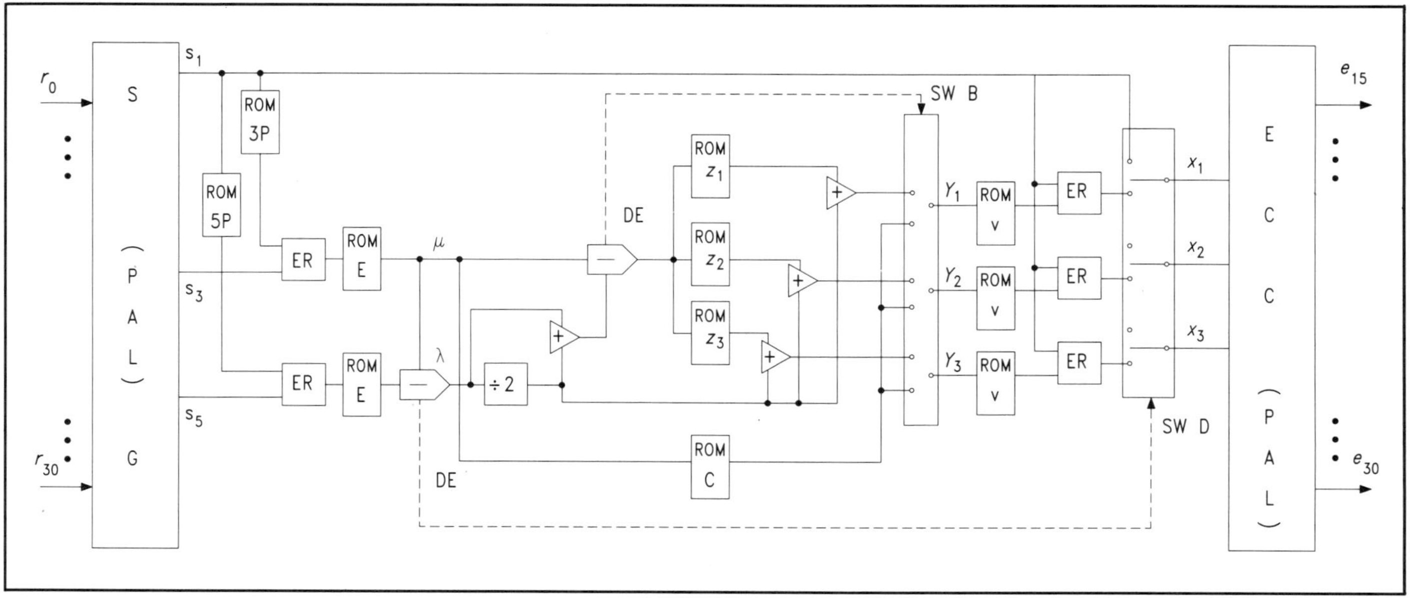

Fig. 7.14 Decoding circuit for the TEC (31, 16) BCH code

$$\lambda = \frac{s_1^5 + s_5}{s_1^3 + s_3} = \frac{1 + \alpha^2 + \alpha^3 + \alpha^4}{\alpha^4 + \alpha^{10}} = \frac{\alpha^{14}}{1} = \alpha^{14} \tag{7.123}$$

$$\mu = s_1^3 + s_3 = \alpha^4 + \alpha^{10} = 1$$

Referring to Eq. 7.104,

$$C_k = \frac{\mu}{\lambda^{3/2}} = \frac{1}{\alpha^{21}} = \alpha^{10} \tag{7.124}$$

Using Table 7.3, we have the roots $z_1 = \alpha^9$, $z_2 = \alpha^{13}$, and $z_3 = \alpha^{19}$ corresponding to $C_k = \alpha^{10}$. Since $y = \lambda^{1/2} z = \alpha^7 z$, the cubic roots for y are

$$\begin{aligned} y_1 &= \alpha^7 z_1 = \alpha^7 \alpha^9 = \alpha^{16} \\ y_2 &= \alpha^7 z_2 = \alpha^7 \alpha^{13} = \alpha^{20} \\ y_3 &= \alpha^7 z_3 = \alpha^7 \alpha^{19} = \alpha^{26} \end{aligned} \tag{7.125}$$

These roots for $C_k = \alpha^{10}$ are stored in memory. Finally, we can obtain the roots $x_i = y_i + s_1$ for $i = 1, 2, 3$, as follows:

$$\begin{aligned} x_1 &= y_1 + s_1 = \alpha^{16} + \alpha^{22} = \alpha + \alpha^2 \alpha^3 = \alpha^{12} \\ x_2 &= y_2 + s_1 = \alpha^{20} + \alpha^{22} = 1 + \alpha^3 + \alpha^4 = \alpha^{25} \\ x_3 &= y_3 + s_1 = \alpha^{26} + \alpha^{22} = \alpha \end{aligned} \tag{7.126}$$

Equation 7.126 represents three random errors occurring in positions x, x^{12}, and x^{25}. Thus, the error pattern becomes

$$e(x) = x + x^{12} + x^{25}$$

as expected. Since $r(x) = e(x)$, $c(x) = r(x) + e(x) = 0$ which indicates correct decoding because $c(x) = 0$ was assumed at the beginning.

Thus, the decoding circuit for the TEC–(31, 16) BCH code can be constructed as shown in Fig. 7.14. ROM E converts the vector expression to the exponent expression, and ROM V converts the exponent expression to the vector expression. Hence, the exponent expression is used between ROM E and ROM V. The vector expression is used throughout in the rest of Fig. 7.14.

REFERENCES

1. Berlekamp, E.R.: *Algebraic Coding Theory*, McGraw-Hill, New York, 1968.

2. Chien, R.T.: "Cyclic decoding procedure for the BCH codes", *IEEE Trans. Inform. Theory*, IT–10, pp 357–363, 1964.
3. Forney, G.D.: "On decoding BCH codes", *IEEE Trans. Inform. Theory*, IT–11, pp 577–580, 1965.
4. Koga, K.: "A new decoding method of binary BCH code", (in Japanes), *Trans. IEICE*, vol. J 66–A, no. 10, pp 925–932, Oct. 1983.
5. Gorenstein, D.C. and N. Zierler: "A class of error-correcting codes in p^m symbols," *J. Soc. Ind. Appl Math*, vol. 9, pp 207–214, 1961.
6. Lin, S. and D.J. Costello, Jr.: *Error Control Coding*, Prentice–Hall, Englewood Cliffs, N J, 1983.
7. Massey, J.L: "Step-by-step decoding of the Bose-Chaudhuri-Hocquenghem codes", *IEEE Trans. Inform. Theory*, IT–11, pp 580–585, 1965.
8. Okano, H. and H. Imai: "A construction method of high-speed decoding using ROM's for Bose-Chaudhuri-Hocquenghem and Reed-Solomon codes", *IEEE Trans Comput.*, C–36, pp 1165–1171, 1987.
9. Peterson, W.W.: "Encoding and error-correction procedures for the Bose-Chaudhuri codes", *IRE Trans. Inform. Theory*, IT–6, pp 459–470, 1960.
10. Peterson, W.W. and E.J. Weldon, Jr.: *Error-Correcting Codes*, 2nd ed., The MIT Press, Cambridge, Mass., 1972.
11. Polkinghorn, F.: "Decoding of double and triple error correcting Bose-Chaudhuri-Hocquenghem code", *IEEE Trans. Inform. Theory*, IT–12, pp 480–481, 1966.
12. Rhee, M.Y.: *Error Correcting Coding Theory*, McGraw-Hill, New York, 1989.
13. ------: *BCH Codes and Reed-Solomon Codes*, Minum Sha, Seoul, 1990.
14. Yamagishi, A. and H. Imai: "A construction method for decoders of BCH codes using ROM", *Trans. IEICE Japan*, vol. J63–D, pp 1034–1041, Dec. 1980.
15. Zierler, N.: "A complete theory for generalized BCH codes", *Proc. 1968 Symp. Error Correcting Codes*, H.B. Mann, Ed., Wiley, New York, 1969.

Chapter

8

Reed-Solomon Codes

In this chapter, we discuss an extremely important and practical class of codes–the Reed-Solomon (RS) codes–which are coming into widespread use in many digital communications and computer systems. These codes are not only used for error control in data storage systems, but in consumer audio products as well like the compact disk (CD) player or the digital audio tape recorder (DAT), to ensure high-quality sound. In particular, a concatenated RS-convolutional encoding system has been adopted for deep-space downlinks. Moreover, secure communication systems commonly use an RS code as one method for protection against jamming. Such codes are also used for ciphertext protection against false data in cryptographic systems.

An RS code is a cyclic symbol-error-correcting code. The importance of these codes lies partly in their superior error-correcting capability but an equally important aspect is the availability of efficient decoding algorithms. A number of decoding algorithms are available for the efficient decoding of RS codes. In what follows, we shall present several RS decoding methods for either random- or burst-error correction.

8.1 ENCODING OF RS CODES

An RS code is a block sequence of the finite field GF (2^m) of 2^m binary symbols, where m is the number of bits per symbol. These symbols can be viewed as the coefficients of a code polynomial $c(x) = c_0 + c_1x + \ldots + c_{n-1}x^{n-1}$ where the field element $c_i \in GF(2^m)$ represents a symbol of m bits.

An (n, k) RS code with symbols from $GF(2^m)$ has the following parameters:

$n = 2^m - 1$	code length in symbols
$k = n - 2t$	number of information symbols
$n - k = 2t$	number of check symbols
$d_0 = 2t + 1 = d_{min}$	designed distance = minimum distance

where t denotes the maximum number of error symbols that can be corrected.

Let $d(x) = c_{n-k}x^{n-k} + c_{n-k+1}x^{n-k+1} + \ldots + c_{n-1}x^{n-1}$ be the information polynomial and $p(x) = c_0 + c_1x + \ldots + c_{n-k-1}x^{n-k-1}$ the check polynomial. Then the encoded RS code polynomial is expressed as

$$c(x) = p(x) + d(x) = \sum_{i=0}^{n-1} c_i x^i \qquad (8.1)$$

where c_i, $0 \leq i \leq n - 1$, represents field elements of $GF(2^m)$.

Thus, a vector of n symbols, $(c_0, c_1, \cdots, c_{n-1})$ is a code word if and only if its corresponding polynomial $c(x)$ is a multiple of the generator polynomial $g(x)$. The common method of encoding a cyclic code is to find $p(x)$ from $d(x)$ and $g(x)$, which is accomplished by dividing $d(x)$ by $g(x)$, which results in an irrelevant quotient $q(x)$ and an important remainder $\gamma(x)$. That is,

$$d(x) = q(x)\,g(x) + \gamma(x) \qquad (8.2)$$

Substituting Eq. 8.2 in Eq. 8.1 gives

$$c(x) = p(x) + q(x)\,g(x) + \gamma(x) \qquad (8.3)$$

If we define the check bits as the negatives of the coefficients of $\gamma(x)$, i.e. if $p(x) = -\gamma(x)$, if follows that

$$c(x) = q(x)\,g(x) \qquad (8.4)$$

This ensures that the code polynomial $c(x)$ is a multiple of $g(x)$. The RS encoder performs the above division process to obtain the check polynomial $p(x)$.

Any conventional $(n, n-2t)$ RS encoder is devised by a bit-parallel multiplication with standard basis. However, we introduce here a bit-serial multiplier algorithm developed by Berlekamp (1982), which is applicable to the design of an RS encoder and is based on dual basis representation. Therefore, in order to comprehend Berlekamp's multiplier algorithm, one has to be familiar with the mathematical concepts of trace and dual basis representation.

8.1.1 Trace and Dual Basis

Designing an RS encoder according to the standard basis comprising powers of α would be somewhat complex. Therefore, we now seek another basis called the dual basis to facilitate bit-serial multiplications.

The trace of an element of β in GF (p^m) of p^m elements is defined as follows:

$$\mathrm{Tr}(\beta) = \sum_{k=0}^{m-1} \beta^{p^k} \tag{8.5}$$

For the binary field of elements $p = 2$, we have

$$\mathrm{Tr}(\beta) = \sum_{k=0}^{m-1} \beta^{2^k} \tag{8.6}$$

Theorem 8.1 If p is a prime, then $(a + b)^p \equiv a^p + b^p \equiv a + b \pmod{p}$ for some integers a and b.

Proof From the binomial theorem, we have

$$(a+b)^p = a^p + \binom{p}{1} a^{p-1} b + \cdots + \binom{p}{k} a^{p-k} b^k + \cdots + \binom{p}{p-1} ab^{p-1} + b^p$$

where the binomial coefficient $\binom{p}{k}$ is

$$\binom{p}{k} = \frac{p(p-1)\cdots(p-k+1)}{k!}$$

or $k!\binom{p}{k} = p(p-1)\cdots(p-k+1) = 0 \pmod{p}$ due to the fact that $p \mid k!$ or $p \mid \binom{p}{k}$. But delete $p \mid k!$ because it implies that $p \mid j$ for some j satisfying $1 \le j \le k \le p-1$ is impossible, Therefore, $p \mid \binom{p}{k}$ converts to a congruence $\binom{p}{k} \equiv 0 \pmod{p}$. Thus, it proves that $(a + b)^p \equiv a^p + b^p \equiv a + b \pmod{p}$ for some integers a and b.

Theorem 8.2 Consider GF (p^m) of characteristic p. Then for some elements β and p in GF (p^m), $(\beta + \gamma)^{p^m} = \beta^{p^m} + \gamma^{p^m}$.

Proof From Theorem 8.1, $(\beta + \gamma))^p = \beta^p + \gamma^p$ modulo p in GF (p^m). Raising this equation to the pth power yields $[(\beta + \gamma)^p]^p = (\beta^p + \gamma^p)^p$, or $(\beta + \gamma)^{p^2} = \beta^{p^2} + \gamma^{p^2}$. If this is done $m - 1$ times, we have

$$(\beta + \gamma)^{p^m} = \beta^{p^m} + \gamma^{p^m} \tag{8.7}$$

However, we must know that $\binom{p}{i} = 1$ for $i = 0$ and p, but $\binom{p}{i} = 0$ for $1 \le i \le p - 1$ simply because $\binom{p}{i} = \frac{p(p-1)!}{i!(p-i)!}$ is a multiple of p, i.e., $p \mid \binom{p}{i}$, and equals zero modulo p. This completes the proof of the theorem.

■ **Example 8.1** Show that a trace has the following properties [11].

1. $\mathrm{Tr}(\beta + \gamma) = \mathrm{Tr}(\beta) + \mathrm{Tr}(\gamma), \quad \beta, \gamma \in \mathrm{GF}(p^m)$
2. $[\mathrm{Tr}(\beta)]^p = \mathrm{Tr}(\beta^p) = \mathrm{Tr}(\beta), \quad \beta \in \mathrm{GF}(p^m)$
3. $\mathrm{Tr}(c\,\beta) = c\,\mathrm{Tr}(\beta), \quad c \in \mathrm{GF}(p)$
4. $\mathrm{Tr}(1) = m \pmod p$

Verification

1. $$\mathrm{Tr}(\beta + \gamma) = \sum_{k=0}^{m-1} (\beta + \gamma)^{p^k} = \sum_{k=0}^{m-1} \left(\beta^{p^k} + \gamma^{p^k}\right)$$
   $$= \sum_{k=0}^{m-1} \beta^{p^k} + \sum_{k=0}^{m-1} \gamma^{p^k} = \mathrm{Tr}(\beta) + \mathrm{Tr}(\gamma)$$

2. $$[\mathrm{Tr}(\beta)]^p = \left[\sum_{k=0}^{m-1} \beta^{p^k}\right]^p = \left[\beta + \beta^p + \beta^{p^2} + \cdots + \beta^{p^{m-1}}\right]^p$$
   $$= \left[\beta^p + \beta^{p^2} + \beta^{p^3} + \cdots + \beta^{p^{m-1}} + \beta^{p^m}\right]$$
   $$= \left[\beta + \beta^p + \beta^{p^2} + \cdots + \beta^{p^{m-1}}\right] = \mathrm{Tr}(\beta)$$

   because $\beta^{p^m} = \beta$.

3. $$\mathrm{Tr}(c\beta) = \sum_{k=0}^{m-1} (c\beta)^{p^k} = \sum_{k=0}^{m-1} c^{p^k} \beta^{p^k}$$

   Since $c^{p^k} \in \mathrm{GF}(p)$, c^{p^k} can be written as $c \in \mathrm{GF}(p)$. Therefore,

$$\text{Tr}(c\beta) = c \sum_{k=0}^{m-1} \beta^{p^k} = c\,\text{Tr}(\beta).$$

4. $\text{Tr}(1) = \sum_{k=0}^{m-1} (1)^{p^k} = (1)(m) = m \pmod{p}$.

A basis $\{\beta_i\}$ in GF (p^m) comprises a set of m linearly independent elements of GF (p^m). Two basis $\{\beta_i\}$ and $\{\mu_i\}$ are said to be dual if and only if

$$\text{Tr}(\beta_i\,\mu_j) = \begin{cases} 1 & \text{if } i = j \\ 0 & \text{otherwise} \end{cases} \tag{8.8}$$

Thus, the basis $\{\beta_i\} = \{\alpha^k\}$, $0 \le k \le m-1$, is called the standard basis of GF (p^m), and the basis $\{\mu_j\}$ is called the dual whose field element is expressed by

$$Z = z_0\,\mu_0 + z_1\mu_1 + \cdots + z_{m-1}\,\mu_{m-1}$$

$$= \sum_{k=0}^{m-1} z_k\,\mu_k \tag{8.9}$$

This new dual basis $\{\mu_i\}$ facilitates bit-serial multiplication. Multiplying Eq. 8.9 by α^k and taking the trace, we have

$$\text{Tr}(Z\alpha^k) = \text{Tr}\left(\alpha^k \sum_{i=0}^{m-1} z_i\,\mu_i\right) = \sum_{i=0}^{m-1} \text{Tr}(z_i\,\mu_i\,\alpha^k)$$

$$= \sum_{i=0}^{m-1} z_i\,\text{Tr}(\mu_i\,\alpha^k) = z_k \tag{8.10}$$

if and only if $i = k$. Thus, Eq. 8.10 represents the kth coefficient of the dual basis.

■ **Example 8.2** Express a field element of a dual basis $\{\mu_j\}$ as

$$Z = z_0\mu_0 + z_1\mu_1 + \cdots + z_{m-1}\,\mu_{m-1}$$

where $z_k = \text{Tr}\,(Z\,\alpha^k)$ for $0 \le k \le m-1$ and α^k is an element of GF (p^m). Multiplying Z of $\{\mu_j\}$ by α yields

$$Z\,\alpha = z_0\,\alpha\,\mu_0 + z_1\,\alpha\,\mu_1 + \cdots + z_{m-1}\,\alpha\,\mu_{m-1}$$

$$= z_0^1\,\mu_0 + z_1^1\,\mu_1 + \cdots + z_{m-1}^1\,\mu_{m-1}$$

where $z_k^1 = z_k\,\alpha$ for $0 \le k \le m-1$ and α is a root of a primitive polynomial of degree m in GF (p^m). Thus, using Eq. 8.10, the coefficients of $Z\alpha$ are

$$z_0^1 = \mathrm{Tr}(Z\,\alpha \cdot \alpha^0) = \mathrm{Tr}(Z\alpha) = z_1$$

$$z_1^1 = \mathrm{Tr}(Z\alpha \cdot \alpha^1) = \mathrm{Tr}(Z\alpha^2) = z_2$$

$$z_2^1 = \mathrm{Tr}(Z\alpha \cdot \alpha^2) = \mathrm{Tr}(Z\alpha^3) = z_3$$

$$\cdot\ \cdot\ \cdot\ \cdot\ \cdot\ \cdot\ \cdot\ \cdot\ \cdot\ \cdot\ \cdot\ \cdot\ \cdot$$

$$z_{m-2}^1 = \mathrm{Tr}(Z\alpha \cdot \alpha^{m-2}) = \mathrm{Tr}(Z\alpha^{m-1}) = z_{m-1}$$

$$z_{m-1}^1 = \mathrm{Tr}(Z\alpha \cdot \alpha^{m-1}) = \mathrm{Tr}(Z\alpha^m)$$

Thus, in summary, we have

$$z_k^1 = \begin{cases} \mathrm{Tr}(Z\alpha^{k+1}) = z_{k+1} & 0 \le k \le m-2 \\ \mathrm{Tr}(Z\alpha^m) & k = m-1 \end{cases} \tag{8.11}$$

Next, consider the multiplication of Z by α^2 such that

$$Z\alpha^2 = z_0\alpha^2\mu_0 + z_1\alpha^2\mu_1 + \cdots + z_{m-1}\,\alpha^2\mu_{m-1}$$

$$= z_0^2\mu_0 + z_1^2\mu_1 + \cdots + z_{m-1}^2\mu_{m-1}$$

where $z_k^2 = z_k\alpha^2$ for $0 \le k \le m-1$. Thus, the coefficients of $Z\,\alpha^2$ are

$$z_0^2 = \mathrm{Tr}(Z\alpha^2) = z_2$$

$$z_1^2 = \mathrm{Tr}(Z\alpha^3) = z_3$$

$$\cdot\ \cdot\ \cdot\ \cdot\ \cdot\ \cdot\ \cdot\ \cdot$$

$$z_{m-2}^2 = \mathrm{Tr}(Z\alpha^m)$$

$$z_{m-1}^2 = \mathrm{Tr}(Z\alpha^{m+1})$$

Let G be a known constant, say from among the coefficients of the generator polynomial $g(x)$ in GF (2^m), expressed in standard basis as

$$G = g_0 + g_1\,\alpha + g_2\,\alpha^2 + \cdots + g_{m-1}\,\alpha^{m-1} \tag{8.12}$$

If we express the product $Y = GZ$ according to dual basis, we have

$$Y = GZ = \sum_{k=0}^{m-1} g_k\, z_k\, \mu_k = \sum_{k=0}^{m-1} \mathrm{Tr}(GZ\alpha^k)\,\mu_k$$

$$= \mathrm{Tr}(GZ)\,\mu_0 + \mathrm{Tr}(GZ\alpha)\,\mu_1 + \cdots + \mathrm{Tr}(GZ\alpha^{m-1})\,\mu_{m-1} \tag{8.13}$$

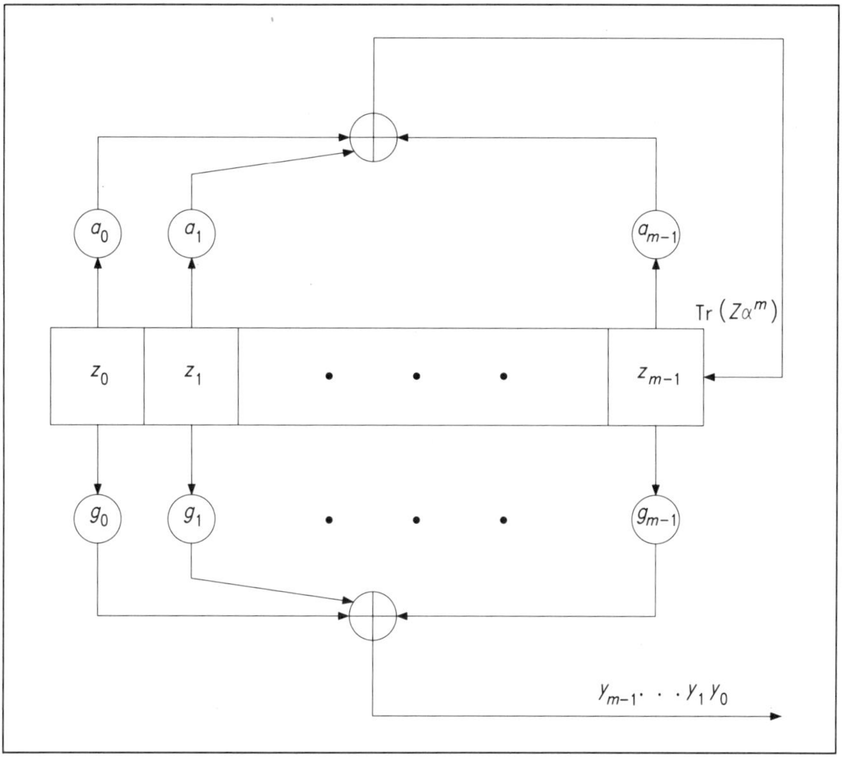

Fig. 8.1 Bit-serial multiplier

Utilizing $g_k z_k = \mathrm{Tr}\ (GZ\,\alpha^k)$ for $0 \le k \le m - 1$, the coefficients of Y are obtained as

$$y_0 = \mathrm{Tr}(GZ\alpha^0) = g_0 z_0 + g_1 z_1 + \cdots + g_{m-1} z_{m-1}$$

$$y_1 = \mathrm{Tr}(GZ\alpha^1) = g_0 z_0^1 + g_1 z_1^1 + \cdots + g_{m-1}\mathrm{Tr}(Z\alpha^m)$$

$$y_2 = \mathrm{Tr}(GZ\alpha^2) = g_0 z_0^2 + g_1 z_1^2 + \cdots + g_{m-1}\mathrm{Tr}(Z\alpha^{m+1}) \tag{8.14}$$

$$\cdots\cdots\cdots\cdots\cdots\cdots$$

$$y_{m-1} = \mathrm{Tr}(GZ\alpha^{m-1})$$

Interpreting Eq. 8.14, $y_0 = \mathrm{Tr}\ (GZ)$ is a single parity-check bit on some subset of the bits in the m-bit Z register; $y_1 = \mathrm{Tr}\ (GZ\,\alpha)$ is obtained from the same parity-check bit simply by shifting Z to $Z\ \alpha$. Thus, $y_k = \mathrm{Tr}\ (GZ\,\alpha^k)$ is easily computed recursively on k for $0 \le k \le m - 1$.

Let $$\alpha^m = a_0 + a_1 \alpha + a_2 \alpha^2 + \cdots + a_{m-1} \alpha^{m-1} \tag{8.15}$$

Then $$\mathrm{Tr}(Z\alpha^m) = z_0 a_0 + z_1 a_1 + \cdots + z_{m-1} a_{m-1} \tag{8.16}$$

By making use of Eqs. 8.14 and 8.16, a bit-serial multiplier can be implemented by shifting and EX-OR operations, as shown in Fig. 8.1.

■ **Example 8.3** Consider the field elements of GF (2^5). Let α be a root of the primitive polynomial $p(x) = 1 + x^2 + x^5$ over GF(2). Then the elements of GF (2^5) are representable by 0 and α^i, $0 \le i \le 30$. If an element Z in GF (2^5) is represented from the standard basis $\{\alpha^k\}$ for $0 \le k \le 4$, it can be expressed as $Z = \lambda_0 + \lambda_1 \alpha + \lambda_2 \alpha^2 + \lambda_3 \alpha^3 + \lambda_4 \alpha^4$, where $\lambda_k \in$ GF (2). Then,

$$\mathrm{Tr}(Z) = \lambda_0 \mathrm{Tr}(1) + \lambda_1 \mathrm{Tr}(\alpha) + \lambda_2 \mathrm{Tr}(\alpha^2) + \lambda_3 \mathrm{Tr}(\alpha^3) + \lambda_4 \mathrm{Tr}(\alpha^4) \tag{8.17}$$

where $\mathrm{Tr}(1) = 5 \pmod 2 = 1$

$$\begin{aligned} \mathrm{Tr}(\alpha) &= \alpha + \alpha^2 + \alpha^4 + \alpha^8 + \alpha^{16} = 0 \\ \mathrm{Tr}(\alpha^2) &= \mathrm{Tr}(\alpha) = 0 \\ \mathrm{Tr}(\alpha^3) &= a^3 + \alpha^6 + \alpha^{12} + \alpha^{24} + \alpha^{17} = 1 \\ \mathrm{Tr}(\alpha^4) &= \mathrm{Tr}(\alpha) = 0 \end{aligned} \tag{8.18}$$

Thus Eq. 8.17 becomes

$$\mathrm{Tr}(Z) = \lambda_0 + \lambda_3$$

A standard basis $\{\beta_i\} = \{\alpha^k\}$ for $0 \le k \le m-1$ and $0 \le i \le 2^m - 2$ is a set of m independent elements. Let us find the dual basis $\{\mu_j) = \{\mu_0, \mu_1, \cdots, \mu_{m-1}\}$ of $\{\alpha^k)$ in GF (2^m). Utilizing Eqs 8.9 and 8.10, we can determine the coefficients of Z which are represented as $z_k = \mathrm{Tr}\,(Z\,\alpha^k)$ for $0 \le k \le m-1$. If we set $Z = \alpha^i$ over $0 \le i \le 2^m - 2$, the coefficients of Z are obtained from $z_k = \mathrm{Tr}(\alpha^{i+k})$ for $0 \le k \le m-1$.

■ **Example 8.4** Let us determine the coefficients z_k of $Z = \alpha^4$ in GF (2^5). The finite field GF (2^5) is generated by α which is a root of the primitive polynomial $p(x) = 1 + x^2 + x^5$ over GF (2). Hence, the coefficients $z_k = \mathrm{Tr}\,(\alpha^{i+k}) = \mathrm{Tr}\,(\alpha^{4+k})$ for $0 \le k \le 4$ are computed as follows:

$$z_0 = \mathrm{Tr}(\alpha^4) = 0$$

$$z_1 = \mathrm{Tr}(\alpha^5) = \mathrm{Tr}(1 + \alpha^2) = 1$$

$$z_2 = \mathrm{Tr}(\alpha^6) = \mathrm{Tr}(\alpha + \alpha^3) = 1 \tag{8.19}$$

$$z_3 = \mathrm{Tr}(\alpha^7) = \mathrm{Tr}(\alpha^2 + \alpha^4) = 0$$

$$z_4 = \mathrm{Tr}(\alpha^8) = \mathrm{Tr}(1 + \alpha^2 + \alpha^3) = 0$$

Thus, the dual basis representation of $Z = \alpha^4$ is (0 1 1 0 0).

■ **Example 8.5** Compute the trace and find the dual basis corresponding to the standard basis $\{\alpha^i\}$, $0 \le i \le 30$, in GF (2^5). Continuous computation of $z_k = \mathrm{Tr}\,(\alpha^{4+k})$ for $5 \le k \le 27$ results in the following trace values:

$$\mathrm{Tr}\,(\alpha^9) = \mathrm{Tr}(\alpha + \alpha^3 + \alpha^4) = 1$$

$$\mathrm{Tr}(\alpha^{10}) = \mathrm{Tr}(1 + \alpha^4) = 1$$

. . . .

$$\mathrm{Tr}(\alpha^{18}) = \mathrm{Tr}(1 + \alpha) = 1$$

$$\mathrm{Tr}(\alpha^{19}) = \mathrm{Tr}(\alpha + \alpha^2) = 0 \tag{8.20}$$

. . . .

$$\mathrm{Tr}(\alpha^{28}) = \mathrm{Tr}(\alpha + \alpha^2 + \alpha^4) = 0$$

$$\mathrm{Tr}(\alpha^{29}) = \mathrm{Tr}(1 + \alpha^3) = 0$$

$$\mathrm{Tr}(\alpha^{30}) = \mathrm{Tr}(\alpha + \alpha^4) = 0$$

Combining Eqs 8.18, 8.19 and 8.20, the trace values Tr (α^i) for $0 \le i \le 30$ are computed and tabulated in the third column of Table 8.1. The elements of the dual basis $\{\mu_j\}$ corresponding to any standard basis $\{\alpha^i\}$, $0 \le i \le 2^m - 2$, can be obtained by counting m digits downward from Tr (α^i) to Tr (α^{i+m-1}). For example, since Tr $(\alpha^{19}) = 0$, Tr $(\alpha^{20}) = 1$, Tr = $(\alpha^{21}) = 1$, Tr $(\alpha^{22}) = 1$, and Tr $(\alpha^{23}) = 0$, the dual basis $(z_0, z_1, z_2, z_3, z_4)$ corresponding to the standard basis (0 1 1 0 0) of $\{\alpha^{19}\}$ over GF (2^5) is (0 1 1 1 0). Thus, the elements of both standard and dual bases over GF(2^5) generated by $\alpha^5 = 1 + \alpha^2$ are tabulated in Table 8.1. In this table, we may observe that the dual basis $\{\mu_0, \mu_1, \mu_2, \mu_3, \mu_4\}$, of the standard basis is the ordered set $\{\alpha^{26}, \alpha^{25}, \alpha^{29}, \alpha^{27}\}$.

8.1.2 Bit-serial RS Encoder

The generator polynomial of an (n, k) RS code is defined as

$$g(x) = \prod_{i=0}^{2t-1} (x + \alpha^{\rho+i}) = \sum_{i=0}^{2t} g_i x_i \tag{8.21}$$

where α is a primitive element of GF (2^m) and ρ is a nonnegative integer. By choosing an appropriate value of ρ, the coefficients of $g(x)$ can be made symmetric, reducing the complexity of the encoder. If $d_{min}-1$ is

Table 8.1 Elements of Standard and Dual Bases over GF (2^5) Generated by $\alpha^5 = 1 + \alpha^2$

Power (i)	Elements of standard base	Tr(α^i)	Elements of dual base
–	00000	0	00000
0	10000	1	10010
1	01000	0	00101
2	00100	0	01011
3	00010	1	10110
4	00001	0	01100
5	10100	1	11001
6	01010	1	10011
7	00101	0	00111
8	10110	0	01111
9	01011	1	11111
10	10001	1	11110
11	11100	1	11100
12	01110	1	11000
13	00111	1	10001
14	10111	0	00011
15	11111	0	00110
16	11011	0	01101
17	11001	1	11011
18	11000	1	10111
19	01100	0	01110
20	00110	1	11101
21	00011	1	11010
22	10101	1	10101
23	11110	0	01010
24	01111	1	10100
25	10011	0	01000
26	11101	1	10000
27	11010	0	00001
28	01101	0	00010
29	10010	0	00100
30	01001	0	01001

even, the preferred value is $\rho = [(2^m-1)-(d_{min}-2)]/2$. If $d_{min}-1$ is odd, $\rho = -(d_{min}-2)/2$. In either case, the preferred value of ρ ensures that $g(x) = x^{2t}g(1/x)$, which makes the coefficients of $g(x)$ symmetric. That is,

$$\begin{aligned} g_0 &= g_{2t} \\ g_1 &= g_{2t-1} \\ &\cdots \\ g_{2t} &= g_0 \end{aligned} \tag{8.22}$$

Hence, making $g(x)$ symmetric (or reversible) ensures reducing the number of coefficients of $g(x)$ by half. In this manner, the complexity of the encoder can be reduced substantially.

An (n, k) RS encoder, using a dual basis over GF (2^m), can be serialized by using Berlekamp's multiplier algorithm as shown in Fig. 8.2. Berlekamp's algorithm requires simply shifting and EX-OR operations. In Fig. 8.2, the trace circuit (or product unit) is used to compute $T_0, T_1, \cdots, T_{2t}$ as follows:

$$\begin{aligned} T_0 &= \mathrm{Tr}(g_0 Z) \\ T_1 &= \mathrm{Tr}(g_1 Z) \\ &\cdots \\ T_{2t} &= \mathrm{Tr}(g_{2t} Z) \end{aligned} \tag{8.23}$$

where Z is a field element of GF (2^m) representing a multiplicand, and g_i, $0 \le i \le 2t$ denotes generator coefficients representing the fixed multiplier. In addition, the output of the trace computation circuit which is fed back into the Z register is

$$T_f = \mathrm{Tr}(\alpha^m Z) \tag{8.24}$$

■ **Example 8.6** Consider a bit-serial (31, 27) RS encoder. Since $n = 31$, we know that $m = 5$ from $2^m = 32$. Therefore, the field element Z is from GF (2^5). Also, since $t = (n-k)/2 = 4/2 = 2$, a (31, 27) RS code is a DSEC code. Because $d_{min} - 1 = 2t$ is even, the preferred value of ρ is $\rho = [(2^m - 1) - (d_{min} - 2)]/2 = 28/2 = 14$.

In general, the generator polynomial of a DSEC (31, 27) RS code is

$$\begin{aligned} g(x) &= (x+\alpha)(x+\alpha^2)(x+\alpha^3)(x+\alpha^4) \\ &= \alpha^{10} + \alpha^{29}x + \alpha^{19}x^2 + \alpha^{24}x^3 + x^4 \end{aligned} \tag{8.25}$$

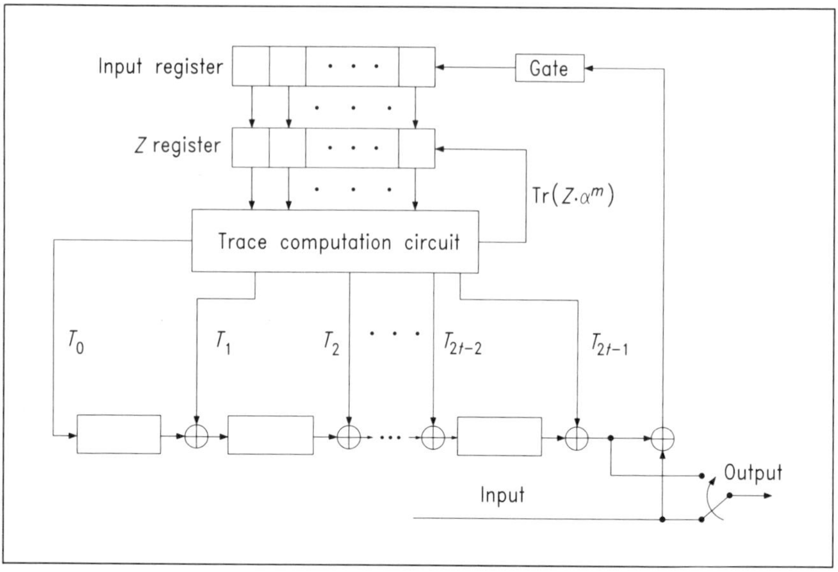

Fig. 8.2 The block diagram of an (n, k) bit-serial RS encoder

In order to make the coefficients of $g(x)$ symmetric, we choose $\rho = 14$ from $2\rho + 2t-1 = 2^m-1$ for $t = 2$ and $m = 5$. Then the generator polynomial for symmetric structure expresses as shown below.

$$g(x) = \prod_{i=0}^{3} (x + \alpha^{14+i})$$

$$= (x + \alpha^{14})(x + \alpha^{15})(x + \alpha^{16})(x + \alpha^{17})$$

$$= 1 + \alpha^6 x + \alpha^{14} x^2 + \alpha^6 x^3 + x^4 \qquad (8.26)$$

where $g_0 = g_4 = 1$, $g_1 = g_3 = \alpha^6$, and $g_2 = \alpha^{14}$, which bears out the symmetry of $g(x)$. Next, the values of T_i, $0 \le i \le 4$, are computed from the trace computation circuit, but we need them only for $i = 0, 1, 2$ because $T_0 = T_4$ and $T_1 = T_3$.

$$T_0 = \mathrm{Tr}(g_0 Z) = \mathrm{Tr}(\alpha^0 Z) = z_0$$

$$T_1 = \mathrm{Tr}(g_1 Z) = \mathrm{Tr}(\alpha^6 Z) = \mathrm{Tr}((\alpha + \alpha^3)Z) = z_1 + z_3$$

$$T_2 = \mathrm{Tr}(g_2 Z) = \mathrm{Tr}(\alpha^{14} Z) = \mathrm{Tr}((1 + \alpha^2 + \alpha^3 + \alpha^4)Z)$$

$$= z_0 + z_2 + z_3 + z_4 \qquad (8.27)$$

$$T_f = \mathrm{Tr}(\alpha^m Z) = \mathrm{Tr}(\alpha^5 Z) = ((1 + \alpha^2)Z) = z_0 + z_2$$

Figure 8.3, shows a DSEC bit-serial (31, 27) RS encoder based on Fig. 8.2 and Eq. 8.27.

The encoder accepts one bit of an information symbol at a time and performs one step of Berlekamp's algorithm. Immediately after all the information symbols are fed into the encoder, the check symbols are available for transmission. Then the encoder is ready to process the next code sequence. Since a bit cycle is defined to be the time interval needed to execute one step of Berlekamp's algorithm, a symbol cycle is the time interval required to perform a complete cycle of this algorithm. Since a symbol has five bits in this example, a symbol cycle contains a 5-bits cycle. Therefore, the computation of a complete code word will require 32 symbol cycles.

Conventional bit-parallel (n, k) RS encoders are covered in detail in several textbooks. An RS code is a block sequence of finite field GF (2^m) of 2^m binary symbols, where m is the number of bits per symbol. A vector of n symbols $(c_0, c_1, \cdots, c_{n-1})$ is a code word if and only if its corresponding polynomial $c(x)$ is a multiple of the generator polynomial $g(x)$. This generator polynomial of a t-error-correcting RS code of length 2^m-1 is defined as:

$$g(x) = (x + \alpha)(x + \alpha^2) \cdot \quad \cdot \quad \cdot (x + \alpha^{2t}) = \sum_{i=0}^{2t} g_i x^i \tag{8.28}$$

where the coefficients g_i, $0 \le i \le 2t$, are from GF (2^m).

■ **Example 8.7** Considerthe conventional DSEC (31, 27) RS code with symbols from GF (2^5). Since $m = 5$ and $t = 2$, we have $k = 31-2t = 31-4 = 27$ information symbols. The generator polynomial of this code is $g(x) = \alpha^{10} + \alpha^{29}x + \alpha^{19}x^2 + \alpha^{24}x^3 + x^4$. Let an information symbol be

$$d(\alpha) = a_0 + a_1\alpha + a_2\alpha^2 + a_3\alpha^3 + a_4\alpha^4$$

where $a_i \in$ GF (2), $0 \le i \le 4$.

Multiplying $d(\alpha)$ by the coefficients of $g(x)$ results in

$$\begin{aligned} \alpha^{10}d(\alpha) &= (a_0 + a_1 + a_4) + (a_1 + a_2)\alpha + (a_1 + a_2 + a_3 + a_4)\alpha^2 + \\ &\quad (a_2 + a_3 + a_4)\alpha^3 + (a_0 + a_3 + a_4)\alpha^4 \\ \alpha^{29}d(\alpha) &= (a_0 + a_2) + (a_1 + a_3)\alpha + a_4\alpha^2 + a_0\alpha^3 + a_1\alpha^4 \\ \alpha^{19}d(\alpha) &= (a_3 + a_4) + (a_0 + a_4)\alpha + (a_0 + a_1 + a_3 + a_4)\alpha^2 + \\ &\quad (a_1 + a_2 + a_4)\alpha^3 + (a_2 + a_3)\alpha^4 \end{aligned} \tag{8.29}$$

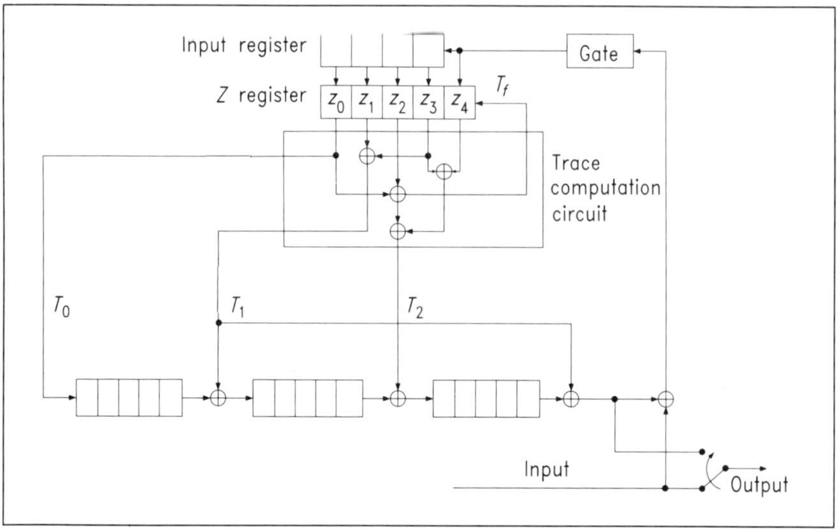

Fig. 8.3 The DSEC bit-serial (31, 27) RS encoder

$$\alpha^{24}d(\alpha) = (a_1 + a_2 + a_3) + (a_0 + a_2 + a_3 + a_4)\,\alpha + (a_0 + a_2 + a_4)$$

$$\alpha^2 + (a_0 + a_1 + a_3)\,\alpha^3 + (a_0 + a_1 + a_2 + a_4)\,\alpha^4$$

Using Eq. 8.29, the GF (2^5) multipliers can be convereted into adders to make implementation straightforward. The layout of this (31, 27) RS encoder is shown in Fig. 8.4.

Next consider again the (31, 27) RS encoder with the symmetrical generator $g(x) = 1 + \alpha^6 x + \alpha^{14} x^2 + \alpha^6 x^3 + x^4$ at $\rho = 14$. Multiplying $d\,(\alpha)$ by the coefficients of $g(x)$ yields:

$$\alpha^6 d(\alpha) = (a_2 + a_4) + (a_0 + a_3)\,\alpha + (a_1 + a_2)\,\alpha^2$$

$$+(a_0 + a_2 + a_3)\,\alpha^3 + (a_1 + a_3 + a_4)\,\alpha^4 \qquad (8.30)$$

$$\alpha^{14} d(\alpha) = (a_0 + a_1 + a_2 + a_3 + a_4) + (a_1 + a_2 + a_3 + a_4)\,\alpha +$$

$$(a_0 + a_1)\,\alpha^2 + (a_0 + a_1 + a_2)\,\alpha^3 + (a_0 + a_1 + a_2 + a_3)\,\alpha^4$$

Utilizing Eq. 8.30, the DSEC (31, 27) RS encoder can be implemented as shown in Fig. 8.5.

We have so far discussed Berlekamp's bit-serial RS encoders, using a dual basis over GF (2^m). A comparative study has also been made between a bit-serial RS encoder and a conventional bit-parallel RS encoder. A comparison of Figs 8.3 and 8.5 reveals that the bit-serial RS

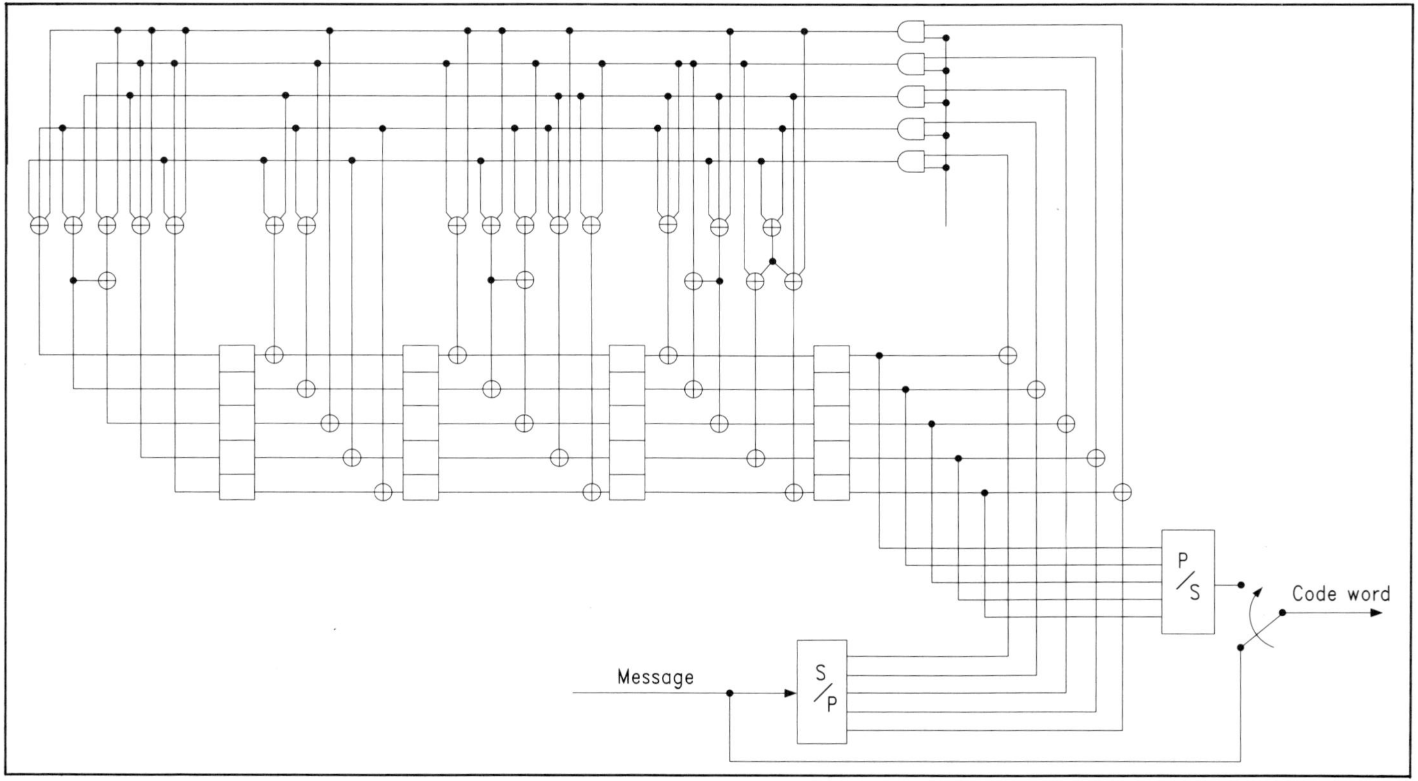

Fig. 8.4 The conventional DSEC (31, 27) RS encoder based on $g(x) = \alpha^{10} + \alpha^{29} + \alpha^{19} x^2 + \alpha^{24} x^3 + x^4$

encoder requires less hardware than the conventional bit-parallel RS encoder even with the symmetrical generator $g(x)$. By making the coefficients of $g(x)$ symmetric, the complexity of the conventional RS encoder can be reduced by choosing an appropriate value of ρ.

8.2 DECODING OF RS CODES

Exactly the same steps as required for decoding a binary BCH code can be applied to RS decoding, except for error-value computation. Several decoding algorithms and methods may be used for RS codes. We shall present the methods of (i) Peterson, Gorenstein and Zierler, (ii) Chien, (iii) Berlekamp, Peterson and Massey, (iv) Digital Fourier Transform (DFT), (v) the Euclidean algorithm coupled with a systolic array cell, and (vi) direct decoding without using the iterative algorithm. Of these six methods, the theory and analysis of (i), (ii) and (iii) have already been covered in Chapter 7. Therefore, we shall discuss methods (iv), (v) and (vi) in detail here.

8.2.1 Error Value Computation

If the error pattern $e(x)$ contains ν errors, $0 \le \nu \le t$, at the locations x^{j_k}, $1 \le k \le \nu$, we have

$$e(x) = e_{j_1} x^{j_1} + e_{j_2} x^{j_2} + \cdots + e_{j_\nu} x^{j_\nu} \tag{8.31}$$

In order to determine $e(x)$, we need to know the error location x^{j_k} and the error values e_{j_k} for $1 \le k \le \nu$.

As with binary BCH codes, the error-locator polynomial $\sigma(x)$ for a ν-error-correcting RS code

$$\begin{aligned}\sigma(x) &= \prod_{\lambda=1}^{\nu} (1 + \alpha^{j_\lambda} x) \\ &= 1 + \sigma_1 x + \sigma_2 x^2 + \cdots + \sigma_{\nu-1} x^{\nu-1} + \sigma_\nu x^\nu \end{aligned} \tag{8.32}$$

can also be derived from Berlekamp's algorithm.

Let the syndrome polynomial be

$$s(x) = s_0 + s_1 x + s_2 x^2 + \cdots + s_\nu x^\nu = \sum_{\lambda=0}^{\nu} s_\lambda x^\lambda \qquad \nu \le 2t \tag{8.33}$$

where $s_0 = 1$. Using Eqs 8.32 and 8.33, the error-evaluator polynomial $\Omega(x)$ is defined as the product of $\sigma(x)$ and $s(x)$ such that

$$\begin{aligned}\Omega(x) = \sigma(x)s(x) = 1 &+ (s_1 + \sigma_1)x + (s_2 + \sigma_1 s_1 + \sigma_2)x^2 + \cdots \\ &+ (s_\nu + \sigma_1 s_{\nu-1} + \cdots + \sigma_\nu)x^\nu \end{aligned} \tag{8.34}$$

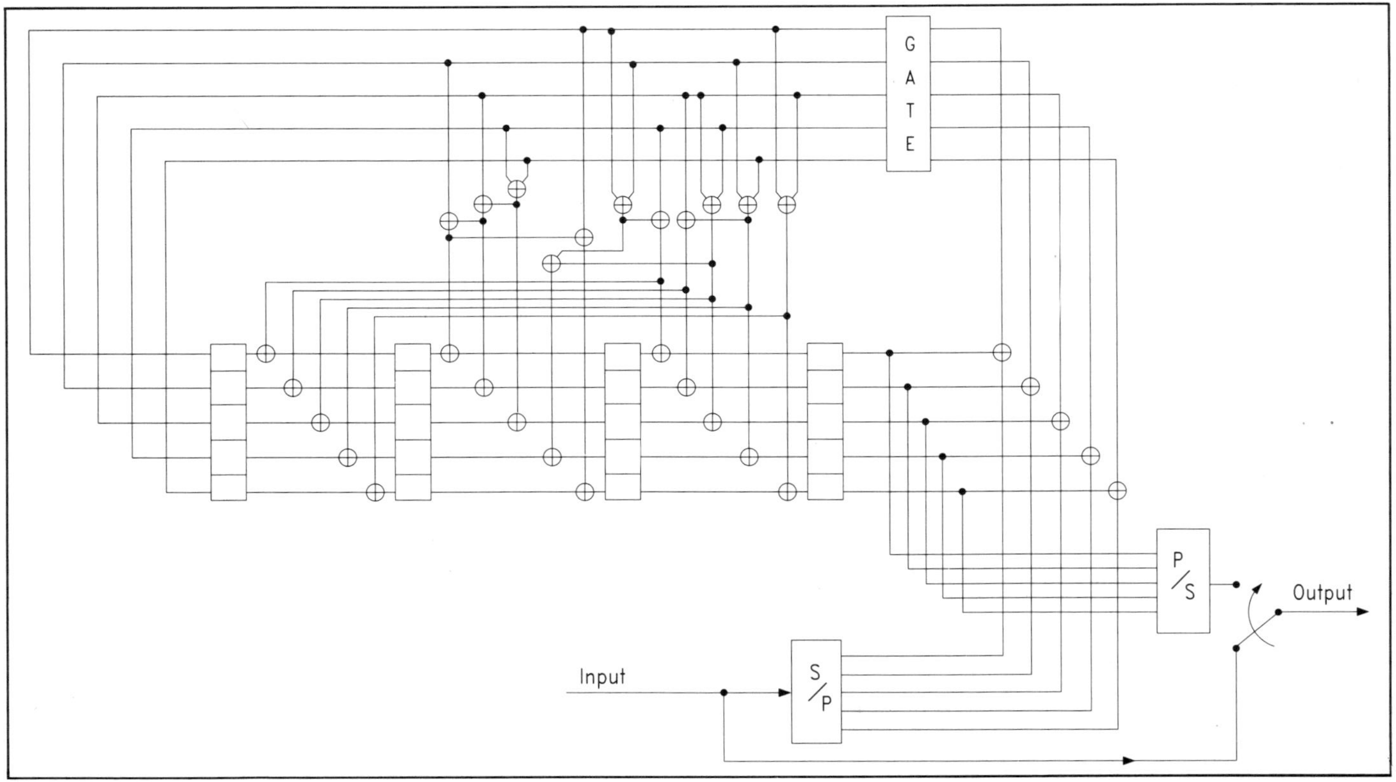

Fig. 8.5 The conventional DSEC (31, 27) RS encoder based on the symmetrical generator $g(x) = 1 + \alpha^6 x + \alpha^{14} x^2 + \alpha^6 x^3 + x^4$

For RS codes, the error-evaluator polynomial $\Omega(x)$ is used to find the error value (or error magnitude) at each error location as described below.

Suppose v errors have occurred in locations corresponding to the indices $j_1 < j_2 < \cdots < j_v \le n - 1$. Then the syndrome components can be expressed as

$$s_\lambda = \sum_{k=1}^{v} e_{j_k} (\alpha^{j_k})^\lambda \qquad 1 \le \lambda \le 2t \tag{8.35}$$

where α^{j_k} for $k = 1, 2, \cdots, v$ are defined as the error-location numbers at position indices j_k. For convenience, let us consider a syndrome polynomial of infinite degree:

$$s(x) = \sum_{\lambda=0}^{\infty} s_\lambda x^\lambda \tag{8.36}$$

Substituting Eq. 8.35 in Eq. 8.36 gives

$$s(x) = \sum_{k=1}^{v} e_{j_k} \sum_{\lambda=0}^{\infty} \left(\alpha^{j_k}\right)^\lambda x^\lambda \tag{8.37}$$

If the following identity

$$\sum_{\lambda=0}^{\infty} \alpha^{\lambda j_k} x^\lambda = 1 + \alpha^{j_k} x + \alpha^{2j_k} x^2 + \cdots = \frac{1}{1 + \alpha^{j_k} x}$$

is utilized, Eq. 8.37 becomes

$$s(x) = \sum_{k=1}^{v} \frac{e_{j_k}}{1 + \alpha^{j_k} x} \tag{8.38}$$

Using Eqs 8.32 and 8.38, the error-evaluator polynomial of degree less than v may be expressed as

$$\Omega(x) = \sum_{k=1}^{v} e_{j_k} \prod_{\substack{\lambda=1 \\ \lambda \ne k}}^{v} \left(1 + \alpha^{j_\lambda} x\right) \tag{8.39}$$

Thus, the error value at location $x = \alpha^{-j_m}$ is easily obtained as

$$e_{j_m} = \frac{\Omega(\alpha^{-j_m})}{\prod_{\substack{\lambda=1 \\ \lambda \ne k}}^{v} (1 + \alpha^{j_\lambda} \alpha^{-j_m})} \tag{8.40}$$

The error values are important because the error-pattern polynomial $e(x)$ is derived from it.

8.2.2 Syndrome Components and Elementary Symmetric Functions

For the sake of simplicity, let $Z_k = \alpha^{j_k}$ represent the error-location numbers and $Y_k = e_{j_k}$ the error values for $1 \le k \le \nu$. Then Eq. 8.35 can be written as

$$s_\lambda = \sum_{k=1}^{\nu} Y_k Z_k^\lambda \qquad 1 \le \lambda \le 2t \tag{8.41}$$

The error-locator polynomial when ν errors actually occur is

$$\sigma(x) = \prod_{k=1}^{\lambda} (1 + Z_k x)$$

$$= \sum_{k=0}^{\nu} \sigma_k x^k = 1 + \sigma_1 x + \sigma_2 x^2 + \cdots + \sigma_\nu x^\nu \tag{8.42}$$

Multiplying $\sigma(x)$ by $Y_i Z_i^{j+\nu}$ first and substituting the root Z_i^{-1}, $1 \le i \le \nu$, of $\sigma(x)$ in Eq. 8.42 results in $\sigma(Z_i^{-1}) = 0$, which means that

$$Y_i Z_i^{j+\nu} \sum_{k=0}^{\nu} \sigma_k Z_i^{-k} = 0$$

or

$$Y_i \sum_{k=0}^{\nu} \sigma_k Z_i^{j+\nu-k} = 0 \tag{8.43}$$

For all the roots of $\sigma(x)$, we have

$$\sum_{i=1}^{\nu} Y_i \sum_{k=0}^{\nu} \sigma_k Z_i^{j+\nu-k} = 0$$

or

$$\sum_{i=1}^{\nu} Y_i Z_i^{j+\nu} + \sigma_1 \sum_{i=1}^{\nu} Y_i Z_i^{j+\nu-1} + \cdots + \sigma_{\nu-1} \sum_{i=1}^{\nu} Y_i Z_i^{j+1}$$

$$+ \sigma_\nu \sum_{i=1}^{\nu} Y_i Z_i^{j} = 0 \tag{8.44}$$

Utilizing Eq. 8.41, Eq. 8.44 can be written as

$$s_{j+\nu} = \sigma_1 s_{j+\nu-1} + \sigma_2 s_{j+\nu-2} + \cdots + \sigma_{\nu-1} s_{j+1} + \sigma_\nu s_j \qquad 1 \le j \le \nu \tag{8.45}$$

Equation 8.45 for $1 \le j \le \nu$ constitutes what are called Newton's identities and relate the syndrome components to the coefficients of $\sigma(x)$. These identities can be represented as follows :

$$\sigma_\nu s_1 + \sigma_{\nu-1} s_2 + \sigma_{\nu-3} s_3 + \cdots + \sigma_2 s_{\nu-1} + \sigma_1 s_\nu = s_{\nu+1}$$

$$\sigma_\nu s_2 + \sigma_{\nu-1} s_3 + \sigma_{\nu-2} s_4 + \cdots + \sigma_2 s_\nu + \sigma_1 s_{\nu+1} = s_{\nu+2}$$

$$\sigma_v s_3 + \sigma_{v-1} s_4 + \sigma_{v-2} s_5 + \cdots + \sigma_2 s_{v+1} + \sigma_1 s_{v+2} = s_{v+3} \qquad (8.46)$$

$$\cdot \quad \cdot \quad \cdot \quad \cdot \quad \cdot \quad \cdot \quad \cdot \quad \cdot \quad \cdot \quad \cdot \quad \cdot \quad \cdot \quad \cdot \quad \cdot \quad \cdot \quad \cdot$$

$$\sigma_v s_v + \sigma_{v-1} s_{v+1} + \sigma_{v-2} s_{v+2} + \cdots + \sigma_2 s_{2v-2} + \sigma_1 s_{2v-1} = s_{2v}$$

This system of Newton's identities is used for RS decoding, as we shall now discuss.

8.3   RS DECODING BY PETERSON-GORENSTEIN-ZIERLER METHOD

The set of equations expressed by Eq. 8.46 can be represented in the following matrix form:

$$
\begin{bmatrix}
s_1 & s_2 & s_3 & \cdots & s_{v-1} & s_v \\
s_2 & s_3 & s_4 & \cdots & s_v & s_{v+1} \\
s_3 & s_4 & s_5 & \cdots & s_{v+1} & s_{v+2} \\
\cdot & & & & & \cdot \\
\cdot & & & & & \cdot \\
\cdot & & & & & \cdot \\
s_v & s_{v+1} & s_{v+2} & \cdots & s_{2v-2} & s_{2v-1}
\end{bmatrix}
\begin{bmatrix}
\sigma_v \\
\sigma_{v-1} \\
\sigma_{v-2} \\
\cdot \\
\cdot \\
\cdot \\
\sigma_1
\end{bmatrix}
=
\begin{bmatrix}
s_{v+1} \\
s_{v+2} \\
s_{v+3} \\
\cdot \\
\cdot \\
\cdot \\
s_{2v}
\end{bmatrix}
\qquad (8.47)
$$

where if we set

$$
\mathbf{M} =
\begin{bmatrix}
s_1 & s_2 & \cdots & s_v \\
s_2 & s_3 & \cdots & s_{v+1} \\
& & \cdot & \\
& & \cdot & \\
& & \cdot & \\
s_v & s_{v+1} & \cdots & s_{2v-1}
\end{bmatrix}
\qquad (8.48)
$$

Eq. 8.47 can be expressed as

$$
\begin{bmatrix}
\sigma_v \\
\sigma_{v-1} \\
\sigma_{v-2} \\
\cdot \\
\cdot \\
\cdot \\
\sigma_1
\end{bmatrix}
= \mathbf{M}^{-1}
\begin{bmatrix}
s_{v+1} \\
s_{v+2} \\
s_{v+3} \\
\cdot \\
\cdot \\
\cdot \\
s_{2v}
\end{bmatrix}
\qquad (8.49)
$$

if and only if the matrix **M** is nonsingular. Equation 8.49 definitely provides the basis of derivation for the error-locator polynomial $\sigma(x)$. If the coefficients σ_k, $1 \le k \le v$ of $\sigma(x)$ are known, the roots of $\sigma(x)$ can be found to obtain the error locations. Therefore, we first need to compute σ_k, $1 \le k \le v$, from the syndrome components s_λ for $1 \le \lambda \le 2t$. The simplest way to find the roots of $\sigma(x)$ is to compute $\sigma(\alpha^i) = 0$ for $x = \alpha^i$, $1 \le i \le 2^m - 2$, from GF (2^m). Another method is Chien search, which has been covered in Sec. 7.5.

Thus, once the roots of $\sigma(x)$ are found, we observe that the error locations are at the reciprocal of the roots.

Considering the determinant of Eq. 8.48 at $v = t$, we have

$$|\mathbf{M}| = \begin{vmatrix} s_1 & s_2 & s_3 & \cdots & s_t \\ s_2 & s_3 & s_4 & \cdots & s_{t+1} \\ & & \cdot & & \\ & & \cdot & & \\ & & \cdot & & \\ s_t & s_{t+1} & s_{t+2} & \cdots & s_{2t-1} \end{vmatrix} \tag{8.50}$$

If $|\mathbf{M}| = 0$, it indicates that the matrix **M** is singular and $v < t$. If $|\mathbf{M}| \ne 0$, then $v = t$ which indicates that the correct value of v has been chosen. v is the number of errors that have actually occurred. Thus, if $|\mathbf{M}| = 0$, we must set $v = t - 1$ by reducing the trial value v by 1 and repeat the process. In this manner, we have to search for the correct value of v until we obtain $|\mathbf{M}| \ne 0$. Once the correct value is determined, we have to invert **M** and compute the coefficients σ_k, $1 \le k \le v$, from Eq. 8.49 and then form the error-locator polynomial $\sigma(x)$. All that remains is finding the roots of $\sigma(x)$ and determining the error-location numbers by taking the reciprocal of the roots.

■ **Example 8.8** Consider the DSEC(31, 27) Reed-Solomon code. Assume that a code word of all zeros is transmitted and that the error pattern $e(x) = \alpha^{29} X^9 + \alpha^{10} X^{18}$ has actually occurred. For finding the error-locator polynomial $\sigma(x)$, let us first compute the syndrome components s_k, $1 \le k \le 4$, as follows:

$$\begin{aligned} s_1 &= e(\alpha) = \alpha^7 + \alpha^{28} = \alpha \\ s_2 &= e(\alpha^2) = \alpha^{16} + \alpha^{15} = \alpha^2 \\ s_3 &= e(\alpha^3) = \alpha^{25} + \alpha^2 = \alpha^{14} \\ s_4 &= e(\alpha^4) = \alpha^3 + \alpha^{20} = \alpha^2 \end{aligned} \tag{8.51}$$

Setting ν = 2, Eq. 8.48 becomes

$$\mathbf{M} = \begin{bmatrix} S_1 & S_2 \\ S_2 & S_3 \end{bmatrix} = \begin{bmatrix} \alpha & \alpha^2 \\ \alpha^2 & \alpha^{14} \end{bmatrix} \tag{8.52}$$

Since the determinant of **M** is not zero, i.e. $|\mathbf{M}| = \alpha^{15} + \alpha^4 = \alpha^{23} \neq 0$, we know that two errors have actually occurred. Thus, the coefficients of the error-locator polynomial $\sigma(x)$ can be found using Eq. 8.49 as follows:

$$\begin{bmatrix} \sigma_2 \\ \sigma_1 \end{bmatrix} = \begin{bmatrix} S_1 & S_2 \\ S_2 & S_3 \end{bmatrix}^{-1} \cdot \begin{bmatrix} S_3 \\ S_4 \end{bmatrix}$$

$$= \frac{1}{S_1S_3 + S_2^2} \begin{bmatrix} S_3 & S_2 \\ S_2 & S_1 \end{bmatrix} \begin{bmatrix} S_3 \\ S_4 \end{bmatrix}$$

from which we have

$$\sigma_2 = \frac{S_3^2 + S_2S_4}{S_1S_3 + S_2^2} \tag{8.53}$$

$$\sigma_1 = \frac{S_2S_3 + S_1S_4}{S_1S_3 + S_2^2}$$

Substituting Eq. 8.51 in Eq. 8.53 yields

$$\sigma_2 = \frac{(\alpha^{28} + \alpha^4)}{\alpha^{23}} = \frac{\alpha^{19}}{\alpha^{23}} = \alpha^{27}$$

$$\sigma_1 = \frac{(\alpha^{16} + \alpha^3)}{\alpha^{23}} = \frac{\alpha^{17}}{\alpha^{23}} = \alpha^{25}$$

Hence, the error-locator polynomial is obtained as

$$\sigma(x) = 1 + \alpha^{25}x + \alpha^{27}x^2 \tag{8.54}$$

Solving for the roots of $\sigma(x)$, we easily obtain two roots at α^{13} and α^{22} by substituting all the field elements of $GF(2^5)$ in $\sigma(x)$. Of course, the Chien search accomplishes computation of the roots without explicitly solving $\sigma(x)$. Thus, the error-location numbers are, respectively, $Z_1 = 1/\alpha^{22} = \alpha^9$ and $Z_2 = 1/\alpha^{13} = \alpha^{18}$. Next, let us evaluate the error-evaluator polynomial $\Omega(x)$. Using Eq. 8.34 for ν = 2,

$$\Omega(x) = 1 + (\alpha + \alpha^{25})x + (\alpha^2 + \alpha^{26} + \alpha^{27})x^2$$

$$= 1 + \alpha^{16}x + \alpha^{21}x^2 \tag{8.55}$$

Utilizing Eq. 8.40, the error values (or error magnitudes) at error locations can be computed as follows:

$$Y_1 = \frac{\Omega(Z_1^{-1})}{1 + Z_2 Z_1^{-1}}$$

$$= \frac{1 + \alpha^7 + \alpha^3}{1 + \alpha^9} = \frac{\alpha^{14}}{\alpha^{16}} = \alpha^{29} \tag{8.56}$$

$$Y_2 = \frac{\Omega(Z_2^{-1})}{1 + Z_1 Z_2^{-1}}$$

$$= \frac{1 + \alpha^{29} + \alpha^{16}}{1 + \alpha^{22}} = \frac{\alpha^{17}}{\alpha^7} = \alpha^{10}$$

Substituting these two error values in Eq. 8.31 for ν=2, we have the error pattern

$$e(x) = \alpha^{29}x^9 + \alpha^{10}x^{18} \tag{8.57}$$

as expected.

The block diagram for the DSEC (31, 27) RS decoder is shown in Fig. 8.6.

At this point it is worth mentioning that the two decoding methods presented in Secs 7.6 and 7.8 are applicable to only binary BCH codes, and not to RS codes.

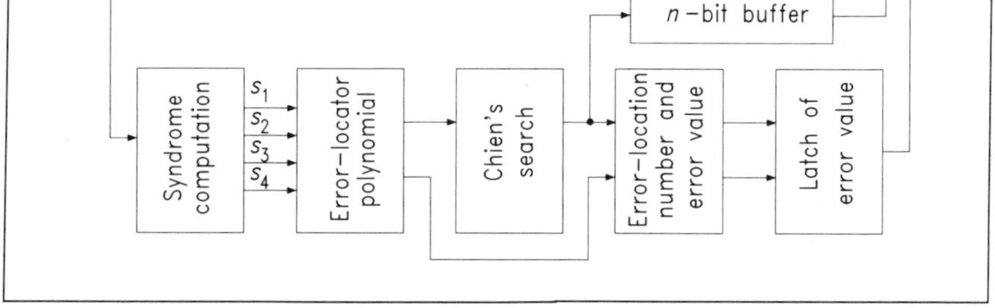

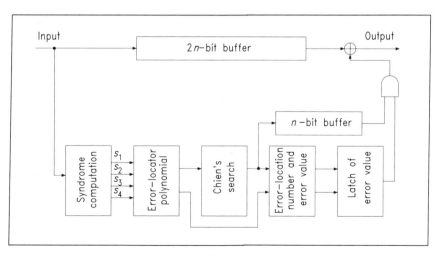

Fig. 8.6 Block diagram for the DSEC (31, 27) RS decoder

8.4 RS DECODING BY BERLEKAMP'S ITERATIVE ALGORITHM

The iterative algorithm for finding the error-locator polynomial $\sigma(x)$ was fully covered in Sec. 7.7. Therefore, we briefly describe the iterative steps for finding a minimum-degree polynomial $\sigma^{(n)}(x)$, $1 \le n \le 2t$, whose coefficients satisfy Newton's identity of Eq. 8.45. Rewriting this identity, we have

$$\sigma_1 s_{j+\nu-1} + \sigma_2 s_{j+\nu-2} + \cdots + \sigma_{\nu-1} s_{j+1} + \sigma_\nu s_j = s_{j+\nu}$$
$$j = 1, 2, \cdots, \nu \tag{8.58}$$

Let

$$\sigma^{(n)}(x) = \sigma_0^{(n)} + \sigma_1^{(n)} x + \cdots + \sigma_{l_n}^{(n)} x^{l_n} \tag{8.59}$$

be the minimum-degree polynomial at the nth step of iteration. The coefficients $\sigma_0^{(n)} = 1$ and $\sigma_i^{(n)}$, $1 \le i \le l_n$, must satisfy the first n Newton's identities of Eq. 8.58. The first step of iteration is to find $\sigma^{(1)}(x)$ and check whether its coefficients satisfy the first two Newton identities of Eq. 8.58. If they satisfy the second Newton identity of this equation we can put $\sigma^{(2)}(x) = \sigma^{(1)}(x)$. If $\sigma^{(2)}(x) \ne \sigma^{(1)}(x)$, a correction term must be added to $\sigma^{(1)}(x)$ to form $\sigma^{(2)}(x)$. The next step is to find $\sigma^{(3)}(x)$ from $\sigma^{(2)}(x)$ such that the coefficients of $\sigma^{(3)}(x)$ satisfy the three Newton identities of Eq. 8.58. If the coefficients of $\sigma^{(2)}(x)$ satisfy the third identity, we know that $\sigma^{(3)}(x) = \sigma^{(2)}(x)$. If they do not, a correction term is added to $\sigma^{(2)}(x)$ to form $\sigma^{(3)}(x)$. Repeating these iterative steps up to $n = 2t$, we obtain $\sigma^{(2t)}(x)$ which will be the error-locator polynomial, i.e. $\sigma(x) = \sigma^{(2t)}(x)$.

The nth discrepancy is defined as

$$d_n = s_{n+1} + \sigma_1^{(n)} s_n + \sigma_2^{(n)} s_{n-1} + \cdots + \sigma_{l_n}^{(n)} s_{n+1-l_n} \tag{8.60}$$

If $d_n = 0$, $\sigma^{(n+1)}(x) = \sigma^{(n)}(x)$ because the coefficients of $\sigma^{(n)}(x)$ satisfy the $(n+1)$st Newton identity. On the other hand, if $d_n \ne 0$, a correction term must be added to $\sigma^{(n)}(x)$ to obtain $\sigma^{(n+1)}(x)$.

To carry out the iterative steps for finding $\sigma(x)$, we refer to Berlekamp's iterative algorithm which was described in Sec. 7.7.

■ **Example 8.9** Consider again the DSEC (31, 27) Reed-Solomon code given in Example 8.8. Assume that the allzero code word is transmitted. We use the same error pattern $e(x) = \alpha^{29} x^9 + \alpha^{10} x^{18}$ and the syndrome components $s_1 = \alpha$, $s_2 = \alpha^2$, $s_3 = \alpha^{14}$, and $s_4 = \alpha^2$. Using the iterative algorithm, we easily obtain Table 8.2.

Thus, the error-locator polynomial $\sigma(x) = \sigma^{(4)}(x) = 1 + \alpha^{25} x + \alpha^{27} x^2$, which is identical to the solution found in Example 8.8. As in Example 8.8,

Table 8.2 Iterative Steps for Finding $\sigma(x)$

n	$\sigma^{(n)}(x)$	d_n	l_n	$n-l_n$	m
−1	1	1	0	−1	
0	1	α	0	0	
1	$1+\alpha x$	0	1	0	−1
2	$1+\alpha x$	0	1	1	
3	$1+\alpha x+\alpha^{21}x^2$	α^7	2	1	0
4	$1+\alpha^{25}x+\alpha^{27}x^2$	–	–	–	

the roots of $\sigma(x)$ are α^{13} and α^{22}. Their inverses are accordingly α^9 and α^{18}. Using Eq. 8.34 for $\nu = 2$, the error-evaluator polynomial is found to be

$$\Omega(x) = 1 + \alpha^{16}x + \alpha^{21}x^2$$

Utilizing Eq. 8.40, the error-values at α^9 and α^{18} are computed as $Y_1 = \alpha^{29}$ and $Y_2 = \alpha^{10}$. From Eq. 8.31, for $\nu = 2$, the error pattern is

$$e(x) = \alpha^{29}x^9 + \alpha^{10}x^{18}$$

Thus, adding $e(x)$ to the received polynomial $r(x)$, we obtain the all zero code word.

8.5 RS DECODING BY SPECTRAL TECHNIQUES

Since the message bearing signal in the digital coded system is discrete, the discrete Fourier transform (DFT) can be applied. Fourier transforms also exist in the vector space of n-tuple code words. In this section, we shall discuss RS decoding based on spectral techniques, which is very different from a time-domain analysis, from a frequency-domain point of view.

Spectral analysis of error-correcting codes has been discussed by many coding theorists over a number of years. Among them, Pollard (1971) discussed Fourier transforms over a finite domain; Gore (1973), and Chien and Choy (1975) introduced and developed Fourier transform techniques applicable to error correcting codes. Particularly, Blahut (1983) treated coding with spectral techniques in his book intensively.

8.5.1 Fourier Transforms in a Vector Space

Let $\mathbf{c} = (c_0, c_1, \ldots, c_{n-1})$ be a code vector and $\mathbf{C} = (C_0, C_1, \ldots, C_{n-1})$ be a corresponding transformed vector. Then, their DFT pair is given by

$$C_k = \sum_{i=0}^{n-1} c_i e^{-j2\pi ik/n} \qquad 0 \le k \le n-1$$

$$c_i = \sum_{k=0}^{n-1} C_k e^{j2\pi ik/n} \qquad 0 \le i \le n-1 \tag{8.61}$$

where $j = \sqrt{-1}$. In the Fourier transform of a Galois field, the spectrum of a vector $\mathbf{v} = (v_0, v_1, \ldots, v_{n-1})$ over GF(q) is represented by a vector $\mathbf{V} = (V_0, V_1, \ldots, V_{n-1})$ defined over GF (q^m) such that

$$V_j = \sum_{i=0}^{n-1} \alpha^{ij} v_i \qquad 0 \le j \le n-1 \tag{8.62}$$

whereas this spectrum is related by

$$v_i = \frac{1}{n} \sum_{j=0}^{n-1} V_j \, \alpha^{-ij} \qquad 0 \le i \le n-1 \tag{8.63}$$

Thus, $\mathbf{v}$ is called the time-domain vector and $\mathbf{V}$ is the spectrum in the frequency domain. Of course, when the block length is $n = q^m - 1$, α is called a primitive element of GF (q^m).

If we represent a vector $\mathbf{v}$ by a polynomial

$$v(x) = v_0 + v_1 x + \ldots + v_{n-1} x^{n-1} = \sum_{i=0}^{n-1} v_i x^i \tag{8.64}$$

the spectrum polynomial $V(z)$ corresponding to $v(x)$ can be expressed as

$$V(z) = V_0 + V_1 z + \ldots. + V_{n-1} z^{n-1} = \sum_{j=0}^{n-1} V_j z^j \tag{8.65}$$

If Eq. 8.64 has a root at α^j, it follows that

$$v(\alpha^j) = \sum_{i=0}^{n-1} v_i (\alpha^j)^i = V_j \qquad 0 \le j \le n-1 \tag{8.66}$$

which agrees with Eq. 8.62, but $V_j = 0$. Whereas, if Eq. 8.65 has a root at α^{-i}, the ith time components of v_i are found as

$$V(\alpha^{-i}) = \sum_{j=0}^{n-1} V_j (\alpha^{-i})^j = v_i \qquad 0 \le i \le n-1 \tag{8.67}$$

where v_i becomes zero. Thus, we conclude that the polynomial $v(x)$ has a root α^j if and only if $V_j = 0$ and the polynomial $V(z)$ has a root α^{-i} if and only if $v_i = 0$.

Consider next the case where the comnponent v_i of a vector $\mathbf{v}$ is in the form of a product of two components of other vectors $\mathbf{A}$ and $\mathbf{B}$ such that $v_i = a_i\, b_i$, $0 \le i \le n-1$. the convolution property is then derived by taking the Fourier transform of $\mathbf{v}$ as follows:

$$V_i = \sum_{i=0}^{n-1} \alpha^{ij} v_i = \frac{1}{n} \sum_{i=0}^{n-1} \alpha^{ij} a_i \left[\sum_{k=0}^{n-1} \alpha^{-ik} B_k \right]$$

$$= \frac{1}{n} \sum_{k=0}^{n-1} B_k \left[\sum_{i=0}^{n-1} \alpha^{i(j-k)} a_i \right] = \frac{1}{n} \sum_{k=0}^{n-1} A_{j-k} B_k$$

$$= \mathbf{A} * \mathbf{B} \qquad 0 \le i \le n-1 \tag{8.68}$$

where all subscripts are defined modulo n. Thus, we see that multiplication in the time domain is equivalent to convolution in the frequency domain, and that the reverse is also true.

8.5.2 Frequency Domain Decoding

Here we shall develop a decoding procedure in the frequency domain, based on the principles discussed in Subsection 8.5.1.

Let $c\,(x)$ be a code polynomial of degree $n-1$ and $d(x)$ an information polynomial of degree $k-1$. Then any code word can be found from the following encoding equation

$$c(x) = d(x)\, g(x) \tag{8.69}$$

where $g(x)$ represents a generator polynomial of degree $n-k$. The polynomial of Eq. 8.69 is equivalent to the following time domain convolution:

$$c_i = \sum_{k=0}^{n-1} g_{i-k}\, d_k \tag{8.70}$$

This is also equivalent to

$$C_j = G_j\, D_j \tag{8.71}$$

in the frequency domain.

A received word $\mathbf{r}$ with components $r_i = c_i + e_i$, $0 \le i \le n-1$ is the sum of a transmitted code word $\mathbf{c}$ and an error pattern $\mathbf{e}$, i.e. $\mathbf{r} = \mathbf{c} + \mathbf{e}$ which has a Fourier transform with components $R_j = C_j + E_j$ for $0 \le j \le n-1$. Since the roots of $g(x)$ are $\alpha, \alpha^2, \ldots, \alpha^{2t}$, α^j's for $1 \le j \le 2t$ are also the roots of $c(x)$, i.e. $c(x) = 0$ at $x = \alpha^j$ for $1 \le j \le 2t$. But since $C_j = c(\alpha^j)$, the coefficients of $C(z)$ are all zeroes in the range $1 < i \le 2t$. Consequently, we have

$$R_j = E_j = e(\alpha^j) \qquad 1 \le j \le 2t \tag{8.72}$$

Thus, we see that each transformed code word **C** is zero in a block of $2t$ consecutive components. From Eq. 8.72, the syndromes of **r** are given by the following set of $2t$ unknown values of E_j:

$$E_j = R_j = S_j \qquad j = 1, 2, \ldots, 2t \tag{8.73}$$

where $$S_j = \sum_{i=0}^{n-1} r_i \alpha^{ij} = r(\alpha^j) \qquad 1 \le j \le 2t$$

The syndromes are then computed as $2t$ components of a Fourier transform. Hence, the syndrome block shows us a window through which we can look at only $2t$ components of the error spectrum, as illustrated in Fig. 8.7.

Now suppose $\nu \le t$ errors have actually occurred at location α^{i_k} for $1 \le k \le \nu$. Let us define the error-locator polynomial $\Phi(z)$ in the frequency domain such that

$$\Phi(z) = \prod_{k=1}^{\nu} \left(1 + z\,\alpha^{i_k}\right)$$

$$= 1 + \Phi_1 z + \Phi_2 z^2 + \cdots + \Phi_\nu z^\nu \tag{8.74}$$

Therefore, the coefficients of the error-locator polynomial in the time domain can be found as

$$\sigma_i = \sum_{j=0}^{n-1} \Phi_j \alpha^{-ij}$$

$$= \Phi(\alpha^{-i}) \tag{8.75}$$

$$= \prod_{k=1}^{\nu} \left(1 - \alpha^{-i} \alpha^{i_k}\right) \qquad 0 \le i \le n-1$$

which is just $\Phi(z)$ evaluated at α^{-i} by taking the inverse Fourier transform of Φ_j. Notice that $\sigma_i = 0$ if and only if $i = i_k$ for $0 \le k \le \nu$, where the indices i_k correspond to the time indices of the ν errors. Hence, in the time domain, $\sigma_i = 0$ wherever $e_i \ne 0$ so that $\sigma_i e_i = 0$ for all $i = i_k$, $k = 1, 2, \ldots, \nu$. Since multiplication in the time domain is equivalent to convolution in the frequency domain, we have

$$\Phi * \mathbf{E} = 0 \tag{8.76}$$

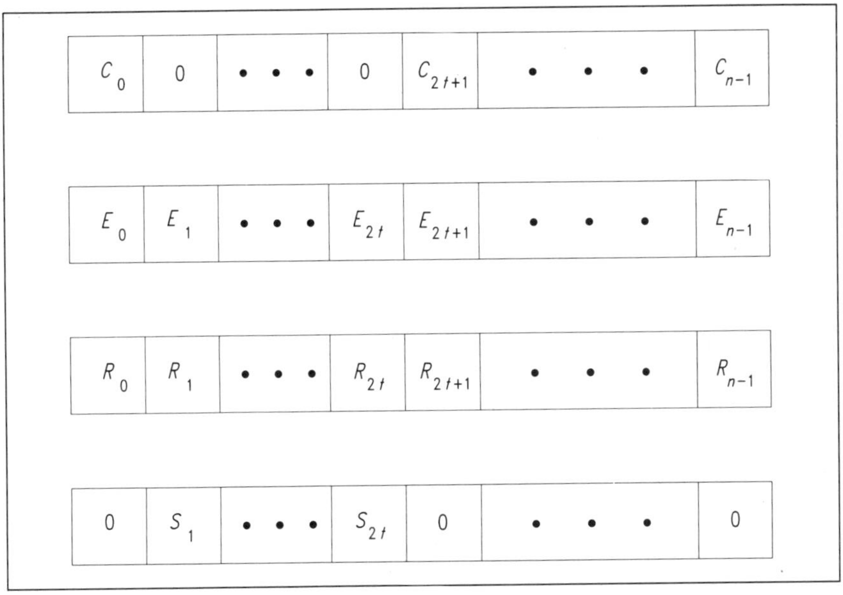

Fig. 8.7 Syndrome window over $2t$ components in the frequency domain

Because $\Phi_j = 0$ for $j > t$ from Eq. 8.74, Eq. 8.76 can be written as

$$\sum_{k=0}^{t} \Phi_k E_{j-k} = 0 \qquad j = 0, 1, \cdots, n-1 \tag{8.77}$$

However, because $\Phi_0 = 1$, Eq. 8.77 can also be expressed as a set of n equations and for $2t$ known values of **E** which are equivalent to the syndromes. They are:

$$E_j = -\sum_{k=1}^{t} \Phi_k E_{j-k} \qquad 0 \le j \le n-1 \tag{8.78}$$

and

$$S_j = -\sum_{k=1}^{t} \Phi_k S_{j-k} \qquad t+1 \le j \le 2t \tag{8.79}$$

Thus, these t equations are solvable for Φ because Eq. 8.79 involves only the known syndromes and the t unknown components of Φ. The set of equations represented by the convolution, namely, Eq. 8.78, plays an important role in solving the decoding problem. The remaining components of $\mathbf{E} = \mathbf{S}$ can also be obtained by iterative techniques. By using the convolution equation (Eq. 8.78), $E_{2t+1} = S_{2t+1}$ is found from the known components of **S** and Φ, after which $E_{2t+2} = S_{2t+2}$ is deter-

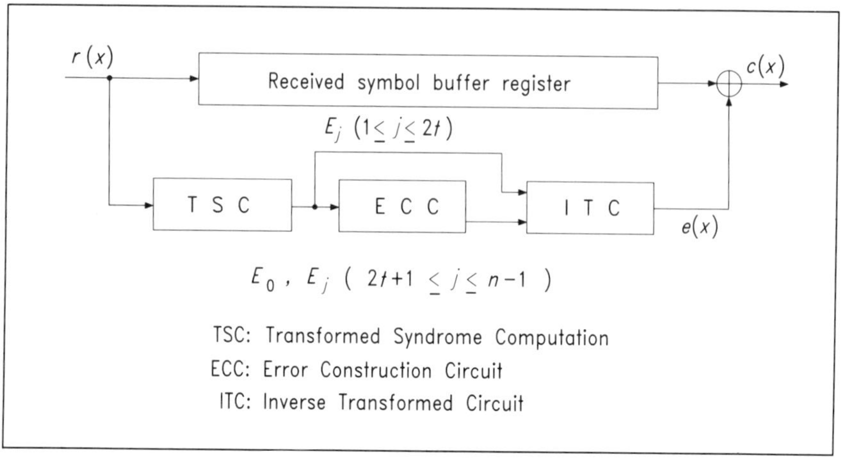

Fig. 8.8 Frequency-domain decoder for RS codes

mined and so on. In this way, if $E_j = S_j$ is computed for all j, the decoder output in the transform domain is

$$C_j = R_j - E_j \qquad \text{for} \quad 0 \le j \le n-1 \tag{8.80}$$

Thus, the decoder output **c** in the time domain would be determined by taking the inverse Fourier transform of **C**. The recursive operation to obtain **E** is easily accomplished using a linear-feedback shift register. The frequency-domain decoder to explain this process is shown in Fig. 8.8.

■ **Example 8.10** Consider the frequency-domain decoding of the DSEC (31, 27) RS code. The syndrome of **r** can be computed using Eq. 8.73 as follows:

$$\begin{aligned} S_1 &= E_1 = \sum_{i=0}^{30} r_i \alpha^i = r(\alpha) \\ S_2 &= E_2 = \sum_{i=0}^{30} r_i \alpha^{2i} = r(\alpha^2) \\ S_3 &= E_3 = \sum_{i=0}^{30} r_i \alpha^{3i} = r(\alpha^3) \\ S_4 &= E_4 = \sum_{i=0}^{30} r_i \alpha^{4i} = r(\alpha^4) \end{aligned} \tag{8.81}$$

From Eq. 8.79, the known syndromes S_j for $j = 3, 4$ are, respectively,

$$-S_3 = \Phi_1 S_2 + \Phi_2 S_1$$

$$-S_4 = \Phi_1 S_3 + \Phi_2 S_2 \tag{8.82}$$

Equation 8.82 may be expressed in matrix form as

$$\begin{bmatrix} \Phi_2 \\ \Phi_1 \end{bmatrix} = \begin{bmatrix} S_1 & S_2 \\ S_2 & S_3 \end{bmatrix}^{-1} \begin{bmatrix} -S_3 \\ -S_4 \end{bmatrix} \tag{8.83}$$

From which the unknown coefficients of $\Phi(z)$ can be determined from the known syndrome components S_i for $1 \le i \le 4$ as follows:

$$\Phi_1 = \frac{S_2 S_3 - S_1 S_4}{S_1 S_3 + S_2^2}$$

$$\Phi_2 = \frac{S_2 S_4 - S_3^2}{S_1 S_3 + S_2^2} \tag{8.84}$$

For the case where a single error has occurred, Eq. 8.79 gives us $S_2 = -\Phi_1 S_1$ or $\Phi_1 = S_2/S_1$. Thus, coefficients Φ_1 and Φ_2 of the error-

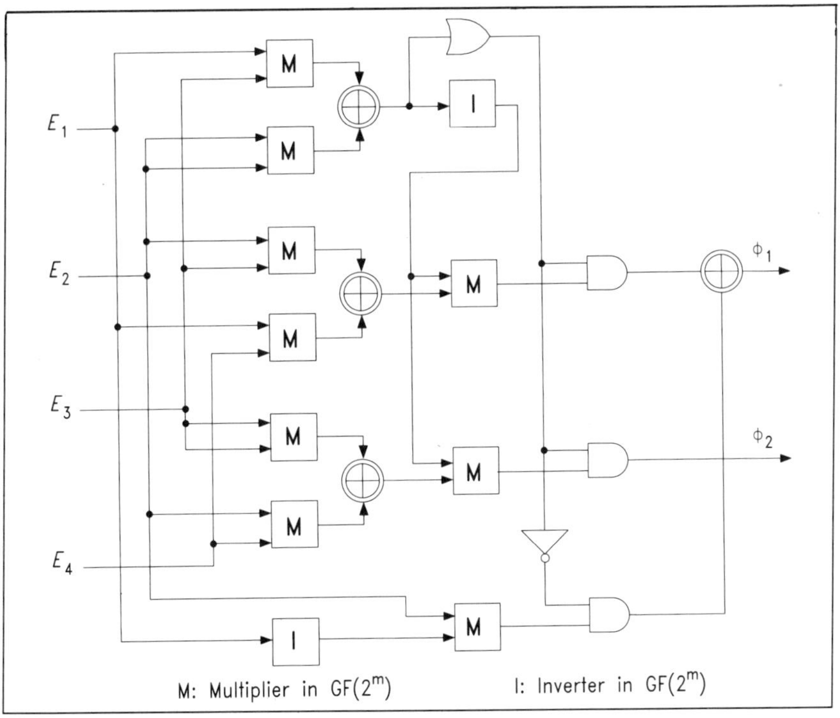

Fig. 8.9 Determination of coefficients Φ_1 and Φ_2 from the syndrome components

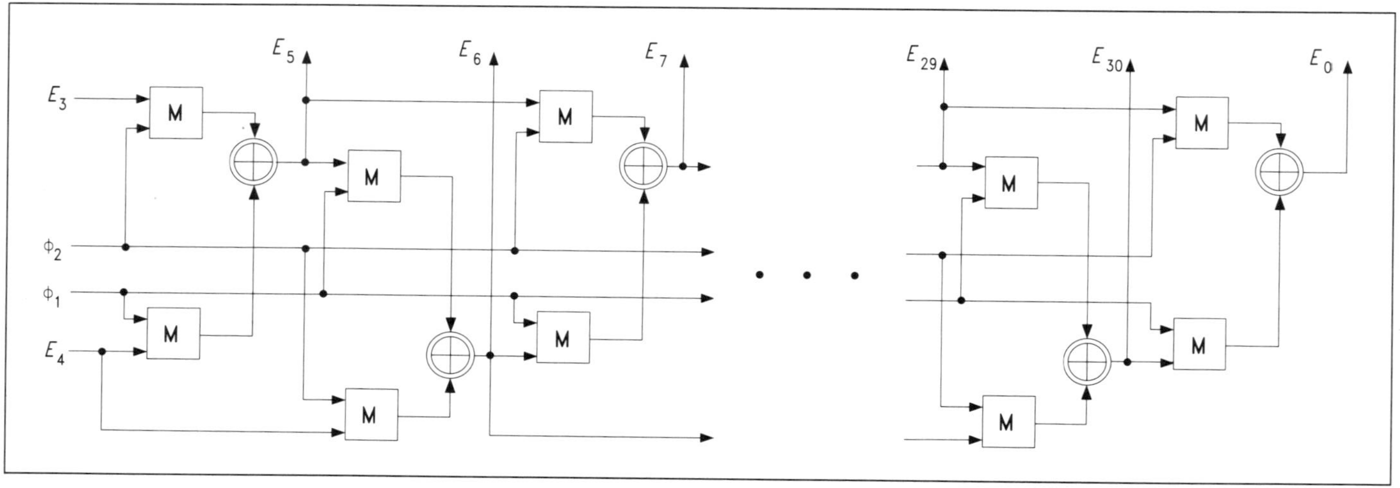

Fig. 8.10 Generation of error symbols in the Fourier transform domain for DSEC (31, 27) RS code

locater polynomial $\Phi(z)$ can be determined as shown in Fig. 8.9. Referring to Eq. 8.78, the error symbols E_j for $j = 0$ and $5 \le j \le 30$ can be computed from the syndromes and coefficients of $\Phi(z)$ as shown below.

$$\begin{aligned}
-E_5 &= \Phi_1 E_4 + \Phi_2 E_3 \\
-E_6 &= \Phi_1 E_5 + \Phi_2 E_4 \\
-E_7 &= \Phi_1 E_6 + \Phi_2 E_5 \\
&\cdots\cdots\cdots\cdots\cdots \\
-E_{30} &= \Phi_1 E_{29} + \Phi_2 E_{28} \\
-E_0 &= \Phi_1 E_{30} + \Phi_2 E_{29}
\end{aligned} \tag{8.85}$$

For a single error, we have

$$\begin{aligned}
-E_5 &= \Phi_1 E_4 \\
-E_6 &= \Phi_1 E_5 \\
&\cdots\cdots\cdots\cdots \\
-E_{30} &= \Phi_1 E_{29} \\
-E_0 &= \Phi_1 E_{30}
\end{aligned} \tag{8.86}$$

The circuit executing Eqs. 8.85 and 8.86 is illustrated in Fig. 8.10.

By taking the inverse Fourier transform of E_j for $0 \le j \le 30$ into the time domain, we can compute the error symbols from the relation

$$\begin{aligned}
e_i &= \sum_{j=0}^{30} \alpha^{-ij} E_j \\
&= E(\alpha^{-i}) \qquad \text{for } 0 \le i \le 30
\end{aligned} \tag{8.87}$$

as shown below.

$$\begin{aligned}
e_{30} &= E(\alpha^{-30}) = E(\alpha) \\
e_{29} &= E(\alpha^{-29}) = E(\alpha^2) \\
&\cdots\cdots\cdots\cdots\cdots \\
e_1 &= E(\alpha^{-1}) = E(\alpha^{29}) \\
e_0 &= E(1) = E(\alpha^{30})
\end{aligned} \tag{8.88}$$

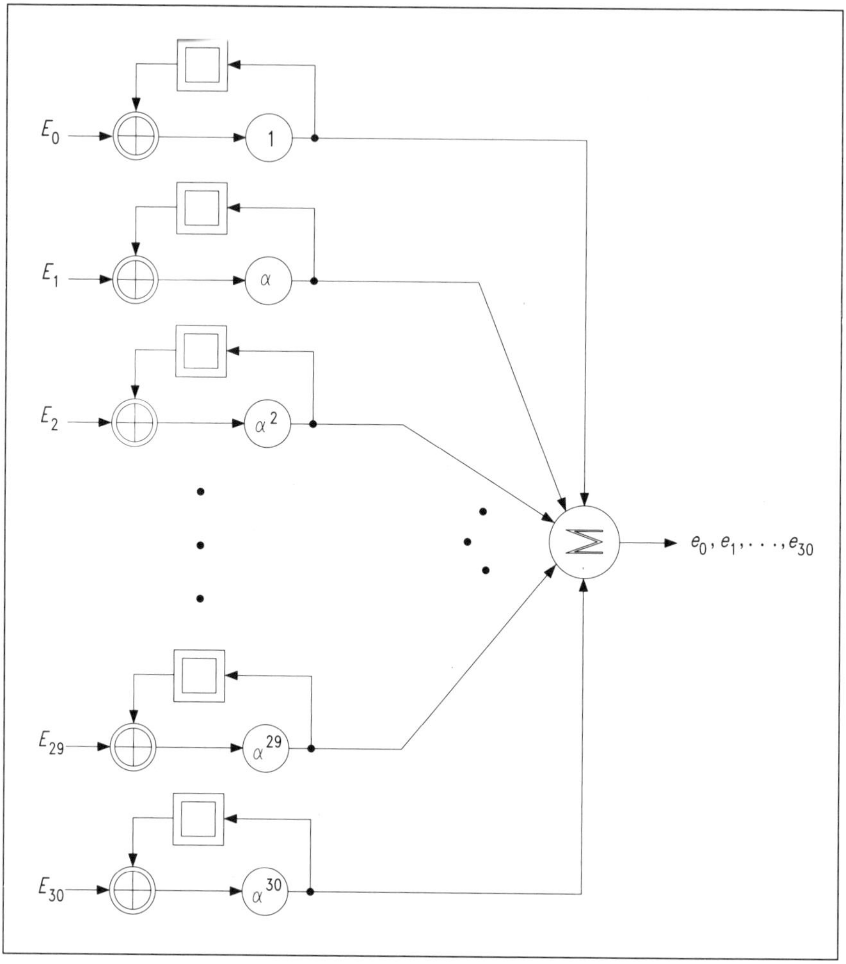

Fig. 8.11 A device for the inverse transform from E_j to e_i

Utilizing Eq. 8.88, the processing circuit for the Fourier inverse transform from E_j to e_i, $0 \le i, j \le 30$, is illustrated in Fig. 8.11. The block diagram of the transform decoder for the DSEC (31, 27) RS code is shown in Fig. 8.12.

8.6 TRANSFORM DECODING WITH EUCLIDEAN ALGORITHM

The Euclidean algorithm can be used to implement another kind of RS decoder which is somewhat different from those we have already dis-

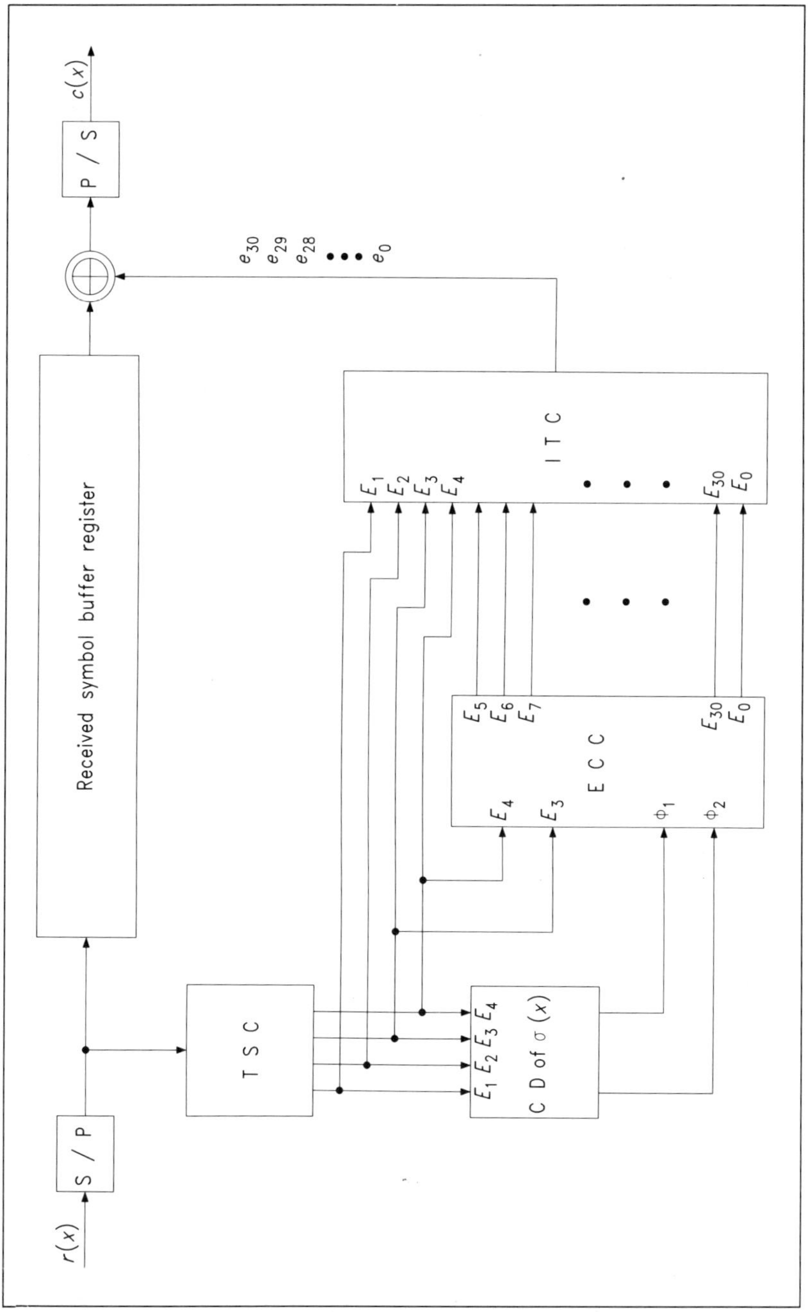

Fig. 8.12 The transform decoder for the DSEC (31, 27) RS code

cussed. The standard transform decoder for decoding RS codes was described in Sec. 8.5.

In this section, we present a pipeline architecture for a transform decoder which can be used to decode an RS code by using a modified form of the Euclidean algorithm. The greatest common divisor (GCD) of two polynomials derived from the Euclidean division algorithm can be used to obtain the error-locator polynomial of an RS code. Computation of the error-locator polynomial by means of the Euclidean algorithm generally requires a calculation of the inverse elements of GF (2^m). However, computation of inverse field elements is completely avoided in this modification of the Euclidean algorithm. By using the Euclidean algorithm, the device well suited to VLSI implementation is to ulitize its modernity. We shall now present the Euclidean algorithm as a recursive procedure for calculating the greatest common divisor of two polynomials.

Theorem 8.3 (Euclidean Algorithm for Polynomials)

Given two polynomials $a(x)$ and $b(x)$ over GF(q), their greatest common divisor (GCD) can be computed by a recursive operation of the division algorithm.

If deg $a(x) \geq$ deg $b(x)$, the computation for GCD $[a(x), b(x)]$ is as follows.

$$
\begin{aligned}
a(x) &= Q_1(x)b(x) + b_1(x) \\
b(x) &= Q_2(x)b_1(x) + b_2(x) \\
b_1(x) &= Q_3(x)b_2(x) + b_3(x) \\
&\cdots\cdots\cdots\cdots\cdots\cdots \qquad (8.89) \\
b_{n-2}(x) &= Q_n(x)b_{n-1}(x) + b_n(x) \\
b_{n-1}(x) &= Q_{n+1}(x)b_n(x)
\end{aligned}
$$

The division process stops when a remainder of zero is reached. We have then $b_n(x) = \lambda$ GCD $[a(x), b(x)]$, where λ is a scalar.

Proof Starting with the first equation, GCD $[a(x), b(x)]$ divides both $a(x)$ and $b(x)$ and must then divide the remainder $b_1(x)$. Since GCD $[a(x), b(x)]$ divides both $b(x)$ and $b_1(x)$, it must also divide $b_2(x)$ in the second equation. Repeating this process down the equations, we see that GCD $[a(x), b(x)]$ divides both $b_{n-1}(x)$ and $b_n(x)$. Starting with the bottom equation we see that $b_n(x)$ divides $b_{n-1}(x)$ because deg $b_{n-1}(x) \geq$ deg $b_n(x)$. In the second equation from the bottom, $b_n(x)$ must divide $b_{n-2}(x)$ because $b_n(x)$ divides $b_{n-1}(x)$ and also deg $b_{n-2}(x) >$ deg $b_n(x)$. Repeating this process upward through the equations, we see that $b_n(x)$ divides $b_1(x)$ and then divides both $b(x)$ and $a(x)$. Thus, we see that $b_n(x)$ divides GCD $[a(x), b(x)]$, i.e. $b_n(x) = \lambda$ GCD $[a(x), b(x)]$.

Theorem 8.4 GCD $[a(x), b(x)] = f(x)\, a(x) + h(x)\, b(x)$, where $a(x)$ and $b(x)$ are polynomials over GF(q).

Proof Since $b_n(x) = \lambda$ GCD $[a(x), b(x)]$ from Theorem 8.3, we can say that

$$\lambda \, \text{GCD}\,[a(x), b(x)] = -Q_n(x)\; b_{n-1}(x) + b_{n-2}(x)$$

From $b_{n-3}(x) = Q_{n-1}(x)\; b_{n-2}(x) + b_{n-1}(x)$, we have $b_{n-1}(x) = -Q_{n-1}(x)$ $b_{n-2}(x) + b_{n-3}(x)$. Substituting this $b_{n-1}(x)$ into the above equation yields

$$\lambda \, \text{GCD}\,[a(x), b(x)] = (Q_n(x)\, Q_{n-1}(x) + 1)\, b_{n-2}(x) - Q_n(x)\, b_{n-3}(x)$$

Similarly, first eliminating $b_{n-2}(x)$, then $b_{n-3}(x)$, and so on, we finally reach

$$\lambda \, \text{GCD}\,[a(x), b(x)] = f_1(x)\, a(x) + h_1(x)\, b(x)$$

which indicates that only $a(x)$ and $b(x)$ remain in the expression for $b_n(x)$. Thus, it proves that

$$\text{GCD}\,[a(x), b(x)] = f(x)\, a(x) + h(x)\, b(x)$$

As we know through Theorems 8.3 and 8.4, the Euclidean algorithm is a recursive procedure for finding the ith remainder $r_i(x)$, i.e. $d(x) =$ GCD $[a(x), b(x)]$ and the quantities $f_i(x)$ and $h_i(x)$ that satisfy

$$f(x)a(x) + h(x)b(x) = d(x) \tag{8.90}$$

When deg $a(x) \geq$ deg $b(x)$, given the initial conditions for the algorithm

$$\begin{aligned} &f_{-1}(x) = 1 \qquad h_{-1}(x) = 0 \qquad r_{-1}(x) = a(x) \\ &f_0(x) = 0 \qquad h_0(x) = 1 \qquad r_0(x) = b(x) \end{aligned} \tag{8.91}$$

$r_i(x)$, $f_i(x)$, and $h_i(x)$ are expressed as follows:

$$\begin{aligned} r_{i-2}(x) &= q_i(x)\, r_{i-1}(x) + r_i(x) \\ f_{i-2}(x) &= q_i(x)\, f_{i-1}(x) + f_i(x) \\ h_{i-2}(x) &= q_i(x)\, h_{i-1}(x) + h_i(x) \end{aligned} \tag{8.92}$$

where deg $r_i(x) <$ deg $r_{i-1}(x)$ for all i, and $q_i(x)$ is the quotient polynomial produced by dividing $r_{i-2}(x)$ by $r_{i-1}(x)$. Thus, the algorithm will always terminate to a zero remainder i.e. $r_{i+1} = 0$, in a finite number of steps. Hence, the resulting $f_i(x)$ and $h_i(x)$ at the termination of the algorithm are the desired polynomials $f(x)$ and $h(x)$.

■ **Example 8.11** Find GCD $[a(x), b(x)]$, where $a(x) = 1 + x^3$ and $b(x) = 1 + x^2$. The initial conditions are:

$$f_{-1}(x) = 1 \qquad h_{-1}(x) = 0 \qquad r_{-1}(x) = 1 + x^3$$

$$f_0(x) = 0 \qquad h_0(x) = 1 \qquad r_0(x) = 1 + x^2$$

Utilizing Eq. 8.92, it follows that:

For $i = 1$,

$$f_1(x) = f_{-1}(x) - q_1(x)\, f_0(x) = 1$$

$$h_1(x) = h_{-1}(x) - q_1(x)\, h_0(x) = q_1(x) = x$$

where

$$q_1(x) \rightarrow \frac{r_{-1}(x)}{r_0(x)} = \frac{(1 + x^3)}{(1 + x^2)}$$

$$= x + \frac{1 + x}{1 + x^2}$$

$$q_1(x) = x \qquad \text{and} \qquad r_1(x) = 1 + x$$

$$r_1(x) = r_{-1}(x) - q_1(x)\, r_0(x)$$

$$= (1 + x^3) - q_1(x)\,(1 + x^2)$$

$$= 1 + x^3 + x(1 + x^2) = 1 + x$$

For $i = 2$,

$$f_2(x) = f_0(x) - q_2(x)\, f_1(x) = q_2(x)$$

where

$$q_2(x) \rightarrow \frac{r_0(x)}{r_1(x)} = \frac{(1 + x^2)}{(1 + x)} = 1 + x$$

$$h_2(x) = h_0(x) - q_2(x)\, h_1(x)$$

$$= 1 - xq_2(x) = 1 + x(1 + x) = 1 + x + x^2$$

$$r_2(x) = r_0(x) - q_2(x)\, r_1(x)$$

$$= 1 + x^2 - q_2(x)\,(1 + x)$$

$$= 1 + x^2 + (1 + x^2) = 0$$

Thus, the last nonzero remainder $r_1(x) = 1 + x$ is GCD $[(1 + x^3), (1 + x^2)]$.

8.6.1 Computation of $\sigma(x)$ by Euclidean Algorithm

Our aim is not to find a greatest common divisor, but calculate the error-locator polynomial $\sigma(x)$ from the syndrome polynomial $s(x)$ by means of the Euclidean algorithm.

Let $s(x)$ be the syndrome polynomial corresponding to the syndrome vector $\mathbf{s} = (s_0, s_1, \ldots, s_{2t-1})$ such that

$$s(x) = \sum_{i=0}^{2t-1} s_i x^i \tag{8.93}$$

Even though we only know the first $2t$ coefficients of $s(x)$, let us consider the infinite-degree syndrome polynomial such that

$$s_\infty(x) = \sum_{i=0}^{\infty} s_i x^i$$

$$= s_0 + s_1 x + s_2 x^2 + \cdots + s_{2t-1} x^{2t-1} + \cdots \tag{8.94}$$

where the syndrome components are expressed by

$$s_i = r(\alpha^i) = e(\alpha^i) \qquad 0 \le i \le 2t - 1 \tag{8.95}$$

Suppose $\nu \le t$ errors actually occur at unknown locations $j_1, j_2, \ldots, j_\nu$. Then, Eq. 8.95 becomes

$$s_i = e(\alpha^i) = e_{j_1}\alpha^{ij_1} + e_{j_2}\alpha^{ij_2} + \cdots + e_{j_\nu}\alpha^{ij_\nu}$$

$$= \sum_{k=1}^{\nu} e_{j_k}\left(\alpha^{j_k}\right)^i \tag{8.96}$$

where e_{j_k} is the magnitude of the kth error.

Substituting Eq. 8.96 in Eq. 8.94 yields

$$s(x) = \sum_{i=0}^{\infty} \left[\sum_{k=1}^{\nu} e_{j_k}\left(\alpha^{j_k}\right)^i\right] x^i$$

$$= \sum_{k=1}^{\nu} \frac{e_{j_k}}{1 + \alpha^{j_k}x} \tag{8.97}$$

Since the error-locator polynomial is expressed as

$$\sigma(x) = \prod_{\lambda=1}^{\nu} \left(1 + \alpha^{j_\lambda}x\right)$$

$$= 1 + \sigma_1 x + \sigma_2 x^2 + \cdots + \sigma_{\nu-1}x^{\nu-1} + \sigma_\nu x^\nu \tag{8.98}$$

the error-evaluator polynomial is given by the formula

$$\Omega(x) = \sigma(x)\, s(x) = \sum_{k=1}^{\nu} e_{j_k} \prod_{\substack{\lambda=1 \\ \lambda \neq k}}^{\nu} \left(1 + \alpha^{j_\lambda} x\right) \qquad \nu \le t \tag{8.99}$$

where deg $\Omega(x) \le \nu - 1$ and deg $\sigma(x) = \nu$.

The applicability of the Euclidean algorithm to Eq.8.99 becomes apparent by noting that $f_i(x)\, a(x) + h_i(x)\, b(x) = r_i(x)$ which may be expressed as

$$h_i(x)\, b(x) \equiv r_i(x) \mod a(x) \tag{8.100}$$

If we set $h_i(x) = \sigma_i(x)$, $b(x) = s(x)$, $r_i(x) = \Omega_i(x)$, and $a(x) = x^{2t}$, Eq. 8.99 has the same form as Eq. 8.100. That is,

$$\sigma(x)\, s(x) \equiv \Omega(x) \mod x^{2t} \tag{8.101}$$

As a result, the error-locator polynomial $\sigma(x)$ can be computed from the Euclidean algorithm by setting $a(x) = x^{2t}$ and $b(x) = s(x)$. Thus, when $\nu \le t$, we see that deg $\Omega(x) <$ deg $\sigma(x) \le t$ and

$$\deg \Omega(x) + \deg \sigma(x) < 2t \tag{8.102}$$

A flowchart for determination of $\sigma(x)$ by the Euclidean algorithm is shown in Fig. 8.13, where $A_{i,22}(x)$ indicates the ith iteration element of $A_i(x)$ in the second row and second column. $A_{i,22}(0)$ is the 0th order coefficient.

8.6.2 Computation of $\sigma(x)$ with a Modified Euclidean Algorithm

Thus far, we have shown that by employing the Euclidean algorithm the greatest common divisor of two polynomials can be used to obtain the error-locator polynomial $\sigma(x)$ of an RS code. But this algorithm requires the computation of inverse elements in GF (2^m). Successive computation of these inverses is difficult to realize in a VLSI implementation. In order to avoid this kind of clumsy operation, a modified form of the Euclidean algorithm can be utilized to find the error-locator polynomial $\sigma(x)$.

■ **Example 8.12** Let α be an element of GF (2^m) such that $\alpha = \alpha^{2^m}$. Then the inverse element is

$$\alpha^{-1} = \alpha^{2^m - 2} = (\alpha^2)(\alpha^{2^2})(\alpha^{2^3}) \cdots (\alpha^{2^{m-1}}) \tag{8.103}$$

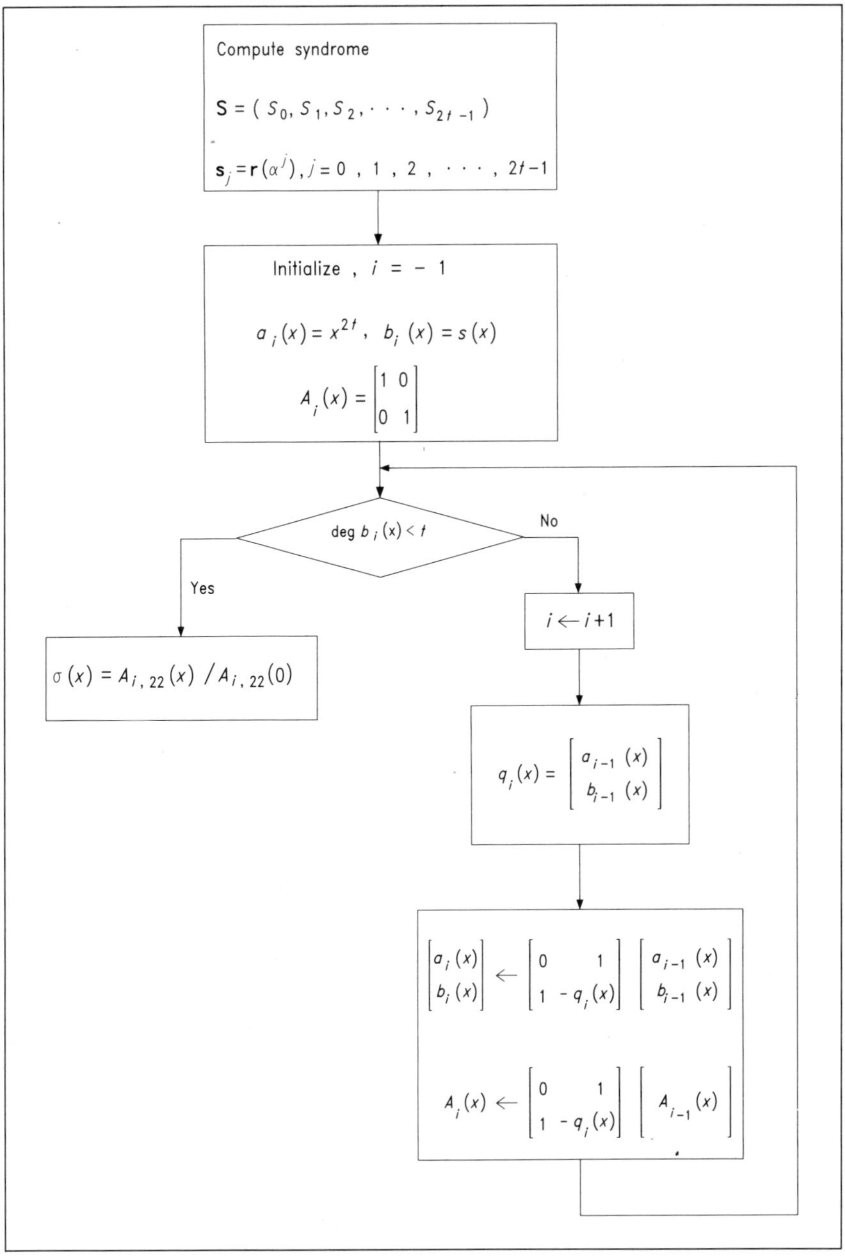

Fig. 8.13 A flowchart for determination of $\sigma(x)$ by the Euclidean algorithm

where α^{2^i} is the ith cyclic shift of α^2. For $m = 5$, the inverse element becomes $\alpha^{-1} = (\alpha^2)(\alpha^4)(\alpha^8)(\alpha^{16})$ which has a form of the normal basis representation. Using Eq. 8.103, the flowchart for computing the inverse element α^{-1} is shown in Fig. 8.14.

Consider the two polynomials

$$A_0(x) = x^{2t} \tag{8.104}$$

and

$$B_0(x) = S(x) = \sum_{k=1}^{2t} S_k x^{k-1} \tag{8.105}$$

Let F_0 be the leading coefficient of $A_0(x)$ and E_0 that of $B_0(x)$. The modified Euclidean algorithm is a recursive procedure for reducing the degrees of both $A_i(x)$ and $B_i(x)$. Figure 8.15 shows a flowchart for determining the error-locator polynomial $\sigma(x)$ by the modified Euclidean algorithm. In this figure, $L_i(0)$ is the zero-degree coefficient of $L_i(x)$ and $M_i(0)$ that of $M_i(x)$. F_{i-1} is the leading coefficient of $A_{i-1}(x)$ and E_{i-1} that of $B_{i-1}(x)$.

8.6.3 The TSEC (31, 25) RS Transform Decoder

The (31, 25) RS code is the triple-symbol-error-correcting (TSEC) code. In this section, we shall present decoding for the TSEC (31, 25) RS code by employing the transform decoding algorithm which utilizes the modified Euclidean algorithm. Transform decoding procedure involves the following steps.

1. Compute the syndrome $S_k = E_k$ in the frequency domain.
2. Determine the error-locator polynomial $\sigma(x)$ by utilizing the modified Euclidean algorithm.
3. Compute the remaining transform errors.
4. Find the inverse transform of E_k over GF (2^m) to obtain the time-domain error pattern e_k.
5. Decode the transmitted code word **c** by subtracting the error pattern **e** from the received word **r**.

Figure 8.16 shows an overall block diagram of the transform decoder based on the decoding procedure described above.

Consider the case where the allzero code word $c(x) = 0$ is transmitted and $r(x) = \alpha^8 x^2 + \alpha^2 x^5 + \alpha x^{10}$ is received. Then we know that three errors occur in the error pattern because $e(x) = r(x)$.

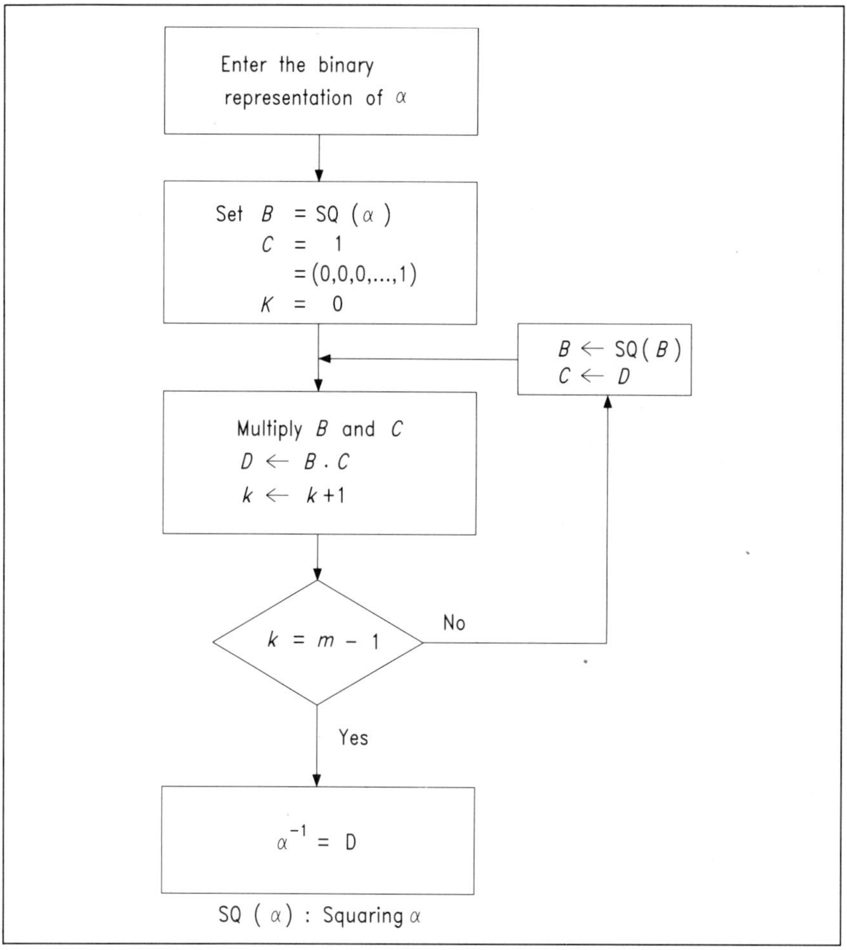

Fig. 8.14 The flowchart for computing the inverse element α^{-1}

Thus, the syndromes of $r(x)$ are

$$S_\lambda = \sum_{j=0}^{30} r_j \alpha^{j\lambda} \qquad 1 \le \lambda \le 6 \tag{8.106}$$

Hence the syndromes in the transform domain yield

$$\begin{aligned} S_1 &= E_1 = r(\alpha) = \alpha \\ S_2 &= E_2 = r(\alpha^2) = \alpha^{21} \\ S_3 &= E_3 = r(\alpha^3) = \alpha^{23} \end{aligned} \tag{8.107}$$

$$S_4 = E_4 = r(\alpha^4) = \alpha^{15}$$

$$S_5 = E_5 = r(\alpha^5) = \alpha^2$$

$$S_6 = E_6 = r(\alpha^6) = \alpha^{13}$$

where S_λ, $1 \le \lambda \le 6$, are the syndrome values in the normal basis.

Let us rewrite Eq. 8.106 in recursive form in order to incorporate S_λ into the systolic cell structure.

$$S_\lambda = r_0 + \alpha^\lambda(r_1 + \alpha^\lambda(r_2 + \cdots + \alpha^\lambda(r_{28} + \alpha^\lambda(r_{29} + r_{30}\alpha^\lambda)))\cdots) \quad 1 \le \lambda \le 6 \quad (8.108)$$

A cell structure for computing Eq. 8.108 is shown in Fig. 8.17. The received word **r** is sent to all the cells simultaneously. After **r** is entered in all the cell registers, the desired syndromes S_λ are computed in registers $B_{7-\lambda}$, $1 \le \lambda \le 6$. Note in this figure that the register B_λ is replaced by $A_\lambda + B_\lambda\,\alpha^{7-\lambda}$. Thus, the computed syndromes are shifted serially from the right end of register B_6 and fed into the next stage which performs a modified Euclidean algorithm.

The second decoding step is to calculate the error-locator polynomial $\sigma(x)$ from the syndrome polynomial $S(x)$ by means of the modified Euclidean algorithm. Starting with the two polynomials $A(x) = x^{2t}$ and $S(x) = \sum_{k=1}^{2t} S_k x^{k-1}$, and applying them to the flowchart shown in Fig. 8.15 according to the modified Euclidean algorithm, we can employ the recursive procedure for finding $\sigma(x)$ as follows.

The initial conditions of the algorithm are

$$i = 0$$

$$U_0 = M_0 = 1 \quad \text{and} \quad L_0 = V_0 = 0$$

$$A_0(x) = x^{2t} = x^6$$

$$B_0(x) = S(x) = \alpha^{13}x^5 + \alpha^2x^4 + \alpha^{15}x^3 + \alpha^{23}x^2 + \alpha^{21}x + \alpha$$

1. If $i = 1$, then $\deg A_0(x) > \deg B_0(x)$.

$$A_1(x) = E_0A_0(x) - F_0B_0(x)\,x^{\deg A_0(x) - \deg B_0(x)}$$

$$= \alpha^{13}x^6 - 1\cdot(\alpha^{13}x^5 + \alpha^2x^4 + \alpha^{15}x^3 + \alpha^{23}x^2 + \alpha^{21}x + \alpha)x$$

$$= \alpha^2x^5 + \alpha^{15}x^4 + \alpha^{23}x^3 + \alpha^{21}x^2 + \alpha x$$

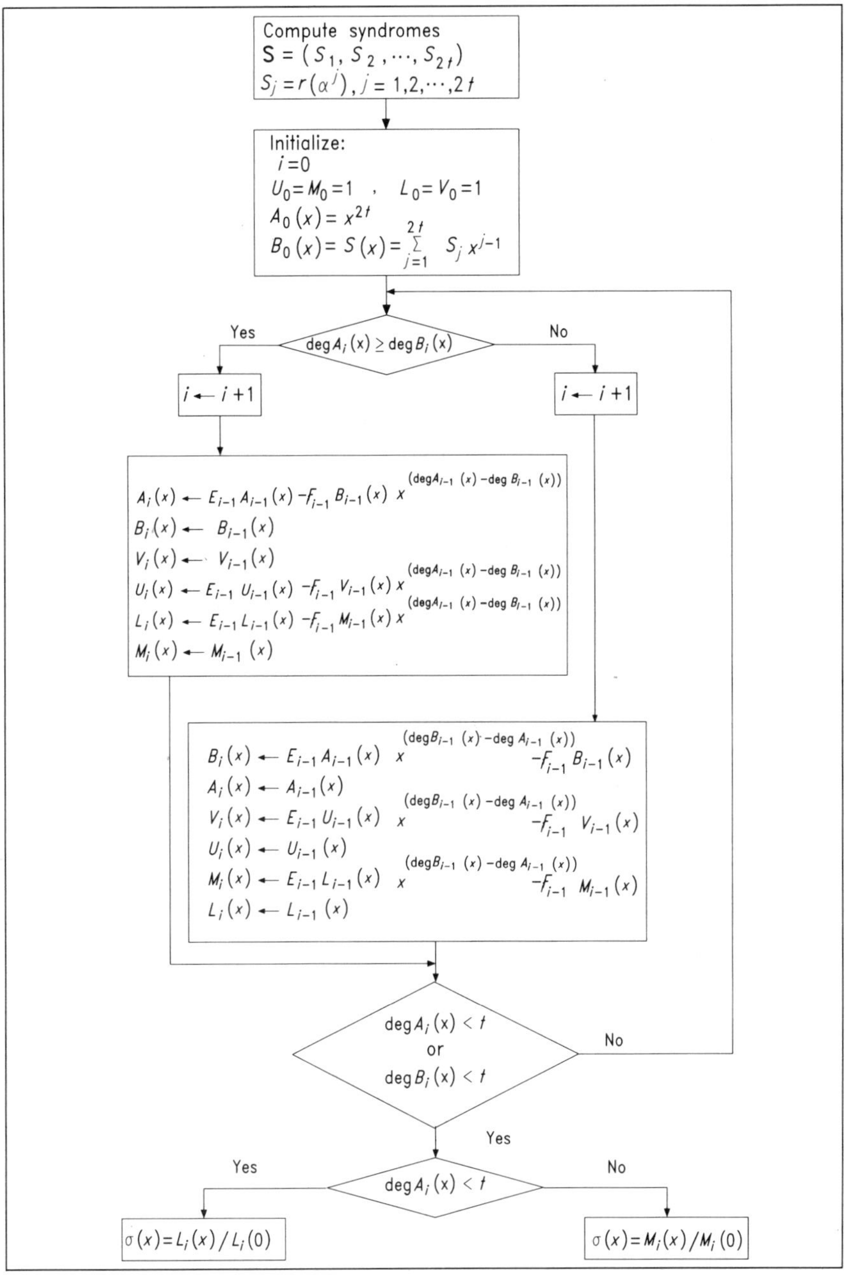

Fig. 8.15 Flowchart for determination of $\sigma(x)$ by the modified Euclidean algorithm

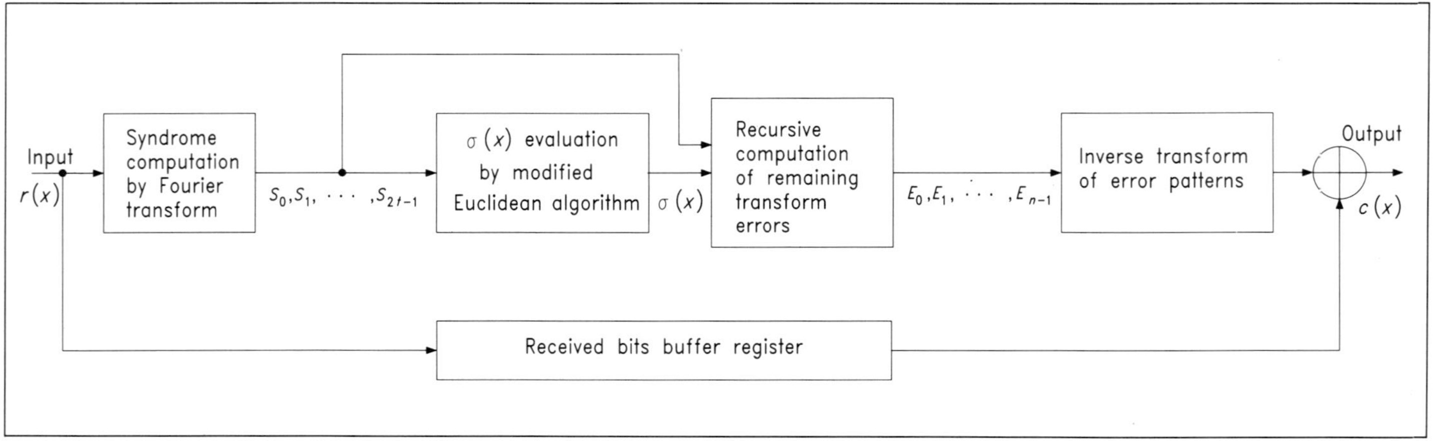

Fig. 8.16 The overall block diagram of an (n, k) RS transform decoder

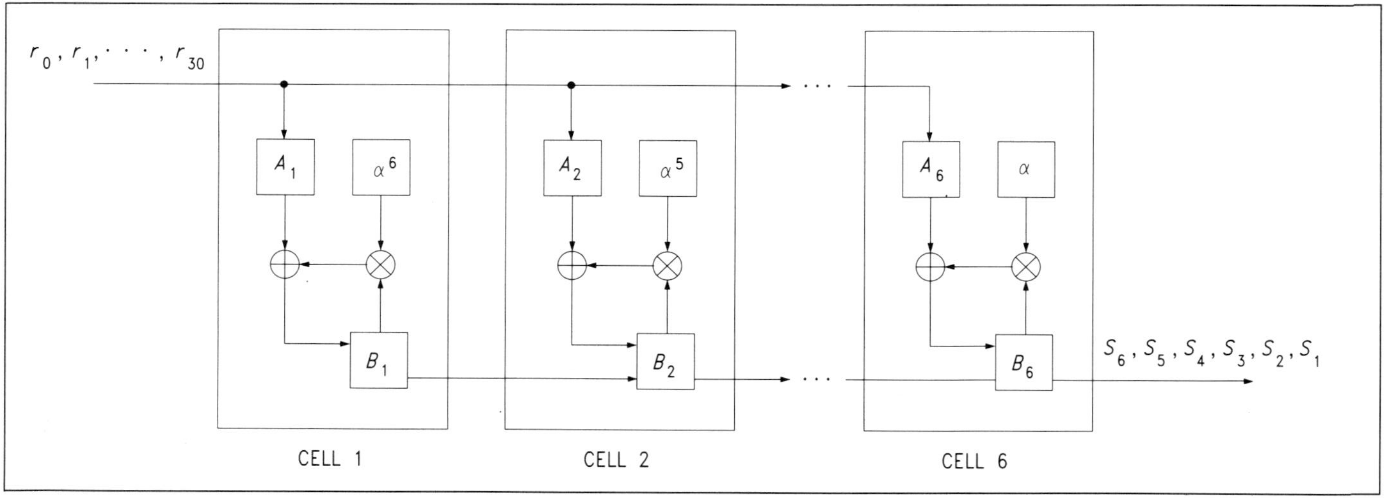

Fig. 8.17 The cell structure for computing syndromes of a (31, 25) RS code

$$B_1(x) = B_0(x) = \alpha^{13}x^5 + \alpha^2x^4 + \alpha^{15}x^3 + \alpha^{23}x^2 + \alpha^{21}x + \alpha$$

$$L_1(x) = E_0M_0(x)\,x^{\deg A_0(x) - \deg B_0(x)}$$

$$= \alpha^{13} \cdot 0 - 1 \cdot 1 \cdot x = x$$

$$M_1(x) = M_0(x) = 1$$

2. If $i = 2$, then $\deg A_1(x) = \deg B_1(x)$.

$$A_2(x) = E_1A_1(x) - F_1B_1(x)\,x^{\deg A_1(x) - \deg B_1(x)}$$

$$= \alpha^{13}A_1(x) - \alpha^2B_1(x)\,x^0$$

$$= \alpha^{19}x^4 + \alpha^{28}x^3 + \alpha^{10}x^2 + \alpha^{30}x + \alpha^3$$

$$B_2(x) = B_1(x) = \alpha^{13}x^5 + \alpha^2x^4 + \alpha^{15}x^3 + \alpha^{23}x^2 + \alpha^{21}x + \alpha$$

$$L_2(x) = E_1L_1(x) - F_1M_1(x)\,x^{\deg A_1(x) - \deg B_1(x)}$$

$$= \alpha^{13}x - \alpha^2 \cdot 1 = \alpha^{13}x + \alpha^2$$

$$M_2(x) = M_1(x) = 1$$

3. If $i = 3$, then $\deg A_2(x) < \deg B_2(x)$.

$$B_3(x) = E_2A_2(x)\,x^{\deg B_2(x) - \deg A_2(x)} - F_2B_2(x)$$

$$= \alpha^{13}A_2(x)x - \alpha^{19}B_2(x)$$

$$= \alpha^{19}x^4 + \alpha^{11}x^3 + \alpha^{29}x^2 + x + \alpha^{20}$$

$$A_3(x) = A_2(x) = \alpha^{19}x^4 + \alpha^{28}x^3 + \alpha^{10}x^2 + \alpha^{30}x + \alpha^3$$

$$M_3(x) = E_2L_2(x)\,x^{\deg B_2(x) - \deg A_2(x)} - F_2M_2(x)$$

$$= \alpha^{13}L_2(x)x - \alpha^{10}M_2(x)$$

$$= \alpha^{26}x^2 + \alpha^{15}x + \alpha^{19}$$

$$L_3(x) = L_2(x) = \alpha^{13}x + \alpha^2$$

4. If $i = 4$, then $\deg A_3(x) = \deg B_3(x)$.

$$A_4(x) = E_3A_3(x) - F_3B_3(x)\,x^{\deg A_3(x) - \deg B_3(x)}$$

$$= \alpha^{29}A_3(x) - \alpha^{19}B_3(x)\,x^0$$

$$= \alpha^5x^3 + \alpha^{24}x^2 + \alpha^4x + \alpha^{23}$$

$$B_4(x) = B_3(x) = \alpha^{29}x^4 + \alpha^{11}x^3 + \alpha^{29}x^2 + x + \alpha^{20}$$

$$L_4(x) = E_3L_3(x) - F_3M_3(x)\,x^{\deg A_3(x) - \deg B_3(x)}$$

$$= \alpha^{29}L_3(x) - \alpha^{19}M_3(x)\,x^0$$

$$= \alpha^{14}x^2 + \alpha^{23}x + \alpha^{22}$$

$$M_4(x) = M_3(x) = \alpha^{26}x^2 + \alpha^{15}x + \alpha^{19}$$

5. If $i = 5$, then $\deg A_4(x) < \deg B_4(x)$.

$$B_5(x) = E_4A_4(x)\,x^{\deg B_4(x) - \deg A_4(x)} - F_4B_4(x)$$

$$= \alpha^{29}A_4(x)x - \alpha^5B_4(x)$$

$$= \alpha^{12}x^3 + \alpha^{20}x^2 + \alpha^{14}x + \alpha^{25}$$

$$A_5(x) = A_4(x) = \alpha^5x^3 + \alpha^{24}x^2 + \alpha^4x + \alpha^{23}$$

$$M_5(x) = E_4L_4(x)\,x^{\deg B_4(x) - \deg A_4(x)} - F_4M_4(x)$$

$$= \alpha^{29}L_4(x)x - \alpha^5M_4(x)$$

$$= \alpha^{12}x^3 + \alpha^{25}x^2 + \alpha^{24}$$

$$L_5(x) = L_4(x) = \alpha^{14}x^2 + \alpha^{23}x + \alpha^{22}$$

6. If $i = 6$, then $\deg A_5(x) = \deg B_5(x)$.

$$A_6(x) = E_5A_5(x) - F_5B_5(x)x^{\deg A_5(x) - \deg B_5(x)}$$

$$= \alpha^{12}A_5(x) - \alpha^5B_5(x)$$

$$= \alpha^{13}x^2 + \alpha^{14}x + \alpha$$

$$B_6(x) = B_5(x) = \alpha^{12}x^3 + \alpha^{20}x^2 + \alpha^{14}x + \alpha^{25}$$

$$L_6(x) = E_5L_5(x) - F_5M_5(x)\,x^{\deg A_5(x) - \deg B_5(x)}$$

$$= \alpha^{12}L_5(x) - \alpha^5 M_5(x)$$

$$= \alpha^{17}x^3 + \alpha^5 x^2 + \alpha^4 x + 1$$

$$M_6(x) = M_5(x) = \alpha^{12}x^3 + \alpha^{25}x^2 + \alpha^{24}$$

Since $\deg A_6(x) < 3$, the error-locator polynomial $\sigma(x)$ can be found as

$$\sigma(x) = L_6(x)/L_6(0) = (\alpha^{17}x^3 + \alpha^5 x^2 + \alpha^4 x + 1)/1$$

$$= \alpha^{17}x^3 + \alpha^5 x^2 + \alpha^4 x + 1 \qquad (8.109)$$

where the coefficients of $\sigma(x)$ are $\sigma_3 = \alpha^{17}$, $\sigma_2 = \alpha^5$, $\sigma_1 = \alpha^4$, and $\sigma_0 = 1$. Note that $U_i(x)$ and $V_i(x)$, indicated in the flowchart in Fig. 8.15, are not needed for computation of $\sigma(x)$.

■ **Example 8.13** To implement the first cell of the systolic array, we look at the initial conditions of the algorithm and the contents of step 1. The inputs to the first cell are

$$A_0(x) = x^6$$

$$B_0(x) = \alpha^{13}x^5 + \alpha^2 x^4 + \alpha^{15}x^3 + \alpha^{23}x^2 + \alpha^{21}x + \alpha$$

$$L_0(x) = 0, \quad \text{and} \quad M_0(x) = 0$$

$$\deg A_0(x) = 6 \quad \text{and} \quad \deg B_0(x) = 5$$

The outputs of cell 1 are

$$A_1(x) = E_0 A_0(x) - F_0 B_0(x)x$$

$$= \alpha^2 x^5 + \alpha^{15}x^4 + \alpha^{23}x^3 + \alpha^{21}x^2 + \alpha x$$

$$B_1(x) = B_0(x) = \alpha^{13}x^5 + \alpha^2 x^4 + \alpha^{15}x^3 + \alpha^{23}x^2 + \alpha^{21}x + \alpha$$

$$L_1(x) = E_0 L_0(x) - F_0 M_0(x) = x$$

$$M_1(x) = M_0(x) = 1$$

The functional block diagram of cell 1 is shown in Fig. 8.18. The leading coefficients of $A_0(x)$ and $B_0(x)$ are aligned with the start signal. The start signal, as well as $xB_0(x)$ and $xM_0(x)$, is delayed by one unit (marked by D) so that the leading coefficients of $A_1(x)$, $B_1(x)$, $L_1(x)$, and $M_1(x)$ can be properly initiated by the start signal at the output of cell 1. Cells 2, 4, and 6 are essentially identical to cell 1. It is left to the reader to devise these individual cells.

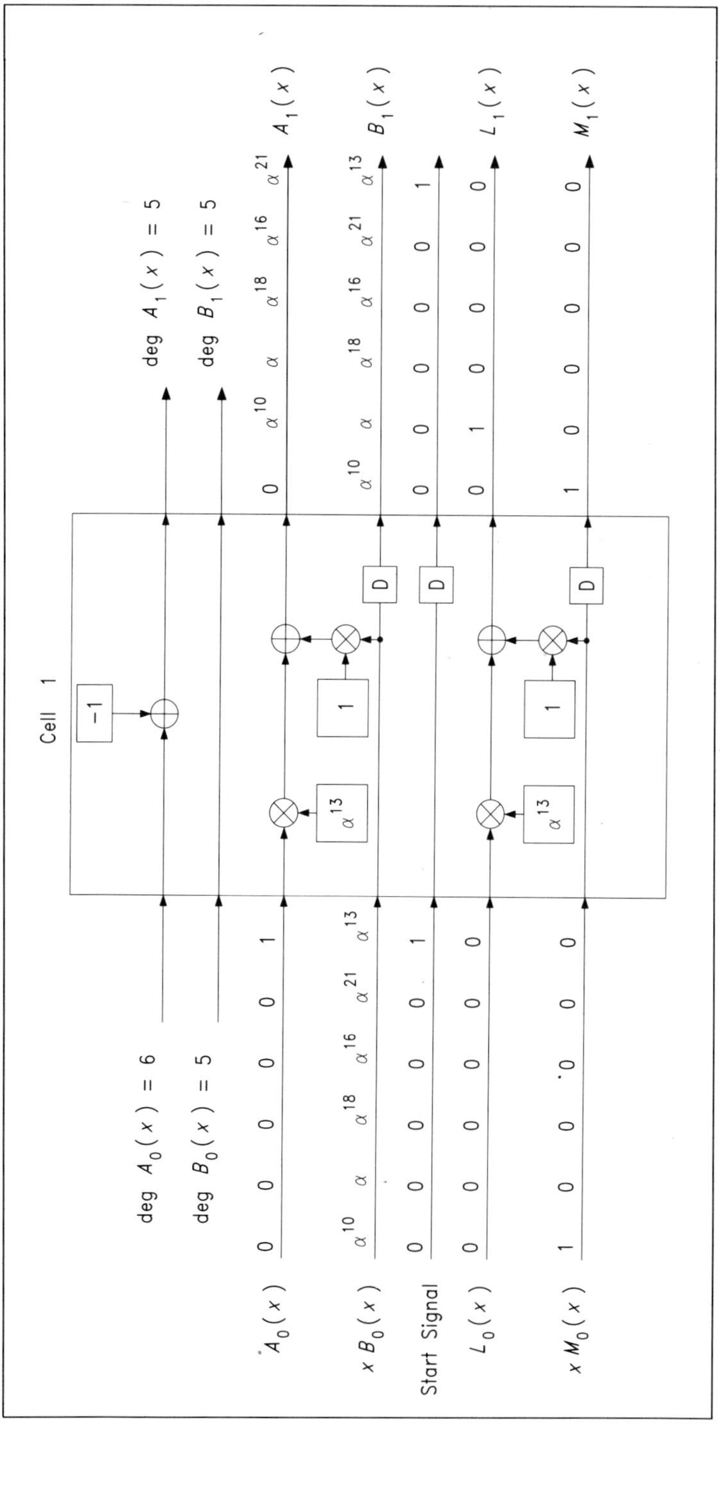
Cell 1
−1
deg $A_0(x) = 6$
deg $B_0(x) = 5$
deg $A_1(x) = 5$
deg $B_1(x) = 5$
$A_0(x)$
$x\,B_0(x)$
Start Signal
$L_0(x)$
$x\,M_0(x)$
$A_1(x)$
$B_1(x)$
$L_1(x)$
$M_1(x)$
0 0 0 0 0 1
α^{10} α α^{18} α^{16} α^{21} α^{13}
0 0 0 0 0 1
0 0 0 0 0 0
1 0 0 0 0 0
0 α^{10} α α^{18} α^{16} α^{21}
α^{10} α α^{18} α^{16} α^{21} α^{13}
0 0 0 0 0 1
0 1 0 0 0 0
1 0 0 0 0 0
α^{13}
1
D

■ **Example 8.14** Consider the functional diagram of cell 5. The inputs to this cell are

$$A_4(x) = \alpha^5 x^3 + \alpha^{24} x^2 + \alpha^4 x + \alpha^{23}$$

$$B_4(x) = \alpha^{29} x^4 + \alpha^{11} x^3 + \alpha^{29} x^2 + x + \alpha^{20}$$

$$L_4(x) = \alpha^{14} x^2 + \alpha^{23} x + \alpha^{22}$$

$$M_4(x) = \alpha^{26} x^2 + \alpha^{15} x + \alpha^{19}$$

$$\deg A_4(x) = 3 \qquad \text{and} \qquad \deg B_4(x) = 4$$

The outputs from cell 5 are

$$A_5(x) = \alpha^5 x^3 + \alpha^{24} x^2 + \alpha^4 x + \alpha^{23}$$

$$B_5(x) = \alpha^{12} x^3 + \alpha^{20} x^2 + \alpha^{14} x + \alpha^{25}$$

$$L_5(x) = \alpha^{14} x^2 + \alpha^{23} x + \alpha^{22}$$

$$M_5(x) = \alpha^{12} x^3 + \alpha^{25} x^2 + \alpha^{24}$$

$$\deg A_5(x) = 3 \text{ and degree } B_5(x) = 3$$

The functional structure of cell 5 is illustrated in Fig. 8.19, which is again identical to cell 3. In this figure, the role-switching operation is implemented by a simple crossover at the inputs of cell 5.

■ **Example 8.15** Cell7 is the last structure of the systolic array. Since $\deg A_6(x) = 2 < t = 3$, the modified Euclidean algorithm stops and the final result $L_6(x) = \alpha^{17}x^3 + \alpha^5 x^2 + \alpha^4 x + 1$ is obtained. Figure 8.20 shows the functional diagram of the last cell, namely cell 7.

The complete systolic array for the TSEC (31, 25) RS code is illustrated in Fig. 8.21. The function for each cell of this array can be realized as shown in Examples 8.12, 8.13, and 8.14.

Consider the third step of the transform decoding procedure. Based on Eq. 8.78, viz. $E_j = \sum_{k=1}^{v} \sigma_k E_{j-k}$, $0 \le j \le n-1$, the remaining transform errors E_j, $7 \le j \le 31$, can be found in terms of the coefficients of $\sigma(x)$ as follows:

$$E_7 = \sigma_1 E_6 + \sigma_2 E_5 + \sigma_3 E_4$$

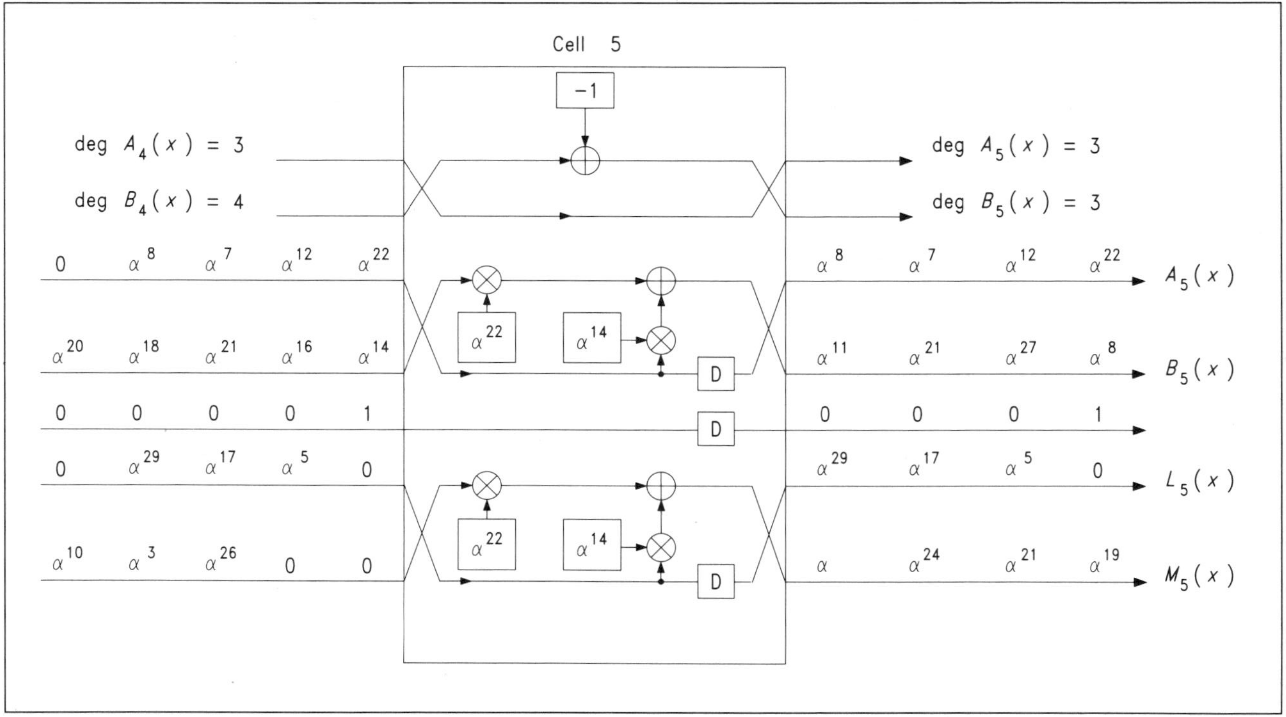

Fig. 8.19 The functional structure of systolic cell 5

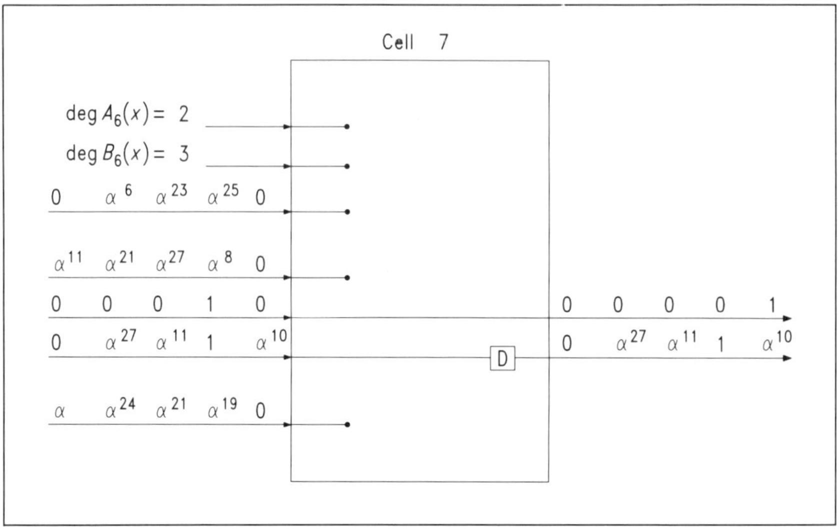

Fig. 8.20 The functional structure diagram of cell 7

$$E_8 = \sigma_1 E_7 + \sigma_2 E_6 + \sigma_3 E_5$$

$$\cdots\cdots\cdots \qquad (8.110)$$

$$E_{30} = \sigma_1 E_{29} + \sigma_2 E_{28} + \sigma_3 E_{27}$$

$$E_{31} = \sigma_1 E_{30} + \sigma_2 E_{29} + \sigma_3 E_{28}$$

Applying Eq. 8.107 and the coefficients $\sigma_1 = \alpha^{21}$, $\sigma_2 = \alpha$, and $\sigma_3 = \alpha^{17}$ of Eq. 8.109 to the set of these equations, the remainders of transform syndromes (or error patterns) E_j for $7 \le j \le 31$ can be easily computed as

$E_7 = \alpha^5$	$E_{16} = \alpha^{13}$	$E_{25} = \alpha^{27}$
$E_8 = \alpha^{15}$	$E_{17} = \alpha^5$	$E_{26} = \alpha^{21}$
$E_9 = \alpha^5$	$E_{18} = \alpha^{25}$	$E_{27} = \alpha^{30}$
$E_{10} = \alpha^{18}$	$E_{19} = \alpha^6$	$E_{28} = \alpha^{18}$
$E_{11} = \alpha^{19}$	$E_{20} = \alpha^{28}$	$E_{29} = \alpha^{10}$
$E_{12} = \alpha^{22}$	$E_{21} = \alpha$	$E_{30} = \alpha^{29}$
$E_{13} = \alpha^{25}$	$E_{22} = \alpha^{12}$	$E_{31} = E_0 = \alpha^{27}$
$E_{14} = \alpha^{11}$	$E_{23} = \alpha^{20}$	
$E_{15} = 0$	$E_{24} = \alpha^{12}$	

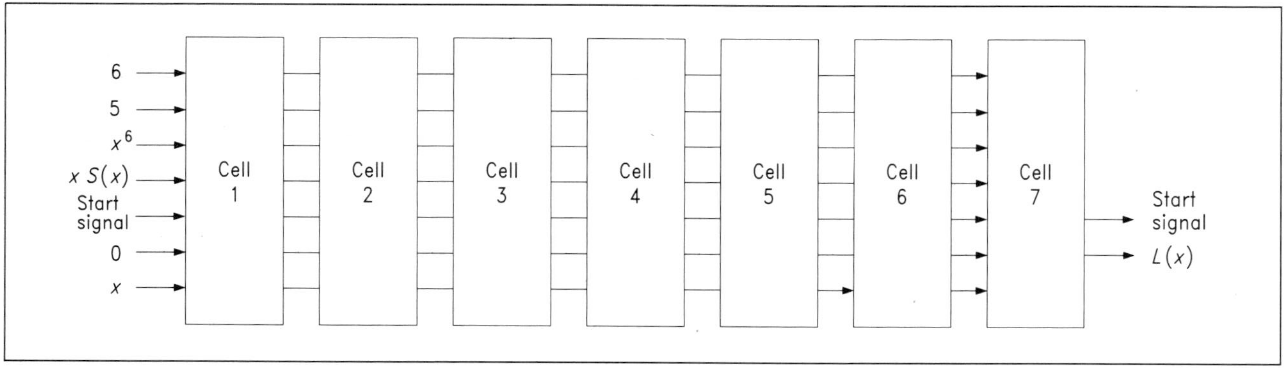

Fig. 8.21 The complete systolic array to compute the error-locator polynomial $\sigma(x)$

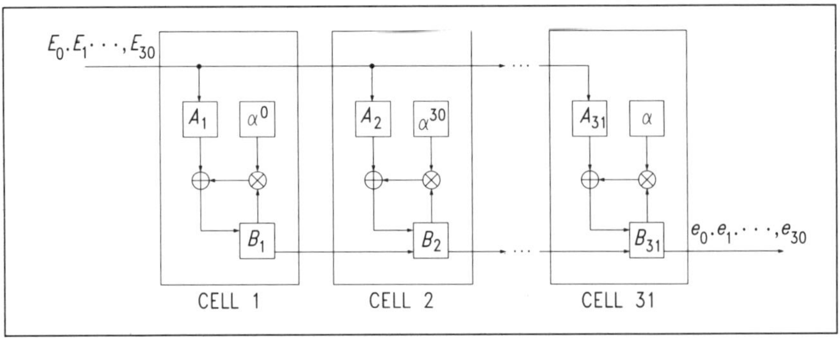

Fig. 8.22 The systolic cell structure for computing the errors of the (31, 25) RS code

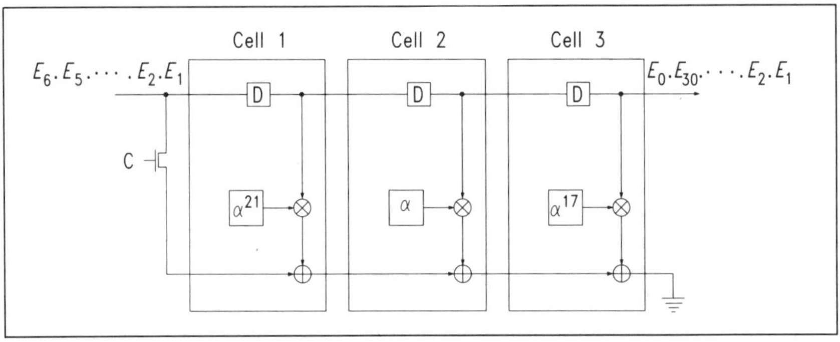

Fig. 8.23 The systolic cell structure for computing the error pattern in a (31, 25) RS code

Thus, a systolic array circuit for computing the transform error can be shown as in Fig. 8.22.

Referring to Eq. 8.87, the inverse transform of the error pattern E_k is

$$e_k = \sum_{j=0}^{30} E_j \, \alpha^{-jk} = E(\alpha^{-k}) \qquad 0 \le k \le 30 \tag{8.111}$$

In order to develop a systolic array for computing e_k, Eq. 8.111 can also be rewritten in recursive form as

$$e_k = (\cdots((E_{30}\,\alpha^{-k} + E_{29})\,\alpha^{-k} + E_{28})\,\alpha^{-k} + \cdots + E_1)\alpha^{-k} + E_0 \tag{8.112}$$

A systolic cell structure for computing Eq. 8.112 is shown in Fig. 8. 23. Using this figure, we obtain $e_2 = \alpha^8$, $e_5 = \alpha^2$ and $e_{10} = \alpha^{10}$ so that the error pattern becomes $e(x) = \alpha^8 x^2 + \alpha^2 x^5 + \alpha x^{10}$ as expected. The number of basic cells needed to compute Eq. 8.112 is 31. Finally the decoding process is accomplished by $c(x) = r(x) + e(x)$.

REFERENCES

1. Berlekamp, E.R.: *Algebraic Coding Theory*, McGraw-Hill, New York, 1968.
2. Berlekamp, E.R.: "Bit-serial Reed-Solomon encoders", *IEEE Trans. Inform. Theory*, vol. IT–28, no. 6, pp 869–874, 1982.
3. Blahut, R.E.: *Theory and Practice of Error Control Codes*, Addison-Wesley, Reading, Mass., 1983.
4. ------: "Transform techniques for error-control codes", *IBM J. Res. Dev.*, vol. 23, pp 299–315, 1970.
5. Gorenstein, D.C. and N. Zierler: "A class of error-correcting codes in p^m symbols" *J. Soc. Ind. Appl. Math.*, vol. 9, pp 207–214, 1961.
6. Hsu, I.K., I.S. Reed, T.K. Troung, K. Wang, C.S. Yeh, and L.J. Deutch: "The VLSI implementation of a Reed-Solomon encoder using Berlekamp's bit-serial multiplier algorithm", *IEEE Trans. Comput.*, vol. C–33, no. 10, pp 906–911, 1984.
7. Miller, R.L., T.K. Troung, and I.S. Reed: "Efficient program for decoding the (255, 223) Reed-Solomon code over GF(2^8) with both errors and erasures, using transform decoding", *Proc. IEEE*, vol. 127, no. 4, July 1980.
8. Murakami, H, I.S. Reed, and L.R. Welch: "A transform decoder for Reed-Solomon codes for multiple-user communication systems", *IEEE Trans. Inform. Theory*, vol. IT–23, pp 675–683, Nov. 1977.
9. Peterson, W.W. and E.J. Weldon, Jr.: *Error-Correcting Codes*, 2nd ed., the MIT Press, Cambridge, Mass., 1972.
10. Rhee, M.Y.: *Error Correcting Coding Theory*, McGraw-Hill, New York, 1989.
11. ------: *BCH Codes and Reed-Solomon Codes*, Minum Sha, Seoul, Korea, 1990.
12. Vries, L.B. and K. Odaka: "CIRC—the error correcting code for compact disc", *AES Premier Conf.* The New World of Digital Audio, New York, pp 3–6, June 1982.
13. Yeh, C.S., I.S. Reed, and T.K. Troung: "Systolic mutipliers for Finite Field GF(2)", *IEEE Trans. Comput.*, vol. C–33, pp 357–360, Apr. 1984.

Chapter

9

Error Control for Cryptosystems

Error-control coding is widely used in digital communications to correct transmission errors as discussed in Chapters 7 and 8. However, not many papers on error-correction techniques for cryptographic protection have been published, although their importance is undisputed. When cryptography and error-correction coding are used together, we may think of two kinds of system configurations as illustrated in Fig. 9.1. In the first type, shown in Fig. 9.1(a), the plaintext is first enciphered and then encoded; after transmission, the coded ciphertext is first decoded and then deciphered. This method is useful for a block cipher because it has the advantage of allowing automatic authentication of received plaintext. The second type is shown in Fig. 9.1(b); where the inner and outer blocks are interchanged so that encoding precedes enciphering and deciphering precedes decoding. In this case, error propagation, if present, may overwhelm beyond the error-correcting capability of the decoder. With this scheme, an opponent can inject false messages which will pass through the error-correcting decoder to create confusion and disrupt the cryptosystem.

Several decoding methods have been described in Chapters 7 and 8. Here we shall mainly cover error corrections for stream cipher

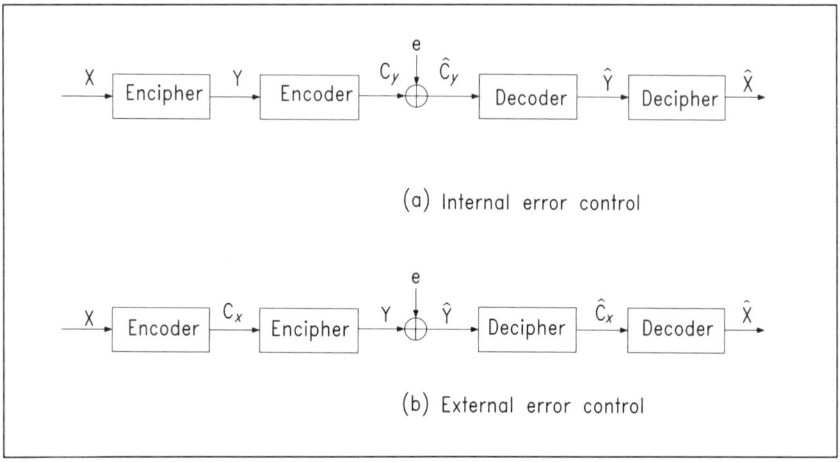

Fig. 9.1 Error-controlled cryptosystems

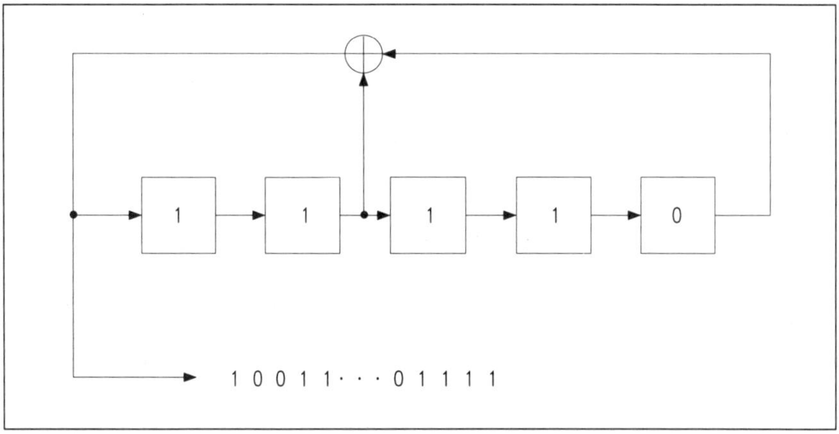

Fig. 9.2 Key stream generator with tap coefficients (01001)

systems by RS decoding using the Peterson-Gorenstein-Zierler (PGZ) method.

9.1 PGZ ALGORITHM FOR RS DECODING

Let the plaintext sequence be $\mathbf{X} = (x_0, x_1, \ldots, x_i, \ldots)$, the key-bit stream $\mathbf{K} = (k_0, k_1, \ldots, k_i, \ldots)$, the ciphertext sequence $\mathbf{Y} = (y_0, y_1, \ldots y_i, \ldots)$, and the initial contents $\boldsymbol{\mu} = (\mu_0, \mu_1, \ldots, \mu_m)$ of the m-stage LFSR. Then the key-bit matrix can be expressed in terms of μ and $\mathbf{T}$:

$$\begin{bmatrix} k_0 \\ k_1 \\ \cdot \\ \cdot \\ \cdot \\ k_{m-1} \\ k_m \end{bmatrix} = \begin{bmatrix} \mu_m & \mu_{m-1} & \cdots & \mu_2 & \mu_1 \\ \mu_{m-1} & \mu_{m-2} & \cdots & \mu_1 & \mu_0 \\ \cdot & \cdot & & \cdot & \cdot \\ \cdot & \cdot & & \cdot & \cdot \\ \cdot & \cdot & & \cdot & \cdot \\ \mu_0 & k_0 & \cdots & k_{m-3} & k_{m-2} \\ k_0 & k_1 & \cdots & k_{m-2} & k_{m-1} \end{bmatrix} \begin{bmatrix} g_m \\ g_{m-1} \\ \cdot \\ \cdot \\ \cdot \\ g_2 \\ g_1 \end{bmatrix} \tag{9.1}$$

where $\mathbf{T} = (g_1, g_2, \ldots, g_m)$ is the tap-coefficient vector.

The following matrix system provides the basis of deriving the error-locator polynomial $\sigma(x)$. If the coefficients σ_k for $1 \le k \le v$ of $\sigma(x)$ are known, the roots of $\sigma(x)$ can be found, in order to determine the error locations.

$$\begin{bmatrix} \sigma_v \\ \sigma_{v-1} \\ \cdot \\ \cdot \\ \cdot \\ \sigma_1 \end{bmatrix} = \mathbf{M}^{-1} \begin{bmatrix} s_{v+1} \\ s_{v+2} \\ \cdot \\ \cdot \\ \cdot \\ s_{2v} \end{bmatrix} \tag{9.2}$$

where $\mathbf{M}$ is the syndrome-component matrix, i.e.

$$\mathbf{M} = \begin{bmatrix} s_1 & s_2 & \cdots & s_v \\ s_2 & s_3 & \cdots & s_{v+1} \\ \cdot & & & \\ \cdot & & & \\ \cdot & & & \\ s_v & s_{v+1} & \cdots & s_{2v-1} \end{bmatrix} \tag{9.3}$$

The syndrome components in Eq. 9.3 are expressed as

$$s_\lambda = \sum_{k=1}^{v} Y_k Z_k^\lambda \qquad 0 \le \lambda \le 2t \tag{9.4}$$

where Z_k denotes the error-location numbers and Y_k the error values for $1 \le k \le v$. Equation 9.4 is rewritten as

$$s_1 = Y_1 Z_1 + Y_2 Z_2 + \cdots + Y_v Z_v$$

$$s_2 = Y_1 Z_1^2 + Y_2 Z_2^2 + \cdots + Y_v Z_v^2$$

. . . .

$$s_{2t} = Y_1 Z_1^{2t} + Y_2 Z_2^{2t} + \cdots + Y_\nu Z_\nu^{2t} \tag{9.5}$$

The unknown error values Y_k for $1 \le k \le \nu$ can be easily determined in terms of the syndrome components s_λ, $0 \le \lambda \le 2t$, and the error-location numbers Z_k, $1 \le k \le \nu$.

The DSEC (31, 27) RS code for GF (2^5) will be used for the error control of the three stream cipher systems, namely (i) the key-autokey synchronous cipher, (ii) the ciphertext-feedback asynchronous cipher, and (iii) the plaintext-feedback asynchronous cipher. As discussed above, there are two error-control schemes depending on whether the decoding methods are internal or external. Consider the case where the plaintext has the following message:

> The aim of cryptography is to hide the clear form of plaintext by making it unreadable.

The encryption process generally begins with the conversion of plaintext into binary numbers representing each plaintext letter. Each bit can take either two values (0 or 1) of a binary (base-2) number system or a decimal (base-10) number system. In some cryptosystems, it is more convenient to work in the ASCII code. Let us convert the plaintext given above into the ASCII code, as shown in the following.

9.2 INTERNAL ERROR CONTROL (IEC) FOR STREAM CIPHERS

If error correction is desired, then internal error control is an ideal scheme to apply. If external error control is used, error propagation in the deciphering operation introduces too many errors so that the error control code prevents error correction. In the following subsections, the DSEC (31, 27) RS code will be used for error control throughout the subsequent sections.

9.2.1 IEC for Key-autokey Synchronous Ciphers

With an internal error control scheme as shown in Fig. 9.1(a), the plaintext is first enciphered with the key stream generated by Fig. 9.2 and then encoded with the RS generator polynomial $g(x) = (x + \alpha)(x + \alpha^2) \ldots (x + \alpha^{2t})$ for $t = 2$.

The key generator with initial contents (11110) is shown in Fig. 9.2. The key-bit stream generated from Fig. 9.2 has a period $2^5 - 1 = 31$ bits, i.e. (1001101001000010101110110001111). The key-bit stream for encipherment is shown in Table 9.2.

Table 9.1 Plaintext Symbols Represented by ASCII Code

01010100	01101000	11100101	00100000	01100001	11101001
01101101	00100000	11101111	11100110	00100000	11100011
11110010	01111001	01110000	11110100	11101111	01100111
11110010	01100001	01110000	01101000	01111001	00100000
11101001	01110011	00100000	11110100	11101111	00100000
01101000	11101001	01100100	11100101	00100000	11110100
01101000	11100101	00100000	11100011	11101100	11100101
01100001	11110010	00100000	11100110	11101111	11110010
01101101	00100000	11101111	11100110	00100000	01110000
11101100	01100001	11101001	01101110	11110100	11100101
11111000	11110100	01100010	01111001	00100000	01101101
01100001	01101011	11101001	01101110	01100111	00100000
11101001	11110100	00100000	01110101	01101110	11110010
11100101	01100001	01100100	01100001	01100010	11101100
11100101	10101110				

Executing modulo-2 addition symbol-by-symbol in Tables 9.1 and 9.2, we can encipher the plaintext into the ciphertext as shown in Table 9.3. Let us assume during transmission two symbol errors occurring at somewhere in the underlined part of Table 9.3.

Consider a DSEC (31, 27) RS code with symbols from GF(2^5). Since $m = 5$ and $t = 2$, there are $k = 31 - 2t = 27$ ciphertext symbols. Therefore, we must arrange the ciphertext listed in Table 9.3 in blocks of 5-bit symbols. For the purpose of illustration, consider only the underlined part of the ciphertext in Table 9.3 for encoding and rearrange it in the form of 27 symbols, each consisting of 5 bits as shown in Table 9.4.

Table 9.2 Key Stream for Encipherment

10011010	01000010	10111011	00011111	00110100	10000101
01110110	00111110	01101001	00001010	11101100	01111100
11010010	00010101	11011000	11111001	10100100	00101011
10110001	11110011	01001000	01010111	01100011	11100110
10010000	10101110	11000111	11001101	00100001	01011101
10001111	10011010	01000010	10111011	00011111	00110100
10000101	01110110	00111110	01101001	00001010	11101100
01111100	11010010	00010101	11011000	11111001	10100100
00101011	10110001	11110011	01001000	01010111	01100011
11100110	10010000	10101110	11000111	11001101	00100001
01011101	10001111	10011010	01000010	10111011	00011111
00110100	10000101	01110110	00111110	01101001	00001010
11101100	01111100	11010010	00010101	11011000	11111001
10100100	00101011	10110001	11110011	01001000	01010111
01100011	11100110				

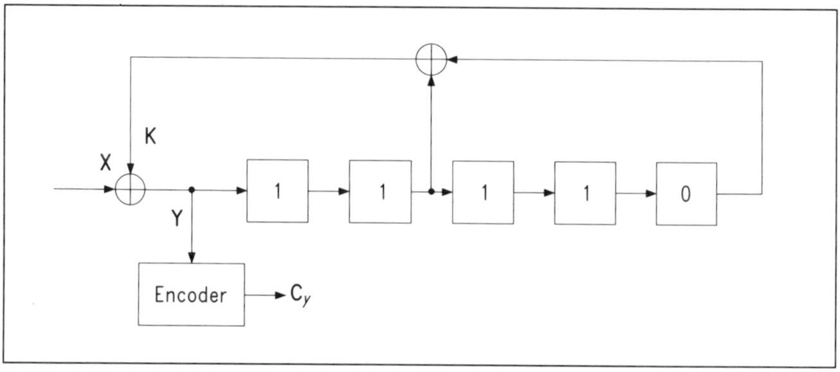

Fig. 9.3 Ciphertext feedback key generator

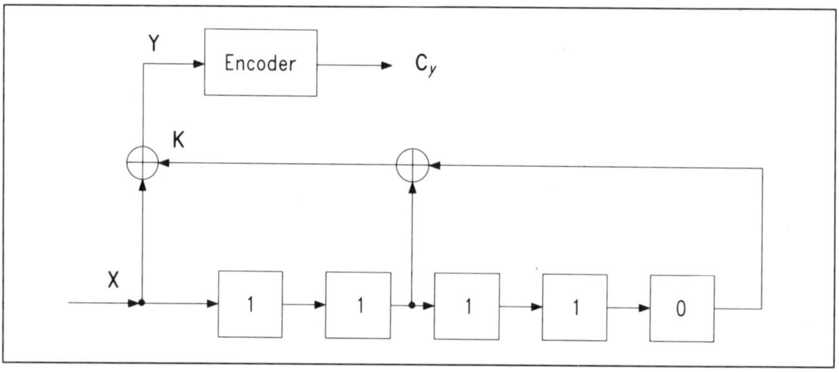

Fig. 9.4 Plaintext feedback key generator

Table 9.3 Ciphertext Symbols Represented by ASCII Code

11001110	00101010	01011110	00111111	01010101	01101100
00011011	00011110	10000110	11101100	11001100	10011111
00100000	01101100	10101000	00001101	01001011	01001100
01000011	10010010	00111000	00111111	00011010	11000110
01111001	11011101	11100111	00111001	11001110	01111101
11100111	01110011	00100110	01011110	00111111	11000000
11101101	10010011	00011110	10001010	11100110	00001001
00011101	00100000	00110101	00111110	00010110	01010110
01000110	10010001	00011100	10101110	01110111	00010011
00001010	11110001	01000111	10101001	00111001	11000100
10100101	01111011	11111000	00111011	10011011	01110010
01010101	11101110	10011111	01010000	00001110	00101010
00000101	10001000	11110010	01100000	10110110	00001011
01000001	01001010	11010101	10010010	00101010	10111011
10000110	01001000				

Table 9.4 Ciphertext for Encoding (Underlined Part in Table 9.3)

10100	11000	10000	11100	10010
00111	00000	11111	10001	10101
10001	10011	11001	11011	10111
10011	10011	10011	10011	10011
11101	11100	11101	11001	10010
01100	10111			

Table 9.5 Encoded Ciphertext $\mathbf{C}_Y$

10100	11000	10000	11100	10010
00111	00000	11111	10001	10101
10001	10011	11001	11011	10111
10011	10011	10011	10011	10011
11101	11100	11101	11001	10010
01100	10111	10001	10110	10000
01000				

Table 9.6 Received Ciphertext $\mathbf{r}_Y$

10100	11000	10000	11100	10010
00111	00000	11111	10001	10101
10001	10011	01000	11011	10111
10011	10011	10011	10011	10011
11101	01110	11101	11001	10010
01100	10111	10001	10110	10000
01000				

These 27 symbols are the enciphered symbols represented by $\mathbf{Y} = (y_0, y_1, \ldots, y_{26})$. The generator polynomial of a double-symbol-error-correcting RS code of length $2^5 - 1 = 31$ symbols is defined as

$$g(x) = (x + \alpha)(x + \alpha^2)(x + \alpha^3)(x + \alpha^4)$$

$$= \alpha^{10} + \alpha^{29}x + \alpha^{19}x^2 + \alpha^{24}x^3 + x^4 \tag{9.6}$$

Using Eq. 9.6, the ciphertext $\mathbf{Y}$ can be encoded into the systematically encoded ciphertext $\mathbf{C}_Y$ as listed in Table 9.5.

The parity-check symbols of encoded ciphertext $\mathbf{C}_Y = (c_{30}, c_{29}, \ldots, c_4, c_3, c_2, c_1, c_0)$ are the last four blocks, i.e. $c_3 = 10001$, $c_2 = 10110$, $c_1 = 10000$ and $c_0 = 01000$. After transmission, assume that $\mathbf{r}_Y = (r_{30}, r_{29}, \ldots r_0)$ is received as tabulated in Table 9.6.

Notice that symbol errors have occurred at $r_9 = 01110$ and $r_{18} = 01000$. Let the error polynomial be $e(x) = \alpha^{29} x^9 + \alpha^{10} x^{18}$ where both α^{29} and α^{10} are the error values at the error positions x^9 and x^{18}. Since $\mathbf{e}_Y = \mathbf{C}_Y + \mathbf{r}_Y$, $e_9 = c_9 + r_9 = (11100) + (01110) = 10010 = \alpha^{29}$ and $e_{18} = c_{18} + r_{18} = (11001) + (01000) = 10001 = \alpha^{10}$. Therefore it is proved that $e(x) = \alpha^{29} x^9 + \alpha^{10} x^{18}$ is the correct expression for the error polynomial. The syndrome components of the received vector $\mathbf{r}_Y$ are symbols computed by substituting $x = \alpha, \alpha^2, \alpha^3$, and α^4, respectively, into $e(x)$. They are:

$$s_1 = e(\alpha) = \alpha^7 + \alpha^{28} = \alpha = (01000)$$

$$s_2 = e(\alpha^2) = \alpha^{16} + \alpha^{15} = \alpha^2 = (00100)$$

$$s_3 = e(\alpha^3) = \alpha^{25} + \alpha^2 = \alpha^{14} = (10111) \tag{9.7}$$

$$s_4 = e(\alpha^4) = \alpha^3 + \alpha^{20} = \alpha^2 = (00100)$$

Since a (31, 27) RS code is a double-symbol-error correcting code, i.e. $\nu = t = 2$, the syndrome-component matrix of Eq. 9.3 becomes

$$\mathbf{M} = \begin{bmatrix} s_1 & s_2 \\ s_2 & s_3 \end{bmatrix} = \begin{bmatrix} \alpha & \alpha^2 \\ \alpha^2 & \alpha^{14} \end{bmatrix} \tag{9.8}$$

the coefficients of the error-locator polynomial $\sigma(x)$ are determined from Eq. 9.2 as shown below.

$$\begin{bmatrix} \sigma_2 \\ \sigma_1 \end{bmatrix} = \begin{bmatrix} s_1 & s_2 \\ s_2 & s_3 \end{bmatrix}^{-1} \begin{bmatrix} s_3 \\ s_4 \end{bmatrix} \tag{9.9}$$

Since $|\mathbf{M}| = \alpha^{23} \neq 0$, σ_2 and σ_1 can be easily obtained as

$$\sigma_2 = \frac{s_3^2 + s_2 s_4}{s_1 s_3 + s_2^2}$$

$$\sigma_1 = \frac{s_2 s_3 + s_1 s_4}{s_1 s_3 + s_2^2} \tag{9.10}$$

Substituting Eq. 9.7 into Eq. 9.10 yields the coefficients of $\sigma(x)$ as shown below.

$$\sigma_2 = \frac{\alpha^{28} + \alpha^4}{\alpha^{23}} = \alpha^{27}$$

$$\sigma_1 = \frac{\alpha^{16} + \alpha^3}{\alpha^{23}} = \alpha^{25} \tag{9.11}$$

Thus, the error-locator polynomial becomes

$$\sigma(x) = 1 + \alpha^{25}x + \alpha^{27}x^2 \tag{9.12}$$

Since $\sigma(x) = 0$ for $x = \alpha^{13}$ and $x = \alpha^{22}$, the error location numbers are

$$Z_1 = \frac{1}{\alpha^{22}} = \alpha^9$$

$$Z_2 = \frac{1}{\alpha^{13}} = \alpha^{18} \tag{9.13}$$

Equation 9.5 for $v = 2$ becomes

$$s_1 = Y_1Z_1 + Y_2Z_2$$

$$s_2 = Y_1Z_1^2 + Y_2Z_2^2 \tag{9.14}$$

From Eq. 9.14, the error values Y_1 and Y_2 can be computed as

$$Y_1 = \frac{s_1Z_2 + s_2}{Z_1Z_2 + Z_1^2}$$

$$Y_2 = \frac{s_1Z_1 + s_2}{Z_1Z_2 + Z_2^2} \tag{9.15}$$

Substituting Z_1, Z_2 from Eq. 9.13 and s_1, s_2 from Eq. 9.7 into Eq.9.15 yields the following error values.

$$Y_1 = \frac{\alpha\alpha^{18} + \alpha^2}{\alpha^8\alpha^{18} + (\alpha^9)^2} = \alpha^{29}$$

$$Y_2 = \frac{\alpha\alpha^9 + \alpha^2}{\alpha^9\alpha^{18} + (\alpha^{18})^2} = \alpha^{10}$$

Therefore, the error-pattern polynomial is

$$e(x) = \alpha^{29}x^9 + \alpha^{10}x^{18} \tag{9.16}$$

which is proved to be the correct assumption. Thus, the received ciphertext $\mathbf{r}_Y = (r_{30}, r_{29}, \ldots, r_0)$ is error-corrected by using the DSEC (31, 27) RS code into the encoded ciphertext $\mathbf{c}_Y = (c_{30}, c_{29}, \ldots, c_0)$. The error symbols occurring at r_9 and r_{18} are completely recovered by error correction such that $r_9 = (01110) \rightarrow c_9 = (11100)$ and $r_{18} = (01000) \rightarrow c_{18} = (11001)$. Finally, the key-autokey decipherment under the same key stream as shown in Table 9.2 recreates ASCII plaintext identical to the one tabulated in Table 9.1. Therefore, conversion of recovered ASCII plaintext into plaintext letters results in the original plaintext as follows.

The aim of cryptography is to hide the clear form of plaintext by making it unreadable.

9.2.2 IEC for Ciphertext Feedback Asynchronous Ciphers

Consider the ciphertext feedback generator for $m = 5$ with tap coefficients (01001) as illustrated in Fig. 9.3. Using again a DSEC (31, 27) RS code with symbols from GF (2^5), let us attempt to correct transmission symbol errors occurring at $e_{23} = (11011) = \alpha^{16}$ and $e_{22} = (11111) = \alpha^{15}$. Suppose the ASCII plaintext is the same as in Table 9.1. Then, the key-bit stream generated from Fig. 9.3 is shown in Table 9.4.

Enciphering the plaintext of Table 9.1 with the key stream of Table 9.7 yields the ciphertext of Table 9.8.

If the ciphertext **Y** corresponding to the underlined part in Table 9.8 is systematically encoded with the generator polynomial $g(x) = \alpha^{10} + \alpha^{29} x + \alpha^{19} x^2 + \alpha^{24} x^3 + x^4$, then the encoded ciphertext $\mathbf{C}_Y$ is as shown in Table 9.9.

If the symbol errors, $e_{23} = (11011) = \alpha^{16}$ and $e_{22} = (11111) = \alpha^{15}$, occur at the respective positions $c_{23} = (00000) = 0$ and $c_{22} = (00110) = \alpha^{20}$ in the underlined part during transmission, then the corresponding received symbols are $r_{23} = (11011) = \alpha^{16}$ and $r_{22} = (11001) = \alpha^{17}$.

Table 9.7 Key Stream for Ciphertext Feedback Scheme

10001001	10010001	10010111	00011110	01110101	10110101
11001101	00001011	10000000	10101001	10010001	11000001
10001100	01110010	10101000	11001111	00101110	01000000
11111010	01001011	11110101	01101000	00011011	10110000
10011110	01111010	00000001	01101011	00000101	11100111
11010011	00101111	10001101	00111001	11011001	10010010
10001110	10100011	10011011	00101101	11110110	01110001
10011001	11001110	11011001	10010111	11000010	00010110
00110100	10101111	10101011	00011000	01100010	10100010
00100100	01001011	11011100	11000111	00111100	01100100
01101000	10011000	01100000	10100000	10101111	10000101
01001011	11110010	10010100	10010000	01110100	01000011
11010110	00000010	00110101	11000000	11000111	00111101
10101001	01100000	01000000	00110111	00100010	00110001
10111100	10000010				

Table 9.8 Ciphertext Symbols for Ciphertext Feedback Scheme

11011101	11111001	01110010	00111110	00010100	01011100
10100000	00101011	01101111	01001111	10110001	00100010
01111110	00001011	11011000	00111011	11000001	00100111
00001000	00101010	10000101	00000000	01100010	10010000
01110111	00001001	00100001	10011111	11101010	11000111
10111011	11000110	11101001	11011100	11111001	01100110
11100110	01000110	10111011	11001110	00011010	10010100
11111000	00111100	11111001	01110001	00101101	11100100
01011001	10001111	01000100	11111110	01000010	11010010
11001000	00101010	00110101	10101001	11001000	10000001
10010000	01101100	00000010	11011001	10001111	11101000
00101010	10011001	01111101	11111110	00010011	01100011
00111111	11110110	00010101	10110101	10101001	11001111
01001100	00000001	00100100	01010110	01000000	11011101
01011001	00101100				

Table 9.9 Encoded Ciphertext Corresponding to the Underlined Part in Table 9.8

10010	01110	00010	00001
01010	10000	10100	00000
00110	00101	00100	00011
10111	00001	00100	10000
11001	11111	11010	10110
00111	10111	01111	00011
01110	10011	10111	01100
01110	11001	00111	

We can now assume that the error-pattern polynomial is $e(x) = \alpha^{15} x^{22} + \alpha^{16} x^{23}$. The syndrome components of the received vector $\mathbf{r}_Y$ are computed from $e(x)$ by substituting $x = \alpha, \alpha^2, \alpha^3$, and α^4 in $e(x)$ as follows:

$$
\begin{aligned}
s_1 &= e(\alpha) = \alpha^6 + \alpha^8 = \alpha^{11} = (11100) \\
s_2 &= e(\alpha^2) = \alpha^{28} + 1 = \alpha^{26} = (11101) \\
s_3 &= e(\alpha^3) = \alpha^{19} + \alpha^{23} = \alpha^{29} = (10010) \\
s_4 &= e(\alpha^4) = \alpha^{10} + \alpha^{15} = \alpha^{12} = (01110)
\end{aligned}
\tag{9.17}
$$

Since $\nu = 2$ in Eq. 9.3, the syndrome-component matrix may be represented as

$$\mathbf{M} = \begin{bmatrix} S_1 & S_2 \\ S_2 & S_3 \end{bmatrix} = \begin{bmatrix} \alpha^{11} & \alpha^{26} \\ \alpha^{26} & \alpha^{29} \end{bmatrix} \tag{9.18}$$

Using Eq. 9.10, the coefficients of the error-locator polynomial $\sigma(x)$ are obtained as

$$\sigma_2 = \frac{\alpha^{27} + \alpha^{7}}{\alpha^{9} + \alpha^{21}} = \frac{\alpha^{15}}{\alpha} = \alpha^{14}$$

$$\sigma_1 = \frac{\alpha^{24} + \alpha^{23}}{\alpha^{9} + \alpha^{21}} = \frac{\alpha^{10}}{\alpha} = \alpha^{9} \tag{9.19}$$

Thus the error-locator polynomial is

$$\sigma(x) = 1 + \alpha^{9}x + \alpha^{14}x^{2} \tag{9.20}$$

Since the roots of $\sigma(x)$ are α^8 and α^9, the error location numbers are obtained as

$$Z_1 = \frac{1}{\alpha^{8}} = \alpha^{23} = (11110)$$

$$Z_2 = \frac{1}{\alpha^{9}} = \alpha^{22} = (10101)$$

The error values Y_1 and Y_2 are computed from Eq. 9.15 as follows:

$$Y_1 = \frac{\alpha^{2} + \alpha^{26}}{\alpha^{14} + \alpha^{15}} = \frac{\alpha^{17}}{\alpha} = \alpha^{16} = (11011) = e_{23}$$

$$Y_2 = \frac{\alpha^{3} + \alpha^{26}}{\alpha^{14} + \alpha^{13}} = \frac{\alpha^{15}}{1} = \alpha^{15} = (11111) = e_{22}$$

Hence, the error-pattern polynomial becomes

$$e(x) = \alpha^{15}x^{22} + \alpha^{16}x^{23} \tag{9.21}$$

Since $\mathbf{C} = \mathbf{e} + \mathbf{r}$, we have $c_{22} = e_{22} + r_{22} = Y_2 + r_{22} = (11111) + (11001) = (00110)$ and $c_{23} = e_{23} + r_{23} = Y_1 + r_{23} = (11011) + (11011) = (00000)$. Thus the encoded ciphertext of Table 9.9 is completely recovered by error correction. Finally, after deletion of parity symbols, we may decrypt the ciphertext under the key stream of Table 9.7 and recover the clear form of the plaintext described in Table 9.1.

Table 9.10 Key Stream for Plaintext Feedback Scheme

10101111	10111001	01111110	01100001	00011011	01110101
00010000	00100001	00111100	10000110	10111001	00111111
11100011	00001101	10010111	10111010	10011100	10100010
11000011	00001011	01010111	10011001	01011101	10000001
00111101	00010111	01010001	00111010	10011100	10110001
00011001	01111101	00010010	00011110	01100001	00111010
10111001	01111110	01100001	00111111	11100100	01011110
01110011	01110011	00011001	00111110	10001100	10000011
00001000	00100001	00111100	10000110	10111001	00011111
10111100	01111011	01110101	00010000	11001010	10011110
01010001	11111010	10111011	10001101	10000001	00011000
00110011	01010001	10100101	00010000	11101010	11110001
00111101	00110010	10101001	00011110	11110000	11001011
00101110	01110011	01010010	00111011	01010011	10101100
01011110	01000110				

9.2.3 IEC for Plaintext Feedback Asynchronous Ciphers

The key generator for the plaintext feedback system is illustrated in Fig. 9.4. Using a DSEC (31, 27) RS code, we shall discuss error-correction problem for plaintext feedback in this section. Assume that symbol errors occur at $e_{24} = Y_1 = (01100) = \alpha^9$ and $e_7 = Y_2 = (10100) = \alpha^5$; let us use the same ASCII plaintext as shown in Table 9.1.

Given the initial contents (11110), the key stream generated from the plaintext feedback generator is shown in Table 9.10.

By enciphering the plaintext shown in Table 9.1 with the key of Table 9.10, we obtain the ciphertext symbols of Table 9.11.

Table 9.11 Ciphertext Symbols for Plaintext Feedback Scheme

11111011	11010001	10011011	01000001	01111010	10011100
01111101	00000001	11010011	01100000	10011001	11011100
00010001	01110100	11100111	01001110	01110011	11000101
00110001	01101010	00100111	11110001	00100100	10100001
11010100	01100100	01110001	11001110	01110011	10010001
01110001	10010100	01110110	11111011	01000001	11001110
11010001	10011011	01000001	11011100	00001000	10111011
00010010	10000001	00111001	11011000	01100011	01110001
01100101	00000001	11010011	01100000	10011001	01101111
01010000	00011010	10011100	01111110	00111110	01111011
10101001	00001110	11011001	11110100	10100001	01110101
01010010	00111010	01001100	01111110	10001101	11010001
11010100	11000110	10001001	01101011	10011110	00111001
11001011	00010010	00110110	01011010	00110001	01000000
10111011	11101000				

Table 9.12 Encoded Ciphertext Corresponding to Underlined Part of Table 9.11

11100	01010	01100	01011	01010
00100	11111	11000	10010	01001
01000	01110	10100	01100	10001
11000	11100	11100	11100	11100
10001	01110	00110	01010	00111
01101	11110	10011	11100	10000
00010				

As assumed before, the ciphertext corresponding to the underlined part in Table 9.11 is encoded with the same generator polynomial $g(x)$ as in previous subsections. Then the corresponding encoded ciphertext $\mathbf{C}_Y$ is as shown in Table 9.12.

If the symbol errors occur at positions 24 and 7 during transmission such that

$$c_{24} = (11111) \rightarrow r_{24} = (01100)$$

$$c_7 = (01010) \rightarrow r_7 = (10100),$$

then the error values will be $e_{24} = Y_1 = (10011) = \alpha^{25}$ and $e_7 = Y_2 = (11110) = \alpha^{23}$. Thus we can assume that the error-pattern polynomial becomes $e(x) = \alpha^{23} x^7 + \alpha^{25} x^{24}$.

The syndrome components are then computed from $e(x)$ as follows:

$$\begin{aligned} s_1 &= e(\alpha) = \alpha^{30} + \alpha^{18} = \alpha^{10} = (10001) \\ s_2 &= e(\alpha^2) = \alpha^6 + \alpha^{11} = \alpha^8 = (10111) \\ s_3 &= e(\alpha^3) = \alpha^{13} + \alpha^4 = \alpha^{20} = (00110) \\ s_4 &= e(\alpha^4) = \alpha^{20} + \alpha^{28} = \alpha^9 = (01011) \end{aligned} \tag{9.22}$$

From Eq. 9.3 for $v = 2$, the syndrome-component matrix can be expressed as

$$\mathbf{M} = \begin{bmatrix} s_1 & s_2 \\ s_2 & s_3 \end{bmatrix} = \begin{bmatrix} \alpha^{10} & \alpha^8 \\ \alpha^8 & \alpha^{20} \end{bmatrix} \tag{9.23}$$

The coefficients of $\sigma(x)$ can be determined by using Eq. 9.10:

$$\sigma_2 = \frac{\alpha^9 + \alpha^{17}}{\alpha^{30} + \alpha^{16}} = \frac{\alpha^{29}}{\alpha^{29}} = 1$$

$$\sigma_1 = \frac{\alpha^{28} + \alpha^{19}}{\alpha^{30} + \alpha^{16}} = \frac{\alpha^4}{\alpha^{29}} = \alpha^6 \tag{9.24}$$

Using Eq. 9.24, we can find the error-locator polynomial as

$$\sigma(x) = 1 + \alpha^6 x + x^2 \tag{9.25}$$

Since $\sigma(x) = 0$ at $x = \alpha^7$ and α^{24}, the error location numbers are easily found by taking the reciprocals of the roots, which are α^7 and α^{24}.

$$Z_1 = \frac{1}{\alpha^7} = \alpha^{24} = (01111)$$

$$Z_2 = \frac{1}{\alpha^{24}} = \alpha^7 = (00101) \tag{9.26}$$

Using Eq. 9.15, the error values can be computed as

$$Y_1 = \frac{\alpha^{17} + \alpha^8}{1 + \alpha^{17}} = \frac{\alpha^{24}}{\alpha^{30}} = \alpha^{25} = (10011)$$

(9.27)

$$Y_2 = \frac{\alpha^3 + \alpha^8}{1 + \alpha^{14}} = \frac{\alpha^5}{\alpha^{13}} = \alpha^{23} = (11110)$$

Thus, the error-pattern polynomial becomes

$$e(x) = \alpha^{23} x^7 + \alpha^{25} x^{24} \tag{9.28}$$

as expected. Once the error symbols are corrected by the (31, 27) RS code, the decoded ciphertext, after removing the parity symbols, is easily decrypted using the key stream of Table 9.10, and the ASCII plaintext shown in Table 9.1 is completely recovered.

We have so far analyzed internal error-control schemes, and have observed that error-control coding is adequate in such modes.

9.3 EXTERNAL ERROR CONTROL (EEC) FOR STREAM CIPHERS

In this section we consider the cases where encoding precedes enciphering and deciphering precedes decoding. We call this kind of system configuration 'external error control'. As in previous subsections, we choose the DSEC (31, 27) RS code for the purpose of external error control. The plaintext used is the same as the one in Sec. 9.2.

9.3.1 EEC for Key-autokey Synchronous Ciphers

In the key-autokey cipher, there is no error propagation due to the deciphering process. Therefore, error correction can be implemented either internally or externally with such a stream cipher. In Fig. 9.5, the key stream **K** is generated from the key-autokey generator with tap coefficients (01001) and initial seed vector (11110). As may be observed, the key-bit stream is generated independently of the plaintext **X**. Since a synchronous stream cipher has the advantage of no propagation of errors, a transmission error affecting one bit will not affect subsequent bits. Therefore, a synchronous stream cipher provides no problem of authentication when used with a fixed error-correcting code.

Consider the problem of encoding the underlined portion in Table 9.13, as before, with the RS generator polynomial $g(x)$ for double-symbol-error correction (DSEC).

The underlined portion is grouped in symbols of 5 bits each because each symbol is from GF (2^5). This portion of plaintext comprises 27 symbols, and may be represented as $\mathbf{X} = (x_0, x_1, \ldots, x_{26})$, as shown in Table 9.14.

Table 9.13 ASCII Plaintext Symbols Including Underlined Portion to Be Encoded

01010100	01101000	11100101	00100000	01100001	11101001
01101101	00100000	11101111	11100110	00100000	11100011
11110010	01111001	01110000	11110100	11101111	01100111
11110010	01100001	01110000	01101000	01111001	00100000
11101001	01110011	00100000	11110100	11101111	00100000
01101000	11101001	01100100	11100101	00100000	11110100
01101000	11100101	00100000	11100011	11101100	11100101
01100001	11110010	00100000	11100110	11101111	11110010
01101101	00100000	11101111	11100110	00100000	01110000
11101100	01100001	11101001	01101110	11110100	11100101
11111000	11110100	01100010	01111001	00100000	01101101
01100001	01101011	11101001	01101110	01100111	00100000
11101001	11110100	00100000	01110101	01101110	11110010
11100101	01100001	01100100	01100001	01100010	11101100
11100101	10101110				

Table 9.14 Regrouped Underlined Portion of Plaintext

10110	01111	11100	10011	00001	01110
00001	10100	00111	10010	01000	00111
01001	01110	01100	10000	01111	01001
11011	11001	00000	01101	00011	10100
10110	01001	11001			

Table 9.15 Encoded Plaintext $\mathbf{C}_x$ Representing Underlined Portion

10110	01111	11100	10011	00001	01110
00001	10100	00111	10010	01000	00111
01001	01110	01100	10000	01111	01001
11011	11001	00000	01101	00011	10100
10110	01001	11001	01001	01001	10110
11010					

Table 9.16 Key Stream **K** for Key-Autokey Encryption

10011	01001	00001	01011	10110	00111
11001	10100	10000	10101	11011	00011
11100	11010	01000	01010	11101	10001
11110	01101	00100	00101	01110	11000
11111	00110	10010	00010	10111	01100
01111					

Table 9.17 Ciphertext **Y** Produced by Encryption

00101	00110	11101	11000	10111	01001
11000	00000	10111	00111	10011	00100
10101	10100	00100	11010	10010	11000
00101	10100	00100	01000	01101	01100
01001	01111	01011	01011	11110	11010
10101					

The encoded plaintext is $\mathbf{C}_x = (c_{30}, c_{29}, \ldots, c_1, c_0)$, and is listed in Table 9.15.

In Table 9.15, the parity symbols are $c_3 = (01001)$, $c_2 = (01001)$, $c_1 = (10110)$, and $c_0 = (11010)$.

The key stream $\mathbf{K} = (k_{30}, k_{29}, \ldots, k_0)$ generated from the key-autokey generator in Fig. 9.5 is tabulated in Table 9.16.

The encryption process is accomplished by symbol-by-symbol, modulo-2 addition, of the encoded plaintext and the key stream tabulated in Tables 9.15 and 9.16, respectively. Thus, the ciphertext $\mathbf{Y} = (y_{30}, y_{29}, \ldots, y_1, y_0)$ is shown in Table 9.17.

Let the received ciphertext be $\hat{\mathbf{Y}} = (\hat{y}_{30}, \hat{y}_{29}, \ldots, \hat{y}_1, \hat{y}_0)$. During transmission of **Y**, assume the two-symbol errors have occurred at two positions, namely $y_{18} = (10101) \rightarrow \hat{y}_{18} = (00100)$ and $y_9 = (01000) \rightarrow \hat{y}_9 = (11010)$. Thus, the received ciphertext symbols are as shown in Table 9.18.

Deciphering the received ciphertext $\hat{\mathbf{Y}}$ of Table 9.18 with the key stream **K** of Table 9.16, we can recover the estimate of the encoded plaintext $\mathbf{C}_x$ as shown in Table 9.19.

Notice from Table 9.19 that c_{18} = (01001) → $\hat{c}_{18}$ – (11000) and c_9 = (01100) → $\hat{c}_9$ = (11111) after deciphering. Now, expecting to restore the original plaintext, the decoding process is to be implemented by using a DSEC (31, 27) RS code in order to correct the two symbol errors $\hat{c}_{18}$ and $\hat{c}_9$.

Let the error-pattern polynomial be $e(x) = \alpha^{29} x^9 + \alpha^{10} x^{18}$, which is the same form as used in Subsection 9.2.1, to facilitate a comparative study of the internal and external schemes. Therefore, the syndrome components of the encoded plaintext $\mathbf{C}_X$ are $s_1 = \alpha$, $s_2 = \alpha^2$, $s_3 = \alpha^{14}$, and $s_4 = \alpha^2$. Since the coefficients of error-locator polynomial $\sigma(x)$ are $\sigma_1 = \alpha^{25}$ and $\sigma_2 = \alpha^{27}$, we have $\sigma(x) = 1 + \alpha^{25}x + \alpha^{27}x^2$. The error location numbers that will be determined by taking the reciprocals of the roots of $\sigma(x)$ are $Z_1 = \alpha^{24}$ and $Z_2 = \alpha^7$, respectively. Applying these values of s_1, s_2, Z_1, and Z_2 to Eq. 9.15, we are able to compute the error values $Y_1 = \alpha^{29}$ and $Y_2 = \alpha^{10}$. Thus, the error-pattern polynomial $e(x)$ can be determined as assumed.

Since the corrected symbol is expressed as $c_i = \hat{c}_i + e_i = \hat{c}_i + Y_i$ for $i = 9$ and 18, we have $c_{18} = \hat{c}_{18} + Y_2$ = (11000) + (10001) = (01001) and $c_9 = \hat{c}_9 + Y_1$ = (11111) + (10010) = (01101). Hence we see that the two symbol errors are completely corrected and thus the original plaintext is recovered by dropping the four parity symbols as listed in Table 9.14.

It is obvious from key-autokey cipher analyses that it is immaterial whether the error corrections are made by the internal control scheme or the external control scheme. Either error-control scheme can be used for error correction.

Table 9.18 Received Ciphertext Symbols $\hat{\mathbf{Y}}$ for Key-Autokey Cipher

00101	00110	11101	11000	10111	01001
11000	00000	10111	00111	10011	00100
00100	10100	00100	11010	10010	11000
00101	10100	00100	11010	01101	01100
01001	01111	01011	01011	11110	11010
10101					

Table 9.19 Encoded Plaintext $\mathbf{C}_x$ Containing Two Symbol Errors

10110	01110	11100	10011	00001	01110
00001	10100	00111	10010	01000	00111
11000	01110	01100	10000	01111	01001
11011	11001	00000	11111	00011	10100
10110	01001	01001	01001	01001	10110
11010					

9.3.2 EEC for Ciphertext Feedback Asynchronous Ciphers

The external error-control system with ciphertext feedback is shown in Fig. 9.6. For a comparative study, we choose again the tap coefficients (01001) and initial seed vector (11110) for the key generator. Since we use the same plaintext as in previous cases, the 27-symbol plaintext is encoded into 31 symbols as shown in Table 9.15. The ciphertext **Y** is obtained by enciphering the coded plaintext $\mathbf{C}_x$ under the key stream **K** generated from the key generator excited by the ciphertext **Y**. The key stream generated at the sending end in the ciphertext feedback stream cipher is shown in Table 9.20.

Encryption of $\mathbf{C}_x$ by **K** produces the ciphertext **Y** as shown in Table 9.21.

Let us assume that two symbol errors have occurred in **Y** during transmission such that $y_{23} = (11001) \rightarrow \hat{y}_{23} = (00110)$ and $y_{22} = (10010) \rightarrow \hat{y}_{22} = (01001)$. Accordingly, the key stream **K** generated at the receiver is not exactly the same as in Table 9.20. But key errors exist in three places in the key stream as marked in Table 9.22.

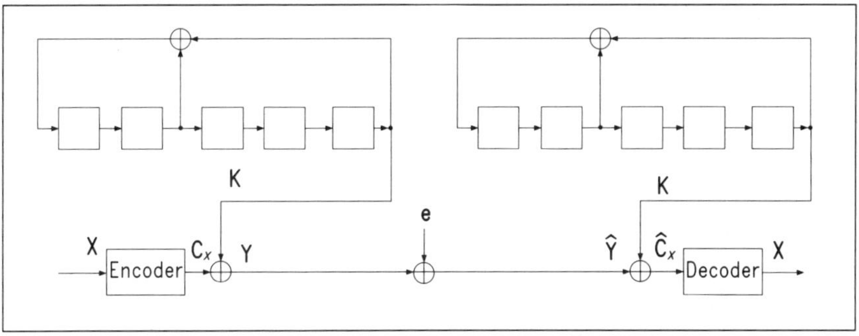

Fig. 9.5 Key-autokey cipher system for external error control

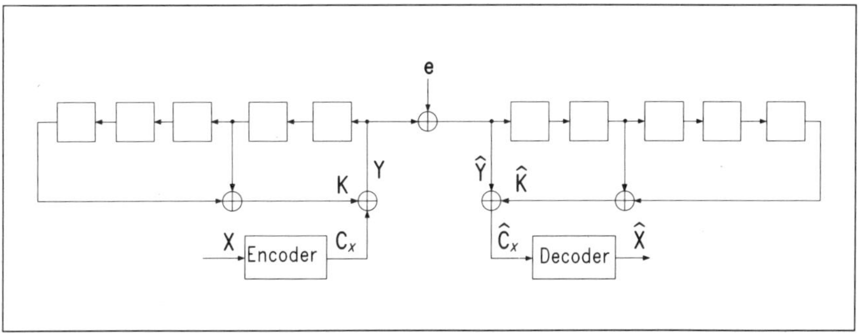

Fig. 9.6 External error control system for ciphertext feedback

Thus, the deciphered plaintext $\hat{\mathbf{C}}_x$ which contains three symbol errors and four redundancy symbols is obtained from modulo-2 sum of **Y** and **K** as indicated in Table 9.23.

Comparing $\mathbf{C}_x$ of Table 9.15 with that of Table 9.23, we may observe three symbol errors as shown below.

$$c_{23} = (10100) \rightarrow \hat{c}_{23} = (01100)$$

$$c_{22} = (00111) \rightarrow \hat{c}_{22} = (11101)$$

$$c_{21} = (10010) \rightarrow \hat{c}_{21} = (10001)$$

Table 9.20 Key Stream Generated at Sender Side

01011	10010	10111	10011	00000	01000
10010	01101	10101	00111	11001	11111
11101	10011	10010	01000	11100	01011
10000	10001	01010	11110	01001	11001
00000	00101	01000	11100	11001	10001
11110					

Table 9.21 Ciphertext **Y** Obtained by Enciphering $\mathbf{C}_x$ with **K**

11101	11101	01011	00000	00001	00110
10011	11001	10010	10101	10001	11000
10100	11101	11110	11000	10011	00010
01011	01000	01010	10011	01010	01101
10110	01100	10001	10101	10000	00111
00100					

Table 9.22 Key Stream **K** Generated at Receiver Side

01011	10010	10111	10011	00000	01000
10010	01010	10100	00100	11001	11111
11101	10011	10010	01000	11100	01011
10000	10001	01010	11110	01001	11001
00000	00101	01000	11100	11001	10001
11110					

Table 9.23 Deciphered Plaintext $\hat{\mathbf{C}}_x$

10110	01111	11100	10011	00001	01110
00001	01100	11101	10001	01000	00111
01001	01110	01100	10000	01111	01001
11011	11001	00000	01101	00011	10100
10110	01001	11001	01001	01001	10110
11010					

Since the error symbol is expressed as $e_i = c_i + \hat{c}_i$, we have

$$e_{23} = c_{23} + \hat{c}_{23} = (11000) = \alpha^{18}$$

$$e_{22} = c_{22} + \hat{c}_{22} = (11010) = \alpha^{27}$$

$$e_{21} = c_{21} + \hat{c}_{21} = (00011) = \alpha^{21}$$

Thus, the error-pattern polynomial can be determined as

$$e(x) = \alpha^{21}x^{21} + \alpha^{27}x^{22} + \alpha^{18}x^{23} \tag{9.29}$$

Using Eq. 9.29, the syndrome components can be obtained as follows:

$$\begin{aligned}
s_1 &= e(\alpha) &= \alpha^{11} &+ \alpha^{18} &+ \alpha^{10} &= \alpha^{22} &= (10101) \\
s_2 &= e(\alpha^2) &= \alpha &+ \alpha^{9} &+ \alpha^{2} &= \alpha^{13} &= (00111) \\
s_3 &= e(\alpha^3) &= \alpha^{22} &+ 1 &+ \alpha^{25} &= \alpha^{8} &= (10110) \\
s_4 &= e(\alpha^4) &= \alpha^{12} &+ \alpha^{22} &+ \alpha^{17} &= \alpha^{3} &= (00010)
\end{aligned} \tag{9.30}$$

Thus, the syndrome-component matrix for $\nu = 2$ is

$$\mathbf{M} = \begin{bmatrix} s_1 & s_2 \\ s_2 & s_3 \end{bmatrix} = \begin{bmatrix} a^{22} & \alpha^{13} \\ \alpha^{13} & \alpha^{8} \end{bmatrix} \tag{9.31}$$

where $|\mathbf{M}| = \alpha^5 \neq 0$.

Substituting the syndrome components obtained in Eq. 9.30 in Eq. 9.10, we can determine the coefficients of $\sigma(x)$ as follows:

$$\sigma_2 = \frac{\alpha^{16} + \alpha^{16}}{\alpha^5} = 0 = (00000)$$

$$\sigma_1 = \frac{\alpha^{21} + \alpha^{25}}{\alpha^5} = \alpha^{26} = (11101) \tag{9.32}$$

Therefore, the error-locator polynomial $\sigma(x)$ becomes

$$\sigma(x) = 1 + \alpha^{26}x \tag{9.33}$$

The root of $\sigma(x)$ is α^5. The error location number is accordingly

$$Z_1 = \frac{1}{\alpha^5} = \alpha^{26} = (\,11101\,)$$

Using Eq. 9.15, the error value is

$$Y_1 = \frac{s_1 Z_2 + s_2}{Z_1 Z_2 + Z_1^2}$$

$$= \frac{\alpha^{13}}{\alpha^{52}} = \alpha^{23} = (11110)$$

because $Z_2 = 0$. Then, the error-pattern polynomial is

$$e(x) = \alpha^{23} x^{26} \tag{9.34}$$

Combining Eqs. 9.29 and 9.34, we may suspect that four symbol errors have occurred at positions x^{21}, x^{22}, x^{23}, and x^{26}. Since $x_i = e_i + \hat{c}_i$, the actually decoded symbols x_i should be:

$$x_{21} = e_{21} + \hat{c}_{21} = (00011) + (10001) = (10010)$$

$$x_{22} = e_{22} + \hat{c}_{22} = (11010) + (11101) = (00111)$$

$$x_{23} = e_{23} + \hat{c}_{23} = (11000) + (01100) = (10100)$$

$$x_{26} = e_{26} + \hat{c}_{26} = (11110) + (11111) = (00001)$$

But, as we may observe from Table 9.24, they are erroneously decoded as $x_{21} = (10001)$, $x_{22} = (11101)$, $x_{23} = (01100)$, and $x_{26} = (11111)$ which are indeed contrary to our expectations.

After dropping the last four parity symbols $x_3 = (01001)$, $x_2 = (01001)$, $x_1 = (10110)$, and $x_0 = (11010)$ from Table 9.24, we obtain Table 9.25 which shows the final decoded plaintext corresponding to the underlined part of Table 9.13.

Replacing the underlined part in Table 9.13 by the contents of Table 9.25, we obtain Table 9.26 which represents the recovered ASCII plaintext.

Table 9.24 Erroneously Decoded Symbols $\hat{x}_i$ for $0 \le i \le 30$

10110	01111	11100	10011	11111	01110
00001	01100	11101	10001	01000	00111
01001	01110	01100	10000	01111	01001
11011	11001	00000	01101	00011	10100
10110	01001	11001	01001	01001	10110
11010					

Table 9.25 Recovered Plaintext after Dropping Parity Symbols

10110	01111	11100	10011	11111	01110
00001	01100	11101	10001	01000	00111
01001	01110	01100	10000	01111	01001
11011	11001	00000	01101	00011	10100
10110	01001	11001			

Table 9.26 Recovered ASCII Plaintext

01010100	01101000	11100101	00100000	01100001	11101001
01101101	00100000	11101111	11100110	00100000	11100011
11110010	01111001	01110000	11110100	11101111	01100111
11110010	01111111	01110000	01011001	11011000	10100000
11101001	01110011	00100000	11110100	11101111	00100000
01101000	11101001	01100100	11100101	00100000	11110100
01101000	11100101	00100000	11100011	11101100	11100101
01100001	11110010	00100000	11100110	11101111	11110010
01101101	00100000	11101111	11100110	00100000	01110000
11101100	01100001	11101001	01101110	11110100	11100101
11111000	11110100	01100010	01111001	00100000	01101101
01100001	01101011	11101001	01101110	01100111	00100000
11101001	11110100	00100000	01110101	01101110	11110010
11100101	01100001	01100100	01100001	01100010	11101100
11100101	10101110				

Comparing Table 9.26 with Table 9.13, we can easily observe that Table 9.26 is erroneously decoded in four different places. Thus the recovered plaintext corresponding to Table 9.26 is as shown below.

> The aim of cryptogrΔ*pYX* is to hide the clear form of plaintext by making it unreadable.

Thus, when double errors occur during transmission, we observe that the external error-control scheme is not effective due to the fact that four symbol errors are created even after the process of decoding by using the DSEC (31, 27) RS code. In contrast, the internal error-control scheme is very efficient to control errors as discussed in Subsection 9.2.2.

9.3.3 EEC for Plaintext Feedback Asynchronous Ciphers

Another external error-control scheme, shown in Fig. 9.7, is based on a cipher system with plaintext feedback. We employ the same plaintext as used previously and also use the same key generator with the tap

Table 9.27 Key Stream **K** at Sender Side

00100	00101	10000	11000	01011	01010
11110	01100	10101	11011	00000	01001
11101	00010	11101	01000	10011	10101
00111	00101	10001	00011	00101	11110
10001	00100	00111	10011	00011	00100
00000					

coefficients (01001) and initial seed vector (11110). The encoded plaintext $\mathbf{C}_x$ is encrypted by the key stream **K** which is generated by the plaintext excitation $\mathbf{C}_x$, and the ciphertext **Y** is obtained as $\mathbf{Y} = \mathbf{C}_x + \mathbf{K}$. The key stream **K** at the sender side is shown in Table 9.27.

Enciphering $\mathbf{C}_x$ by **K** yields the ciphertext **Y** listed in Table 9.28.

Table 9.28 Ciphertext **Y** in Case of Plaintext Feedback

10010	01010	01100	01011	01010	00100
11111	11000	10010	01001	01000	01110
10100	01100	10001	11000	11100	11100
11100	11100	10001	01110	00110	01010
00111	01101	11110	11010	01010	10010
11010					

Table 9.29 Key Stream $\hat{\mathbf{K}}$ at Receiver Side

00100	00101	10000	11000	01011	01010
11011	01011	01100	01111	10000	11100
00110	00001	00001	10010	11011	11111
11010	10100	01111	01110	00001	11101
00000	11010	01010	10111	00110	01010
11000					

Table 9.30 Deciphered Plaintext $\hat{\mathbf{C}}_x$ at Receiver Side

10110	01111	11100	10011	00001	01110
10111	10011	11110	00110	11000	10010
10010	01101	10000	01010	00111	00011
00110	01000	11110	00000	00111	01001
00111	10111	10100	01101	01100	11000
00010					

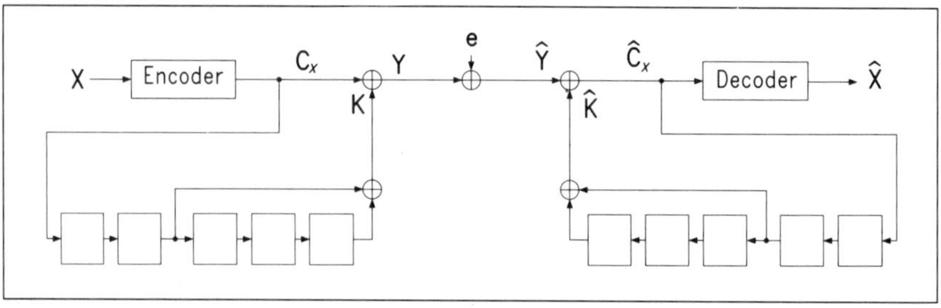

Fig. 9.7 External error-control scheme with plaintext feedback

Due to the symbol errors caused by e_{24} and e_7, the two positions at y_{24} = (11111) and y_7 = (01010) in the transmitted ciphertext **Y** will have altered values $\hat{y}_{24}$ = (01100) and $\hat{y}_7$ = (10100) respectively in the received ciphertext $\hat{\mathbf{Y}}$. The key stream $\hat{\mathbf{K}}$ derived from the key generator at the receiver side is obtained by $\hat{\mathbf{K}} = \hat{\mathbf{Y}} + \hat{\mathbf{C}}_x$, where $\hat{\mathbf{K}}$ is shown in Table 9.29. Of course, the key generator is excited by the deciphered plaintext $\hat{\mathbf{C}}_x$.

The modulo-2 sum of $\hat{\mathbf{Y}}$ and $\hat{\mathbf{K}}$ will be the deciphered plaintext $\hat{\mathbf{C}}_x$ shown in Table 9.30.

This deciphered plaintext is now subject to decoding by the DSEC (31, 27) RS decoder for elimination of errors. Thus, we are hoping to recover the original ASCII plaintext **X**. But, comparing $\mathbf{C}_x$ of Table 9.15 (which is common to all three error-control schemes) with $\hat{\mathbf{C}}_x$ of Table 9.30, we immediately find a great difference between them except for the top row. This fact implies that any externally controlled cipher system with plaintext feedback is infeasible owing to the fact that a plaintext feedback scheme involves indefinite error propagation. Therefore, there is really no point in further analysis for recovering the clear form of plaintext; we shall nevertheless proceed with decoding for this scheme in the following.

Using $\mathbf{C}_x$ and $\hat{\mathbf{C}}_x$, the error symbols are represented by $\mathbf{e} = \mathbf{C}_x + \hat{\mathbf{C}}_x$. Therefore the error pattern polynomial becomes

$$e(x) = \alpha^{18} + \alpha^{12}x + \alpha^{7}x^{2} + \ldots + \alpha^{17}x^{22} + \alpha^{13}x^{23} + \alpha^{8}x^{24} \qquad (9.35)$$

Substituting $x = \alpha^i$ for $1 \le i \le 4$ in $e(x)$, we obtain the syndrome components as $s_1 = e(\alpha) = \alpha^{10}$ = (10001), $s_2 = e(\alpha^2) = \alpha^8$ = (10110), $s_3 = e(\alpha^3) = \alpha^{21}$ = (00011), and $s_4 = e(\alpha^4) = \alpha^{23}$ = (11110). The coefficients of $\sigma(x)$ are computed as σ_1 = (01001) = α^{30} and σ_2 = (10001) = α^{10}, based on double-error correction. But the error-location numbers are useless because symbol errors have occurred in as many as 25 different places in $\hat{\mathbf{C}}_x$. Thus, it is meaningless to attempt to determine the error values. The DSEC (31, 27) RS decoder passes all the 25 error symbols without error correction. The decoded symbol sequence, after stripping the parity symbols, is shown in Table 9.31.

Finally, the completely recovered ASCII plaintext $\hat{\mathbf{X}}$ is shown as listed in Table 9.32.

Table 9.31 Decoded Plaintext after Stripping Parity Symbols

10110	01111	11100	10011	00001	01110
10111	10011	11110	00110	11000	10010
10010	01101	10000	01010	00111	00011
00110	01000	11110	00000	00111	01001
00111	10111	10100			

Table 9.32 Erroneously Recovered ASCII Plaintext $\hat{\mathbf{X}}$

01010100	01101000	11100101	00100000	01100001	11101001
01101101	00100000	11101111	11100110	00100000	11100011
11110010	01111001	01110000	11110100	11101111	01100111
11110010	01100001	01110101	11100111	11100011	01100010
01010010	01101100	00010100	01110001	10011001	00011110
00000001	11010010	01111011	11010010	11000110	01100100
11000110	00100010	11101101	11000010	10110001	01101010
11111011	10110000	10011011	11111001	11011011	01110111
00011011	00011110	10000000	00101011	00000001	00101101
01100011	11111011	10101011	11010101	11101011	11010001
01111101	10000010	01011100	00010000	00101010	10000001
00011101	10110100	01110011	00101100	11011100	00111111
11011101	01110001	01010110	01001011	00000111	11111000
00001001	00011101	10110110	01110100	10111010	00010101
01011010	10011010				

An attempt to translate Table 9.32 into plaintext **X** fails miserably, and results in the following garbled message.

The aim of cryptograugcbRlq |→ ⌈ R{RF dF"mB1j {0 [w → + ¬ – c {+ UkQ}⌉

A comparative study of the various schemes shows that the key-autokey stream cipher is the best system regardless of whether internal or external correction is used. The ciphertext-feedback stream cipher is the second best, because the external error control somewhat impairs the ability of the system to correct errors. The plaintext feedback stream cipher is undoubtedly the worst because of its potential for indefinite error propagation.

REFERENCES

1. Berlekamp, E.R.: *Algebraic Coding Theory*, McGraw-Hill, New York, 1968.
2. Blahut, R.E.: *Theory and Practice of Error Control Codes*, Addison-Wesley, Reading, Mass., 1983.
3. Clark, G.C. and J.B. Cain: *Error-Correction Coding for Digital Communications*, Plenum Press, New York, 1981.
4. Diffie, W. and M.E. Hellman: "Privacy and authentication: An introduction to cryptography", *Proc. IEEE*, vol. 67, no. 3, p. 419, Mar. 1979.
5. Gorenstein, D.C. and N. Zierler: "A class of error-correction codes in P^m symbols", *J. Soc. Ind. Appl. Math.*, vol. 9, pp. 207–214, 1961.
6. Lin, S. and D.J. Costello, Jr.: *Error Control Coding : Fundamentals and Applications*, Prentice-Hall, Englewood Cliffs, NJ, 1983.

7. Michelson, A.M. and A.H. Levesque: *Error-Control Techniques for Digital Communication*, Wiley, New York, 1985.
8. Peterson, W.W. and E.J. Weldon, Jr.: *Error-Correcting Codes*, 2nd ed., The MIT Press, Cambridge, Mass., 1972.
9. Rhee, M.Y.: *Error Correcting Coding Theory*, McGraw-Hill, New York, 1989.

Chapter

10

Authentication, Digital Signature, ZKIP, and Cryptographic Applications

Data security embraces the problems of both privacy and authentication. The privacy problem is concerned with the task of preventing an opponent from extracting message information from the channel. On the other hand, authentication deals with preventing the injection of false data into the channel or altering of messages that change their meaning. Privacy problems related to providing adequate protection have been considered in Chapters 3, 4, and 5. This chapter deals with a variety of authentication and signature schemes.

In computerised communication systems, it is important to provide an adequate method by which communicators can identify themselves to each other in an unforgeable manner. Authentications can be classified under two distinct categories—user authentication and message authentication. The validity of business contracts and agreements is guaranteed by signatures. Business applications, such as bank transactions, military command and control orders, contract negotiations using computer communication networks, require digital signatures. Digital signature schemes can be classified into one of two categories, namely arbitrated signatures and true signatures.

We outline a general authentication protocol between users A and B using a conventional secret-key cryptosystem, where A and B use a common secret key **K** to encipher and decipher the message plaintext.

1. B picks a random identifier IB and sends its encryption function E_K (IB) to A.

2. A deciphers E_k (IB) first and picks a random identifier IA. After these steps, A sends its encryption function E_K (IB, IA) to B.

3. B deciphers E_K (IB, IA) to get IB′ and IA′ and compare IB with IB′. If they match, i.e. if IB = IB′, then B identifies A as the legitimate user. B subsequently sends E_K (IA′) to A.

4. A deciphers E_K (IA′) to get IA′. If IA = IA′, then A confirms receipt of B. Thus, users A and B have identified themselves to each other.

Public-key cryptosystems make the problem of authentication easier due to the simplification of key distribution. An authentication protocol using a public-key cryptosystem is given below:

1. A sends to B the cryptogram E_{K_pB} (IA, A) encrypted with public key $K_p B$ of B.

2. B deciphers E_{K_pB} (IA, A) using its secret key K_sB and obtains IA and A. B then sends E_{K_pA} (IA, IB) to A.

3. A deciphers E_{K_pA} (IA, IB) using its secret key $K_s A$ to get IA′ and IB′. If IA = IA′, then A confirms the identity of B. A next sends E_{K_pB} (IB) to B.

4. B deciphers E_{K_pB} (IB) using its secret key K_sB and compares IB with IB′. If IB = IB′, then B confirms the identity of A.

Thus, users A and B have identified themselves to each other, because IA and IB are matched.

In an arbitrated signature scheme, signed messages produced by a sender S are sent to a receiver R via an arbitrator A, who serves as a witness. In a true signature scheme, S sends signed messages directly to R, who checks their validity and authenticity. Both conventional secret-key and public-key cryptosystems can be applied to produce true signatures. But a solution using a public-key cryptosystem is simpler and is given below.

1. The user A enciphers the message plaintext X with his secret key $K_s A$ to get a signed message $Y = E_{K_sA}(X)$ and then enciphers Y again with B's public key $K_p B$ to produce $Y' = E_{K_pB}$ (Y). Now A sends Y′ to B.

2. User B deciphers Y' first with his own secret key $K_s B$ to get Y and then deciphers Y again with A's public key $K_p A$ to obtain **X**.

3. B saves Y as proof that A has sent the message plaintext **X** to him.

In the following sections, we shall examine several authentication schemes built using public-key cryptosystems as well as conventional symmetric cipher systems, and also cover many signature schemes meant for conformation of alleged messages.

10.1 ELGAMAL'S AUTHENTICATION (OR SIGNATURE) SCHEME

The authentication (or signature) we shall discuss in this section is due to ElGamal's algorithm [15]. The security of this scheme relies on the difficulty of computing discrete logarithms over the finite field GF (p), where p is a prime. ElGamal's technique used here relies upon sending messages in clear form along with a secret authenticator.

Let X be a message plaintext signed, where $X \in$ GF (p), or $0 \leq X \leq p - 1$. The sender picks a primitive element α of GF (p) and selects an arbitrary element $r \in$ GF (p) such that

$$K \equiv \alpha^r \pmod{p} \tag{10.1}$$

where K represents a key in the public file. To authenticate a message $X \in$ GF (p), the sender selects another field element $s \in$ GF (p) such that gcd $(s, p - 1) = 1$ and computes

$$W \equiv \alpha^s \pmod{p} \tag{10.2}$$

Using the Euclidean algorithm, we have

$$X \equiv rW + sV \pmod{(p-1)} \tag{10.3}$$

which has a solution for V if s is chosen such that gcd $(s, p - 1) = 1$. Given X, W, and V, the sender transmits X along with the secret pair (W, V), $0 \leq W, V < p - 1$, which is sometimes called an authenticator, to the receiver and forms at the receiver the following relation

$$\alpha^X \equiv K^W W^V \pmod{p}$$

or

$$\alpha^X \equiv \alpha^{rW} \alpha^{sV} \pmod{p} \tag{10.4}$$

$$\equiv \alpha^{rW+sV} \pmod{p}$$

which can be solved for V by using Eq. 10.3. Thus, Eq. 10.3 has a solution for V if s is chosen such that gcd $(s, p - 1) = 1$.

Upon receiving the cryptogram (X, W, V), we calculate $\alpha^X \equiv \alpha^{rW+sV} \pmod p$ using the public key (K, α, p) and accept the plaintext X as authentic because the secret pair (W, V) matches the message plaintext X.

■ **Example 10.1** Let us prove Eq. 10.3. Knowing that $\beta = \gamma + k(p-1)$ is $\beta \equiv \gamma \pmod{p-1}$, we have $\alpha^\beta \equiv \alpha^\gamma \pmod p$. If we put $\beta = X$ and $\gamma = rW + sV$, it follows that $\alpha^X \equiv \alpha^{rW+sV} \pmod p$, i.e. $X \equiv rW + sV \pmod{p-1}$.

■ **Example 10.2** Consider the prime field GF (11). Then the set of its primitive elements is {2, 6, 7, 8}. Take one primitive element $\alpha = 7$ from the set. Then we can generate all the nonzero elements $\alpha^i \pmod{11}$, $0 \le i \le 10$, of GF (11) with respect to $\alpha = 7$ as follows:

$\alpha^0 = 1$	$\alpha^6 = 4$
$\alpha^1 = 7$	$\alpha^7 = 6$
$\alpha^2 = 5$	$\alpha^8 = 9$
$\alpha^3 = 2$	$\alpha^9 = 8$
$\alpha^4 = 3$	$\alpha^{10} = 1$
$\alpha^5 = 10$	

If the sender selects $r = 3$, then $K \equiv \alpha^r \pmod p \equiv 7^3 \pmod{11} \equiv 2$. Thus, we obtain the public key $(K, \alpha, p) = (2, 7, 11)$. Suppose the message plaintext is $X = 6$. Let the sender choose another random number $s = 7$ such that $\gcd(s, p-1) = \gcd(7, 10) = 1$. Next, calculate $W = \alpha^s \pmod p \equiv 7^7 \pmod{11} \equiv 6$. Now, the sender solves Eq. 10.3 for V such that

$$X \equiv rW + sV \pmod{(p-1)}$$

$$6 \equiv 3 \times 6 + 7V \pmod{10}$$

from which we get $V = 4$. The sender now transmits the cryptogram $Y = (X, W, V) = (6, 6, 4)$ to the receiver. This cryptogram consists of actually the clear form of the message X along with the secret authenticator (W, V). The receiver calculates $\alpha^X \equiv K^W W^V \pmod p$ as follows:

Right member: $K^W W^V \pmod p \equiv 2^6 \cdot 6^4 \pmod{11} \equiv 82944 \pmod{11} \equiv 4$

Left member: $\alpha^X \pmod p \equiv 7^6 \pmod{11} \equiv 4$

Since both sides are equal, the message $X = 6$ is accepted as authentic.

10.2 ANOTHER SCHEME OF ELGAMAL'S SYSTEM

The sender chooses a finite field GF (p) where p is a prime. Let α be a primitive element of GF (p). Both α and p are publicly known. Under this scheme, the sender randomly selects a key r which is kept secret by both the sender and the receiver. Let X denote a message plaintext which is relatively prime to p. Assume that the sender forms

$$W \equiv \alpha^X \pmod p \tag{10.5}$$

Let Y denote a ciphertext with gcd $(Y, p) = 1$; and consider the following congruence for V such that

$$Y \equiv rW + XV \pmod{(p-1)} \tag{10.6}$$

Now, the cryptogram (Y, W, V) is transmitted to the receiver.

On receipt of (Y, W, V), the receiver computes

$$\begin{aligned} A &\equiv (\alpha^r)^W W^V \pmod p \\ &\equiv \alpha^{Y-XV} (\alpha^X)^V \pmod p \\ &\equiv \alpha^Y \pmod p \end{aligned} \tag{10.7}$$

Thus, the ciphertext Y is accepted as authentic if $A \equiv \alpha^Y \pmod p$. Once this ciphertext has been accepted, the message X is recovered by means of Eq. 10.6, so that

$$X \equiv V^{-1}(Y - rW) \pmod{(p-1)} \tag{10.8}$$

The algorithm given above is illustrated in the following example.

■ **Example 10.3** If we take the finite field GF (11), the set of primitive elements is {2, 6, 7, 8} as before. Choose a primitive element $\alpha = 7$ from the set. Define the public key as $(p, \alpha) = (11, 7)$ and $r = 5$ as the chosen secret key which is shared by both the sender and the receiver. If the sender now wants to transmit the message $X = 3$, gcd (X, p) = gcd (3, 11) = 1, by means of the ciphertext $Y = 7$, then

$$W \equiv \alpha^X \pmod p \equiv 7^3 \pmod{11} \equiv 2$$

Next, let us compute V by solving Eq. 10.6 as shown below.

$$7 \equiv (5)(2) + 3V \pmod{10}$$

$$3V \equiv 7 \pmod{10}$$

from which we obtain $V = 9$. The sender is now ready to send the cryptogram $(Y, W, V) = (7, 2, 9)$ to the receiver. On receipt of (7, 2, 9), the receiver starts to compute

$$A \equiv (\alpha^r)^W \cdot W^V \pmod p$$

$$\equiv (7^5)^2 \cdot 2^9 \pmod{11}$$

$$\equiv (10^2)(2^9) \pmod{11} \equiv 6$$

and

$$\alpha^Y \pmod p \equiv 7^7 \pmod{11} \equiv 6$$

$A = \alpha^Y \pmod p = 6$ agrees with the original value of A and the cryptogram (7, 2, 9) is accepted, and $Y = 7$ is authentic. Finally the message plaintext is recovered in the following manner.

$$X \equiv V^{-1}(Y - rW) \pmod{(p-1)}$$

$$\equiv 9^{-1}(7 - 5 \cdot 2) \pmod{10}$$

$$\equiv (9^{-1})(7) \pmod{10} \equiv 3$$

Now, we can see that the message $X = 3$ is completely recovered.

10.3 ONG-SCHNORR-SHAMIR SIGNATURE (OR AUTHENTICATION) SCHEME

Ong, Schnorr, and Shamir [38] proposed a signature scheme based on the polynomial equation $P(x_1, x_2, \ldots, x_\lambda)$ modulo n. In 1984, this scheme using a polynomial P of degree 2 was proposed, and drew a great deal of interest. However, this system has been broken by J.M. Pollard [39].

In the quadratic OSS system, the public key consists of two integers n and k. The modulus n is a large composite number, whose factorization is kept secret: k has also a large size similar to that of n. To forge a signature to the message M, $0 < M < n$, it is necessary to find x and y such that

$$x^2 + \lambda y^2 \equiv M \pmod n \tag{10.9}$$

A random integer λ is picked such that $\gcd(\lambda, n) = 1$, and λ is given as the secret key such that $k \equiv \sqrt{-1/\lambda} \pmod n$, from which

$$\lambda \equiv -k^{-2} \pmod n \tag{10.10}$$

The pair (k, n) constitutes the public key. To authenticate a message M, where gcd $(M, n) = 1$, a random integer r, with r relatively prime to n, must be selected in order to compute

$$x \equiv \frac{1}{2}\left(\frac{M}{r} + r\right) \pmod n$$

$$y \equiv \frac{k}{2}\left(\frac{M}{r} - r\right) \pmod n \tag{10.11}$$

Now, the cryptogram $Y = (x, y)$ is transmitted to the receiver. Thus, the message M should be recreated by using Eq. 10.9.

To illustrate the operation of the OSS system, we shall now present a small example.

■ **Example 10.4** Prove that $x^2 + \lambda y^2 \equiv M \pmod n$ by substituting Eqs. 10.10 and 10.11 into the following quadratic equation.

$$x^2 + \lambda y^2 = \left[\frac{1}{2}\left(\frac{M}{r} + r\right)\right]^2 + \lambda\left[\frac{1}{2}k\left(\frac{M}{r} - r\right)\right]^2$$

$$= \frac{1}{4}\left(\frac{M}{r} + r\right)^2 - \frac{1}{4}k^{-2} \cdot k^2\left(\frac{M}{r} - r\right)^2$$

$$= \frac{1}{4}\left[\left(\frac{M}{r} + r\right)^2 - \left(\frac{M}{r} - r\right)^2\right]$$

$$= \frac{1}{4}\left[4\left(\frac{M}{r}\right)r\right] = M$$

■ **Example 10.5** Choose $n = 12$ and $k = 5$ such that gcd (k, n) = gcd (5, 12) = 1. The pair (n, k) constitutes the public key. Knowing $k = 5$ which is the first part of the public key, the secret key λ can be calculated by using Eq. 10.10 as well as $kk^{-1} \equiv 1 \pmod n$ as follows.

From $\lambda \equiv -(k^{-1})^2 \pmod n$, we have $\lambda \equiv -(5)(5) \pmod{12}$ if and only if $k = k^{-1} = 5$. Hence $\lambda \equiv -25 \pmod{12} \equiv (-25 + 36) \pmod{12} \equiv 11$. Thus, the secret key is formed as $(\lambda, n) = (11, 12)$. Next, if the plaintext $M = 7$, gcd (M, n) = gcd (7, 12) = 1, is to be transmitted, it is required to first compute x and y in Eq. 10.11 by picking a random integer $r = 5$, subsequently as $r^{-1} = 5$ for mod 12.

$$x \equiv \frac{1}{2}(7 \cdot 5 + 5) \pmod{12} \equiv 20 \pmod{12} \equiv 8$$

$$y \equiv \frac{5}{2}(7 \cdot 5 - 5)\ (\text{mod } 12) \equiv 75\ (\text{mod } 12) \equiv 3$$

Thus, the cryptogram $Y = (x, y) = (8, 3)$ is sent to the receiver. Upon receipt of Y, the message M is recreated using Eq. 10.9 in the following manner.

$$\begin{aligned} M &\equiv x^2 + \lambda y^2\ (\text{mod } n) \\ &\equiv (8^2 + (11)\, 3^2)\ (\text{mod } 12) \\ &\equiv 163\ (\text{mod } 12) \equiv 7 \end{aligned}$$

as expected.

The quadratic version of the OSS system proposed in [37] [38] used the polynomial $x^2 + \lambda y^2 = M$ where the secret key is an integer λ such that $\lambda \equiv -k^{-2}$ (mod n). It is worth noting that this signature scheme is multiplicative. If $x_1{}^2 + \lambda y_1{}^2 = M_1$ and $x_2{}^2 + \lambda y_2{}^2 = M_2$, then the quadratic form $x^2 + \lambda y^2 = M_1 M_2$ has a solution of $x = x_1 x_2 - \lambda y_1 y_2$ and $y = x_1 y_2 + x_2 y_1$.

Pollard cryptanalysed the quadratic and cubic OSS schemes in his paper [39], thus raising doubts about the security of any such signature schemes.

10.4 MODIFIED VERSION OF OSS SCHEME

As for the original OSS scheme in Sec. 10.3, we choose a secret key λ such that gcd $(\lambda, n) = 1$ where n is the modulus for additive and multiplicative operation. Suppose a message M is transmitted by means of ciphertext Y such that gcd $(M, n) = 1$ where $M = 1, 2, \ldots, n - 1$ and gcd $(Y, n) = 1$ where $Y = 1, 2, \ldots, n - 1$.

The pair of authenticators is defined as follows:

$$x \equiv \frac{1}{2}\left(\frac{Y}{M} + M\right)\ (\text{mod } n)$$

$$y \equiv \frac{\lambda}{2}\left(\frac{Y}{M} - M\right)\ (\text{mod } n) \tag{10.12}$$

and the sender transmits the triple cryptogram (Y, x, y) to the receiver. Upon receiving it, the receiver starts to authenticate it with the following equation:

$$Y' \equiv x^2 - \frac{y^2}{\lambda^2}\ (\text{mod } n) \tag{10.13}$$

and checks whether $Y' = Y$. The cryptogram (Y, x, y) is accepted as authentic if and only if $Y' = Y$. But it is rejected if $Y' \neq Y$. Once the cryptogram has been accepted to be authentic, the receiver can recover the message as

$$M \equiv \frac{Y}{x + \lambda^{-1}y} \pmod{n} \tag{10.14}$$

We shall illustrate this scheme in Example 10.7.

■ **Example 10.6** Prove that $Y' = Y$ from $Y' \equiv x^2 - (y^2/\lambda^2) \pmod{n}$ by substituting Eq. 10.12 in Eq. 10.13.

$$Y' \equiv \left(\frac{1}{4}\right)\left(\frac{Y}{M} + M\right)^2 - \left(\frac{\lambda^{-2}}{4}\right)\left[\lambda^2\left(\frac{Y}{M} - M\right)^2\right]$$

$$\equiv \left(\frac{1}{4}\right)\left[\left(\frac{Y}{M}\right)^2 + 2Y + M^2\right] - \left(\frac{1}{4}\right)\left[\left(\frac{Y}{M}\right)^2 - 2Y + M^2\right]$$

$$\equiv Y \pmod{n}$$

Show that $M \equiv Y/(x + \lambda^{-1} y) \pmod{n}$ by substituting Eq.10.12 in Eq.10.14.

$$\frac{Y}{x + \lambda^{-1}y} \equiv \frac{Y}{(1/2)[(Y/M) + M] + \lambda^{-1}(\lambda/2)[(Y/M) - M]} \pmod{n}$$

$$\equiv \frac{Y}{Y/M} \equiv M \pmod{n}$$

■ **Example 10.7** Choose the modulus $n = 15$ and the secret key $\lambda = 2$ such that $\gcd(\lambda, n) = \gcd(2, 15) = 1$. Since $\lambda \cdot \lambda^{-1} \equiv 1 \pmod{n}$ or $2\lambda^{-1} \equiv 1 \pmod{15}$, we have $\lambda^{-1} = 8$. For transmitting the message $M = 7$ by means of the ciphertext $Y = 13$ such that $\gcd(Y, n) = \gcd(13, 12) = 1$, we first calculate $M^{-1} = 13$ from $7M^{-1} \equiv 1 \pmod{15}$. Now, using Eq. 10.12, let us compute the two authenticators x and y as follows:

$$x \equiv \frac{1}{2}\left(\frac{Y}{M} + M\right) \pmod{n}$$

$$\equiv \frac{1}{2}(13 \times 13 + 7) \pmod{15} \equiv 88 \pmod{15} \equiv 13$$

$$y \equiv \left(\frac{\lambda}{2}\right)\left(\frac{Y}{M} - M\right) \pmod{n}$$

$$\equiv \left(\frac{2}{2}\right)\left(\frac{13}{7} - 7\right) \pmod{15}$$

$$\equiv (169 - 7) \pmod{15} \equiv 12$$

Once the authenticators are calculated, the sender transmits the cryptogram $(Y, x, y) = (13, 13, 12)$ to the receiver. Having received the cryptogram, the receiver starts to compute the message M for authentication.

$$Y' \equiv x^2 - \frac{y^2}{\lambda^2} \pmod{n}$$

$$\equiv \left(13^2 - \frac{12^2}{4}\right) \pmod{15}$$

$$\equiv 133 \pmod{15} \equiv 13$$

Thus, we get $Y' = 13 = Y$ so that the receiver can accept it as authentic. Finally the receiver recovers the message M applying Eq. 10.14 as follows:

$$M \equiv \frac{Y}{x + \lambda^{-1} y} \pmod{n}$$

$$\equiv \frac{13}{13 + 8 \times 12} \pmod{15}$$

$$\equiv 52 \pmod{15} \equiv 7$$

This completes our illustration.

10.5 SHAMIR'S FAST SIGNATURE SCHEME

The cryptanalysis of Shamir's fast signature scheme is in some ways similar to the attacks on the multiplicative knapsack system. In 1984, Odlyzko [35] devised a method of attacks to break Shamir's scheme which is designed for authentication.

We now consider the original Shamir scheme in detail. The sender creates a $n \times 2n$ matrix $\mathbf{K}$ whose elements $k_{ij} \in GF(2)$ are chosen at random. We call $\mathbf{K}$ a secret key. The sender selects a prime p for $p \geq 2^n - 1$ where n is the length of the plaintext. Consider the following matrix congruence system for solving the vector $\mathbf{A} = (a_1, a_2, \ldots, a_{2n})$, where $a_i \in GF(p)$, $i = 1, 2, \ldots, 2n$.

$$\mathbf{K}_{n \times 2n} \cdot \mathbf{A}^T_{2n \times 1} \equiv \begin{bmatrix} 1 \\ 2 \\ \cdot \\ \cdot \\ \cdot \\ 2^{n-1} \end{bmatrix} \pmod{p} \tag{10.15}$$

The sender chooses n random elements $(a_1, a_2, \ldots, a_n)$ of $\mathbf{A}$ and computes the rest, $(a_{n+1}, a_{n+2}, \ldots, a_{2n})$, using Eq. 10.15 because he has only n equations with $2n$ unknown variables. Let us define the pair $(\mathbf{A}, p)$ as the public key. We can convert a given message plaintext $\mathbf{X} \in \mathrm{GF}(p)$ to the binary sequence $\mathbf{X} = (x_1, x_2, \ldots, x_n)$, when $x_i \in \mathrm{GF}(2)$. If arranged backwards, $\mathbf{X} = (x_n, x_{n-1}, \ldots, x_1)$, that is, $X(x) = x_n z^0 + x_{n-1} z^1 + \ldots + x_1 z^{n-1}$.

The cryptogram $\mathbf{Y}$ corresponding to $\mathbf{X}$ is now determined as

$$\mathbf{Y} = \mathbf{X} \cdot \mathbf{K} \tag{10.16}$$

or

$$(y_1, y_2, \ldots, y_{2n}) = (x_n, x_{n-1}, \ldots, x_1) \begin{bmatrix} k_{11} & k_{12} & \cdots & k_{1,2n} \\ k_{21} & k_{22} & \cdots & k_{2,2n} \\ \cdot & & & \cdot \\ \cdot & & & \cdot \\ \cdot & & & \cdot \\ \cdot & & & \cdot \\ k_{n,1} & k_{n,2} & \cdots & k_{n,2n} \end{bmatrix}$$

from which we get

$$y_j = \sum_{i=1}^{n} x_{n-i+1} k_{ij} \tag{10.17}$$

On receipt of $\mathbf{Y}$, the receiver computes the message $\mathbf{X}$ using the cryptogram $\mathbf{Y}$ and public key $(\mathbf{A}, p)$ such that

$$\mathbf{X} \equiv \mathbf{Y} \cdot \mathbf{A}^T \pmod{p} \tag{10.18}$$

or

$$D_A(\mathbf{Y}) = (y_1, y_2, \ldots, y_{2n}) \begin{bmatrix} a_1 \\ a_2 \\ \cdot \\ \cdot \\ \cdot \\ \cdot \\ a_{2n} \end{bmatrix}$$

$$= \sum_{j=1}^{2n} y_j a_j \tag{10.19}$$

Substituting y_j of Eq. 10.17 in Eq. 10.19 yields

$$D_A(\mathbf{Y}) = \sum_{j=1}^{2n} \left(\left(\sum_{i=1}^{n} x_{n-i+1} k_{ij} \right) a_j \right)$$

$$= \sum_{i=1}^{n} x_{n-i+1} \left(\sum_{j=1}^{2n} k_{ij} a_j \right) \tag{10.20}$$

Equation 10.15 can also be expressed as

$$\begin{bmatrix} k_{11} & k_{12} & \dots & k_{1,2n} \\ k_{21} & k_{22} & \dots & k_{2,2n} \\ \cdot & & & \cdot \\ \cdot & & & \cdot \\ \cdot & & & \cdot \\ k_{n,1} & k_{n,2} & \dots & k_{n,2n} \end{bmatrix} \begin{bmatrix} a_1 \\ a_2 \\ \cdot \\ \cdot \\ \cdot \\ a_{2n} \end{bmatrix} = \begin{bmatrix} 2^0 \\ 2^1 \\ \cdot \\ \cdot \\ \cdot \\ 2^{n-1} \end{bmatrix}$$

from which we obtain

$$\sum_{j=1}^{2n} k_{ij} a_j = 2^{i-1} \qquad i = 1, 2, \dots, n \tag{10.21}$$

Coupling Eqs. 10.21 and 10.20, we have

$$D_A(\mathbf{Y}) = \sum_{i=1}^{n} x_{n-i+1} \, (2^{i-1}) \tag{10.22}$$

Since the message plaintext **X** is expressed in polynomial form, it follows that

$$X(x) = x_n 2^0 + x_{n-1} 2^1 + x_{n-2} 2^2 + \dots + x_1 2^{n-1}$$

$$= \sum_{i=1}^{n} x_{n-i+1} 2^{i-1} \tag{10.23}$$

Comparing Eq. 10.22 with Eq. 10.23, we can see that

$$D_A(\mathbf{Y}) \equiv X(x) \equiv \sum_{i=1}^{n} x_{n-i+1} \cdot 2^{i-1} \pmod{p} \tag{10.24}$$

Observing Eq. 10.16, we see that each message plaintext yields a set of $2n$ linear equations, which lead to the discovery of some elements of the secret key **K**. But it will only take n messages prior to determination of the $n \times 2n$ unknown elements of **K**. We now give a small example to illustrate the above theory.

■ **Example 10.8** Let us consider Shamir's system for message authentication using GF (7) by choosing $p = 7$. Since $p \geq 2^n - 1$, we must select $n = 3$. Consequently, we can assume the secret key **K** to have the following matrix form:

$$\mathbf{K} = \begin{bmatrix} 1 & 1 & 1 & 0 & 0 & 1 \\ 0 & 0 & 1 & 1 & 0 & 1 \\ 0 & 1 & 1 & 1 & 1 & 0 \end{bmatrix}$$

Randomly selecting $a_i \in$ GF (7) for $i = 1, 2, 3$ such that $a_1 = 2$, $a_2 = 5$, and $a_3 = 6$, the remaining elements a_4, a_5, a_6 of **A** can be determined by using Eq. 10.15.

$$\begin{bmatrix} 1 & 1 & 1 & 0 & 0 & 1 \\ 0 & 0 & 1 & 1 & 0 & 1 \\ 0 & 1 & 1 & 1 & 1 & 0 \end{bmatrix} \begin{bmatrix} 2 \\ 5 \\ 6 \\ a_4 \\ a_5 \\ a_6 \end{bmatrix} \equiv \begin{bmatrix} 1 \\ 2 \\ 4 \end{bmatrix} \pmod 7$$

$$2 + 5 + 6 + a_6 \equiv 1 \pmod 7$$

$$6 + a_4 + a_6 \equiv 2 \pmod 7$$

$$5 + 6 + a_4 + a_5 \equiv 4 \pmod 7$$

From this congruence system, we obtain $a_6 = 2$, $a_4 = 1$, and $a_5 = 6$. Thus, the public key can be determined as $\mathbf{A} = (2, 5, 6, 1, 6, 2)$. Assuming message $\mathbf{X} = 5 \in$ GF (7), its binary representation is $\mathbf{X} = (1 \;\; 0 \;\; 1)$. Using Eq. 10.16, the cryptogram becomes

$$\mathbf{Y} = (1 \;\; 0 \;\; 1) \begin{bmatrix} 1 & 1 & 1 & 0 & 0 & 1 \\ 0 & 0 & 1 & 1 & 0 & 1 \\ 0 & 1 & 1 & 1 & 1 & 0 \end{bmatrix} = (1\;2\;2\;1\;1\;1)$$

At the receiver end, the message plaintext is recreated using the public key $(\mathbf{A}, p)$ as follows:

$$\mathbf{X} = (1 \quad 2 \quad 2 \quad 1 \quad 1 \quad 1)\begin{bmatrix} 2 \\ 5 \\ 6 \\ 1 \\ 6 \\ 2 \end{bmatrix} = 2 + 10 + 12 + 1 + 6 + 2$$

$$\equiv 33 \pmod 7 \equiv 5$$

Hence, the message $\mathbf{X} = 5$ is completely recovered as it is. To repulse cryptanalytic attack, Shamir made his scheme more secure by adding a random factor with each original message. In this method, the sender forms the modified message as

$$\mathbf{X}' \equiv \mathbf{X} - \mathbf{R} \cdot \mathbf{A}^T \pmod p \tag{10.25}$$

where the original message $\mathbf{X} \in GF(p)$, a random vector $\mathbf{R} = (r_1, r_2, \ldots, r_{2n})$ where $r_i \in GF(2)$, and the public key $\mathbf{A} = (a_1, a_2, \ldots, a_{2n})$. If the modified message is arranged in the descending order of subscripts such that $\mathbf{X}' = (x_n', x'_{n-1}, \ldots, x_1')$, its polynomial form can be written as $X'(x) = x_n' \, 2^0 + x'_{n-1} \, 2^1 + x'_{n-2} \, 2^2 + \ldots + x_1' \, 2^{n-1}$ as done before. Thus, the intermediate ciphertext is represented as

$$\mathbf{Y}' \equiv \mathbf{X}' \cdot \mathbf{K} \pmod p \tag{10.26}$$

The final ciphertext to be transmitted assumes the following form:

$$\mathbf{Y} \equiv \mathbf{Y}' + \mathbf{R} \pmod p \tag{10.27}$$

At the receiver end, authentication is performed by checking if the following relation holds good.

$$\mathbf{X} \equiv \mathbf{Y} \cdot \mathbf{A}^T \pmod p \tag{10.28}$$

■ **Example 10.9** Show that $\mathbf{X} \equiv \mathbf{Y} \cdot \mathbf{A}^T \pmod p$.

$$\mathbf{Y} \cdot \mathbf{A}^T = (\mathbf{Y}' + \mathbf{R})\,\mathbf{A}^T = \mathbf{Y}' \cdot \mathbf{A}^T + \mathbf{R} \cdot \mathbf{A}^T \tag{10.29}$$

where $\mathbf{R} \cdot \mathbf{A}^T = \mathbf{X} - \mathbf{X}'$ from Eq. 10.25.

Using Eq. 10.26, we have

$$(y_1', y_2', \ldots, y'_{2n}) = (x_n', x'_{n-1}, \ldots, x_1')\begin{bmatrix} k_{11} & k_{12} & \cdots & k_{1,2n} \\ k_{21} & k_{22} & \cdots & k_{2,2n} \\ \cdot & & & \cdot \\ \cdot & & & \cdot \\ \cdot & & & \cdot \\ k_{n,1} & k_{n,2} & & k_{n,2n} \end{bmatrix}$$

or

$$y_j' = \sum_{i=1}^{n} x'_{n-i+1} k_{ij} \quad i \le j \le 2n \tag{10.30}$$

The first term of Eq. 10.29 may be expressed as

$$\mathbf{Y}' \cdot \mathbf{A}^T = (y_1', y_2', \ldots, y'_{2n}) \begin{bmatrix} a_1 \\ a_2 \\ \cdot \\ \cdot \\ \cdot \\ a_{2n} \end{bmatrix}$$

$$= \sum_{j=1}^{2n} y_j' a_j \tag{10.31}$$

Combining Eqs 10.31 and, 10.30 we have

$$\mathbf{Y}' \cdot \mathbf{A}^T = \sum_{i=1}^{n} x'_{n-i+1} \left(\sum_{j=1}^{2n} k_{ij} a_j \right)$$

$$= \sum_{i=1}^{n} x'_{n-i+1} (2^{i-1}) = \mathbf{X}' \tag{10.32}$$

Thus, using the equalities $\mathbf{Y}' \cdot \mathbf{A}^T = \mathbf{X}'$ and $\mathbf{R} \cdot \mathbf{A}^T = \mathbf{X} - \mathbf{X}'$, Eq. 10.29 becomes

$$\mathbf{Y} \cdot \mathbf{A}^T \equiv \mathbf{X}' + (\mathbf{X} - \mathbf{X}') \equiv \mathbf{X} \pmod{p}$$

The following example is based on the more secure version of Shamir's scheme.

■ **Example 10.10** Consider here the improved version of Shamir's scheme. Let us choose the same data: $n = 3$, $p = 7$, $\mathbf{X} = 5$, and $\mathbf{K}$ as used in Example 10.8. If we take the random vector $\mathbf{R} = (r_1, r_2, \ldots, r_{2n}) = (1\ 1\ 0\ 1\ 0\ 0)$ for $n = 3$, the modified message becomes

$$\mathbf{X}' \equiv \mathbf{X} - \mathbf{R} \cdot \mathbf{A}^T \pmod{p}$$

$$\equiv 5 - (1\,1\,0\,1\,0\,0) \begin{bmatrix} 2 \\ 5 \\ 6 \\ 1 \\ 6 \\ 2 \end{bmatrix} \pmod{7}$$

$$\equiv 5 - (2 + 5 + 1) \pmod 7$$

$$\equiv 4$$

The modified message $\mathbf{X}' = 4$ is converted into the binary sequence $(1\ 0\ 0)$ and its inverse order is $(0\ 0\ 1)$. Using Eq. 10.26, the intermediate ciphertext is calculated as

$$\mathbf{Y}' \equiv \mathbf{X}' \cdot \mathbf{K} \pmod p$$

$$\equiv (0\,0\,1)\begin{bmatrix} 1 & 1 & 1 & 0 & 0 & 1 \\ 0 & 0 & 1 & 1 & 0 & 1 \\ 0 & 1 & 1 & 1 & 1 & 0 \end{bmatrix} \pmod 7$$

$$\equiv (0\,1\,1\,1\,1\,0) \pmod 7$$

Thus, the final ciphertext to be transmitted is

$$\mathbf{Y} \equiv \mathbf{Y}' + \mathbf{R} \pmod p$$

$$\equiv (0\quad 1\quad 1\quad 1\quad 1\quad 0) + (1\quad 1\quad 0\quad 1\quad 0\quad 0) \pmod 7$$

$$\equiv (1\quad 2\quad 1\quad 2\quad 1\quad 0) \pmod 7$$

At the receiver end, the original plaintext is recreated by the authentication process as follows:

$$\mathbf{X} \equiv \mathbf{Y} \cdot \mathbf{A}^T \pmod p$$

$$\equiv (1\,2\,1\,2\,1\,0)\begin{bmatrix} 2 \\ 5 \\ 6 \\ 1 \\ 6 \\ 2 \end{bmatrix} \pmod 7$$

$$\equiv 12 \pmod 7 \equiv 5$$

Therefore, the message plaintext $\mathbf{X} = 5$ is completely recovered by using the public key $\mathbf{A}$.

10.6 SEBERRY-JONES AUTHENTICATION SCHEME

Jones and Seberry extended Shamir's original idea of the fast signature scheme [24]. As discussed in Sec. 10.5, the sender creates an $n \times 2n$ matrix $\mathbf{K}$ whose elements are $k_{ij} \in GF(p)$. The sender also chooses n

random elements of $\mathbf{A} = (a_1, a_2, \ldots, a_{2n})$. Recall that $(\mathbf{A}, p)$ is a public key. Seberry [42] proposed to calculate the secret vector $\mathbf{B} = (b_1, b_2, \ldots, b_n)$ by using the following congruence.

$$\mathbf{K} \cdot \mathbf{B}^T \equiv 0 \pmod{p} \tag{10.33}$$

where $\mathbf{B}$ is called the secret key, and is known only to both the users. Assuming a subliminal message $\mathbf{X} \in GF(p)$ to be sent, the vector $\mathbf{R} = (r_1, r_2, \ldots, r_{2n})$ is to be determined by means of the congruence

$$\mathbf{X} \equiv \mathbf{R} \cdot \mathbf{B}^T \pmod{p} \tag{10.34}$$

where $r_i \in GF(2)$ for $1 \le i \le 2n$ are the components of $\mathbf{R}$.

As done by Shamir, the sender now forms the modified message $\mathbf{X}'$ such that

$$\mathbf{X}' \equiv \mathbf{M} - \mathbf{R} \cdot \mathbf{A}^T \pmod{p}$$

$$\equiv \mathbf{M} - (r_1, r_2, \ldots, r_{2n}) \begin{bmatrix} a_1 \\ a_2 \\ \cdot \\ \cdot \\ \cdot \\ a_{2n} \end{bmatrix} \pmod{p} \tag{10.35}$$

where the modified message $\mathbf{X}' = (x_n', x'_{n-1}, \ldots, x_1')$ for $x_i' \in GF(2)$, $1 \le i \le n$, is expressed as

$$\mathbf{X}' = \sum_{i=0}^{n} x'_{n-i+1} 2^{i-1}$$

and $\mathbf{M} = (m_1, m_2, \ldots, m_n)$ is the vector randomly generated at the sender side. Since the intermediate ciphertext $\mathbf{Y}'$ and final ciphertext $\mathbf{Y}$ are represented as $\mathbf{Y}' \equiv \mathbf{X}' \cdot \mathbf{K} \pmod{p}$ and $\mathbf{Y} \equiv \mathbf{Y}' + \mathbf{R} \pmod{p}$, respectively, the authenticator $(\mathbf{M}, \mathbf{Y})$ is accordingly sent to the receiver.

Upon receiving the authenticator $(\mathbf{M}, \mathbf{Y})$, the receiver computes $\mathbf{Y} \cdot \mathbf{A}^T \pmod{p}$. If $\mathbf{Y} \cdot \mathbf{A}^T \pmod{p} \equiv \mathbf{M}$, the pair $(\mathbf{M}, \mathbf{Y})$ is considered to be authentic. But it is rejected if $\mathbf{Y} \cdot \mathbf{A}^T \pmod{p} \not\equiv \mathbf{M}$. Finally, the subliminal message $\mathbf{X}$ can be recovered by solving the following congruence:

$$\mathbf{X} \equiv \mathbf{Y} \cdot \mathbf{B}^T \pmod{p} \tag{10.36}$$

■ **Example 10.11** Prove that $\mathbf{X} \equiv \mathbf{Y} \cdot \mathbf{A}^T \equiv \mathbf{Y} \cdot \mathbf{B}^T \pmod{p}$.

Consider $\mathbf{Y} \cdot \mathbf{A}^T \pmod{p}$:

$$\mathbf{Y} \cdot \mathbf{A}^T = (\mathbf{Y}' + \mathbf{R})\,\mathbf{A}^T = \mathbf{Y}' \cdot \mathbf{A}^T + \mathbf{R} \cdot \mathbf{A}^T \tag{10.37}$$

From Eq. 10.35, we have

$$\mathbf{R} \cdot \mathbf{A}^T = \mathbf{M} - \mathbf{X}' \tag{10.38}$$

and

$$\mathbf{Y}' \cdot \mathbf{A}^T = (y_1', y_2', \ldots, y'_{2n}) \begin{bmatrix} a_1 \\ a_2 \\ \cdot \\ \cdot \\ \cdot \\ a_{2n} \end{bmatrix} = \sum_{j=1}^{2n} y_j' a_j \tag{10.39}$$

Since the intermediate ciphertext is $\mathbf{Y}' \equiv \mathbf{X}' \cdot \mathbf{K} \pmod p$, it follows that

$$(y_1', y_2', \ldots, y'_{2n}) = (x_n', x'_{n-1}, \ldots, x_1') \begin{bmatrix} k_{11} & k_{12} & \ldots & k_{1,2n} \\ k_{21} & k_{22} & \ldots & k_{2,2n} \\ \cdot & & & \cdot \\ \cdot & & & \cdot \\ \cdot & & & \cdot \\ k_{n,1} & k_{n,2n} & & k_{n,2n} \end{bmatrix}$$

where the jth element of $\mathbf{Y}'$ expresses

$$y_j' = x_n' k_{1j} + x_n{}'_{-1} k_{2j} + \ldots + x_1' k_{nj}$$

$$= \sum_{i=1}^{n} x_n{}'_{-i+1} k_{ij} \tag{10.40}$$

Substituting Eq. 10.40 in Eq. 10.39, we have

$$\mathbf{Y}' \cdot \mathbf{A}^T = \sum_{j=1}^{2n} \left(\sum_{i=1}^{n} x_n{}'_{-i+1} k_{ij} \right) a_j$$

$$= \sum_{i=1}^{n} x'_{n-i+1} \sum_{j=1}^{2n} k_{ij} a_j$$

$$= \sum_{i=1}^{n} x'_{n-i+1} (2^{i-1}) = \mathbf{X}' \tag{10.41}$$

Substituting Eqs. 10.38 and 10.41 in Eq. 10.37 yields

$$\mathbf{Y} \cdot \mathbf{A}^T \equiv \mathbf{M} \pmod p \tag{10.42}$$

Next, let us show $\mathbf{X} = \mathbf{Y} \cdot \mathbf{B}^T$ as follows:

$$\mathbf{Y} \cdot \mathbf{B}^T = (\mathbf{Y}' + \mathbf{R})\mathbf{B}^T = \mathbf{Y}' \cdot \mathbf{B}^T + \mathbf{R} \cdot \mathbf{B}^T = (\mathbf{X}' \cdot \mathbf{K})\mathbf{B}^T + \mathbf{R} \cdot \mathbf{B}^T$$

Since $\mathbf{K} \cdot \mathbf{B}^T \equiv 0 \pmod p$ from Eq. 10.33, we have

$$\mathbf{Y} \cdot \mathbf{B}^T \equiv \mathbf{X}' \cdot \mathbf{0} + \mathbf{R} \cdot \mathbf{B}^T \equiv \mathbf{R} \cdot \mathbf{B}^T \equiv \mathbf{X} \pmod p \tag{10.43}$$

by using Eq. 10.34.

This scheme is illustrated in the following simple example.

■ **Example 10.12** If the length n of plaintext is known, the prime $p \geq 2^n - 1$ can be determined. Hence, we have $p \geq 2^3 - 1 = 7$ for $n = 3$. Let us choose *a* 3×6 matrix at random as shown below.

$$\mathbf{K} = \begin{bmatrix} 1 & 4 & 3 & 1 & 3 & 1 \\ 2 & 2 & 2 & 4 & 0 & 2 \\ 4 & 1 & 1 & 1 & 2 & 0 \end{bmatrix}$$

Consider the public vector $\mathbf{A} = (a_1, a_2, \ldots, a_6)$ in which a_i, $1 \leq i \leq 3$, are chosen at random such that $a_1 = 3$, $a_2 = 2$, and $a_3 = 1$. Using Eq. 10.15, we have

$$\mathbf{K} \cdot \mathbf{A}^T \equiv \begin{bmatrix} 1 & 4 & 3 & 1 & 3 & 1 \\ 2 & 2 & 2 & 4 & 0 & 2 \\ 4 & 1 & 1 & 1 & 2 & 0 \end{bmatrix} \begin{bmatrix} 3 \\ 2 \\ 1 \\ a_4 \\ a_5 \\ a_6 \end{bmatrix} \equiv \begin{bmatrix} 1 \\ 2 \\ 4 \end{bmatrix} \pmod 7$$

from which we obtain the following linear congruence system.

$$3 + 8 + 3 + a_4 + 3a_5 + a_6 \equiv 1 \pmod 7$$

$$6 + 4 + 2 + 4a_4 \quad + 2a_6 \equiv 2 \pmod 7$$

$$12 + 2 + 1 + a_4 + 2a_5 \quad \equiv 4 \pmod 7$$

or

$$a_4 + 3a_5 + a_6 \equiv 1 \pmod 7$$

$$4a_4 \quad + 2a_6 \equiv 4 \pmod 7$$

$$a_4 + 2a_5 \quad \equiv 3 \pmod 7$$

From the last congruence, it follows that

$$a_4 \equiv 3 - 2a_5 \pmod 7$$

Substituting this a_4 in the first two congruences yields

$$a_5 + a_6 \equiv 5 \pmod 7$$

and

$$-4a_5 + a_6 \equiv 3 \pmod 7$$

Solving the last three congruences, we can easily obtain $a_5 = 6$, $a_6 = 6$, and $a_4 = 5$, respectively. Thus we get $\mathbf{A} = (3, 2, 1, 5, 6, 6)$. Hence the public key is represented as $(\mathbf{A}, p) = [(3, 2, 1, 5, 6, 6), 7)]$. Now, the secret vector **B** is calculated using Eq. 10.33 as follows:

$$\mathbf{K} \cdot \mathbf{B}^T \equiv \begin{bmatrix} 1 & 4 & 3 & 1 & 3 & 1 \\ 2 & 2 & 2 & 4 & 0 & 2 \\ 4 & 1 & 1 & 1 & 2 & 0 \end{bmatrix} \begin{bmatrix} b_1 \\ b_2 \\ b_3 \\ b_4 \\ b_5 \\ b_6 \end{bmatrix} \equiv 0 \pmod 7$$

Since this congruence system has three congruences and six unknowns, we have to randomly fix three of them; for instance, as $b_1 = 1$, $b_2 = 3$, $b_3 = 2$. The remaining three elements can be computed as follows:

$$1 + 12 + 6 + b_4 + 3b_5 + b_6 \equiv 0 \pmod 7$$

$$2 + 6 + 4 + 4b_4 \qquad +2b_6 \equiv 0 \pmod 7$$

$$4 + 3 + 2 + b_4 + 2b_5 \qquad \equiv 0 \pmod 7$$

or

$$b_4 + 3b_5 + b_6 \equiv 2 \pmod 7$$

$$4b_4 \qquad +2b_6 \equiv 2 \pmod 7$$

$$b_4 + 2b_5 \qquad \equiv 5 \pmod 7$$

Solving this congruence system, we have $b_5 = 4$, $b_4 = 4$, $b_6 = 0$. Thus, the secret key can be determined as $\mathbf{B} = (1, 3, 2, 4, 4, 0)$. **B** must now be sent to the receiver before the transmission of a subliminal message **X**.

If the sender now intends to send $\mathbf{X} = 3 \in GF(7)$, he first calculates the vector $\mathbf{R} = (r_1, r_2, r_3, r_4, r_5, r_6)$ where $r_i \in GF(2)$ such that

$$\mathbf{X} \equiv \mathbf{R} \cdot \mathbf{B}^T \pmod p$$

$$\equiv (r_1, r_2, r_3, r_4, r_5, r_6)\begin{bmatrix}1\\3\\2\\4\\4\\0\end{bmatrix} \pmod 7$$

$$\equiv 3$$

One possible solution for **R** to satisfy the congruence is **R** = (0 0 1 1 1 0). But **R** may have another solution of binary sequence; for example, i.e., **R** = (1 1 1 1 0 0). We call **R** a carrier of **X**.

Suppose the sender generates the authenticator $\mathbf{M} \equiv 6 \pmod 7$ at random. Then he forms the modified message $\mathbf{X}'$ such that

$$\mathbf{X}' \equiv \mathbf{M} - \mathbf{R} \cdot \mathbf{A}^T \pmod p$$

$$\equiv 6 - (0\quad 0\quad 1\quad 1\quad 1\quad 0)\begin{bmatrix}3\\2\\1\\5\\6\\6\end{bmatrix} \pmod 7$$

$$\equiv 6 - 5 \equiv 1$$

$\mathbf{X}'$ may be expressed in binary form as (1 0 0). Next, the intermediate ciphertext is computed as follows:

$$\mathbf{Y}' \equiv \mathbf{X}' \cdot \mathbf{K} \pmod p$$

$$\equiv (1\ 0\ 0)\begin{bmatrix}1 & 4 & 3 & 1 & 3 & 1\\2 & 2 & 2 & 4 & 0 & 2\\4 & 1 & 1 & 1 & 2 & 0\end{bmatrix} \pmod 7$$

$$\equiv (1, 4, 3, 1, 3, 1) \pmod 7$$

The final cryptogram **Y** is calculated as

$$\mathbf{Y} \equiv \mathbf{Y}' + \mathbf{R} \pmod p$$

$$\equiv (1, 4, 3, 1, 3, 1) + (0, 0, 1, 1, 1, 0) \pmod 7$$

$$\equiv (1, 4, 4, 2, 4, 1) \pmod 7$$

The pair $(\mathbf{M}, \mathbf{Y}) = [6, (1, 4, 4, 2, 4, 1)]$ is now directed to the receiver. On receipt of $(\mathbf{M}, \mathbf{Y})$, the receiver performs the following calculation:

$$\mathbf{Y} \cdot \mathbf{A}^T \equiv (1,4,4,2,4,1) \begin{bmatrix} 3 \\ 2 \\ 1 \\ 5 \\ 6 \\ 6 \end{bmatrix} \pmod 7$$

$$\equiv 55 \pmod 7 \equiv 6$$

Using Eq. 10.42, $\mathbf{Y} \cdot \mathbf{A}^T = \mathbf{M} = 6$ is obtained as expected. Hence, the pair $(\mathbf{M}, \mathbf{Y})$ is considered to be authentic. Finally, using Eq. (10.43), the subliminal message $\mathbf{X}$ is recovered as follows:

$$\mathbf{X} \equiv \mathbf{Y} \cdot \mathbf{B}^T \pmod p$$

$$\equiv (1,4,4,2,4,1) \begin{bmatrix} 1 \\ 3 \\ 2 \\ 4 \\ 4 \\ 0 \end{bmatrix} \pmod 7$$

$$\equiv 45 \pmod 7 \equiv 3$$

Thus, the message $\mathbf{X}$ is completely recreated.

As computers accept information only in digital form, any signatures in question must also be digital. In current practice, a written signature is physically appended to a given document which contains both a message and a signature. But in a computer environment, it is impossible to directly print messages along with suitable signatures without storing and sending them via communication channels where illegal users may come into the picture. Therefore, digital signatures must fulfil the authenticity of signed messages by confirming mutual identification.

In the following sections, we shall discuss authentication processes which use conventional private-key cryptosystems.

10.7 RABIN SIGNATURE SCHEME

The Rabin signature scheme is based on symmetric crypto-operations. A sender randomly generates 2λ keys for constructing the signature such that

$$\mathbf{K} = (k_1, k_2, \ldots, k_{2\lambda}) \tag{10.44}$$

This key set is secret and only the sender knows it. He also creates the following two sequences which have to be validated by the receiver

$$\mathbf{S} = (S_1, S_2, \ldots, S_{2\lambda}) \tag{10.45}$$

and

$$\mathbf{R} = (R_1, R_2, \ldots, R_{2\lambda}) \tag{10.46}$$

The second sequence **R** is generated by enciphering the first sequence **S** such that

$$R_i = E_{k_i}(S_i) \qquad 1 \le i \le 2\lambda \tag{10.47}$$

or

$$\begin{aligned} R_1 &= E_{k_1}(S_1) \\ R_2 &= E_{k_2}(S_2) \\ &\cdots\cdots \\ R_{2\lambda} &= E_{k_{2\lambda}}(S_{2\lambda}) \end{aligned} \tag{10.48}$$

These two sequences **S** and **R** are stored in a public register with their individual binary blocks S_i and R_i depending upon the cryptographic algorithm used; for example, 56 bits is the block size for the DES algorithm. In general, data compression (DC) from an n-bit message **X** to an m-bit sequence is called the message digest DC (**X**), where $n > m$. If the data compression method is applied, a shorter signature is possible. Let us first compress a message plaintext **X**. If the resulting digest DC (**X**) is enciphered under keys k_i, $1 \le i \le 2\lambda$, then the signature SG (**X**) of the message plaintext **X** is formed by the following cryptograms:

$$\mathrm{SG}(\mathbf{X}) = \{E_{k_1}[DC(\mathbf{X})], E_{k_2}[\mathrm{DC}(\mathbf{X})], \ldots, E_{k_{2\lambda}}[\mathrm{DC}(\mathbf{X})]\} \tag{10.49}$$

Hence, the length of SG (**X**) will be $(2\lambda)\,m$. Now, the signature SG (**X**) along with the message **X** is sent to the receiver. Creation of signatures in the Rabin scheme is shown in Fig. 10.1.

To validate the signature, the receiver selects a 2λ–bit sequence **T** of λ ones and λ zeros as follows:

$$\mathbf{T} = (t_0, t_1, \ldots, t_{2\lambda}) \qquad t_i \in \mathrm{GF}(2) \tag{10.50}$$

where the weight of **T** is $w(\mathbf{T}) = \lambda$. The receiver now sends this binary sequence **T** to the sender. Upon receipt, the sender examines whether the ith element t_i of **T** is "1". The sender thus forms a λ-element subset of the secret key. Since the weight of **T** is λ, the subset of keys is

$$\mathbf{K}_T = (k_{i1}, k_{i2}, \ldots, k_{i\lambda})$$

$$= k_{ij} \qquad 1 \le j \le \lambda \tag{10.51}$$

For example, if $\mathbf{T} = (1, 0, 0, 1, \ldots, 1, 0, 1)$, then $\mathbf{K}_T = (k_1, k_4, \ldots, k_{2\lambda-2}, k_{2\lambda})$. Now, using **S**, **R**, **T**, and $\mathbf{K}_T$, the receiver starts authenticating the key

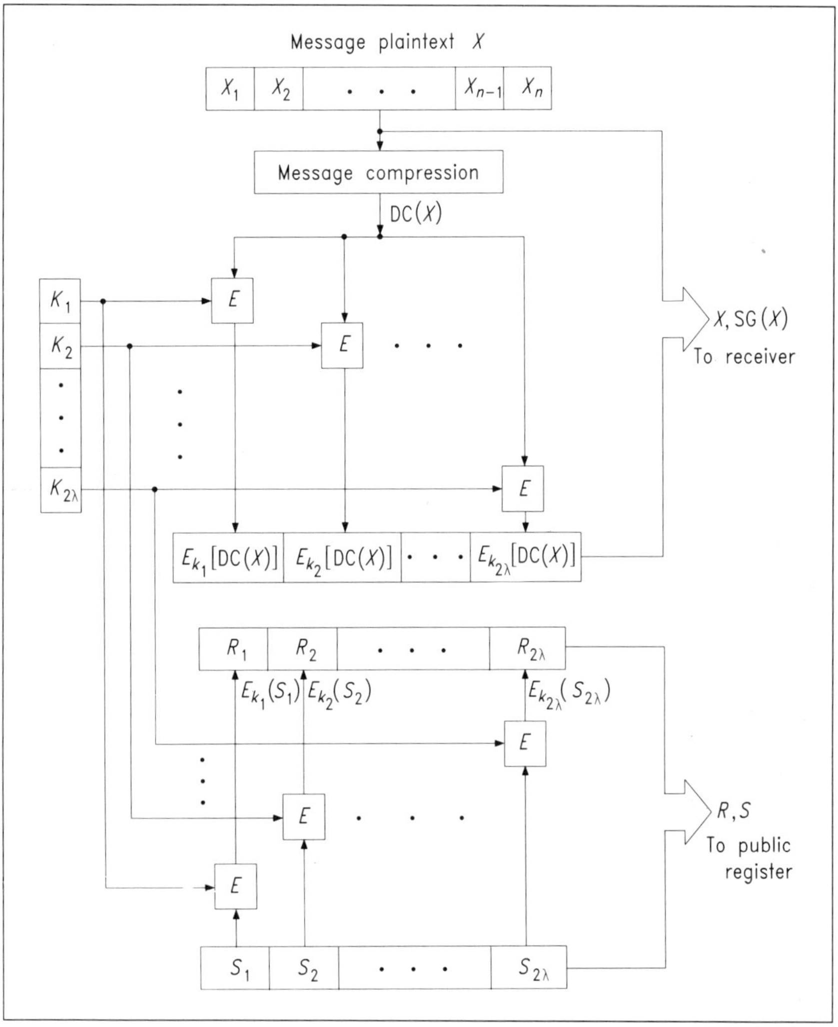

Fig. 10.1 Generation of signature SG (**X**) of message plaintext **X** in the Rabin scheme

subset by generating and comparing the λ cryptograms of $\mathbf{S}'$ to the original cryptograms of $\mathbf{S}$ as follows:

Let the locations of $t_i = 1$ in $\mathbf{T}$ be denoted as $(i1, i2, \ldots, i\lambda)$. Then we have

$$\mathbf{R}' = (R_{i1}, R_{i2}, \ldots, R_{i\lambda}) \tag{10.52}$$

where

$$\begin{aligned} R_{i1} &= E_{k_{i1}}(S_{i1}) \\ R_{i2} &= E_{k_{i2}}(S_{i2}) \\ &\cdots\cdots \\ R_{i\lambda} &= E_{k_{i\lambda}}(S_{i\lambda}) \end{aligned} \tag{10.53}$$

For example, when $\mathbf{T} = (1, 0, 0, 1, \ldots, 1, 0, 1)$, we get

$$\begin{aligned} R_1 &= E_{k_1}(S_1) \\ R_4 &= E_{k_4}(S_4) \\ &\cdots\cdots \\ R_{2\lambda-2} &= E_{k_{2\lambda-2}}(S_{2\lambda-2}) \\ R_{2\lambda} &= E_{k_{2\lambda}}(S_{2\lambda}) \end{aligned}$$

The elements of Eq. 10.52 are compared to those of Eq. 10.46. If these two element sets are equal, we obtain $R_{i1} = R_1, R_{i2} = R_2, \ldots, R_{i\lambda} = R_\lambda$. If these conditions are met, we conclude that the key subset $\mathbf{K}_T = (k_{i1}, k_{i2}, \ldots, k_{i\lambda})$ is authentic. If this is so, the receiver produces the data digest DC($\mathbf{X}$) of the message $\mathbf{X}$ and calculates the corresponding cryptograms in order to form the signature SG′ ($\mathbf{X}$) as follows:

$$\begin{aligned} \mathrm{SG}'(\mathbf{X}) &= \{E_{k_{i1}}[\mathrm{DC}(\mathbf{X})], E_{k_{i2}}[\mathrm{DC}(\mathbf{X})], \ldots, E_{k_{i\lambda}}[\mathrm{DC}(\mathbf{X})]\} \\ &= \{E'_{k_1}[\mathrm{DC}(\mathbf{X})], E'_{k_2}[\mathrm{DC}(\mathbf{X})], \ldots, E'_{k_{2\lambda}}[\mathrm{DC}(\mathbf{X})]\} \end{aligned} \tag{10.54}$$

For instance, when Eqs 10.54 and 10.49 are equal, the receiver declares the authenticity of the signature. Validation of signatures in the Rabin scheme is illustrated in Fig. 10.2.

10.8 THE DIFFIE-LAMPORT SIGNATURE SCHEME

Cryptographic operations used in the Diffie-Lamport scheme (1979) [29] [33] are based on symmetric encryption and decryption. Data compression for short signatures is not used in this scheme.

Let an n-bit message be represented as $\mathbf{X} = (X_1, X_2, \ldots, X_n)$ where $X_i \in$ GF (2) for $1 \le i \le n$. Let the signature of this message be denoted as SG ($\mathbf{X}$).

The sender must first choose n key pairs at random if he desires to sign n-bit messages $\mathbf{X}$ such that

$$\mathbf{K} = [(K_{10}, K_{11}), (K_{20}, K_{21}), \ldots, (K_{n0}, K_{n1})] \tag{10.55}$$

where K_{ij} for $1 \le i \le n$ and $j = 0, 1$ is the key length. For example, $K_{ij} = 56$ bits for DES. The sender must keep $\mathbf{K}$ secret. Next, the sender randomly selects n pairs of (S_{i0}, S_{i1}) for $1 \le i \le n$ such that

$$\mathbf{S} = [(S_{10}, S_{11}), (S_{20}, S_{21}), \ldots, (S_{n0}, S_{n1})] \tag{10.56}$$

where the elements of $\mathbf{S}$ are S_{ij} for $1 \le i \le n$ and $j = 0, 1$. For example, $S_{ij} =$ 64 bits for DES.

The sender encrypts $\mathbf{S}$ under $\mathbf{K}$ into the cryptogram $\mathbf{R}$ such that

$$R_{ij} = E_{k_{ij}}(S_{ij}) \qquad 1 \le i \le n, j = 0, 1 \tag{10.57}$$

This may also be represented as

$$\begin{aligned} R_{10} &= E_{K_{10}}(S_{10}) \\ R_{11} &= E_{K_{11}}(S_{11}) \\ &\cdots\cdots\cdots \\ R_{n0} &= E_{K_{n0}}(S_{n0}) \\ R_{n1} &= E_{K_{n1}}(S_{n1}) \end{aligned} \tag{10.58}$$

Equation 10.58 represents the elements of $\mathbf{R}$ which are the cryptograms of $\mathbf{S}$. Thus, the cryptogram sequence $\mathbf{R}$ is represented as

$$\mathbf{R} = [(R_{10}, R_{11}), (R_{20}, R_{21}), \ldots, (R_{n0}, R_{n1})] \tag{10.59}$$

where, for example, $R_{ij} = 64$ bits for DES.

These two sequences of $\mathbf{S}$ and $\mathbf{R}$, as shown in Eqs 10.56 and 10.59, are being used to authenticate the signatures. Since $\mathbf{S}$ and $\mathbf{R}$ are public, the receivers know them. They are stored in a public register, but only the authorized person can write into it even though anyone can read it.

The signature SG ($\mathbf{X}$) of an n-bit message $\mathbf{X} = (X_1, X_2, \ldots, X_n)$, $X_i \in$ GF (2) for $1 \le i \le n$ is described by a sequence of cryptographic keys as shown below.

$$\mathrm{SG}(\mathbf{X}) = (K_{1\mu_1}, K_{2\mu_2}, \ldots, K_{n\mu_n}) \tag{10.60}$$

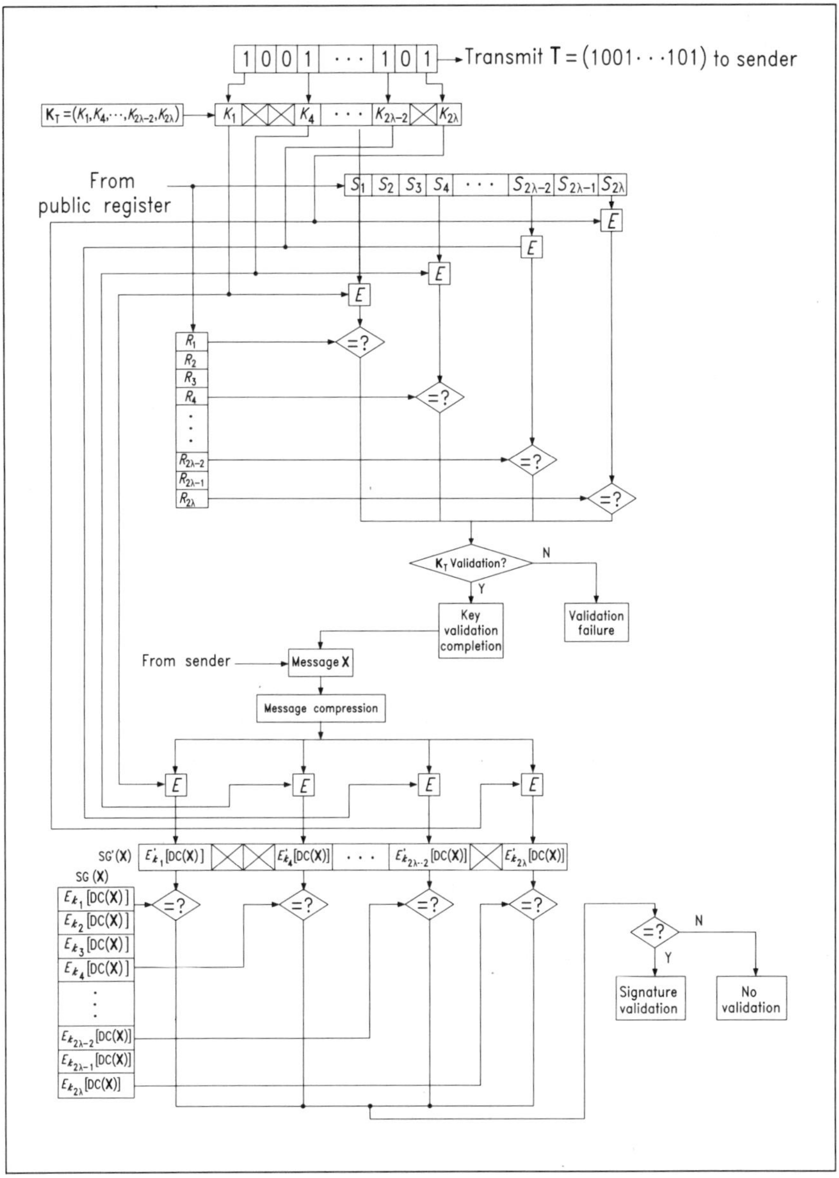

Fig. 10.2 Validation of signatures in the Rabin scheme

where

$$\mu_j = \begin{cases} 0 & \text{for } X_j = 0 \\ 1 & \text{for } X_j = 1 \end{cases} \qquad 1 \le j \le n$$

For example, for the 6-bit message $\mathbf{X} = (1, 1, 0, 1, 0, 0)$, the signature will takc the form SG $(\mathbf{X}) = (K_{11}, K_{21}, K_{30}, K_{41}, K_{50}, K_{60})$.

Now, the sender transmits ($\mathbf{X}$, SG($\mathbf{X}$)) to the receiver, who verifies the signature SG ($\mathbf{X}$) by using $\mathbf{S}$ and $\mathbf{R}$ from the public register in the following manner.

Since $X_1 = \mu_1 \in$ GF (2), the receiver reads $S_{1\mu_1}$ from the public register and produces its cryptogram $R_{1\mu_1} = E_{K_{1\mu_1}}(S_{1\mu_1})$. Similarly, he also obtains the cryptogram $R_{2\mu_2} = E_{K_{2\mu_2}}(S_{2\mu_2})$ for $X_2 = \mu_2 \in$ GF (2). Thus, in general, the receiver will produce $R_{j\mu_j} = E_{K_{j\mu_j}}(S_{j\mu_j})$ for $X_j = \mu_j$ where $1 \le j \le n$. In summary,

$$
\begin{aligned}
R_{1\mu_1} &= E_{K_{1\mu_1}}(S_{1\mu_1}) \\
R_{2\mu_2} &= E_{K_{2\mu_2}}(S_{2\mu_2}) \\
&\cdot \quad \cdot \quad \cdot \quad \cdot \quad \cdot \quad \cdot \\
R_{n\mu_n} &= E_{K_{n\mu_n}}(S_{n\mu_n})
\end{aligned}
\tag{10.61}
$$

Thus, if Eq. 10.61 between $\mathbf{R}$ and $\mathbf{S}$ under the keys $K_{j\mu_j}$ for $1 \le j \le n$ is satisfied, the receiver accepts the signature as legitimate. Otherwise the signature is not authentic.

■ **Example 10.13** Consider the Diffie-Lamport scheme where the message plaintext is $\mathbf{X} = (1\ 0\ 0\ 1\ 1\ 0)$. The receiver knows the two sequences $\mathbf{S}$ and $\mathbf{R}$ that are stored in a public register. The signature is of the form SG $(\mathbf{X}) = (K_{11}, K_{20}, K_{30}, K_{41}, K_{51}, K_{60})$. Now, the receiver enciphers $\mathbf{S} = (S_{ij}, 1 \le i \le 6$ and $j = 0, 1)$ under the keys $\mathbf{K} = (K_{ij}, 1 \le i \le 6$ and $j = 0, 1)$ into the respective cryptograms $\mathbf{R} = (R_{ij}, 1 \le i \le 6$ and $j = 0, 1)$ such that

$$
\begin{aligned}
R_{11} &= E_{K_{11}}(S_{11}) \\
R_{20} &= E_{K_{20}}(S_{20}) \\
R_{30} &= E_{K_{30}}(S_{30}) \\
R_{41} &= E_{K_{41}}(S_{41}) \\
R_{51} &= E_{K_{51}}(S_{51}) \\
R_{60} &= E_{K_{60}}(S_{60})
\end{aligned}
$$

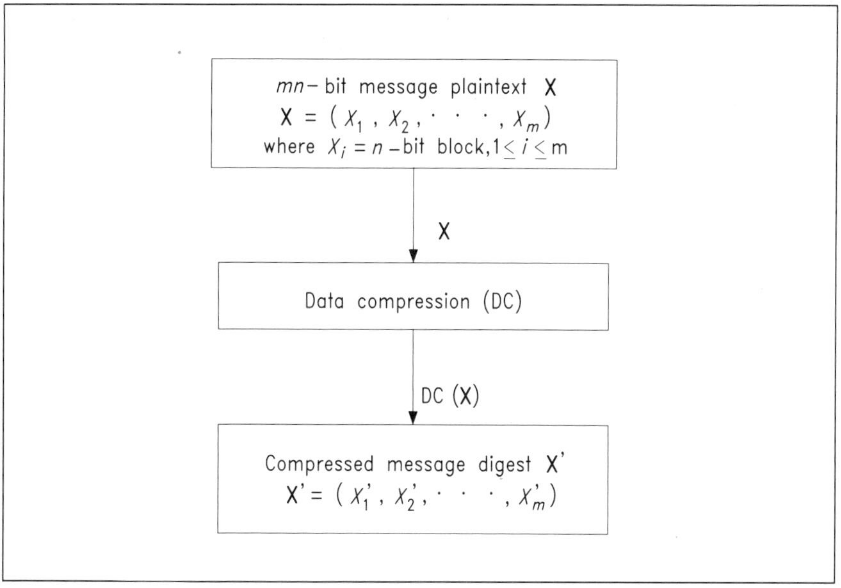

Fig. 10.3 Data compression to obtain an r-bit digest of the mn-bit message **X**

The encryptions are used to authenticate the signature. If they match, SG (**X**) is authentic.

The drawback of the Diffie-Lamport scheme is the excessive length of the signatures. Consider an n-bit message of m blocks and an r-bit key. Here, the length of the signatures SG (**X**) is equal to (mnr) bits. For example, for the case of DES, the length of SG (**X**) is 56 mn bits for an n-bit message. To meet such a situation, the compression method can be used to reduce the length of SG (**X**). Let $\mathbf{X} = (X_1, X_2, \ldots, X_m)$ be an mn-bit message. The flowchart of compression is shown in Fig. 10.3.

The signature creation and validation procedures when data compression is applied in the Diffie-Lamport scheme are shown in Figs. 10.4 and 10.5, respectively.

For example, since the signature required an r-bit encryption key, the length of SG (**X**) for DES is nr = (64) (56) bits.

10.9 MATYAS-MEYER SIGNATURE SCHEME

The signature scheme invented by Matyas and Meyer in 1981 is based on the DES algorithm [32]. The digital signature is a list of 31 keys selected from a 31 × 31 matrix of secret keys as indicated in Eq. 10.63. First of all, the sender generates a 30 × 31 matrix of

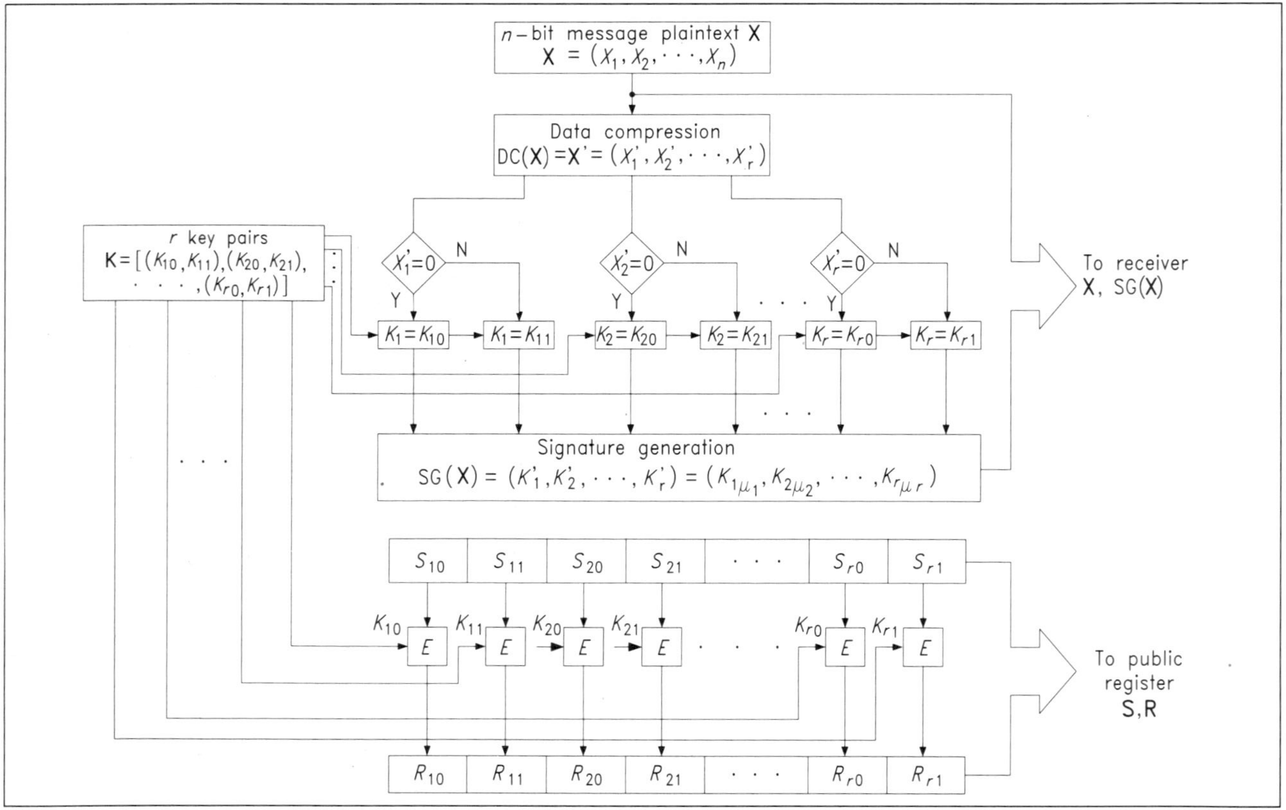

Fig. 10.4 Signature generation procedure in the Diffie-Lamport compressing scheme

nonsecret code words as shown below.

$$\mathbf{U} = \begin{bmatrix} u(1,1) & u(1,2) & \ldots & u(1,31) \\ u(2,1) & u(2,2) & \ldots & u(2,31) \\ \cdot & \cdot & & \cdot \\ \cdot & \cdot & & \cdot \\ \cdot & \cdot & & \cdot \\ u(30,1) & u(30,2) & \ldots & u(30,31) \end{bmatrix} \tag{10.62}$$

$$= [u(i,j)] \quad \text{for} \quad 1 \le i \le 30 \quad \text{and} \quad 1 \le j \le 31$$

where $u\ (i, j)$ are 64-bit sequences generated from pseudorandom generators. The sender then creates a 31 × 31 secret key matrix

$$\mathbf{K} = \begin{bmatrix} k(1,1) & k(1,2) & \ldots & k(1,31) \\ k(2,1) & k(2,2) & \ldots & k(2,31) \\ \cdot & \cdot & & \cdot \\ \cdot & \cdot & & \cdot \\ \cdot & \cdot & & \cdot \\ k(31,1) & k(31,2) & \ldots & k(31,31) \end{bmatrix} \tag{10.63}$$

$$= [k(i,j)] \quad \text{for} \quad 1 \le i,j \le 31$$

where $k\ (i, j)$ are also 64-bit sequences. The first row of **K** contains 31 initial keys produced via pseudorandom generators. The other rows are evaluated by the following encryptions:

$$k\ (i+1, j) = E_{k(i,j)}[u(i,j)] \tag{10.64}$$

where $1 \le i \le 30$ and $1 \le j \le 31$.

Equation 10.64 can also be written as

$$\begin{aligned} k(2,j) &= E_{k(1,j)}[u(1,j)] && \text{for} \quad i = 1 \text{ and } 1 \le j \le 31 \\ k(3,j) &= E_{k(2,j)}[u(2,j)] && \text{for} \quad i = 2 \text{ and } 1 \le j \le 31 \\ &\cdots\cdots\cdots\cdots \\ k(31,j) &= E_{k(30,j)}[u(30,j)] && \text{for} \quad i = 30 \text{ and } 1 \le j \le 31 \end{aligned} \tag{10.65}$$

After calculating **K**, the sender delivers all elements of **U** along with the last row of the matrix **K**, namely $k\ (31, 1), k\ (31, 2), \ldots, k\ (31, 31)$, to a public register and the receiver.

Before the sender generates his signature for a message **X**, he needs to compress it in the manner described in previous sections. The data compression, or DC (**X**), of **X** is used together with 31 nonsecret keys, $k_1, k_2, \ldots, k_{31}$, to produce 31 unique encryptions b_i for $1 \leq i \leq 31$ such that

$$b_i = E_{k_i} [DC\ (\mathbf{X})] \qquad 1 \leq i \leq 31 \tag{10.66}$$

That is,

$$\begin{aligned} b_1 &= E_{k_1} [\text{DC}\ (\mathbf{X})] \\ b_2 &= E_{k_2} [\text{DC}\ (\mathbf{X})] \\ &\ldots\ldots\ldots \\ b_{31} &= E_{k_{31}} [\text{DC}\ (\mathbf{X})] \end{aligned} \tag{10.67}$$

where the keys k_i for $1 \leq i \leq 31$ are public and kept in a public register. These 31 b-values are now sorted into numerical sequence. The sequence b_i, $1 \leq i \leq 31$, can be ordered according to increasing value as $b_{i1}, b_{i2}, \ldots, b_{i31}$. Each b-value has a position in the sorted and unsorted sequences, and therefore constitutes an index that can be used to select a key from the key matrix. Once the preliminary steps have been completed, the sender can generate the signature for the message **X** by selecting 31 keys from the matrix **K**. Since the ordered sequence of elements b_i takes the form $(b_{i1}, b_{i2}, \ldots, b_{i31})$, the signature has the following form:

$$\text{SG}\ (\mathbf{X}) = [k\ (i1, 1), k\ (i2, 2), \ldots, k\ (i31, 31)] \tag{10.68}$$

Now, the sender forwards the message **X** and the signature SG(**X**) to the receiver.

Upon receiving **X** and SG(**X**), the receiver authenticates SG(**X**) by repeating the same steps performed by the sender. First, the receiver must obtain the data compression DC(**X**) of the message **X**. Then he has to compute the 31 b-values and sort them in numerical order. Using b_{ij} for $1 \leq j \leq 31$, $u\ (i, j)$ of **U** from the public register, and $k\ (i\ \lambda, j)$ for $1 \leq \lambda, j \leq 31$, the receiver generates $k'\ (i\ \lambda, j)$ for $1 \leq \lambda, j \leq 31$, so as to check the signature. Thus, comparing $k'\ (31, j)$ with $k\ (31, j)$ for $1 \leq j \leq 31$, the message **X** and its signature SG(**X**) are accepted as valid if and only if $k'\ (31, j) = k\ (31, j)$: otherwise **X** and SG(**X**) are rejected. The Matyas-Meyer scheme for generation of authentication parameters and signature SG(**X**) is illustrated in Figs 10.6 (a) and (b).

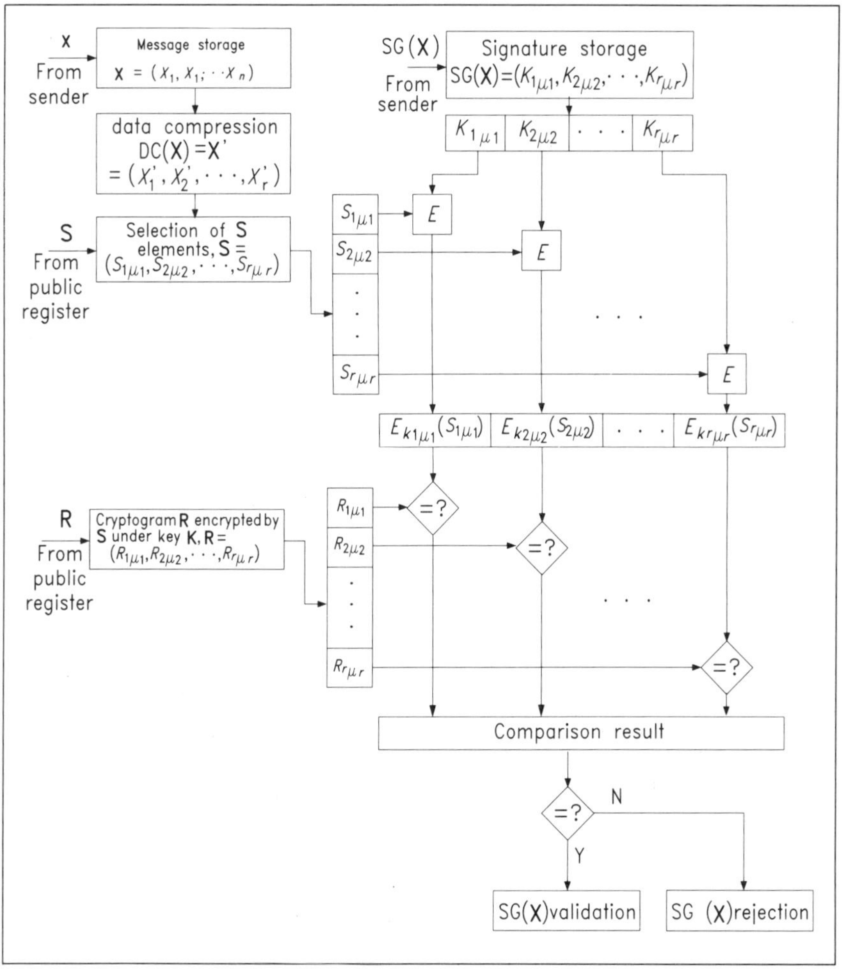

Fig. 10.5 Signature validation procedure in the Diffie-Lamport compressing scheme

10.10 ID-BASED CRYPTOSYSTEM AND SIGNATURE SCHEME

In 1984, Shamir proposed an innovative cryptographic scheme called the 'Identity (ID)-Based Cryptosystem and Signature Scheme' [44]. This system enables two communicators to exchange their messages securely and verify each other's signatures without exchanging secret or public keys. Consequently, this scheme does not require a key directory, or the use of any service from a third party. But the key generation centers in this scheme must provide each user an individual

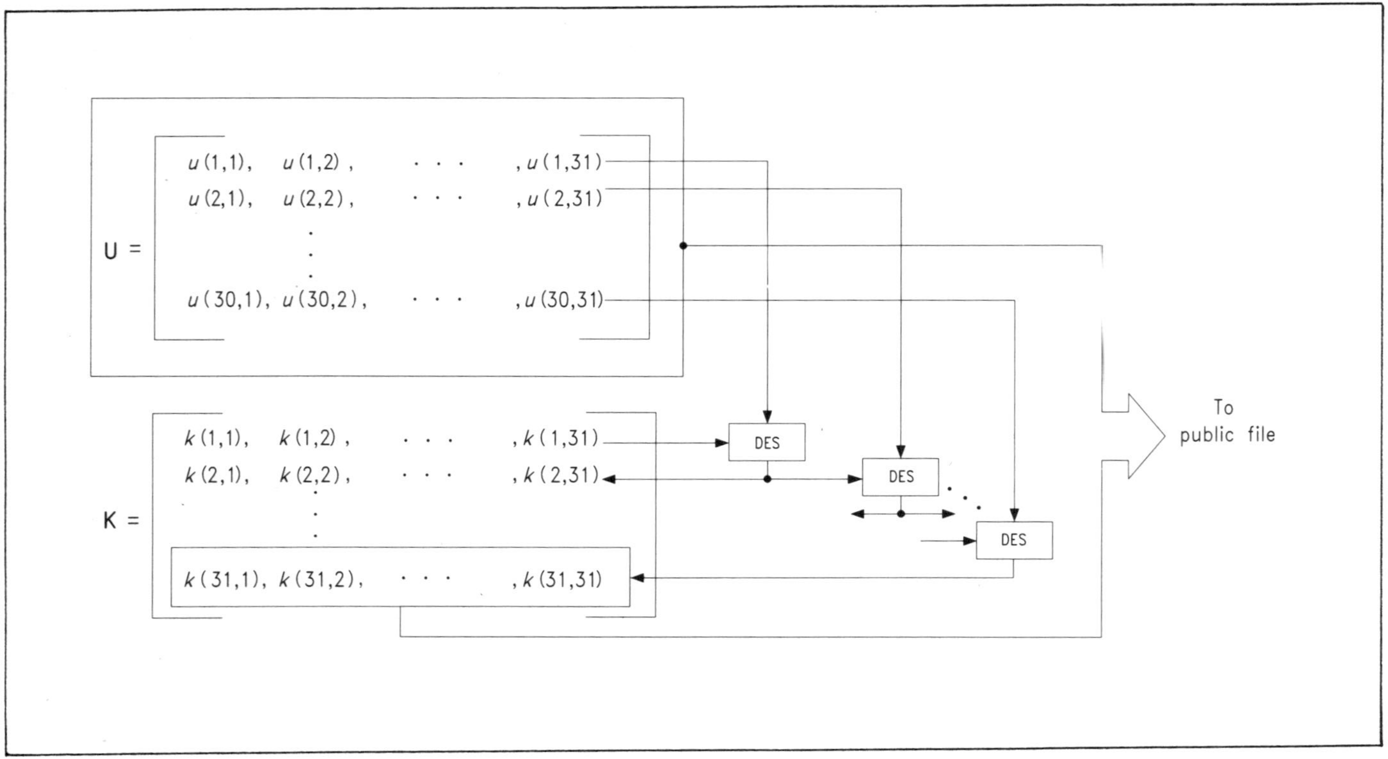

(a) Generation of authentication parameters **U** and **K**

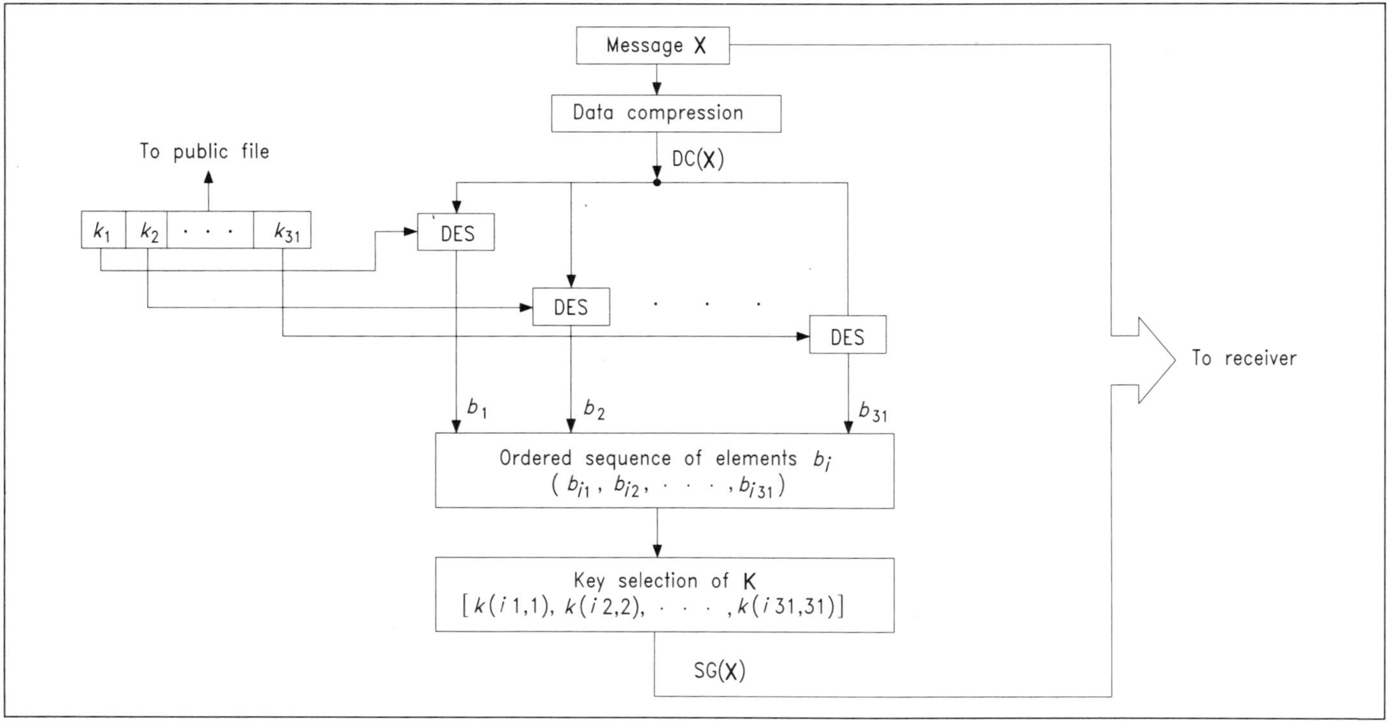

(b) Signature generation SG (**X**)

Fig. 10.6 The Matyas-Meyer scheme for generation of authentication parameters and signature SG(**X**)

smart card with which he can sign and encrypt messages to be sent and also decrypt and verify messages received.

The scheme is ideal for closed groups of users, and is based on a public-key cryptosystem for which the user chooses his name and network address as his public key. The secret key is computed by a key generation centre and issued to the user in the form of a smart card. This card contains a microprocessor, an I/O port, an RAM, an ROM with the secret key, and programs for message encryption and decryption, as also signature generation and verification. Thus, the smart card is intended to be a truly multiservice card because creation of unforgeable ID cards will be an important issue to numerous commercial and military applications (see Sec. 10.12).

In order to implement a public-key cryptosystem based on the discrete logarithm problem, the public and secret keys have to be determined. Let X be a message for $0 \le X \le p - 1$ where p is a very large prime number. The sender picks a primitive element α from the set of primitive numbers from GF (p). He selects the secret key K_s for $0 \le K_s \le p - 2$ and computes the public key such that

$$K_p \equiv \alpha^{K_s} \pmod p \tag{10.69}$$

where K_p, p and α are publicly known, and are kept in a public file by both parties. When user A wants to send a message X to user B, encryption proceeds as follows:

$$Y_1 \equiv \alpha^r \pmod p \tag{10.70}$$

$$Y_2 \equiv X \cdot K_{pB}^r \pmod p \tag{10.71}$$

where r is a random number selected by A, and K_{pB} denotes the public key of B. A sends the cryptogram (Y_1, Y_2) to B. Upon receiving it, B first deciphers Y_1 using his secret key K_{sB} as follows:

$$\begin{aligned} Y_1' &\equiv Y_1^{K_{sB}} \pmod p \\ &\equiv (\alpha^r)^{K_{sB}} \pmod p \\ &\equiv K_{pB}^r \pmod p \end{aligned} \tag{10.72}$$

Thus, B can restore the message X by utilizing Y_1' and Y_2 such that

$$(Y_1')^{-1} \cdot Y_2 \pmod p \equiv (K_{pB}^r)^{-1} \cdot X \cdot K_{pB}^r \pmod p \equiv X \pmod p \tag{10.73}$$

For restoring the message X from Y_1, Y_2, and K_{pB}, it is required to find the random number $r \equiv \log_\alpha Y_1 \pmod p$ which is based on the discrete logarithm problem.

Even though the ID-based scheme is fundamentally based on a public-key cryptosystem, the user can employ any combination of his name, social security number, telephone number, or network address as his public key without the generation of a random pair of public and secret keys. As shown in Fig. 10.7, the secret keys must be computed by a key generation center rather than by the users. Therefore, the key generation center should process some secret information, such as the factorization of a large number, so as to be able to compute the secret keys of all users in the network. In ID-based schemes, the encryption key K_E is usually the user's identity ID and the decryption key K_D is derived from the ID and some seed S via $K_D = f(ID, S)$. The security of the scheme largely depends on the secret information stored by the key generation centre and the thoroughness of the identity check performed by it before issuing the card to the user.

Before considering a specific ID-based cryptosystem, let us take a look at a key generation center. Let ID_A denote user A's identity. Then,

$$\text{ID}_A = f(\text{name,address,}\ldots\text{,etc.})]$$

$$= (\text{ID}_{A1}, \text{ID}_{A2}, \ldots, \text{ID}_{Ak}) \qquad (10.74)$$

where $\text{ID}_{Ai} \in \text{GF}(2)$ for $1 \le i \le k$.

The key generation center selects two large primes q_1 and q_2 whose product is $N = q_1 q_2$. Choosing the encryption exponent e such that gcd $(e, \phi(N)) = 1$, where $\phi(N) = (q_1 - 1)(q_2 - 1)$, the key generation center computes the extended identity (EID) of A as follows:

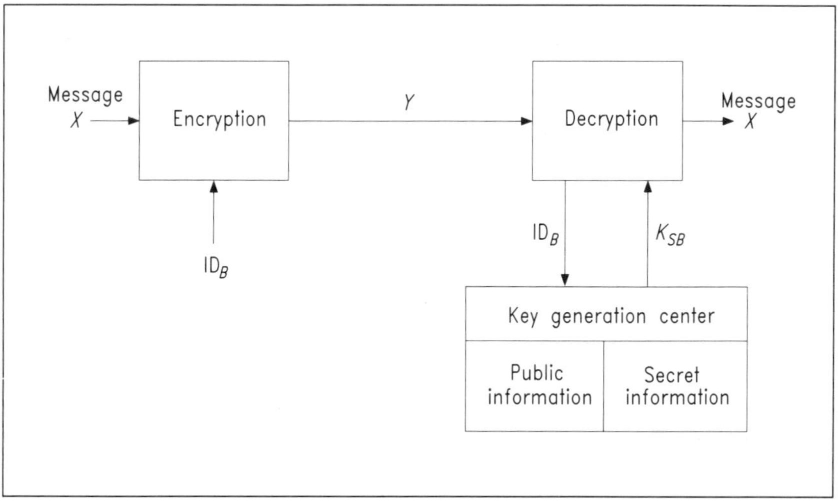

Fig. 10.7 ID-based cryptosystem

$$\mathrm{EID}_A \equiv (\mathrm{ID}_A)^e \pmod N$$

$$\equiv (\mathrm{EID}_{A1}, \mathrm{EID}_{A2}, \ldots, \mathrm{EID}_{An}) \tag{10.75}$$

where n denotes the number of bits when N is represented by $\{0, 1\}$.

Consider the superincreasing sequence

$$\mathbf{a}' = (a_1', a_2', \ldots, a_n') \tag{10.76}$$

which satisfies

$$a_i' \geq t \sum_{j=1}^{i-1} a_j' \tag{10.77}$$

where t is an arbitrary integer, and

$$\sum_{i=1}^{n} a_i' < p - 1 \tag{10.78}$$

Selecting w which is relatively prime to $p-1$, i.e. gcd $(w, p-1) = 1$, the center must determine the secret information

$$\mathbf{a} = (a_1, a_2, \ldots, a_n) \tag{10.79}$$

such that

$$a_i \equiv a_i' \cdot w \pmod{p-1}, 1 \leq i \leq n. \tag{10.80}$$

After selecting an element α from the primitive set of GF (p), the centre computes the public key $\mathbf{K}_p$ as

$$\mathbf{K}_p = (k_{p_1}, k_{p_2}, \ldots, k_{p_n}) \tag{10.81}$$

where $k_{p_i} \equiv \alpha^{a_i} \pmod p$, $1 \leq i \leq n$.

Using the center's secret information $\mathbf{a}$ and the user's EID, the secret key K_s is computed as

$$K_{sA} \equiv \sum_{i=1}^{n} a_i \cdot \mathrm{EID}_{Ai} \pmod{p-1} \tag{10.82}$$

where K_{sA} represents user A's secret key.

Let us consider the encryption process for the ID-based cryptosystem. Suppose user A sends a message X to user B. A computes EID_B by using ID_B (B's ID) such that

$$\mathrm{EID}_B \equiv (\mathrm{ID}_B)^e \pmod N$$

$$\equiv (\mathrm{EID}_{B1}, \mathrm{EID}_{B2}, \ldots, \mathrm{EID}_{Bn}) \tag{10.83}$$

where $\mathrm{EID}_{Bi} \in \{0, 1\}$ for $1 \leq i \leq n$.

Using the center's public key $\mathbf{K}_p$, A computes the public key K_{pB} of B as follows:

$$K_{pB} \equiv \prod_{i=1}^{n} k_{p_i}^{\mathrm{EID}_{Bi}} \pmod{p}$$

$$\equiv \prod_{i=1}^{n} \left(\alpha^{a_i}\right)^{\mathrm{EID}_{Bi}} \pmod{p}$$

$$\equiv \alpha^{\sum_{i=1}^{n} a_i(\mathrm{EID}_{Bi})} \pmod{p}$$

$$\equiv \alpha^{K_{sB}} \pmod{p} \tag{10.84}$$

User A picks a random number r, $0 \le r \le p-2$, and encrypts the message X, $0 \le X \le p-1$, into the cryptogram (Y_1, Y_2) as follows:

$$Y_1 \equiv \alpha^r \pmod{p}$$

$$Y_2 \equiv X \cdot (K_{pB})^r \pmod{p} \tag{10.85}$$

A now transmits the pair (Y_1, Y_2) to B.

We shall now show the decryption process. Upon receiving the ciphertext pair (Y_1, Y_2), user B computes Y'_1 by means of his secret key K_{sB} as

$$Y_1' \equiv Y^{K_{sB}} \pmod{p}$$

$$\equiv (\alpha^r)^{K_{sB}} \pmod{p} \tag{10.86}$$

Using Eqs. 10.72 and 10.85, B can recover the message X by utilizing Y'_1 and Y_2 as follows:

$$(Y_1')^{-1} Y_2 \pmod{p} \equiv \left[(\alpha^r)^{K_{sB}}\right]^{-1} \cdot X \cdot (K_{pB})^r \pmod{p}$$

$$\equiv \left[(\alpha^r)^{K_{sB}}\right]^{-1} \cdot X \cdot \left(\alpha^{K_{sB}}\right)^r \pmod{p}$$

$$\equiv X \pmod{p} \tag{10.87}$$

This completes the restoring process for the message X.

Let us consider the following example to see how the ID-based scheme operates.

■ **Example 10.14** Assume that the identity of the user B is $\mathrm{ID}_B = (\mathrm{ID}_{B1}, \mathrm{ID}_{B2}, \mathrm{ID}_{B3}) = (1, 0, 1) = 5$ for $k = 3$. Suppose the sender A has chosen

$q_1 = 3$ and $q_2 = 5$. Then $N = (3)(5) = 15$ and $\phi(N) = 8$. Choosing $e = 7$ from gcd $(e, 8) = 1$, B's extended identity for $n = 4$ becomes

$$\begin{aligned} EID_B &\equiv (ID_B)^e \quad (\text{mod } N) \\ &\equiv 5^7 \qquad (\text{mod } 15) \\ &\equiv 5 \\ &= (0101) \end{aligned}$$

Letting $p = 23$, $t = 1$, and $\mathbf{a}' = (a_1', a_2', a_3', a_4') = (1, 2, 4, 8)$, the center's secret information $\mathbf{a} = (a_1, a_2, a_3, a_4)$ can be determined by selecting w in such a manner as to satisfy gcd $(w, p - 1)$. Therefore, from gcd $(w, 22) = 1$, we can choose $w = 7$. Using a_i' for $1 \le i \le 4$ and $w = 7$, we can compute the secret information vector $\mathbf{a}$ as follows:

$$a_1 \equiv a_1'w \ (\text{mod } p-1) \equiv (1)(7) \ (\text{mod } 22) \equiv 7$$

$$a_2 \equiv a_2'w \ (\text{mod } p-1) \equiv (2)(7) \ (\text{mod } 22) \equiv 14$$

$$a_3 \equiv a_3'w \ (\text{mod } p-1) \equiv (4)(7) \ (\text{mod } 22) \equiv 6$$

$$a_4 \equiv a_4'w \ (\text{mod } p-1) \equiv (8)(7) \ (\text{mod } 22) \equiv 12$$

Thus, we get $\mathbf{a} = (7, 14, 6, 12)$.

Next, we try to determine the center's public key $\mathbf{K}_p$. When the primitive element of GF (p) is chosen as $\alpha = 7$, the elements of $\mathbf{K}_p$ are calculated as follows:

$$k_{p_1} \equiv \alpha^{a_1} \ (\text{mod } p) \equiv 7^7 \ (\text{mod } 23) \equiv 5$$

$$k_{p_2} \equiv \alpha^{a_2} \ (\text{mod } p) \equiv 7^{14} \ (\text{mod } 23) \equiv 2$$

$$k_{p_3} \equiv \alpha^{a_3} \ (\text{mod } p) \equiv 7^{6} \ (\text{mod } 23) \equiv 4$$

$$k_{p_4} \equiv \alpha^{a_4} \ (\text{mod } p) \equiv 7^{12} \ (\text{mod } 23) \equiv 16$$

Hence, the center's public key is computed as $\mathbf{K}_p = (5, 2, 4, 16)$.

The secret key of B is determined as

$$\begin{aligned} K_{sB} &\equiv \mathbf{a} \cdot EID_B \ (\text{mod } p-1) \\ &\equiv (7, 14, 6, 12) \cdot (0, 1, 0, 1) \ (\text{mod } 22) \\ &\equiv 26 \ (\text{mod } 22) \equiv 4 \end{aligned}$$

Suppose A sends a message X to B. Then, A must first determine EID_B from ID_B such that

$$EID_B \equiv (ID_B)^e \pmod N \equiv 5^7 \pmod{15} = (0101)$$

as calculated before.

Using Eq. 10.84, the public key of B is easily obtained as

$$K_{pB} \equiv \prod_{i=1}^{n} k_{p_i}^{EID_{Bi}} \pmod p$$

$$\equiv 5^0 \cdot 2^1 \cdot 4^0 \cdot 16^1 \pmod{23}$$

$$\equiv 32 \pmod{23} \equiv 9$$

Assume that sender A wants to send the message $X = 7$ and to choose the random number $r = 8$. Then, the pair of cryptograms (Y_1, Y_2) can be computed from Eq. 10.85.

$$Y_1 \equiv \alpha^r \pmod p \equiv 7^8 \pmod{23} \equiv 12$$

$$Y_2 \equiv X \cdot (K_{pB})^r \pmod p \equiv 7 \cdot 9^8 \pmod{23} \equiv 22$$

Now, A sends the pair (12, 22) to B.
Upon receiving the cryptogram (12, 22), B starts to compute Y_1' using Eq. 10.86 such that

$$Y_1' \equiv Y_1^{K_{sB}} \pmod p \equiv (12)^4 \pmod{23} \equiv 13$$

Using Eq. 10.87, the message X will be recovered as follows.

$$(Y_1')^{-1} \cdot Y_2 \pmod p \equiv (13^{-1})(22) \pmod{23} \equiv (16)(22) \pmod{23} \equiv 7$$

as expected.

At this point, let us consider only the implementation protocol for an ID-based signature scheme. The ElGamal signature scheme [15], based on the difficulty of solving the discrete logarithm problem, may be used as an ID-based scheme. The message is signed with a signature generation key, transmitted along with its signature and sender identity, and verified by means of a signature verification key.

Let X be the message of user A and (R, S), $0 \le R, S \le p - 1$, be the signature corresponding to X. Choose a random integer r, $0 \le r \le p - 2$, satisfying $\gcd(r, p - 1) = 1$ and a primitive element α of GF (p), where p is prime. Then, the first signature is computed as

$$R \equiv \alpha^r \pmod p \qquad (10.88)$$

The sender uses the Euclidean algorithm to solve the following congruence for the second signature S.

$$X \equiv K_{sA}R + rS \pmod{p-1} \tag{10.89}$$

Observing that $rS \pmod{p-1} \equiv X - K_{sA}R \pmod{p-1}$ from Eq. 10.89, S certainly exists since the light of gcd $(r, p-1) = 1$.

Now sender A transmits the message X along with the signature pair (R, S) to receiver B.

Upon receiving X, B computes α^X and p as well as EID_A as follows:

$$\text{EID}_A \equiv (\text{ID}_A)^e \pmod{N}$$

$$\equiv (\text{EID}_{A1}, \text{EID}_{A2}, \ldots, \text{EID}_{An}) \tag{10.90}$$

B now computes A's public key K_{pA} by utilizing the centre's public key $\mathbf{K}_p$ and EID_A as

$$K_{pA} \equiv \prod_{i=1}^{n} \left(k_{p_i}\right)^{\text{EID}_{Ai}} \pmod{p}$$

$$\equiv \alpha^{\sum_{i=1}^{n} a_i(\text{EID}_{Ai})} \pmod{p}$$

$$\equiv \alpha^{K_{sA}} \pmod{p}$$

Thus, the receiver B calculates

$$\alpha^X \equiv \alpha^{K_{sA}R + rS} \pmod{p}$$

$$\equiv \left(\alpha^{K_{sA}}\right)^R \cdot (\alpha^r)^S \pmod{p}$$

$$\equiv (K_{pA})^R \cdot R^S \pmod{p}$$

Therefore, the pair (R, S) is accepted as the genuine signature if and only if α^X matches $(K_{pA})^R \cdot R^S$.

The following example illustrates an ID-based signature scheme.

■ **Example 10.15** As in Example 10.14, sender A chooses $N = q_1q_2 = (3)(5) = 15$ and the primitive element $\alpha = 7$ from the Z_p^* of GF (p) where $p = 23$. A selects a random number r, $0 \le r \le p - 2$, such that gcd $(r, p-1) = 1$, from which we obtain $r = 7$.

Let (R, S) be a pair of signatures corresponding to the message X of user A. Then, the first signature R is computed as

$$R \equiv \alpha^r \pmod{p} \equiv 7^7 \pmod{23} \equiv 5$$

Assuming $X = 7$, the second signature is calculated using Eq. 10.89 as follows:

$$X \equiv K_{sA}R + rS \pmod{p-1}$$

$$7 \equiv (4)(5) + (7)S \pmod{22}$$

$$7S \equiv 9 \pmod{22}$$

from which we obtain $S = 17$.

Now A sends the triple $(X, R, S) = (7, 5, 17)$ to user B.

Upon receiving (X, R, S), B must compute $\alpha^x \pmod{p} \equiv 7^7 \pmod{23} \equiv 5$ and $\mathrm{EID}_A \equiv (\mathrm{ID}_A)^e \pmod{N} = 5^7 \pmod{15} \equiv 5 = (0101)$.

Using the public key $\mathbf{K}_p$ and EID_A, K_{pA} can be computed as

$$K_{pA} \equiv \prod_{i=1}^{n} (k_{p_i})^{\mathrm{EID}_{Ai}} \pmod{p} \equiv 5^0\, 2^1\, 4^0\, 16^1 \pmod{23} \equiv 9$$

B also calculates

$$(K_{pA})^R R^S \pmod{p} \equiv 9^5\, 5^{17} \pmod{23} \equiv 5$$

and

$$\alpha^X \equiv 7^7 \pmod{23} \equiv 5$$

Hence, since $\alpha^X \equiv (K_{pA})^R R^S \pmod{23} = 5$, the signature pair $(R, S) = (5, 17)$ is accepted as legitimate.

Since Shamir introduced ID-based cryptosystems in 1984, several cryptologists have investigated and promoted such systems through their researches. Tsujii, Itho, and Kurosawa [46] presented a paper on an ID-based cryptosystem based on the discrete logarithm problem. Okamoto and Tanaka [36] introduced an ID-based information security management system for personal computer networks. Matsumoto and Imai [31] discussed the security of some key sharing schemes. Koyama and Ohta [28] presented a paper on the security of improved ID-based conference key distribution systems. Youm and Rhee [47] published a paper on an ID-based cryptosystem and digital signature scheme using the discrete logarithm problem.

10.11 ZERO-KNOWLEDGE INTERACTIVE PROOFS (ZKIPs)

Considerable attention has been focussed on ZKIPs since 1984. Goldwasser, Micali, and Rackoff [22] examined how much knowledge should be communicated in order to convince a polynomial-time verifier for the validity of a theorem. Such a proof is known as a zero-knowledge interactive proof. The ZKIPs are based on the difficulty of computing the discrete logarithm modulo a large prime, quadratic residuosity of numbers, modular square roots, and the factorization of a composite number. ZKIP techniques are useful in many application areas, such as identifications and digital signatures in authentication systems. The application of a ZKIP to identification schemes has, for example, been demonstrated in [5], [18], and [21] among others.

Consider simple identification and signature schemes which enable any user to prove his identity and the authenticity of his messages to any other user without the need for shared or public keys. Fiat and Shamir (FS) claim that their identification scheme is a combination of the ZKIP by Goldwasser, Micali, and Rackoff (1985) and identity-based schemes by Shamir (1984). The FS scheme is based on the difficulty of computing square roots modulo a composite n when the factorization of n is unknown.

In the following section, we shall discuss a typical ZKIP based on the Fiat-Shamir scheme presented in 1986 [18].

10.11.1 Fiat-Shamir (FS) Identification Scheme

Let n be a modulus and f denote a pseudorandom function. Before the trusted centre starts issuing the smart cards, n and f are chosen and made public. The modulus n is the product of two secret primes p and q, but only the centre knows the factorization of n and thus every user can use the same n. The function f should be indistinguishable from a truly random function by any polynomially bounded computation.

When an eligible user applies for a smart card, the centre prepares a string I containing all relevant information about the user (name, address, ID number, physical description, etc) and about the card (expiry date, limitations on validity, etc). Now the centre performs the preparatory steps as shown below.

1. For an eligible user j, $v_j = f(I, j) = I\,\mathrm{D}_j$ for $j = 1, 2, \ldots$ is computed such that

$$v_1 = f(I, 1)$$

$$v_2 = f(I, 2)$$

$$\cdots\cdots$$

$$v_\lambda = f(I, \lambda)$$

2. Quadratic residues v_j are considered for small values of indices $j = 1, 2, \ldots, k$, and the square roots of v_j^{-1} (mod n), viz. s_j, are computed as follows:

$$s_j^2 \equiv v_j^{-1} \pmod{n} \qquad 1 \le j \le k$$

from which

$$s_1 \equiv v_1^{-1/2} \pmod{n}$$

$$s_2 \equiv v_2^{-1/2} \pmod{n}$$

$$\cdots\cdots\cdots\cdots$$

$$s_k \equiv v_k^{-1/2} \pmod{n}$$

3. A smart card containing the user information I, modular square roots s_j, and their indices $j = 1, 2, \ldots, k$, is issued.

It is recommended that the center be eliminated by the user choosing his own n and publishing it in a public key directory. For typical implementations, it is recommended that $1 \le k \le 18$ and n at least 512 bits long be chosen.

Creating unforgeable smart cards is an important problem with numerous commercial and military applications. The problem becomes particularly challenging when the two parties (the prover P and the verifier V) compose an interactive proof system (P $\leftrightarrow$ V). The FS interactive proof is based on the following protocol.

1. P sends I to V.
2. V generates $v_j = f(I, j)$ when $j = 1, 2, \ldots, k$. Steps 3 to 6 are repeated for $i = 1, 2, \ldots, t$.
3. P chooses a random number $r_i \in [0, n-1]$, computes $x_i \equiv r_i^2 \pmod{n}$ and sends x_i to V.
4. V sends a random binary vector $(e_{i1}, e_{i2}, \ldots, e_{ik})$ to P.
5. P computes

$$y_i \equiv r_i \prod_{\substack{j=1 \\ e_{ij}=1}}^{k} s_j \pmod{n}$$

and sends y_i to V.

6. V checks that

$$x_i \equiv y_i^2 \prod_{\substack{j=1 \\ e_{ij}=1}}^{k} v_j \pmod{n}$$

Thus, the verifier V accepts the prover P's proof of identity only if all the t checks are successful.

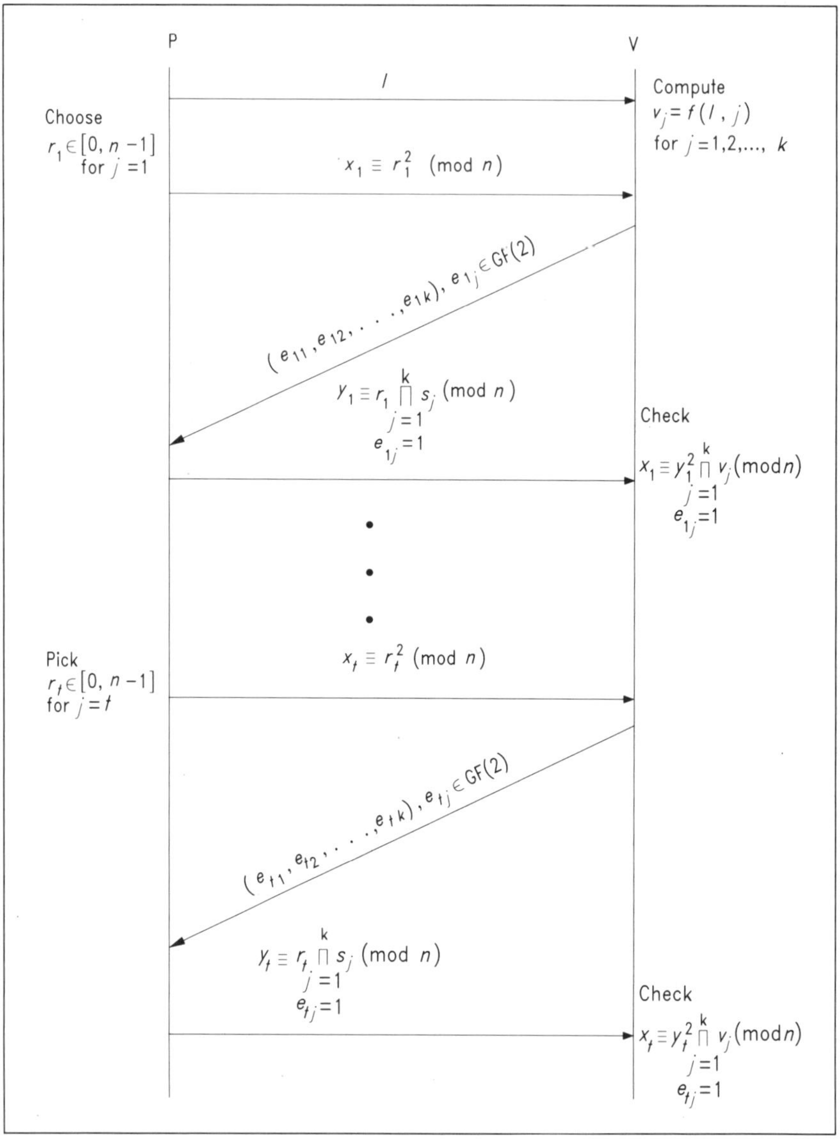

Fig. 10.8 FS interactive identification protocol

We have so far discussed the process of interactive identification. This FS identification protocol is sketched in Fig. 10.8.

Proposition (I) If (P ↔ V) follows the protocol, then V always accepts the proof as valid.

Proof From step 6, we have

$$y_i^2 \prod_{\substack{j=1 \\ e_{ij}=1}}^{k} v_j = r_i^2 \prod_{\substack{j=1 \\ e_{ij}=1}}^{k} s_j^2 v_j$$

Using $s_j^2 v_j \equiv 1 \pmod{n}$, we have

$$y_i^2 \prod_{\substack{j=1 \\ e_{ij}=1}}^{k} v_j = r_i^2 = x_i$$

Proposition (II) Assume that P does not know s_j for $1 \le j \le k$ and cannot compute in polynomial time the square root of any product form $\prod_{j=1}^{k} v_j^{c_j}$ (mod n) where $c_j = \{-1, 0, +1\}$. If V follows the protocol, he will accept the proof as valid with probability bounded by 2^{-kt}.

Proof Without receiving $e_{ij} \in \{0, 1\}$ from V, P guesses an arbitrary binary vector $\mathbf{e}_{ij} = (e_{i1}, e_{i2}, \ldots, e_{ik})$ and sends

$$x_i \equiv r_i^2 \prod_{\substack{j=1 \\ e_{ij}=1}}^{k} v_j \pmod{n}$$

to V. V sends a random binary vector $\mathbf{e}_{ij}' = (e_{i1}' \, e_{i2}', \ldots, e_{ik}')$ to P. P then compares $\mathbf{e}_{ij}$ with $\mathbf{e}_{ij}'$ and sends $y_i = r_i$ to V only if $e_{ij} = e_{ij}'$ for $1 \le j \le k$. Using step 6, V computes

$$y_i^2 \prod_{\substack{j=1 \\ e_{ij}=1}}^{k} v_j \pmod{n}$$

$$\equiv r_i^2 \prod_{\substack{j=1 \\ e_{ij}=1}}^{k} v_j \pmod{n}$$

$$= x_i$$

Thus, V accepts the proof as valid.
However, the probability of this event per iteration is

$$p[\text{event}] = p[e_{ij} = e_{ij}', 1 \le j \le k; e_{ij} \text{ or } e_{ij}' \in \text{GF}(2)]$$

$$= 2^{-k}$$

Hence, the probability of t iterations for the whole operation is

$$p_t = (2^{-k})^t = 1/2^{kt}$$

To increase this probability, P must choose the x_i values such that he can compute the square roots y_i' and y_i'' of $x_i / \prod_{\substack{j=1 \\ e_{ij}=1}}^{k} v_j \pmod n$ for $e_{ij} \rightarrow e_{ij}'$ and e_{ij}''. That is

$$y_i' \equiv \left[x_i / \prod_{\substack{j=1 \\ e'_{ij}=1}}^{k} v_j \right]^{1/2} \pmod n$$

$$y_i'' = \left[x_i / \prod_{\substack{j=1 \\ e''_{ij}=1}}^{k} v_j \right]^{1/2} \pmod n$$

The ratio y_i'/y_i'' (mod n) will be of the form $\prod_{j=1}^{k} s_j^{c_j}$ (mod n):

$$\frac{y_i'}{y_i''} = \left[\prod_{\substack{j=1 \\ e''_{ij}=1}}^{k} v_j \Big/ \prod_{\substack{j=1 \\ e'_{ij}=1}}^{k} v_j \right]^{1/2}$$

Since $v_j^{-1/2} = s_j$, we have

$$\frac{y_i'}{y_i''} \equiv \prod_{j=1}^{k} s_j^{c_j} \pmod n \quad \text{where } c_j \in \{-1, 0, +1\}.$$

This contradicts the assumption.

To help readers better understand Proposition (II), we shall consider the following practical example.

■ **Example 10.16** Let us examine the premise that P cannot compute a square root of the form $\prod_{j=1}^{k} v_j^{c_j}$ (mod n) where $c_j = (-1, 0, +1)$.

$$\frac{y_i'}{y_i''} \equiv \prod_{j=1}^{3} s_j^{c_j} \pmod n \quad \text{for } k = 3$$

Since $s_j^2 = v_j^{-1}$, we have $v_1 = s_1^{-2}$, $v_2 = s_2^{-2}$, and $v_3 = s_3^{-2}$.

Let us compute

$$\left(\prod_{j=1}^{3} v_j \right)^{1/2} = (v_1^1 v_2^0 v_3^1)^{1/2} = (s_1^{-1} s_2^0 s_3^{-1}) \quad \text{for } \mathbf{e}'_{ij} = (1, 0, 1)$$

and $\left(\prod_{j=1}^{3} v_j\right)^{1/2} = (v_1^1 v_2^1 v_3^0)^{1/2} = (s_1^{-1} s_2^{-1} s_3^0)$ for $\mathbf{e}_{ij}'' = (1, 1, 0)$

Thus
$$\frac{y'_i}{y''_i} = (s_1^{-1} s_2^{-1} s_3^0)/(s_1^{-1} s_2^0 s_3^{-1})$$

$$= s_2^{-1} s_3^1 = s_1^0 s_2^{-1} s_3^1$$

Therefore, we can find $c_j = (0, -1, 1)$

This contradicts our assumption.

Proposition (III) For a fixed k and arbitrary t, this is a zero-knowledge proof.

Proof From step 5, namely

$$y_i \equiv r_i \prod_{\substack{j=1 \\ e_{ij}=1}}^{k} s_j \pmod n$$

we see that y_i consists of the product of r_i and s_j. But each y_i contains an independent random variable r_i which masks s_j. All the messages $x_i \equiv r_i^2 \pmod n$ sent from P to V are thus random numbers with uniform probability distribution, and cheating by V cannot change this fact. But our intuitive reasoning is not sufficiently rigorous to prove this claim.

We have thus far seen that the probability of forgery is 2^{-kt}. For attaining a security level of 2^{-20}, it is clear that one has to choose $k = 5$ and $t = 4$. Assuming an equally likely distribution for binary bits, i.e. $p[e_{ij} = 1] = 1/2$ and $p[e_{ij} = 0] = 1/2$, the average number of modular multiplications required to generate or verify this identity proof can be computed as follows: The modular multiplication for $x_i \equiv r_i^2 \pmod n$ is 1 and that for $y_i \equiv r_i \prod_{\substack{j=1 \\ e_{ij}=1}}^{k} s_j \pmod n = r_i s_1^{e_{i1}} s_2^{e_{i2}} \cdots s_k^{e_{ik}} \pmod n$ is $k/2$. Hence, the average modular multiplication of t iterations required for the whole protocol is $[1 + (k/2)]t = t(k + 2)/2$. For example, for $k = 5$ and $t = 4$, the average number of modular multiplications is $4(5 + 2)/2 = 14$.

Assuming $n = 512$ bits = 64 bytes, we have 64 bytes for the user's information string I, 64 bytes for x_i, 64 bytes for y_i and $k/8$ bytes for e_{ij}. Therefore, the number of bytes exchanged by the parties during the entire protocol is $64 + t\,[64 + 64 + (k/8)]$ bytes. For $k = 5$ and $t = 4$, we have $64 + 4\,[128 + (5/8)] \cong 579$ bytes. The number of bytes for the secret values s_j, $1 \le j \le 4$, is computed as $64k = 320$ for $k = 5$ which can be stored in a 320-byte ROM. Even better performance can be expected by increasing k to 18. In this case, the secret s_j is determined as $64k = 64 \times 18 = 1152$ bytes. These bytes of s_j can be stored in a 1152-byte ROM. If we use $\mathbf{e}_{ij}$ with at the most three 1's in them, the number of possible $\mathbf{e}_{ij}$s in each iteration is $\binom{18}{3} + \binom{18}{2} + \binom{18}{1} + \binom{18}{0} = 988$. With $t = 2$ iterations, $\mathbf{e}_{ij}$ vectors become $988 \times 988 \sim 1 \times 10^6$, i.e. the security level remains about one in a million, but the number of transmitted bytes drops to $64 + 2 [64 + 64 + (18/8)] = 325$ bytes and the average number of modular multiplications drops to $t(k + 2)/2 = 20$ for $t = 2$ and $k = 18$.

Finally, we would like to comment that the sequential version of the interactive identification scheme is zero-knowledge, but the parallel identification scheme cannot be rigorously proved to be so because ($P \leftrightarrow V$) are not allowed to share a randomly selected string back and forth interactively.

10.11.2 FS Signature Scheme

The role of the trusted center in this case is the same as that in the identification scheme. In the FS identification scheme, the random vector $\mathbf{e}_{ij}$ which V sends contains no information, but its unpredictability prevents P from cheating. Switching an FS identification scheme to an FS signature scheme, we replace V's role by the function f and obtain the following signature protocol.

1. To sign a message **m**, the prover P:

(i) Chooses random numbers $r_1, r_2, \ldots, r_t \in [0, n-1]$ and computes $x_i \equiv r_i^2 \pmod{n}$.

(ii) Computes $f(\mathbf{m}, x_1, x_2, \ldots, x_t)$ and uses its first kt bits as $\{e_{ij}\}$, $0 \le i \le t$ and $1 \le j \le k$.

(iii) Computes

$$y_i \equiv r_i \prod_{\substack{j=1 \\ e_{ij}=1}}^{k} s_j \pmod{n} \quad \text{for } 1 \le i \le t$$

and sends I, **m**, $\{e_{ij}\}$, and $\{y_i\}$ to V.

2. To verify P's signature on **m**, the verifier V:

(i) Computes $v_j = f(I, j)$ for $1 \le j \le k$.

(ii) Computes

$$z_i \equiv y_i^2 \prod_{\substack{j=1 \\ e_{ij}=1}}^{k} v_j \pmod n \quad \text{for } 1 \le i \le t$$

(iii) Verifies whether the first kt bits of $f(\mathbf{m}, z_1, z_2, \ldots, z_t)$ are $\{e_{ij}\}$ or not. V accepts the message **m** as genuine if and only if $\{e_{ij}\}$ equals to the first kt bits.

As may be observed from the protocol we have discussed the signature scheme is not zero-knowledge. If everyone can recognize valid signatures but no one can forge them, V cannot regenerate P's messages with the same probability distribution. But the information about $\{s_i\}$ that V gets from signatures generated by P is so implicit that it is impossible to forge new signatures, and thus the signature scheme is probably secure even if it is not zero-knowledge. To increase security and not be vulnerable to specialized attacks, we have to pick a sufficiently large n and a truly random function f. According to Fiat and Shamir, when n is at least 512 bits long and f is sufficiently strong, such attacks are quite unlikely.

Proposition (IV) If P and V follow their protocols, V always accepts the signature as valid.

Proof From the definition,

$$z_i \equiv y_i^2 \prod_{\substack{j=1 \\ e_{ij}=1}}^{k} v_j \pmod n$$

$$\equiv r_i^2 \prod_{\substack{j=1 \\ e_{ij}=1}}^{k} s_j^2 v_j \pmod n$$

Since $s_j^2 v_j = 1, z_i \equiv r_i^2 \equiv x_i \pmod n$.

Thus, $$f(\mathbf{m}, z_1, z_2, \ldots, z_t) = f(\mathbf{m}, x_1, x_2, \ldots, x_t)$$

The desired security level is $2^{-kt} = 2^{-72}$ and is obtained by choosing $k = 9$ and $t = 8$. The number of bytes for the private key is computed as $64k = 64 \times 9 = 576$. Thus, the key can be stored in a 576-byte ROM. Each signature required $64t + (kt)/8 = 64 \times 8 + 72/8 = 521$ bytes. The average number of modular multiplications for this choice is t for $x_i \equiv r_i^2 \pmod n$ plus $kt/2$ for $y_i \equiv r_i \prod_{\substack{j=1 \\ e_{ij}=1}}^{k} s_j \pmod n$. Hence, we have $t + (kt/2) = 8 + 36 = 44$.

One of the most basic issues to be considered in complexity theory and cryptography is how much knowledge should be yielded in order to convince a polynomial-time verifier of the validity of a theorem. In the interaction between the prover and the verifier, the prover sends an NP statement and the verifier computes polynomial time to satisfy himself that it is indeed a proof. It is well known that zero-knowledge proofs for all languages in NP have enormous implications in cryptography. Intuitively, a zero-knowledge proof is a proof which yields nothing but its validity.

Goldwasser, Micali, and Rackoff (GMR) [22] and also Babai [2] introduced the basic concept of an interactive proof (IP) system. The IP system they proposed is a two-party protocol through which one party (the prover) can convince another (the verifier) of the validity of some statement concerning a common input $x \in L$. Such proofs have been shown to be zero-knowledge and have been a principal focus of attention since 1985. Even though Babai's model is similar to that of GMR, it is seemingly more limited due to the fact that the verifier is required to reveal to the prover all of his coin flips. This lack of privacy seems an important restriction, but these two interactive models are basically equivalent in respect of language recognition. The wide applicability of zero-knowledge proof systems has been demonstrated by Goldreich, Micali, and Wigderson (GMW) [21]. They have shown that under the assumption that secure bit commitment schemes exist, any NP language has a ZKIP system. Ben-Or, Goldreich, Goldwasser, Hastad, Kilian, Micali, and Rogaway [7] extended the result of GMW that, under the same assumption, all of NP admits ZKIPs. Furthermore, assuming envelopes for bit commitment, they claimed that every language which admits an interactive proof admits a perfect ZKIP.

An interactive proof system for membership is a two-party protocol whereby a prover convinces a verifier that the input string x is actually in a language L, i.e. $x \in L$. Ben-Or, Goldwasser, Kilian, and Wigderson [8] introduced the idea of multi-prover interactive proofs for showing how to achieve perfect ZKIPs for the entire IP system without using any intractability assumptions. Instead of one prover attempting to convince the verifier that x is in L, the two-prover model involves two separate provers who jointly agree on a strategy to convince the verifier that x is in the language L. Theoretically, the two-prover scheme seems much more efficient than those known for the one-prover model. There are quite a few powerful methodologies for developing secure two-party and multiparty protocols. Recent developments in ZKIP methodologies seem to indicate that it is easier for a prover to cheat the verifier in a single prover IP system than in a multiprover IP system.

Brassard and Crepeau [10] proposed ZKIPs for all languages in NP, which rely heavily on the intractability of quadratic residuosity, as well as showing "zero-information proofs" if factoring is intractable. Independently, Chaum [12] also proposed a protocol, very similar to the one due to Brassard and Crepeau, involving zero-information proofs.

There are two very useful and applicable notions of zero-knowledge proofs, namely interactive proofs (ZKIP) and non-interactive proofs (NIZK). As stated above, ZKIP was introduced by GMR [22], and developed by GMW [21] and Impagliazzo and Yung [23], while NIZK was introduced by Blum, Feldman, and Micali [9] and also discussed by De Santis, Micali, and Persiano [14]. BFM and DMP describe concrete implementations of their NIZK models based on the computational difficulty of distinguishing products of two primes from those of three primes, and quadratic residues from quadratic non-residues, respectively. Under the assumption that 'oblivious transfer' protocols exist, Kilian, Micali and Ostrovsky [27] showed how, after an initial preprocessing stage, the prover can noninteractively prove many NP-statements polynomially, these proofs not being publicly verifiable and all of them being directed to a particular verifier. Feige and Shamir [17] solved the problem of zero-knowledge for NP in a constant number of rounds, under the assumption that one-way functions exist. Brassard, Crepeau, and Yung [11] showed the existence of parallel perfect zero-knowledge arguments for NP under the certified discrete log assumption. Bellare, Micali, and Ostrovsky [6] exhibited perfect zero-knowledge proofs for quadratic residuosity and graph isomorphism in five rounds. Fortnow, Rompel, and Siper [20] claimed to obtain the perfect zero-knowledge problem by exhibiting a parallel two-prover protocol, but Fortnow [19] later showed their proof of soundness to be faulty. No alternative parallel protocol is currently known to be perfect in this respect. But Lapidot and Shamir [30] presented a simplified parallel protocol for Hamiltonicity, and its correctness has so far not been challenged.

Lapidot and Shamir [30] proposed the first publicly verifiable NIZK proof for any NP statement under the general assumption that one-way permutations exist. If the prover P and verifier V have a common random string and P is polynomially bounded, then the LS scheme can be based on the stronger assumption that trapdoor permutations exist. Such NIZK proofs have important cryptographic applications, such as digital signature and message authentication by Bellare and Goldwasser [5], and protection of public key cryptosystems against chosen ciphertext attacks by Naor and Yung [34].

Beaver, Feigenbaum, and Shoup [4] formalized the notion of zero-knowledge for an instance-hiding proof system with several provers and showed that all such systems can be made zero-knowledge. Consider an instance-hiding scheme for a Boolean function f on x, where the input x is on a private tape, accessible only to the querier V. The protocol allows V to obtain the value of $f(x)$ without revealing to any prover any information about x. In an instance-hiding multiprover interactive proof system for a function f on the input x, the provers P_1, $P_2, \ldots, P_m$ do not know x, nor can they infer anything about x, from the messages they receive from the verifier V. That is, the provers learn nothing about x and the verifier learns nothing but the value of $f(x)$. As in ordinary MIP, the verifier V is a probabilistic polynomial-time Turing Machine, the provers $P_1, P_2, \ldots, P_m$ are computationally unbounded, and the provers cannot communicate with each other. Also the provers have a shared random tape (that is only required in the construction of zero-knowledge instance-hiding proof systems) to which the verifier does not have access. Unlike in ordinary MIP, the input x in an instance-hiding proof system is known only to the verifier. The output produced by V after interacting with the many provers is an element of the set {0, 1, reject}. We recommend the works on hiding information in multioracle queries by Beaver and Feigenbaum [3], and on hiding information from an oracle by Abadi, Feigenbaum, and Kilian [1] for further reading on this subject.

Thus far, no robust transformation is known for converting interactive proof systems into the Arthur-Merlin form. Kilian [25] proposed that there exists a robust transformation that converts interactive proofs to satisfiable ZKIPs. A robust transformation Φ takes an interactive proof system (P, V) for a large L and produces a new interactive proof system (P*, V*). To elucidate a more evolutional notion of a protocol transformation, a robust transformation may be described as follows: Let Φ denote a transformation from (P, V) to (P*, V*). Then we say that Φ is robust if (i) Φ (P, V) = (P*, V*) for all (P*, V*) accepts the same language as (P, V) and (ii) P* can be evaluated by a probabilistic polynomial-time Turing Machine M with access to a black-box evaluator for P.

Since 1985, interest has been shown by the new idea on zero-knowledge proofs. A great deal of theoretical research has been done on ZKIPs since then. This new area provides cryptologists with fascinating protocols for achieving provably secure communications. Almost all the proposed protocols are based on the difficulty of: (i) factorizing a composite number, (ii) determining quadratic residuosity,

(iii) computing a discrete logarithm, (iv) calculating of square roots modulo n (a composite), and (v) computing the exponent of a modulo exponentiation trapdoor one-way function.

10.12 SMART CARDS

A smart card is an improved version of the traditional credit card, and is superior to a magnetic strip card. Smart cards are IC cards in credit format, and are widely used nowadays. Embedded in such a card is a built-in microcontroller that can be programmed to execute practical applications within its processing power (CPU) and memory capacity (ROM).

Smart cards (sometimes called tamper-resistant security devices) rely on VLSI chip technology not only for data storage, but for information processing as well. They store, process, and control internal cryptographic algorithms, and are thus eminently suitable for establishing identity, and enhancing logical security. Smart cards in general have three fundamental elements, namely, processing power, data storage elements, and a means to input and output data. The processing power is supplied by a microprocessor chip, the storage elements by a memory chip, and I/O data through metallic contacts on the card's surface. Those cards which have metallic contacts are inserted in a slot in the read/write unit so that a link is made with a connector inside the unit. Through this connector data can flow into or out of the card. Contactless smart cards that transfer data between a card and a read/write unit do not require the use of external contacts, but need only be placed on or near the surface of the unit. Smart cards can be used in such areas as financial transactions, medical records relating to the cardholder, pay televisions, public phones, train season tickets establishing identification at ticket barriers, equipment maintenance records, and many more.

10.12.1 Cardholder Identification (User Authentication)

In this section we will focus on the identification of the cardholder by the card, considering that the card itself is authenticated by other means. It is most important that the smart card identifies the person attempting to use it as the authorized cardholder. Such identification involves the input of a Personal Identification Number (PIN) and verification in the smart card. The smart card internally compares the PIN presented by the user with the reference PIN written in a secret area of its nonvolatile programmable memory (NVM). Up to more than three tries are usually allowed for a PIN input. If the test results are incorrect after three successive erroneous attempts, the card is blocked and cannot be used thereafter. For certain system configurations, the PIN also needs to be encrypted for transportation from the key pad to the smart card in order to foil attempts to eavesdrop on confidential information. However, PIN systems have some drawbacks even though they are in widespread use because of their simplicity. Since the memorization process entails some risk of disclosure, certain smart cards are designed to cooperate with an external biometric identification device, increasing the authentication abilities in a system.

To link the cardholder positively to the card requires some alternative method of personal identification. Therefore, the memory capacity of the smart card makes the use of alternatives possible. These alternatives are known as biometrics and involve the identification of a unique personal characteristic of the cardholder. This may be based on the fingerprints, hand geometry, retinal eye patterns, dynamic signature verification, voice patterns, and any other physical characteristic of the individual user. For this purpose, the card must deliver a reference pattern to the external checking device; the dialogue between the card and the checking device has to be randomized and encrypted.

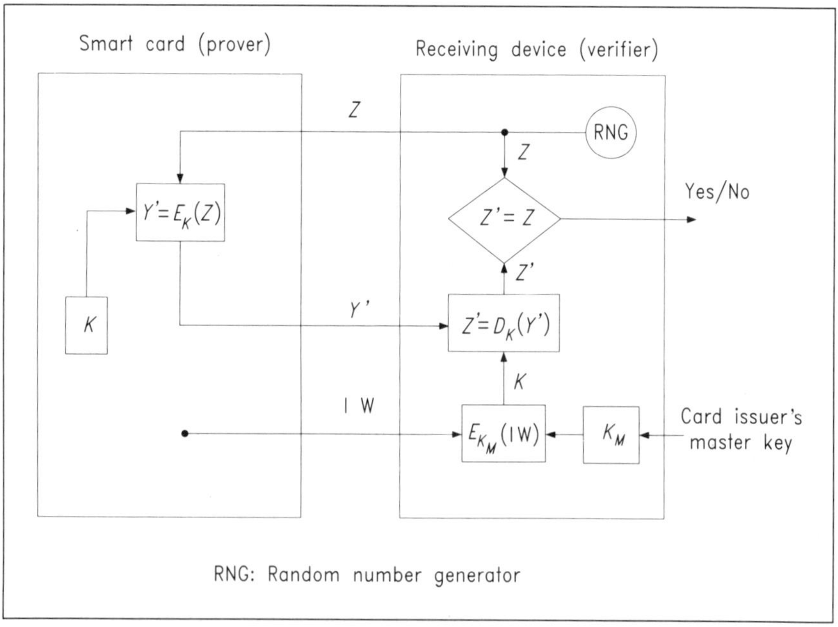

Fig. 10.9 Card authentication with symmetric key algorithm

10.12.2 Card Authentication

An authentication process between the smart card (prover) and the receiving device (verifier) takes place at the commencement of any transaction, for example, banking or retail. The cryptographic identification process between these two is called card (or node) authentication. Through this process, the receiving device verifies the authenticity of the smart card and the smart card proves its identity to the verifier. This assurance thus establishes mutual authentication.

Interrogation protocols for card authentication can be categorized on the basis of cryptographic principles to be applied. They are: (i) symmetric one-key algorithms, (ii) asymmetric public-key algorithms, and (iii) zero-knowledge-based protocols.

Card authentication with symmetric key algorithms

The smart card proves its identity by enciphering a random number obtained from the verifier with the secret card key and returning the enciphered result to the verifier. As shown in Fig. 10.9, this procedure consists of the following steps.

1. The receiving device (verifier) transmits a random number Z to the smart card (prover).
2. The smart card transmits back the random number Z enciphered with the secret card key K, $Y' = E_k(Z)$, as well as its identification word (IW) to the verifier.
3. The verifier's secret key K must be derived using the card issuer's master key K_M which is housed in the protected security zone of the verifier. The secret key of the verifier is obtained by enciphering IW under the master key K_M such that $K = E_{K_M}(\text{IW})$.
4. The check in the verifier is then carried out by deciphering the cryptogram Y' with the derived secret key K such that $Z' = D_K(Y')$ and comparing Z' with the original random number Z sent to the smart card.

The identification word IW consists of an issuer identification number, a user identification number, and the expiry date of the card.

Card authentication with public key algorithms

If any public key system is cryptographically strong, it is not feasible to deduce the secret key from either the enciphered random number or the public key. The RSA algorithm is an extremely important contribution to public key cryptography, in that it supports both secrecy and authentication problems simultaneously. This algorithm is based on the difficulty of factoring the product of two large prime numbers, which appears computationally infeasible. We shall now briefly illustrate how it can be used for authentication of a smart card. For this purpose, the random number Z is first deciphered by the smart card with the card's secret key d. Verification by enciphering is carried out with the public key (n, e) at the verifier. The product n of p and q is made publicly known to the verifier during the authentication process.

If $n = pq$ is the product of two large primes and d is secretly chosen at the card such that $\gcd(d, \Phi(n)) = 1$, where $\Phi(n) = (p - 1)(q - 1)$, then the modular exponentiation function $Y \equiv Z^d \pmod{n}$ is a trapdoor one-way function. If $Y \equiv Z^d \pmod{n}$ for some random number Z, then the only practical way to determine Z is to use the public exponent e with $de \equiv 1 \pmod{\Phi(n)}$, and calculate $Y^e \pmod{n}$.

The procedure of card authentication with the RSA algorithm is shown in Fig. 10.10, as described below.

1. The verifier transmits a random number Z to the smart card.
2. The smart card sends back both the identification word IW and the random number Z deciphered with the card's secret key d, $Y \equiv Z^d \pmod{n}$.
3. The checking in the verifier is then carried out by enciphering the random number previously deciphered by the card, $Z' \equiv Y^e \pmod{n}$, and comparing it with the random number Z originally sent.

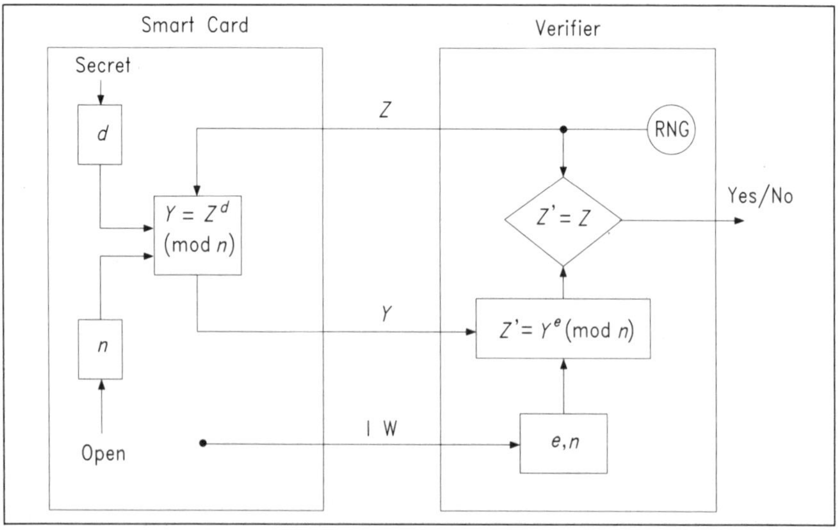

Fig. 10.10 Card authentication with RSA algorithm

Card authentication with zero-knowledge-based protocols

A practical zero-knowledge-based scheme suited to smart cards was published in 1988 by Guillou and Quisquater. ZKIPs are extremely useful for verification of identity. After Goldwasser, Micali, and Rackoff introduced their theoretical protocol, Fiat and Shamir proposed a first practical identification scheme which was covered in Sec. 10.11. Guillou and Quisquater proposed a new scheme involving minimum storage and exchange the storage of only one authentication number B in each security microprocessor and the check of only one witness number t. Thus the authentication transaction between the card and the verifier is limited to a unique interaction. Therefore, this scheme requires less memory in the chip card and less communication than the Fiat-Shamir scheme for the same level of security. However, it consumes more processing time.

For card identification, the card issuer chooses two large prime numbers p and q (each 256 bits long) and forms the product $n = pq$. This composite integer n represents a public constant which is also known to the verifier. Two prime numbers p and q are secret and known only to the card issuer. Together with n, an exponent v is published by the card issuer and known to the verifier. The size of v (at about 30 bits) represents a compromise between speed and security. J, a number as large as n, is the shadowed identity of the card. How to construct J, from the card identity I is specified by publicly known redundancy rules; $J =$ Red (I). The authentication number B must be secretly constructed to satisfy the equation $JB^{v} \equiv 1 \pmod{n}$ with $J =$ Red (I).

Figure 10.11 illustrates of the Guillou-Quisquater scheme. The protocol to be observed by the card and the verifier for proving card identification is as follows.

1. The card processor secretly selects an integer r at random over $0 < r < n - 1$ and computes a test $T \equiv r^{v} \pmod{n}$. This T is called a test number and is computed as the vth power modulo n of r. Now, the card transmits T with the card identity I to the verifier.
2. The verifier randomly selects an integer d from 0 to $v - 1$ and sends it to the card(prover).
3. The card then computes the product mod n of r by dth power of B, i.e. $t \equiv rB^{d} \pmod{n}$ where t is called a witness number. The card transmits t to the verifier.
4. In order to verify t, the verifier computes $J^{d}t^{v} \pmod{n}$ and compares it with the test number T as follows:

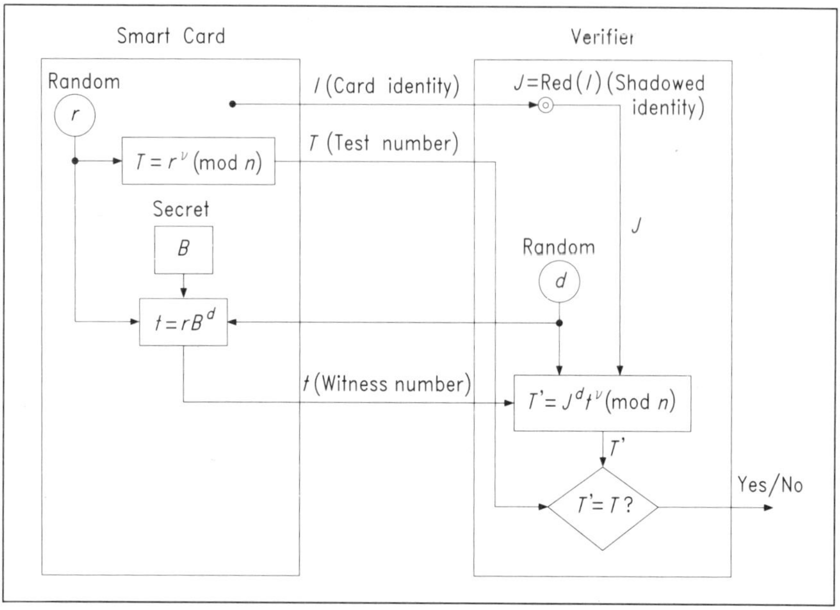

Fig. 10.11 Card authentication with Guillou-Quisquater scheme

$$J^d t^\nu \pmod n \equiv J^d (rB^d)^\nu \pmod n$$
$$\equiv (JB^\nu)^d \cdot r^\nu \pmod n$$
$$\equiv T$$

because $JB^\nu \pmod n \equiv 1$.

10.12.3 Smart Card Structure

Memory

The memory types consist of an ROM, RAM, EPROM and EEPROM configured for use in different ways within a smart card. (The last two stand for Electrically Programmable Read Only Memory, and Electrically Erasable Programmable Read Only Memory, respectively.)

A general-purpose program is stored in an ROM which is nonvolatile but not reprogrammable. An RAM is used as temporary storage for intermediate calculations, and is reprogrammable and volatile. There are two principal types of PROM, namely EPROM and EEPROM. The first is used for storage of data under control of the software program in the ROM. Once each location has been programmed it cannot be changed, so the card has to be discarded when the memory is full. The EEPROM contains the application program and an area for data that has to be retained when the power is removed from the card. It is a more recently developed type than EPROM, with the significant advantage that is not necessary to erase the entire memory as each memory cell can be reprogrammed individually. The order of magnitude of present-day smart card memories ranges from 128–256 bytes for RAMs, 2–4 Kbytes for ROMs and 6–8 Kbytes for EPROMs or EEPROMs.

Microprocessor

The microprocessor used determines the processing power of the smart card. Its functions are to manipulate and interpret data according to instructions stored in the card's memory. It can read the contents of a memory location or write data to a given location by executing appropriate instructions in its program. The sequence of instructions stored in the memory is called a program which is usually classified into an operating system and an application program. The operating system comprises various groups of instructions, involving initiation of sequence, transmission and reception of data, and so on. The application program comprises a set of instructions defining functions such as financial transactions or security identification of the card.

I/O Port

The I/O port is a means by which the smart card can receive and send data. Smart cards can be broadly divided into three different categories—contact, contactless and super-smart.

A contact smart card communicates data through metallic contacts on its surface. This is the type most commonly used. There are eight contacts on the card's surface and the allocation of its individual functions has been standardized. In 1985 the ISO set up an international steering committee to standardize contact smart cards to cover such items as contact position, interface protocol, and data content and control. Since 1983, French PTT Minitel models have undertaken trials using smart cards with videotexts, telephone directory terminals, and public telephones. They were also used to pay for telephone calls, control access to banking facilities, and to record transactions. The success of this trial encouraged replacement of existing coin-operated public phones by new systems operated by contact cards. Since the mid-1980's, interest in smart cards has increased in Japan and other countries (France, UK, USA). In 1985, the Bull CP8 card (an EPROM-based card) containing a single chip incorporating an 8-bit microprocessor and memory was developed for the French banking system. Besides EPROM, the chip embedded in CP8 type has an RAM for temporary storage memory, and an ROM.

A contactless smart card transmits and receives data to and from a read/write unit by operating at a small distance away from the surface of the card. Such cards have been further developed by AT&T in the United States, GEC in Britain, and Toppan in Japan. The AT&T card employs two forms of contactless coupling in one card—inductive and capacitive. An inductive coil is used to power the card. There are also four capacitive plates, two for data transmission and reception, and two for communication. The GEC contactless card is one of the card leaders and is operated by inductive coupling between coils embedded in the card and the read/write unit. The two coils perform the functions of transferring power to the card and transferring data to and from the card. In 1988, Toppan produced a contactless smart card which operated using three induction coils in the card and three in the read/write unit. One set of coils in the card and one in the read/write unit are used for power transfer and the clock. A second set of coils is used for data input and a third for data output, enabling simultaneous data transmission and reception.

The super card is a third category of smart card. The super smart card incorporates a keyboard and liquid crystal display (LCD), which make it quite different from other smart cards. It functions more a stand-alone device, not requiring a read/write unit. Visa International of the USA in collaboration with Toshiba of Japan brought out the first super card. In order to meet thickness specifications set by ISO for plastic cards, Toshiba had to develop a number of new manufacturing techniques. These cards were made using very high density CMOS technology which has the advantage of requiring low power. The functions available to the cardholder include financial services, clock and calendar, electronic notepad and calculator. Before access to financial services or purchase with the card, the cardholder has to enter the PIN for the amount he requires.

In conclusion, the interested reader should be consulted with the following identification schemes which are well suited for use in smart cards. Schnorr's scheme (1989), based on the difficulty of computing discrete logarithms, may be regarded as a practical refinement of the zero-knowledge protocols of Chaum, Evertse, and Graaf (1987). Brickell and McCurley (1990) presented a modification of Schnorr's identification scheme for use in smart cards. Beth (1988) also proposed another interesting identification scheme based on discrete logarithms. However, the security of Beth's scheme is more likely related to the ElGamal signature scheme.

REFERENCES

1. Abadi, M., J. Feigenbaum, and J. Kilian: "On hiding information from an Oracle", *J. Comp. System Sci.*, vol. 39, pp 21–50, 1989.
2. Babai, L.: "Trading group theory for randomness", *Proc. 17th Annual ACM Symp. Theory of Computing*, pp 421–429, 1985.
3. Beaver, D. and J. Feigenbaum: "Hiding instances in multioracle queries", *Proc. 7th STACS*, LNCS 415, pp 37-48, Springer-Verlag, 1990.
4. Beaver, D., J. Feigenbaum, and V. Shoup: "Hiding instances in zero-knowledge proof systems", *Proc. Crypto 90*, pp 309–320, Santa Barbara, CA, Aug. 1990.
5. Bellare, M. and S. Goldwasser: "New paradigms for digital signatures and message authentication based on non-interactive zero-knowledge proofs", *Proc. Crypto 89*, LNCS 435, pp 194–210, Springer-Verlag, New York, 1989.
6. Bellare, M., S. Micali, and R. Ostrovsky: "Perfect zero-knowledge in constant rounds", *Proc. 22nd STOC*, pp 482–493, 1990.
7. Ben-Or, M., O. Goldreich, S. Goldwasser, J. Hastad, J. Kilian, S. Micali, and P. Rogaway: "Everything provable is provable in zero-knowledge", *Proc. Crypto 88*, LNCS 403, pp 37–56, Springer-Verlag, New York, 1989.
8. Ben-Or, M., S. Goldwasser, J. Kilian, and A. Wigderson: "Multi-prover interactive proofs: How to remove intractability assumptions", *Proc. 20th STOC*, pp 113–131, 1988.
9. Blum, M., P. Feldman, and S. Micali: "Non-interactive zero-knowledge and its applications", *Proc. 20th STOC*, pp 103–112, 1988.
10. Brassard, G. and C. Crepeau: "Non-transitive transfer of confidence: A perfect zero-knowledge interactive protocol for SAT and beyond", *Proc. 27th Annual IEEE Symp. Foundation of Computer Science*, pp 188–195, Oct. 1986.
11. Brassard, G.,C. Crepeau, and M. Yung: "Everything in NP can be argued in perfect zero-knowledge in a bounded number of rounds", *Proc. 16th ICLP*, Stresa, Italy, 1989.
12. Chaum, D.: "Demonstrating that a public predicate can be satisfied without revealing any information about how", *Proc Crypto 86*, LNCS 263, pp 195–199, Springer-Verlag, New York, 1987.
13. Chaum, D., I. Damgard, and J. Van de Graaf: "Multiparty computations ensuring secrecy of each party's input and correctness of the output", *Proc. Crypto 85*, Santa Barbara, LNCS 218, pp 477–488, Springer-Verlag, New York, 1986.
14. De Santis, A., S. Micali, and G. Persiano: "Non-interactive zero-knowledge proof systems", *Proc. Crypto 87*, Santa Barbara, pp 52–72, 1987.

15. ElGamal, T.: "A public key cryptosystem and a signature scheme based on discrete logarithm", *IEEE Trans. Inform, Theory*, vol, IT-31, no. 4, pp 469–472, July 1985.
16. Feige, U., A. Fiat, and A. Shamir: "Zero-knowledge proofs of identity", *ACM Annual Symp. Theory of Computing*, pp 210–217, May 1988.
17. Feige, U. and A. Shamir: "Zero-knowledge proofs of knowledge in two rounds", *Proc. Crypto 89*, LNCS 435, pp 526-542, Springer-Verlag, 1989.
18. Fiat, M. and A. Shamir: "How to prove yourself: Practical solution to identification and signature problems", *Proc. Crypto 86*, Santa Barbara, Springer-Verlag, LNCS vol. 263, pp 186–199, 1986.
19. Fortnow, L.: "The complexity of perfect zero-knowledge", *Proc. 19th STOC*, pp 204–209, 1987.
20. Fortnow, L., J. Rompel, and M. Siper: "On the power of multiprover interactive protocols", *Proc. IEEE 3rd Structure Complexity Theory Conf.*, pp 156–161, 1988.
21. Goldreich, O., S. Micali, and A. Wigderson: "How to prove all NP statements in zero-knowledge and a methodology of cryptographic protocol design", *Proc. 27th Annual IEEE Symp. Foundations of Computer Science*, pp 174–187, 1986.
22. Goldwasser, S., S. Micali, and C. Rackoff: "The knowledge complexity of interactive proof systems", *Proc. 17th Annual ACM Symp. Theory of Computing*, pp 291–304, 1985.
23. Impagliazzo, R. and M. Yung: "Direct minimum-knowledge computations", *Proc. Crypto 87*, Santa Barbara, Springer-Verlag, LNCS 293, pp 40–51, 1988.
24. Jones, T.C., and J. Seberry: "Authentication without secrecy", *Ars Combinatoria*, vol. 21A, pp 115–121, 1986.
25. Kilian, J.: "Achieving zero-knowledge robustly", *Proc. Crypto 90*, pp 295–307, Santa Barbara, CA, Aug. 1990.
26. Kilian, J.: "Founding cryptography on oblivious transfer", *Proc. 20th STOC*, pp 20–31, 1988.
27. Kilian, J., S. Micali, and R. Ostrovsky: "Efficient zero-knowledge proofs with bounded interaction", *Proc. Crypto 89,* Santa Barbara, Springer-Verlag, LNCS 435, pp 545–546, 1990.
28. Koyama, K. and K. Ohta: "Security of improved identity-based conference key distribution systems", *Proc. Eurocrypt 88*, Davos, pp 11–18, 1988.
29. Lamport, L.: "Constructing digital signatures from a one-way function", *SRI Int. Computer Science Lab. Report No. CSL-98*, Oct. 1979.
30. Lapidot, D. and A. Shamir: "Publicly verifiable non-interactive zero-knowledge proofs", *Proc. Crypto 90*, pp 339–354, Santa Barbara, Aug. 1990.
31. Matsumoto, T. and H. Imai: "On the key predistribution system: A practical solution to the key distribution problem", *Proc. Crypto 87*, Santa Barbara, pp 185–193, Aug. 1987.
32. Matyas, S.M. and C.H. Meyer: "Electronic signature for data encryption standard", *IBM Tech. Disc. Bull.*, vol. 24, no. 5, pp 2332–2334, 1981.

33. Meyer, C.H. and S.M. Matyas: *Cryptography: A New Dimension in Computer Data Security*, Wiley, New York, 1982.
34. Naor, M. and M. Yung: "Public-key cryptosystems provably secure against chosen ciphertext attacks", *Proc. 22nd Annual ACM Symp. Theory of Computing*, pp 427–437, Baltimore, Maryland, 1990.
35. Odlyzko, A.M.: "Cryptanalytic attacks on the multiplicative knapsack cryptosystem and on Shamir's fast signature scheme", *IEEE Trans. Inform. Theory*, vol. IT-30, no. 4, pp 594–601, July 1984.
36. Okamoto, E. and K. Tanaka: "Identity-based information security management system for personal computer networks", *IEEE J. Selected Area Comm.*, Feb. 1989.
37. Ong, H., and C.P. Schnorr: "Signatures through approximate representations by quadratic forms", *Advances in Cryptology—Proc. Crypto 83*, D. Chaum (Ed.), pp 117–132, Plenum Press, New York, 1984.
38. Ong, H., C.P. Schnorr, and A. Shamir: "An efficient signature scheme based on quadratic equations", *Proc. 16th Symp. Theory of computing*, Washington, DC, Apr. 1984.
39. Pollard, J.M. and C.P. Schnorr: "An efficient solution of the congruence $x^2 + ky^2 = m \pmod{n}$", *IEEE Trans. Inform. Theory*, vol. IT-33, no. 5, pp 702–709, Sep. 1987.
40. Rabin, M.O.: "Digitalized signatures", *Foundations of Secure Computation*, R. Lipton and R.DeMillo (Eds), pp 155–166, Academic Press, New York, 1978.
41. Rabin, M.O.: "Signature and certification by coding", *IBM Tech. Disc. Bull.*, vol. 20, no. 8, pp 3337–3338, Jan. 1978.
42. Seberry, J.: "A subliminal channel in codes for authentication without secrecy", *Ars combinatoria*, vol. 19A, pp 337–342, 1985.
43. Seberry, J. and J. Pieprzyk: *Cryptography : An Introduction to Computer Security*, Prentice-Hall, Sydney, 1989.
44. Shamir, A.: "Identity-based cryptosystems and signature schemes", *Proc. Crypto 84*, Santa Barbara, Springer-Verlag, LNCS 196, pp 47–53, 1985.
45. Tompa, M. and H. Woll: "Random self-reducibility and zero-knowledge interactive proofs for possession of information", *Proc. 28th FOCS*, pp 472–482, 1987.
46. Tsujii, S., T. Itho, and K. Kurosawa: "ID-Based cryptosystem using discrete logarithm problem", *Electronic Letters*, vol. 23, pp 1318–1320, Nov. 1987.
47. Youm, H.Y. and M.Y. Rhee: "ID-based cryptosytem and digital signature scheme using discrete logarithm problem", *Proc. Workshop Data security, KIISC Korea*, pp 161–177, 1991.

Chapter

11

Key Management for Key Generation, Distribution, Storage, and Updation

Key management is an important aspect to be considered in the design for secure cryptosystems. Data encryption and authentication require the management of a large set of cryptographic keys. Such keys are enciphered and sent to suitable users in the form of cryptograms. The function of key management is to securely distribute and update keys whenever required, to ensure cryptographic protection of data transmission as also file security.

Meyer and Matyas have described a complete key management scheme for communication and file security [13]. This chapter deals mainly with key management incorporating a conventional symmetric cryptosystem, such as DES, to provide for communication and file security. The key distribution protocol for implementing public-key algorithms is also described in this chapter.

11.1 NETWORK ENCRYPTION MODES

Data protected with encryption are transmitted over several links before arriving at their final destination. In a computer communications network, data are transmitted from one node on the network to another for processing or storage. In this section, we show how cryptographic keys can be distributed between nodes where a message is being enciphered and deciphered. There are three different ways of incorporating cryptography into a communication network using link-by-link, node-to-node, and end-to-end encryption.

Link-by-link encryption (Fig. 11.1) protects data between adjacent network nodes equipped with identical keys. Node-to-node encryption (Fig. 11.2) is similar to link-by-link encryption in that each pair of nodes shares a key to protect data communicated between nodes. However, the enciphered data at an intermediate node are deciphered under one key and re-enciphered under another key within a security module attached to that particular node. End-to-end encryption (Fig. 11.3) continuously protects data during transmission between two nodes at the source and destination. Data are enciphered under one key and never appear in clear form at intermediate nodes. At the destination node, data are deciphered under the same key as the source node used. Since end-to-end encryption enciphers and deciphers a message at the source and destination only, this scheme provides a high level of data security because data are not deciphered until they reach their final destination. Whereas, with link-by-link or node-to-node encryption, data may be exposed to secrecy and authenticity threats when they are in the form of plaintext at the intermediate nodes. Thus, end-to-end encryption is preferable for electronic mail (EM) and electronic funds transfer (EFT) requiring a high level of security.

End-to-end encryption is preferred for purposes of communication because it provides maximum security. In terms of cost, flexibility, and security, such encryption is the most suitable for systems requiring many protected links. Therefore, considerable research is being done on the design of cryptographic operational architecture for end-to-end encryption as well as encryption of file data.

11.2 KEY HIERARCHY

There are key layers at each host, i.e. one master key and two of its variants at the highest level, key encryption keys at the second level, and data encryption keys at third, as shown in Fig. 11.4. Each host contains the highest level (Level 1) of key organization which creates one master key K_M and two of its variants K_{M1} and K_{M2}. The second

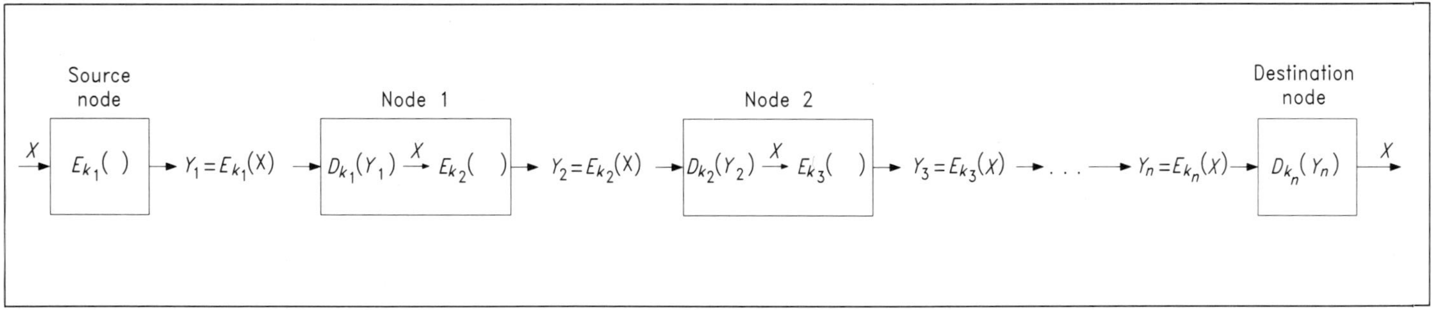

Fig. 11.1 Link-by-link encryption

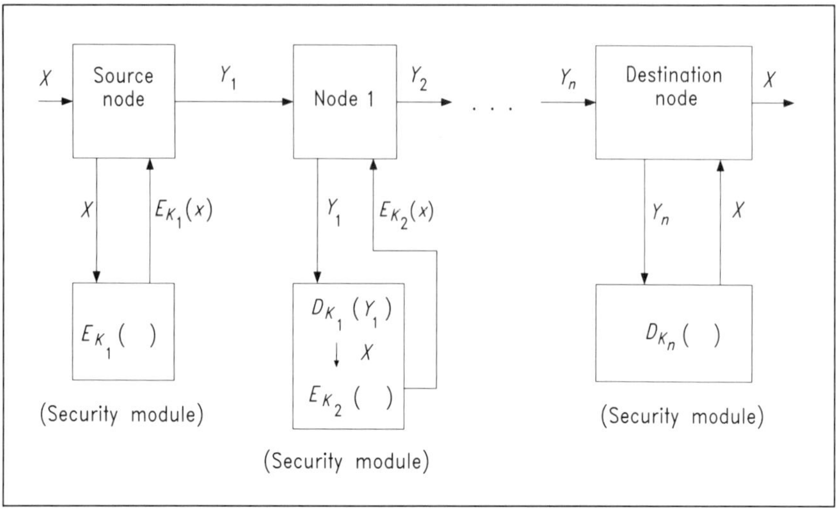

Fig. 11.2 Node-to-node encryption

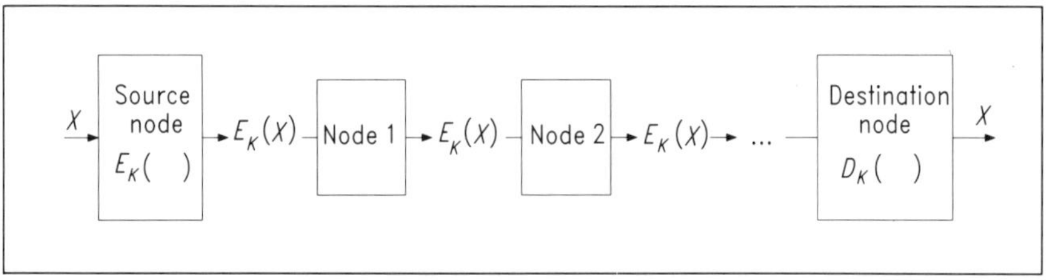

Fig. 11.3 End-to-end encryption

level comprises secondary communication keys K_{SC} and secondary file keys K_{SF}, which are stored as cryptograms obtained by applying K_{M1} and K_{M2}. The third level comprises data encryption keys K_C or K_F which are protected by applying the key encryption keys or the host master key.

Data encryption keys, sometimes called primary or session keys, are used to protect large amounts of data or messages in symmetric cryptosystems such as DES. These keys are generated by a pseudorandom generator and enciphered for protection through the key encryption keys (secondary keys) or under the host master key. Different types of primary keys for data encryption and authentication must always be encrypted under different versions of the key encryption keys. The key encryption keys are, in turn, protected under the variants of the host master key. Secondary keys, one for each direction per link, used to

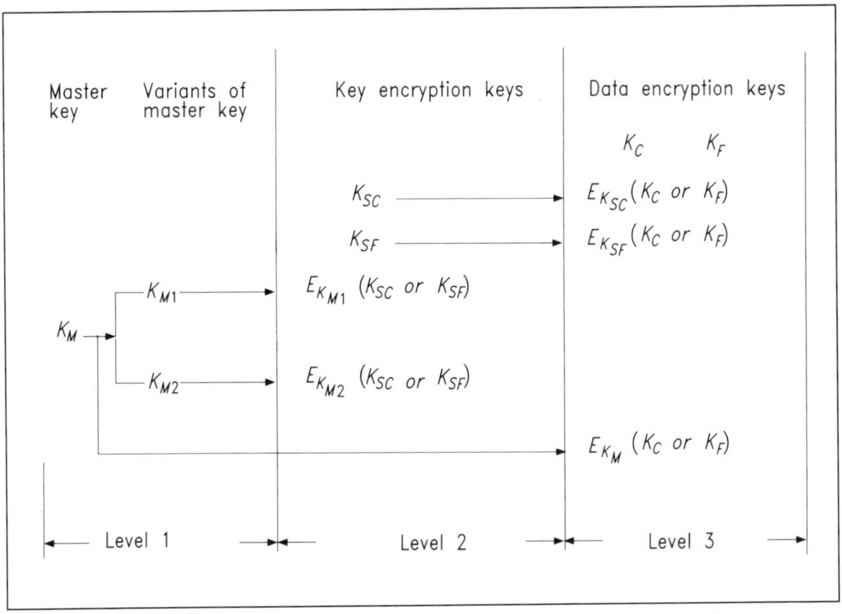

Fig. 11.4 Hierarchy of keys in a host

transport keys between two nodes in a communications network are known as cross-domain keys. The master key is used to encrypt the key encryption keys when they are required to be stored outside a secure cryptographic facility, such as disk. There is generally only one master key at each computer site.

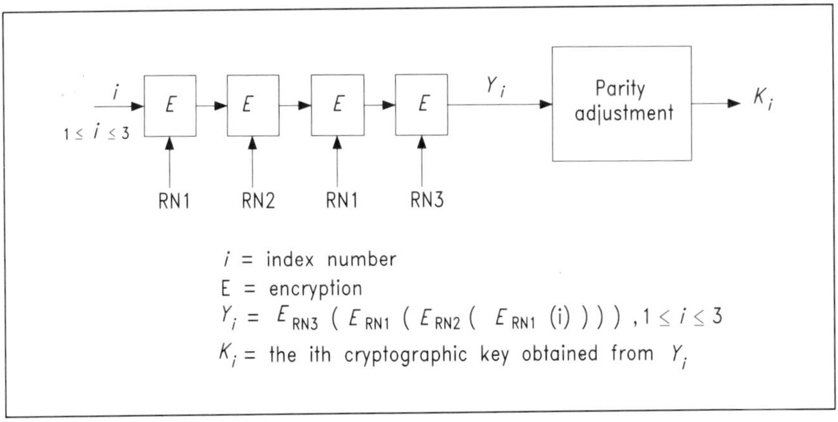

Fig. 11.5 Key generation procedure using DES

11.3 KEY GENERATION AND STORAGE

Suppose a key generation procedure uses DES as a generator of pseudorandom numbers, RNi for $1 \leq i \leq n$. Let RN be a 64-bit random number produced by DES. Consider that RNi, $1 \leq i \leq 3$, represents the entire set of keys consisting of three 64-bit random values. RN1 and RN2 are the random numbers supplied externally by the user, and RN3 is a random number generated internally within the host processor. Then Ki, $1 \leq i \leq n$, denotes the ith cryptographic key obtained by adjusting each byte in Y_i for odd parity. The key generation procedure for key encryption keys using RNi, $1 \leq i \leq 3$, is illustrated in Fig.11.5 [13].

The data encryption keys must not be exposed in clear form. This is ensured by using the DES algorithm as a random-number generator (Fig. 11.5). A data encryption key is produced from a 64-bit random number RN, which is deciphered under a key encryption key known to the cryptographic system. For example, in communication security, RN is defined as the session key K_S enciphered under the host master key K_{MH} such that RN = $E_{K_{MH}}(K_S)$, while, in file security, RN is defined as a file key K_F enciphered under a secondary file key K_{SF} such that RN = $E_{K_{SF}}(K_F)$.

One way to generate RNis which represent enciphered data-encryption keys is using a nonresettable counter that can be incremented only by the cryptographic facility (CF). That is, RN (an enciphered data-encryption key) is generated by incrementing the counter and enciphering the result value C + 1 with a special variant of the host master key K_{M4}, as shown in Fig. 11.6. Thus, RN is also defined as a data encryption key enciphered under a key enciphering key known to the CF. Since the counter is accessed only by the CF, an opponent cannot reset its values and therefore the prior data-encryption keys cannot be regenerated.

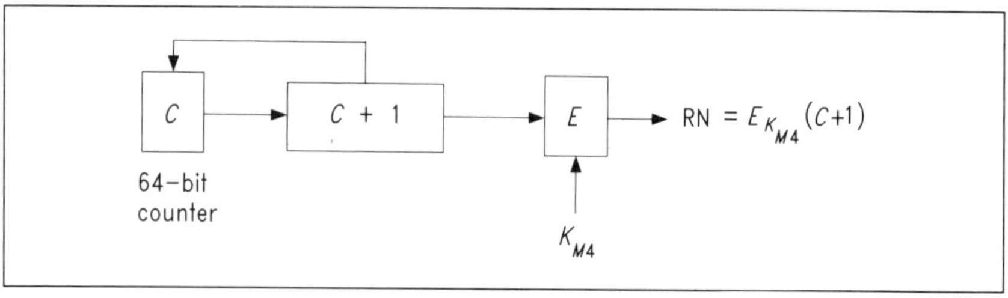

Fig. 11.6 Procedure for generating data encryption keys

Finally, the host master key is generated by a random process such as tossing coins or throwing dice. It is desirable that the master key remains unchanged for a relatively long time. Since this key protects all other keys stored at the host processor, special care should be taken to ensure that it is generated and installed in the CF in a secure manner.

As discussed before, keys used to encipher all subsidiary keys (primary and secondary) comprise what is called a host master key K_{MH} and its variants K_{MH1} and K_{MH2}. These master keys reside at a given host and a given terminal in clear form. Therefore, disclosure or destruction of their values implies that all other enciphered keys are wrongly deciphered and, in turn, that all enciphered data become unreadable.

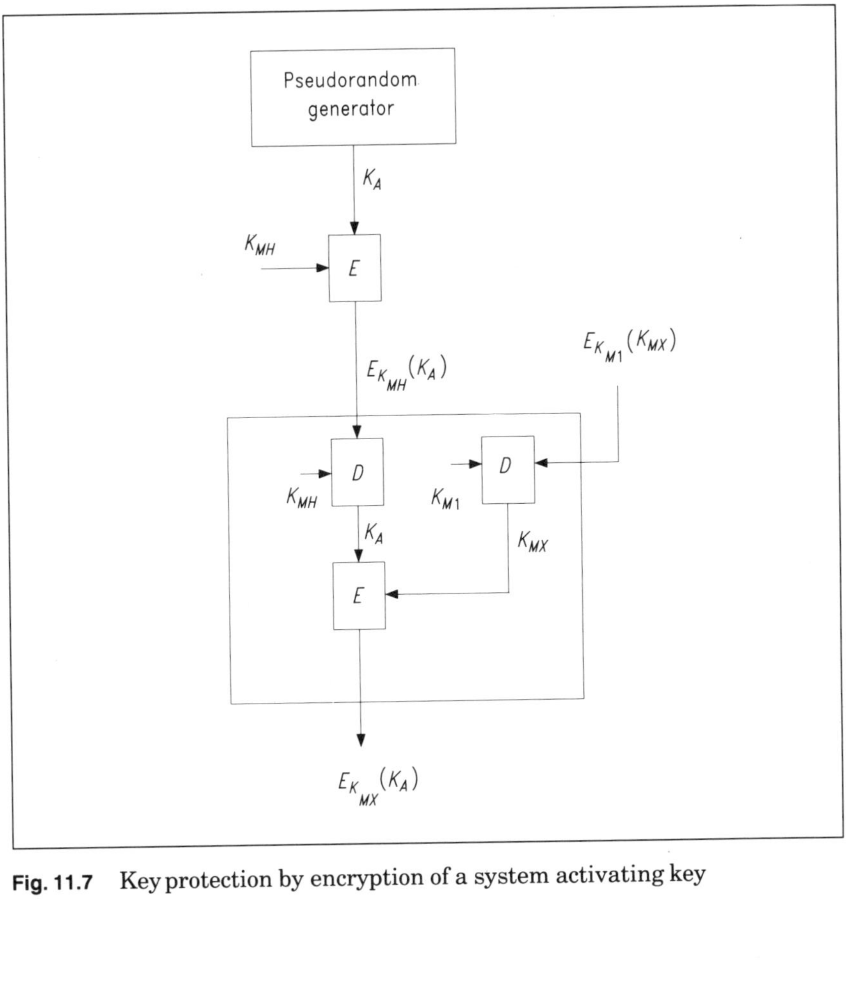

Fig. 11.7 Key protection by encryption of a system activating key

■ **Example 11.1** Let K_A denote a system subsidiary key, which can be either a primary or a secondary key. These subsidiary keys are usually created by means of a pseudorandom generator and can be stored in an unprotected place. But, rather than as a key K_A itself, it is generated in the form of a cryptogram $E_{K_{MH}}(K_A)$ under a host master key K_{MH}. If we want to encipher a key K_A under a variant of master key K_{MX}, $X = 1$ or 2, we put both the cryptogram $E_{K_{MH}}(K_A)$ and a variant master key K_{MX} into the cryptographic system, as shown in Fig. 11.7.

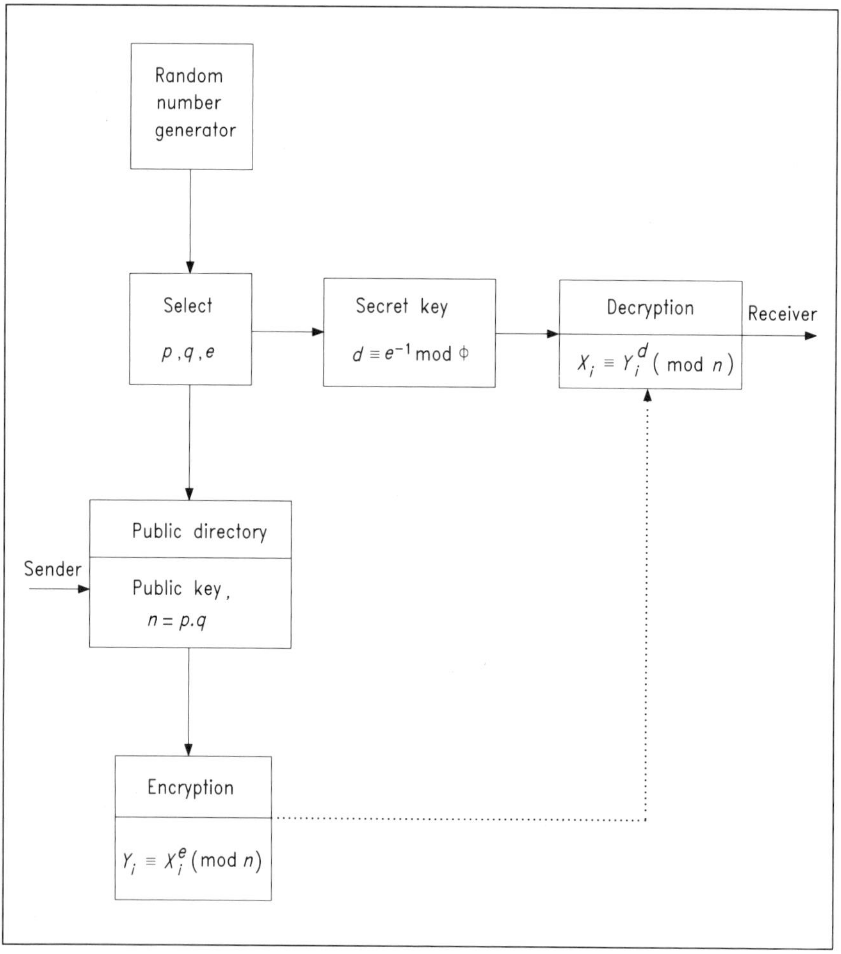

Fig. 11.8 RSA key generation

Public key cryptosystems are asymmetric algorithms used for secrecy and authentication. In the case of communication networks with protection based on an asymmetric cryptographic algorithm, generation of a pair of keys, secret key and public key depends on the asymmetric algorithm used.

In the RSA algorithm [20], either the public key e or secret key d is an integer selected at random. Two large primes p and q are generated and the sender calculates $n = pq$. Then the sender finds integers e and d such that

$$e \cdot d \equiv 1 \bmod \phi(n)$$

where $\phi(n) = (p - 1)(q - 1)$ is called Euler's totient function, and $\gcd(\phi(n), e) = 1$. Thus, the public key (n, e) can be placed in a public directory, whereas the secret key d must be kept privately. RSA key generation is illustrated in Fig. 11.8.

To derive a common key between two users A and B, Diffie and Hellman [7] proposed that user A select a secret key X_A from the set of integers $\{1, 2, \ldots, q - 1\}$ and place a public key $Y_A \equiv \alpha^{X_A} \pmod q$ in a public directory. They should define their common key as

$$K_{AB} \equiv Y_B^{X_A} \pmod q \equiv \alpha^{X_B X_A} \pmod q$$

for communication privately. Similarly, user B obtains the common key K_{AB} such that

$$K_{AB} \equiv Y_A^{X_B} \pmod q \equiv \alpha^{K_A K_B} \pmod q$$

But each user must compute the common key from Y_A and Y_B by determining

$$K_{AB} \equiv Y_A^{(\log_\alpha Y_B)} \pmod q$$

In 1978, Merkle and Hellman [17] proposed the M–H public key cryptosystem based on the trapdoor knapsack problem. A simple knapsack vector $\mathbf{K}_p' = (k_1', k_2', \ldots, k_n')$, where k_i' for $1 \le i \le n$ are integers, is a superincreasing vector. The designer chooses two large secret integers m and w such that $m > w$ and $\gcd(m, w) = 1$ (relatively prime). Moreover, m must be an integer larger than $\Sigma k_i'$, i.e. $m > \Sigma k_i'$ for $1 \le i \le n$. Now, the trapdoor knapsack vector $\mathbf{K}_p$ is induced from the simple knapsack vector $\mathbf{K}_p'$ via v which is the multiplicative inverse of w modulo m such that $v\,w \equiv 1 \pmod m$, where $v = w^{-1}$. Thus, a trapdoor knapsack $\mathbf{K}_p$ is generated by multiplying each component of a simple knapsack vector $\mathbf{K}_p'$ by w modulo m such that

$$k_i \equiv wk_i' \pmod m \qquad 1 \le i \le m$$

or $$\mathbf{K}_p \equiv w\mathbf{K}_p' \pmod{m}$$

Thus, a trapdoor knapsack vector $\mathbf{K}_p$ is published by the user as his public key, whereas the parameters $v = w^{-1}$ and m, and a knapsack vector $\mathbf{K}_p'$ are kept as his secret keys. M–H key generation is illustrated in Fig. 11.9.

11.4 KEY DISTRIBUTION

Consider a communication network in which cryptographic protection is based on either a symmetric or an asymmetric algorithm. Either of

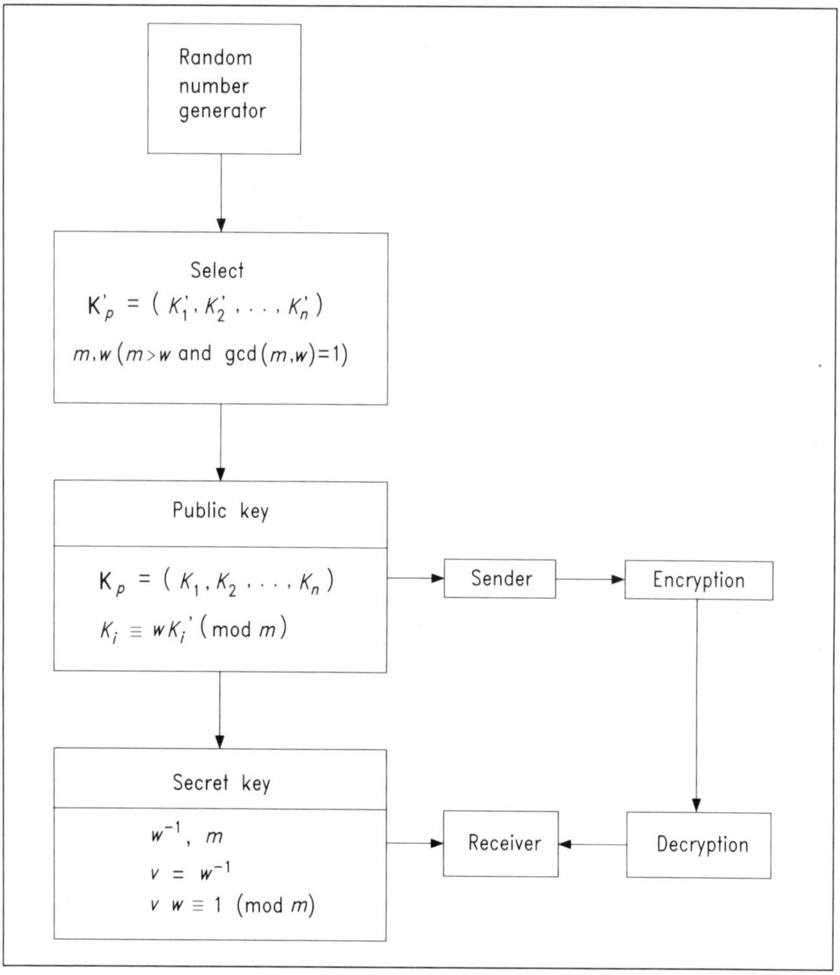

Fig. 11.9 M–H key generation

these requires a key control center that verifies the authenticity of keys and initiates communication between users. However, key distribution problems for symmetric cryptographic algorithms are more sensitive to illegal activity because a key distribution center (KDC) stores all cryptographic keys. All keys are stored in the form of cryptograms which have been generated using the master key and its variants. Whereas, in case of an asymmetric algorithm, a key directory (KD) distributes public keys whose protection is not needed.

We shall first consider the situation where cryptographic protection is based on conventional symmetric cryptosystems in which keys are sent in the form of suitable cryptograms. In such a case, the key distribution may be either centralized or decentralized. The former is controlled by a single host computer, and latter by a group of host computers. As stated before, cryptographic protection may be also based on asymmetric algorithms. We shall discuss key distribution in both situations in the following subsections.

11.4.1 Key Distribution Protocol for Symmetric Algorithms

In this subsection, we consider the case where key distribution is controlled by a single host computer, i.e. a centralized key distribution facility (CKDF). Assume that each user shares with CKDF a prearranged pair of secret message keys. Let us describe a protocol for obtaining session keys from CKDF [18] [21]. If two users want to communicate, one of them obtains a session key K_S from CKDF and transmits it to the other. But for n users there are $\binom{n}{2} = n\,(n-1)/2$ possible key pairs which would be enormous.

CKD protocol is as follows.

1. User A sends a suitable request R_A along with A's identity ID_A to CKDF in clear form.
2. CKDF sends to user A the following cryptogram:

$$E_{K_A}(K_{AB}, ID_A, R_A, E_{K_B}(K_{AB}, ID_A))$$

   where K_{AB} is a cross-domain key to protect transmission between users A and B; K_A and K_B are the secondary communication keys between A and CKDF and between B and CKDF, respectively; and E_{K_B} (K_{AB}, ID_A) is a cryptogram of (K_{AB}, ID_A) obtained under B's secret key K_B.
3. Upon receiving the cryptogram, A deciphers it and checks whether the identifier ID_A and the request R_A are identical to the

original. If so, A forwards the cryptogram $E_{K_B}(K_{AB}, ID_A)$ to the user B.

4. B deciphers the received cryptogram under the key K_B and recovers the clear form of both K_{AB} and ID_A. As a result, users A and B can have the same key K_{AB}. Since B has obtained K_{AB}, he initiates an authentication procedure in order to eliminate any possibility of a false cryptogram. Thus, B directs the cryptogram $E_{K_{AB}}$ (RN), i.e. encryption of a random number RN with K_{AB}, to A.
5. A deciphers the received cryptogram to obtain RN and modifies it in some predetermined way to get f(RN) = (RN)′ which depends on the time. The sequence f(RN) is encrypted under K_{AB} and returns $E_{K_{AB}}(f(\text{RN}))$ to B.
6. If B confirms receipt of the legitimate RN and the use of K_{AB}, with the handshake, A can begin transmitting the message to B.

The general scheme of key distribution protocol between two users A and B for symmetric cryptosystems is given in Fig. 11.10.

The protocol scheme involving decentralized key distribution is controlled by a group of host computers. Therefore, the CKDF is distributed over the network so that all keys do not have to be registered at a single CKDF [8]. The host computers for the users exchange an enciphered session key, RN = $E_{K_M}(K_S)$. Each host uses the reencipher-from-master-key (RFMK) instruction to transmit K_S to its respective user's terminal, enciphered under the terminal master key K_{MT}. The host systems exchange K_S using the RFMK and RTMK operations as shown below. Let H_A denote host A and H_B the host B, and let K_{MA} and K_{MB} be their respective master keys. H_A and H_B share a secondary communication key K_{SC} which is stored as $S_A = E_{K_{MA1}}(K_{SC})$ at H_A and as $S_B = E_{K_{MB2}}(K_{SC})$ at H_B. The encrypted key of K_S at host A is given by $RNA = E_{K_{MA}}(K_S)$. H_A uses the RFMK instruction to send K_S to H_B, and H_B uses the RTMK instruction to receive K_S. The complete protocol for key distribution by host systems is as follows:

1. H_A generates $RNA = E_{K_{MA}}(K_S)$ and sends it to H_B using the following RFMK operation:

$$\text{RFMK}: \{ S_A, RNA \} \rightarrow E_{K_{SC}}(K_S)$$

2. H_B computes RNB by using the following RTMK operation:

$$\text{RTMK}: \{ S_B, E_{K_{SC}}(K_S) \} \rightarrow E_{K_{MB}}(K_S)$$

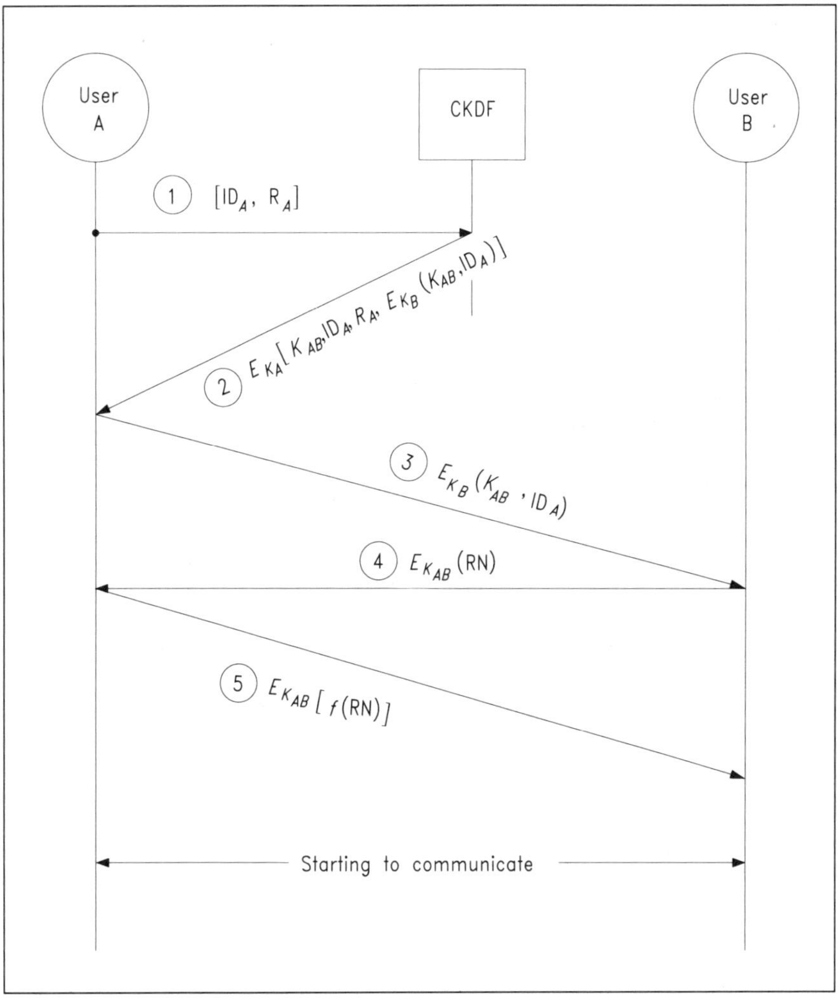

Fig. 11.10 A general scheme of key distribution protocol for a conventional symmetric cryptosystem

3. H_A sends to user A

$$U_A = \text{RFMK} : \{ Z_A, \text{RNA} \} \rightarrow E_{K_{MTA}} (K_S)$$

where K_{MTA} desginates A's terminal master key, and $Z_A = E_{K_{MA1}} (K_{MTA})$.

A computes K_S by deciphering U_A.

4. Similarly, H_B sends to user B

$$U_B = \text{RTMK} : \{ Z_B, \text{RN}B \} \rightarrow E_{K_{MTB}} (K_S)$$

where K_{MTB} is B's terminal master key, and $Z_B = E_{K_{MB2}} (K_{MTB})$. Thus B obtains K_S by deciphering U_B.

This key distribution protocol may be also used to distribute session keys to nodes rather than terminals.

11.4.2 Key Distribution Protocol for Asymmetric Algorithms

Let us consider the case where a computer network with cryptographic protection utilizes an asymmetric algorithm. Two users A and B in a network generate their key pairs–public and secret keys. All public keys are kept in a key directory (KD) within the computer network. The KD is responsible for maintaining, updating, and distributing all public keys used in the computer network. In asymmetric cryptosystems, a public key can be sent via an insecure channel without endangering the security of a secret key. But any user receiving a key should check whether the key is authentic. Thus, the problem of key authenticity must take into consideration for asymmetric cryptographic algorithms.

Using the time-stamping technique, let us design a key distribution protocol between two users A and B belonging to the same key directory. Let K_A be the public key of user A and K_B that of user B. They are registered in the KD. Assume also that public key K_{KD} of the KD is known to all its users. The protocol for establishing a key distribution between A and B is as follows:

1. User A initiates the procedure to obtain the public key of B, K_B, by sending the request RQ_A, along with the current time T_1 in clear form to the KD.
2. The KD then finds K_B on the basis of the request RQ_A and transmits K_B, along with a copy of (RQ_A, T_1) to A in the form of the cryptogram $E_{K_{KD}} [K_B, (\text{RQ}_A, T_1)]$, enciphered under a public key of the KD.
3. Knowing K_{KD}, A can decipher the cryptogram and extract an authentic public key K_B, a copy of the request RQ_A, and the time T_1. The pair (RQ_A, T_1) is then compared with the original. Now, having the public key K_B, A sends B a cryptogram $E_{K_B} (N_A, \text{RS}, T_2)$ where N_A is A's name, RS is a random sequence chosen by A, and T_2 is the current time.

4. Upon receiving the cryptogram, B recreates the clear form of messages using the secret key K_B. Since B knows the name N_A, B can ask for A's authentic public key from the KD by sending the appropriate request RQ_B and the current time T_3.
5. In response, the KD transmits to B the cryptogram $E_{K_{KD}}$ $[K_A, (RQ_B, T_3)]$ enciphered under the KD's public key.

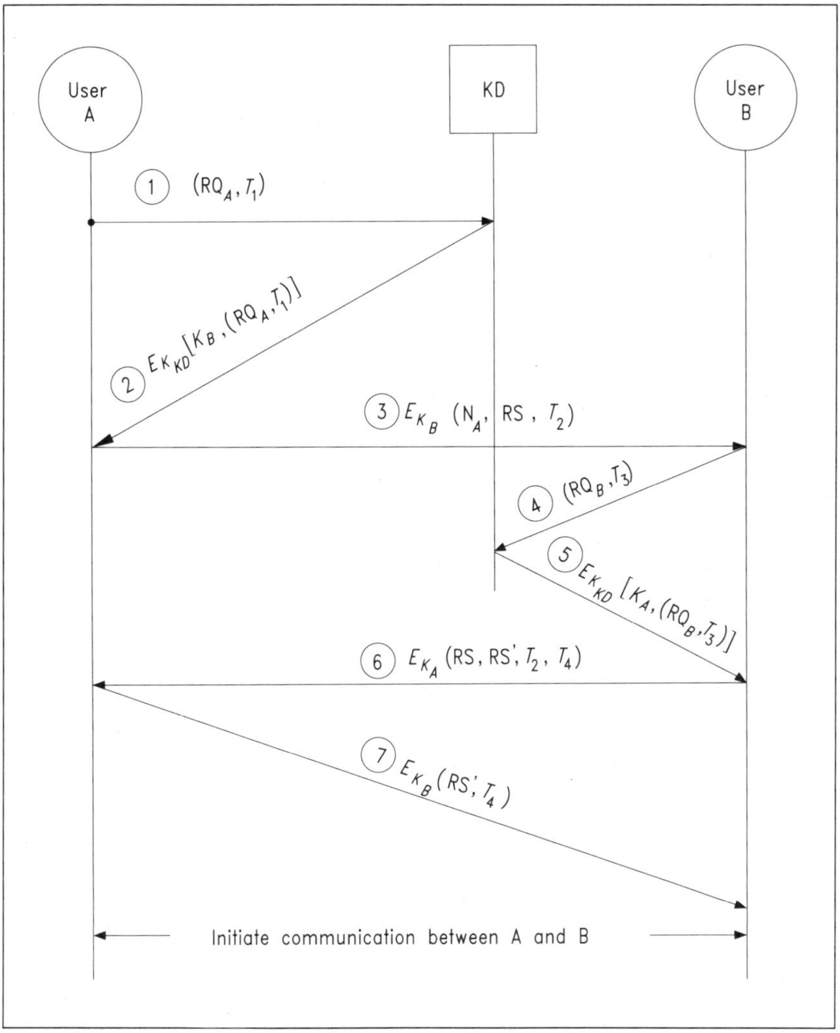

Fig. 11.11 Key distribution protocol with KD for an asymmetric cryptosystem

6. After deciphering the cryptogram, B obtains the authentic public key of A, but the pair (RQ_B, T_3) must be compared with the original. Next, B creates the cryptogram E_{K_A} (RS, RS′, T_2, T_4), enciphered under A's public key, where the random sequence RS is obtained from the user A, a random sequence RS′ is self-generated, and T_4 is the current time. Subsequently, this cryptogram is sent to A.
7. A decrypts the cryptogram and compares (RS, T_2) with the original. If these sequences are the same, A is sure that user B is authentic. Finally, A retransmits the random sequence RS′ in the form of the cryptogram E_{K_B} (RS′, T_4) to B.
8. After decrypting, B also compares the original RS′ with that recreated from the cryptogram. If they match, B confirms the authenticity of A. It can now initiate communication with A.

The key distribution protocol for an asymmetric algorithm is shown in Fig. 11.11.

11.5 KEY MANAGEMENT OPERATION

Since the host processor has an active role in managing the system's cipher keys (data encryption and key encryption keys), key-ciphering operations at the host node are more complex than those at the terminal node. Cryptographic operations performed by a CF can be described in terms of their input parameters and output which are either keys or data parameters in either clear or cryptographic form.

The set-master-key (SMK) operation is used to write a key into the master key storage of the host's cryptographic facility.

The encipher-under-master-key (EMK) operation provides a means for enciphering a data encryption key K under the host's master key K_{MH}, expressed by the notation

$$\text{EMK} : \{ K \} \rightarrow E_{K_{MH}} (K)$$

The re-encipher-from-master key (RFMK) operation is used to transform a primary key K (which could be the session key K_S, communication key K_C or file key K_F) from encryption under the host master key K_{MH} to encryption under a secondary key K_N (secondary communication key K_{SC}, secondary file key K_{SF}, or terminal master key K_{MT}) by the notation

$$\text{RFMK} : \{ E_{K_{MH1}} (K_N), E_{K_{MH}} (K) \} \rightarrow E_{K_N} (K)$$

The re-encipher-to-master-key (RTMK) operation is used with the key program to transform a primary key K from encryption under a

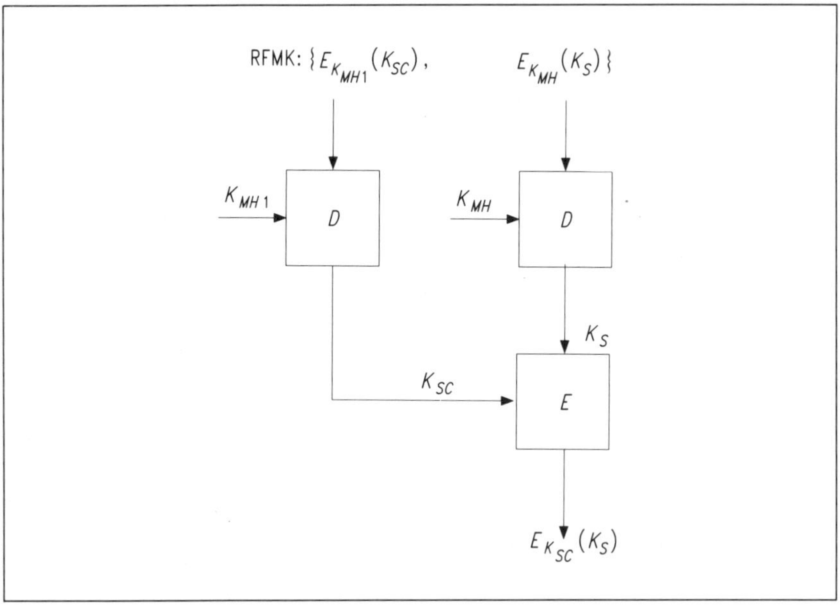

Fig. 11.12 RFMK operation at a host system

secondary key K_N to encryption under the host master key K_{MH}, and is expressed as follows:

$$\text{RTMK} : \{ E_{K_{MH2}}(K_N), E_{K_N}(K) \} \rightarrow E_{K_{MH}}(K)$$

■ **Example 11.2** Consider the RFMK operation procedure. Let the primary key K be the session key K_S and the secondary key K_N the secondary communication key K_{SC}. Then the RFMK operation at the host system can be illustrated as shown in Fig. 11.12.

■ **Example 11.3** Let us consider another example involving RFMK operation. Let the primary key K be the session key K_S between the host and terminal, and the secondary key K_N the terminal master key K_{MT1}. Recovery of K_S at the terminal's cryptographic facility (TCF) is shown in Fig. 11.13.

■ **Example 11.4** Let us now examine a case involving RTMK operation. Let the session key K_S be the primary key and let K_N designate the secondary key. We try to transform the session key K_S from encryption under a secondary key K_N to encryption under the host master key K_{MH}, as illustrated in Fig. 11.14.

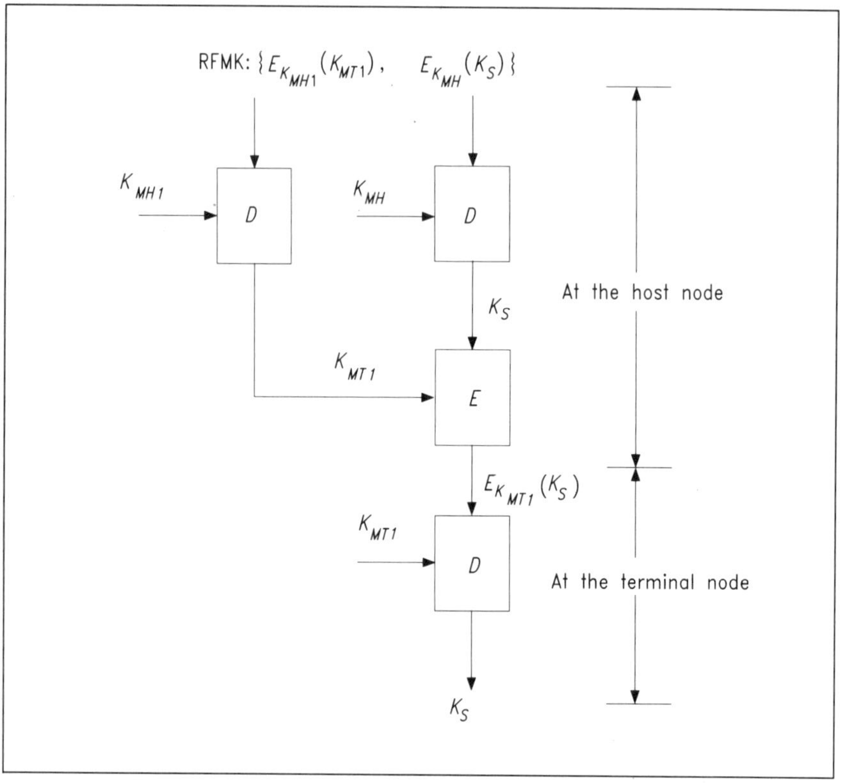

Fig. 11.13 Recovery of a session key at the terminal node

11.6 KEY INSTALLATION AND RECOVERY

To achieve communication security, the host processor generates a session key K_S and transmits it to the terminal. In this process, K_S is protected by enciphering it under the terminal master key K_{MT} which is resident within the terminal's cryptographic facility. Since the session key (or the primary communication key) is encrypted by K_{MT}, this terminal master key is often called the secondary communication key K_{SC}. Therefore, a terminal master key provides a means for the host to transmit a common session key (or a primary communication key) to a terminal securely. For example, a 64-bit pseudorandom number (RN) is generated at the host system and is defined to be the session key K_S enciphered under the host master key K_{MH}, i.e. RN = $E_{K_{MH}}(K_S)$. Since K_{MH} is unavailable at the terminal, $E_{K_{MH}}(K_S)$ must be transformed into a

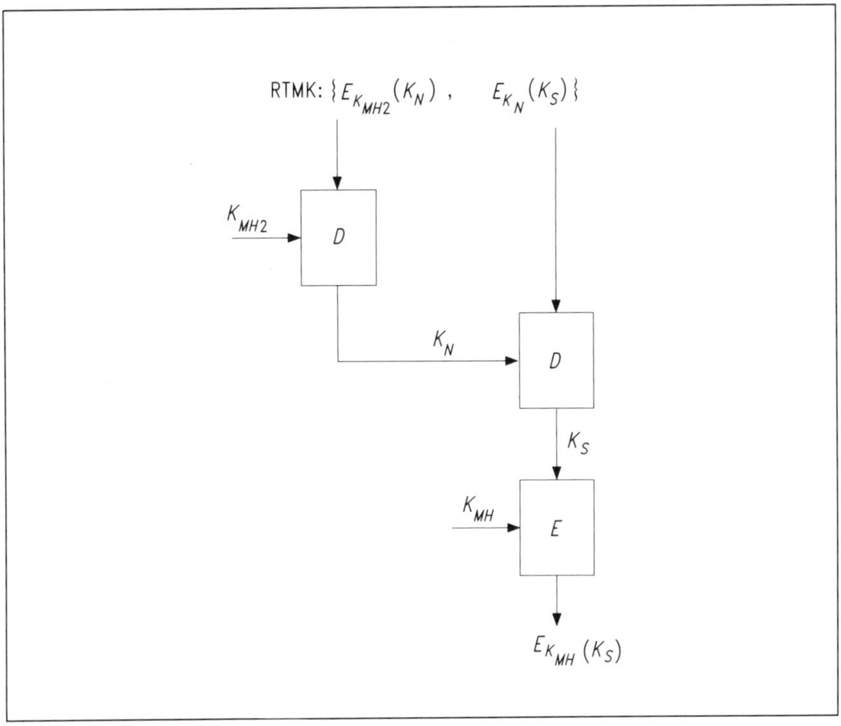

Fig. 11.14 RTMK operation at the host system

usable form at the terminal, i.e., into the form $E_{K_{MT}}(K_S)$. This is accomplished through the RTMK operation we have discussed. Then $E_{K_{MT}}(K_S)$ is transmitted to the terminal, where K_S is recovered in the TCF.

Consider a multidomain network consisting of many host and terminal nodes. The set of cryptographic operations permits communication security and file security to be achieved within a multidomain network. Let i and j denote two host nodes whose master keys are K_{MHi} and K_{MHj}, respectively. The first variant of the host master key, K_{MH1i}, for the domain i is used to protect terminal master key K_{MTik}, $k = 1, 2, \ldots, n$, and the secondary communication key K_{SCij} from domain i to domain j. The second variant of the host master key K_{MH2i} is used to protect the secondary communication key K_{SCji} from j to i. Similarly, for the domain j, the terminal master keys K_{MTjk}, $k = 1, 2, \ldots, n$, are encrypted under the first variant of the host master key K_{MH1j} for protection of K_{MTjk}. The process of recovering a session key at a terminal is illustrated in Fig. 11.15.

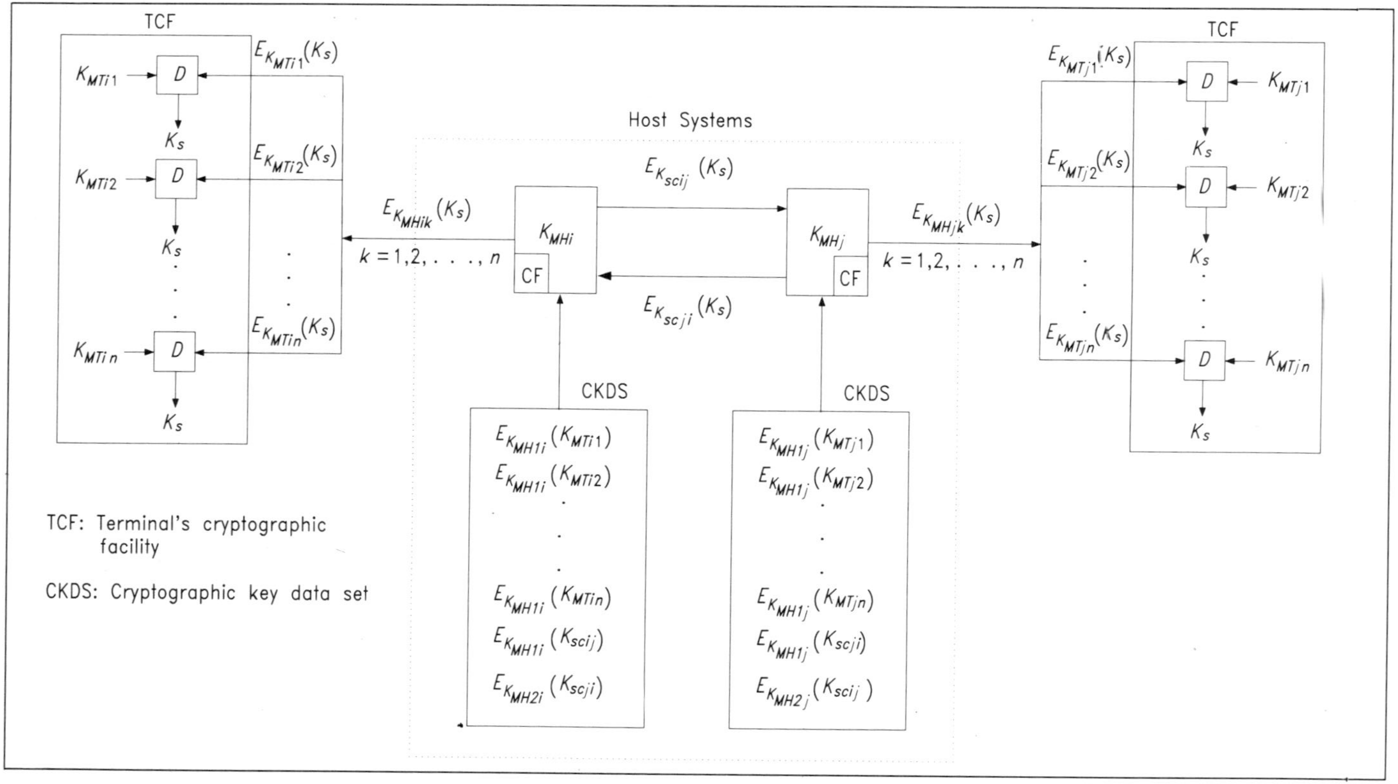

Fig. 11.15 Session key recovery procedure for communication security within a multidomain network

We have so far discussed the set of basic cryptographic operations that permits communication security to be achieved within a multiple-domain communications network. In the following, we shall show that this same set of cryptographic operations is sufficient to achieve file security within a multidomain network. First, to establish a common primary file key K_F between domains i and j, the host systems must share a common key called secondary file key K_{NF}.

In the protocol we shall discuss, the secondary file keys are defined as follows:

K_{NFij} is the secondary file key shared by host nodes i and j and protects the primary file key K_F to be transmitted from node i to node j. K_{NFji} is the secondary file key from node j to node i to protect a file key K_F to be transmitted. K_{NFii} permits a file key K_F generated at host node i to be recovered at host node i. K_{NFjj} is similarly defined at host node j.

At host node i, a pseudorandom number RN is generated and defined as

$$\text{RN} = E_{K_{MHi}}(K_F)$$

RN can be used directly into the encipher data (ECPH) operation to encrypt the file data such that

$$\text{ECPH}: \{\ \text{RN, Data}\ \} \rightarrow E_{K_F}(\text{Data})$$

Next, to send K_F from host processor i to domain j, the RFMK operation is first employed in order to transform K_F as follows. K_{NFij} which is enciphered under K_{MH1i} is stored in the key storage at host processor i. The RFMK operation is then used for allowing K_F to be transmitted to host processor j such that

$$\text{RFMK}: \{\ E_{K_{MH1i}}(K_{NFij}), E_{K_{MHi}}(K_F)\ \} \rightarrow E_{K_{NFij}}(K_F)$$

Thus, the cryptogram of K_F under K_{NFij}, viz. $E_{K_{NFij}}(K_F)$, is recorded in the file header and sent to host node j, where the RTMK operation is used to transform K_F from encryption under K_{NFij} to encryption under K_{MHj} such that

$$\text{RTMK}: \{\ E_{K_{MH2j}}(K_{NFij}), E_{K_{NFij}}(K_F)\ \} \rightarrow E_{K_{MHj}}(K_F)$$

Thus, in order to recover the file data at host node j, $E_{K_{MHj}}(K_F)$ is directly used for the decipher data (DCPH) operation such that

$$\text{DCPH}: \{\ E_{K_{MHj}}(K_F), E_{K_F}(\text{Data})\ \} \rightarrow \text{Data}$$

File security protocol between domains i and j can be illustrated as shown in Fig. 11.16. Notice that the RFMK and RTMK operations are

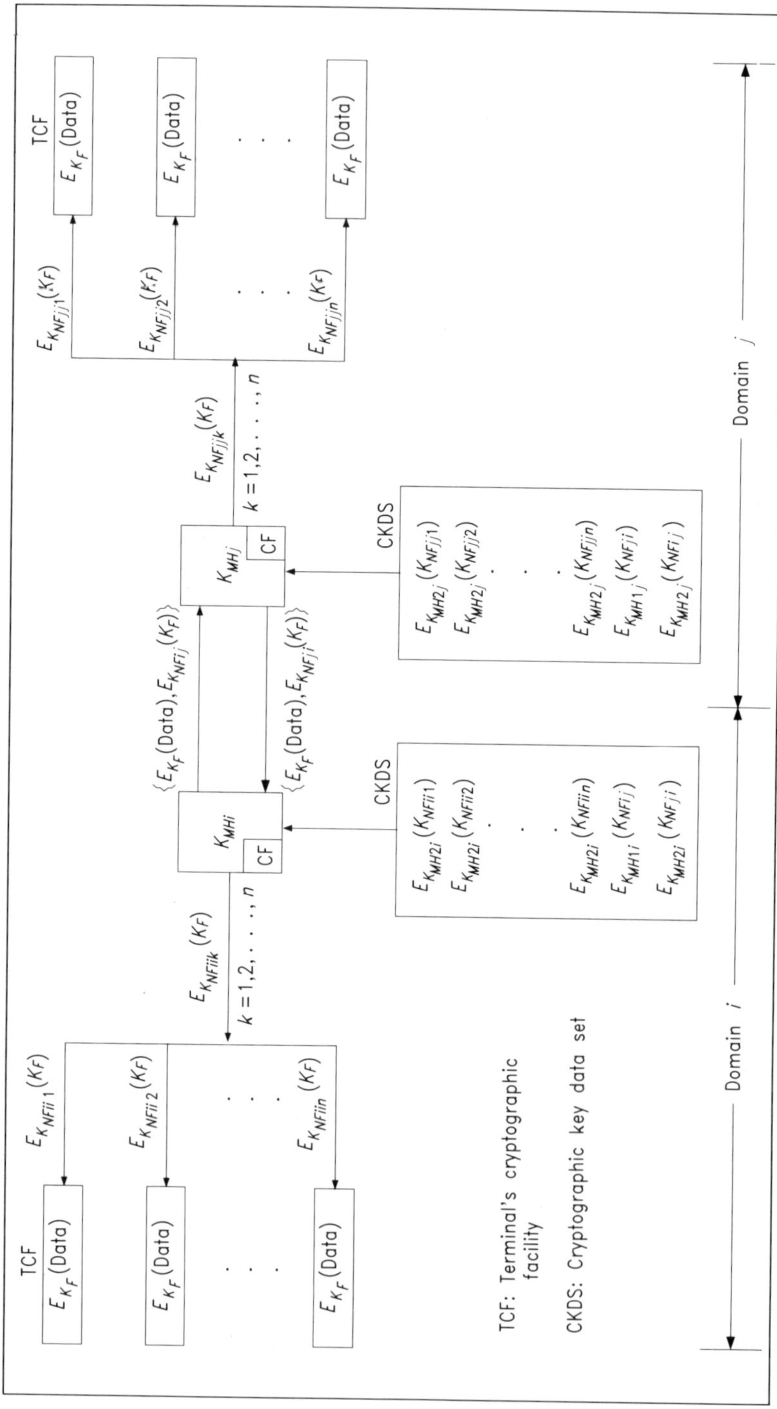

Fig. 11.16 File security protocol between domains i and j

designed for using only the first and second variants of the host master key. To help the reader understand Fig. 11.16 better we shall now present a few examples.

■ **Example 11.5** Let RN be a pseudorandom number generated at host node i and defined as RN = $E_{K_{MHi}}(K_F)$. Encipher the file data under K_F through the ECPH operation as shown in Fig. 11.17.

■ **Example 11.6** For transmitting a file key K_F to domain j, the RFMK operation, using the host's first variant K_{MH1i}, is used as illustrated in Fig. 11.18. Therefore, to send K_F to domain j we have to first transform K_F from encipherment under K_{MHi} (host master key) to encipherment under K_{NFij} (secondary file key). This enciphered file key $E_{K_{NFij}}(K_F)$ is recorded in the file header and then sent to host node j.

■ **Example 11.7** Use the RTMK operation at host node j to transform K_F from encryption under K_{NFij} to that under K_{MHj} as shown in Fig. 11.19.

■ **Example 11.8** Recover the file data by the DCPH operation using $E_{K_{MH_j}}(K_F)$ which was obtained from Example 11.7. (See Fig. 11.20.)

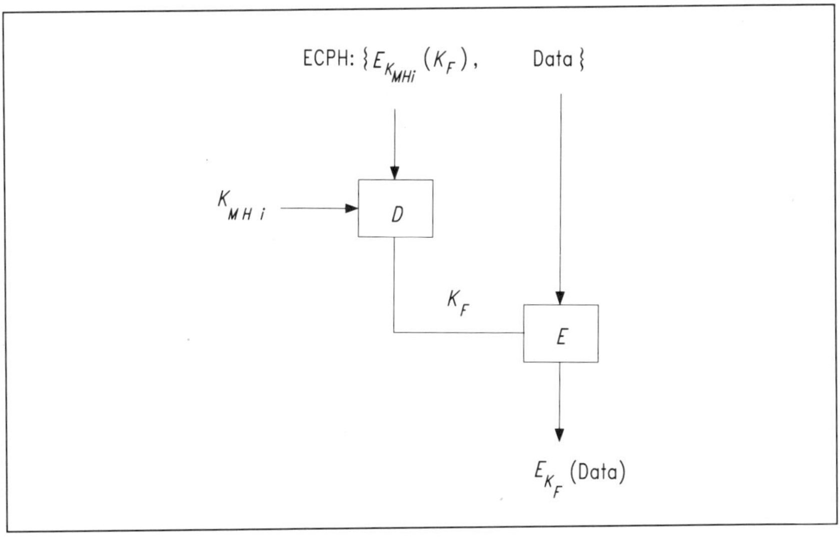

Fig. 11.17 Encipherment of file data under K_F

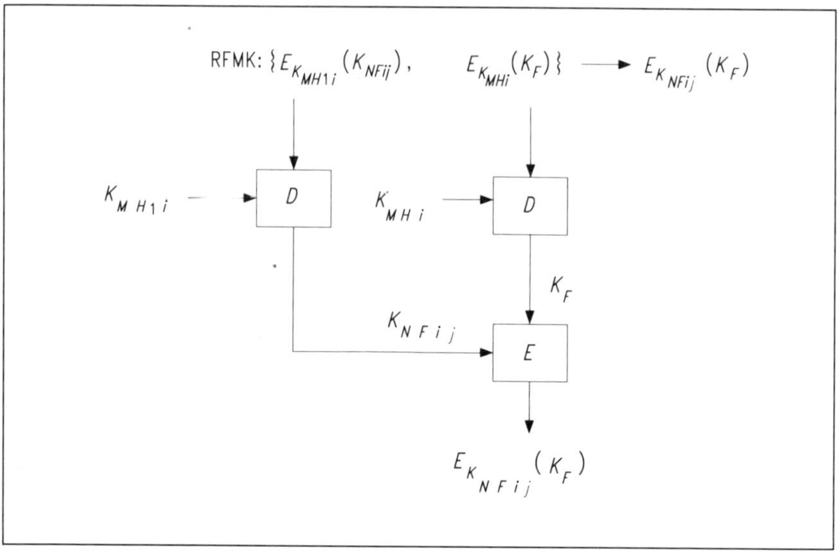

Fig. 11.18 Encryption of K_F under K_{NFij}

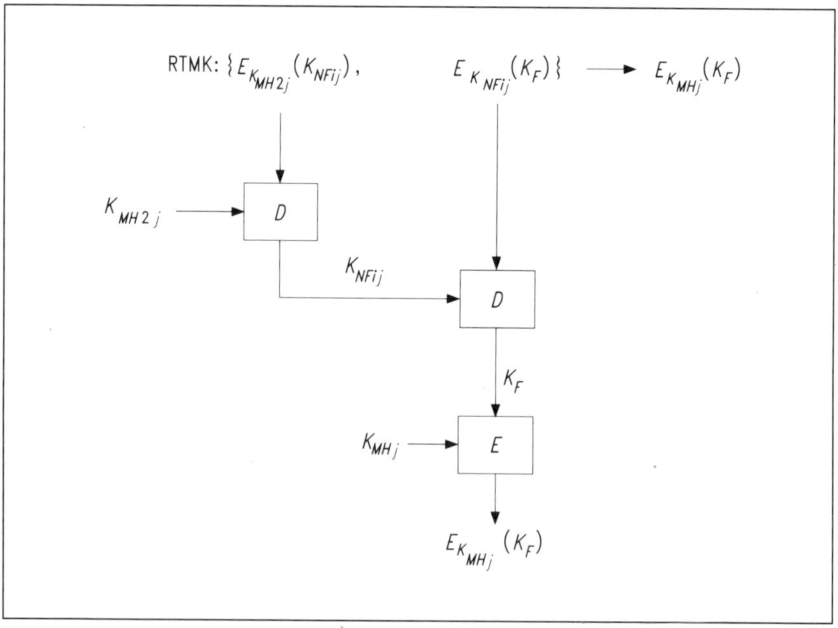

Fig. 11.19 Encryption of K_F under K_{MHj}

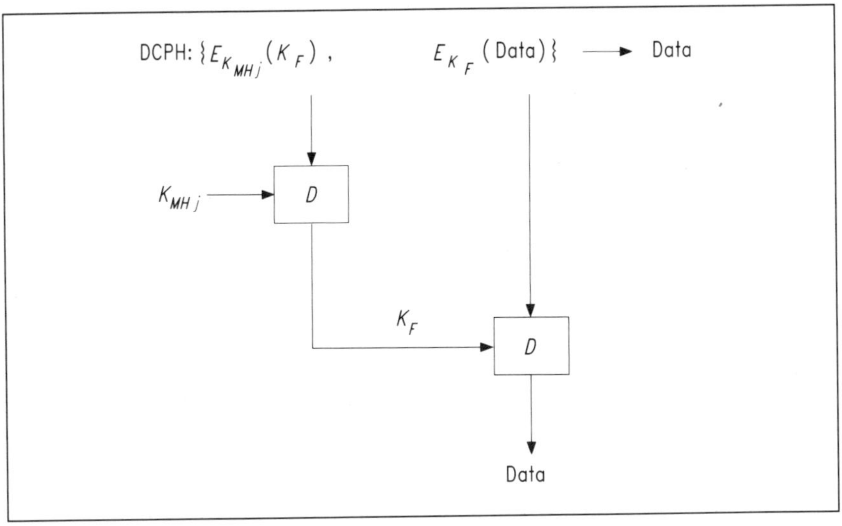

Fig. 11.20 Recovery of file data by DCPH operation

■ **Example 11.9** We can show how file data can be sent to host node i by merely replacing $E_{K_{NFji}}(K_F)$ with $E_{K_{NFii}}(K_F)$ in the file header as shown in Fig. 11.21. But the assumptions we have made are that (i) at host i, the secondary file key K_{NFij} can be enciphered under the host master key K_{MHi} such that $E_{K_{MHi}}(K_{NFij})$; and (ii) that it is possible to obtain $E_{K_{MH1i}}(K_{MH1i})$ from the ECPH operation such that

$$\text{ECPH}: \{E_{K_{MHi}}(K_{MH1i}), K_{MH1i}\} \rightarrow E_{K_{MH1i}}(K_{MH1i})$$

11.7 UPDATION OF CRYPTOGRAPHIC KEYS

The host master key can be changed within the cryptographic system keeping the other keys unchanged. Let K^*_{MH} and K_{MH} represent the old and new master keys, respectively. K^*_{MH} and K_{MH} are read into the main memory of the host system where the variants K^*_{MH1}, K^*_{MH2}, K_{MH1} and K_{MH2} are derived by inverting appropriate bits in K^*_{MH} and K_{MH}, respectively [18].

The encipher-under-master-key (EMK) operation is used to generate

$$\text{EMK}:\{K_{MH1}\} \rightarrow E_{K_{MH}}(K_{MH1})$$

$$\text{EMK}:\{K_{MH2}\} \rightarrow E_{K_{MH}}(K_{MH2})$$

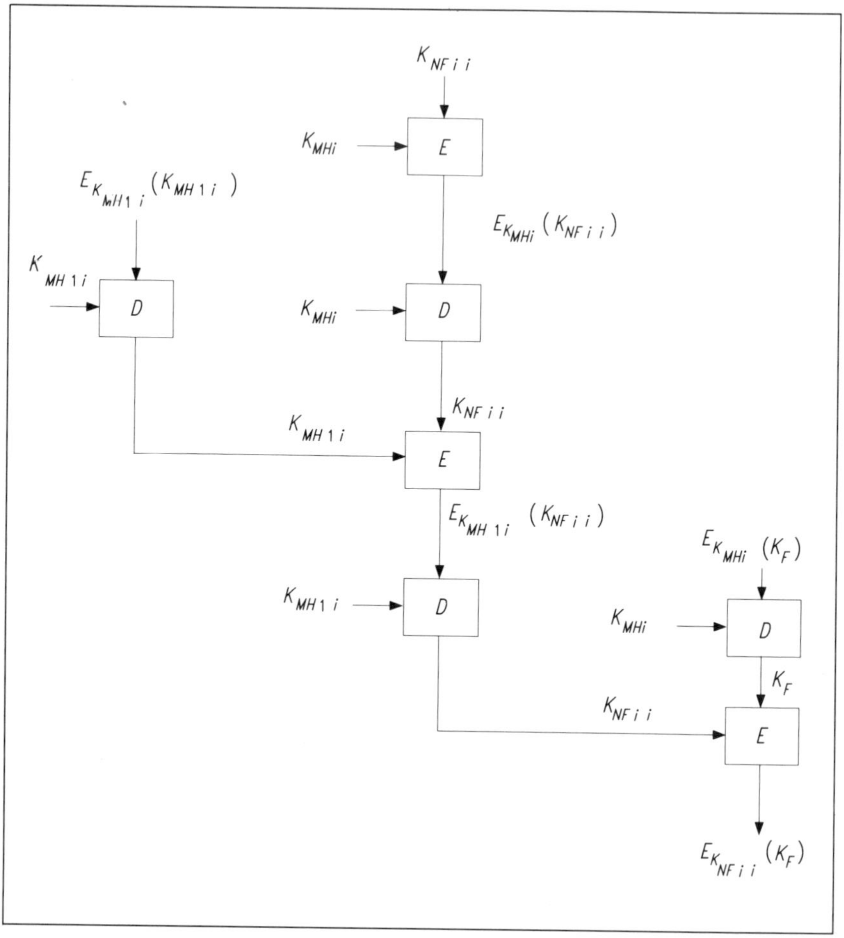

Fig. 11.21 Replacement of $E_{K_{NFji}}(K_F)$ by $E_{K_{NFii}}(K_F)$ in file header

Using these quantities, we generate additional quantities under the ECPH operation as follows:

$$\text{ECPH: } \{E_{K_{MH}}(K_{MH1}), K_{MHX}\} \rightarrow E_{K_{MH1}}(K_{MHX}) \qquad \text{where } X = 1 \text{ or } 2$$

$$\text{ECPH: } \{E_{K_{MH}}(K_{MH2}), K^*_{MHX}\} \rightarrow E_{K_{MH2}}(K^*_{MHX}) \qquad \text{where } X = 1 \text{ or } 2$$

Let α be a secondary key enciphered under the first variant of the host master key. Then reencipherment is accomplished as follows:

$$\text{RTMK: } \{E_{K_{MH2}}(K^*_{MH1}), E_{K^*_{MH1}}(\alpha)\} \rightarrow E_{K_{MH}}(\alpha)$$

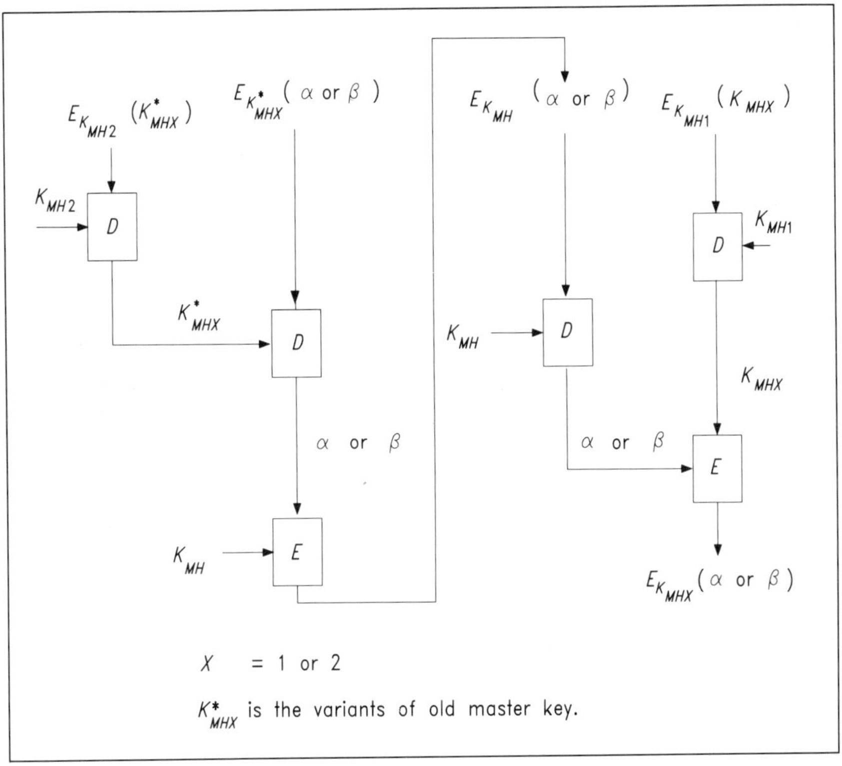

Fig. 11.22 Reencipherment of a secondary key α or β from an old to a new master key

$$\text{RFMK: } \{E_{K_{MH1}}(K_{MH1}), E_{K_{MH}}(\alpha)\} \rightarrow E_{K_{MH1}}(\alpha)$$

Let β denote a secondary key enciphered under the second variant of the host master key. Then reencipherment can be done as shown below.

$$\text{RTMK: } \{E_{K_{MH2}}(K^*_{MH2}), E_{K^*_{MH2}}(\beta)\} \rightarrow E_{K_{MH}}(\beta)$$

$$\text{RFMK:} \{E_{K_{MH1}}(K_{MH2}), E_{K_{MH}}(\beta)\} \rightarrow E_{K_{MH2}}(\beta)$$

Thus far, we have briefly discussed the general procedure for reencipherment of cryptographic keys.

■ **Example 11.10** Consider, using the RTMK and RFMK operations, reencipherment of cryptographic keys from an old to a new master key as illustrated in Fig. 11.22.

11.8 SECRET KEY SHARING METHODS

Shamir [22] showed how to share a secret based on the (k, n) threshold scheme. McEliece and Sarwate [16] proved that Shamir's scheme for sharing secrets was closely related to Reed-Solomon coding schemes. Blom [2] proposed a method of constructing a key generation scheme that is based on a maximum distance separable (MDS) code, as well as on the polynomial in two variables. Since 1987, Matsumoto and Imai have done intensive research on Key Predistribution Systems (KPSs) for practical implementation. We are going to explore their study in what follows.

In addition, it is worthwhile to mention that Brickell (1989), Rabin and Ben-Or (1989), Simmons (1990), Ingemarson and Simmons (1990) and some other researchers have made significant contributions in the area of shared secret schemes. We recommend that the reader go through their recent studies. This will help him understand how they can be applied to key sharing problems.

11.8.1 On Sharing Secrets

Shamir [22] showed how to implement secret sharing of a robust key based on a (k, n) threshold scheme, where k is the minimum number of entities (users) required to construct the cryptographic key K; and n is the number of total entities. Dividing the cryptographic key K into n pieces $K_1, K_2, \ldots, K_n$ in such a way that K is easily reconstructable from any k pieces of it. The so-called (k, n) threshold scheme has the following features:

1. Knowledge of any k or more K_i pieces makes K easily computable.
2. Knowledge of any $k - 1$ or fewer K_i pieces leaves K completely undetermined.

Such a scheme is very helpful in the management of cryptographic keys. By using a (k, n) threshold scheme with $n = 2k - 1$, a robust key management scheme can recover the original key K even if $\lfloor n/2 \rfloor = k - 1$ of n pieces are destroyed. Nevertheless the opponents cannot reconstruct the key even when security breaches expose $k - 1$ of the remaining k pieces. Therefore, threshold schemes are ideally suited to applications in which a group of mutually suspicious individuals with conflicting interests must cooperate.

Let us consider a (k, n) threshold scheme based on polynomial interpolation. Given any subset of k of K_i values, we can find the coefficients of a random polynomial $f(x) = a_0 + a_1x + \ldots + a_{k-1}x^{k-1}$ of degree $(k - 1)$ interpolation, and evaluate

$$K_i = f(X_i), \qquad i = 1, 2, \ldots, n$$

This may be expressed as follows.

$$K_1 = f(X_1) = a_0 + a_1X_1 + \ldots + a_{k-1}X_1^{k-1}$$

$$K_2 = f(X_2) = a_0 + a_1X_2 + \ldots + a_{k-1}X_2^{k-1}$$

....

$$K_n = f(X_n) = a_0 + a_1X_n + \ldots + a_{k-1}X_n^{k-1}$$

in which $a_0 = f(0) = K$. We thus see that we have chosen the distinct X_is $i = 1, 2, \ldots, n$ in order to generate the interpolation key information K_i. However, knowledge of just $k - 1$ of these values does not suffice in order to compute K.

To make this claim more precise, we use modular arithmetic. We pick a prime p which is larger than K and n. The coefficients of $f(x)$, $\{a_1, a_2, \ldots, a_{k-1}\} \in Z_p = \{0, 1, \ldots, p-1\}$ are chosen randomly and the values $K_1, K_2, \ldots, K_n$ are computed modulo p. If K is long, it is advisable to break it into shorter blocks of bits in order to avoid multiprecision arithmetic operations. However, the blocks cannot be arbitrarily short, because the smallest usable value of p is $n + 1$. For a 16-bit modulo, it suffices for applications with up to $2^{16} > 64{,}000$ K_i pieces.

Given any k or more K_i pieces in the two-dimensional plane (X_{i_1}, K_{i_1}), (X_{i_2}, K_{i_2}), $\ldots$, (X_{i_k}, K_{i1_k}), where $i_1, i_2, \ldots, i_k \in \{1, 2, \ldots, n\}$. Then we can compute the polynomial $f(x)$ of degree $k - 1$ by using the Lagrange interpolation polynomial

$$f(x) = \sum_{\lambda=1}^{k} K_{i_\lambda} \prod_{\substack{j=1 \\ j \neq \lambda}}^{k} \frac{(x - X_{i_j})}{(X_{i_\lambda} - X_{i_j})} \quad \text{over GF}(p)$$

Assuming $k - 1$ of these n pieces, there is absolutely nothing the opponent can deduce about the real value of K.

McEliece and Sarwate [16] showed that Shamir's scheme for sharing secrets was closely related to Reed-Solomon coding schemes. Consider Reed-Solomon codes with code symbols from GF (2^m). If α denotes a primitive element in GF (2^m), then $(\alpha_1, \alpha_2, \ldots, \alpha_{m-1})$ represents a set of nonzero elements from GF (2^m) with m elements. The generator polynomial of a t-symbol-error-correcting $(n, n - 2t)$ RS code of length $n = 2^m - 1$ is $g(x) = (x + \alpha)(x + \alpha^2) \cdots (x + \alpha^{2t})$. Let $a(x) = a_0 + a_1x + \ldots + a_{k-1}x^{k-1}$ be the message, where $k = n - 2t$. Then the message symbols

$\mathbf{a} = (a_0, a_1, \ldots, a_{k-1})$ where $a_i \in GF(2^m)$ is encoded into the code word $\mathbf{K} = (K_1, K_2, \ldots, K_{n-1})$, where $K_i = \sum_{j=0}^{k-1} a_j \alpha_i^j$. The secret key is $a_0 = -\sum_{i=1}^{n-1} K_i$, while the pieces of the secret are K_is. Suppose s of the pieces are given but t of these are in error. Then by applying an erasure and error decoding algorithm, it is possible to recover **K** and **a** provided that $s - 2t \geq k$. Thus, Shamir scheme corresponds to a special case of this result where m is a prime, $\alpha_i = i$ and $t = 0$.

11.8.2 Key Sharing Technique Based on a Symmetrical Square Matrix

There is no doubt that secure communications can be achieved if a common key distribution is obtainable between entities (users) in large open networks. In the following, we present a key sharing technique based on the symmetrical square matrix.

Assume that the key managing center generates a symmetrical square matrix **G** and keeps it secret. When entity A joins the system, A sends his ID vector $\mathbf{I}_A = (I_{A1}, I_{A2}, \ldots, I_{An})$ to the centre, which computes the secret matrix $\mathbf{S}_A = \mathbf{I}_A \cdot \mathbf{G}$ upon receiving $\mathbf{I}_A$ (see Fig. 11.23).

Let us look at the problem of common key sharing between entities A and B. The centre's secret information **G** has the following $n \times n$ symmetrical matrix form.

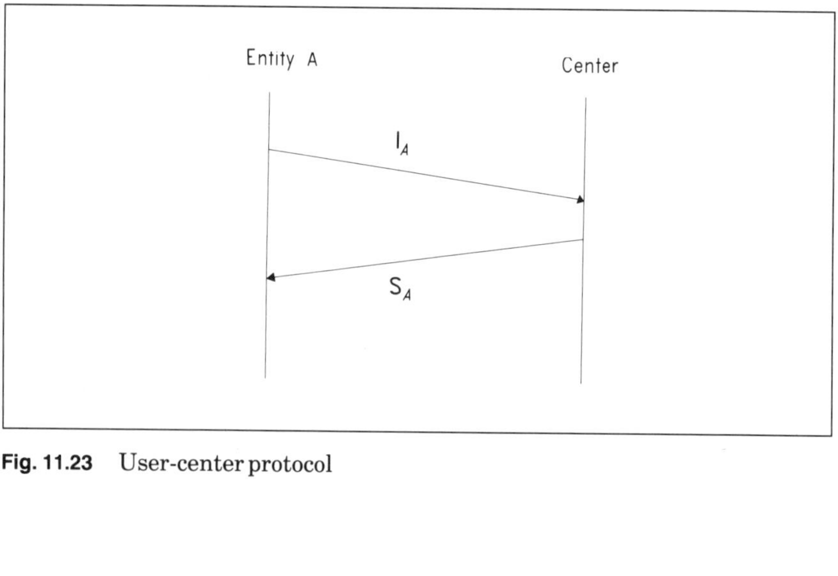

Fig. 11.23 User-center protocol

$$\mathbf{G} = \begin{bmatrix} g_{11} & g_{12} & g_{13} & \cdots & & g_{1n} \\ g_{12} & g_{22} & g_{23} & \cdots & & g_{2n} \\ g_{13} & g_{23} & g_{33} & \cdots & & g_{3n} \\ \cdot & \cdot & \cdot & g_{44} & \cdots & g_{4n} \\ \cdot & \cdot & & \cdot & & \cdot \\ \cdot & \cdot & & & \cdot & \cdot \\ & & & & \cdot & \cdot \\ g_{1n} & g_{2n} & g_{3n} & \cdots & & g_{nn} \end{bmatrix}$$

At this point, our main objective is how we should construct some schemes that give a unique common key for each entity pair (A, B).

We shall now consider the most simple scheme involving key sharing:

1. The centre computes user A's secret information $\mathbf{S}_A$ as follows:

$$\mathbf{S}_A = \mathbf{I}_A \cdot \mathbf{G}$$

$$= (I_{A1}, I_{A2}, \cdots, I_{An}) \begin{bmatrix} g_{11} & g_{12} & g_{13} & \cdots & g_{1n} \\ g_{12} & g_{22} & g_{23} & \cdots & g_{2n} \\ \cdot & \cdot & \cdot & & \cdot \\ \cdot & \cdot & & \cdot & \cdot \\ \cdot & \cdot & & \cdot & \cdot \\ g_{1n} & g_{2n} & g_{3n} & \cdots & g_{nn} \end{bmatrix}$$

User A stores the secret information $\mathbf{S}_A$ in his IC card.

2. He then computes the common key k_{AB} using user B's $\mathbf{I}_B$ such that

$$k_{AB} = \mathbf{S}_A \cdot \mathbf{I}_B^{\mathrm{T}}$$

$$= \mathbf{I}_B \cdot \mathbf{G} \cdot \mathbf{I}_B^{\mathrm{T}}$$

3. User B likewise computes the common key k_{BA} using user A's $\mathbf{I}_A$ such that

$$k_{BA} = \mathbf{S}_B \cdot \mathbf{I}_A^{\mathrm{T}}$$

$$= \mathbf{I}_B \cdot \mathbf{G} \cdot \mathbf{I}_A^{\mathrm{T}}$$

4. Thus the common key is obtained as $k_{AB} = k_{BA}$.

■ **Example 11.11** Prove that $k_{AB} = k_{BA}$ (common key) by applying commutativity.

$$k_{AB} = \mathbf{I}_A \cdot \mathbf{G} \cdot \mathbf{I}_B^{\mathrm{T}}$$

$$= (I_{A1}, I_{A2}, \cdots, I_{An}) \begin{bmatrix} g_{11} & g_{12} & g_{13} & \cdots & g_{1n} \\ g_{12} & g_{22} & g_{23} & \cdots & g_{2n} \\ \cdot & \cdot & \cdot & & \cdot \\ \cdot & \cdot & & \cdot & \cdot \\ \cdot & \cdot & & \cdot & \cdot \\ g_{1n} & g_{2n} & g_{3n} & \cdots & g_{nn} \end{bmatrix} \begin{bmatrix} I_{B1} \\ I_{B2} \\ \cdot \\ \cdot \\ \cdot \\ I_{Bn} \end{bmatrix}$$

$$= (I_{A1}g_{11} + I_{A2}g_{12} + \dots + I_{An}g_{1n}) I_{B1} + (I_{A1}g_{12} + I_{A2}g_{22} + \dots$$

$$+ I_{An}g_{2n}) I_{B2} + \dots + (I_{A1}g_{1n} + I_{A2}g_{2n} + \dots + I_{An}g_{nn}) I_{Bn}$$

$$= I_{A1}g_{11}I_{B1} + I_{A2}g_{12}I_{B1} + \dots + I_{An}g_{1n}I_{B1}$$

$$+ I_{A1}g_{12}I_{B2} + I_{A2}g_{22}I_{B2} + \dots + I_{An}g_{2n}I_{B2} + \dots$$

$$+ I_{A1}g_{1n}I_{Bn} + I_{A2}g_{2n}I_{Bn} + \dots + I_{An}g_{nn}I_{Bn}$$

Regrouping terms, we have k_{AB} as follows:

$$k_{AB} = (I_{B1}g_{11} + I_{B2}g_{12} + \dots + I_{Bn}g_{1n}) I_{A1} + (I_{B1}g_{12} + I_{B2}g_{22} + \dots$$

$$+ I_{Bn}g_{2n}) I_{A2} + \dots + (I_{B1}g_{1n} + I_{B2}g_{2n} + \dots + I_{Bn}g_{nn}) I_{An}$$

$$= [(I_{B1}g_{11} + I_{B2}g_{12} + \dots + I_{Bn}g_{1n}), (I_{B1}g_{12} + I_{B2}g_{22} + \dots + I_{Bn}g_{2n}), \dots,$$

$$(I_{B1}g_{1n} + I_{B2}g_{2n} + \dots + I_{Bn}g_{nn})] \cdot \begin{bmatrix} I_{A1} \\ I_{A2} \\ \cdot \\ \cdot \\ \cdot \\ I_{An} \end{bmatrix}$$

$$= (I_{B1}, I_{B2}, \dots, I_{Bn}) \begin{bmatrix} g_{11} & g_{12} & g_{13} & \cdots & g_{1n} \\ g_{12} & g_{22} & g_{23} & \cdots & g_{2n} \\ \cdot & \cdot & \cdot & & \cdot \\ \cdot & \cdot & & \cdot & \cdot \\ \cdot & \cdot & & \cdot & \cdot \\ g_{1n} & g_{2n} & g_{3n} & \cdots & g_{nn} \end{bmatrix} \begin{bmatrix} I_{A1} \\ I_{A2} \\ \cdot \\ \cdot \\ \cdot \\ I_{An} \end{bmatrix}$$

$$= \mathbf{I}_B \cdot \mathbf{G} \cdot \mathbf{I}_A^T = k_{BA}$$

Thus, it is proved that $k_{AB} = k_{BA}$ which is the key in common between users A and B.

The number of unknown elements of **G** is $1 + 2 + \ldots + n = n(n+1)/2$. From $\mathbf{S}_A = (s_{A1}, s_{A2}, \ldots, s_{An}) = \mathbf{I}_A \cdot \mathbf{G}$, we can obtain the components of user A's secret information as follows:

$$s_{A1} = I_{A1}g_{11} + I_{A2}g_{12} + \ldots + I_{An}g_{1n}$$

$$s_{A2} = I_{A1}g_{12} + I_{A2}g_{22} + \ldots + I_{An}g_{2n}$$

$$\cdots\cdots\cdots\cdots\cdots\cdots\cdots\cdots$$

$$s_{An} = I_{A1}g_{1n} + I_{A2}g_{2n} + \ldots + I_{An}g_{nn}$$

Thus, we can see that each user induces n simultaneous equations with unknown elements g_{ij}. Consequently, if $\lfloor (n(n+1)/2)/n \rfloor = \lfloor (n+1)/2 \rfloor$ entities disclose their own secret information S_i, i = A, B, C, . . ., to one another, then the secret centre matrix **G** can be found. This is a major weakness.

11.8.3 KPS Key Sharing Scheme

As a typical application of key distribution, the following key sharing method is of intersect. After introducing the key sharing method in CRYPTO 87, Matsumoto and Imai have been developing the Key Predistribution System (KPS) method, which is meant for application to a ciphered communication system designed for large-scale networks such as smart card based key-sharing and facsimile systems. KPS is applicable to end-to-end cryptographic communication systems comprising a large number of entities. In 1990, Matsumoto and Imai proposed a prototype implementation of KPSL1CARD and a KPS interface adapter to be connected to a facsimile terminal [15].

KPS is a mechanism which on request brings a common key to each member of any group U in a network. The network is assumed to have one or several managing centres (KPS centres). Let y_i denote to KPS-ID of entity i, i = A, B, C, . . . , where ID can be specified as a fixed identifier composed of the entity's name and address or telephone number.

We shall now describe a KPS method for producing a common key among the same group members.

1. Each KPS center p (p = 1 or 2 or . . . , or n for n centers) in the system generates its respective center algorithm G_p and keeps it secret.
2. When an entity i joins the system, the KPS-ID y_i of each entity i in each KPS centre p can be applied to the centre algorithm G_p to obtain an algorithm $X_{pi} = G_p(y_i)$ where i = A, B, C, . . . ; and passes X_{pi} only to entity i. Entity i incorporates the algorithm X_{pi} into the

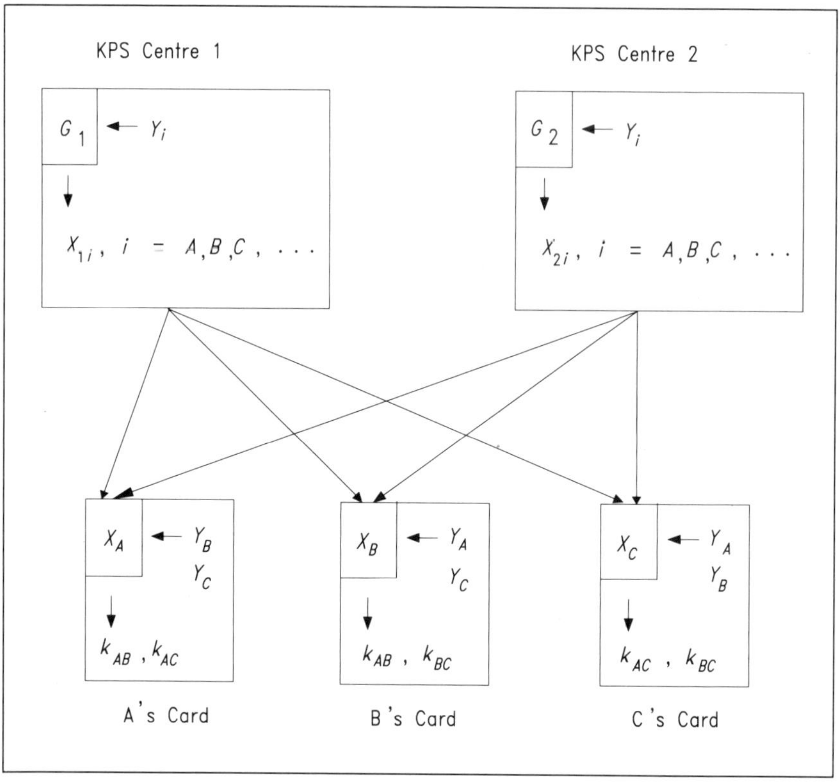

Fig. 11.24 Key sharing among the group {A, B, C}

secret algorithm X_i and keeps it secret. The distribution of X_{pi} as well as generation of X_i implemented in the smart card should be done by some interactive procedure among the KPS centers and a smart card owned by entity i.

3. After steps (1) and (2) have been completed, any group U of the entire entities can share a common key k_U. Each member $i \in U$ can compute the same key k_U by feeding an input y_j, $j \in U - i$, of KPS-IDs to its secret-algorithm X_i, as shown in Fig. 11.24.

Key sharing among the same group members can be achieved by the linear schemes with which G_p and X_i can be implemented by multi-linear mappings and pseudorandom transformations.

11.8.4 ID-based Key Exchange Protocol

The problem of key distribution among many users has been an important area of research in the past. Günther and Boveri [11] proposed a solution to be exchanged authenticated session keys for closed user groups and public communication systems of arbitrary size. They adopted Shamir's approach for the construction of an identity-based key exchange scheme. In their protocol, the two parties construct keys which agree if both of them are legitimate and do both conform to the protocol. Their scheme is some kind of a mixture of the Diffie-Hellman key-exchange scheme and the ElGamal signature scheme.

ID based protocol consists of two phases: a primary preauthentication phase and a key exchange phase. The first phase involves a key authentication center (KAC) which is trusted by all parties. Since the KAC lays down all the system parameters, all users who wish to join the communication network should contact the KAC and identify themselves. After verifying the user's identity, the KAC sends him the signature of his name and system parameters. But the user should verify the authenticity of the signature.

The most important feature of ID-based protocol is that a user is able to authenticate himself in the key exchange phase to any other user without further communication with the KAC and without exposing the secret signature of his name.

The KAC chooses a one-way function $f(D_A)$, a primitive element $g \in$ GF (p) where p is a prime, a random number $X \in \mathbf{Z}_{p-1}$ such that $\gcd(X, p-1) = 1$. X is the KAC's secret key which is used to compute the public key $Y \equiv g^X \pmod{p}$. Now, user A contacts the KAC and identifies himself. If the centre accepts him, it provides A with f, GF (p), g, and Y.

Let us consider the protocol between the KAC and user A in the following procedure.

1. User A sends D_A to the centre, where D_A denotes the description of A, including A's name, birthday, physical description, etc.
2. The KAC chooses a random number $K_A \in \mathbf{Z}_{p-1}$ such that $\gcd(K_A, p - 1) = 1$, and computes R_A such that $R_A \equiv g^{K_A} \pmod{p}$. The KAC computes $\mathrm{ID_A}$ such that $\mathrm{ID_A} = f(\mathrm{D_A})$. The center also solves the equation $\mathrm{ID}_A \equiv XR_A + K_A S_A \pmod{p-1}$ for S_A which is A's secret key.
3. The center now transmits A's public key R_A and secret key S_A to A.
4. Upon receipt of R_A and S_A, user A establishes whether they are legitimate:

$$g^{\mathrm{ID}_A} \equiv Y^{R_A} \cdot R_A^{S_A} \pmod{p}$$

which can be proved as follows:

$$Y^{R_A} R_A^{S_A} \equiv (g^X)^{R_A} \cdot (g^{K_A})^{S_A} \pmod p$$

$$\equiv g^{XR_A + K_A S_A} \pmod p$$

$$\equiv g^{\mathrm{ID}_A} \pmod p, \quad \text{where} \quad \mathrm{ID}_A = f(\mathrm{D}_A)$$

Reinterpretation of this equation leads us to an identity-based ElGamal signature scheme.

Making R_A public does not compromise the secret key S_A. That is,

$$R_A^{S_A} \equiv g^{\mathrm{ID}_A} \cdot Y^{-R_A} \pmod p$$

We cannot compute the discrete logarithm of S_A to the base R_A such that

$$S_A \equiv \log_{R_A} b \pmod p, \qquad \text{where} \quad b = g^{\mathrm{ID}_A} \cdot Y^{-R_A}$$

By sharing their secret keys S_A and S_B, we can determine the common session key such that $S_{KA} = S_{KB}$. The Diffie-Hellman algorithm must be adapted to accommodate different bases for two parties. We shall now illustrate the key exchange protocol between two users.

1. User A sends (ID_A, R_A) to user B.

2. Upon receipt of (ID_A, R_A), B computes $R_A^{S_A} \pmod p$ as follows:

$$g^{\mathrm{ID}_A} \cdot Y^{-R_A} \pmod p \equiv g^{\mathrm{ID}_A} \cdot g^{-XR_A} \pmod p \equiv g^{\mathrm{ID}_A - XR_A} \pmod p$$

$$\equiv g^{K_A S_A} \pmod p \equiv R_A^{S_A}$$

B sends (ID_B, R_B) to A.

3. After receiving (ID_B, R_B) from B, A computes $R_B^{S_B}$ using g and Y as follows:

$$g^{\mathrm{ID}_B} \cdot Y^{-R_B} \pmod p \equiv g^{\mathrm{ID}_B - XR_B} \pmod p$$

$$\equiv g^{K_B S_B} \pmod p \equiv R_B^{S_B}$$

4. A selects $T_A \in \mathbf{Z}_{p-1}$ such that gcd $(p - 1, T_A) = 1$. Compute U_A utilizing R_B and T_A, such that $U_A \equiv R_B^{T_A} \pmod p$. A then sends U_A to B.

5. B selects T_B so as to satisfy gcd $(p - 1, T_B) = 1$. Using R_A and T_B, B computes $U_B \equiv R_A^{T_B} \pmod p$. B sends U_B to A.

6. Utilizing U_B, S_A, $R_B^{S_B}$, and T_A, A computes the common session key S_{KA} such that

$$S_{KA} \equiv U_B^{S_A} \left(R_B^{S_B}\right)^{T_A} \pmod p \equiv R_A^{S_A T_B} \cdot R_B^{S_B T_A} \pmod p$$

7. B computes the common session key S_{KB} by using U_A, S_B, $R_A^{S_A}$, and T_B as follows:

$$S_{KB} \equiv U_A^{S_B} \left(R_A^{S_A}\right)^{T_B} \pmod p \equiv R_B^{S_B T_A} \cdot R_A^{S_A T_B} \pmod p$$

Thus, since it has been proved that $S_{KA} = S_{KB}$, two users can share their common keys S_{KA} and S_{KB}.

Besides the Günther-Boveri algorithm, we can also find a few more protocols involving the key-sharing algorithm, based on the Diffie-Hellman key-exchange. Such protocols include those of Okamoto and Tanaka (1989), and Banspieβ and Konbloch (1989). The former transforms the D-H key-exchange scheme into an ID-based one by using the RSA scheme, and the latter obtains a key-sharing scheme which introduces the zero-knowledge identification concept.

REFERENCES

1. Benaloh, J. and J. Leighter: "Generalized secret sharing and monotone functions", *LCNS*, vol. 403, pp 27–35, 1990.
2. Blom, R.: "Non-public key distribution," *Proc. Crypto 82*, Santa Barbara, pp 231–236, 1982.
3. Brickell, E.F.: "Some ideal secret sharing scheme", *J. Combin. Math. and Combin. Comput.*, vol. 9, pp 105–113, 1989.
4. Brickell, E.F. and D.M. Davenport: "On the classification of ideal secret sharing schemes", *LCNS*, vol. 435, pp 278–285, 1989.
5. Davies, D.W. and W.L. Price: *Security for Computer Networks : An Introduction to Data Security in Teleprocessing and Electronic Funds Transfer*, Wiley, New York, 1984.
6. Denning, D.E. and G.M. Sacco: "Time stamps in key-distribution protocols", *CACM*, vol. 24, no. 8, pp 533–536, Aug. 1981.
7. Diffie, W. and M.E. Hellman: "New direction in cryptography", *IEEE Trans. Inform. Theory*, vol. IT–22, pp 644–654, 1976.
8. Ehrsam, W.F., S.M. Matyas, C.H. Meyer, and W.L. Tuchman: "A cryptographic key management scheme for implementing the data encryption standard", *IBM Syst. J.*, vol. 17, no. 2, pp 106–125, 1978.

9. ElGamal, T. : "A public key cryptosystem and a signature scheme based on discrete logarithms", *IEEE Trans. Inform. Theory*, vol. IT-31, pp 469–472, July 1985.
10. Guillou, L.C. and J.J. Quisquater: "A practical zero-knowledge protocol fitted to security microprocessor minimizing both transmission and memory", *Advances in Cryptology—Eurocrypt 88, LNCS*, vol. 330, pp 123–128, Springer-Verlag, 1988.
11. Günther, C.G. and A.B. Boveri: "An identity-based key-exchange protocol", *Advances in Cryptology—Eurocrypt 89, LNCS*, vol. 434, pp 29–37, Springer-Verlag, 1989.
12. Karnin, E.D., J.W. Greene, and M.E. Hallman: "On secret sharing systems", *IEEE Trans. Inform. Theory*, vol. IT-29, no. 1, pp 35–41, Jan. 1983.
13. Matyas, S.M. and C.H. Meyer: "Generation, distribution, and installation of cryptographic keys", *IBM Syst. J.*, vol. 17, no. 2, pp 126–137, 1978.
14. Matsumoto, T. and H. Imai: "On the key predistribution system: A practical solution to the key distribution problèm", *Advances in cryptology—Proc. Crypto 87*, Santa Barbara, Springer-Verlag *LNCS,* vol. 293, pp 185–193, 1987.
15. Matsumoto, T., Y. Takashima, H. Imai, M. Sasaki, H. Yoshikawa, and S. Watanabe: "A prototype KPS and its application-IC card based key sharing and cryptographic communication (in Japanese)", *Trans. IEICE*, vol. E73, no. 7, 1990.
16. McEliece, R.J. and D.V. Sarwate: "On sharing secrets and Reed-Solomon codes", *CACM*, vol. 24, no. 9, pp 583–584, Sept. 1981.
17. Merkle, R.C. and M.E. Hellman: "Hiding information and signatures in trapdoor knapsacks", *IEEE Trans. Inform. Theory*, vol. IT-24, no. 5, pp 525–530, 1978.
18. Meyer, C.H. and S.M. Matyas: *Cryptograph: A new dimension in computer data security,* Wiley, New York, 1982.
19. Rabin, T. and M. Ben-Or: "Verifiable secret sharing and multiparty protocols with honest majority", *Proc. 21st ACM Symp. Theory of Computing*, pp 73–85, 1989.
20. Rivest, R., A. Shamir, and L. Adleman: "A method for obtaining signatures and public-key cryptosystems", *CACM*, vol. 21, no. 2, pp 120–128, Feb. 1978.
21. Seberry, J. and J. Pieprzyk: *Cryptography: An Introduction to Computer Security*, Prentice-Hall, Sydney, 1989.
22. Shamir, A.: "How to share a secret", *CACM*, vol. 22, no. 11, pp 612–613, November 1979.
23. Simmons, G.J.: "How to (really) share a secret", Springer-Verlag, *LNCS*, vol. 403, pp 390–448, 1988.
24. Simmons, G.J.: "Prepositioned shared secret and/or shared control schemes", Springer-Verlag, *LNCS*, vol. 434, pp 436–467, 1989.

Index

RI

RE

N

REC